My Little Monster

13

Robico

CONTENTS

STORY

Through their awkwardness, Shizuku Mizutani
and Haru Yoshida have come to understand
and respect each other, and have taken a new
step forward. The rest of the cast are also each
striving to take their own steps forward through
their own conflicts! Everyone is the hero of his
or her own story. And everyone's story goes on,
never ending!!

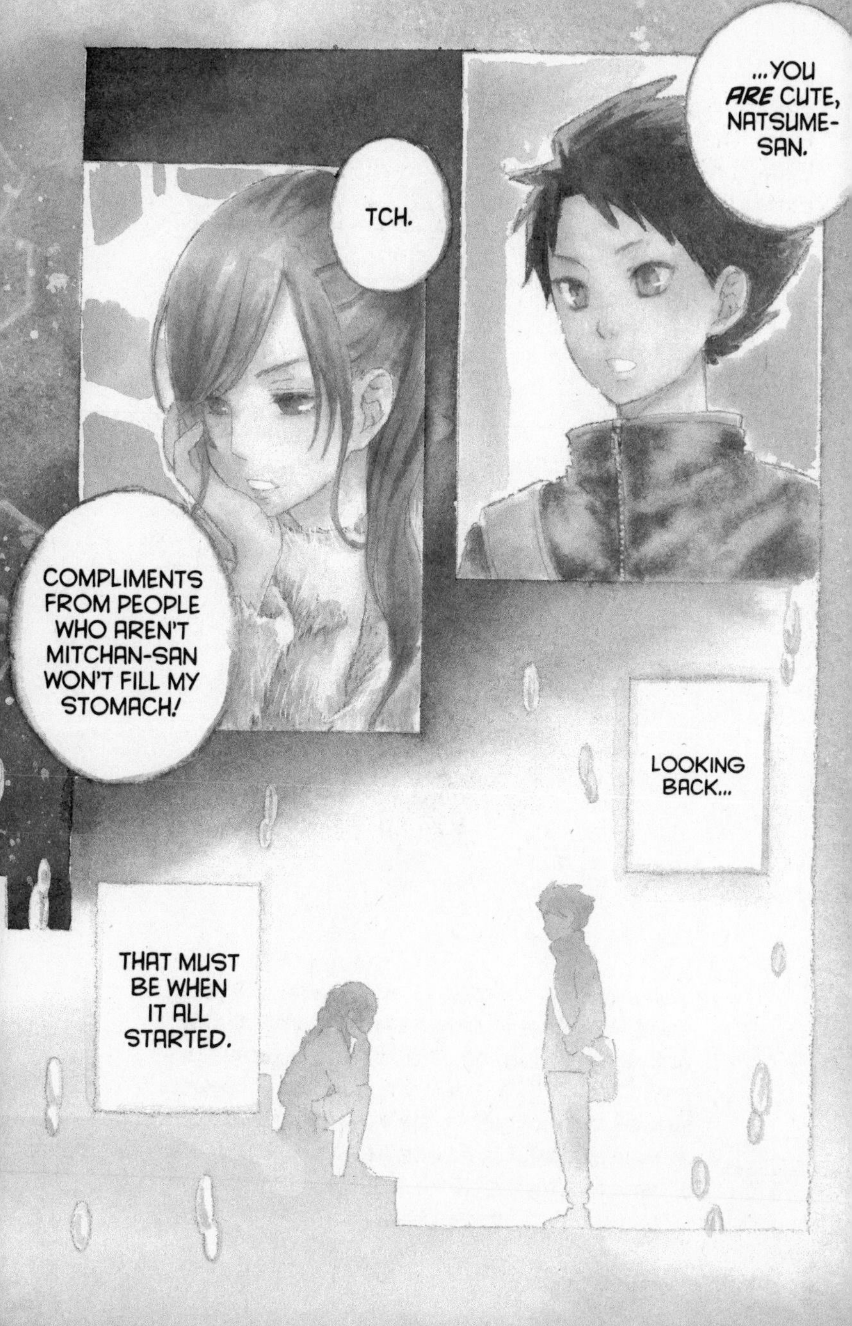
...YOU ARE CUTE, NATSUME-SAN.
TCH.
COMPLIMENTS FROM PEOPLE WHO AREN'T MITCHAN-SAN WON'T FILL MY STOMACH!
LOOKING BACK...
THAT MUST BE WHEN IT ALL STARTED.

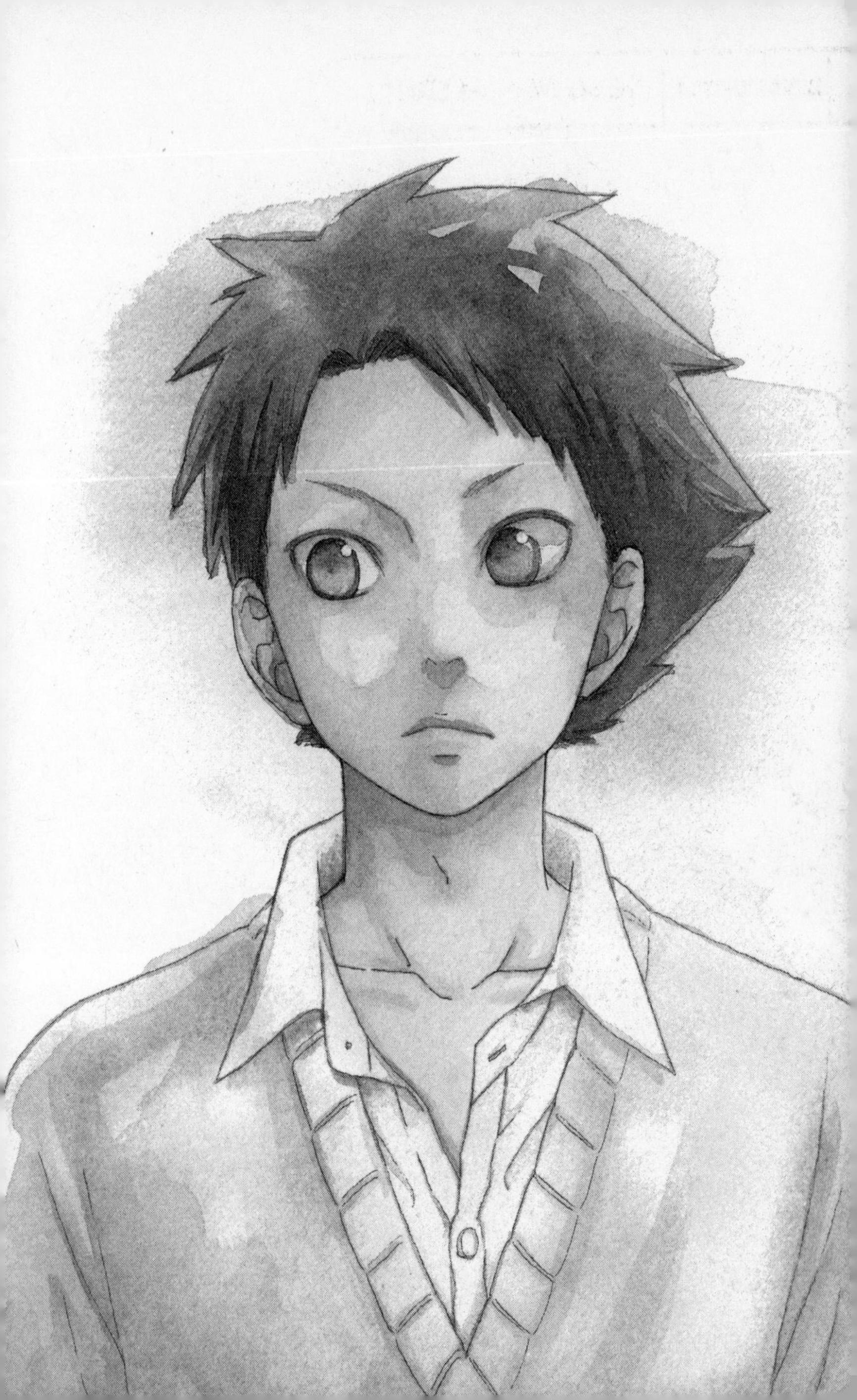

EXTRA CHAPTER 1: THE SASAYAN-KUN STORY 2

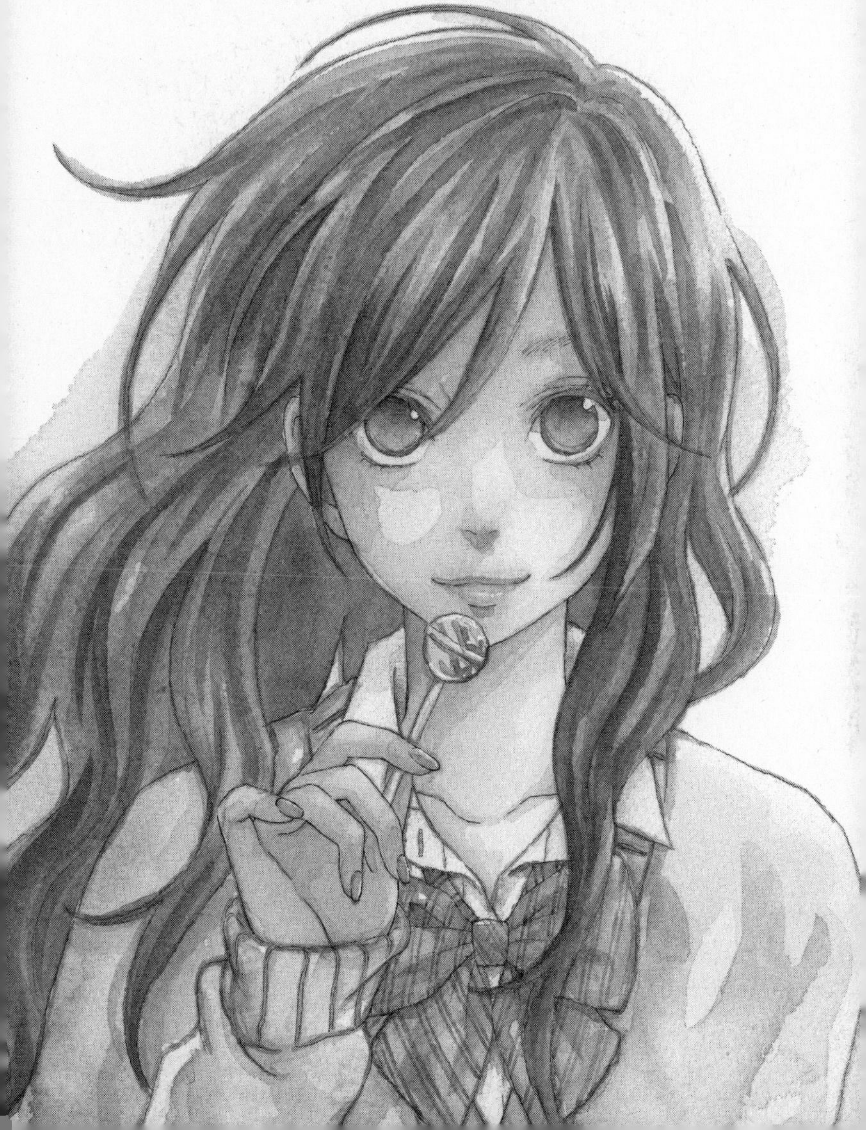

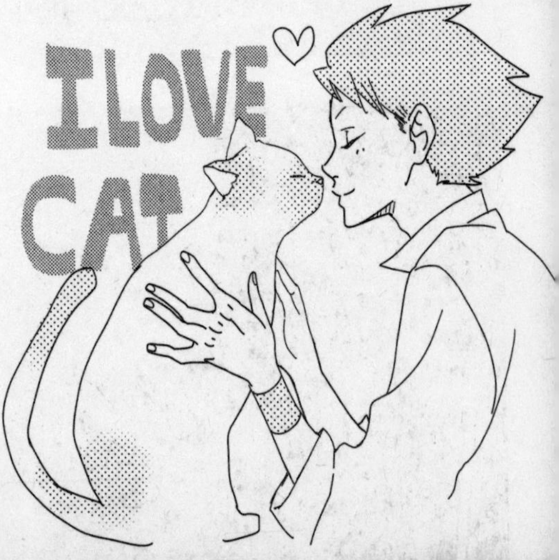
I LOVE
CAT

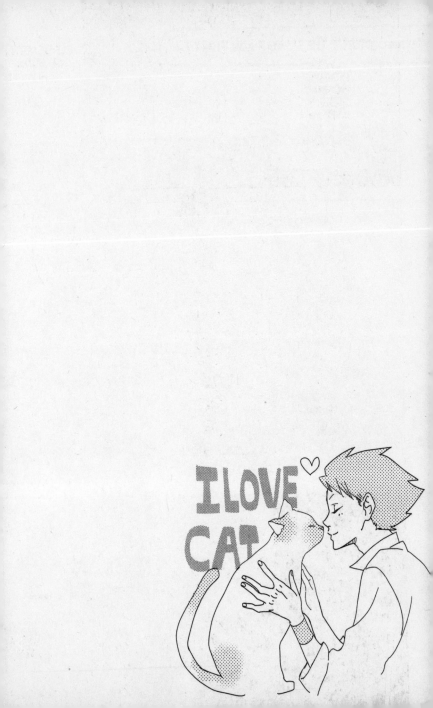

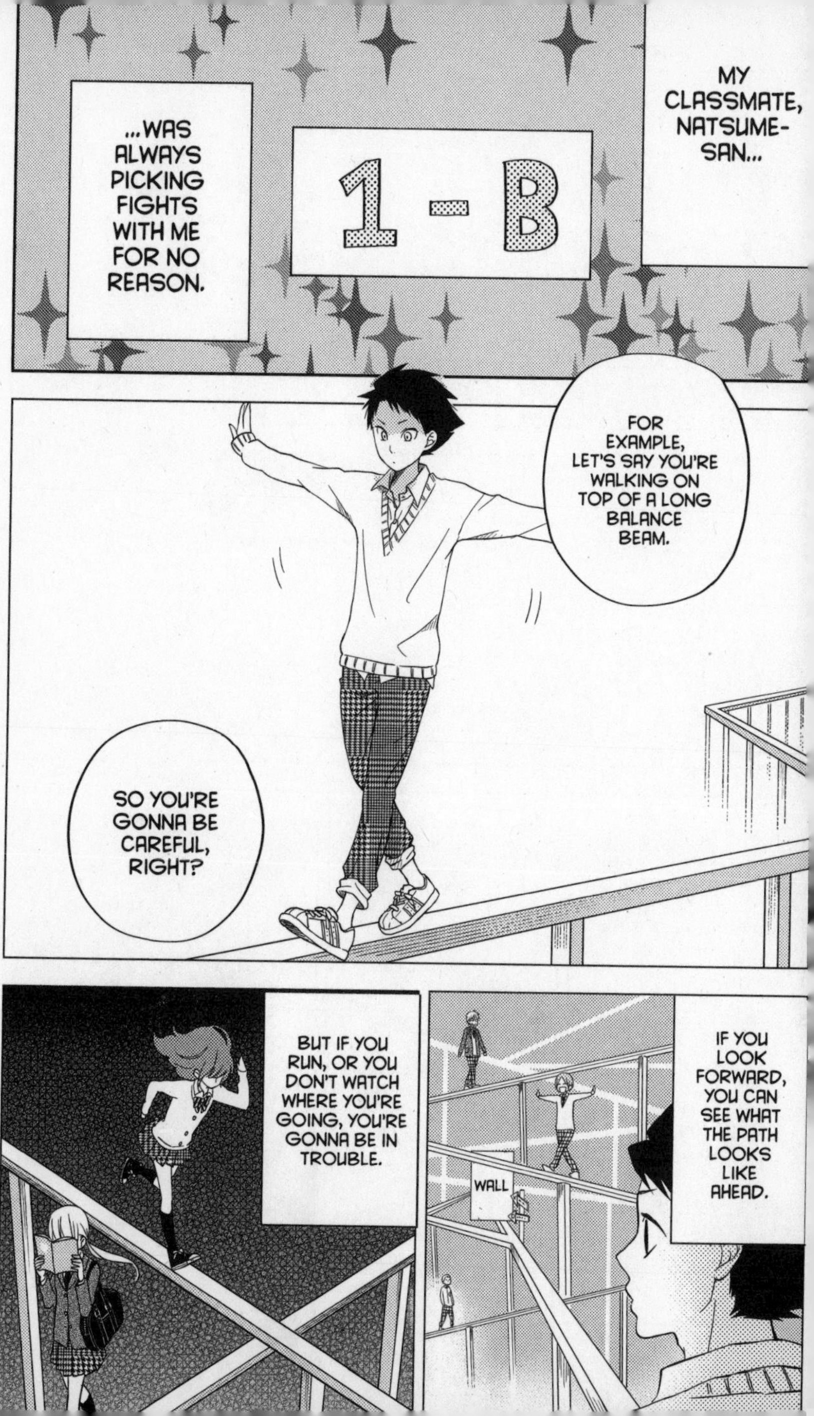
MY CLASSMATE, NATSUME-SAN...
1-B
...WAS ALWAYS PICKING FIGHTS WITH ME FOR NO REASON.
FOR EXAMPLE, LET'S SAY YOU'RE WALKING ON TOP OF A LONG BALANCE BEAM.
SO YOU'RE GONNA BE CAREFUL, RIGHT?
IF YOU LOOK FORWARD, YOU CAN SEE WHAT THE PATH LOOKS LIKE AHEAD.
WALL
BUT IF YOU RUN, OR YOU DON'T WATCH WHERE YOU'RE GOING, YOU'RE GONNA BE IN TROUBLE.

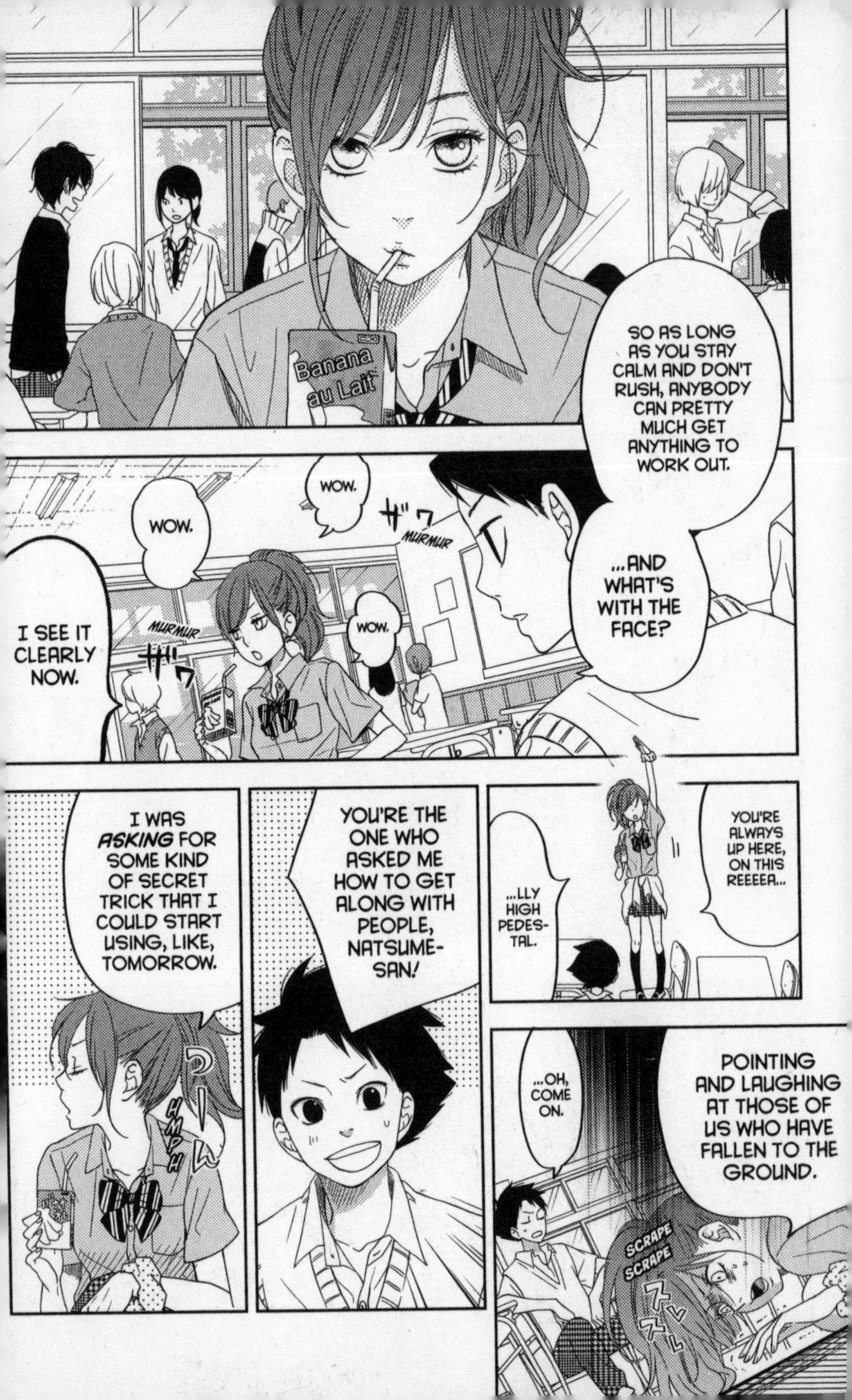
Banana au Lait
SO AS LONG AS YOU STAY CALM AND DON'T RUSH, ANYBODY CAN PRETTY MUCH GET ANYTHING TO WORK OUT.
...AND WHAT'S WITH THE FACE?
WOW.
ザワ
MURMUR
WOW.
WOW.
MURMUR
ザワ
I SEE IT CLEARLY NOW.
YOU'RE ALWAYS UP HERE, ON THIS REEEEA...
...LLY HIGH PEDES-TAL.
POINTING AND LAUGHING AT THOSE OF US WHO HAVE FALLEN TO THE GROUND.
...OH, COME ON.
SCRAPE SCRAPE
YOU'RE THE ONE WHO ASKED ME HOW TO GET ALONG WITH PEOPLE, NATSUME-SAN!
I WAS *ASKING* FOR SOME KIND OF SECRET TRICK THAT I COULD START USING, LIKE, TOMORROW.
HMPH

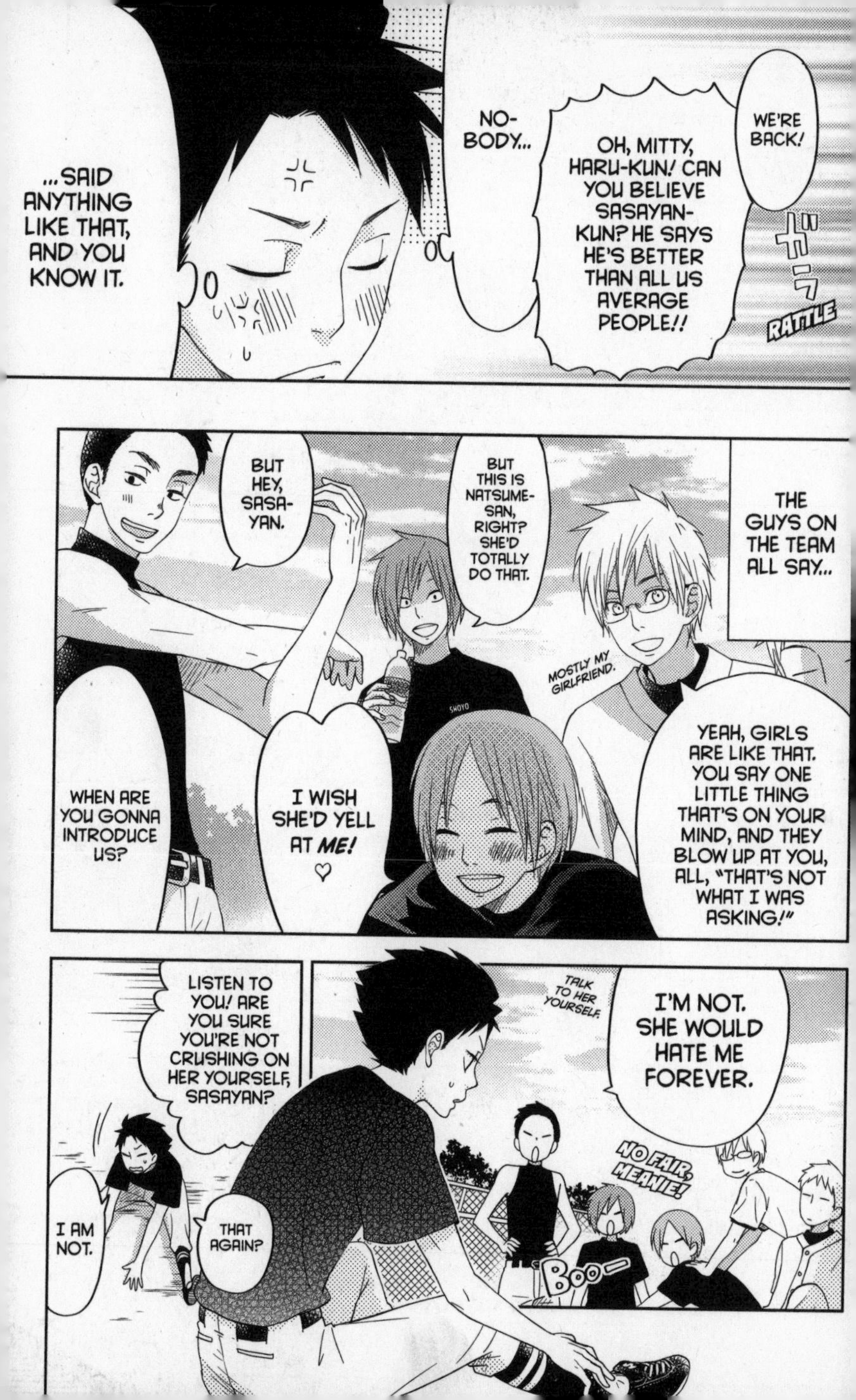
WE'RE BACK!
ガラ
RATTLE
OH, MITTY, HARU-KUN! CAN YOU BELIEVE SASAYAN-KUN? HE SAYS HE'S BETTER THAN ALL US AVERAGE PEOPLE!!
NO-BODY...
...SAID ANYTHING LIKE THAT, AND YOU KNOW IT.
THE GUYS ON THE TEAM ALL SAY...
BUT THIS IS NATSUME-SAN, RIGHT? SHE'D TOTALLY DO THAT.
BUT HEY, SASA-YAN.
MOSTLY MY GIRLFRIEND.
YEAH, GIRLS ARE LIKE THAT. YOU SAY ONE LITTLE THING THAT'S ON YOUR MIND, AND THEY BLOW UP AT YOU, ALL, "THAT'S NOT WHAT I WAS ASKING!"
I WISH SHE'D YELL AT ME! ♡
WHEN ARE YOU GONNA INTRODUCE US?
I'M NOT. SHE WOULD HATE ME FOREVER.
TALK TO HER YOURSELF.
NO FAIR, MEANIE!
BOO—
LISTEN TO YOU! ARE YOU SURE YOU'RE NOT CRUSHING ON HER YOURSELF, SASAYAN?
THAT AGAIN?
I AM NOT.

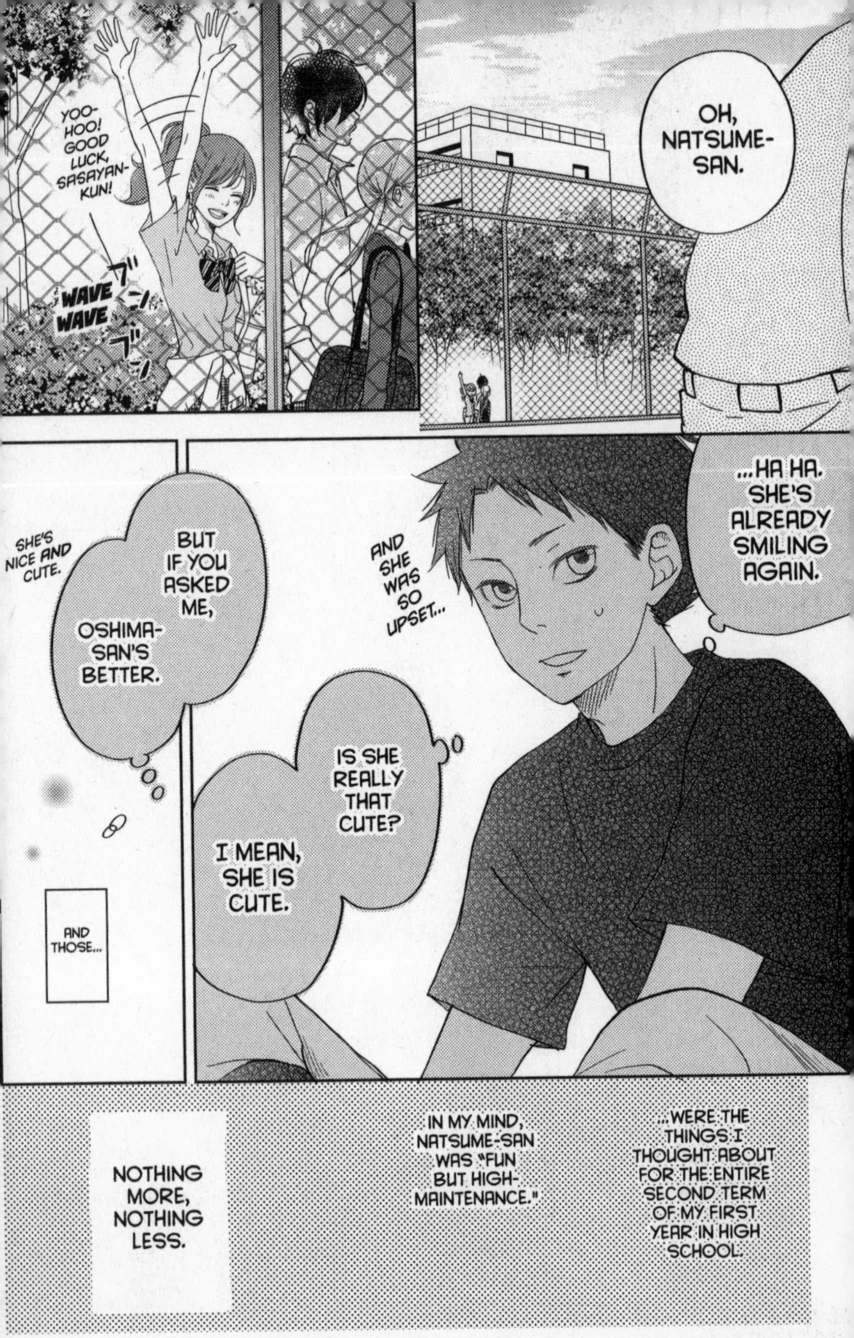
OH, NATSUME-SAN.
YOO-HOO! GOOD LUCK, SASAYAN-KUN!
WAVE WAVE
...HA HA. SHE'S ALREADY SMILING AGAIN.
AND SHE WAS SO UPSET...
IS SHE REALLY THAT CUTE?
I MEAN, SHE IS CUTE.
BUT IF YOU ASKED ME,
OSHIMA-SAN'S BETTER.
SHE'S NICE AND CUTE.
AND THOSE...
...WERE THE THINGS I THOUGHT ABOUT FOR THE ENTIRE SECOND TERM OF MY FIRST YEAR IN HIGH SCHOOL.
IN MY MIND, NATSUME-SAN WAS "FUN BUT HIGH-MAINTENANCE."
NOTHING MORE, NOTHING LESS.

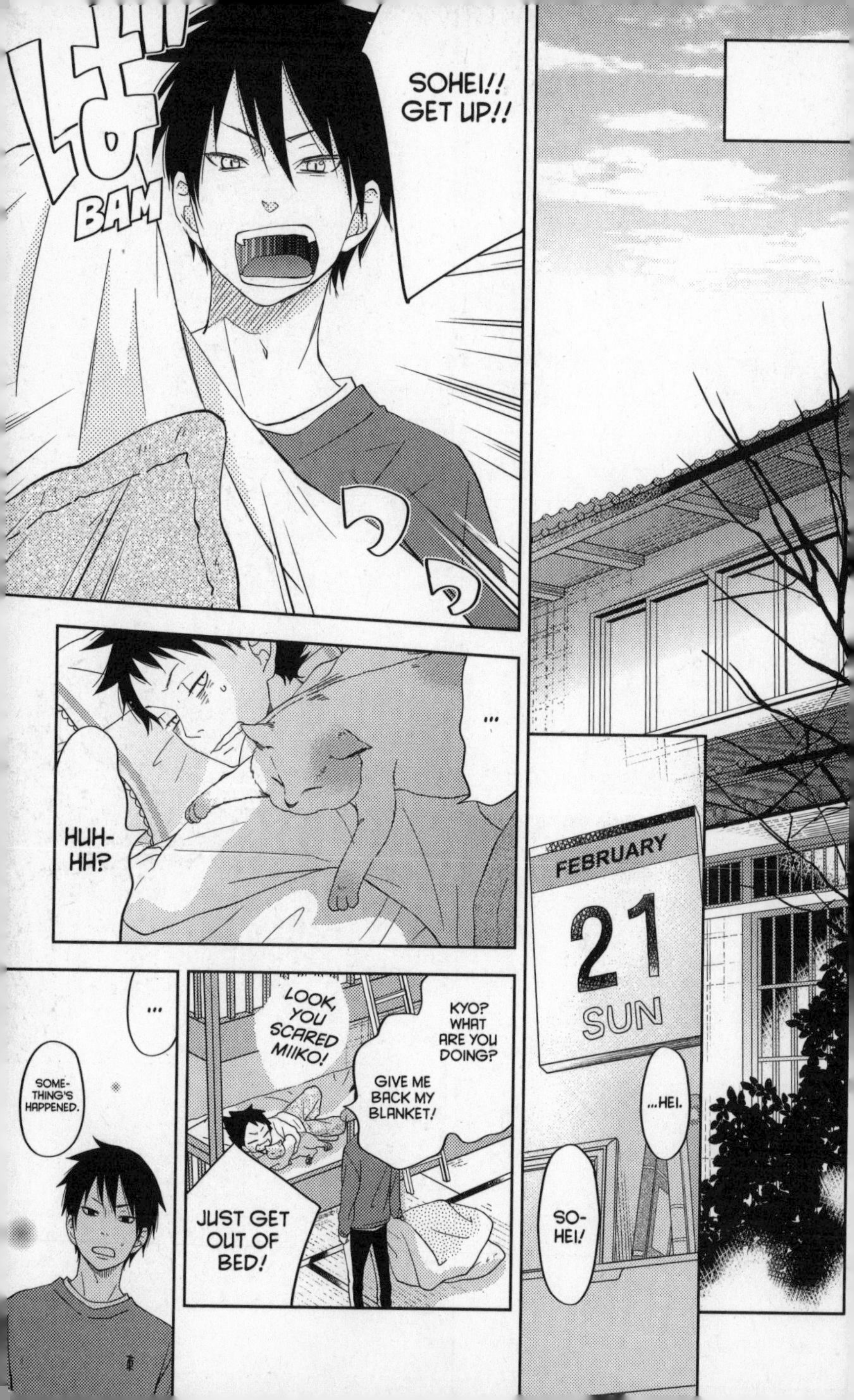
FEBRUARY
21
SUN
...HEI.
SO-HEI!
BAM
SOHEI!! GET UP!!
...
HUH-HH?
KYO? WHAT ARE YOU DOING?
LOOK, YOU SCARED MIIKO!
GIVE ME BACK MY BLANKET!
JUST GET OUT OF BED!
...
SOME-THING'S HAPPENED.

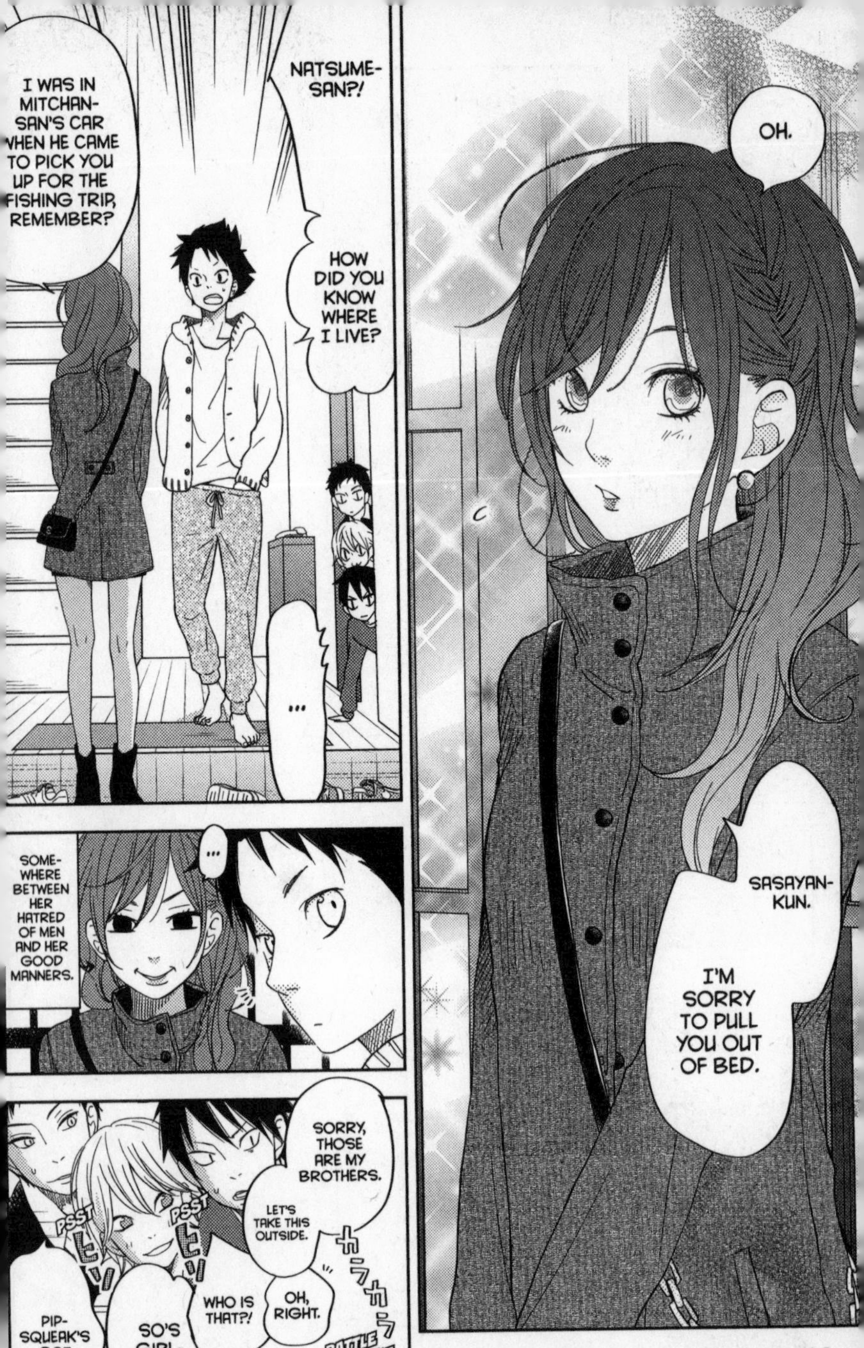
OH.
SASAYAN-KUN.
I'M SORRY TO PULL YOU OUT OF BED.
NATSUME-SAN?!
HOW DID YOU KNOW WHERE I LIVE?
I WAS IN MITCHAN-SAN'S CAR WHEN HE CAME TO PICK YOU UP FOR THE FISHING TRIP, REMEMBER?
...
...
SOMEWHERE BETWEEN HER HATRED OF MEN AND HER GOOD MANNERS.
SORRY, THOSE ARE MY BROTHERS.
LET'S TAKE THIS OUTSIDE.
RATTLE RATTLE
OH, RIGHT.
WHO IS THAT?!
PSST
PSST
SO'S GIRLFRIEND?!
PIP-SQUEAK'S GOT GAME.

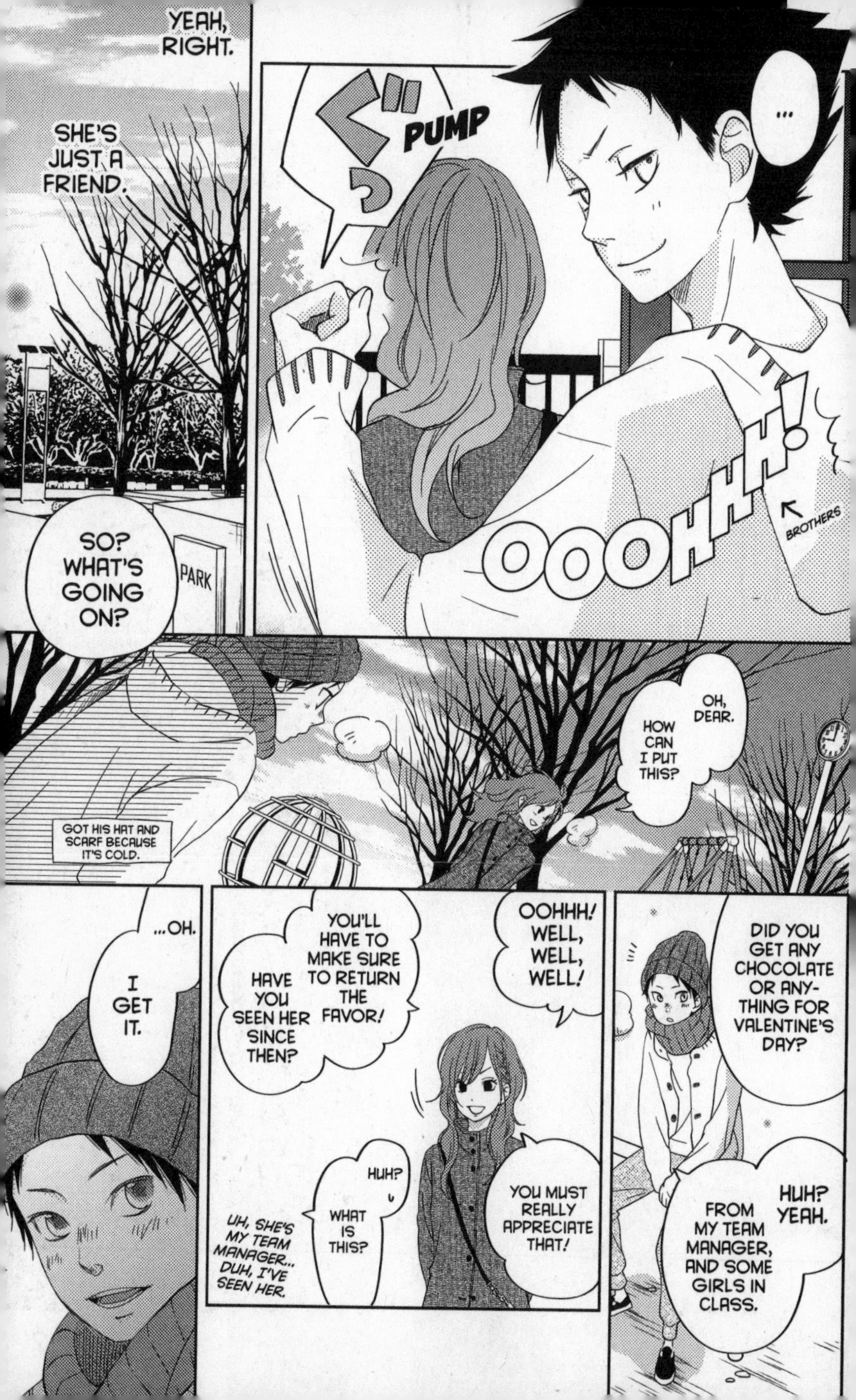
...
ぐっ
PUMP
OOOHHH!
BROTHERS
YEAH, RIGHT.
SHE'S JUST A FRIEND.
PARK
SO? WHAT'S GOING ON?
OH, DEAR.
HOW CAN I PUT THIS?
GOT HIS HAT AND SCARF BECAUSE IT'S COLD.
DID YOU GET ANY CHOCOLATE OR ANY-THING FOR VALENTINE'S DAY?
HUH? YEAH.
FROM MY TEAM MANAGER, AND SOME GIRLS IN CLASS.
OOHHH! WELL, WELL, WELL!
YOU MUST REALLY APPRECIATE THAT!
YOU'LL HAVE TO MAKE SURE TO RETURN THE FAVOR!
HAVE YOU SEEN HER SINCE THEN?
HUH?
WHAT IS THIS?
UH, SHE'S MY TEAM MANAGER... DUH, I'VE SEEN HER.
...OH.
I GET IT.

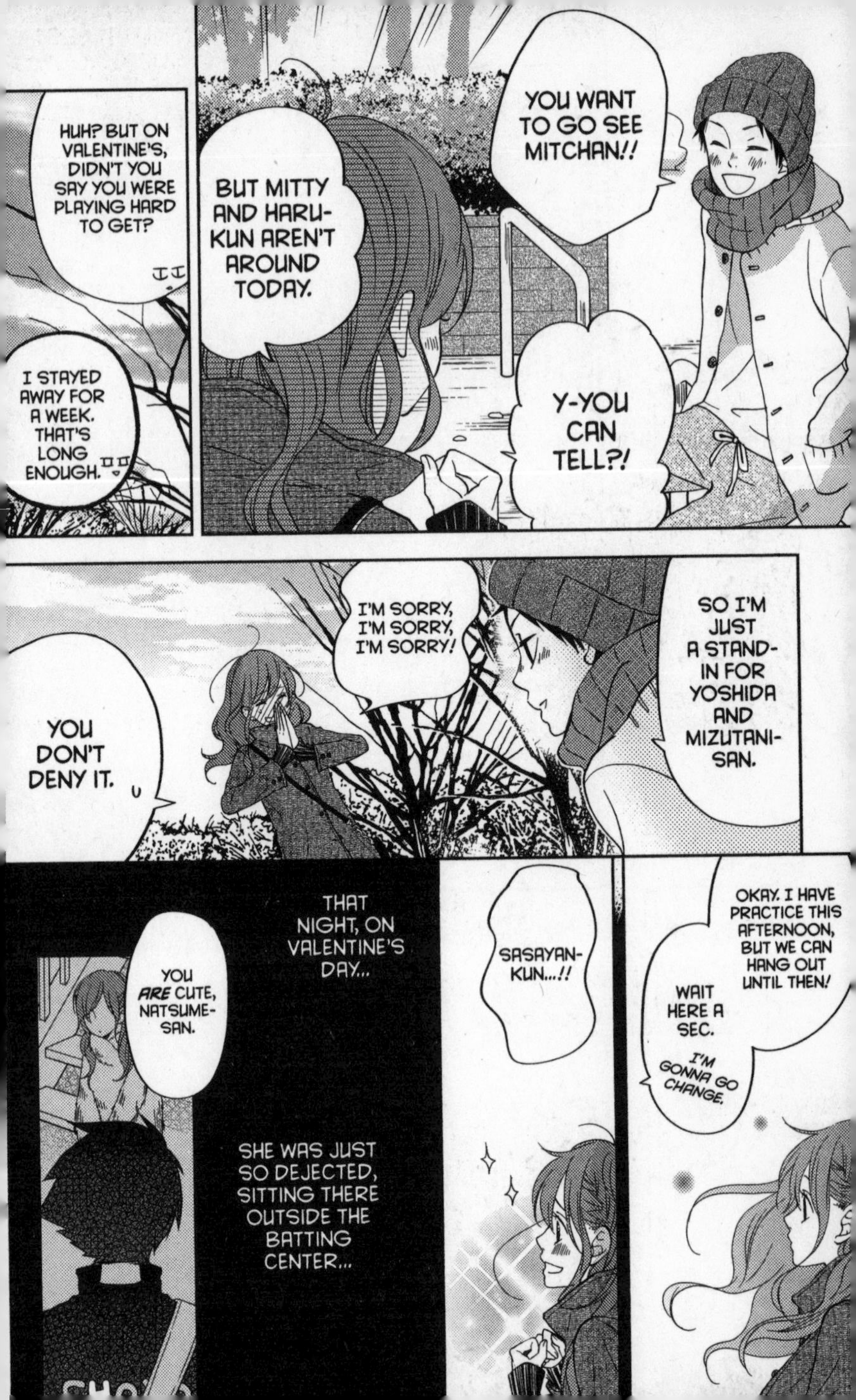
YOU WANT TO GO SEE MITCHAN!!
Y-YOU CAN TELL?!
BUT MITTY AND HARU-KUN AREN'T AROUND TODAY.
HUH? BUT ON VALENTINE'S, DIDN'T YOU SAY YOU WERE PLAYING HARD TO GET?
I STAYED AWAY FOR A WEEK. THAT'S LONG ENOUGH.
SO I'M JUST A STAND-IN FOR YOSHIDA AND MIZUTANI-SAN.
I'M SORRY, I'M SORRY, I'M SORRY!
YOU DON'T DENY IT.
OKAY. I HAVE PRACTICE THIS AFTERNOON, BUT WE CAN HANG OUT UNTIL THEN!
WAIT HERE A SEC.
I'M GONNA GO CHANGE.
SASAYAN-KUN...!!
THAT NIGHT, ON VALENTINE'S DAY...
YOU ARE CUTE, NATSUME-SAN.
SHE WAS JUST SO DEJECTED, SITTING THERE OUTSIDE THE BATTING CENTER...

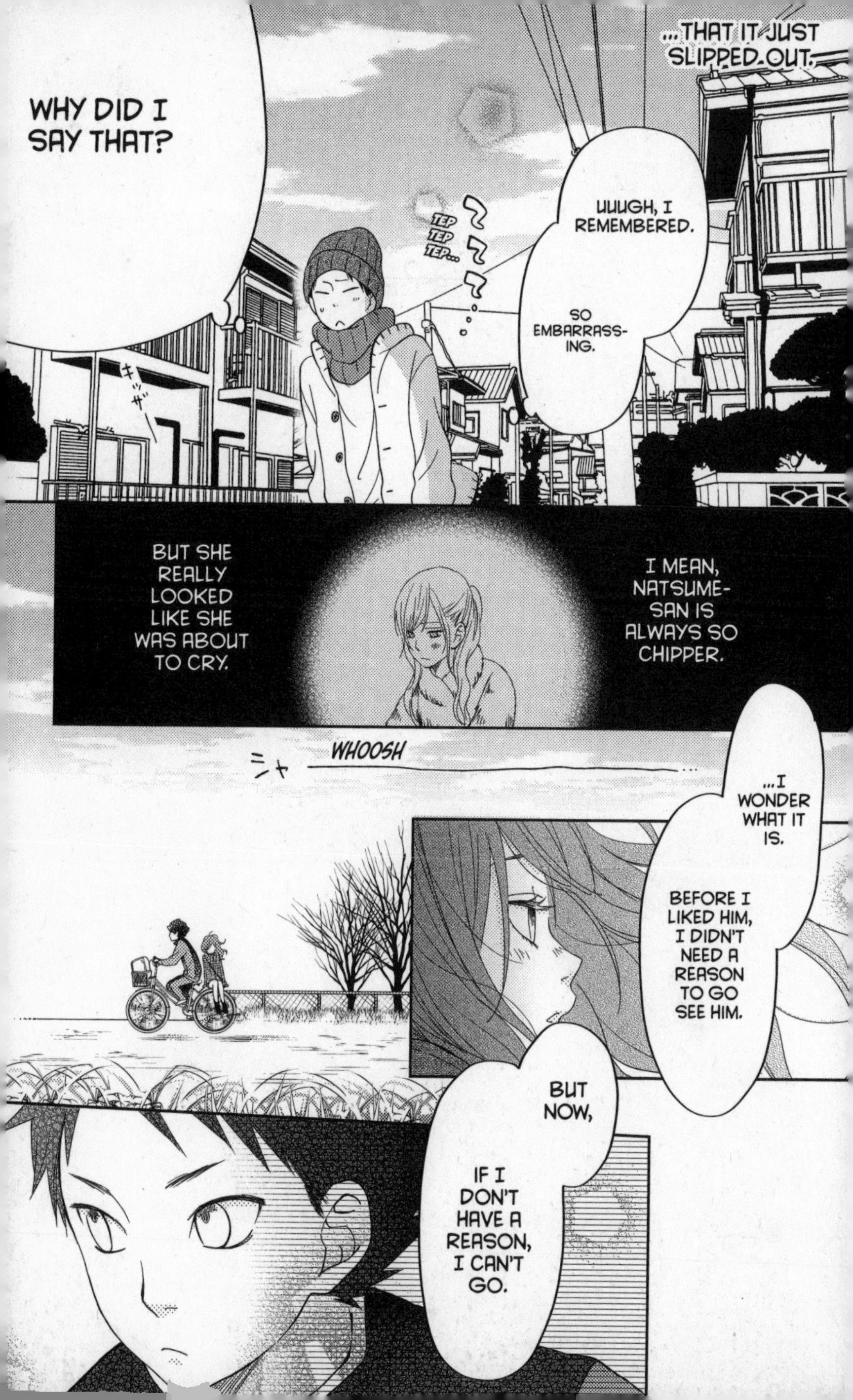

...THAT IT JUST SLIPPED OUT.
UUUGH, I REMEMBERED.
SO EMBARRASSING.
TEP TEP TEP...
WHY DID I SAY THAT?
I MEAN, NATSUME-SAN IS ALWAYS SO CHIPPER.
BUT SHE REALLY LOOKED LIKE SHE WAS ABOUT TO CRY.
WHOOSH
...I WONDER WHAT IT IS.
BEFORE I LIKED HIM, I DIDN'T NEED A REASON TO GO SEE HIM.
BUT NOW,
IF I DON'T HAVE A REASON, I CAN'T GO.

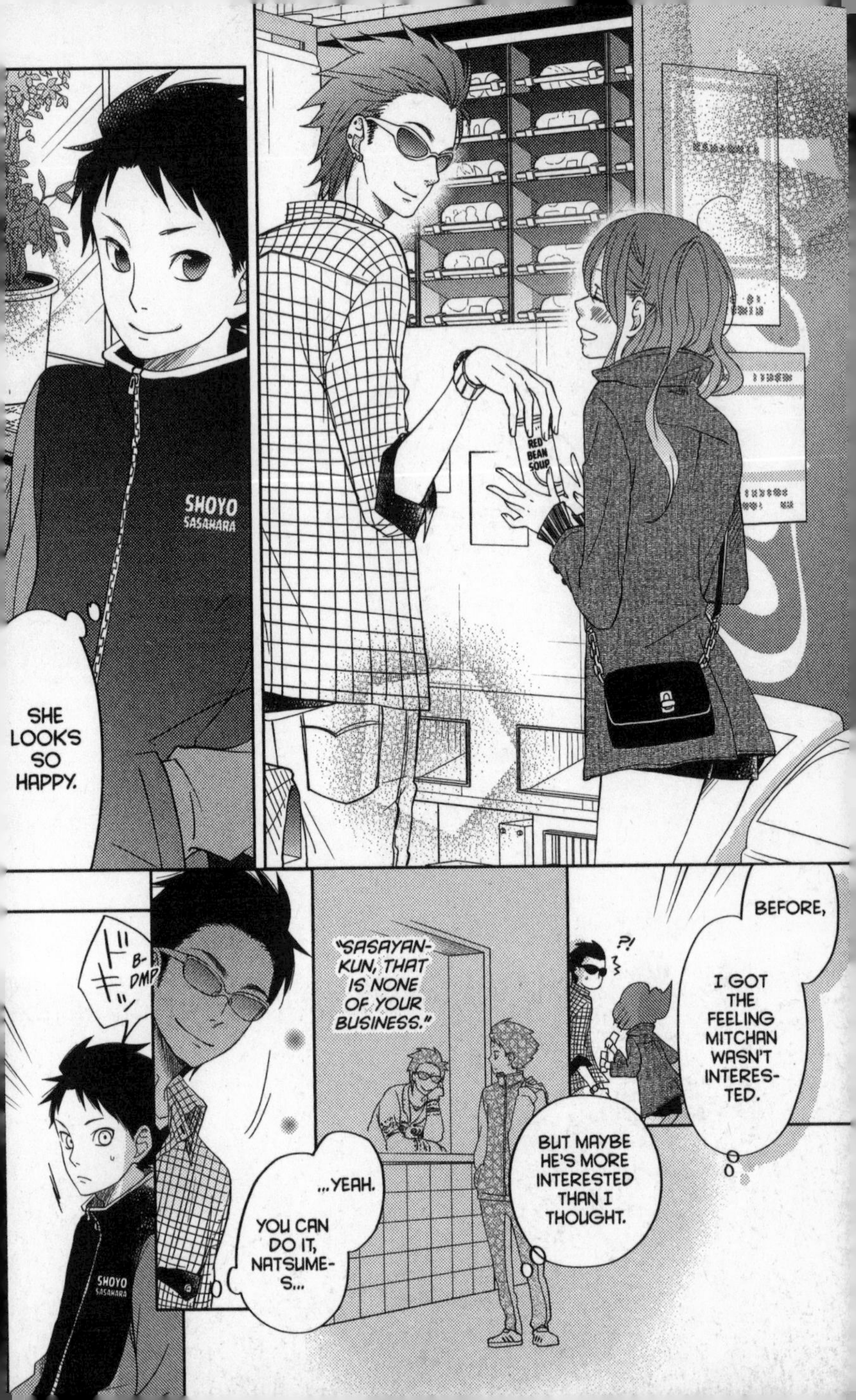
RED BEAN SOUP
SHOYO SASAHARA
SHE LOOKS SO HAPPY.
?!
BEFORE,
I GOT THE FEELING MITCHAN WASN'T INTERES-TED.
"SASAYAN-KUN, THAT IS NONE OF YOUR BUSINESS."
BUT MAYBE HE'S MORE INTERESTED THAN I THOUGHT.
ドキッ
B-DMP
...YEAH.
YOU CAN DO IT, NATSUME-S...
SHOYO SASAHARA

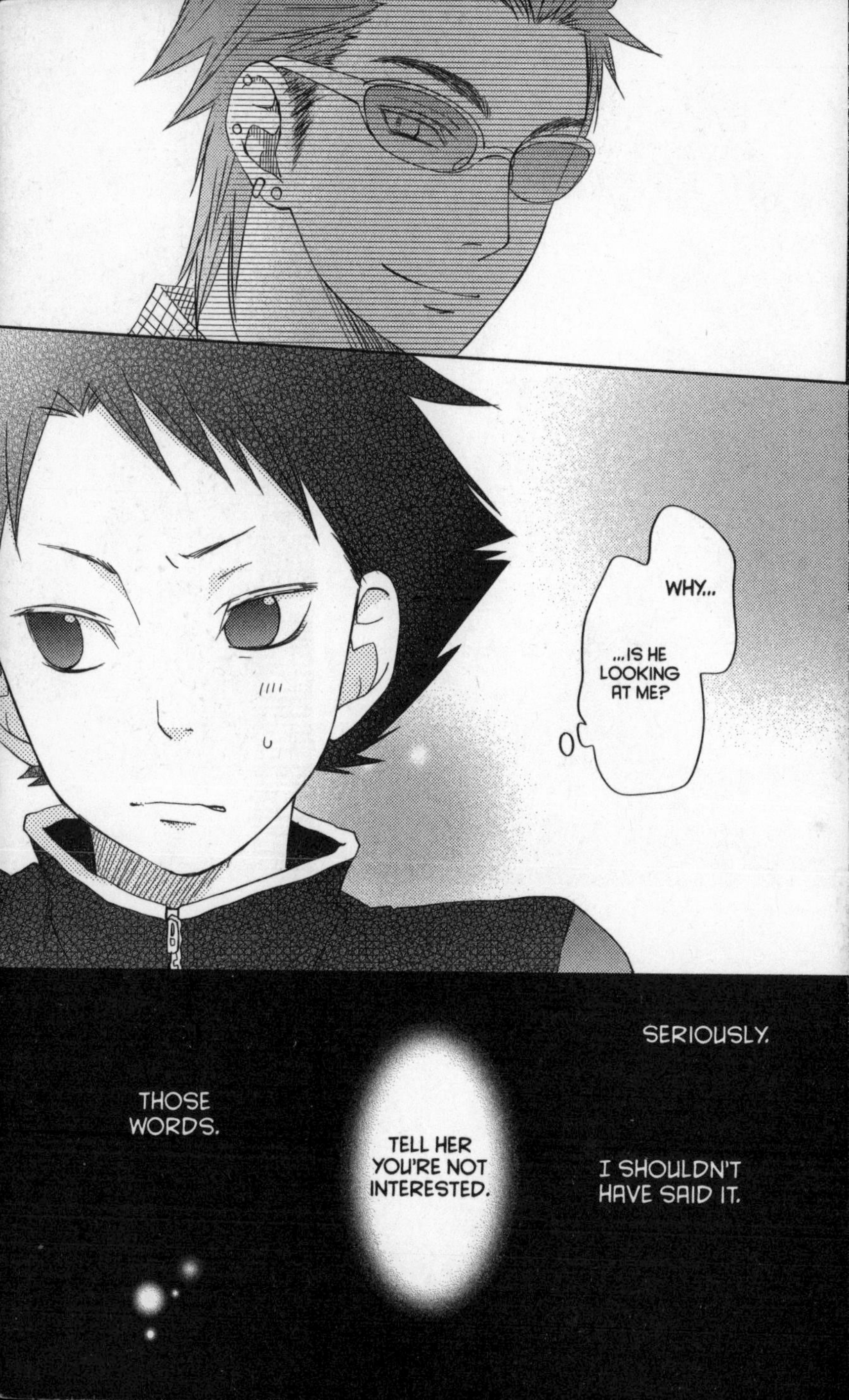
WHY...
...IS HE LOOKING AT ME?
SERIOUSLY.
I SHOULDN'T HAVE SAID IT.
TELL HER YOU'RE NOT INTERESTED.
THOSE WORDS.

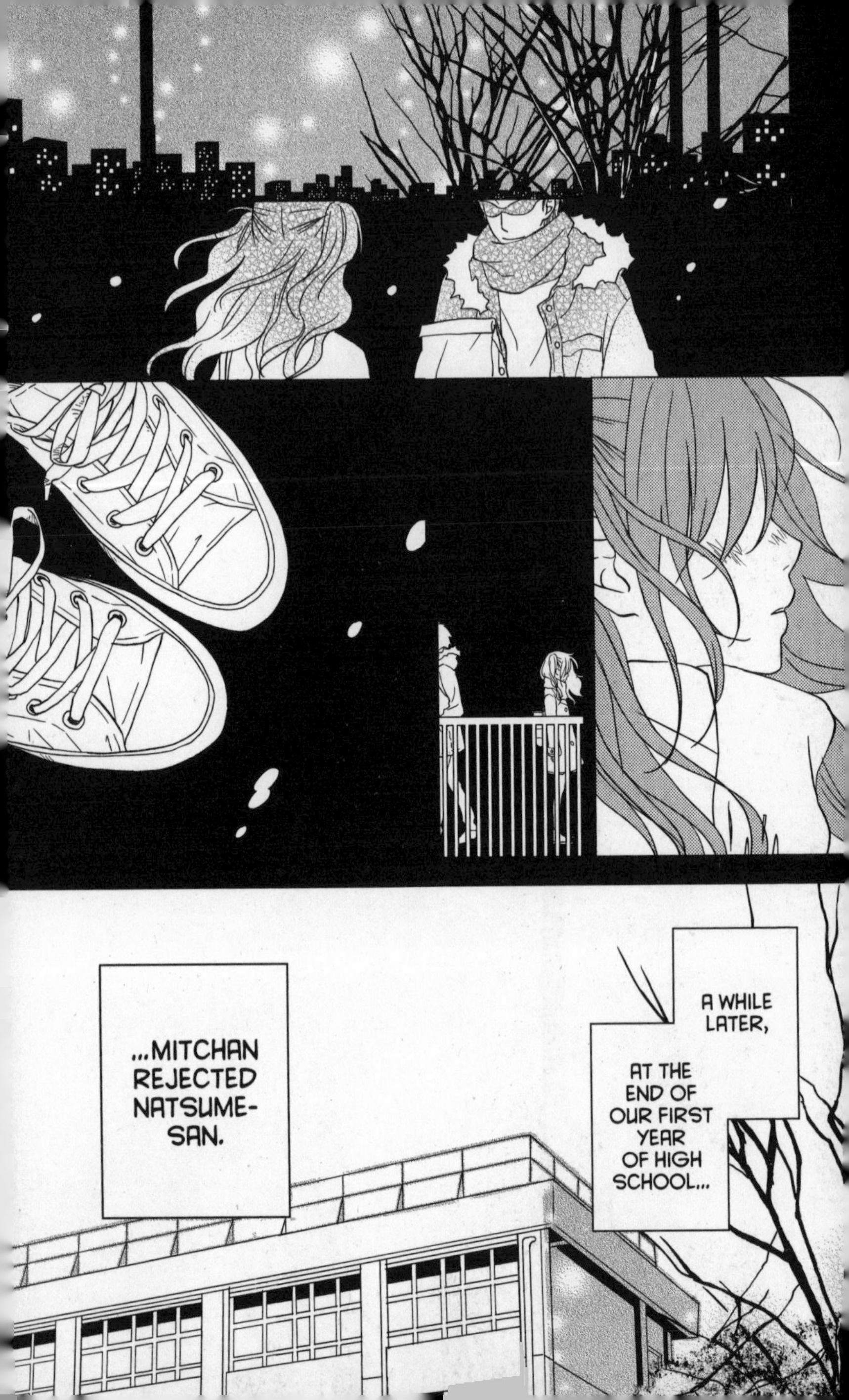
A WHILE LATER,
AT THE END OF OUR FIRST YEAR OF HIGH SCHOOL...
...MITCHAN REJECTED NATSUME-SAN.

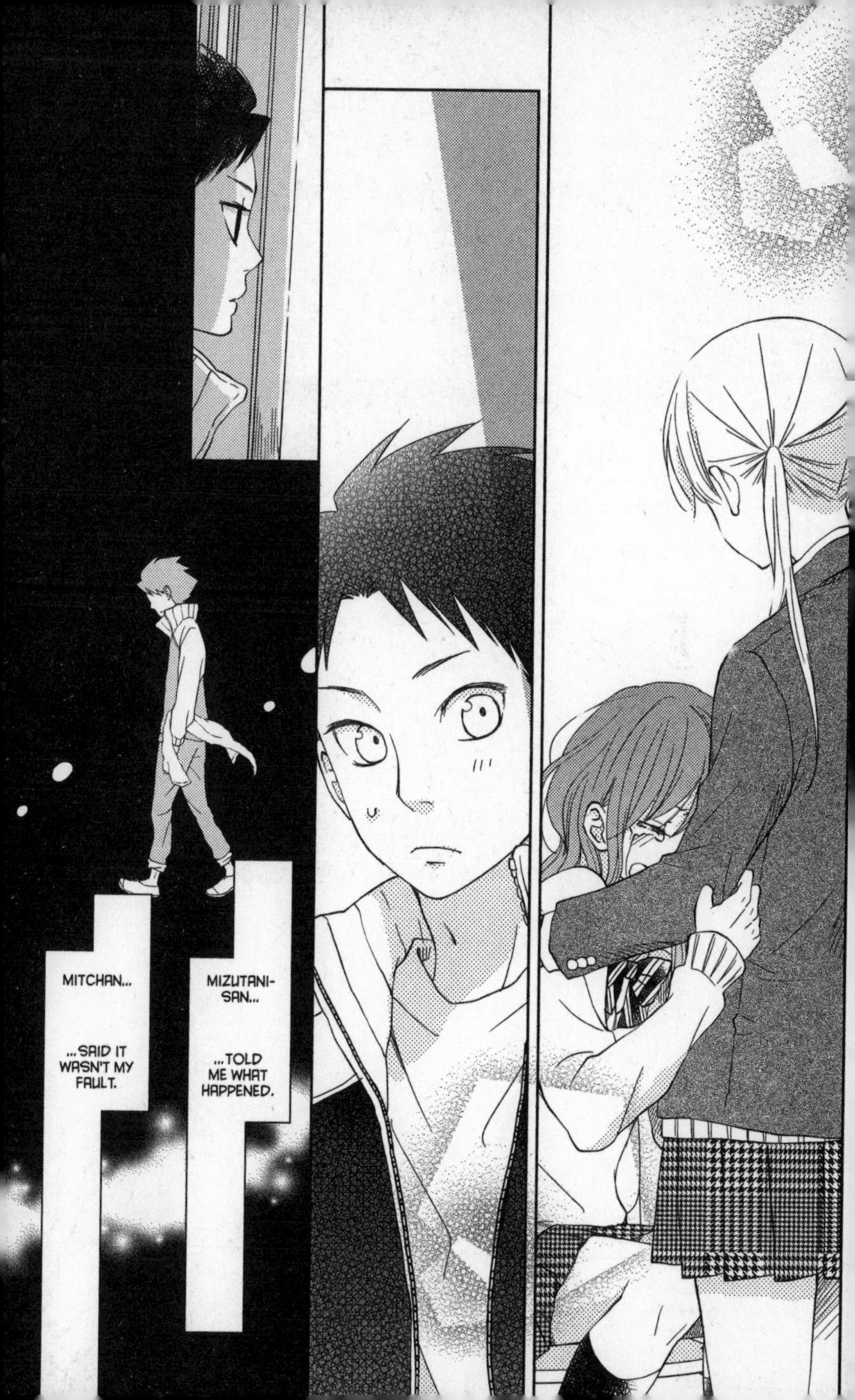
MIZUTANI-SAN...
...TOLD ME WHAT HAPPENED.
MITCHAN...
...SAID IT WASN'T MY FAULT.

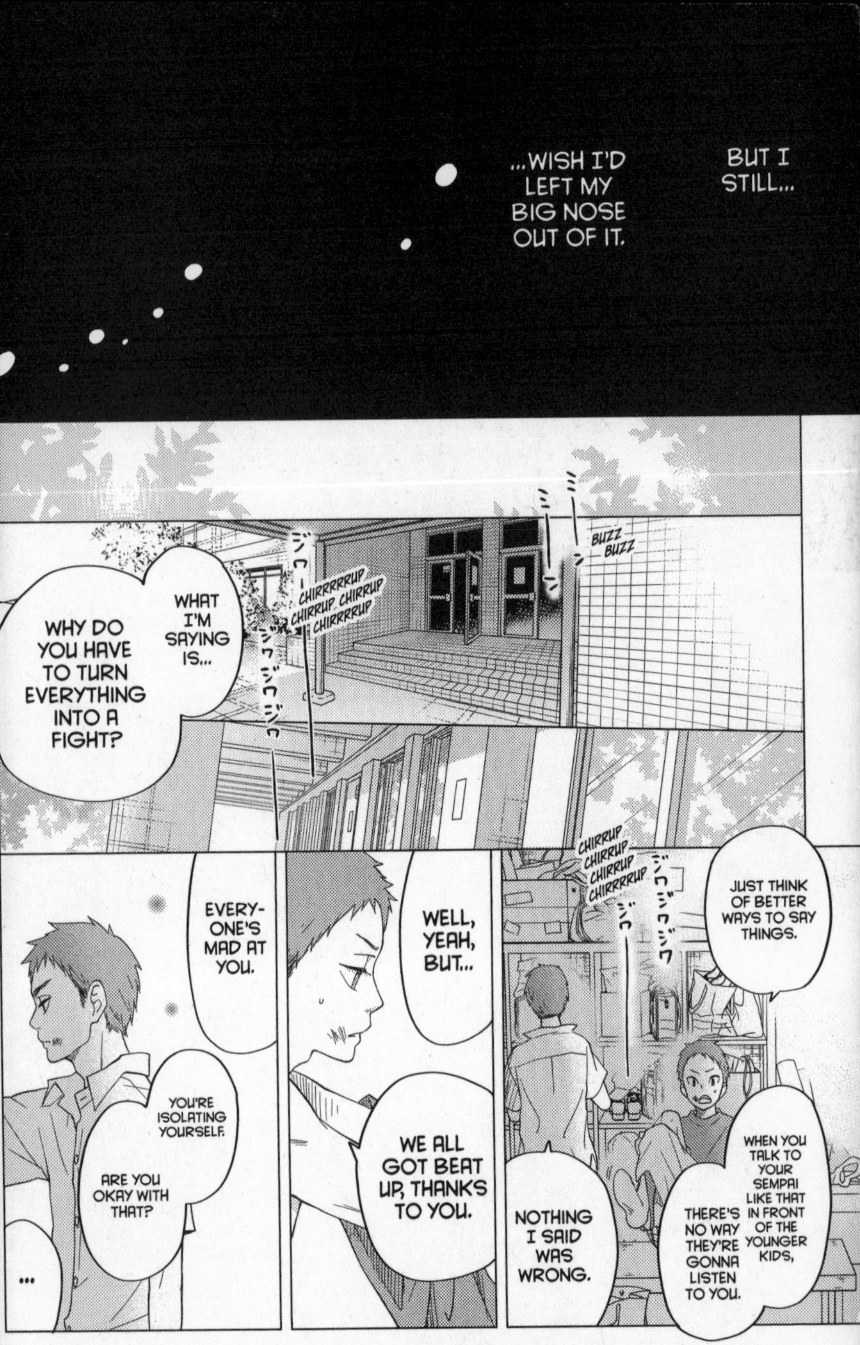
BUT I STILL...
...WISH I'D LEFT MY BIG NOSE OUT OF IT.
BUZZ BUZZ
CHIRRRRRUP CHIRRUP CHIRRUP CHIRRRRUP
WHAT I'M SAYING IS...
WHY DO YOU HAVE TO TURN EVERYTHING INTO A FIGHT?
JUST THINK OF BETTER WAYS TO SAY THINGS.
CHIRRUP CHIRRUP CHIRRUP CHIRRRRUP
WHEN YOU TALK TO YOUR SEMPAI LIKE THAT IN FRONT OF THE YOUNGER KIDS,
THERE'S NO WAY THEY'RE GONNA LISTEN TO YOU.
NOTHING I SAID WAS WRONG.
WELL, YEAH, BUT...
WE ALL GOT BEAT UP, THANKS TO YOU.
EVERY-ONE'S MAD AT YOU.
YOU'RE ISOLATING YOURSELF.
ARE YOU OKAY WITH THAT?
...

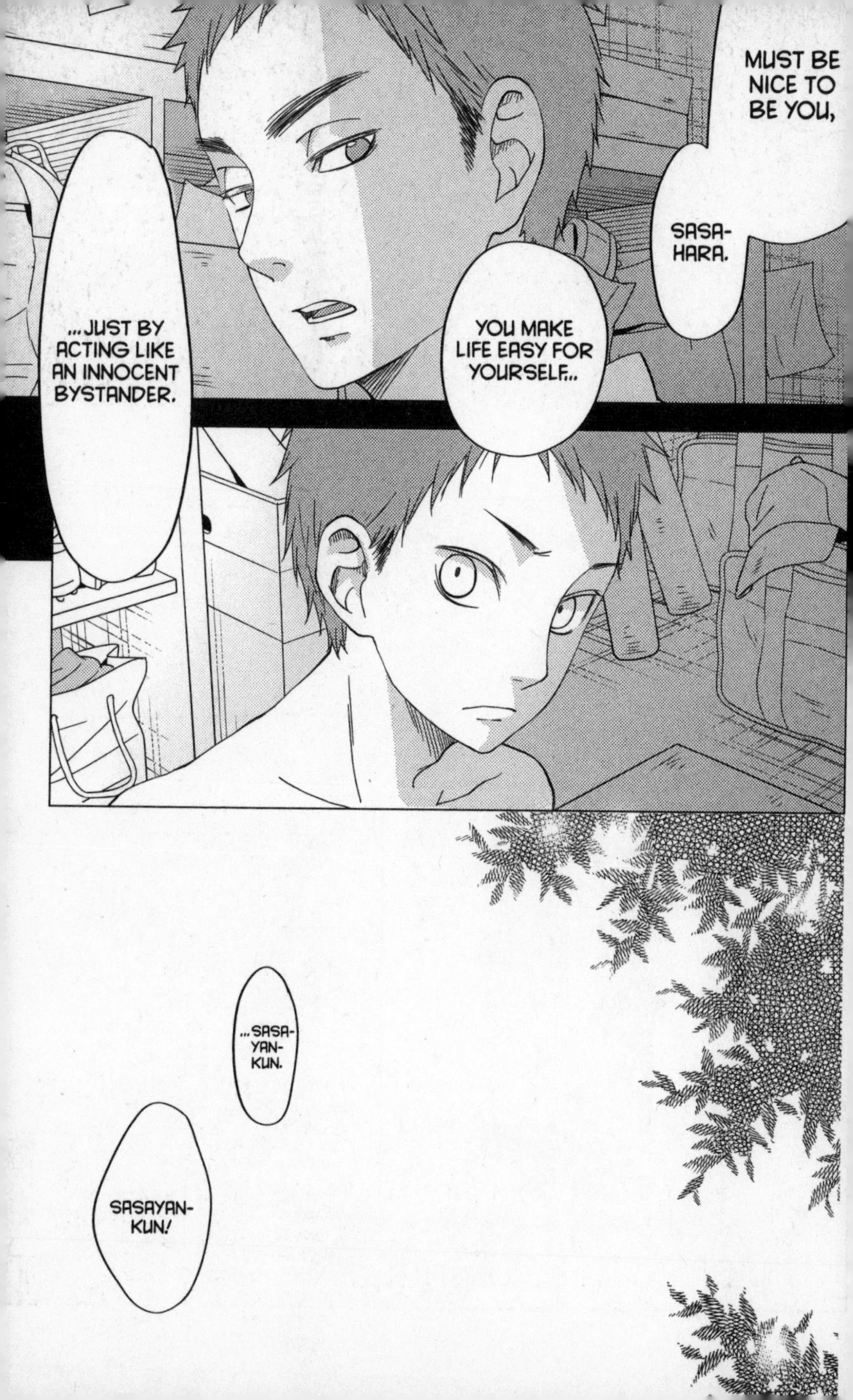
MUST BE NICE TO BE YOU,
SASA-HARA.
YOU MAKE LIFE EASY FOR YOURSELF...
...JUST BY ACTING LIKE AN INNOCENT BYSTANDER.
...SASA-YAN-KUN.
SASAYAN-KUN!

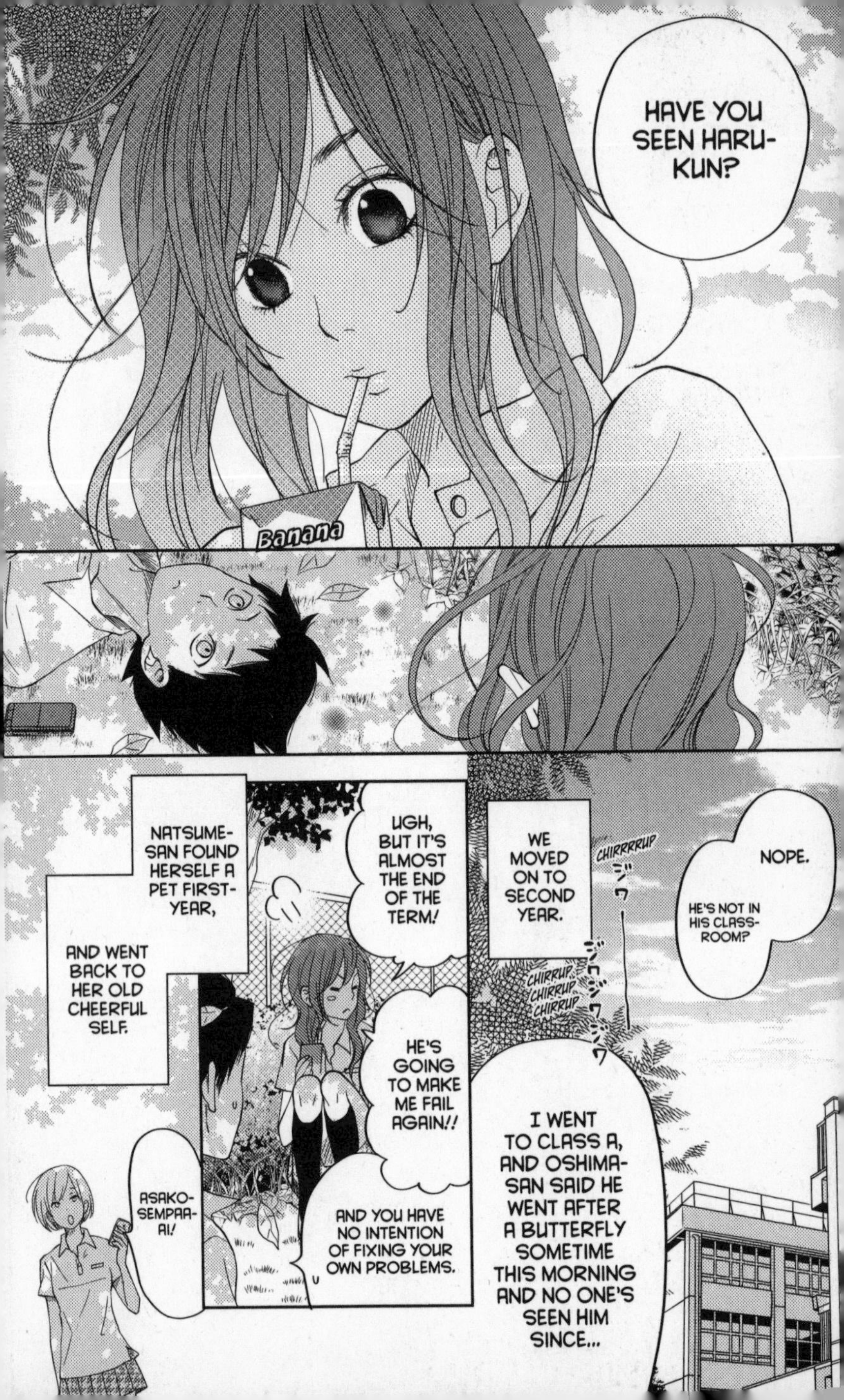
HAVE YOU SEEN HARU-KUN?
Banana
NOPE.
HE'S NOT IN HIS CLASSROOM?
WE MOVED ON TO SECOND YEAR.
CHIRRRRUP
ジワー
CHIRRUP CHIRRUP CHIRRUP
ジワジワジワ
I WENT TO CLASS A, AND OSHIMA-SAN SAID HE WENT AFTER A BUTTERFLY SOMETIME THIS MORNING AND NO ONE'S SEEN HIM SINCE...
UGH, BUT IT'S ALMOST THE END OF THE TERM!
NATSUME-SAN FOUND HERSELF A PET FIRST-YEAR,
HE'S GOING TO MAKE ME FAIL AGAIN!!
AND WENT BACK TO HER OLD CHEERFUL SELF.
AND YOU HAVE NO INTENTION OF FIXING YOUR OWN PROBLEMS.
ASAKO-SEMPAA-AI!

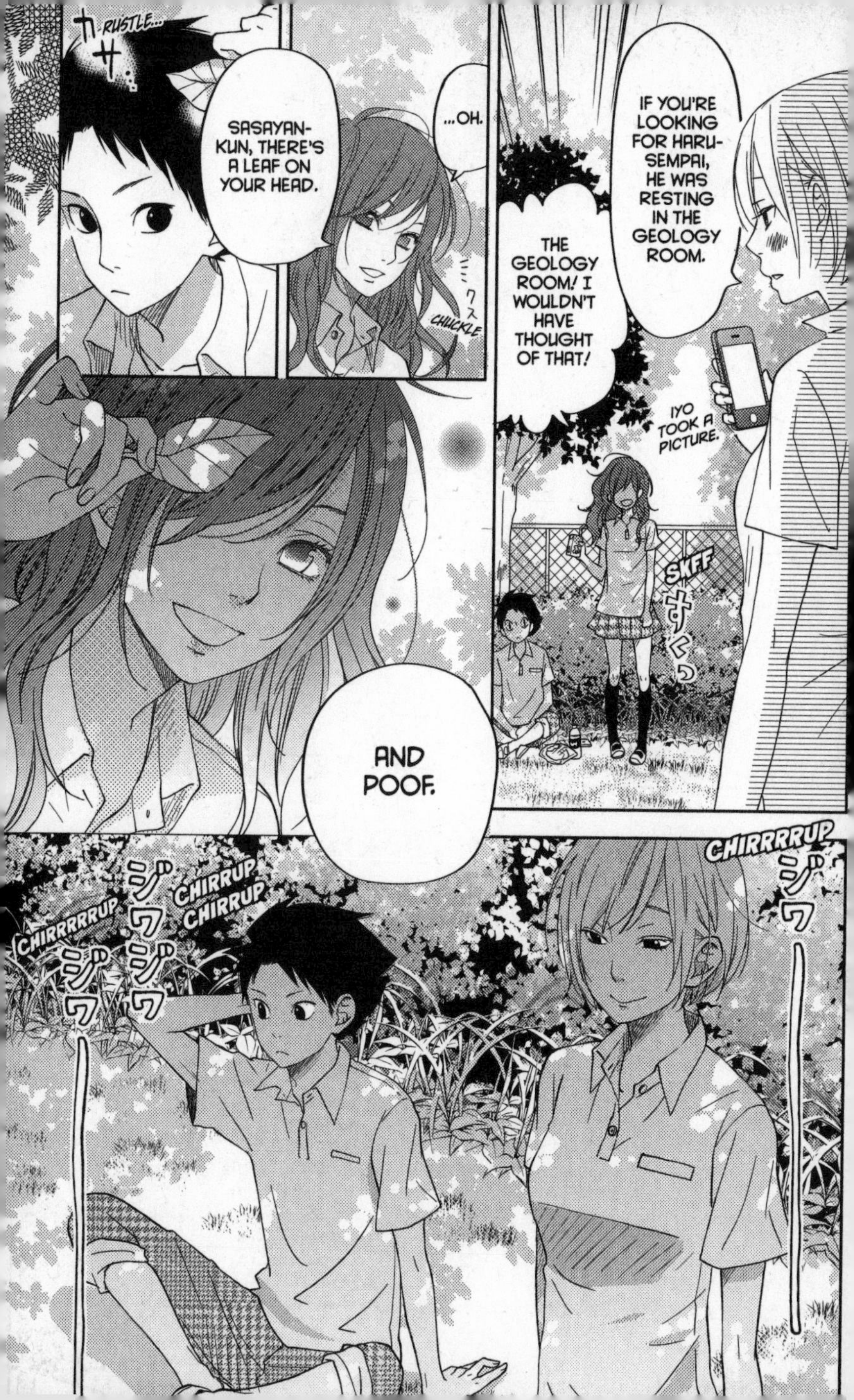
IF YOU'RE LOOKING FOR HARU-SEMPAI, HE WAS RESTING IN THE GEOLOGY ROOM.
THE GEOLOGY ROOM! I WOULDN'T HAVE THOUGHT OF THAT!
IYO TOOK A PICTURE.
SKFF
すくっ
...OH.
クス
CHUCKLE
カサ
RUSTLE...
SASAYAN-KUN, THERE'S A LEAF ON YOUR HEAD.
AND POOF.
CHIRRRRUP
ジワ
CHIRRUP CHIRRUP
ジワジワ
CHIRRRRRUP
ジワジワ

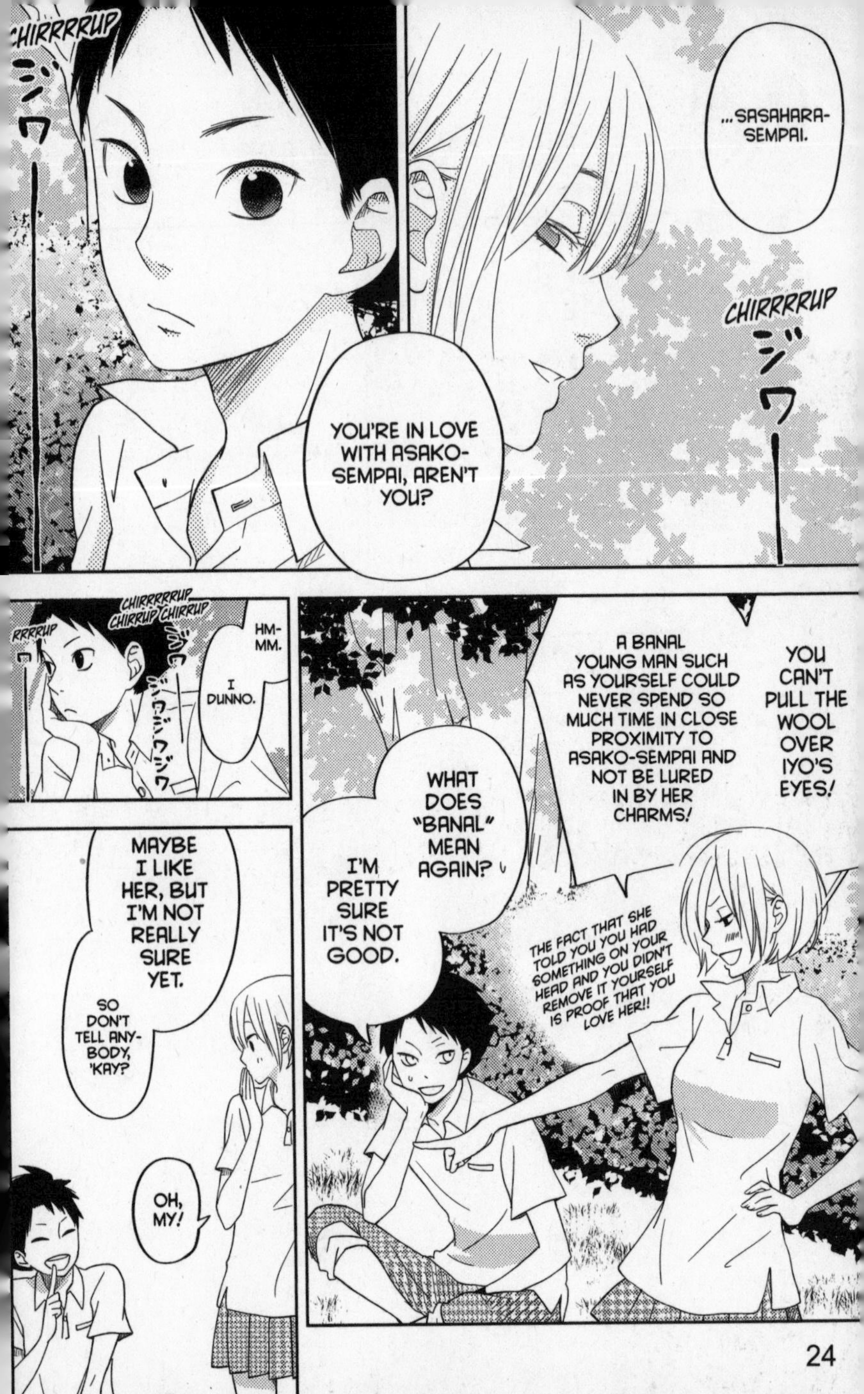
...SASAHARA-SEMPAI.
CHIRRRRUP
ジワー
YOU'RE IN LOVE WITH ASAKO-SEMPAI, AREN'T YOU?
CHIRRRRUP
ジワー
YOU CAN'T PULL THE WOOL OVER IYO'S EYES!
A BANAL YOUNG MAN SUCH AS YOURSELF COULD NEVER SPEND SO MUCH TIME IN CLOSE PROXIMITY TO ASAKO-SEMPAI AND NOT BE LURED IN BY HER CHARMS!
THE FACT THAT SHE TOLD YOU YOU HAD SOMETHING ON YOUR HEAD AND YOU DIDN'T REMOVE IT YOURSELF IS PROOF THAT YOU LOVE HER!!
WHAT DOES "BANAL" MEAN AGAIN?
I'M PRETTY SURE IT'S NOT GOOD.
CHIRRRRRUP CHIRRUP CHIRRUP
RRRRUP
HM-MM.
I DUNNO.
MAYBE I LIKE HER, BUT I'M NOT REALLY SURE YET.
SO DON'T TELL ANYBODY, 'KAY?
OH, MY!

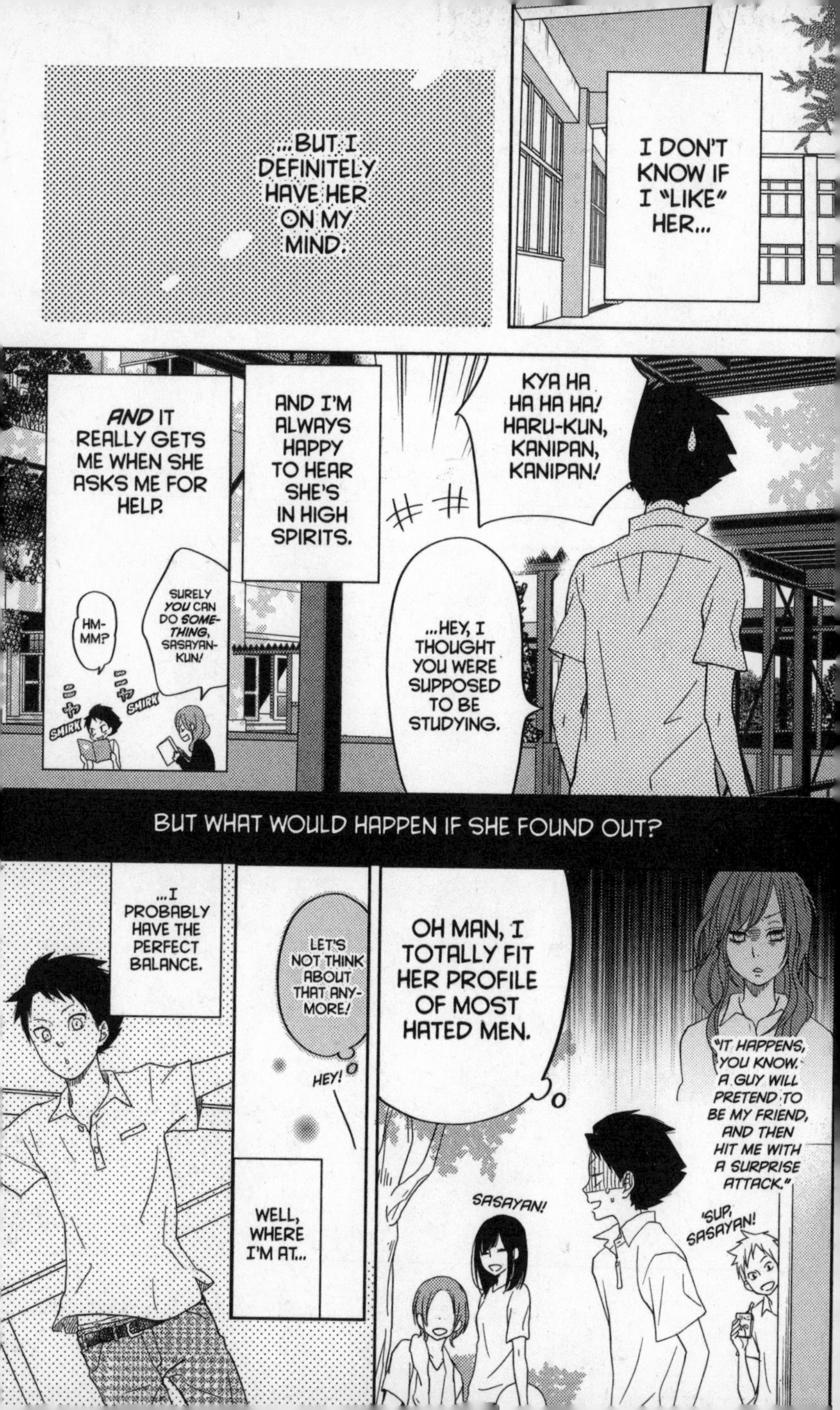
I DON'T KNOW IF I "LIKE" HER...
...BUT I DEFINITELY HAVE HER ON MY MIND.
KYA HA HA HA HA! HARU-KUN, KANIPAN, KANIPAN!
...HEY, I THOUGHT YOU WERE SUPPOSED TO BE STUDYING.
AND I'M ALWAYS HAPPY TO HEAR SHE'S IN HIGH SPIRITS.
AND IT REALLY GETS ME WHEN SHE ASKS ME FOR HELP.
SURELY YOU CAN DO SOMETHING, SASAYAN-KUN!
HM-MM?
SMIRK
SMIRK
BUT WHAT WOULD HAPPEN IF SHE FOUND OUT?
OH MAN, I TOTALLY FIT HER PROFILE OF MOST HATED MEN.
"IT HAPPENS, YOU KNOW. A GUY WILL PRETEND TO BE MY FRIEND, AND THEN HIT ME WITH A SURPRISE ATTACK."
'SUP, SASAYAN!
SASAYAN!
LET'S NOT THINK ABOUT THAT ANY-MORE!
HEY!
WELL, WHERE I'M AT...
...I PROBABLY HAVE THE PERFECT BALANCE.

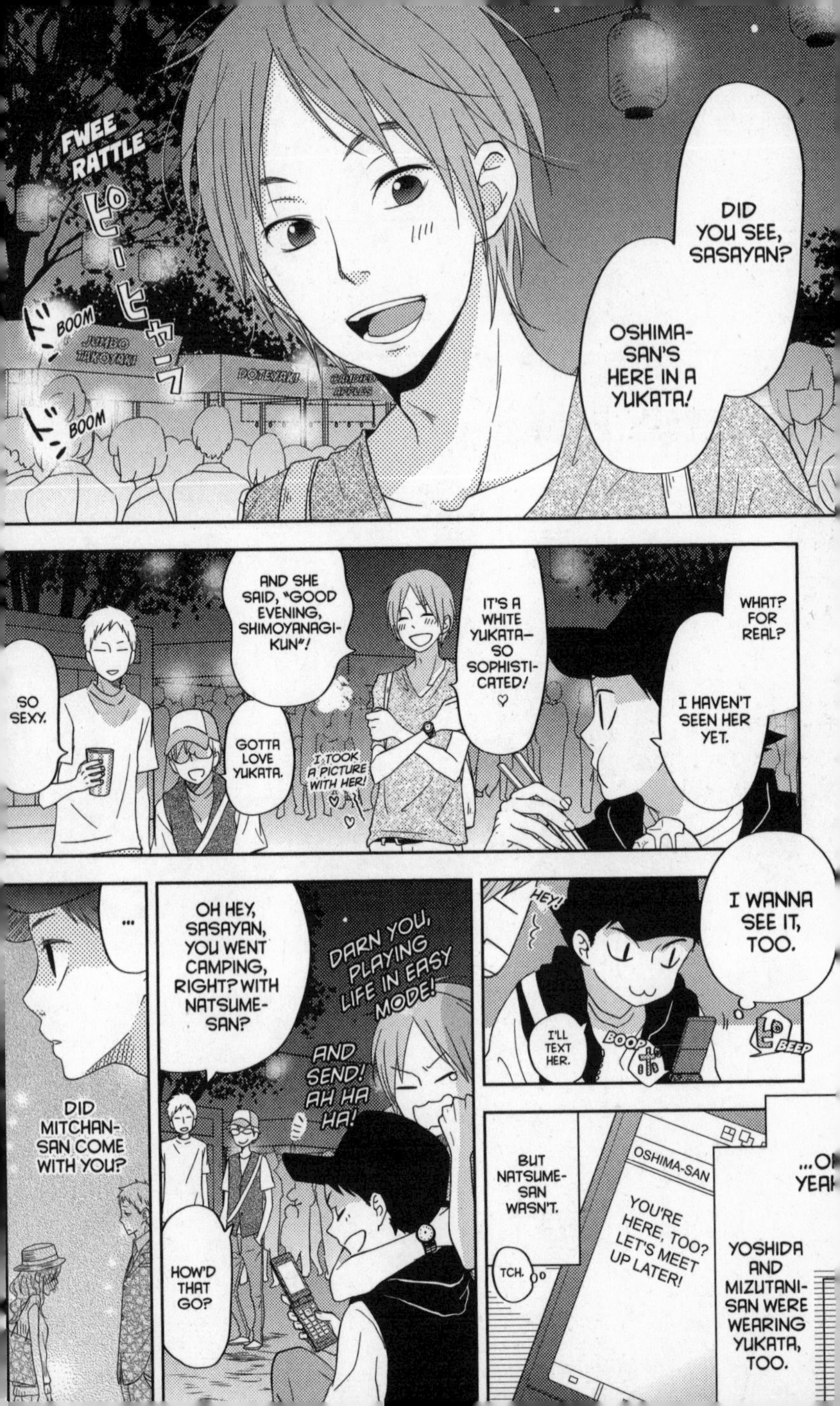
FWEE RATTLE
ピーヒャラ
BOOM
BOOM
JUMBO TAKOYAKI
DOTEYAKI
CANDIED APPLES
DID YOU SEE, SASAYAN?
OSHIMA-SAN'S HERE IN A YUKATA!
WHAT? FOR REAL?
I HAVEN'T SEEN HER YET.
IT'S A WHITE YUKATA—SO SOPHISTICATED! ♡
AND SHE SAID, "GOOD EVENING, SHIMOYANAGI-KUN"!
I TOOK A PICTURE WITH HER! ♡
GOTTA LOVE YUKATA.
SO SEXY.
I WANNA SEE IT, TOO.
HEY!
I'LL TEXT HER.
BOOP
BEEP
...O
YEA
YOSHIDA AND MIZUTANI-SAN WERE WEARING YUKATA, TOO.
OSHIMA-SAN
YOU'RE HERE, TOO? LET'S MEET UP LATER!
BUT NATSUME-SAN WASN'T.
TCH.
OH HEY, SASAYAN, YOU WENT CAMPING, RIGHT? WITH NATSUME-SAN?
DARN YOU, PLAYING LIFE IN EASY MODE!
AND SEND! AH HA HA!
HOW'D THAT GO?
...
DID MITCHAN-SAN COME WITH YOU?

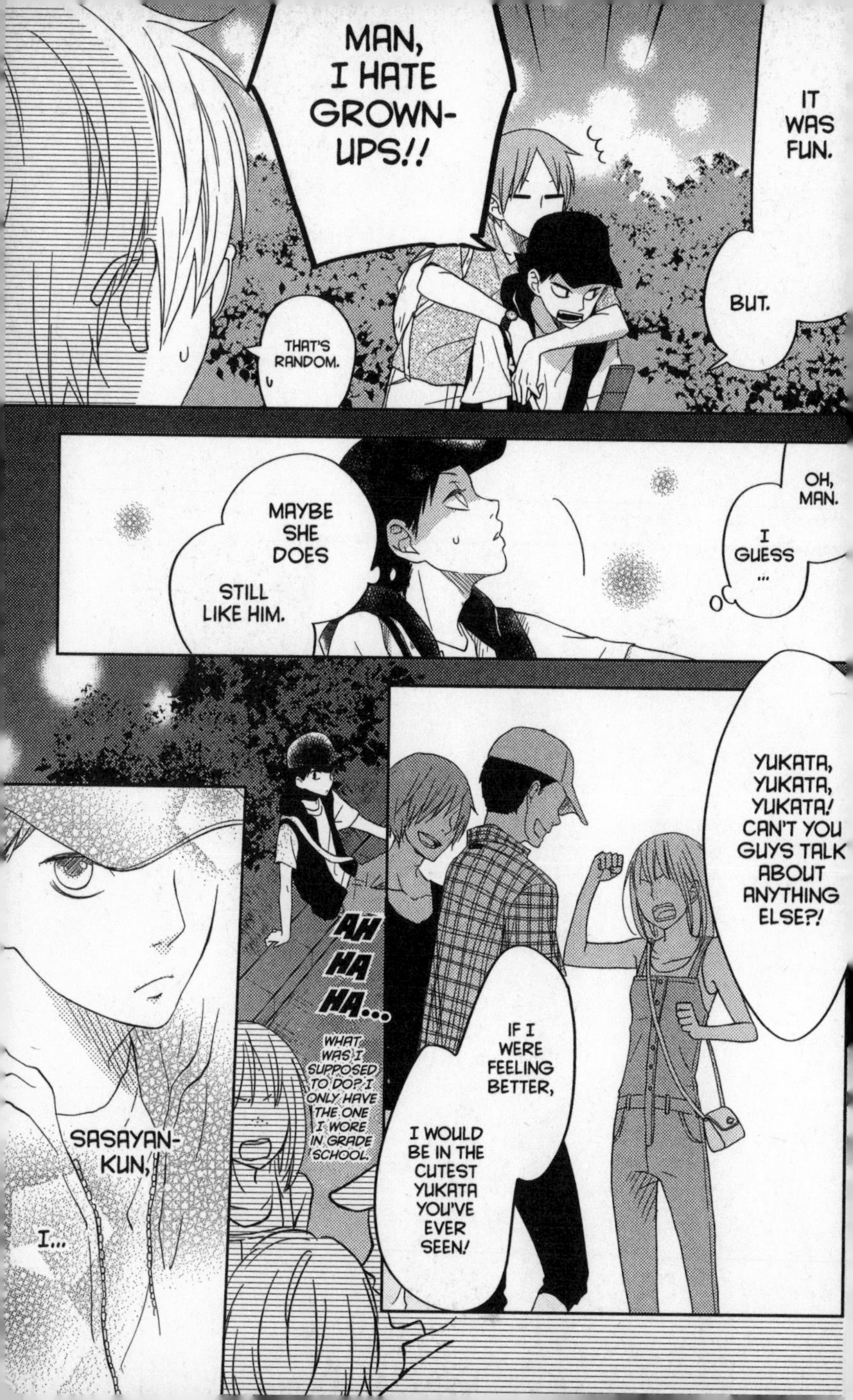
IT WAS FUN.
BUT.
MAN, I HATE GROWN-UPS!!
THAT'S RANDOM.
OH, MAN. I GUESS ...
MAYBE SHE DOES STILL LIKE HIM.
YUKATA, YUKATA, YUKATA! CAN'T YOU GUYS TALK ABOUT ANYTHING ELSE?!
IF I WERE FEELING BETTER,
I WOULD BE IN THE CUTEST YUKATA YOU'VE EVER SEEN!
AH HA HA...
WHAT WAS I SUPPOSED TO DO? I ONLY HAVE THE ONE I WORE IN GRADE SCHOOL.
SASAYAN-KUN,
I...

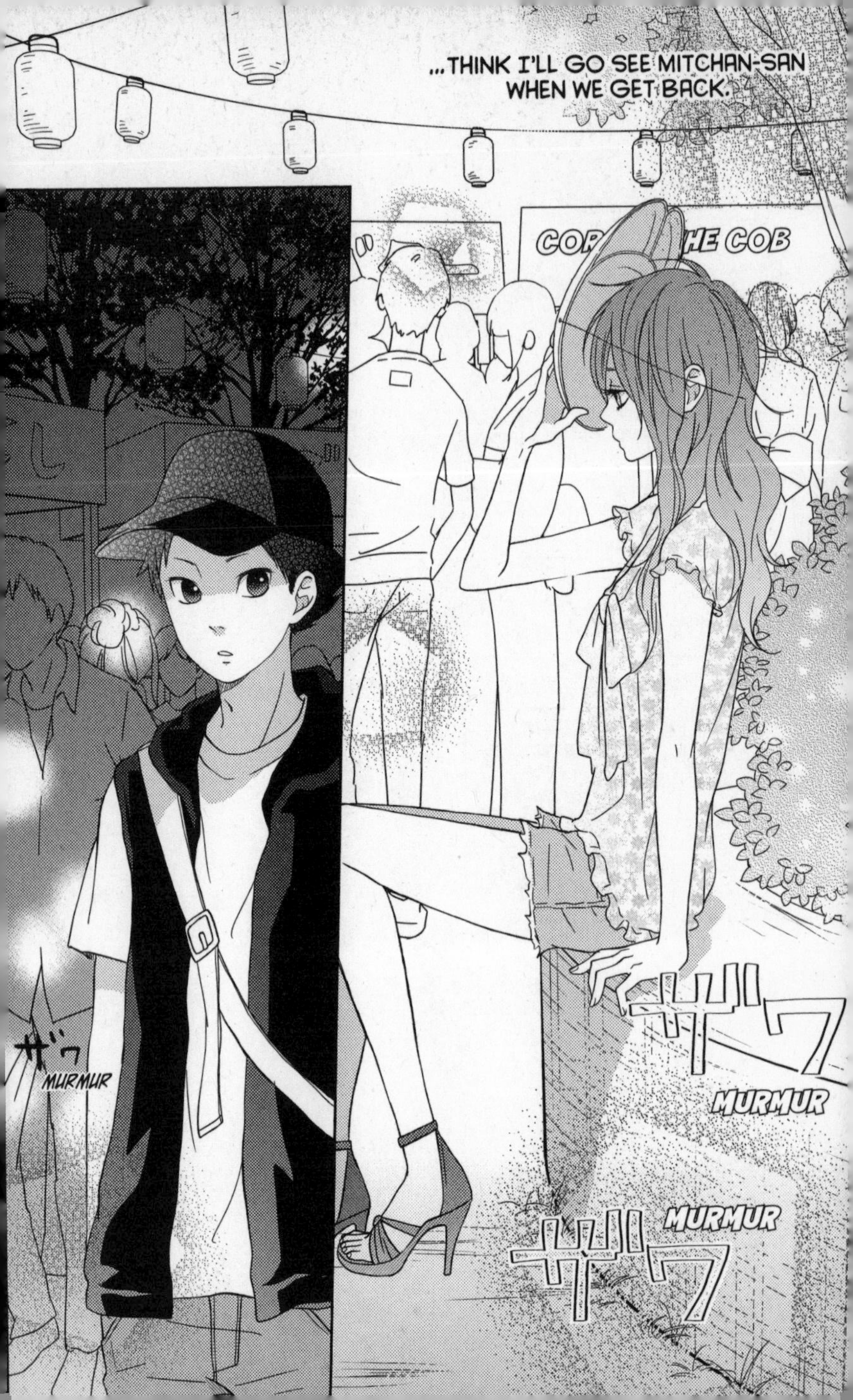
...THINK I'LL GO SEE MITCHAN-SAN WHEN WE GET BACK.
COR
HE COB
ザワ
MURMUR
MURMUR
ザワ
ザワ
MURMUR

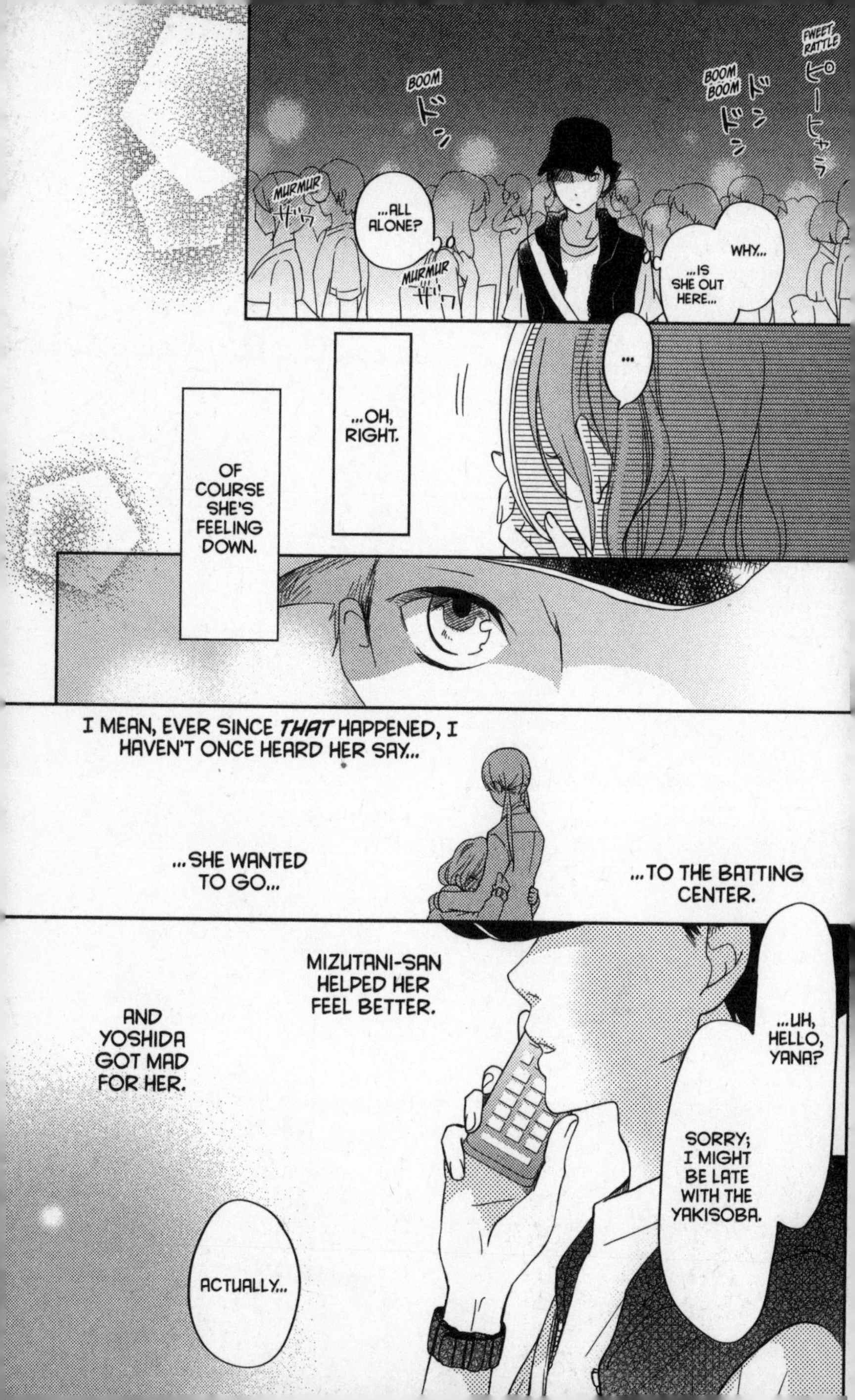
FWEET RATTLE
ピーヒャラ
BOOM BOOM
ドン ドン
WHY...
...IS SHE OUT HERE...
BOOM
ドン
...ALL ALONE?
MURMUR
ザワ
MURMUR
ザワ
...
...OH, RIGHT.
OF COURSE SHE'S FEELING DOWN.
I MEAN, EVER SINCE *THAT* HAPPENED, I HAVEN'T ONCE HEARD HER SAY...
...SHE WANTED TO GO...
...TO THE BATTING CENTER.
...UH, HELLO, YANA?
SORRY; I MIGHT BE LATE WITH THE YAKISOBA.
MIZUTANI-SAN HELPED HER FEEL BETTER.
AND YOSHIDA GOT MAD FOR HER.
ACTUALLY...

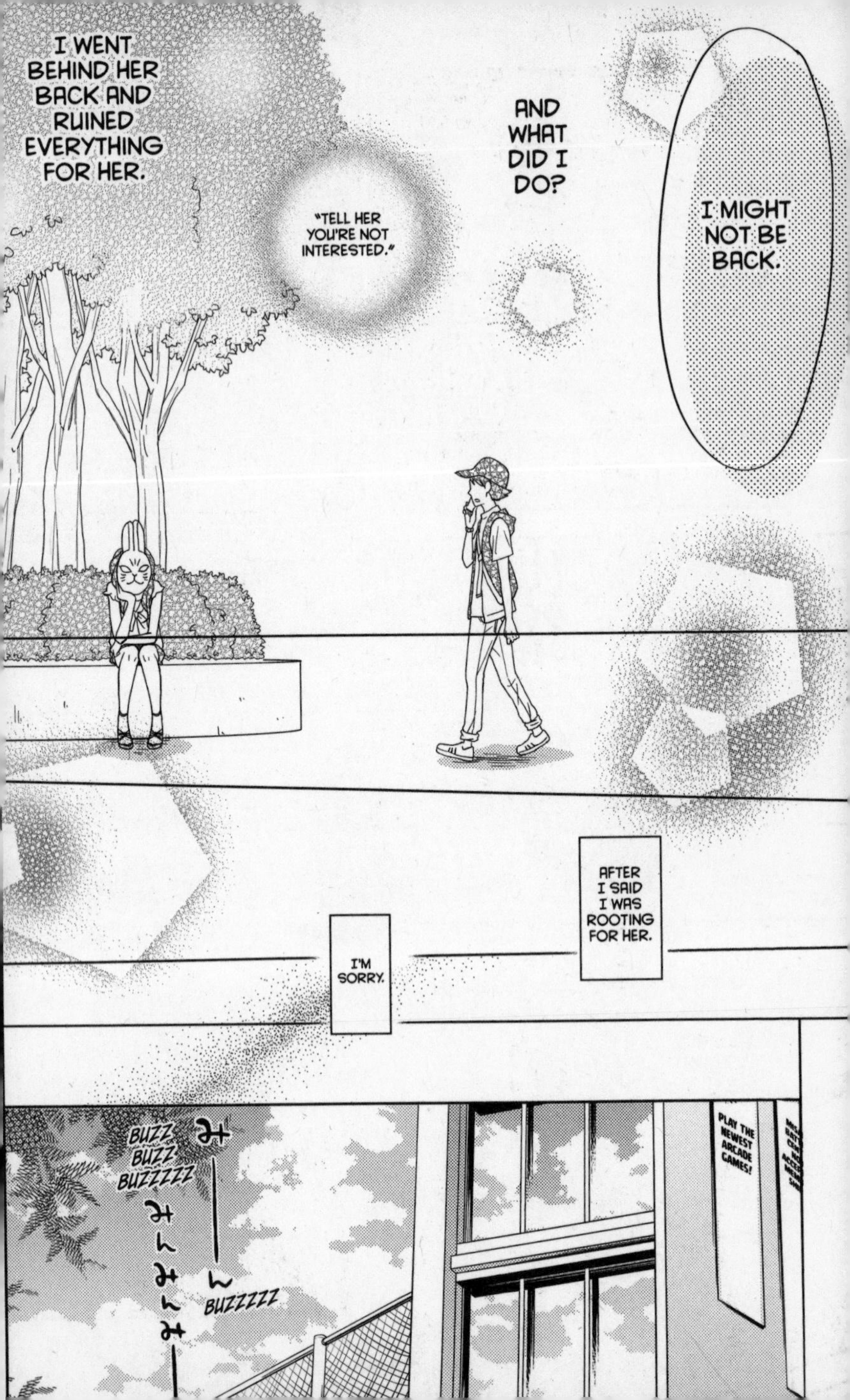
I MIGHT NOT BE BACK.
AND WHAT DID I DO?
"TELL HER YOU'RE NOT INTERESTED."
I WENT BEHIND HER BACK AND RUINED EVERYTHING FOR HER.
AFTER I SAID I WAS ROOTING FOR HER.
I'M SORRY.
PLAY THE NEWEST ARCADE GAMES!
みーーん
BUZZ BUZZ BUZZZZZ
みんみんみー
BUZZZZZ

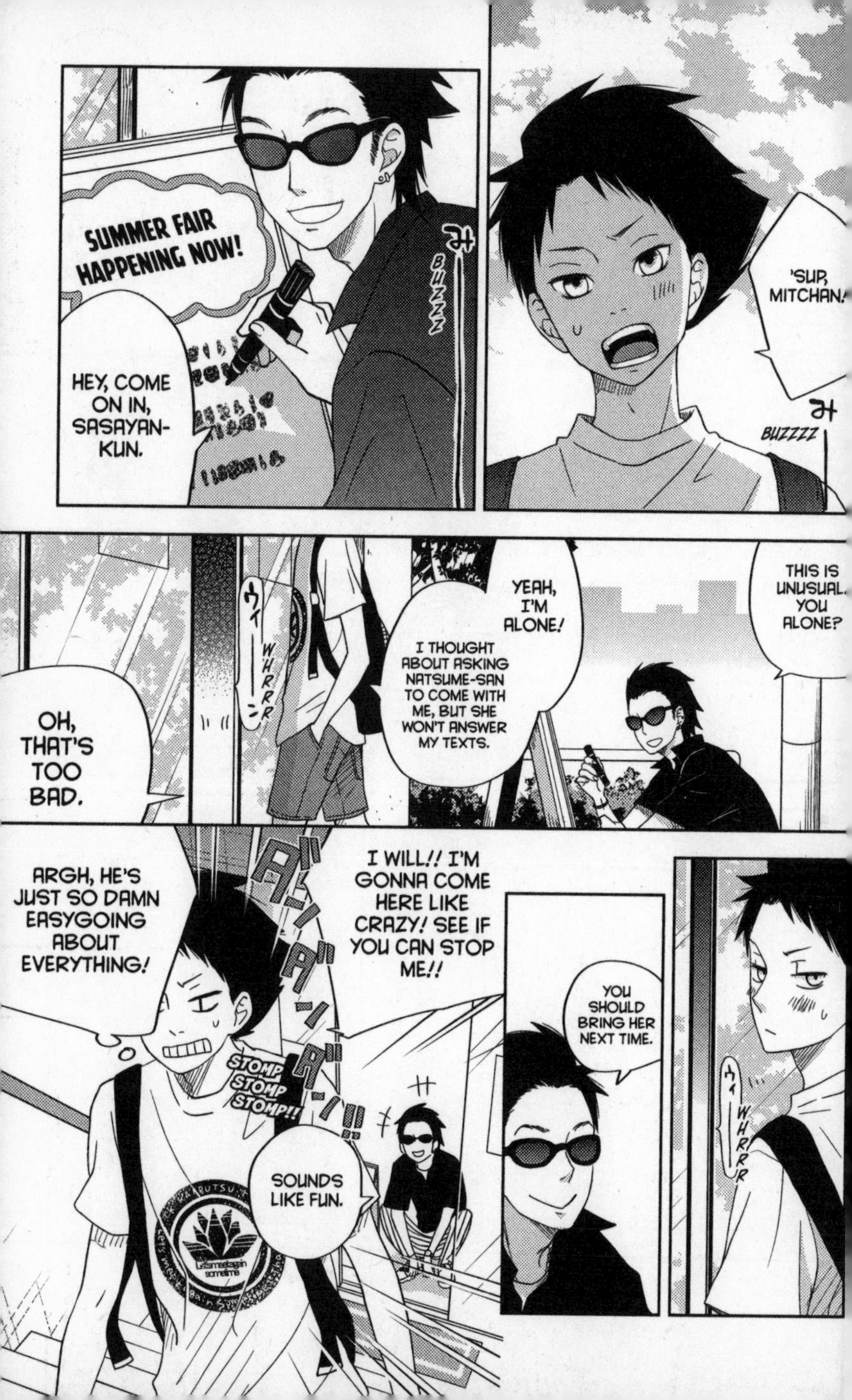
'SUP, MITCHAN!
み
BUZZZZ
SUMMER FAIR HAPPENING NOW!
み
BUZZZZ
HEY, COME ON IN, SASAYAN-KUN.
THIS IS UNUSUAL. YOU ALONE?
YEAH, I'M ALONE!
I THOUGHT ABOUT ASKING NATSUME-SAN TO COME WITH ME, BUT SHE WON'T ANSWER MY TEXTS.
ウィーン
WHRRR
OH, THAT'S TOO BAD.
ウィーン
WHRRR
YOU SHOULD BRING HER NEXT TIME.
I WILL!! I'M GONNA COME HERE LIKE CRAZY! SEE IF YOU CAN STOP ME!!
ARGH, HE'S JUST SO DAMN EASYGOING ABOUT EVERYTHING!
STOMP STOMP STOMP!!
SOUNDS LIKE FUN.

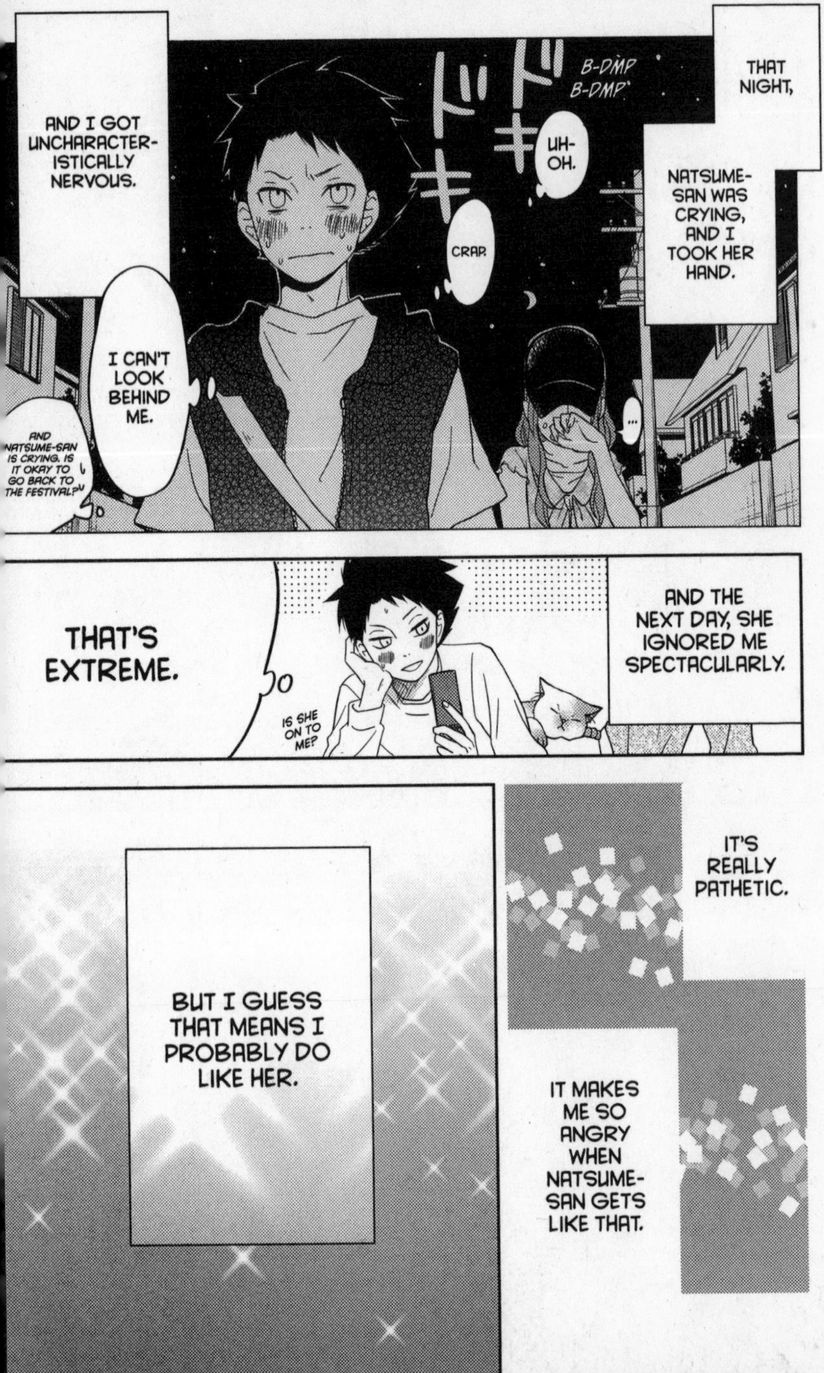
THAT NIGHT,
NATSUME-SAN WAS CRYING, AND I TOOK HER HAND.
ドキドキ
B-DMP B-DMP
UH-OH.
CRAP.
...
AND I GOT UNCHARACTERISTICALLY NERVOUS.
I CAN'T LOOK BEHIND ME.
AND NATSUME-SAN IS CRYING. IS IT OKAY TO GO BACK TO THE FESTIVAL?
AND THE NEXT DAY, SHE IGNORED ME SPECTACULARLY.
IS SHE ON TO ME?
THAT'S EXTREME.
IT'S REALLY PATHETIC.
IT MAKES ME SO ANGRY WHEN NATSUME-SAN GETS LIKE THAT.
BUT I GUESS THAT MEANS I PROBABLY DO LIKE HER.

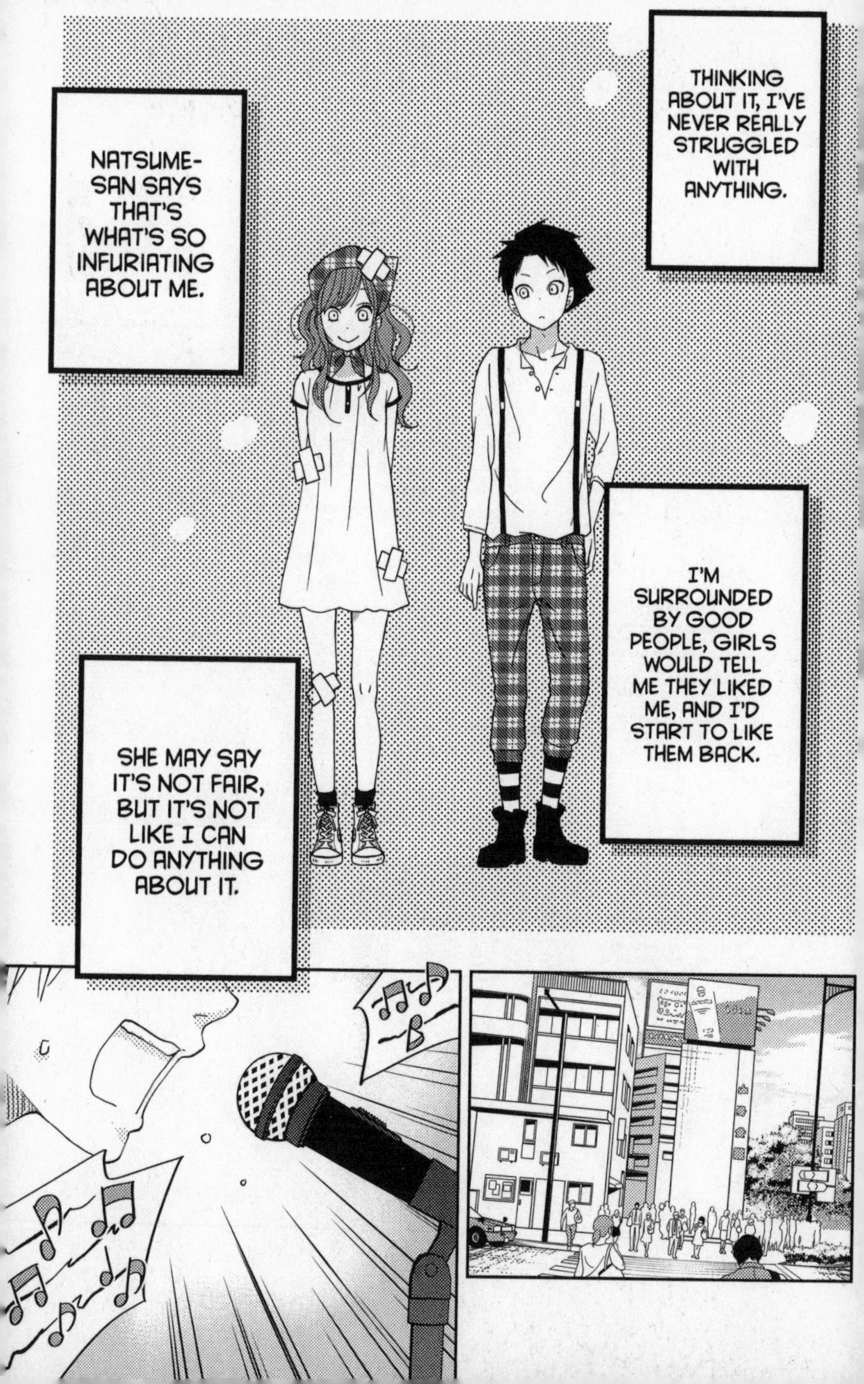
THINKING ABOUT IT, I'VE NEVER REALLY STRUGGLED WITH ANYTHING.
I'M SURROUNDED BY GOOD PEOPLE, GIRLS WOULD TELL ME THEY LIKED ME, AND I'D START TO LIKE THEM BACK.
NATSUME-SAN SAYS THAT'S WHAT'S SO INFURIATING ABOUT ME.
SHE MAY SAY IT'S NOT FAIR, BUT IT'S NOT LIKE I CAN DO ANYTHING ABOUT IT.

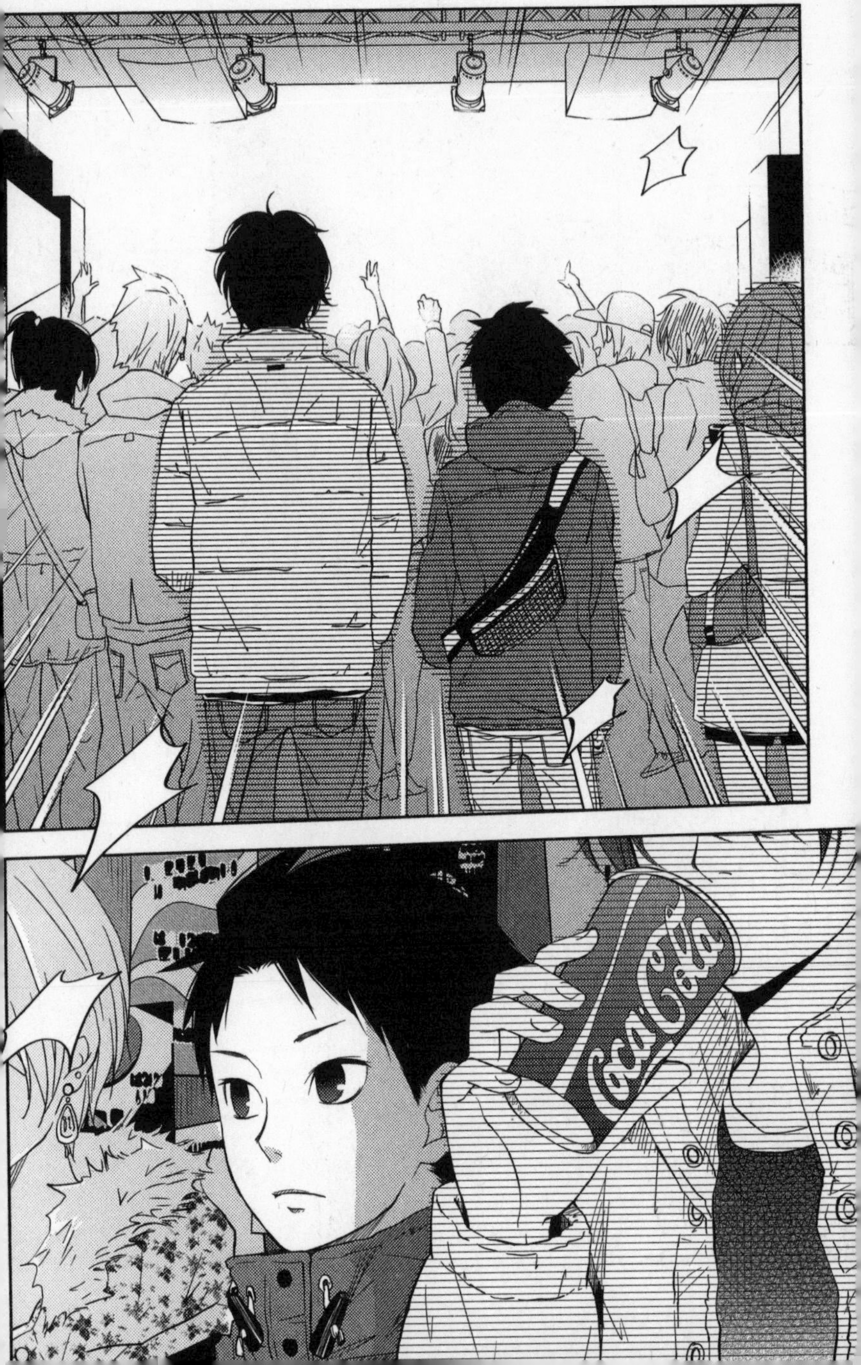
Coca-Cola

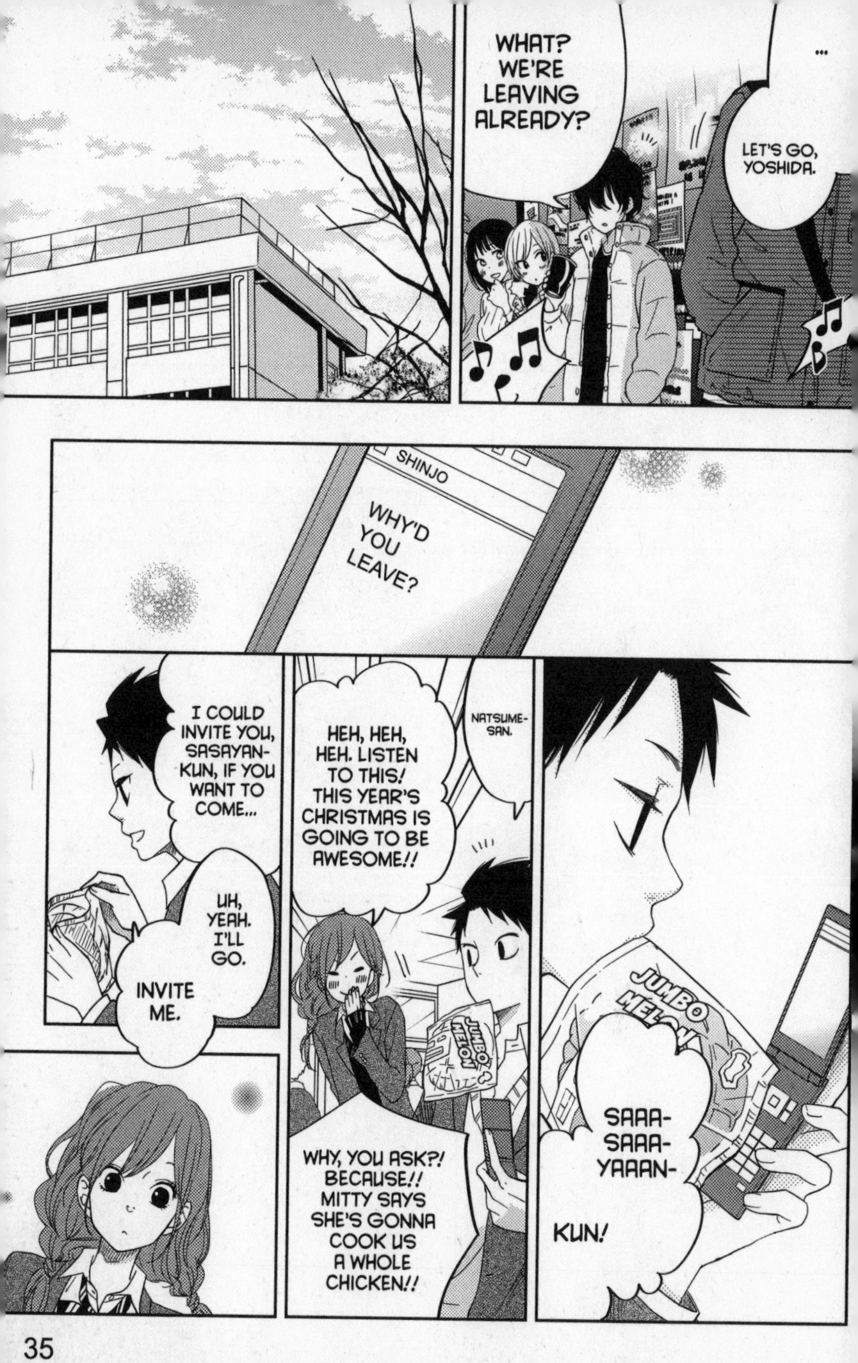
...
LET'S GO, YOSHIDA.
WHAT? WE'RE LEAVING ALREADY?
SHINJO
WHY'D YOU LEAVE?
JUMBO MELON
SAAA-SAAA-YAAAN-
KUN!
NATSUME-SAN.
HEH, HEH, HEH. LISTEN TO THIS! THIS YEAR'S CHRISTMAS IS GOING TO BE AWESOME!!
WHY, YOU ASK?! BECAUSE!! MITTY SAYS SHE'S GONNA COOK US A WHOLE CHICKEN!!
I COULD INVITE YOU, SASAYAN-KUN, IF YOU WANT TO COME...
UH, YEAH. I'LL GO.
INVITE ME.

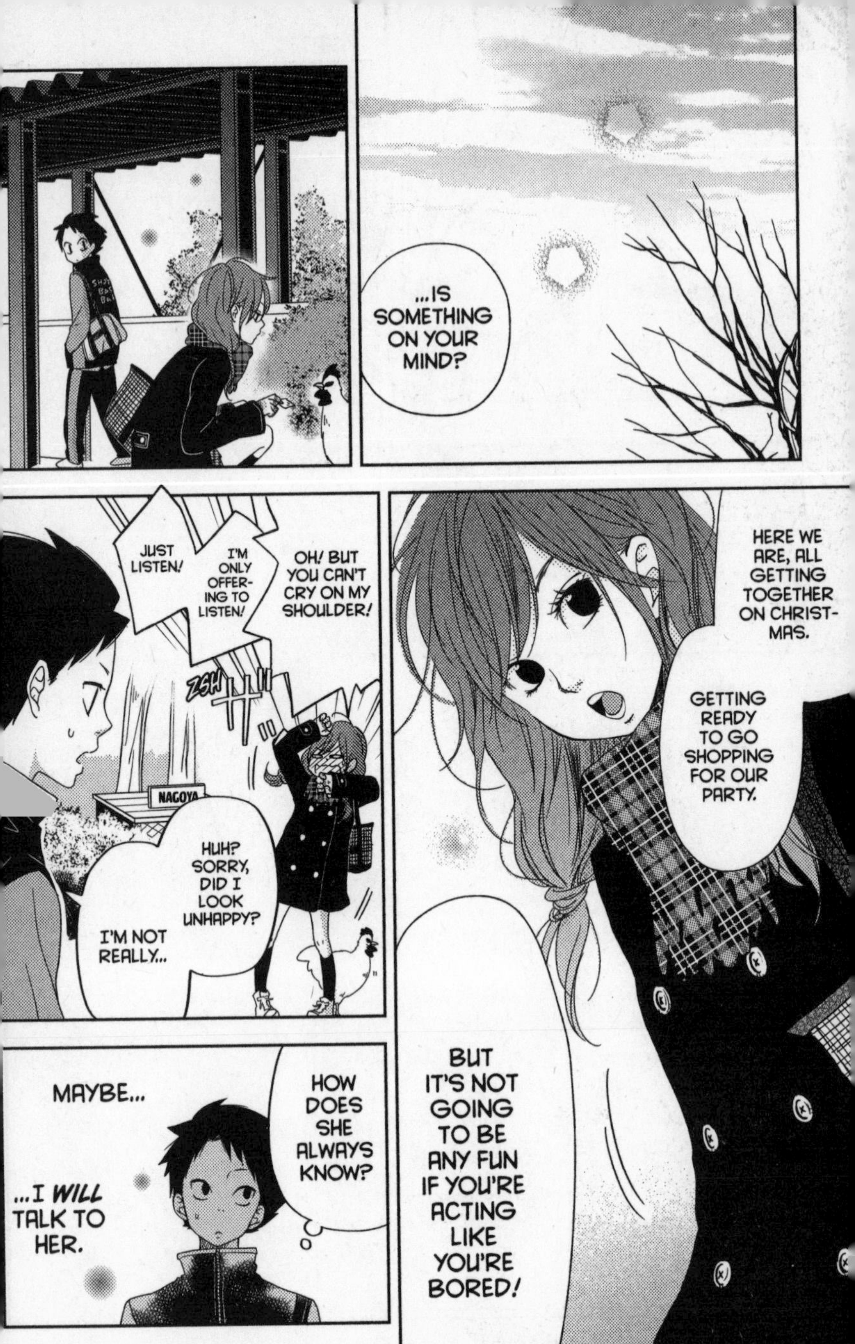
...IS SOMETHING ON YOUR MIND?
HERE WE ARE, ALL GETTING TOGETHER ON CHRISTMAS.
GETTING READY TO GO SHOPPING FOR OUR PARTY.
BUT IT'S NOT GOING TO BE ANY FUN IF YOU'RE ACTING LIKE YOU'RE BORED!
OH! BUT YOU CAN'T CRY ON MY SHOULDER!
I'M ONLY OFFERING TO LISTEN!
JUST LISTEN!
ZSH
NAGOYA
HUH? SORRY, DID I LOOK UNHAPPY?
I'M NOT REALLY...
HOW DOES SHE ALWAYS KNOW?
MAYBE...
...I *WILL* TALK TO HER.

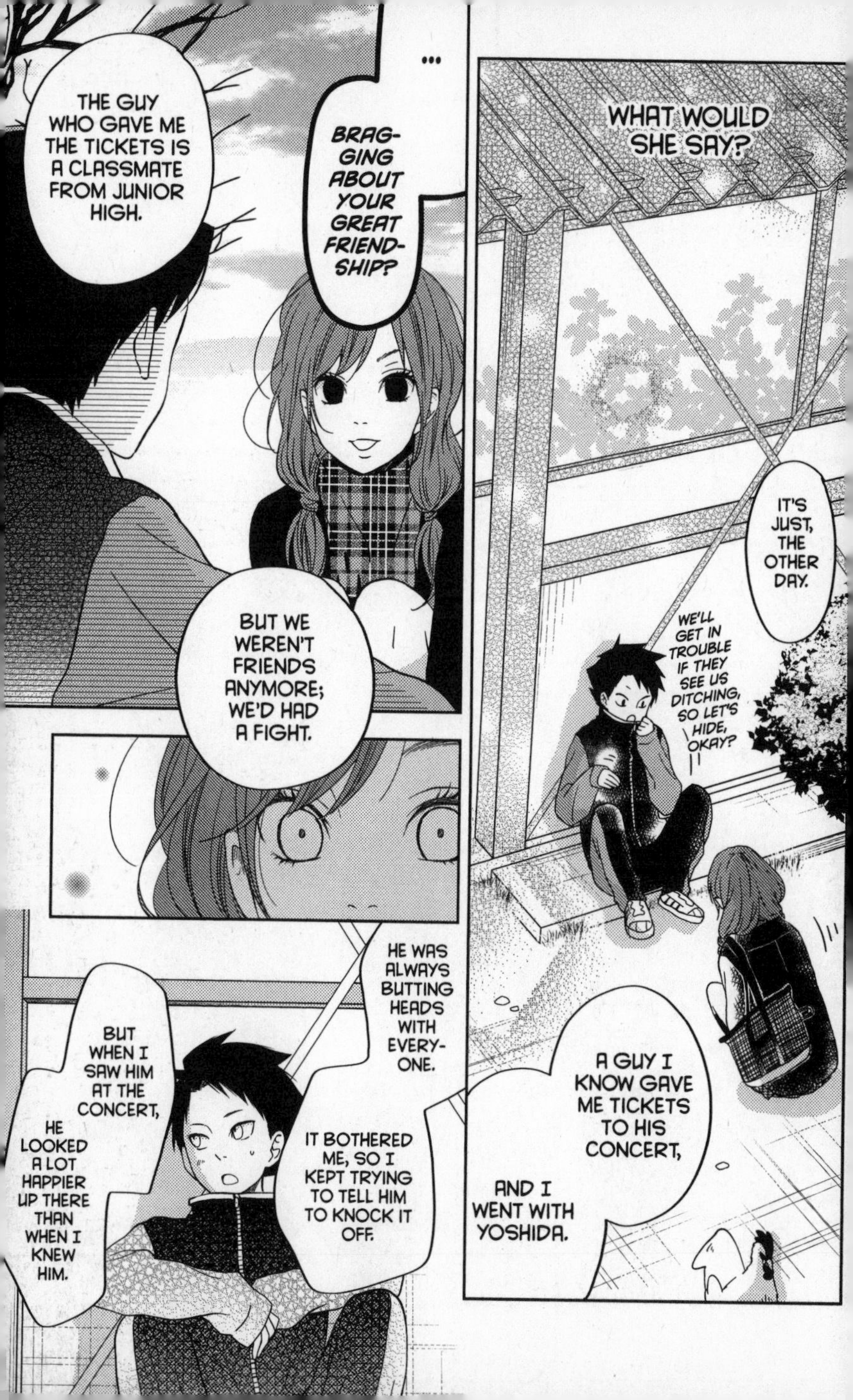
WHAT WOULD SHE SAY?
IT'S JUST, THE OTHER DAY.
WE'LL GET IN TROUBLE IF THEY SEE US DITCHING, SO LET'S HIDE, OKAY?
A GUY I KNOW GAVE ME TICKETS TO HIS CONCERT,
AND I WENT WITH YOSHIDA.
...
BRAG-GING ABOUT YOUR GREAT FRIEND-SHIP?
THE GUY WHO GAVE ME THE TICKETS IS A CLASSMATE FROM JUNIOR HIGH.
BUT WE WEREN'T FRIENDS ANYMORE; WE'D HAD A FIGHT.
HE WAS ALWAYS BUTTING HEADS WITH EVERY-ONE.
IT BOTHERED ME, SO I KEPT TRYING TO TELL HIM TO KNOCK IT OFF.
BUT WHEN I SAW HIM AT THE CONCERT,
HE LOOKED A LOT HAPPIER UP THERE THAN WHEN I KNEW HIM.

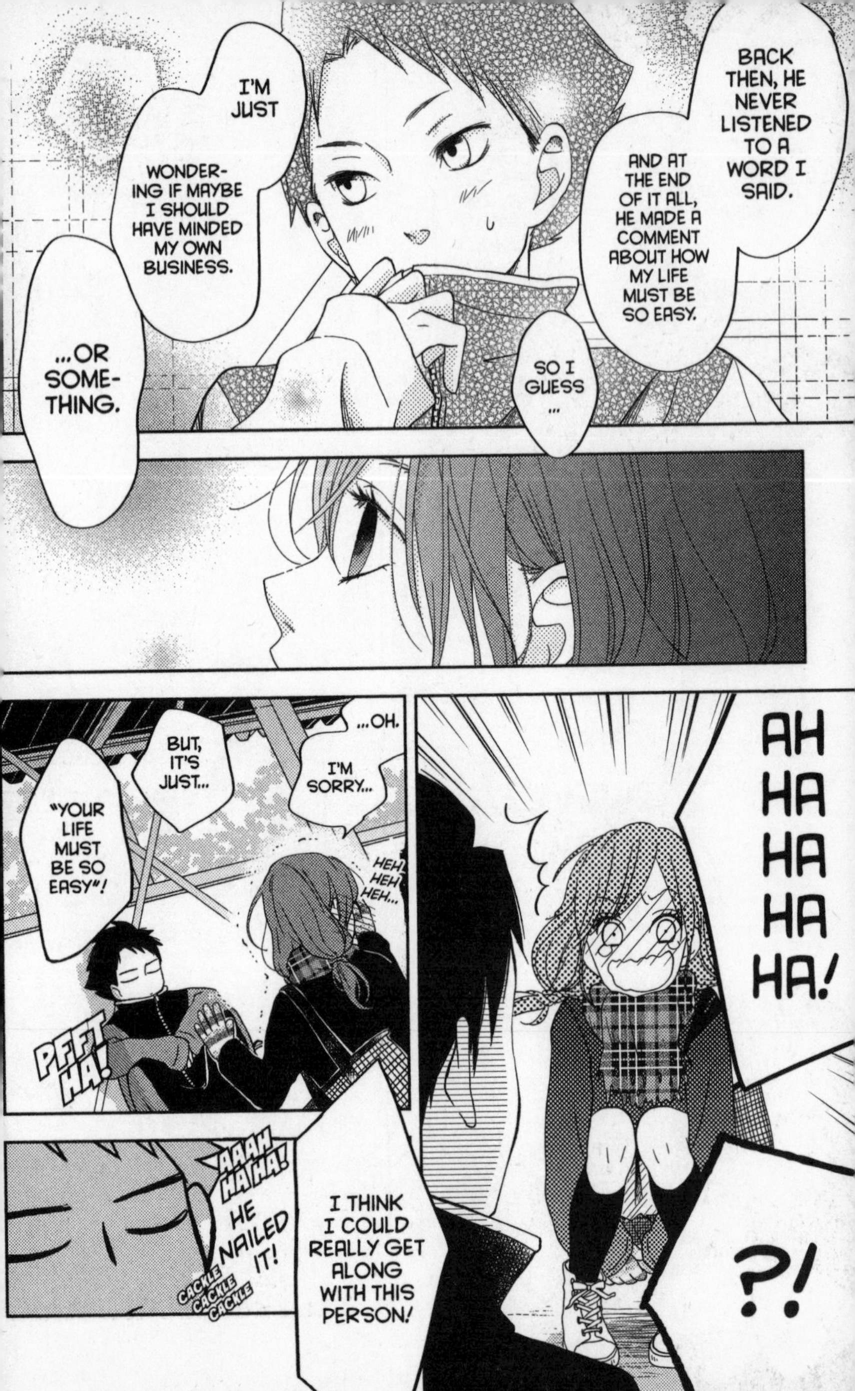
BACK THEN, HE NEVER LISTENED TO A WORD I SAID.
AND AT THE END OF IT ALL, HE MADE A COMMENT ABOUT HOW MY LIFE MUST BE SO EASY.
SO I GUESS ...
I'M JUST
WONDERING IF MAYBE I SHOULD HAVE MINDED MY OWN BUSINESS.
...OR SOMETHING.
AH HA HA HA HA HA!
?!
...OH.
I'M SORRY...
HEH HEH HEH...
BUT, IT'S JUST...
"YOUR LIFE MUST BE SO EASY"!
PFFT HA!
I THINK I COULD REALLY GET ALONG WITH THIS PERSON!
AAAH HA HA!
HE NAILED IT!
CACKLE CACKLE CACKLE

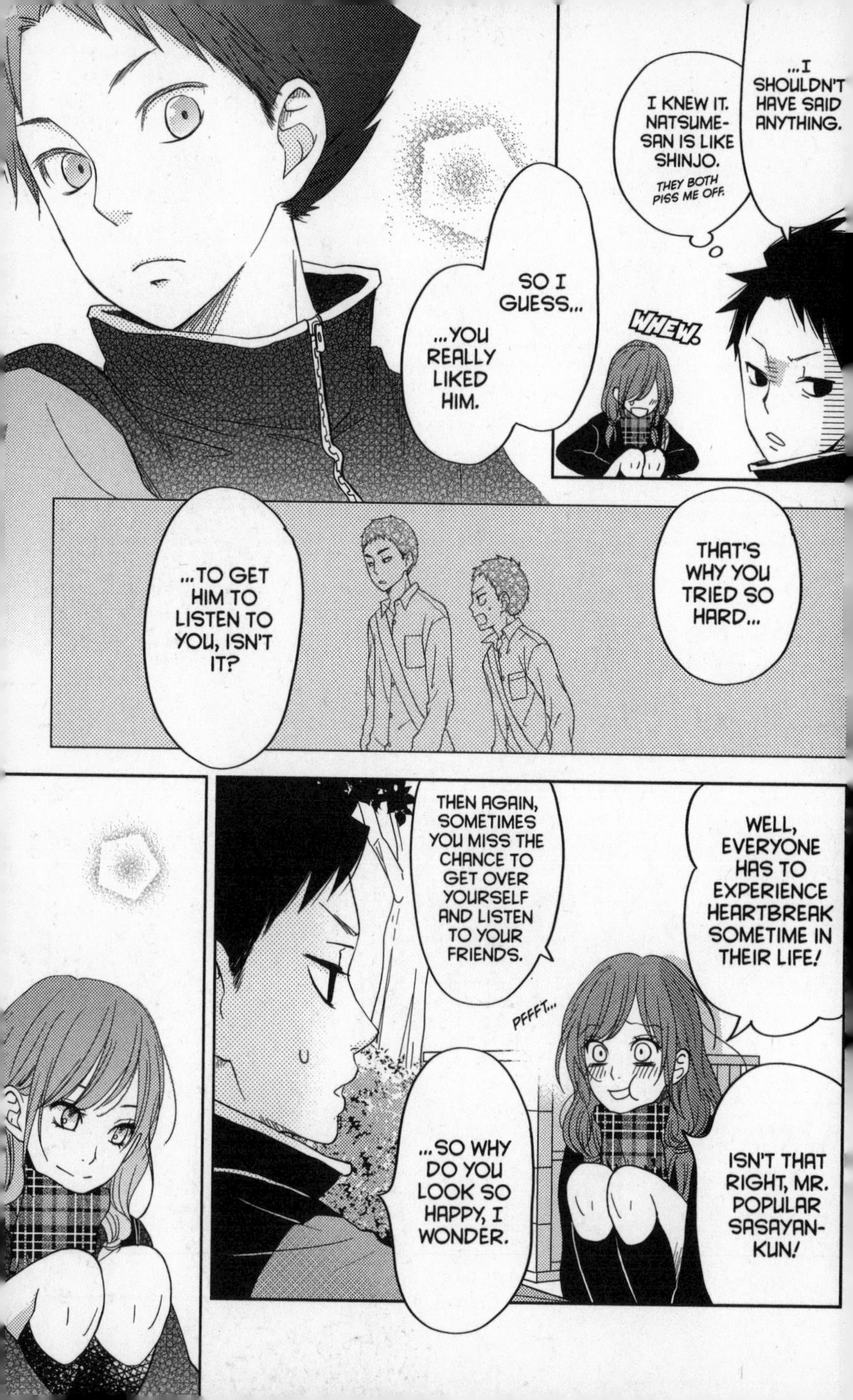
...I SHOULDN'T HAVE SAID ANYTHING.
I KNEW IT. NATSUME-SAN IS LIKE SHINJO.
THEY BOTH PISS ME OFF.
WHEW.
SO I GUESS...
...YOU REALLY LIKED HIM.
THAT'S WHY YOU TRIED SO HARD...
...TO GET HIM TO LISTEN TO YOU, ISN'T IT?
WELL, EVERYONE HAS TO EXPERIENCE HEARTBREAK SOMETIME IN THEIR LIFE!
ISN'T THAT RIGHT, MR. POPULAR SASAYAN-KUN!
THEN AGAIN, SOMETIMES YOU MISS THE CHANCE TO GET OVER YOURSELF AND LISTEN TO YOUR FRIENDS.
PFFFT...
...SO WHY DO YOU LOOK SO HAPPY, I WONDER.

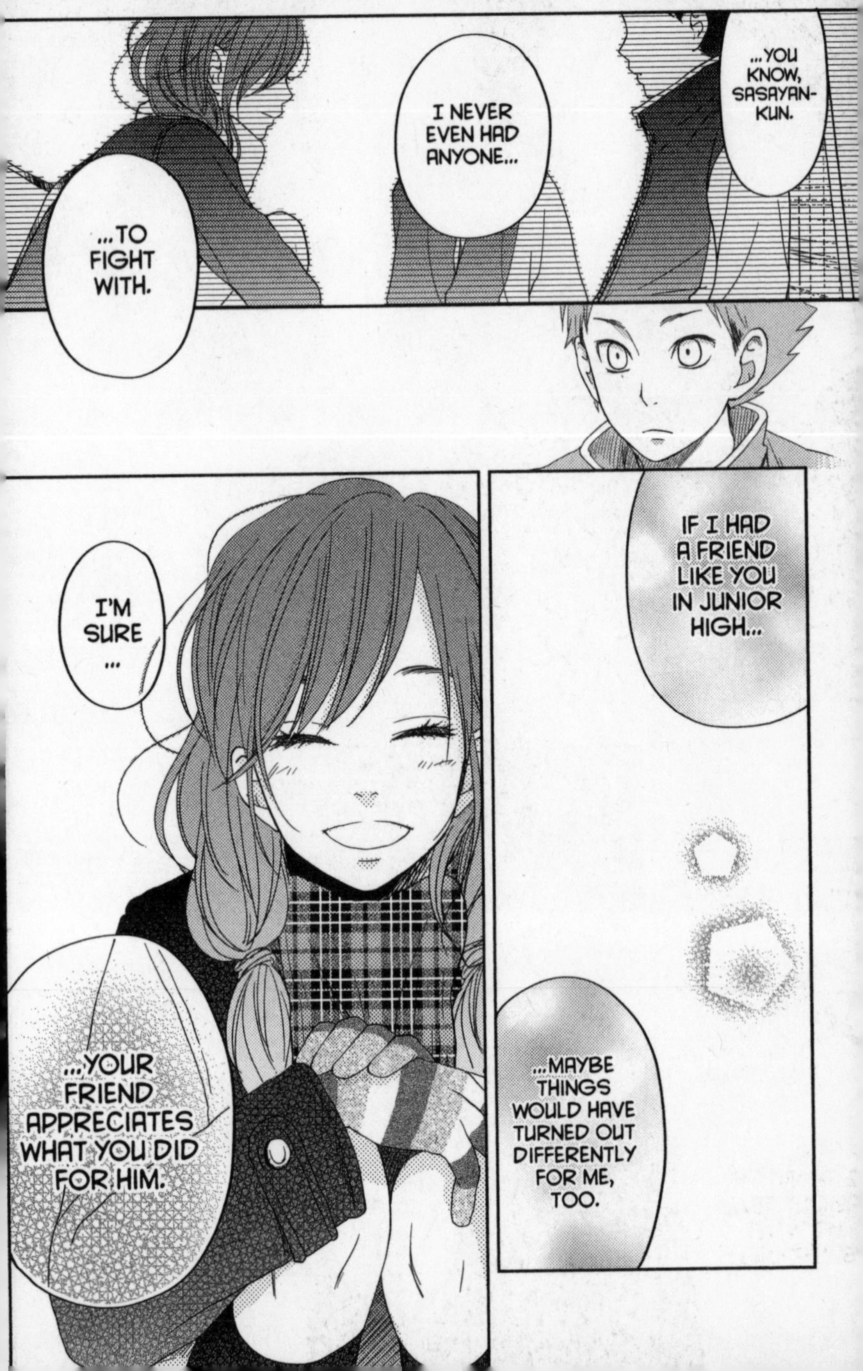
...YOU KNOW, SASAYAN-KUN.
I NEVER EVEN HAD ANYONE...
...TO FIGHT WITH.
IF I HAD A FRIEND LIKE YOU IN JUNIOR HIGH...
...MAYBE THINGS WOULD HAVE TURNED OUT DIFFERENTLY FOR ME, TOO.
I'M SURE...
...YOUR FRIEND APPRECIATES WHAT YOU DID FOR HIM.

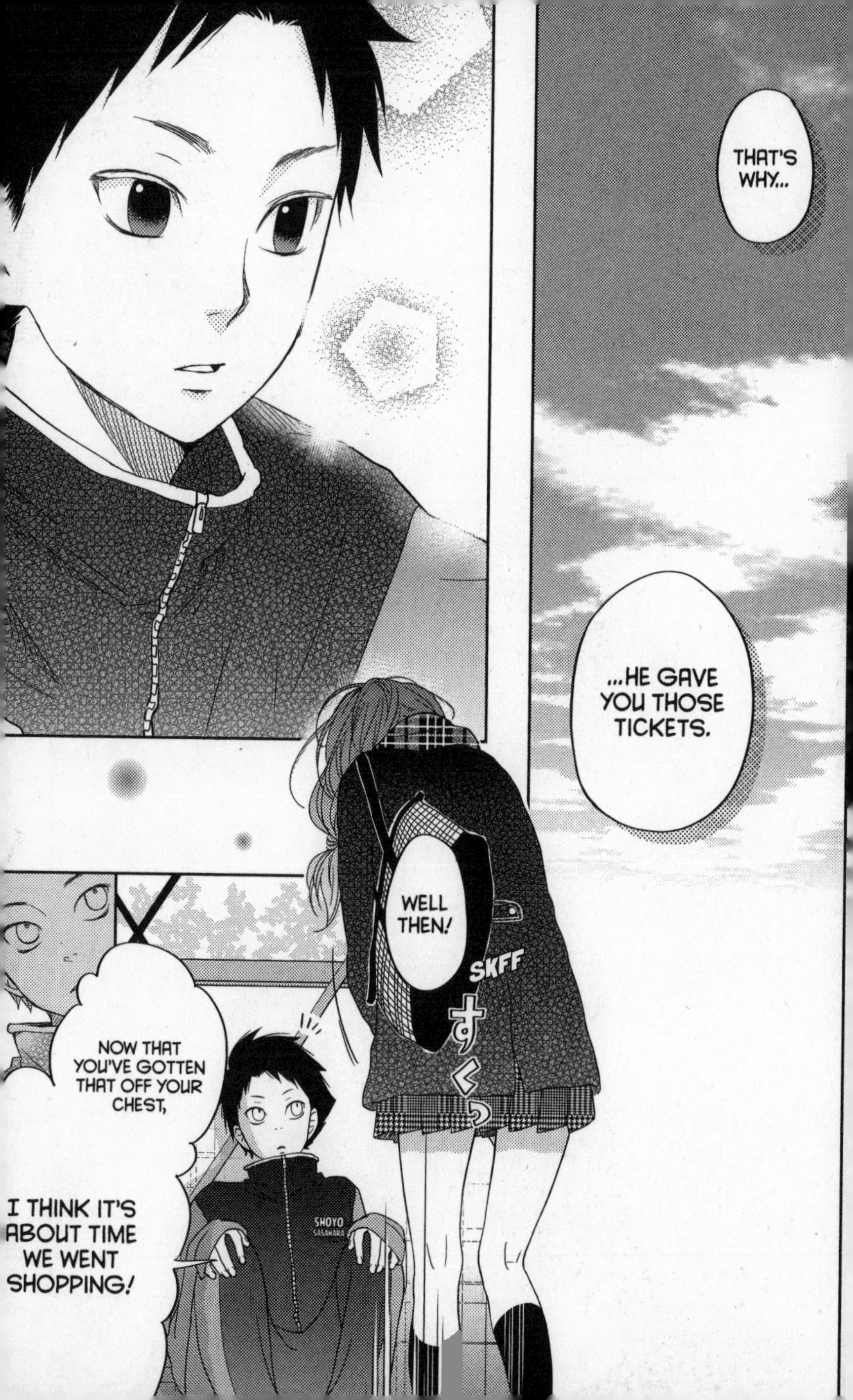
THAT'S WHY...
...HE GAVE YOU THOSE TICKETS.
WELL THEN!
SKFF
すくっ
NOW THAT YOU'VE GOTTEN THAT OFF YOUR CHEST,
I THINK IT'S ABOUT TIME WE WENT SHOPPING!
SHOYO
SASAHARA

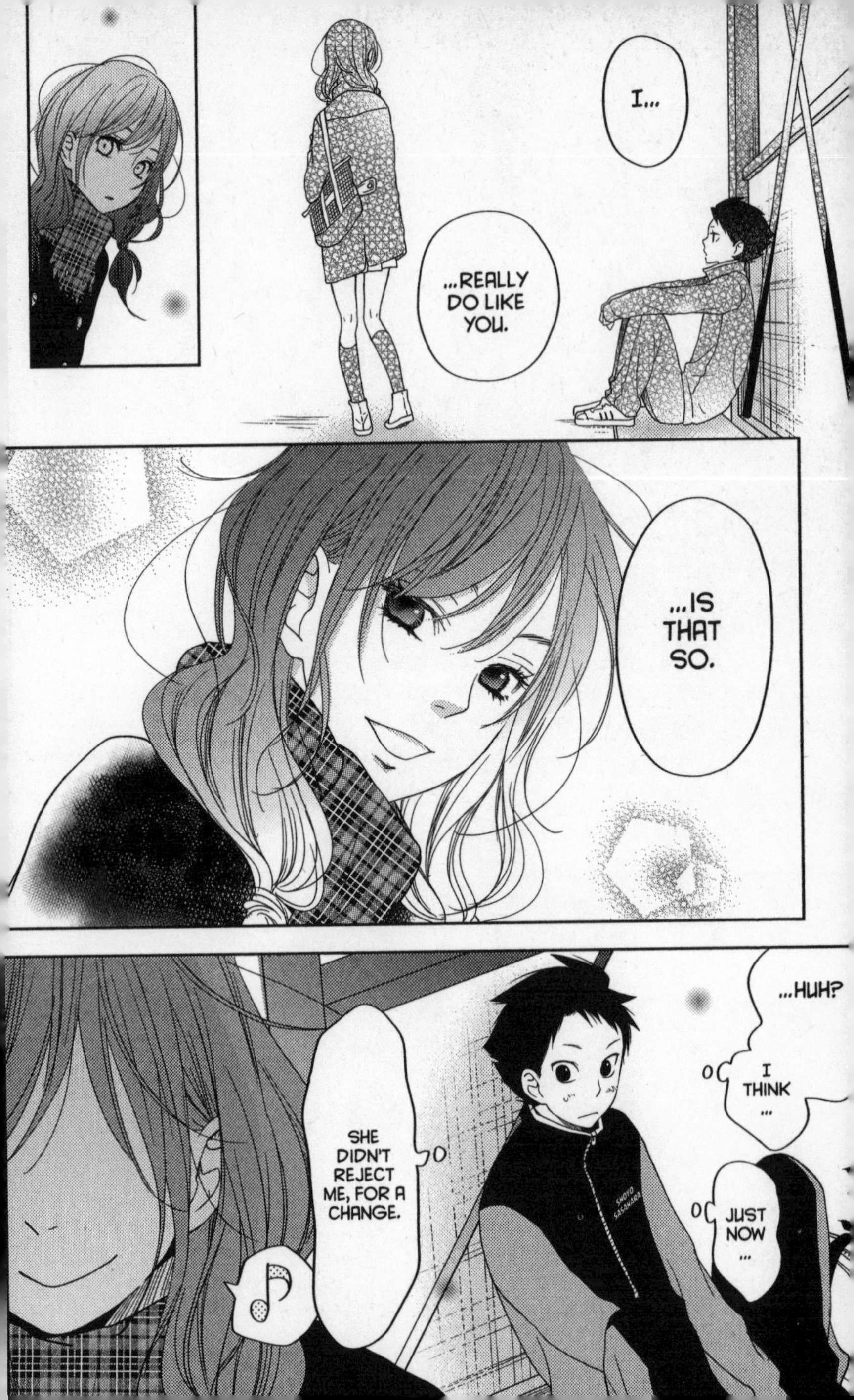
I...
...REALLY DO LIKE YOU.
...IS THAT SO.
...HUH?
I THINK ...
JUST NOW ...
SHE DIDN'T REJECT ME, FOR A CHANGE.

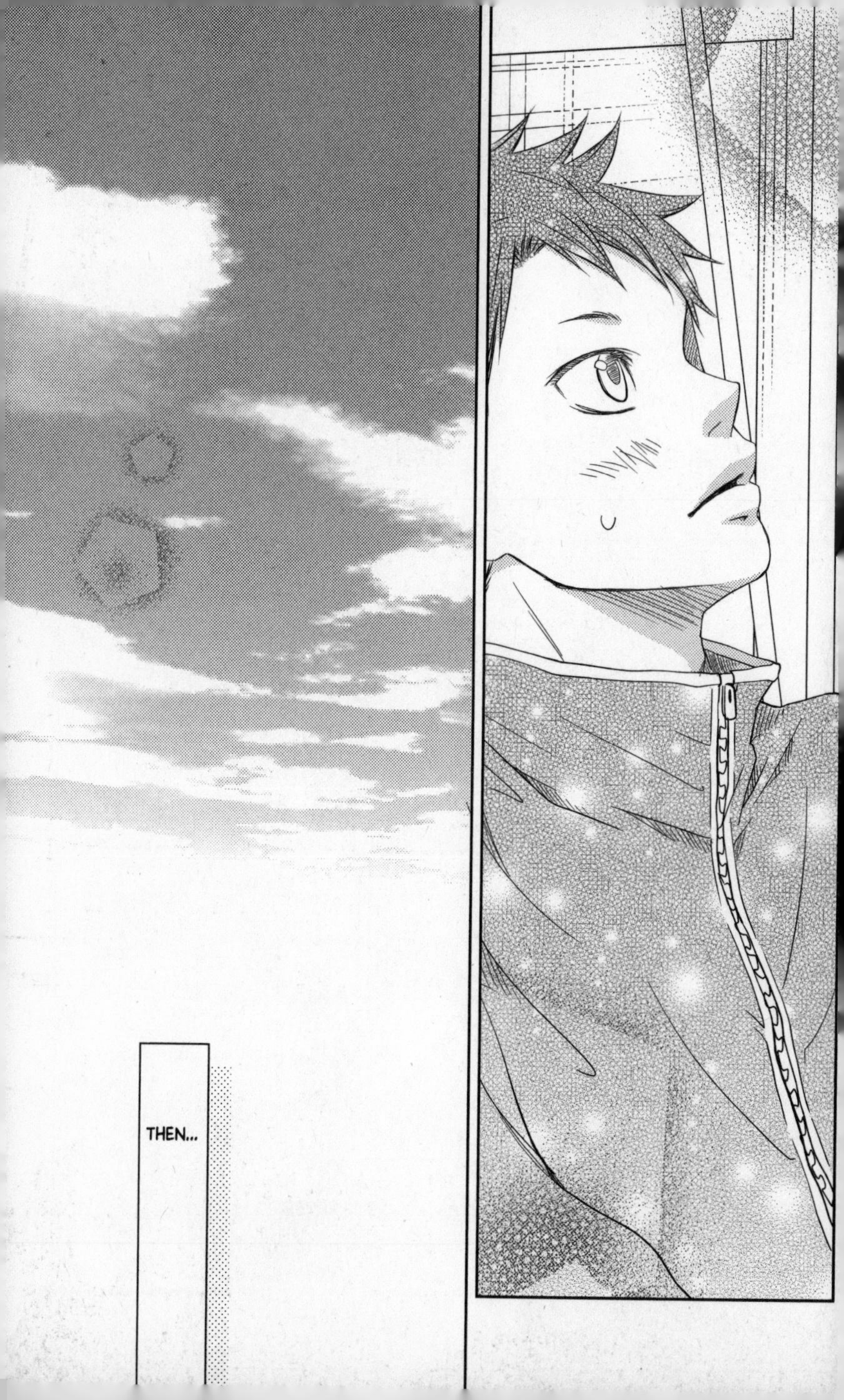
THEN...

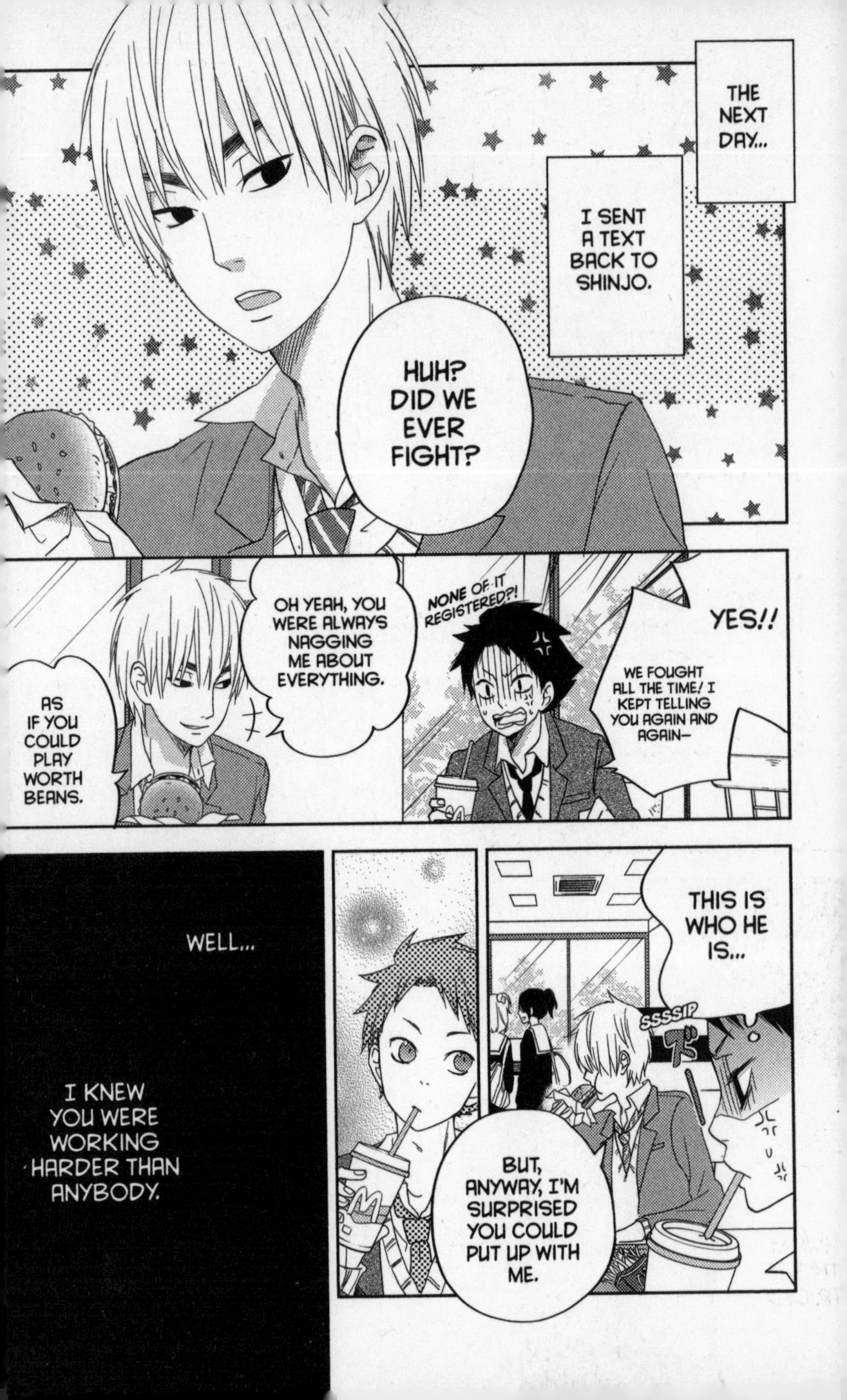
THE NEXT DAY...
I SENT A TEXT BACK TO SHINJO.
HUH? DID WE EVER FIGHT?
YES!!
WE FOUGHT ALL THE TIME! I KEPT TELLING YOU AGAIN AND AGAIN—
NONE OF IT REGISTERED?!
OH YEAH, YOU WERE ALWAYS NAGGING ME ABOUT EVERYTHING.
AS IF YOU COULD PLAY WORTH BEANS.
THIS IS WHO HE IS...
SSSSIP
BUT, ANYWAY, I'M SURPRISED YOU COULD PUT UP WITH ME.
WELL...
I KNEW YOU WERE WORKING HARDER THAN ANYBODY.

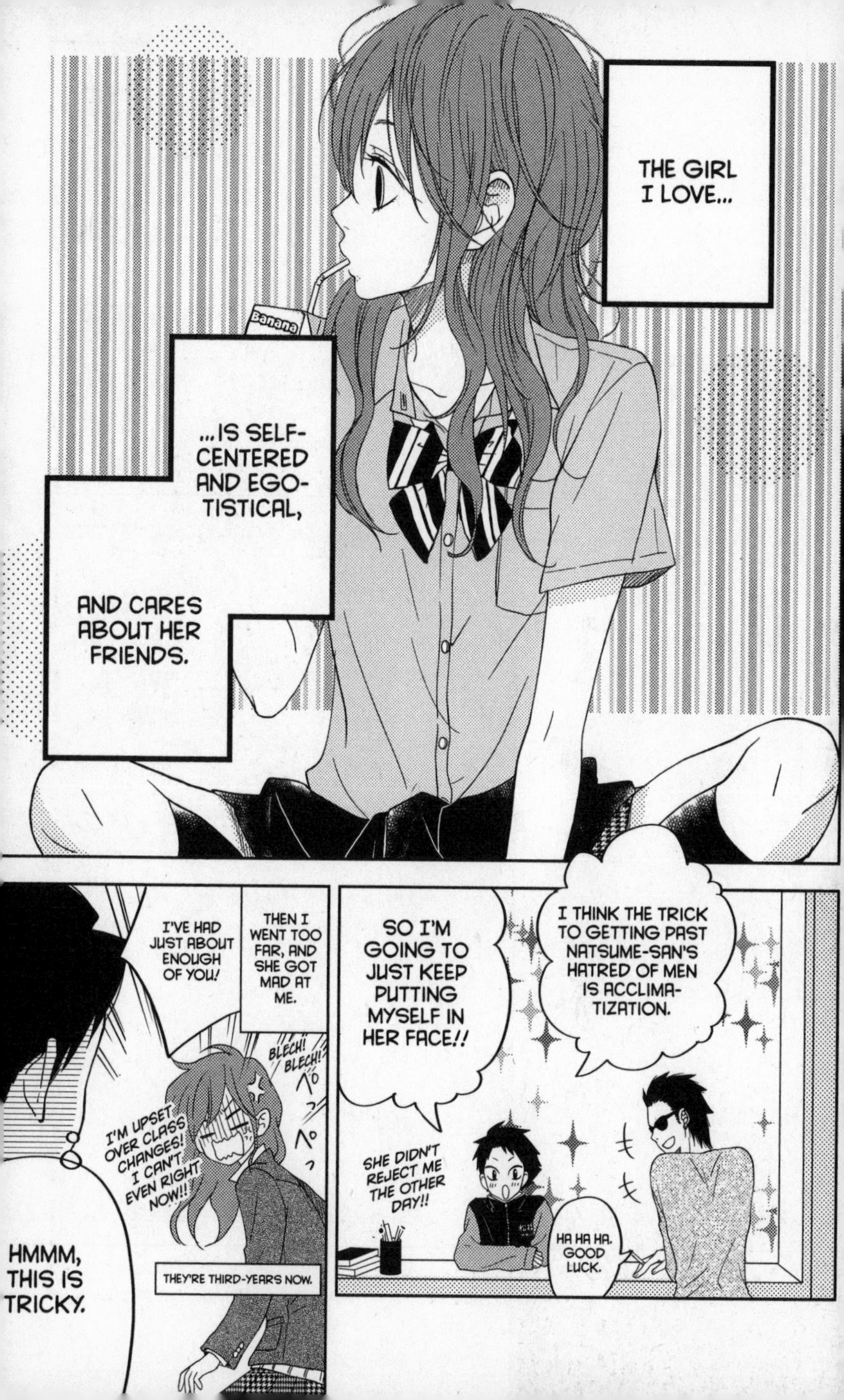
THE GIRL I LOVE...
...IS SELF-CENTERED AND EGO-TISTICAL,
AND CARES ABOUT HER FRIENDS.
I THINK THE TRICK TO GETTING PAST NATSUME-SAN'S HATRED OF MEN IS ACCLIMA-TIZATION.
SO I'M GOING TO JUST KEEP PUTTING MYSELF IN HER FACE!!
HA HA HA. GOOD LUCK.
SHE DIDN'T REJECT ME THE OTHER DAY!!
THEN I WENT TOO FAR, AND SHE GOT MAD AT ME.
I'VE HAD JUST ABOUT ENOUGH OF YOU!
BLECH! BLECH!
I'M UPSET OVER CLASS CHANGES! I CAN'T EVEN RIGHT NOW!!
THEY'RE THIRD-YEARS NOW.
HMMM, THIS IS TRICKY.

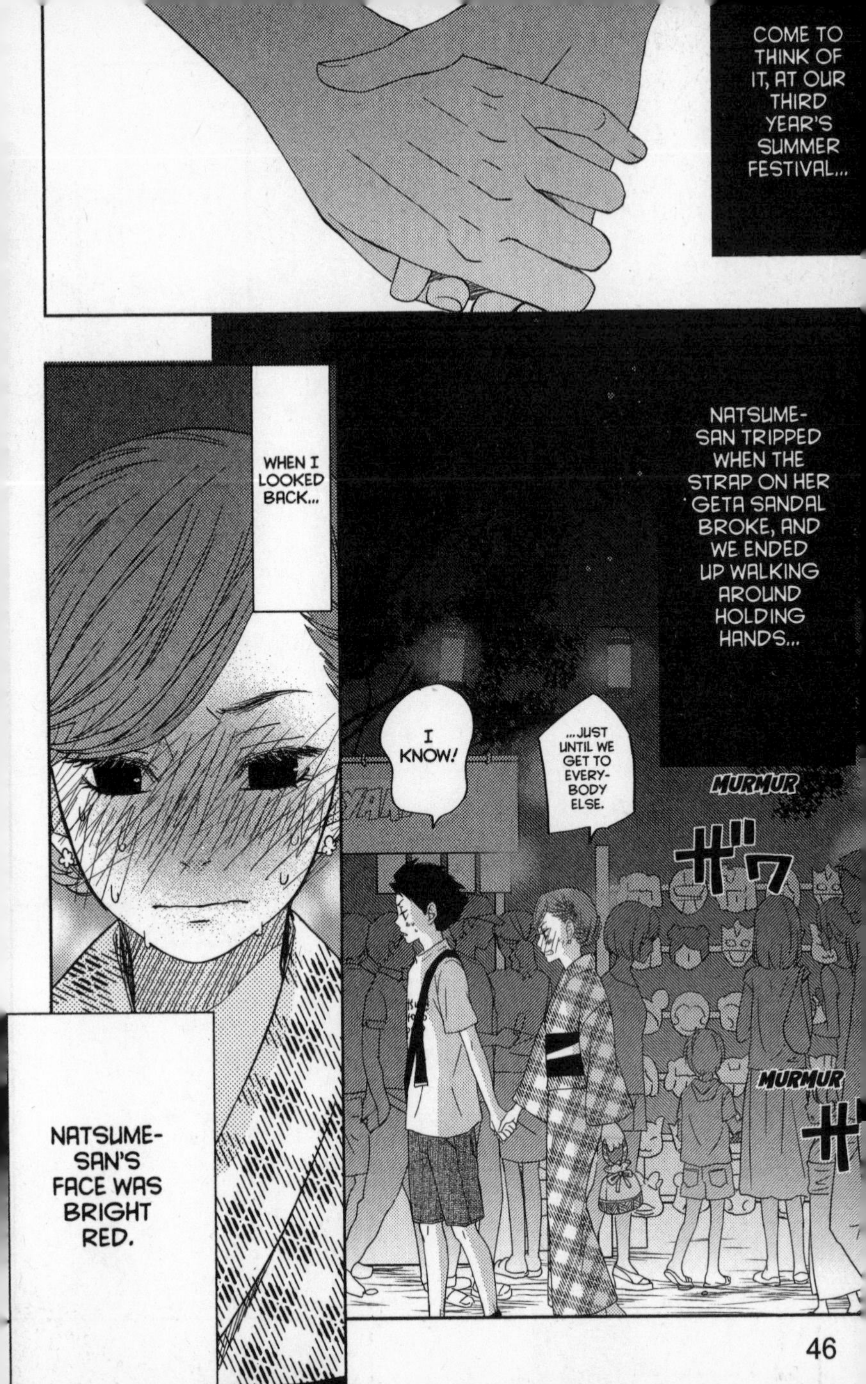
COME TO THINK OF IT, AT OUR THIRD YEAR'S SUMMER FESTIVAL...
NATSUME-SAN TRIPPED WHEN THE STRAP ON HER GETA SANDAL BROKE, AND WE ENDED UP WALKING AROUND HOLDING HANDS...
...JUST UNTIL WE GET TO EVERYBODY ELSE.
I KNOW!
MURMUR
ザワ
MURMUR
ザ
WHEN I LOOKED BACK...
NATSUME-SAN'S FACE WAS BRIGHT RED.

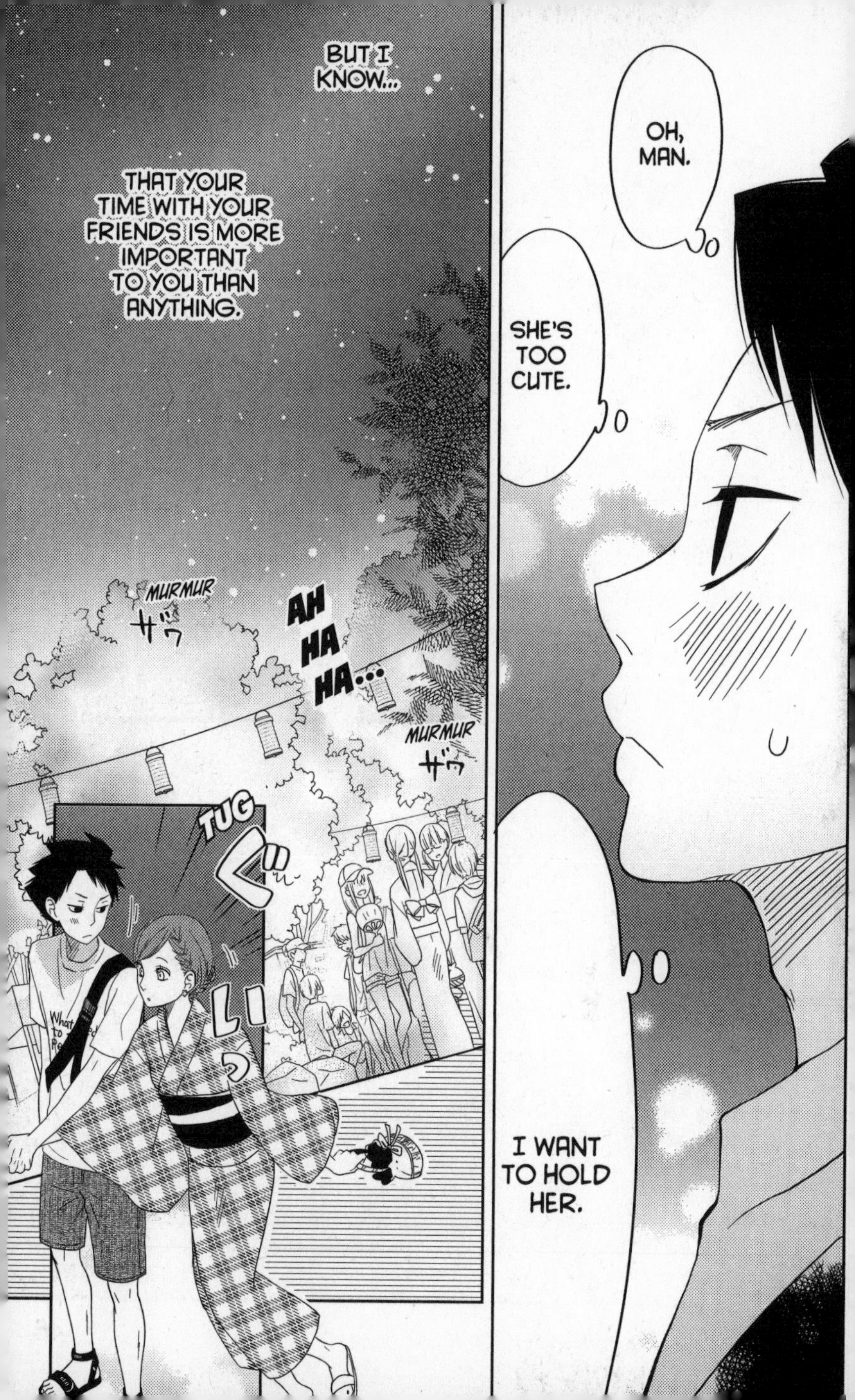
OH, MAN.
SHE'S TOO CUTE.
I WANT TO HOLD HER.
BUT I KNOW...
THAT YOUR TIME WITH YOUR FRIENDS IS MORE IMPORTANT TO YOU THAN ANYTHING.
MURMUR
AH HA HA...
MURMUR
TUG

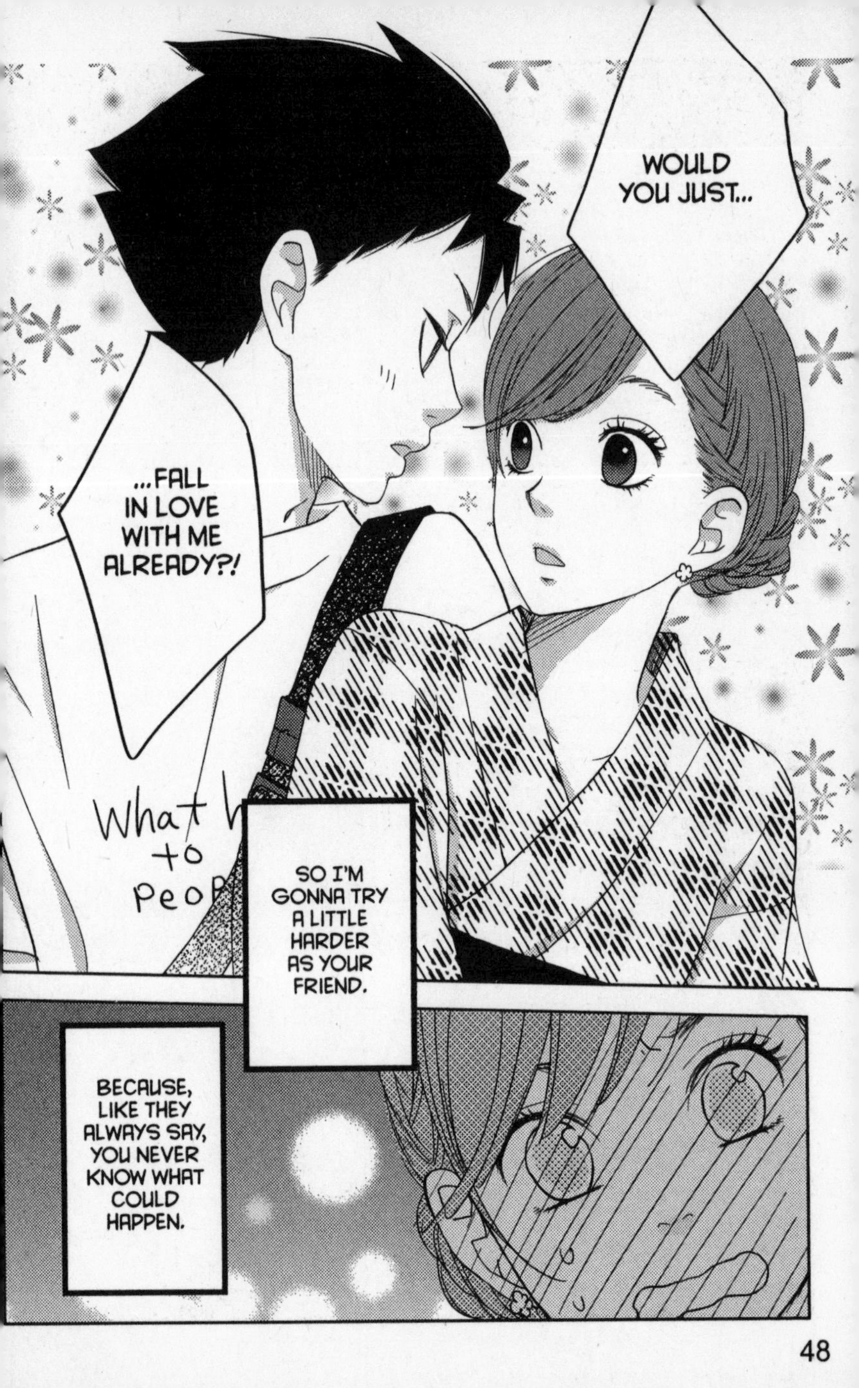
WOULD YOU JUST...
...FALL IN LOVE WITH ME ALREADY?!
SO I'M GONNA TRY A LITTLE HARDER AS YOUR FRIEND.
BECAUSE, LIKE THEY ALWAYS SAY, YOU NEVER KNOW WHAT COULD HAPPEN.

EXPERIMENT

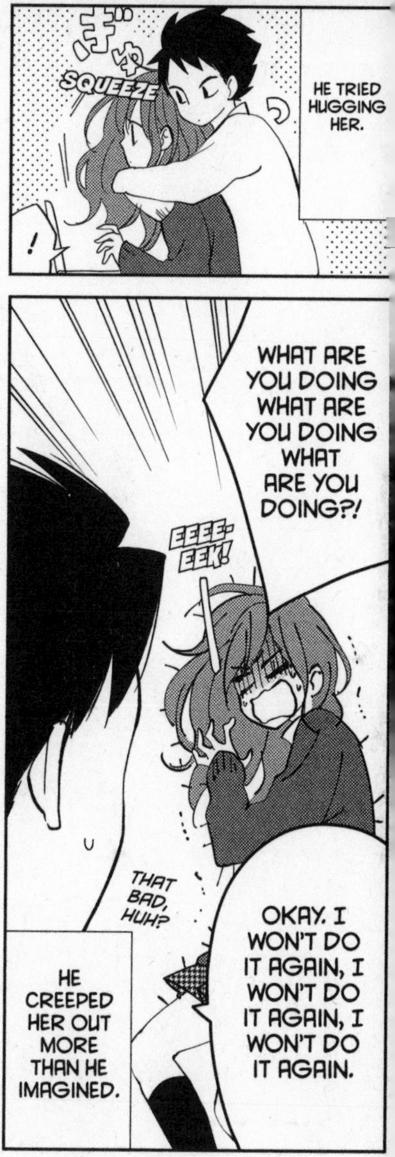
SQUEEZE
HE TRIED HUGGING HER.
WHAT ARE YOU DOING WHAT ARE YOU DOING WHAT ARE YOU DOING?!
EEEE-EEK!
THAT BAD, HUH?
OKAY. I WON'T DO IT AGAIN, I WON'T DO IT AGAIN, I WON'T DO IT AGAIN.
HE CREEPED HER OUT MORE THAN HE IMAGINED.

EXPERIMENT 2

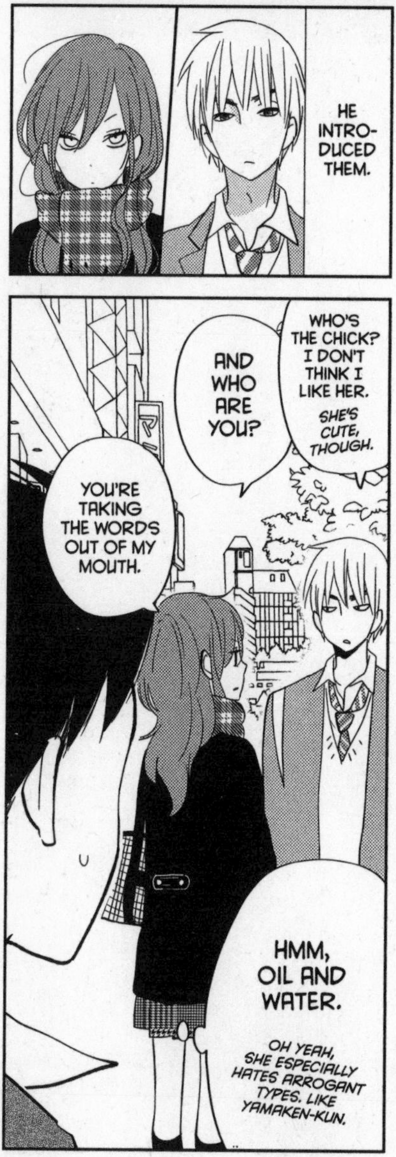
HE INTRODUCED THEM.
WHO'S THE CHICK? I DON'T THINK I LIKE HER.
SHE'S CUTE, THOUGH.
AND WHO ARE YOU?
YOU'RE TAKING THE WORDS OUT OF MY MOUTH.
HMM, OIL AND WATER.
OH YEAH, SHE ESPECIALLY HATES ARROGANT TYPES. LIKE YAMAKEN-KUN.

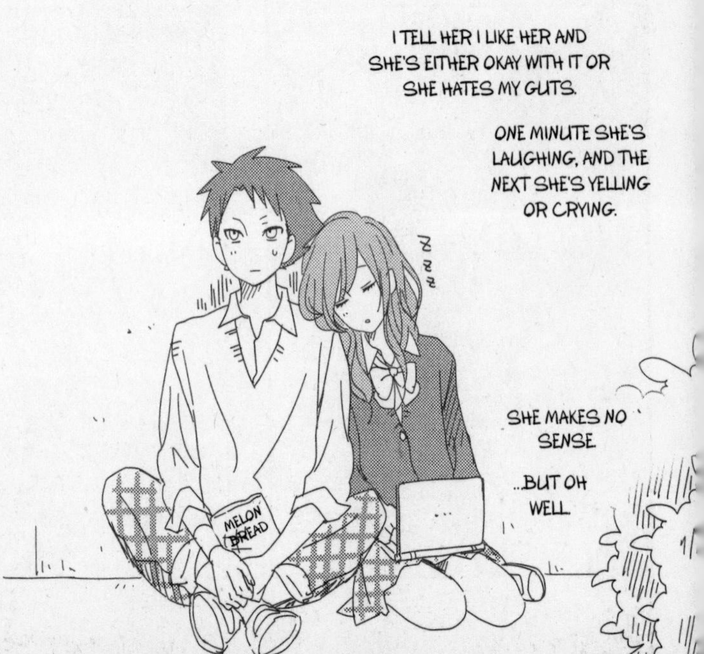
I TELL HER I LIKE HER AND SHE'S EITHER OKAY WITH IT OR SHE HATES MY GUTS.
ONE MINUTE SHE'S LAUGHING, AND THE NEXT SHE'S YELLING OR CRYING.
ZZZ
SHE MAKES NO SENSE.
...BUT OH WELL.
MELON BREAD
...

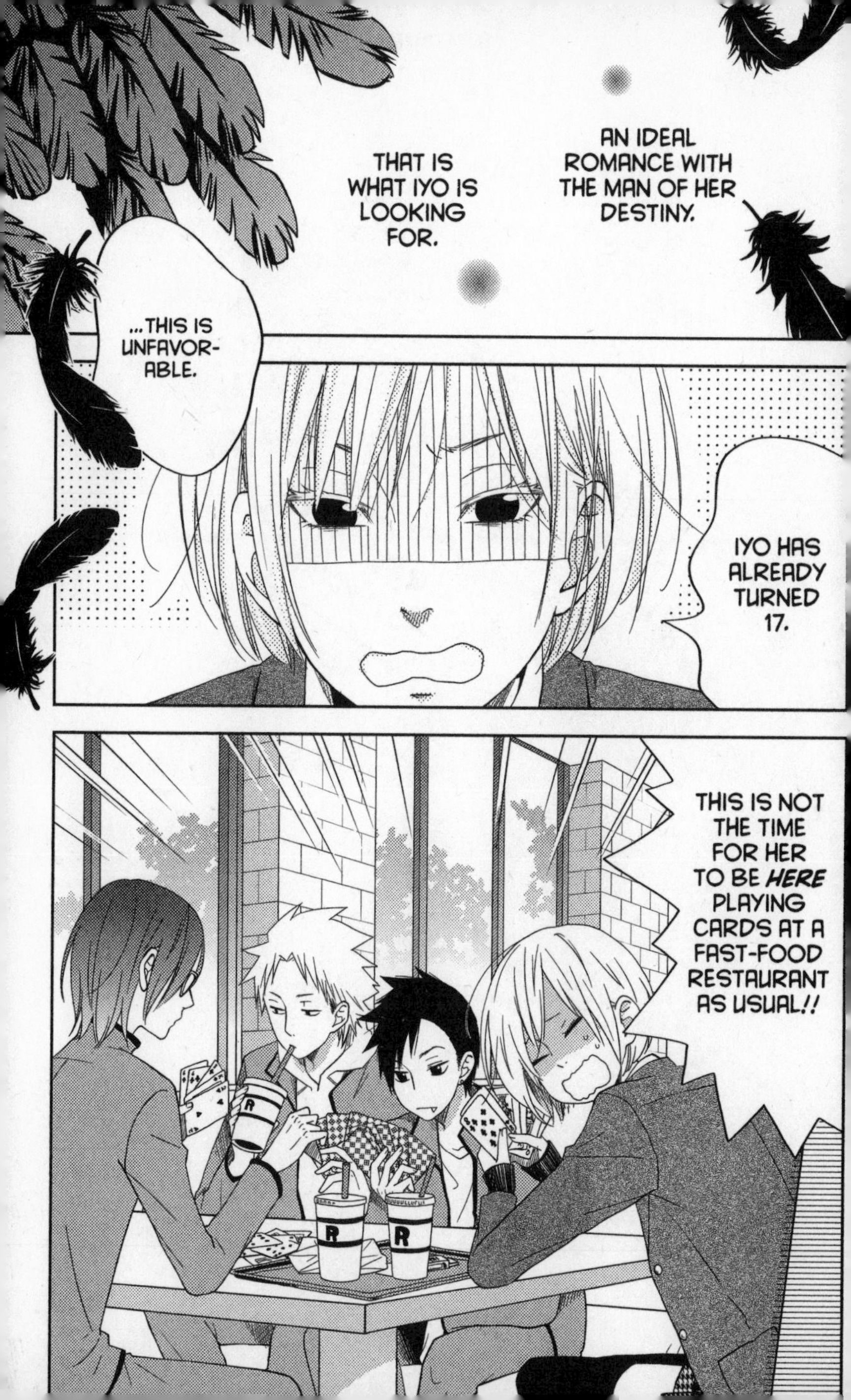
AN IDEAL ROMANCE WITH THE MAN OF HER DESTINY.
THAT IS WHAT IYO IS LOOKING FOR.
...THIS IS UNFAVOR-ABLE.
IYO HAS ALREADY TURNED 17.
THIS IS NOT THE TIME FOR HER TO BE *HERE* PLAYING CARDS AT A FAST-FOOD RESTAURANT AS USUAL!!

EXTRA CHAPTER 2: IYO'S OPERATION: PRINCE CHARMING!

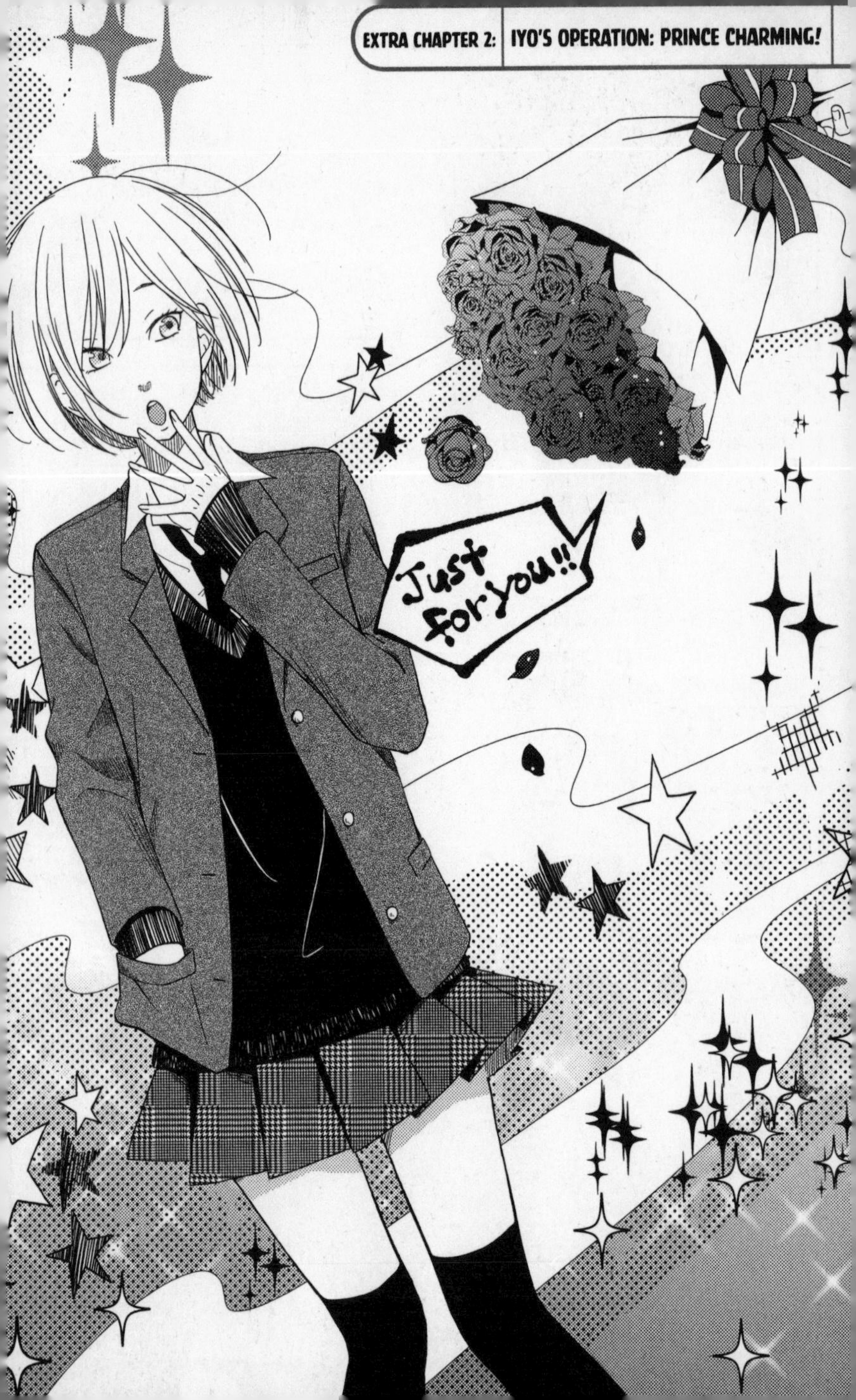
Just for you!!

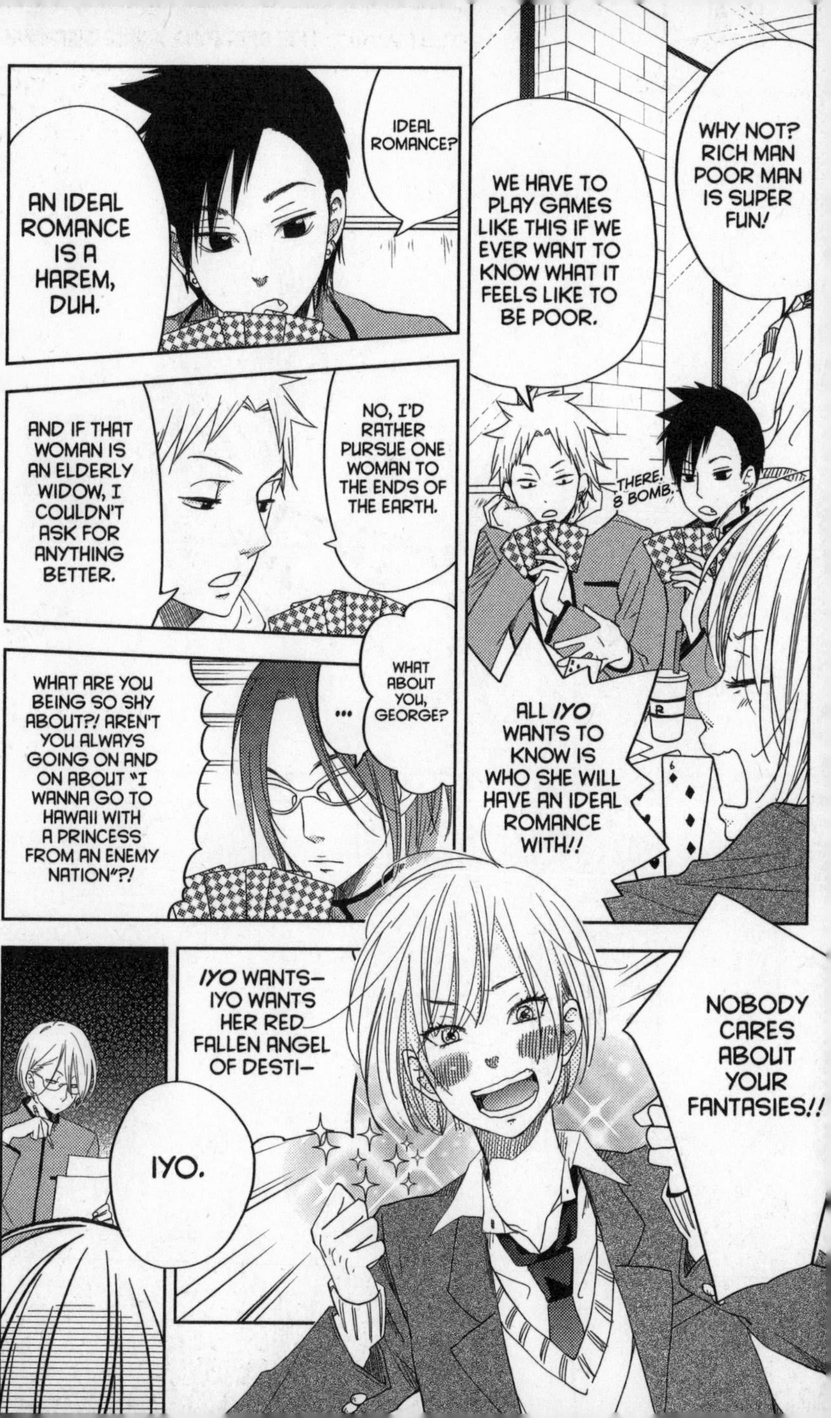
WHY NOT? RICH MAN POOR MAN IS SUPER FUN!
WE HAVE TO PLAY GAMES LIKE THIS IF WE EVER WANT TO KNOW WHAT IT FEELS LIKE TO BE POOR.
THERE. 8 BOMB.
ALL *IYO* WANTS TO KNOW IS WHO SHE WILL HAVE AN IDEAL ROMANCE WITH!!
IDEAL ROMANCE?
AN IDEAL ROMANCE IS A HAREM, DUH.
NO, I'D RATHER PURSUE ONE WOMAN TO THE ENDS OF THE EARTH.
AND IF THAT WOMAN IS AN ELDERLY WIDOW, I COULDN'T ASK FOR ANYTHING BETTER.
WHAT ABOUT YOU, GEORGE?
...
WHAT ARE YOU BEING SO SHY ABOUT?! AREN'T YOU ALWAYS GOING ON AND ON ABOUT "I WANNA GO TO HAWAII WITH A PRINCESS FROM AN ENEMY NATION"?!
NOBODY CARES ABOUT YOUR FANTASIES!!
IYO WANTS— IYO WANTS HER RED FALLEN ANGEL OF DESTI—
IYO.

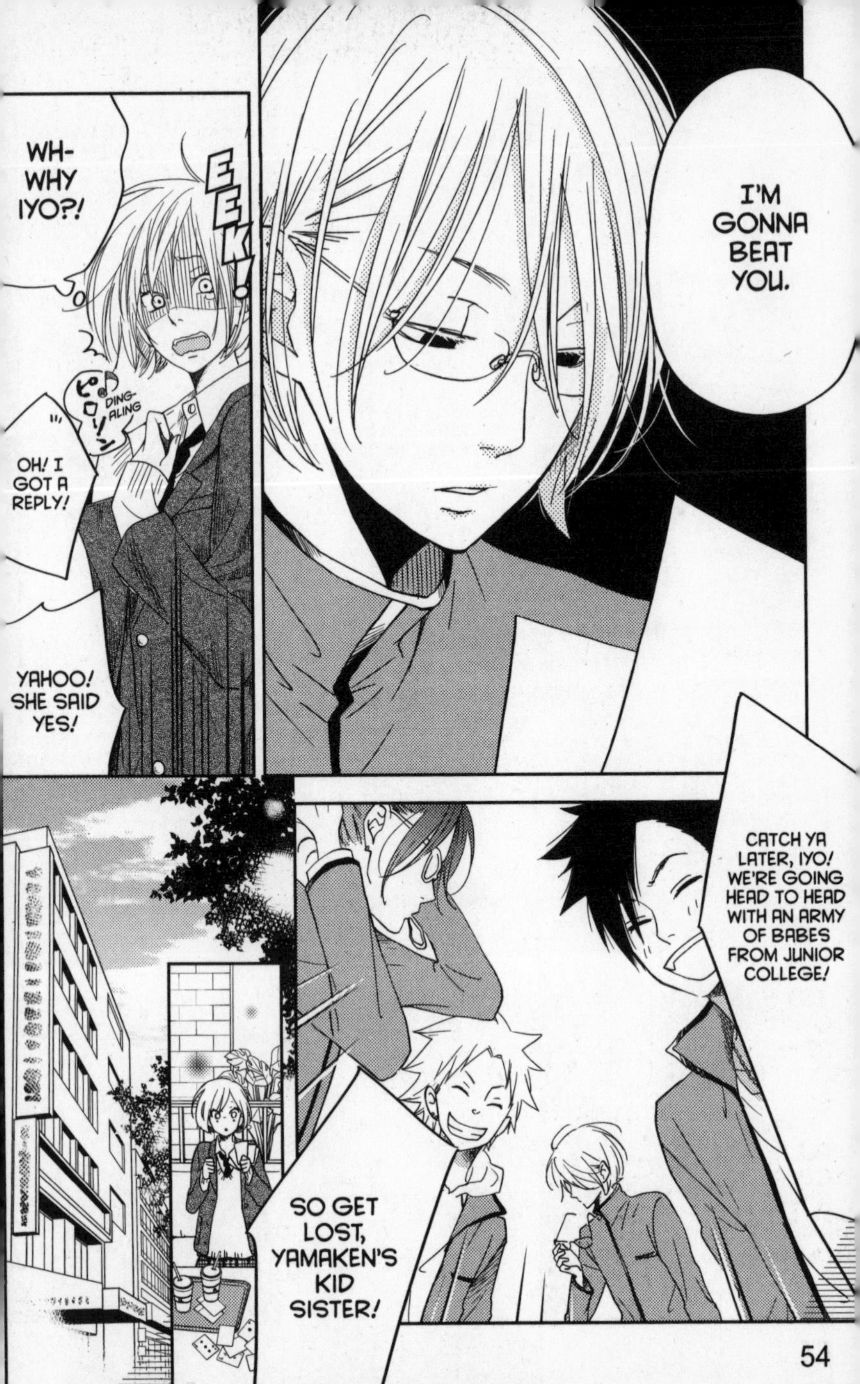
I'M GONNA BEAT YOU.
EEK!
WH- WHY IYO?!
DING-ALING
OH! I GOT A REPLY!
YAHOO! SHE SAID YES!
CATCH YA LATER, IYO! WE'RE GOING HEAD TO HEAD WITH AN ARMY OF BABES FROM JUNIOR COLLEGE!
SO GET LOST, YAMAKEN'S KID SISTER!

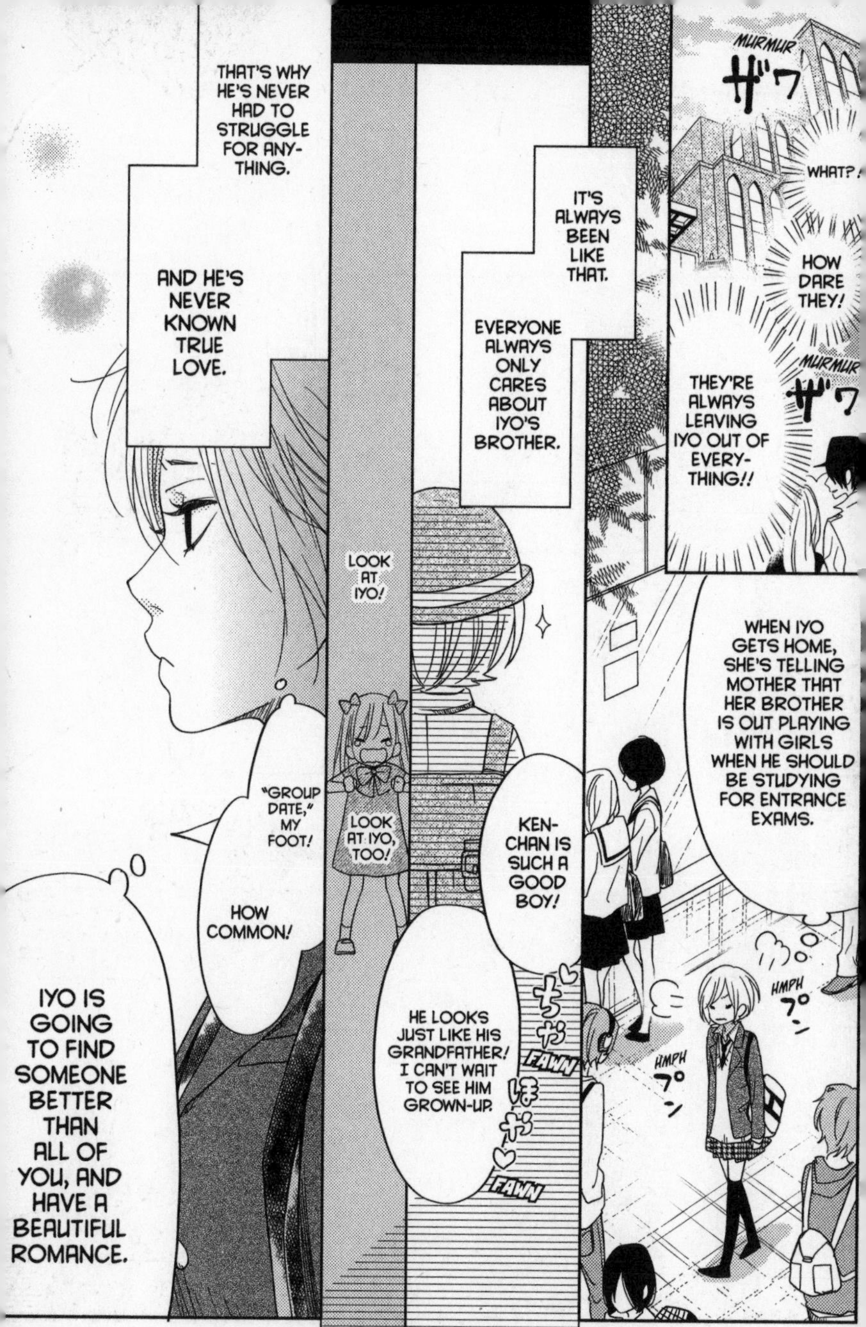
MURMUR
ザワ
WHAT?!
HOW DARE THEY!
MURMUR
ザワ
THEY'RE ALWAYS LEAVING IYO OUT OF EVERY-THING!!
WHEN IYO GETS HOME, SHE'S TELLING MOTHER THAT HER BROTHER IS OUT PLAYING WITH GIRLS WHEN HE SHOULD BE STUDYING FOR ENTRANCE EXAMS.
HMPH
プン
HMPH
プン
IT'S ALWAYS BEEN LIKE THAT.
EVERYONE ALWAYS ONLY CARES ABOUT IYO'S BROTHER.
LOOK AT IYO!
LOOK AT IYO, TOO!
KEN-CHAN IS SUCH A GOOD BOY!
HE LOOKS JUST LIKE HIS GRANDFATHER! I CAN'T WAIT TO SEE HIM GROWN-UP.
FAWN
FAWN
THAT'S WHY HE'S NEVER HAD TO STRUGGLE FOR ANY-THING.
AND HE'S NEVER KNOWN TRUE LOVE.
"GROUP DATE," MY FOOT!
HOW COMMON!
IYO IS GOING TO FIND SOMEONE BETTER THAN ALL OF YOU, AND HAVE A BEAUTIFUL ROMANCE.

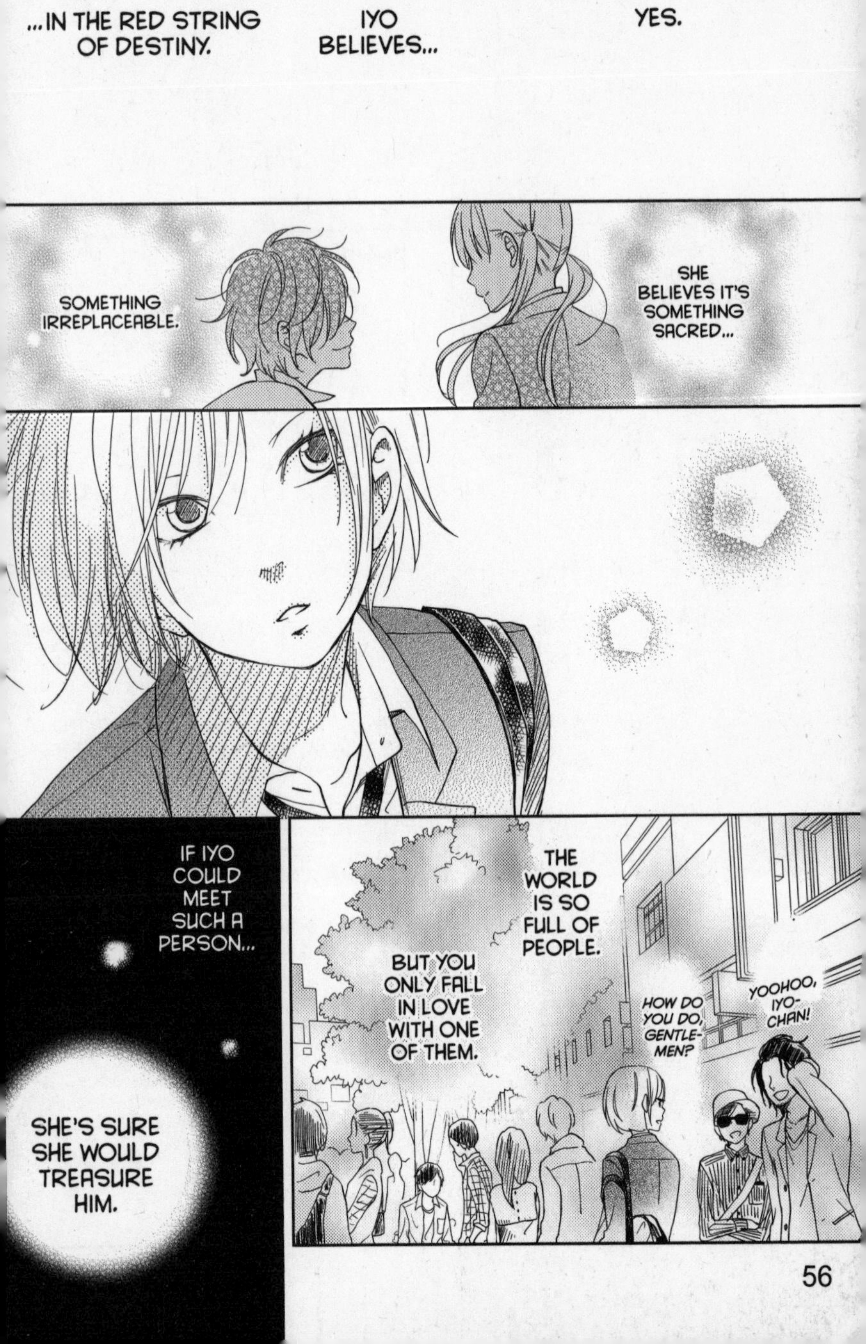
YES.
IYO BELIEVES...
...IN THE RED STRING OF DESTINY.
SHE BELIEVES IT'S SOMETHING SACRED...
SOMETHING IRREPLACEABLE.
THE WORLD IS SO FULL OF PEOPLE.
BUT YOU ONLY FALL IN LOVE WITH ONE OF THEM.
YOOHOO, IYO-CHAN!
HOW DO YOU DO, GENTLEMEN?
IF IYO COULD MEET SUCH A PERSON...
SHE'S SURE SHE WOULD TREASURE HIM.

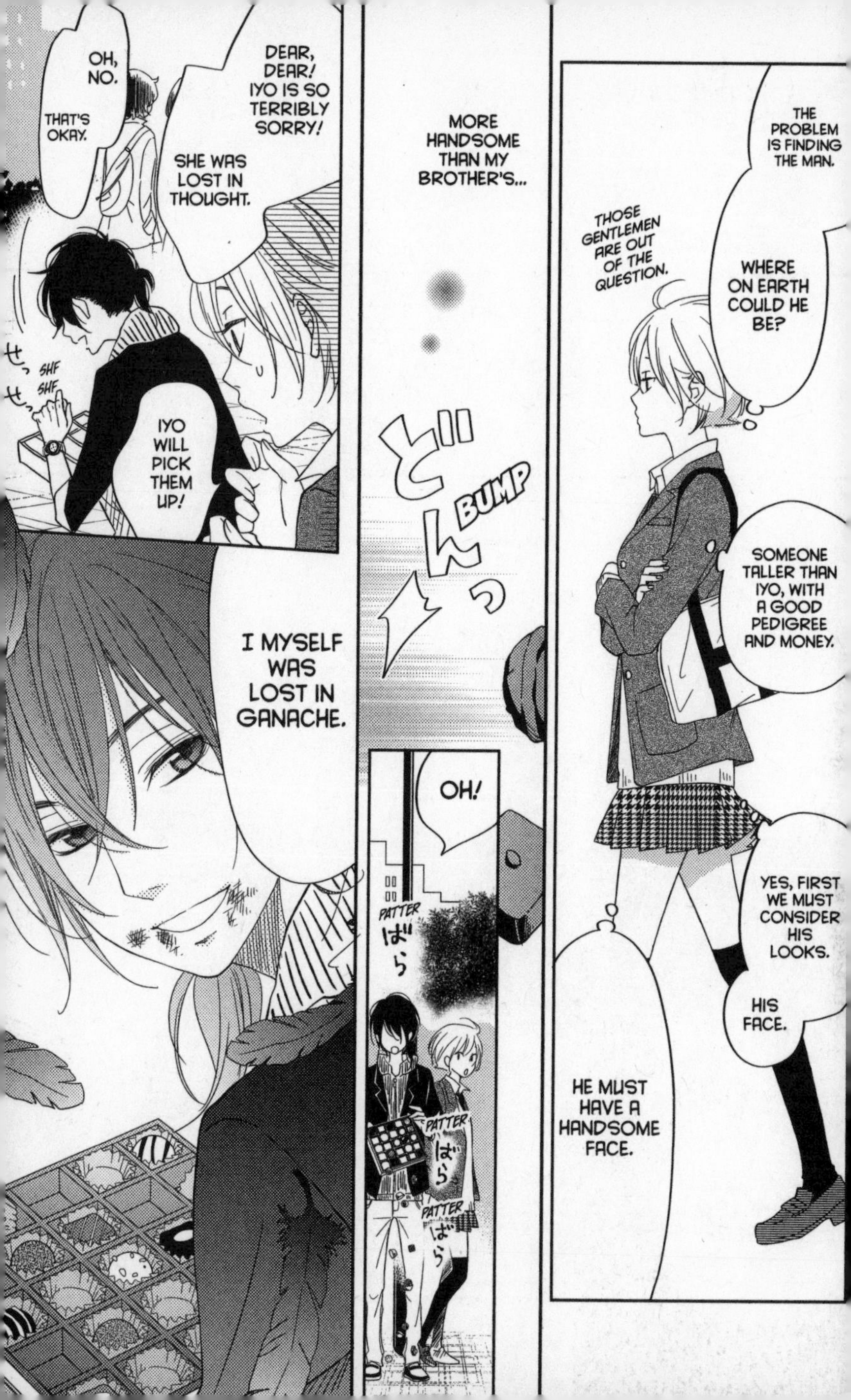
THE PROBLEM IS FINDING THE MAN.
WHERE ON EARTH COULD HE BE?
THOSE GENTLEMEN ARE OUT OF THE QUESTION.
SOMEONE TALLER THAN IYO, WITH A GOOD PEDIGREE AND MONEY.
YES, FIRST WE MUST CONSIDER HIS LOOKS.
HIS FACE.
HE MUST HAVE A HANDSOME FACE.
MORE HANDSOME THAN MY BROTHER'S...
どんっ
BUMP
OH!
PATTER
ばら
PATTER
ばら
PATTER
ばら
DEAR, DEAR! IYO IS SO TERRIBLY SORRY!
SHE WAS LOST IN THOUGHT.
OH, NO.
THAT'S OKAY.
せっ
SHF
せっ
SHF
IYO WILL PICK THEM UP!
I MYSELF WAS LOST IN GANACHE.

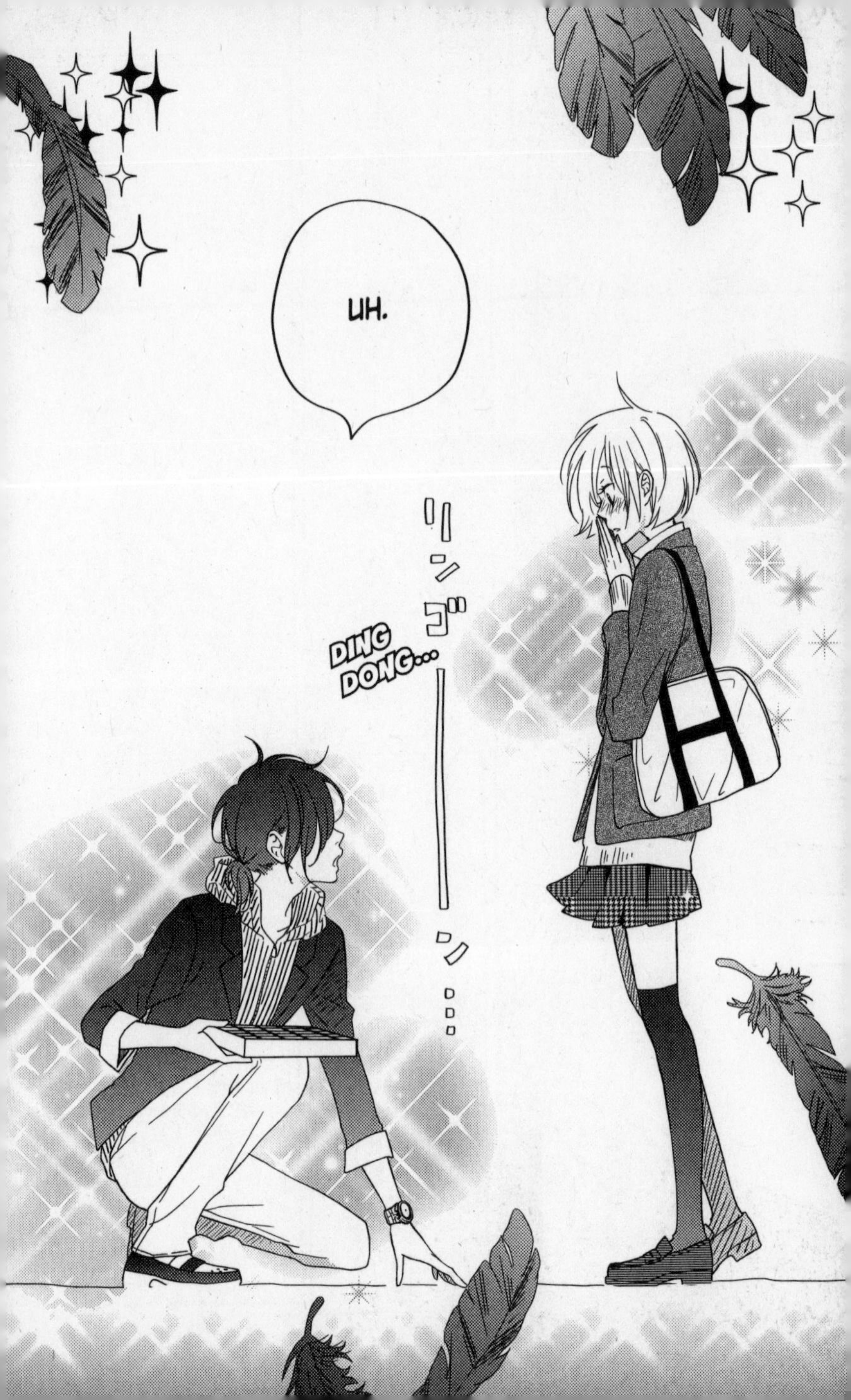
UH.
リンゴーン...
DING DONG...

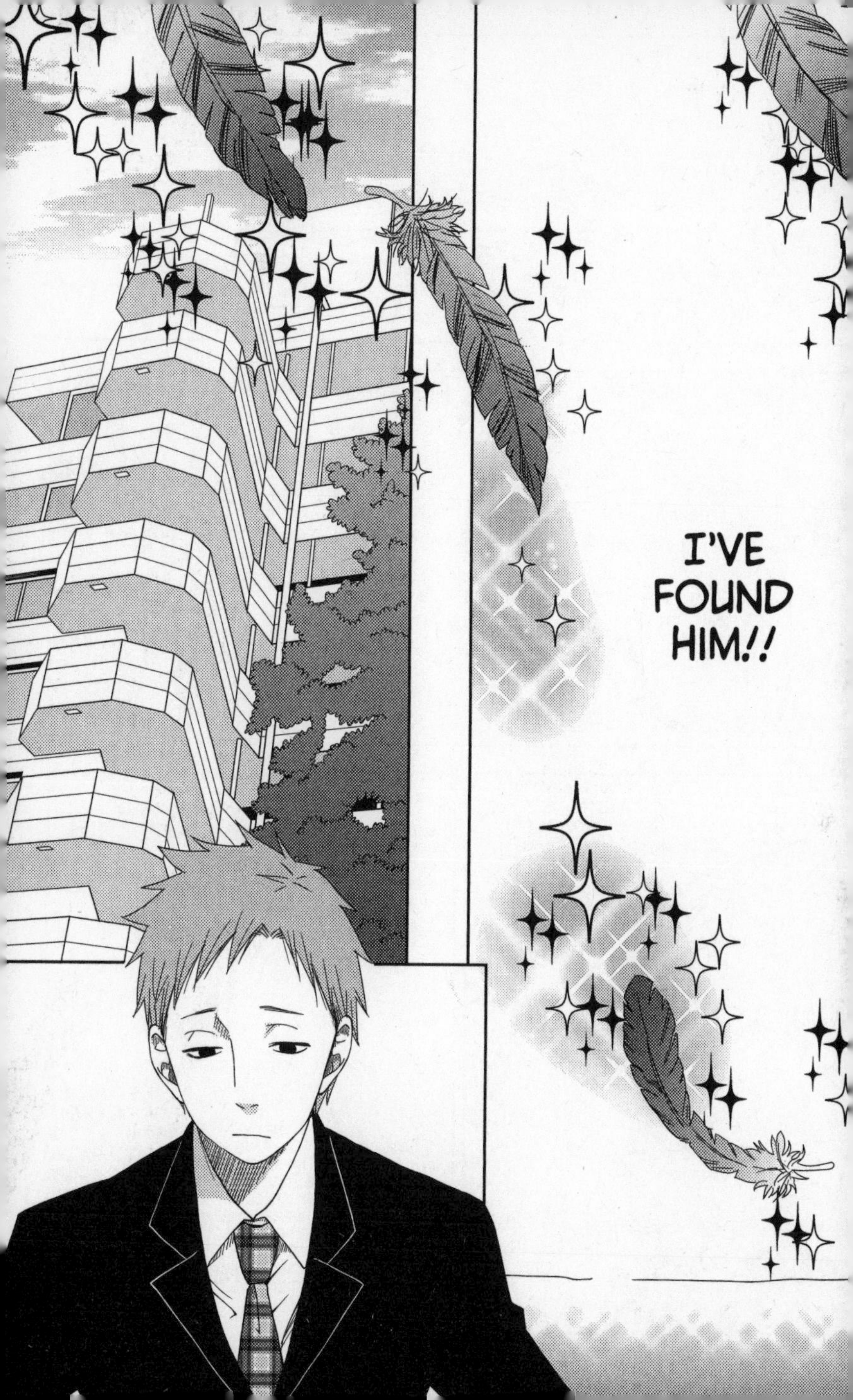
I'VE FOUND HIM!!

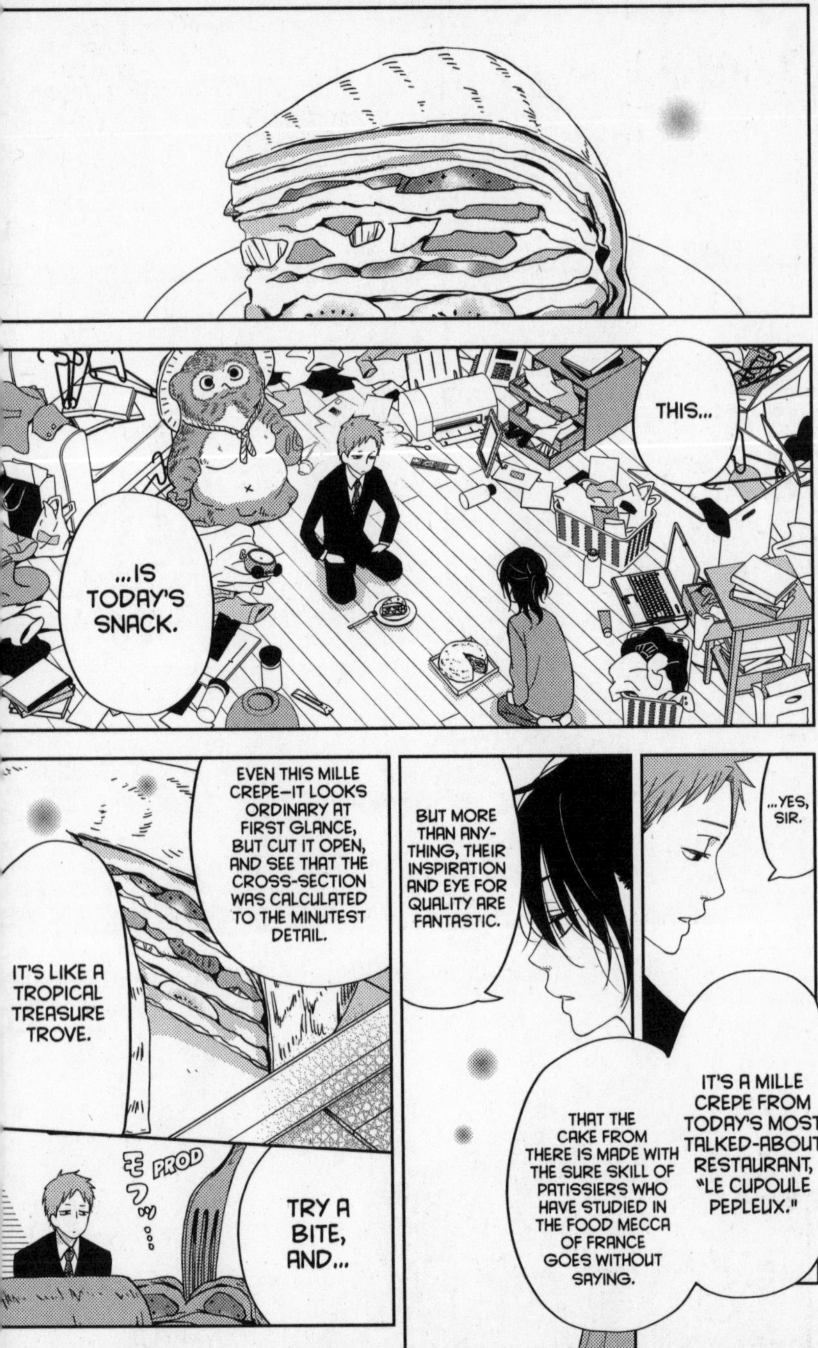
THIS...
...IS TODAY'S SNACK.
...YES, SIR.
IT'S A MILLE CREPE FROM TODAY'S MOST TALKED-ABOUT RESTAURANT, "LE CUPOULE PEPLEUX."
THAT THE CAKE FROM THERE IS MADE WITH THE SURE SKILL OF PATISSIERS WHO HAVE STUDIED IN THE FOOD MECCA OF FRANCE GOES WITHOUT SAYING.
BUT MORE THAN ANYTHING, THEIR INSPIRATION AND EYE FOR QUALITY ARE FANTASTIC.
EVEN THIS MILLE CREPE—IT LOOKS ORDINARY AT FIRST GLANCE, BUT CUT IT OPEN, AND SEE THAT THE CROSS-SECTION WAS CALCULATED TO THE MINUTEST DETAIL.
IT'S LIKE A TROPICAL TREASURE TROVE.
PROD
TRY A BITE, AND...

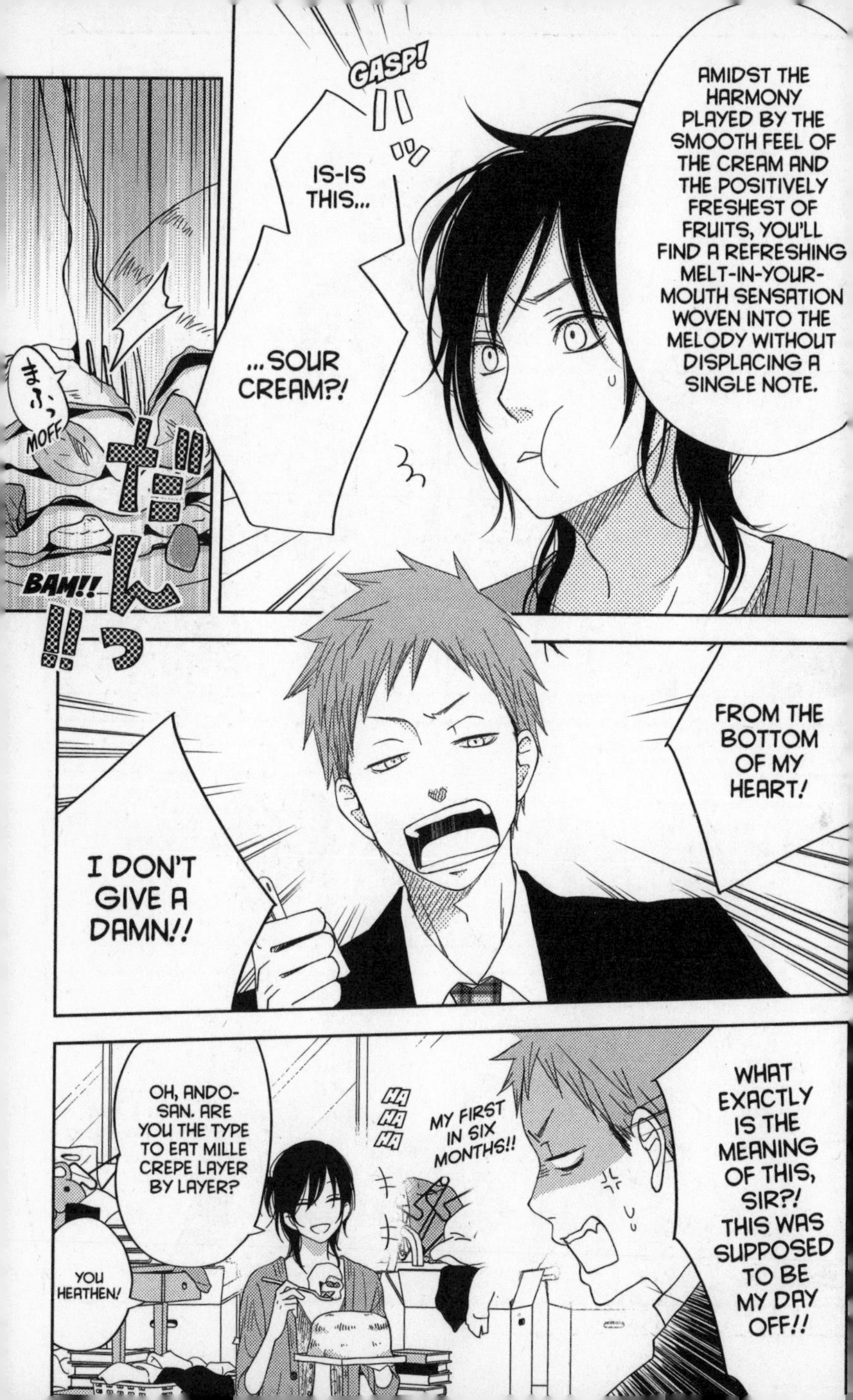
AMIDST THE HARMONY PLAYED BY THE SMOOTH FEEL OF THE CREAM AND THE POSITIVELY FRESHEST OF FRUITS, YOU'LL FIND A REFRESHING MELT-IN-YOUR-MOUTH SENSATION WOVEN INTO THE MELODY WITHOUT DISPLACING A SINGLE NOTE.
GASP!
IS-IS THIS...
...SOUR CREAM?!
まふっ
MOFF
ずだん!!っ
BAM!!
FROM THE BOTTOM OF MY HEART!
I DON'T GIVE A DAMN!!
WHAT EXACTLY IS THE MEANING OF THIS, SIR?! THIS WAS SUPPOSED TO BE MY DAY OFF!!
MY FIRST IN SIX MONTHS!!
HA HA HA
OH, ANDO-SAN. ARE YOU THE TYPE TO EAT MILLE CREPE LAYER BY LAYER?
YOU HEATHEN!

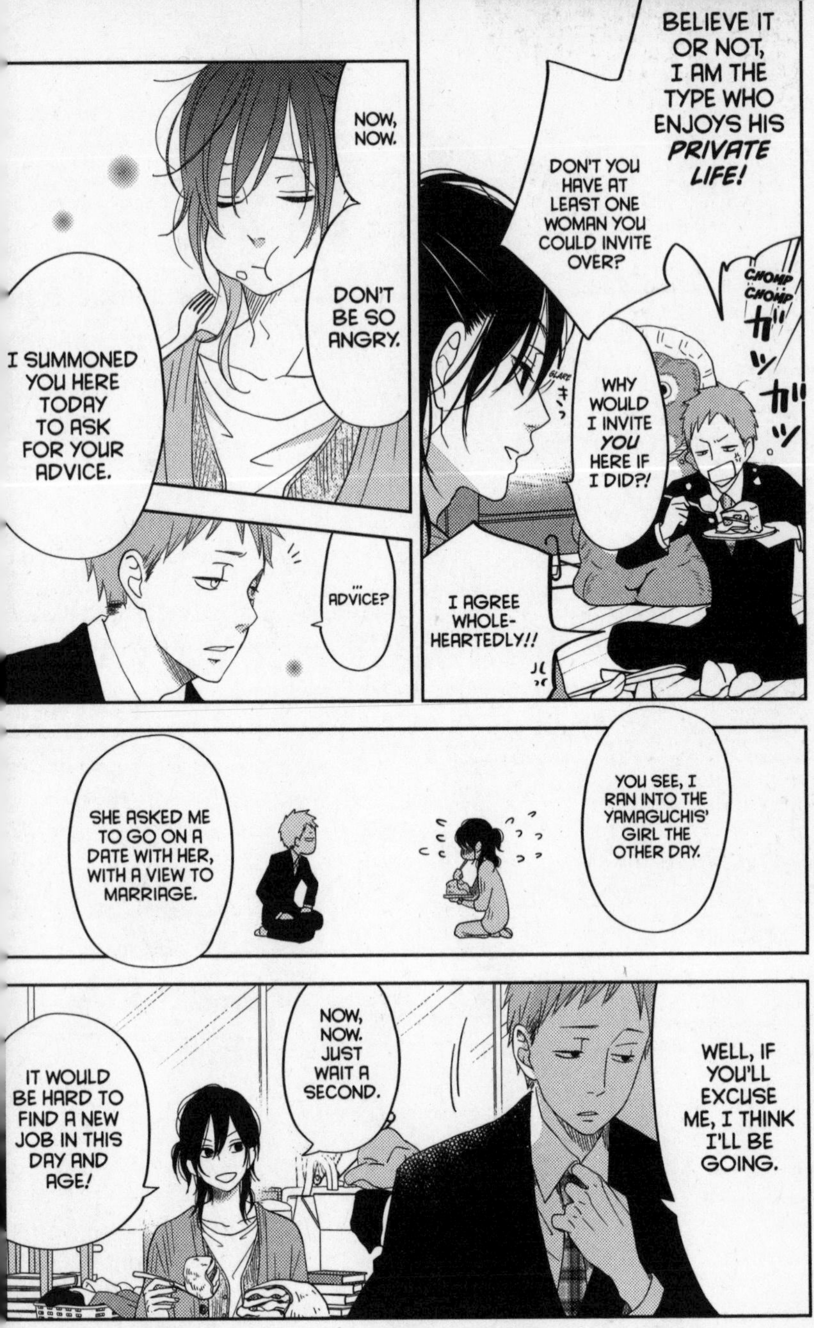
BELIEVE IT OR NOT, I AM THE TYPE WHO ENJOYS HIS *PRIVATE LIFE!*
DON'T YOU HAVE AT LEAST ONE WOMAN YOU COULD INVITE OVER?
CHOMP CHOMP
ガッ ガッ
WHY WOULD I INVITE *YOU* HERE IF I DID?!
GLARE
I AGREE WHOLE-HEARTEDLY!!
NOW, NOW.
DON'T BE SO ANGRY.
I SUMMONED YOU HERE TODAY TO ASK FOR YOUR ADVICE.
...ADVICE?
YOU SEE, I RAN INTO THE YAMAGUCHIS' GIRL THE OTHER DAY.
SHE ASKED ME TO GO ON A DATE WITH HER, WITH A VIEW TO MARRIAGE.
WELL, IF YOU'LL EXCUSE ME, I THINK I'LL BE GOING.
NOW, NOW. JUST WAIT A SECOND.
IT WOULD BE HARD TO FIND A NEW JOB IN THIS DAY AND AGE!

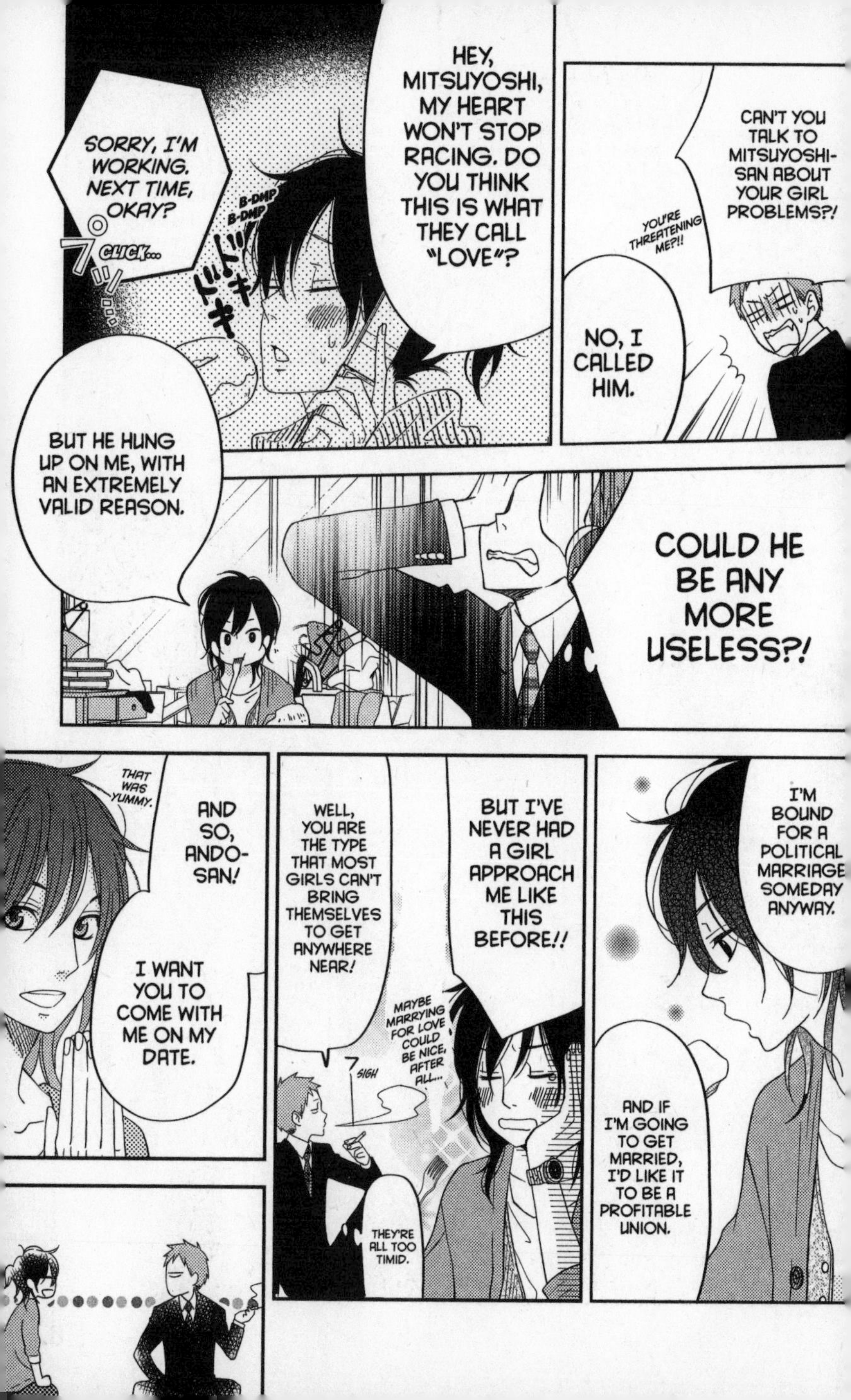
CAN'T YOU TALK TO MITSUYOSHI-SAN ABOUT YOUR GIRL PROBLEMS?!
YOU'RE THREATENING ME?!!
NO, I CALLED HIM.
HEY, MITSUYOSHI, MY HEART WON'T STOP RACING. DO YOU THINK THIS IS WHAT THEY CALL "LOVE"?
B-DMP B-DMP
SORRY, I'M WORKING. NEXT TIME, OKAY?
CLICK...
BUT HE HUNG UP ON ME, WITH AN EXTREMELY VALID REASON.
COULD HE BE ANY MORE USELESS?!
I'M BOUND FOR A POLITICAL MARRIAGE SOMEDAY ANYWAY.
AND IF I'M GOING TO GET MARRIED, I'D LIKE IT TO BE A PROFITABLE UNION.
BUT I'VE NEVER HAD A GIRL APPROACH ME LIKE THIS BEFORE!!
WELL, YOU ARE THE TYPE THAT MOST GIRLS CAN'T BRING THEMSELVES TO GET ANYWHERE NEAR!
MAYBE MARRYING FOR LOVE COULD BE NICE, AFTER ALL...
SIGH
THEY'RE ALL TOO TIMID.
THAT WAS YUMMY.
AND SO, ANDO-SAN!
I WANT YOU TO COME WITH ME ON MY DATE.

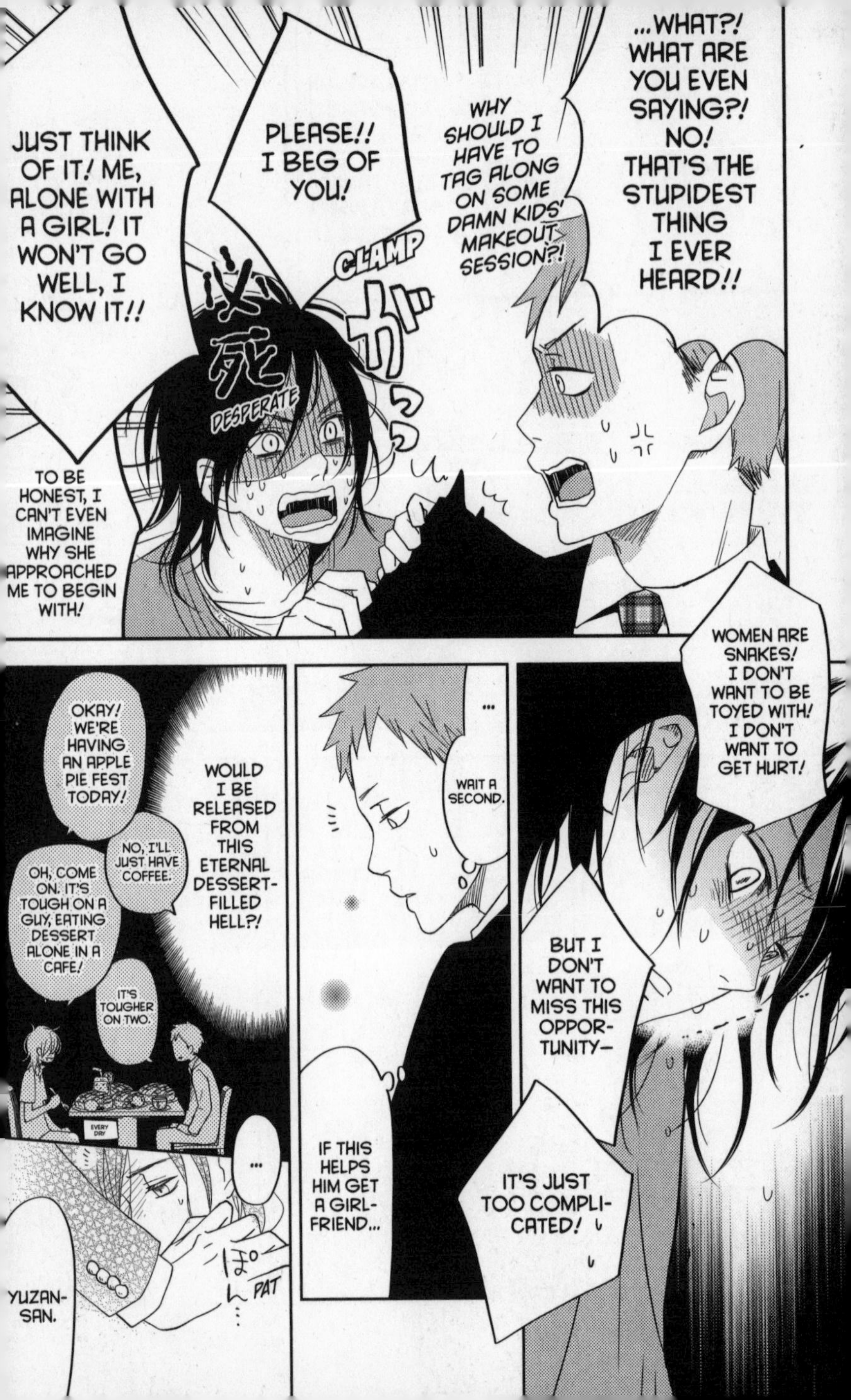

...WHAT?! WHAT ARE YOU EVEN SAYING?! NO! THAT'S THE STUPIDEST THING I EVER HEARD!!
WHY SHOULD I HAVE TO TAG ALONG ON SOME DAMN KIDS' MAKEOUT SESSION?!
PLEASE!! I BEG OF YOU!
カッ
CLAMP
JUST THINK OF IT! ME, ALONE WITH A GIRL! IT WON'T GO WELL, I KNOW IT!!
必死
DESPERATE
TO BE HONEST, I CAN'T EVEN IMAGINE WHY SHE APPROACHED ME TO BEGIN WITH!
WOMEN ARE SNAKES! I DON'T WANT TO BE TOYED WITH! I DON'T WANT TO GET HURT!
BUT I DON'T WANT TO MISS THIS OPPORTUNITY—
IT'S JUST TOO COMPLICATED!
...
WAIT A SECOND.
IF THIS HELPS HIM GET A GIRLFRIEND...
WOULD I BE RELEASED FROM THIS ETERNAL DESSERT-FILLED HELL?!
OKAY! WE'RE HAVING AN APPLE PIE FEST TODAY!
NO, I'LL JUST HAVE COFFEE.
OH, COME ON. IT'S TOUGH ON A GUY, EATING DESSERT ALONE IN A CAFE!
IT'S TOUGHER ON TWO.
EVERY DAY
...
ぽん
PAT
YUZAN-SAN.

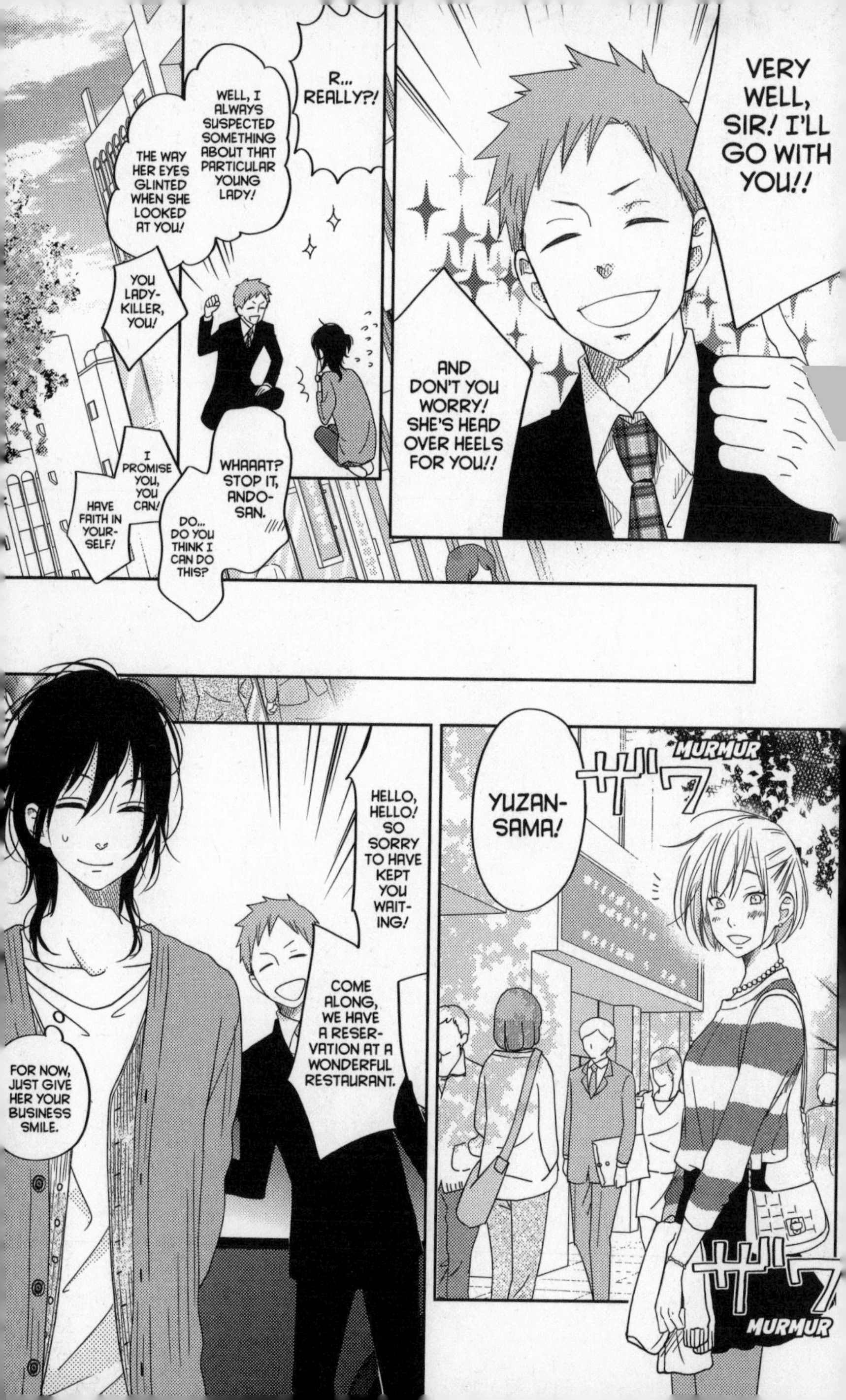
VERY WELL, SIR! I'LL GO WITH YOU!!
AND DON'T YOU WORRY! SHE'S HEAD OVER HEELS FOR YOU!!
R... REALLY?!
WELL, I ALWAYS SUSPECTED SOMETHING ABOUT THAT PARTICULAR YOUNG LADY!
THE WAY HER EYES GLINTED WHEN SHE LOOKED AT YOU!
YOU LADY-KILLER, YOU!
WHAAAT? STOP IT, ANDO-SAN.
I PROMISE YOU, YOU CAN!
DO... DO YOU THINK I CAN DO THIS?
HAVE FAITH IN YOURSELF!
MURMUR
YUZAN-SAMA!
MURMUR
HELLO, HELLO! SO SORRY TO HAVE KEPT YOU WAITING!
COME ALONG, WE HAVE A RESERVATION AT A WONDERFUL RESTAURANT.
FOR NOW, JUST GIVE HER YOUR BUSINESS SMILE.

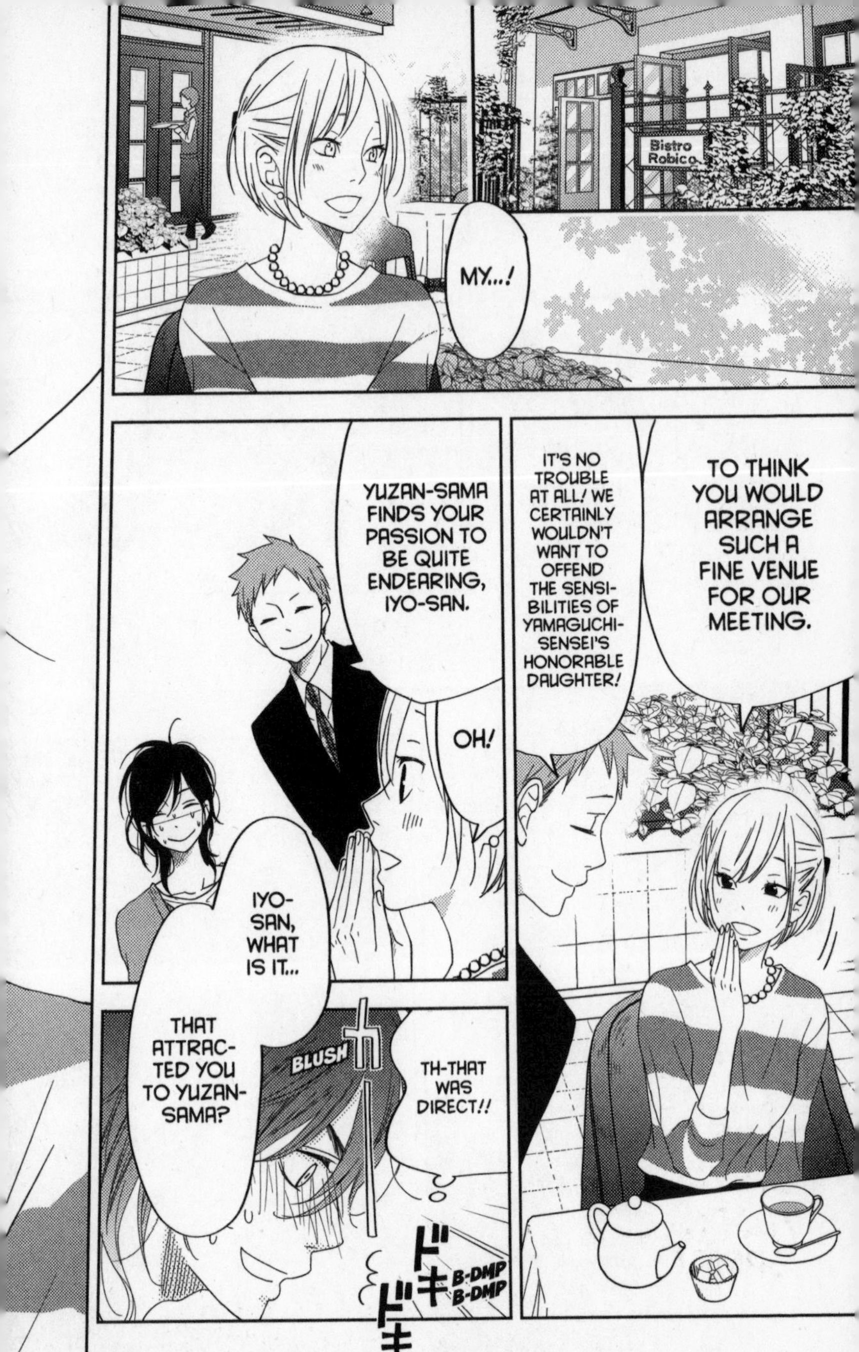
Bistro Robico
MY...!
TO THINK YOU WOULD ARRANGE SUCH A FINE VENUE FOR OUR MEETING.
IT'S NO TROUBLE AT ALL! WE CERTAINLY WOULDN'T WANT TO OFFEND THE SENSI-BILITIES OF YAMAGUCHI-SENSEI'S HONORABLE DAUGHTER!
YUZAN-SAMA FINDS YOUR PASSION TO BE QUITE ENDEARING, IYO-SAN.
OH!
IYO-SAN, WHAT IS IT...
THAT ATTRAC-TED YOU TO YUZAN-SAMA?
BLUSH
TH-THAT WAS DIRECT!!
B-DMP
B-DMP

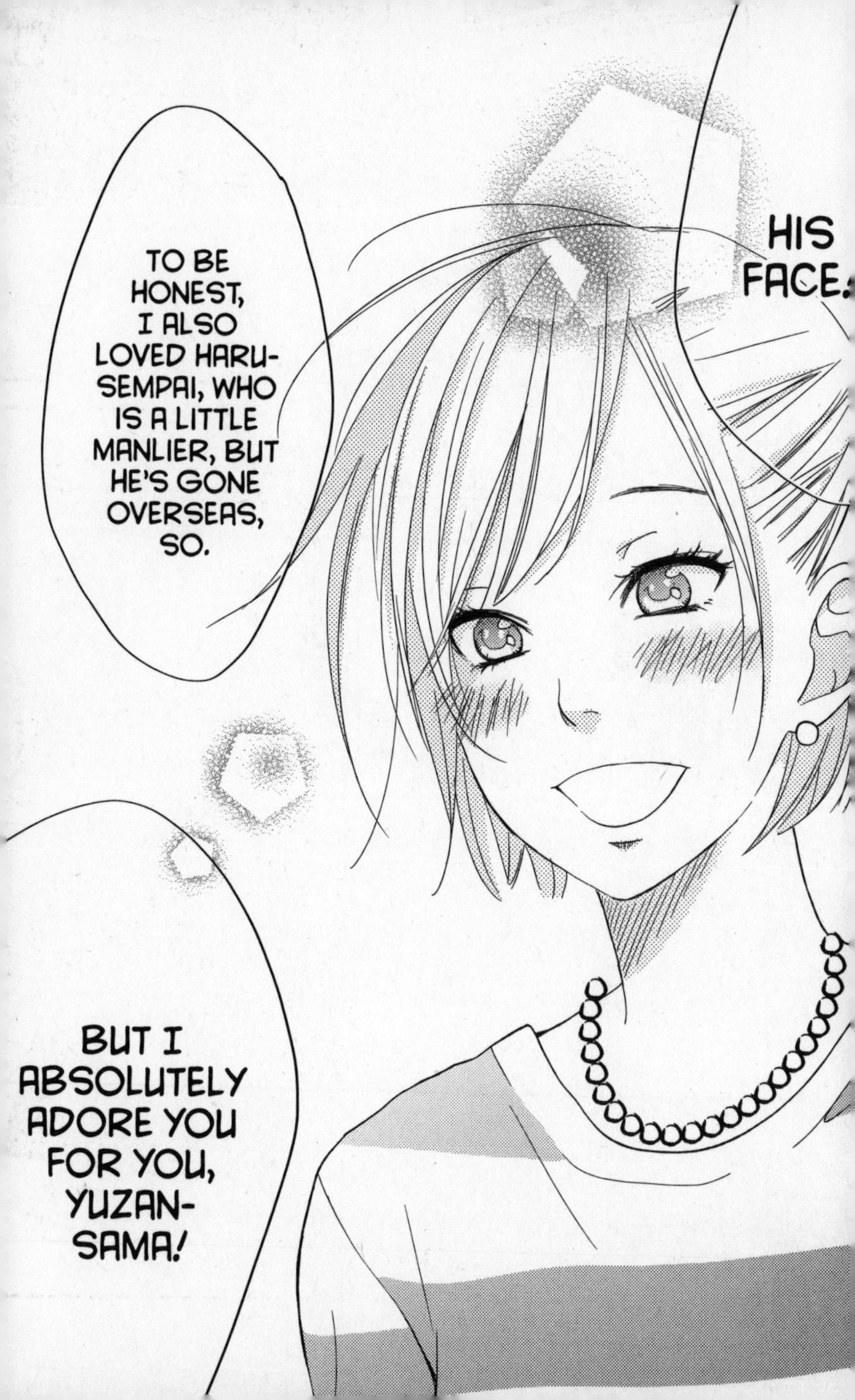
HIS FACE.
TO BE HONEST, I ALSO LOVED HARU-SEMPAI, WHO IS A LITTLE MANLIER, BUT HE'S GONE OVERSEAS, SO.
BUT I ABSOLUTELY ADORE YOU FOR YOU, YUZAN-SAMA!

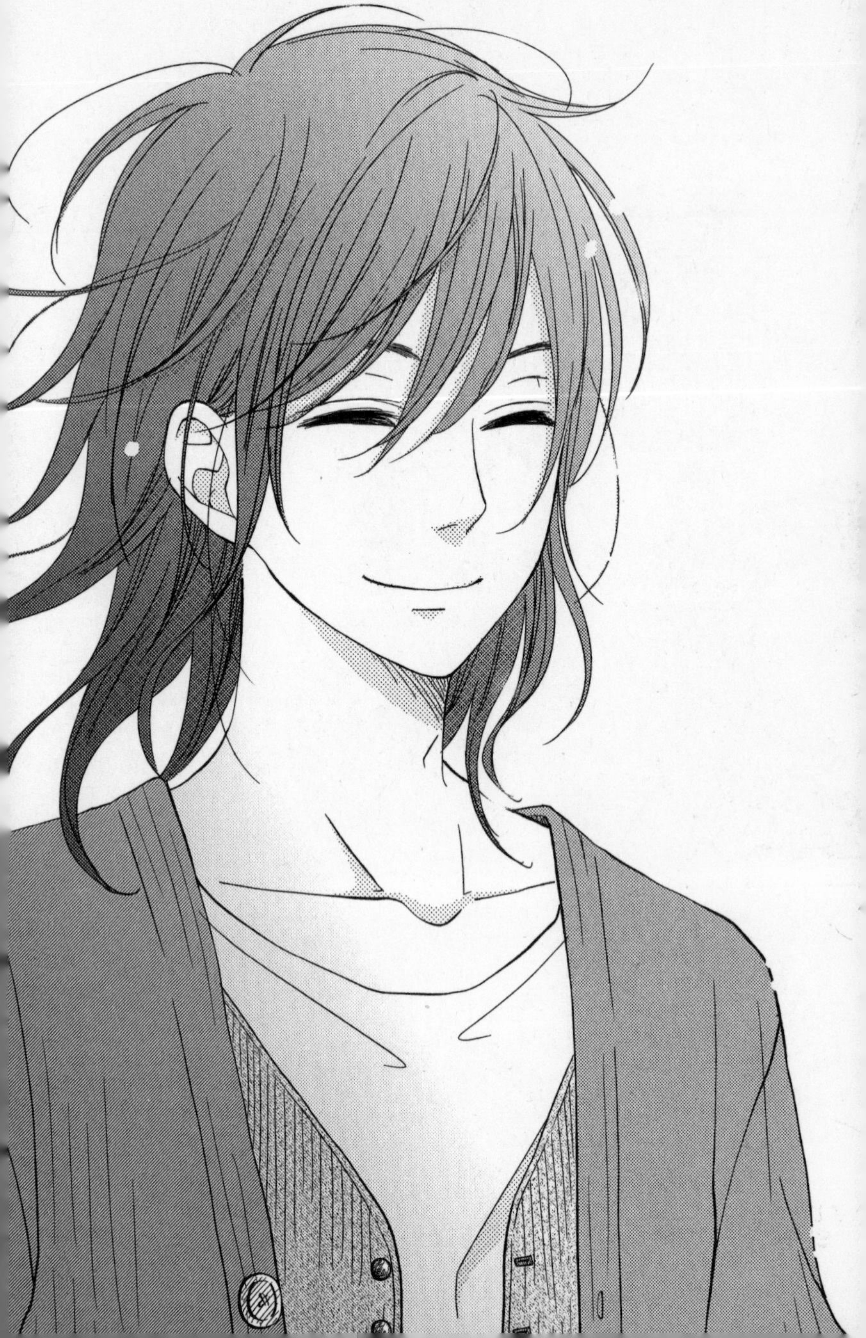

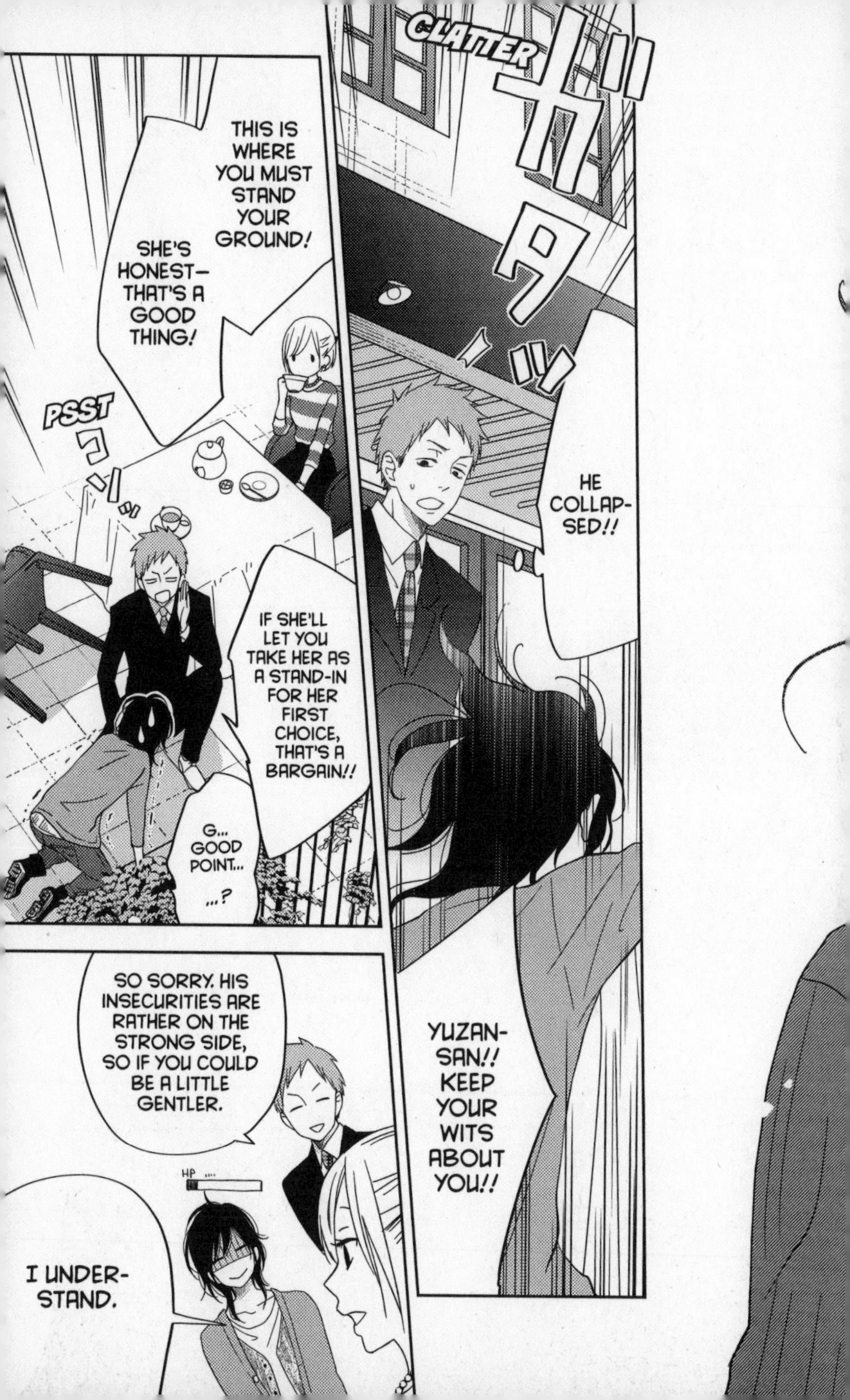

CLATTER
HE COLLAPSED!!
YUZAN-SAN!! KEEP YOUR WITS ABOUT YOU!!
THIS IS WHERE YOU MUST STAND YOUR GROUND!
SHE'S HONEST—THAT'S A GOOD THING!
PSST
IF SHE'LL LET YOU TAKE HER AS A STAND-IN FOR HER FIRST CHOICE, THAT'S A BARGAIN!!
G... GOOD POINT...
...?
SO SORRY. HIS INSECURITIES ARE RATHER ON THE STRONG SIDE, SO IF YOU COULD BE A LITTLE GENTLER.
HP
I UNDERSTAND.

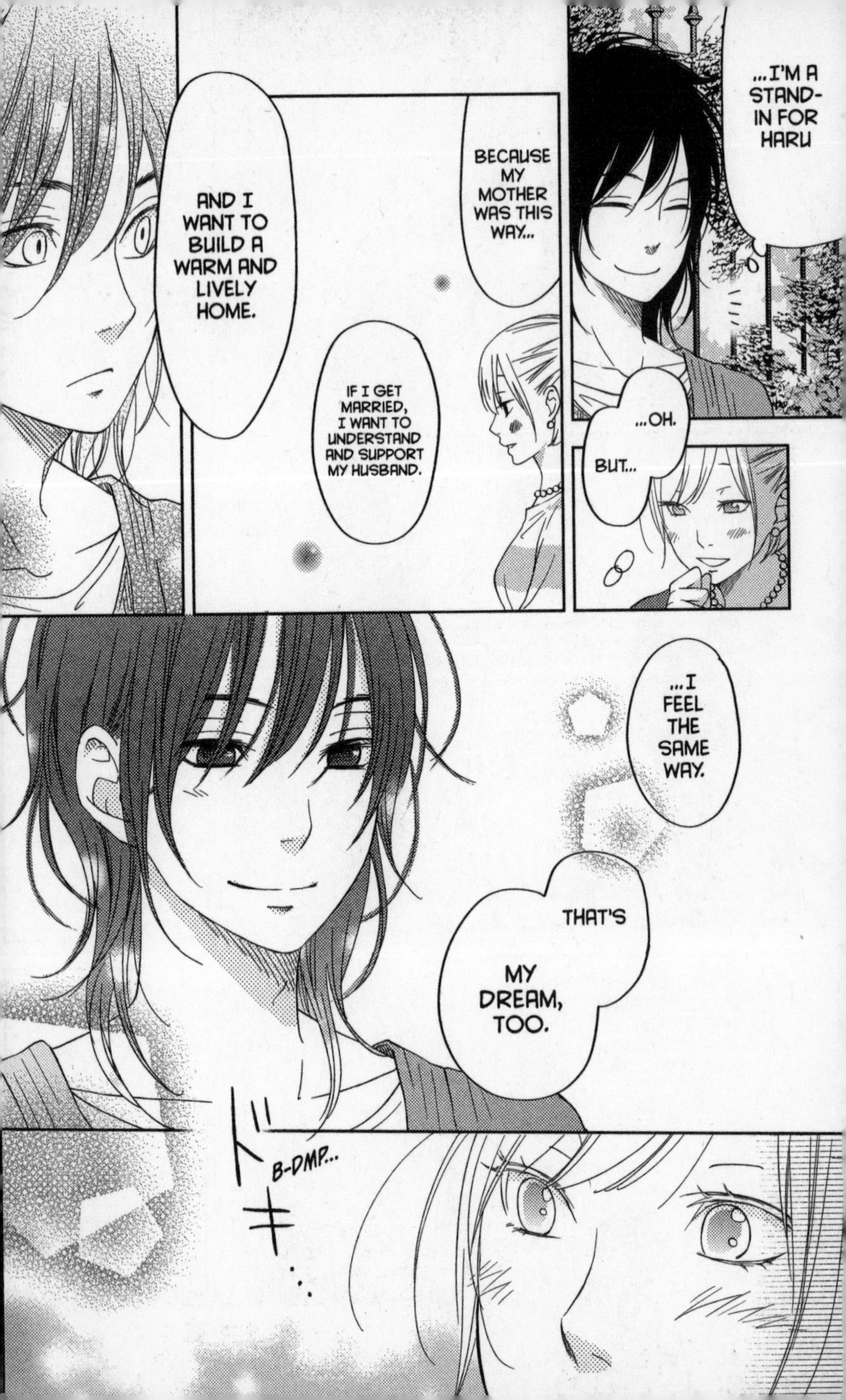
...I'M A STAND-IN FOR HARU
...OH.
BUT...
BECAUSE MY MOTHER WAS THIS WAY...
IF I GET MARRIED, I WANT TO UNDERSTAND AND SUPPORT MY HUSBAND.
AND I WANT TO BUILD A WARM AND LIVELY HOME.
...I FEEL THE SAME WAY.
THAT'S MY DREAM, TOO.
ドキ…
B-DMP...

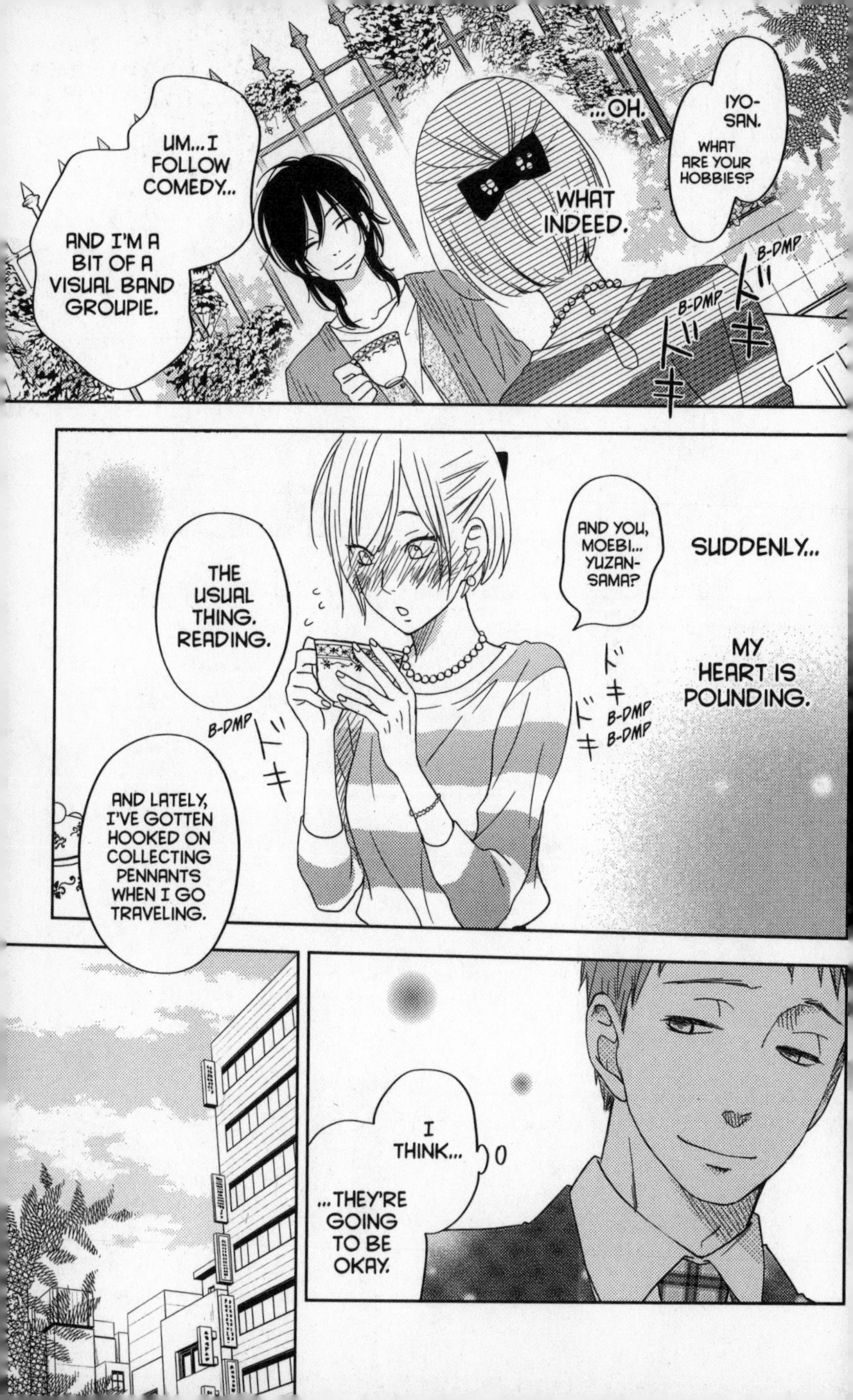
IYO-SAN.
WHAT ARE YOUR HOBBIES?
B-DMP ドキ
B-DMP ドキ
...OH.
WHAT INDEED.
UM...I FOLLOW COMEDY...
AND I'M A BIT OF A VISUAL BAND GROUPIE.
SUDDENLY...
MY HEART IS POUNDING.
AND YOU, MOEBI... YUZAN-SAMA?
ドキ B-DMP
ドキ B-DMP
THE USUAL THING. READING.
B-DMP ドキ
AND LATELY, I'VE GOTTEN HOOKED ON COLLECTING PENNANTS WHEN I GO TRAVELING.
I THINK...
...THEY'RE GOING TO BE OKAY.

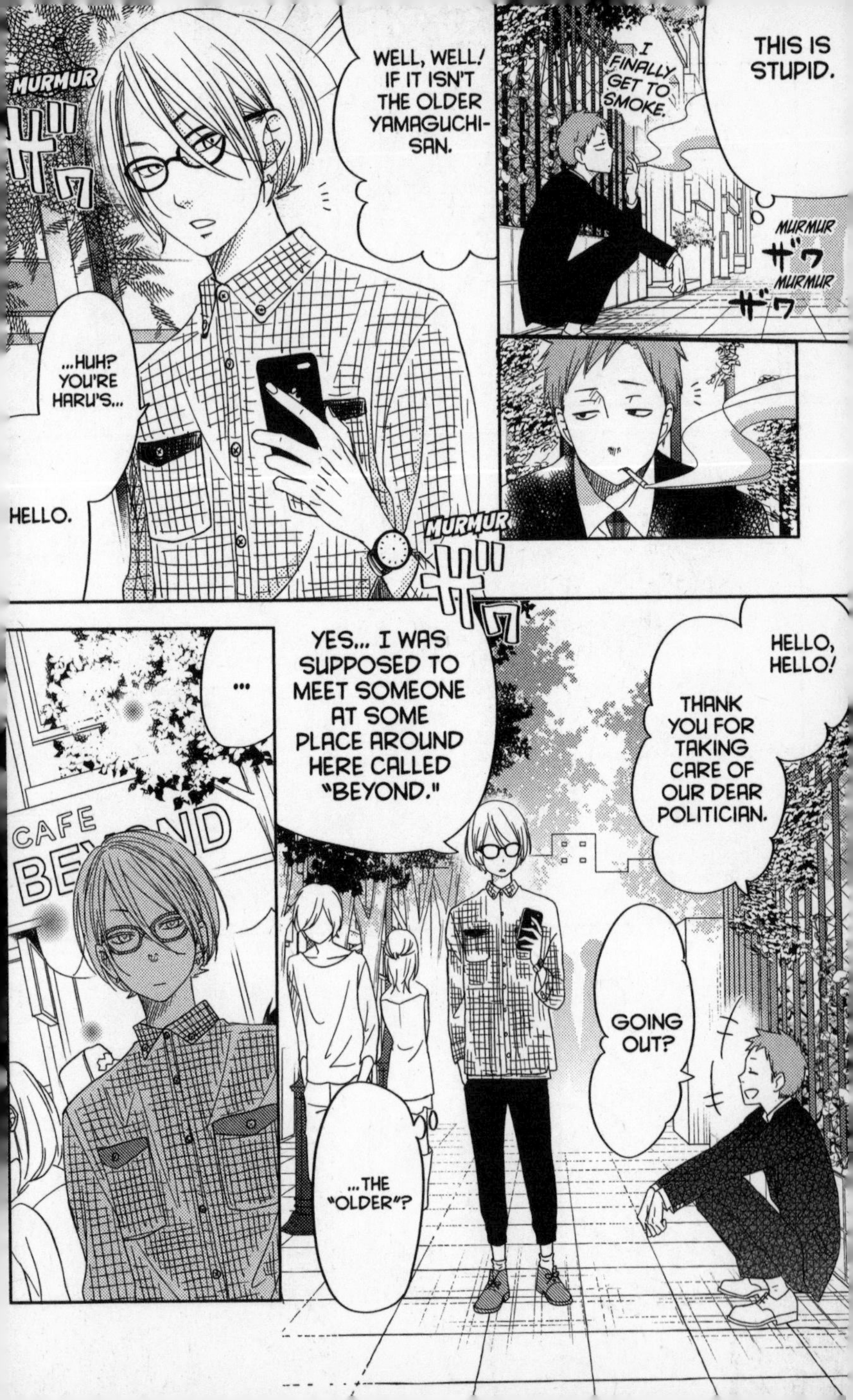
THIS IS STUPID.
I FINALLY GET TO SMOKE.
MURMUR
ザワ
MURMUR
ザワ
WELL, WELL! IF IT ISN'T THE OLDER YAMAGUCHI-SAN.
MURMUR
ザワ
...HUH? YOU'RE HARU'S...
HELLO.
MURMUR
ザワ
HELLO, HELLO!
THANK YOU FOR TAKING CARE OF OUR DEAR POLITICIAN.
GOING OUT?
YES... I WAS SUPPOSED TO MEET SOMEONE AT SOME PLACE AROUND HERE CALLED "BEYOND."
...THE "OLDER"?
...
CAFE

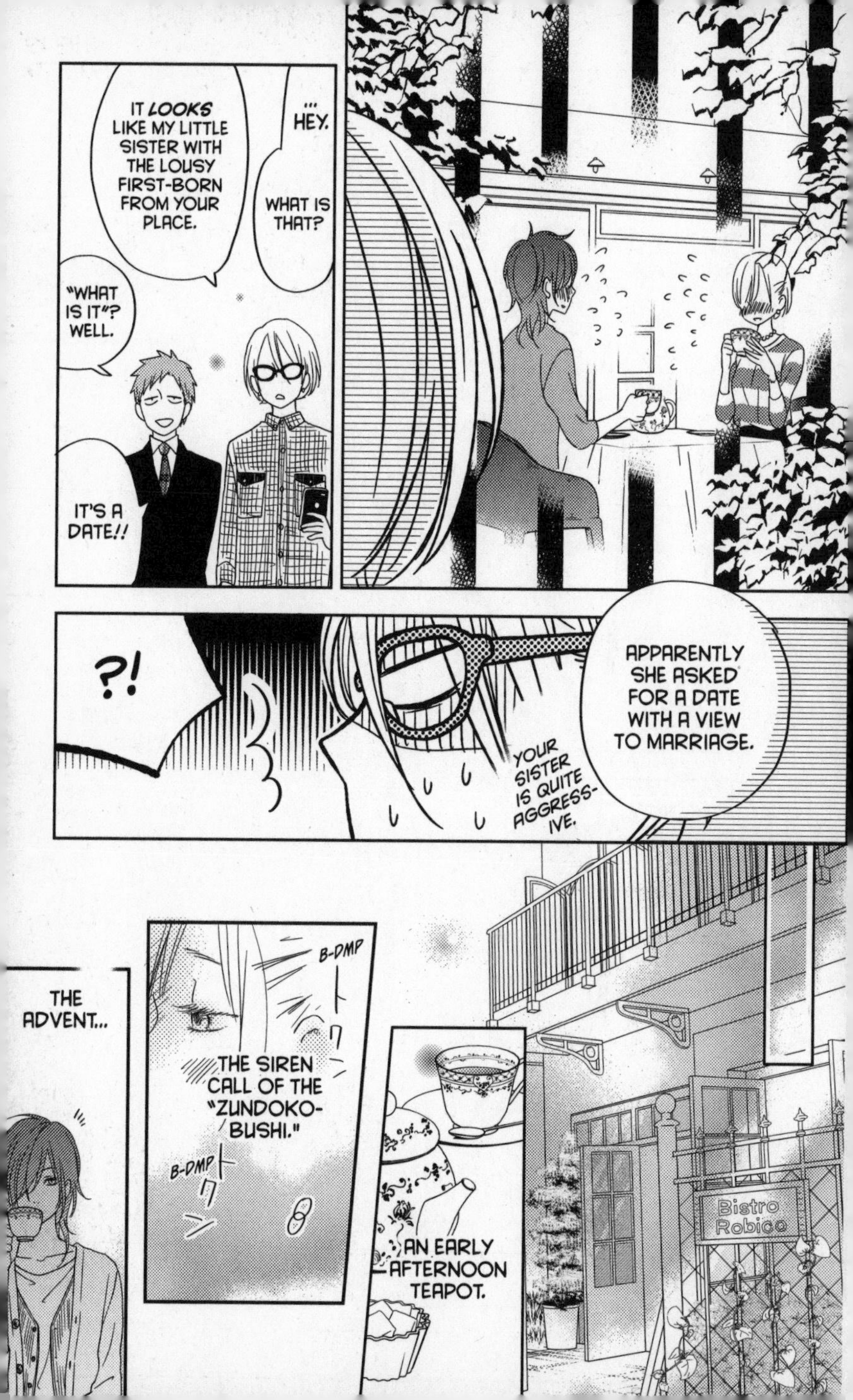

...HEY.
WHAT IS THAT?
IT *LOOKS* LIKE MY LITTLE SISTER WITH THE LOUSY FIRST-BORN FROM YOUR PLACE.
"WHAT IS IT"? WELL.
IT'S A DATE!!
APPARENTLY SHE ASKED FOR A DATE WITH A VIEW TO MARRIAGE.
YOUR SISTER IS QUITE AGGRESS-IVE.
?!
Bistro Robico
AN EARLY AFTERNOON TEAPOT.
B-DMP
THE SIREN CALL OF THE "ZUNDOKO-BUSHI."
B-DMP
THE ADVENT...

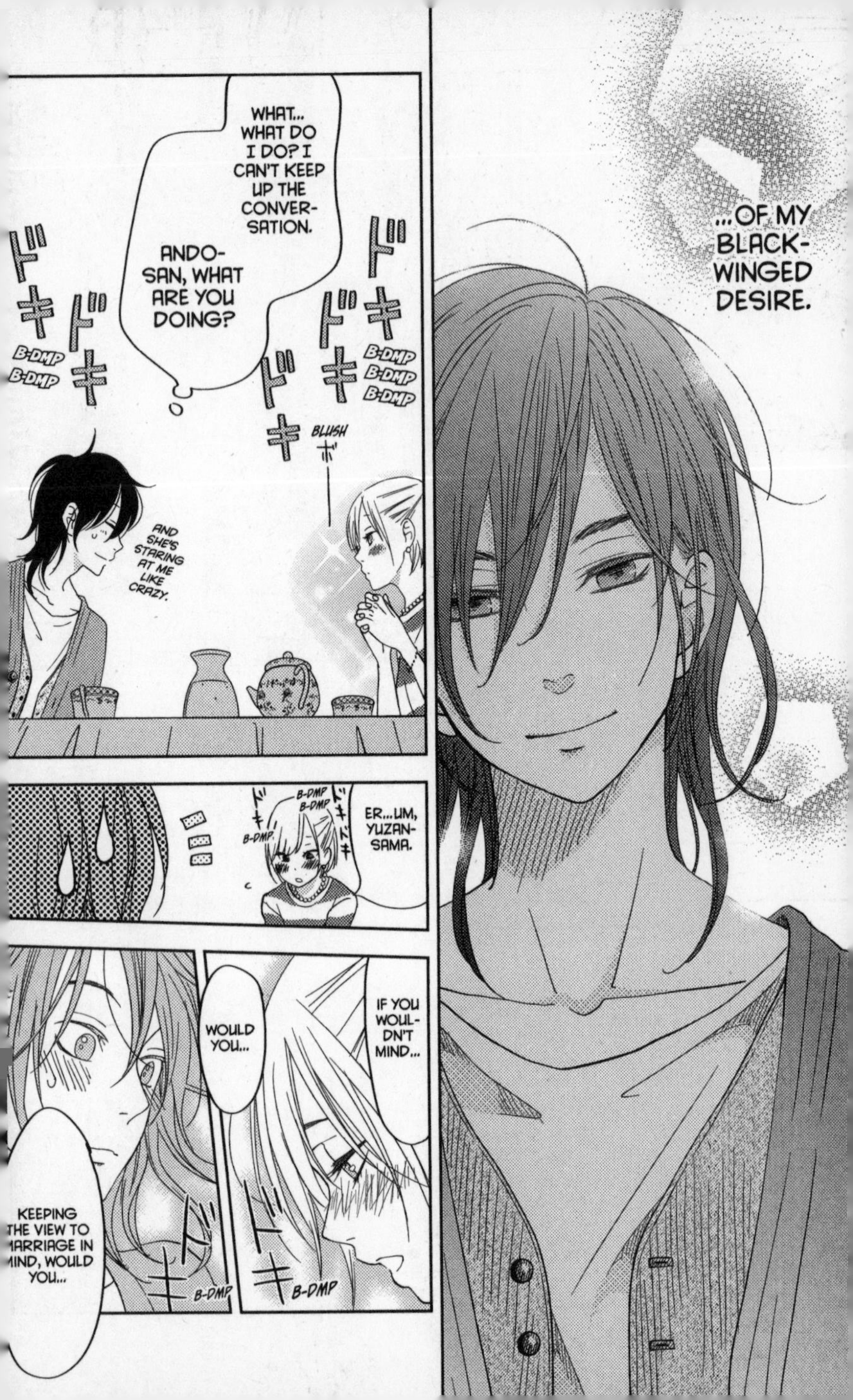
...OF MY BLACK-WINGED DESIRE.
WHAT... WHAT DO I DO? I CAN'T KEEP UP THE CONVERSATION.
ANDO-SAN, WHAT ARE YOU DOING?
ドキドキドキ
B-DMP B-DMP B-DMP
ドキドキ
B-DMP B-DMP
BLUSH ボ
AND SHE'S STARING AT ME LIKE CRAZY.
ER...UM, YUZAN-SAMA.
ドキドキ
B-DMP B-DMP B-DMP
IF YOU WOULDN'T MIND...
WOULD YOU...
ドキ B-DMP
KEEPING THE VIEW TO MARRIAGE IN MIND, WOULD YOU...
ドキ B-DMP

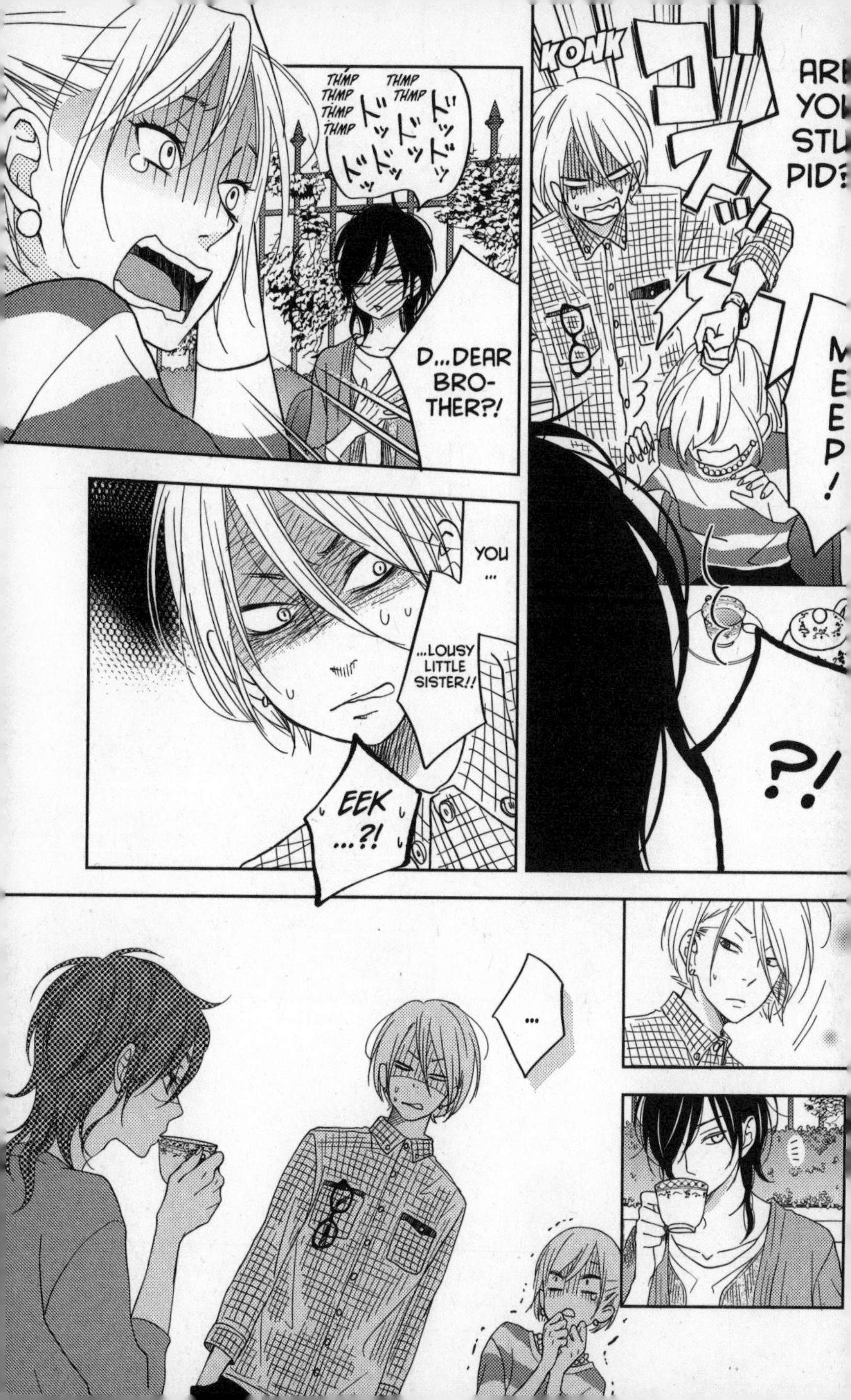
KONK
ARE YOU STUPID?!
MEEP!
THMP THMP THMP THMP
THMP THMP
D...DEAR BROTHER?!
?!
YOU...
...LOUSY LITTLE SISTER!!
EEK...?!
...

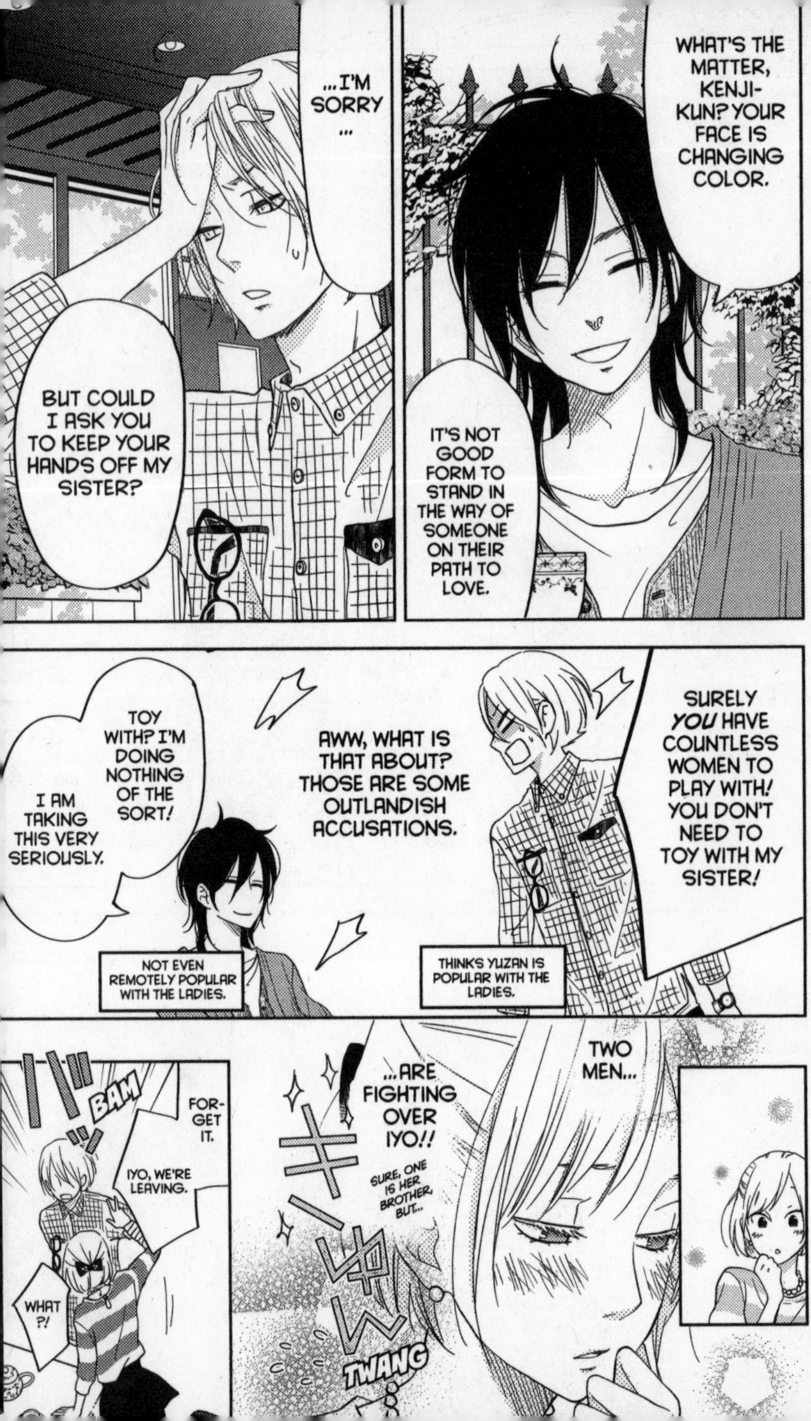
WHAT'S THE MATTER, KENJI-KUN? YOUR FACE IS CHANGING COLOR.
IT'S NOT GOOD FORM TO STAND IN THE WAY OF SOMEONE ON THEIR PATH TO LOVE.
...I'M SORRY...
BUT COULD I ASK YOU TO KEEP YOUR HANDS OFF MY SISTER?
SURELY *YOU* HAVE COUNTLESS WOMEN TO PLAY WITH! YOU DON'T NEED TO TOY WITH MY SISTER!
THINKS YUZAN IS POPULAR WITH THE LADIES.
AWW, WHAT IS THAT ABOUT? THOSE ARE SOME OUTLANDISH ACCUSATIONS.
TOY WITH? I'M DOING NOTHING OF THE SORT!
I AM TAKING THIS VERY SERIOUSLY.
NOT EVEN REMOTELY POPULAR WITH THE LADIES.
TWO MEN...
...ARE FIGHTING OVER IYO!!
SURE, ONE IS HER BROTHER, BUT...
TWANG
BAM
FOR-GET IT.
IYO, WE'RE LEAVING.
WHAT?!

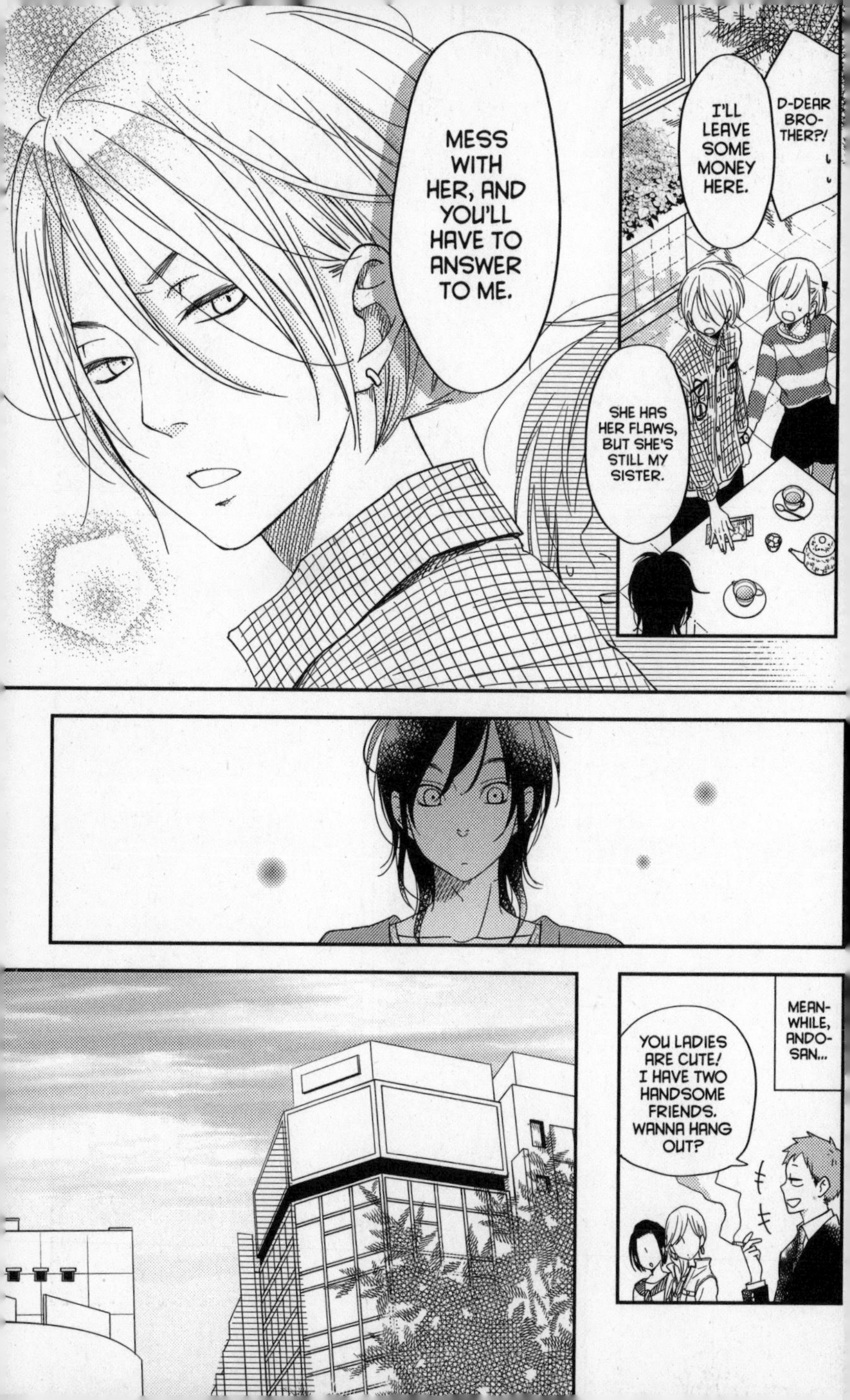
D-DEAR BRO-THER?!
I'LL LEAVE SOME MONEY HERE.
SHE HAS HER FLAWS, BUT SHE'S STILL MY SISTER.
MESS WITH HER, AND YOU'LL HAVE TO ANSWER TO ME.
MEAN-WHILE, ANDO-SAN...
YOU LADIES ARE CUTE! I HAVE TWO HANDSOME FRIENDS. WANNA HANG OUT?

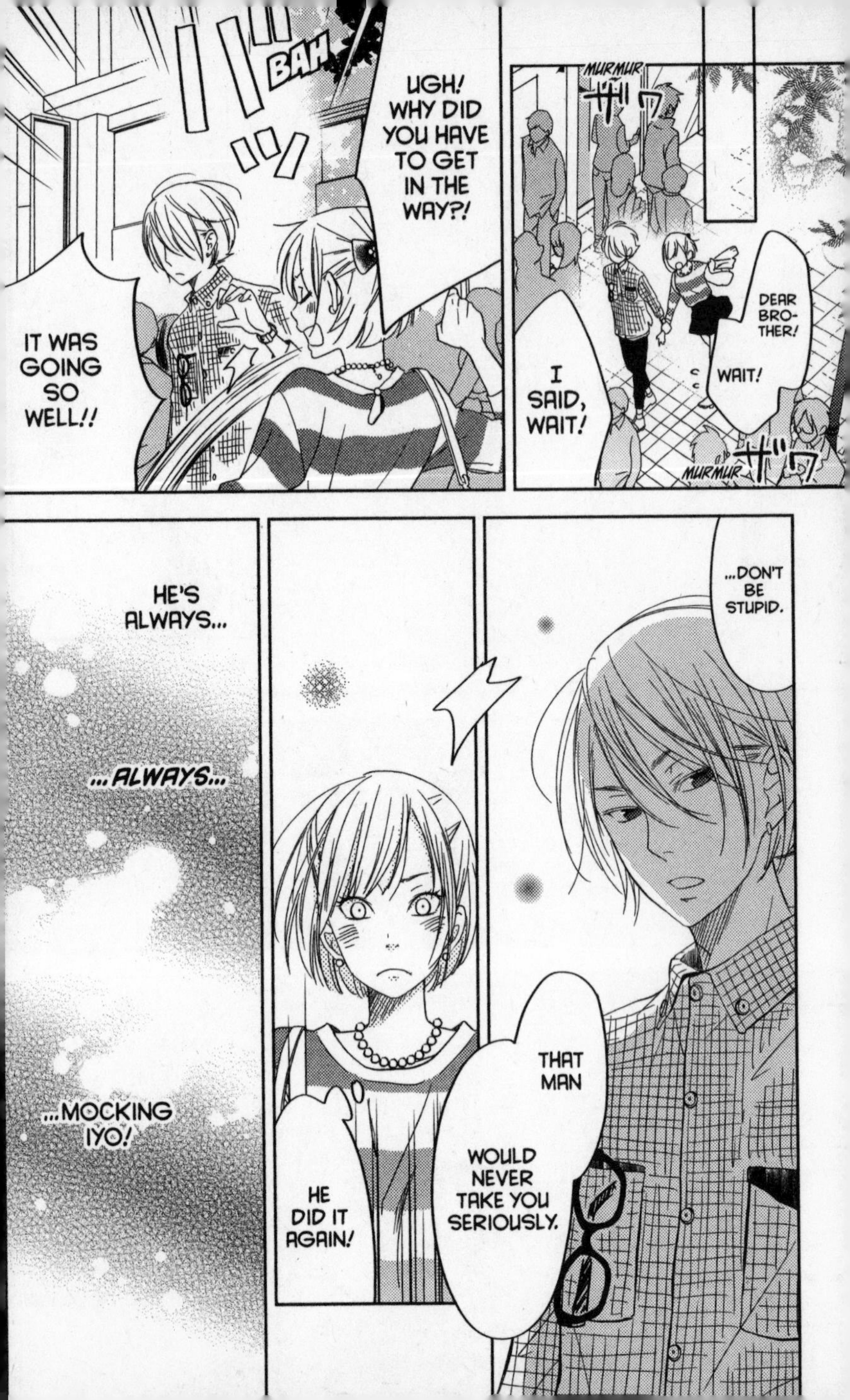
MURMUR ザワ
DEAR BROTHER!
WAIT!
I SAID, WAIT!
MURMUR ザワ
BAH
UGH! WHY DID YOU HAVE TO GET IN THE WAY?!
IT WAS GOING SO WELL!!
...DON'T BE STUPID.
THAT MAN
WOULD NEVER TAKE YOU SERIOUSLY.
HE DID IT AGAIN!
HE'S ALWAYS...
...ALWAYS...
...MOCKING IYO!

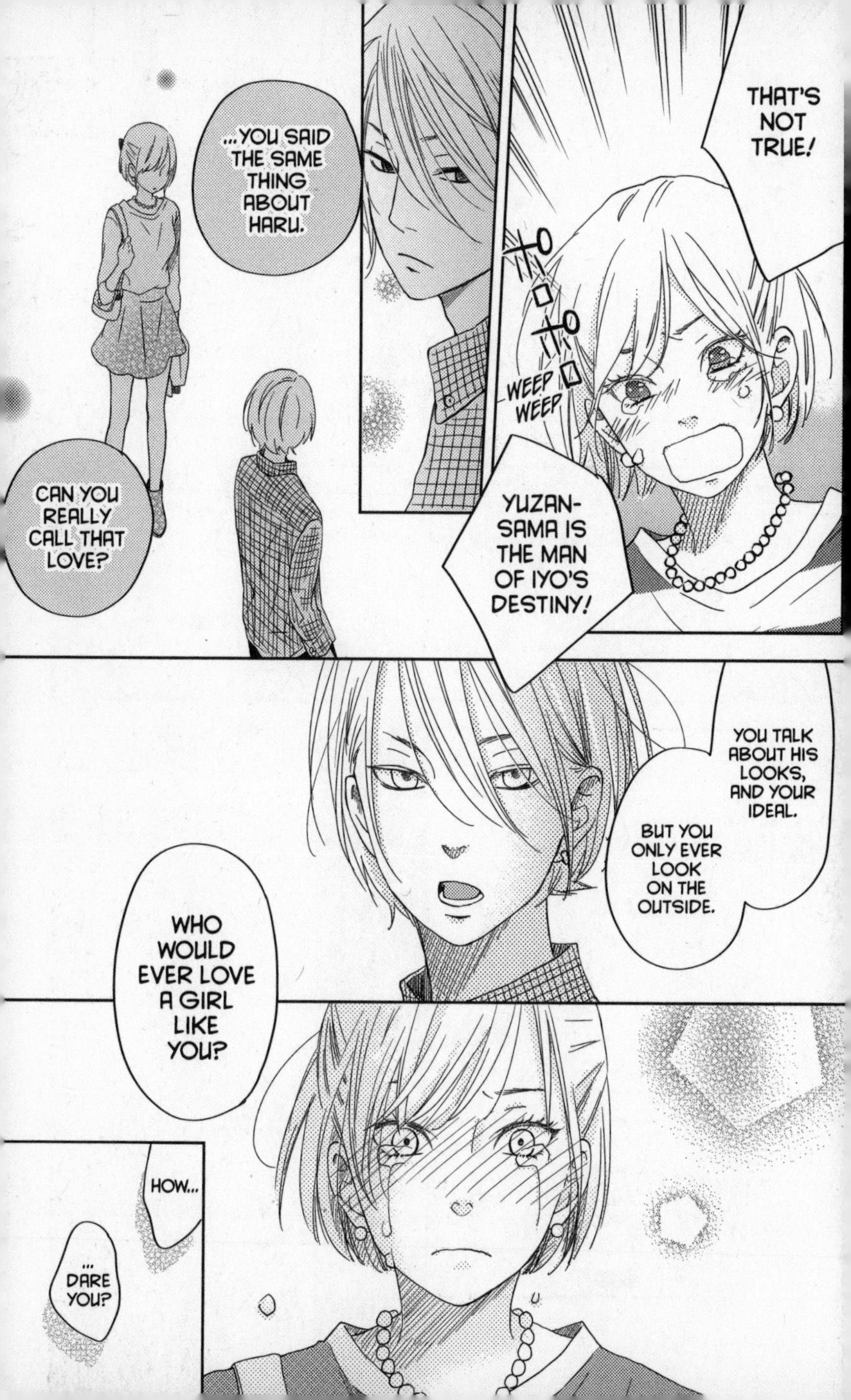
THAT'S NOT TRUE!
WEEP WEEP
YUZAN-SAMA IS THE MAN OF IYO'S DESTINY!
...YOU SAID THE SAME THING ABOUT HARU.
CAN YOU REALLY CALL THAT LOVE?
YOU TALK ABOUT HIS LOOKS, AND YOUR IDEAL.
BUT YOU ONLY EVER LOOK ON THE OUTSIDE.
WHO WOULD EVER LOVE A GIRL LIKE YOU?
HOW...
...DARE YOU?

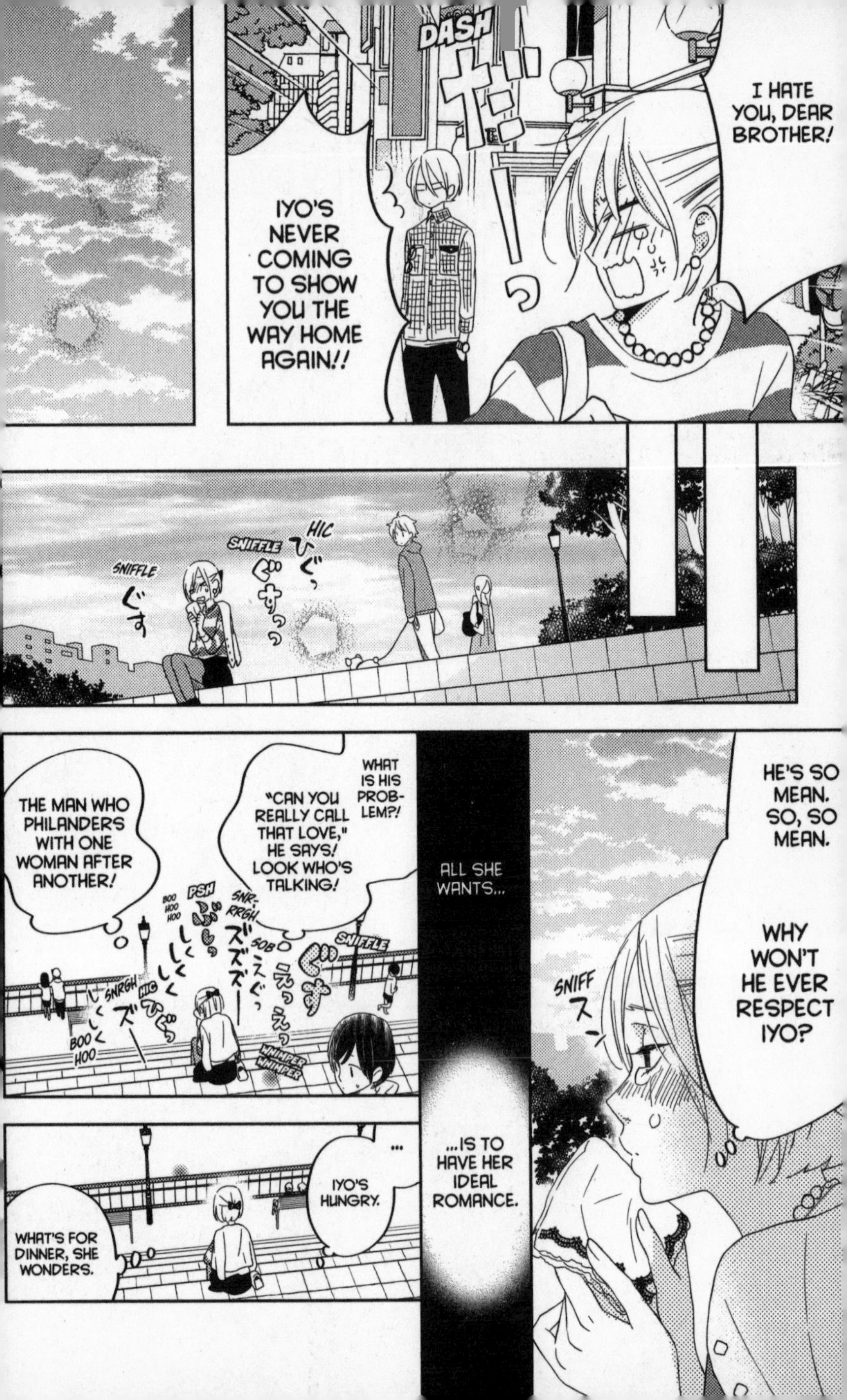

I HATE YOU, DEAR BROTHER!
DASH
IYO'S NEVER COMING TO SHOW YOU THE WAY HOME AGAIN!!
HIC
ひぐっ
SNIFFLE
ぐすっ
SNIFFLE
ぐす
HE'S SO MEAN. SO, SO MEAN.
WHY WON'T HE EVER RESPECT IYO?
SNIFF
ス－
ALL SHE WANTS...
...IS TO HAVE HER IDEAL ROMANCE.
WHAT IS HIS PROBLEM?!
"CAN YOU REALLY CALL THAT LOVE," HE SAYS! LOOK WHO'S TALKING!
THE MAN WHO PHILANDERS WITH ONE WOMAN AFTER ANOTHER!
SNIFFLE
SOB
SNR-RRGH
PSH
BOO HOO HOO
WHIMPER WHIMPER
HIC
SNRGH
BOO HOO
...
IYO'S HUNGRY.
WHAT'S FOR DINNER, SHE WONDERS.

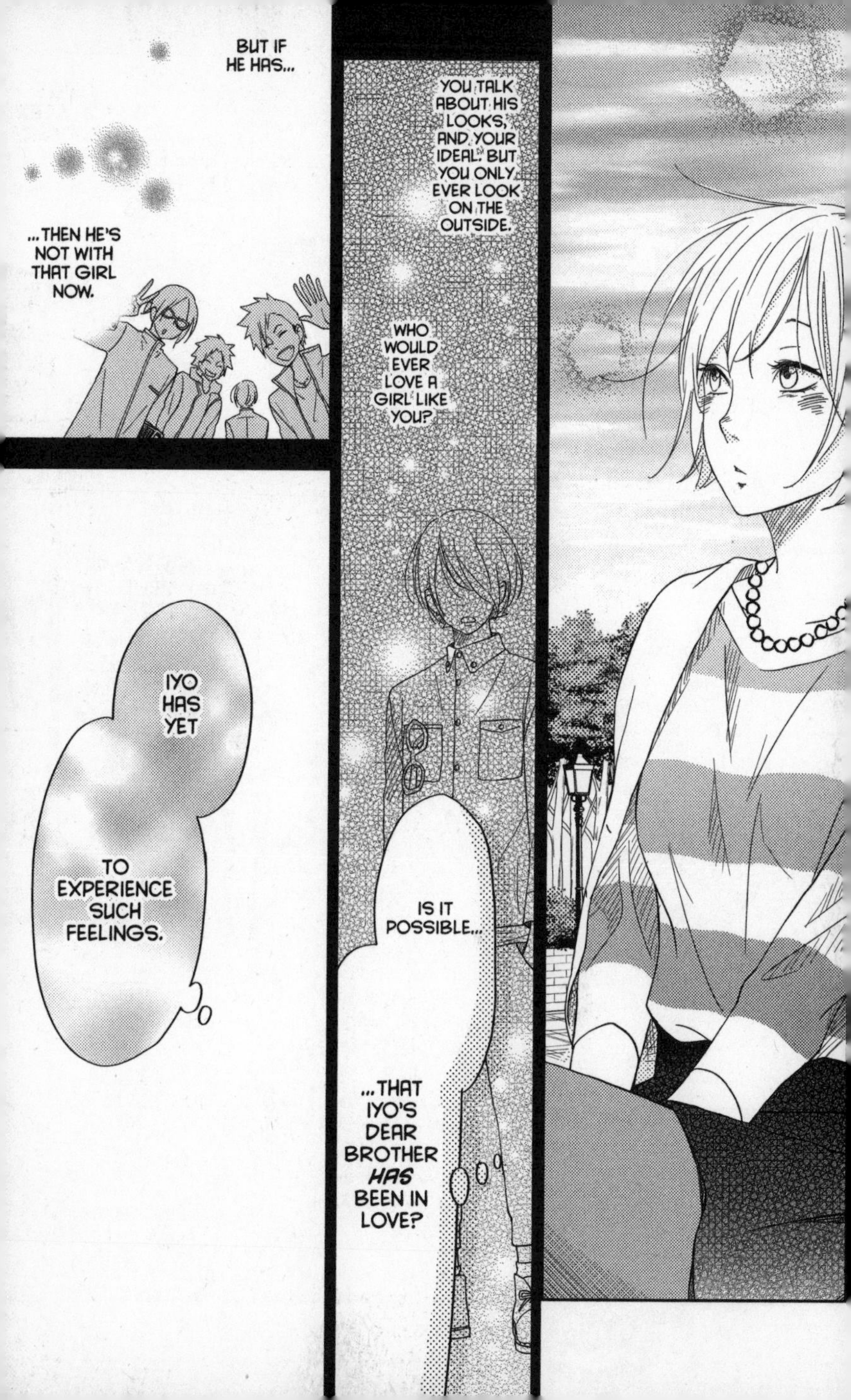
YOU TALK ABOUT HIS LOOKS, AND YOUR IDEAL. BUT YOU ONLY EVER LOOK ON THE OUTSIDE.
WHO WOULD EVER LOVE A GIRL LIKE YOU?
IS IT POSSIBLE...
...THAT IYO'S DEAR BROTHER *HAS* BEEN IN LOVE?
BUT IF HE HAS...
...THEN HE'S NOT WITH THAT GIRL NOW.
IYO HAS YET
TO EXPERIENCE SUCH FEELINGS.

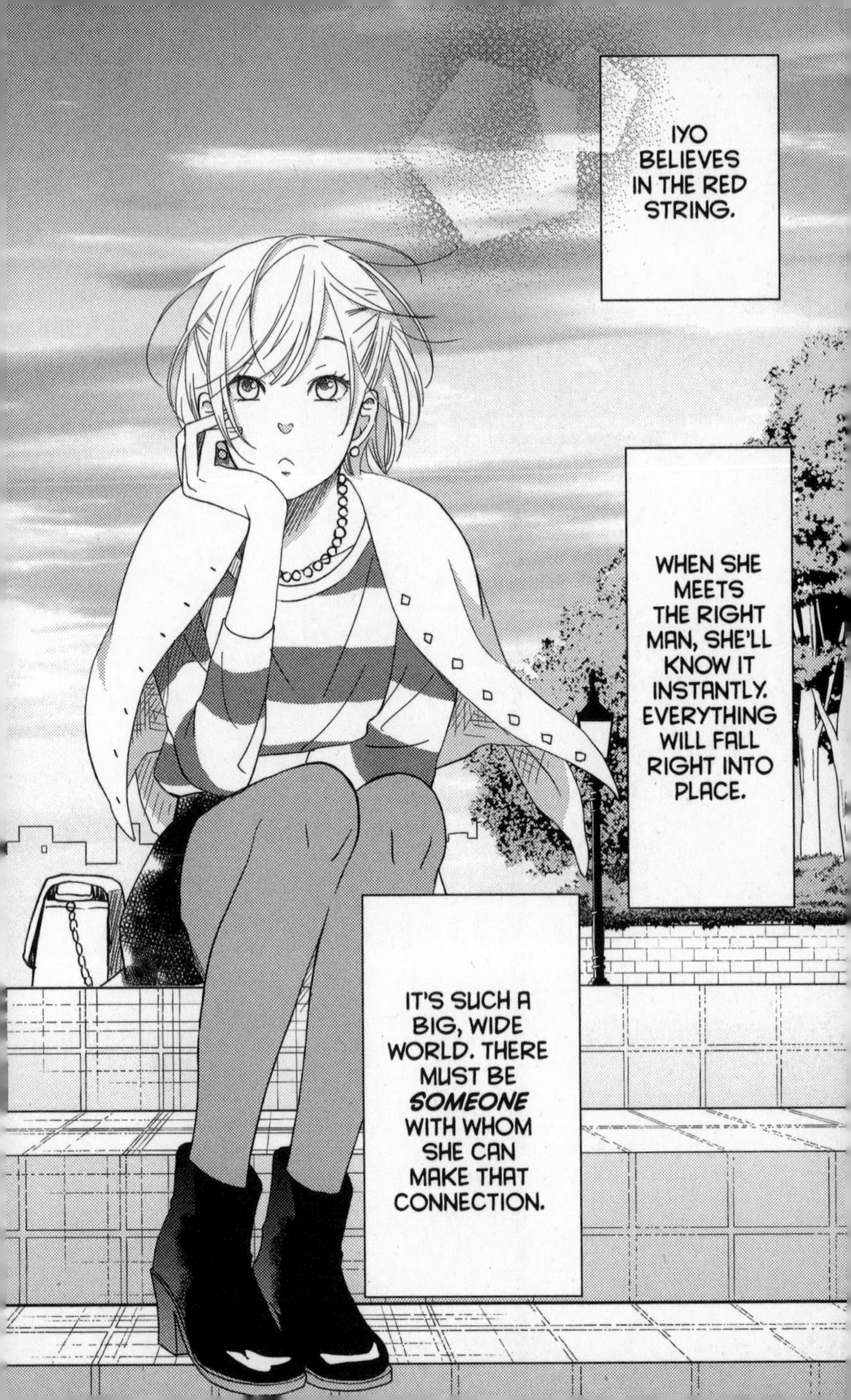
IYO BELIEVES IN THE RED STRING.
WHEN SHE MEETS THE RIGHT MAN, SHE'LL KNOW IT INSTANTLY. EVERYTHING WILL FALL RIGHT INTO PLACE.
IT'S SUCH A BIG, WIDE WORLD. THERE MUST BE *SOMEONE* WITH WHOM SHE CAN MAKE THAT CONNECTION.

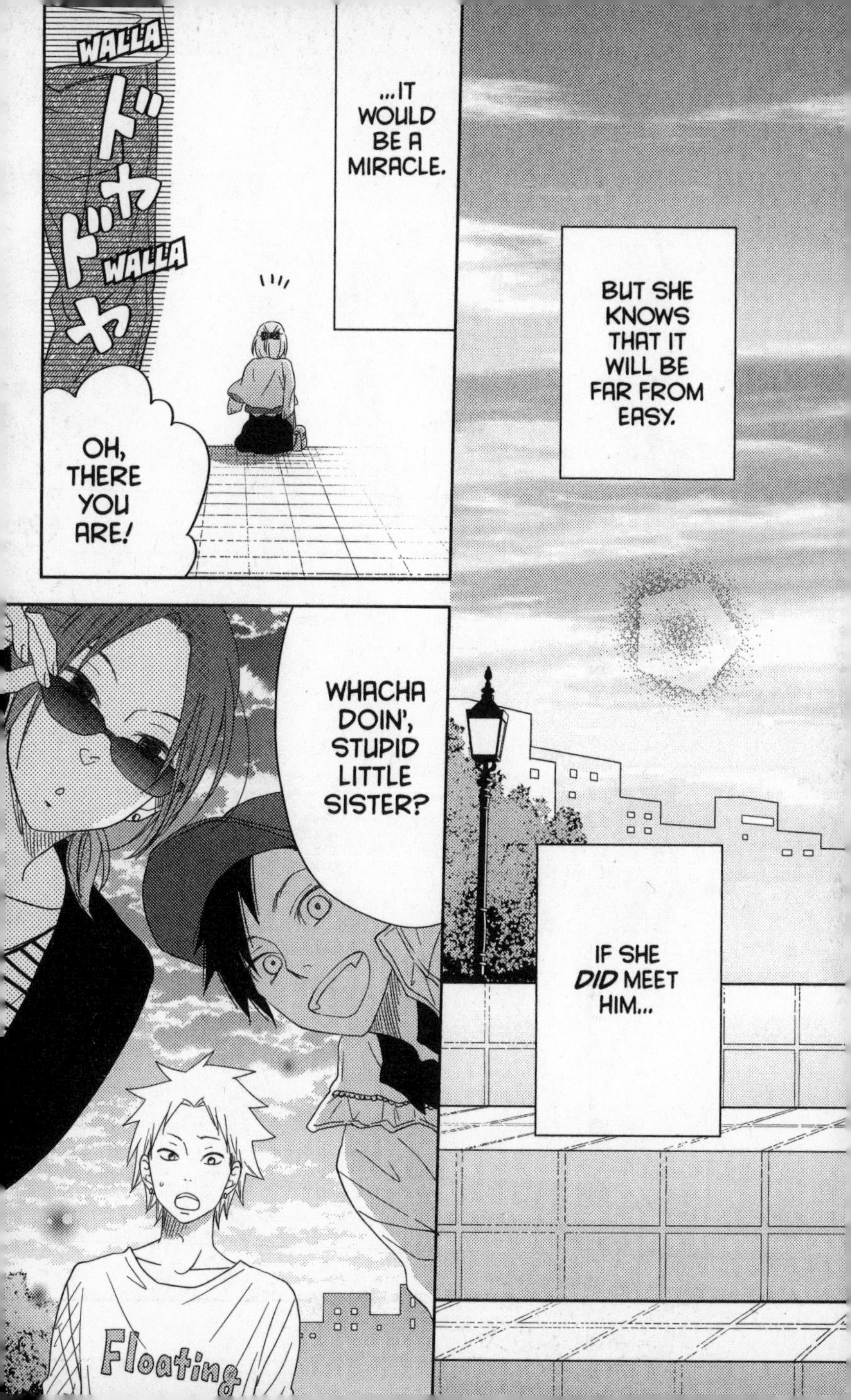
BUT SHE KNOWS THAT IT WILL BE FAR FROM EASY.
IF SHE *DID* MEET HIM...
...IT WOULD BE A MIRACLE.
WALLA
ドヤドヤ
WALLA
OH, THERE YOU ARE!
WHACHA DOIN', STUPID LITTLE SISTER?
Floating

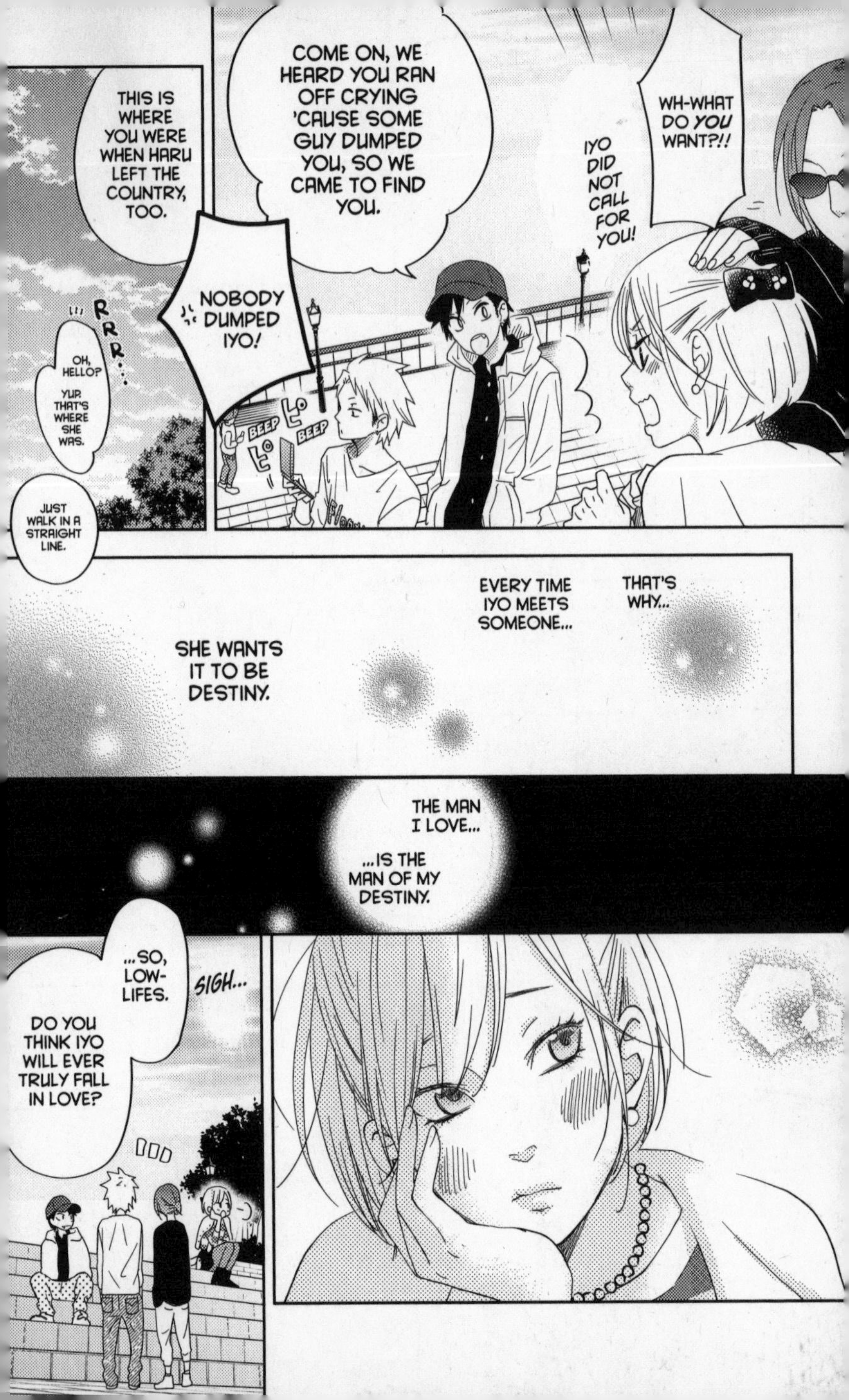
WH-WHAT DO YOU WANT?!!
IYO DID NOT CALL FOR YOU!
COME ON, WE HEARD YOU RAN OFF CRYING 'CAUSE SOME GUY DUMPED YOU, SO WE CAME TO FIND YOU.
NOBODY DUMPED IYO!
BEEP
BEEP
THIS IS WHERE YOU WERE WHEN HARU LEFT THE COUNTRY, TOO.
RRR...
OH, HELLO?
YUP. THAT'S WHERE SHE WAS.
JUST WALK IN A STRAIGHT LINE.
THAT'S WHY...
EVERY TIME IYO MEETS SOMEONE...
SHE WANTS IT TO BE DESTINY.
THE MAN I LOVE...
...IS THE MAN OF MY DESTINY.
SIGH...
...SO, LOW-LIFES.
DO YOU THINK IYO WILL EVER TRULY FALL IN LOVE?

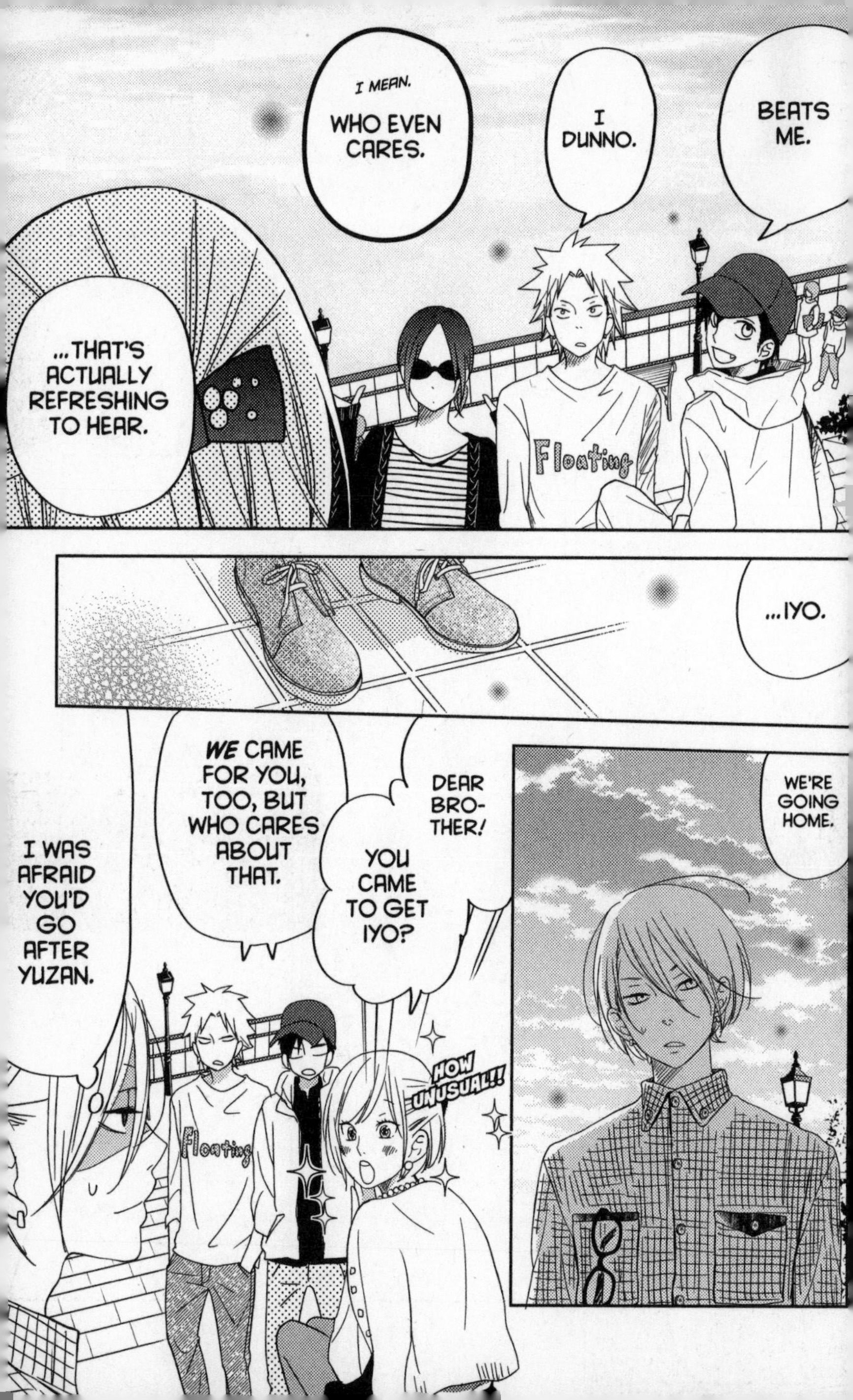
BEATS ME.
I DUNNO.
I MEAN. WHO EVEN CARES.
...THAT'S ACTUALLY REFRESHING TO HEAR.
...IYO.
WE'RE GOING HOME.
DEAR BROTHER!
YOU CAME TO GET IYO?
WE CAME FOR YOU, TOO, BUT WHO CARES ABOUT THAT.
HOW UNUSUAL!!
I WAS AFRAID YOU'D GO AFTER YUZAN.

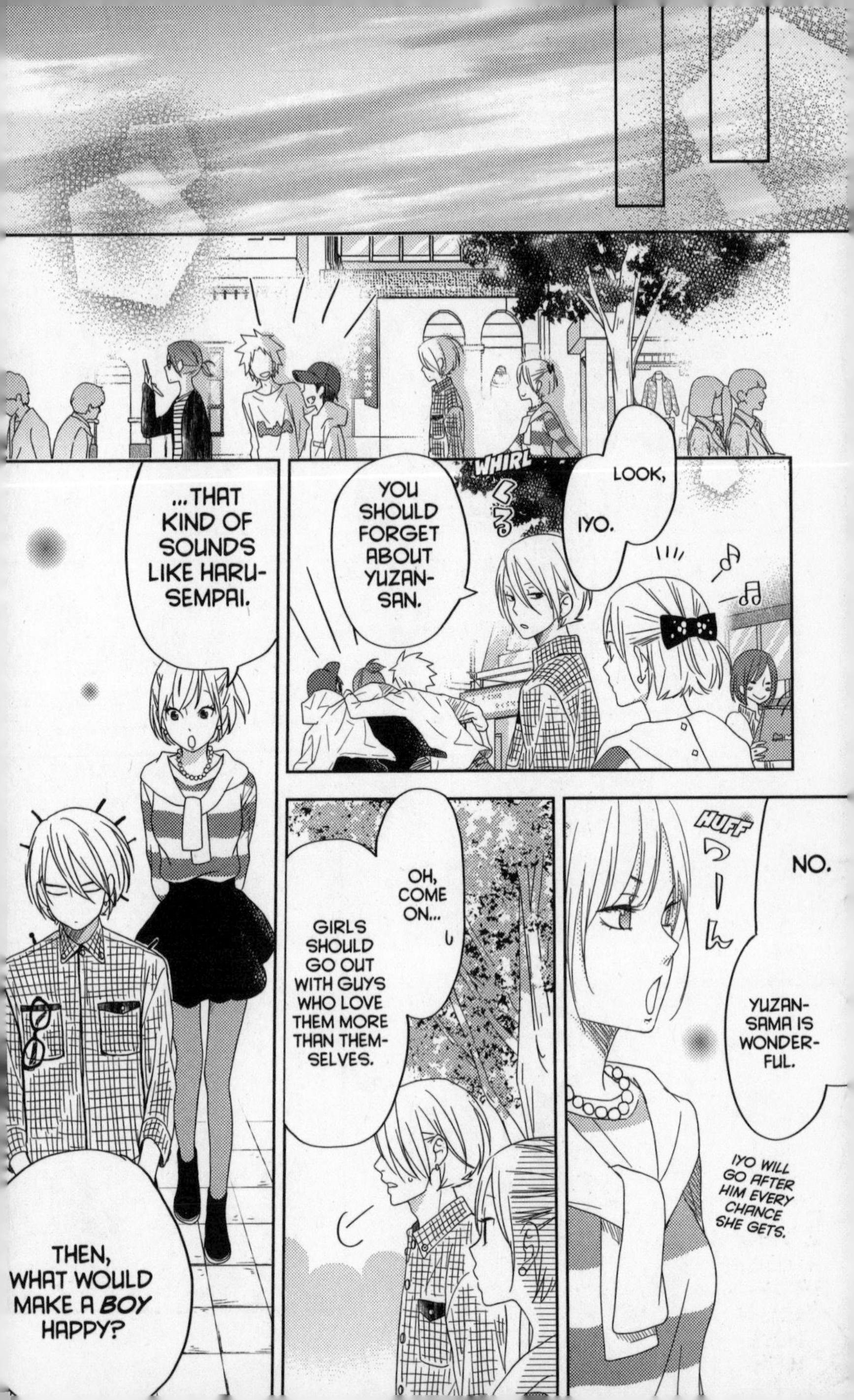
LOOK,
IYO.
WHIRL
YOU SHOULD FORGET ABOUT YUZAN-SAN.
HUFF
NO.
YUZAN-SAMA IS WONDERFUL.
IYO WILL GO AFTER HIM EVERY CHANCE SHE GETS.
OH, COME ON...
GIRLS SHOULD GO OUT WITH GUYS WHO LOVE THEM MORE THAN THEMSELVES.
...THAT KIND OF SOUNDS LIKE HARU-SEMPAI.
THEN, WHAT WOULD MAKE A *BOY* HAPPY?

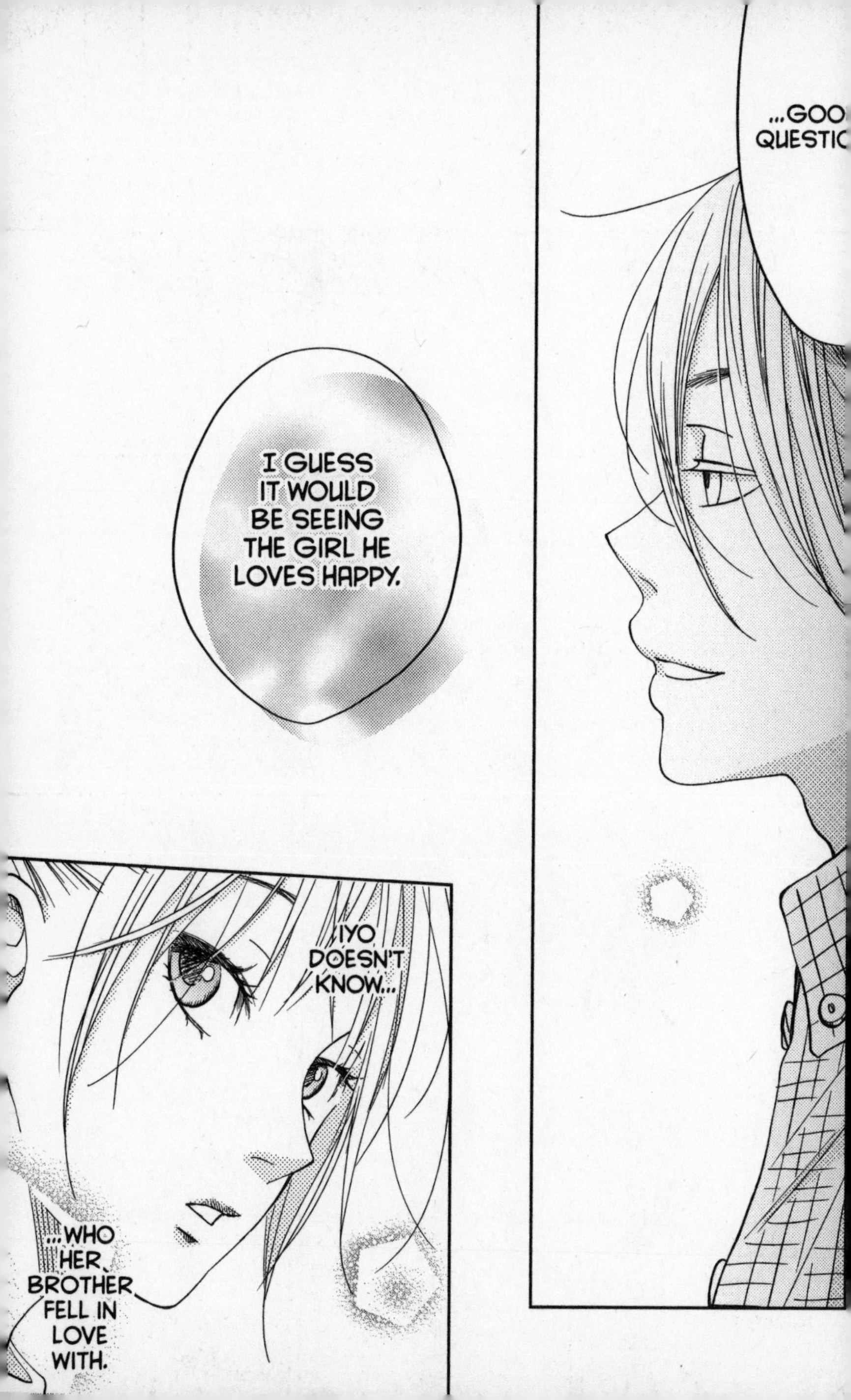
...GOO QUESTI
I GUESS IT WOULD BE SEEING THE GIRL HE LOVES HAPPY.
IYO DOESN'T KNOW...
...WHO HER BROTHER FELL IN LOVE WITH.

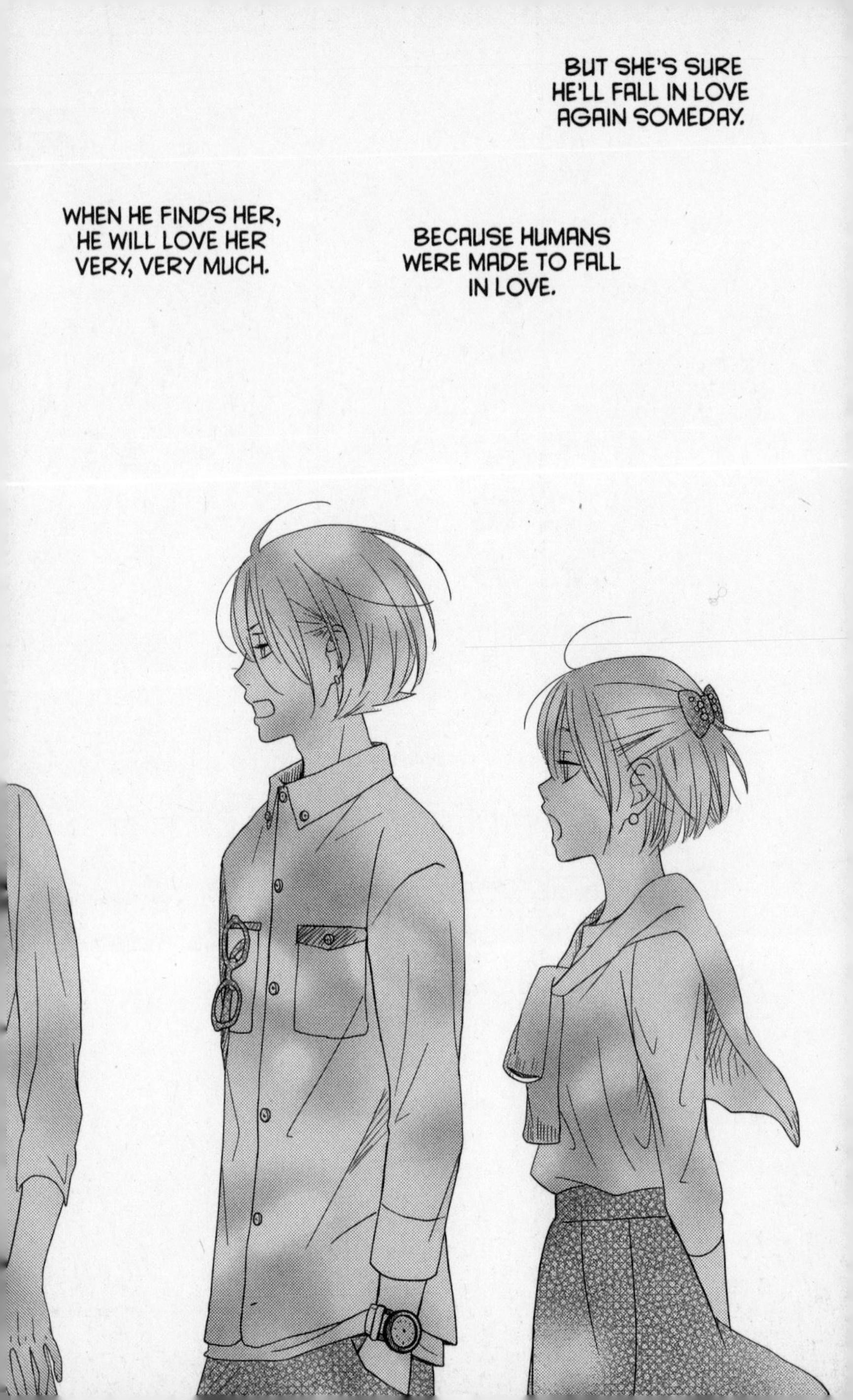
BUT SHE'S SURE HE'LL FALL IN LOVE AGAIN SOMEDAY.
BECAUSE HUMANS WERE MADE TO FALL IN LOVE.
WHEN HE FINDS HER, HE WILL LOVE HER VERY, VERY MUCH.

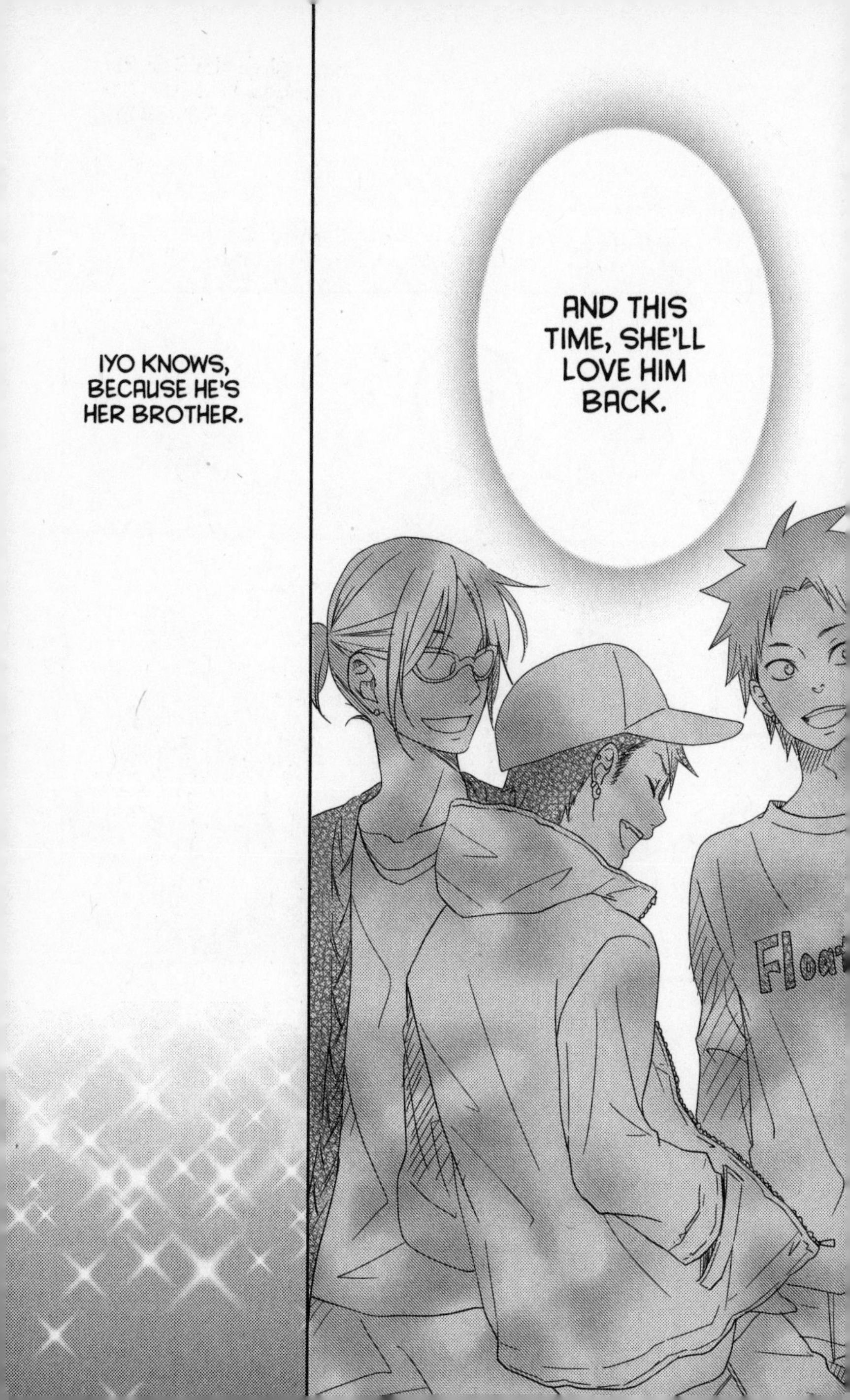
AND THIS TIME, SHE'LL LOVE HIM BACK.
IYO KNOWS, BECAUSE HE'S HER BROTHER.

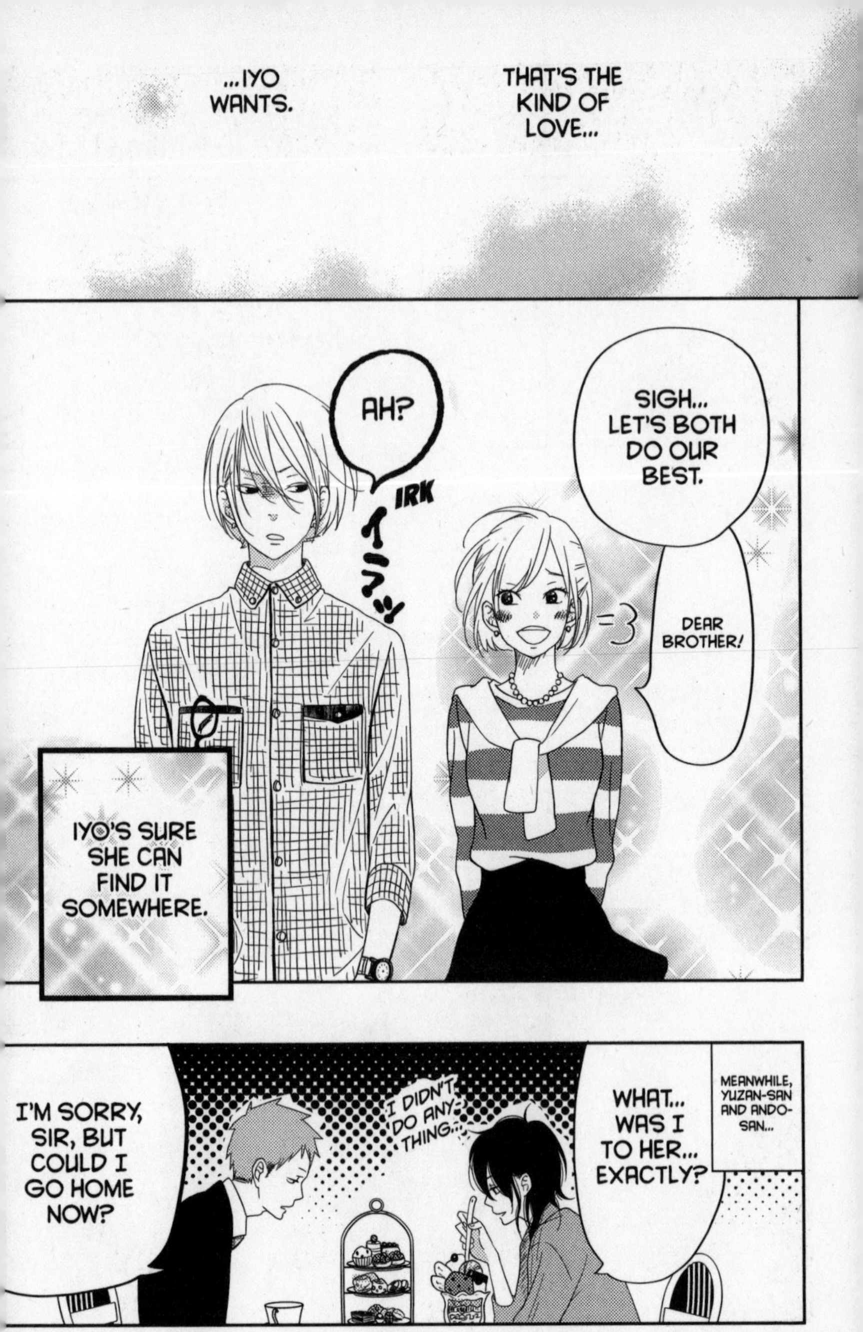
THAT'S THE KIND OF LOVE...
...IYO WANTS.
SIGH... LET'S BOTH DO OUR BEST.
DEAR BROTHER!
AH?
IRK
イラッ
IYO'S SURE SHE CAN FIND IT SOMEWHERE.
MEANWHILE, YUZAN-SAN AND ANDO-SAN...
WHAT... WAS I TO HER... EXACTLY?
I DIDN'T DO ANYTHING...
I'M SORRY, SIR, BUT COULD I GO HOME NOW?

WHAT ABOUT THE BOYS YOU KNOW?

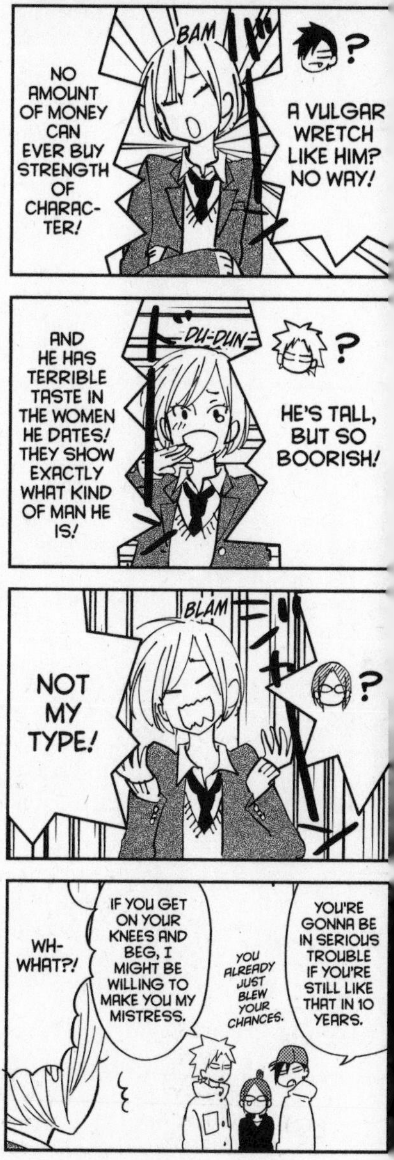
BAM
NO AMOUNT OF MONEY CAN EVER BUY STRENGTH OF CHARACTER!
A VULGAR WRETCH LIKE HIM? NO WAY!
DU-DUN
AND HE HAS TERRIBLE TASTE IN THE WOMEN HE DATES! THEY SHOW EXACTLY WHAT KIND OF MAN HE IS!
HE'S TALL, BUT SO BOORISH!
BLAM
NOT MY TYPE!
IF YOU GET ON YOUR KNEES AND BEG, I MIGHT BE WILLING TO MAKE YOU MY MISTRESS.
WH-WHAT?!
YOU'RE GONNA BE IN SERIOUS TROUBLE IF YOU'RE STILL LIKE THAT IN 10 YEARS.
YOU ALREADY JUST BLEW YOUR CHANCES.

ARGUMENT: WON

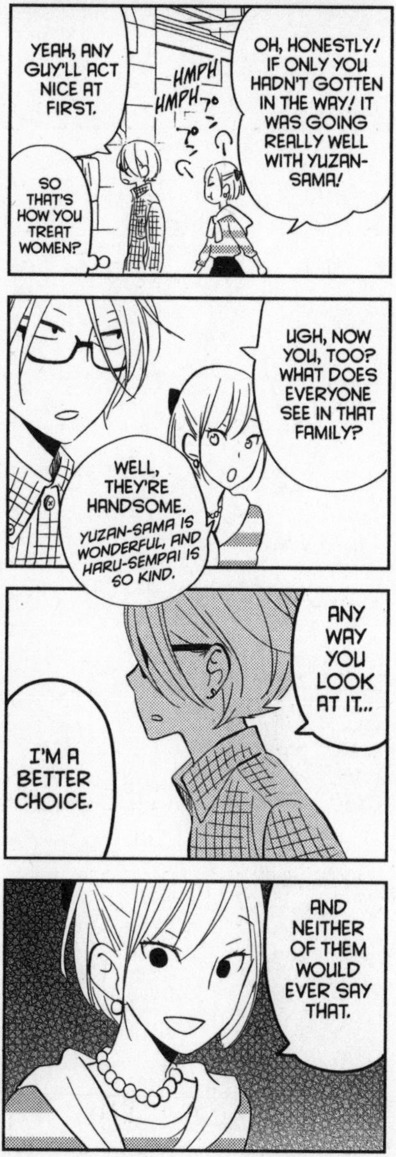
OH, HONESTLY! IF ONLY YOU HADN'T GOTTEN IN THE WAY! IT WAS GOING REALLY WELL WITH YUZAN-SAMA!
HMPH
HMPH
YEAH, ANY GUY'LL ACT NICE AT FIRST.
SO THAT'S HOW YOU TREAT WOMEN?
UGH, NOW YOU, TOO? WHAT DOES EVERYONE SEE IN THAT FAMILY?
WELL, THEY'RE HANDSOME. YUZAN-SAMA IS WONDERFUL, AND HARU-SEMPAI IS SO KIND.
ANY WAY YOU LOOK AT IT...
I'M A BETTER CHOICE.
AND NEITHER OF THEM WOULD EVER SAY THAT.

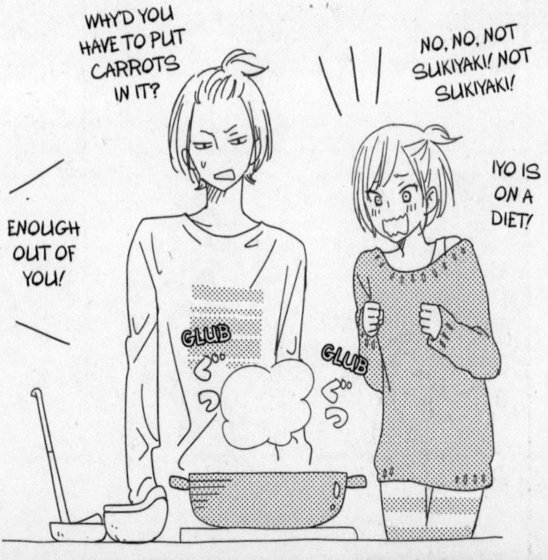
NO, NO, NOT SUKIYAKI! NOT SUKIYAKI!
IYO IS ON A DIET!
WHY'D YOU HAVE TO PUT CARROTS IN IT?
ENOUGH OUT OF YOU!
GLUB
GLUB

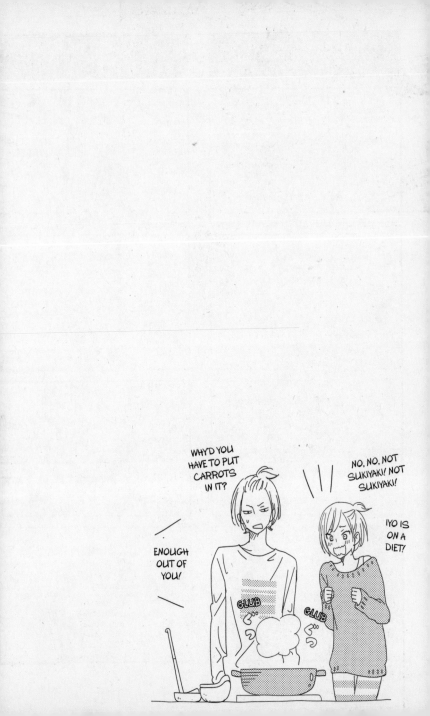

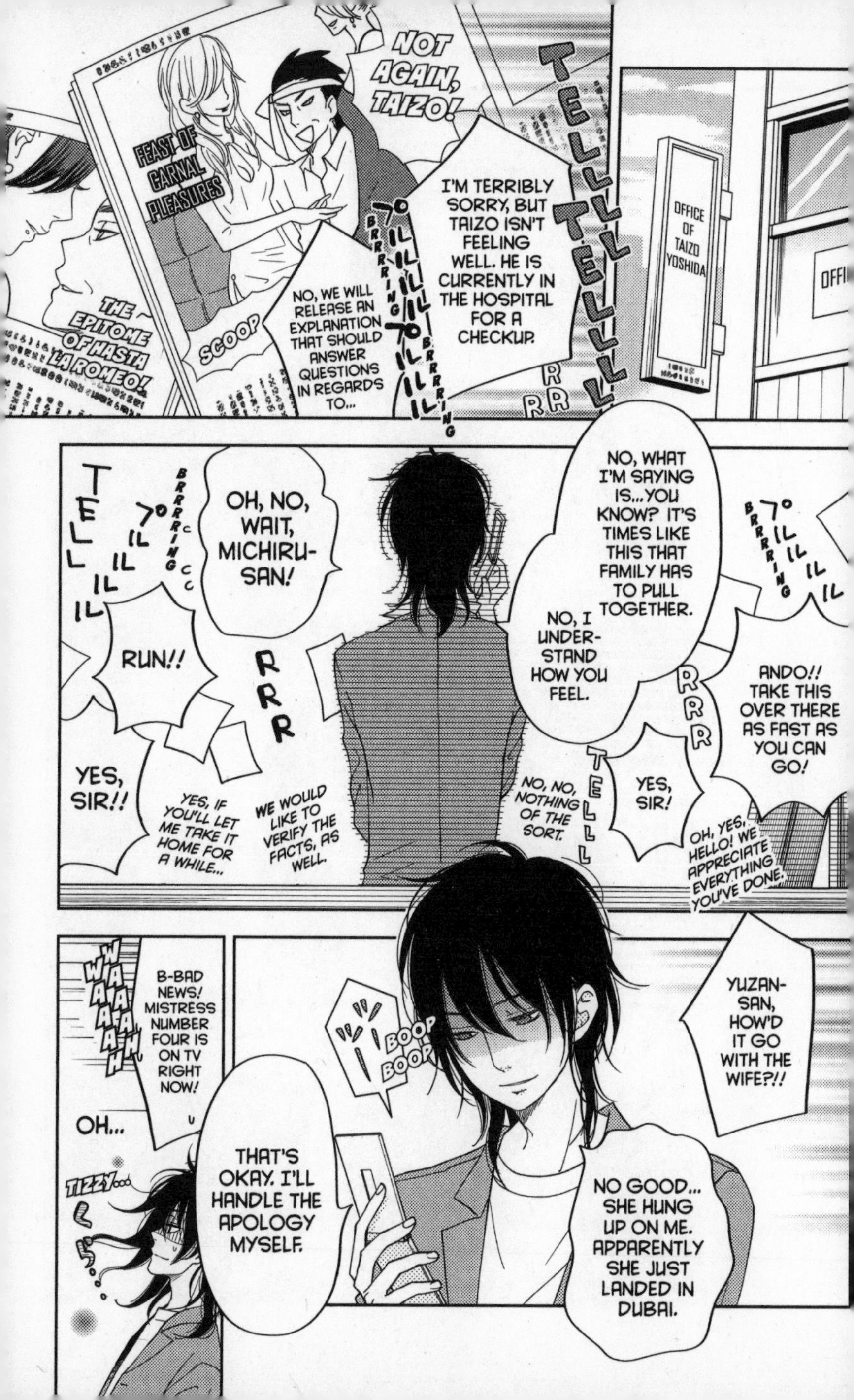
OFFICE OF TAIZO YOSHIDA
OFFI
TELLLLL TELLLLL
RRR
I'M TERRIBLY SORRY, BUT TAIZO ISN'T FEELING WELL. HE IS CURRENTLY IN THE HOSPITAL FOR A CHECKUP.
BRRRRING BRRRRING
NO, WE WILL RELEASE AN EXPLANATION THAT SHOULD ANSWER QUESTIONS IN REGARDS TO...
NOT AGAIN, TAIZO!
FEAST OF CARNAL PLEASURES
THE EPITOME OF HASTA LA ROMEO!
SCOOP
BRRRRING
NO, WHAT I'M SAYING IS...YOU KNOW? IT'S TIMES LIKE THIS THAT FAMILY HAS TO PULL TOGETHER.
ANDO!! TAKE THIS OVER THERE AS FAST AS YOU CAN GO!
RRR
YES, SIR!
NO, I UNDER-STAND HOW YOU FEEL.
OH, YES, HELLO! WE APPRECIATE EVERYTHING YOU'VE DONE.
TELL
NO, NO, NOTHING OF THE SORT.
OH, NO, WAIT, MICHIRU-SAN!
BRRRRING
TELLLL
RRR
WE WOULD LIKE TO VERIFY THE FACTS, AS WELL.
YES, IF YOU'LL LET ME TAKE IT HOME FOR A WHILE...
RUN!!
YES, SIR!!
YUZAN-SAN, HOW'D IT GO WITH THE WIFE?!!
NO GOOD... SHE HUNG UP ON ME. APPARENTLY SHE JUST LANDED IN DUBAI.
BOOP BOOP
THAT'S OKAY. I'LL HANDLE THE APOLOGY MYSELF.
WAAAAAH WAAAAH
B-BAD NEWS! MISTRESS NUMBER FOUR IS ON TV RIGHT NOW!
OH...
TIZZY...

EXTRA CHAPTER 3: CHILDREN BY THE RIVERSIDE

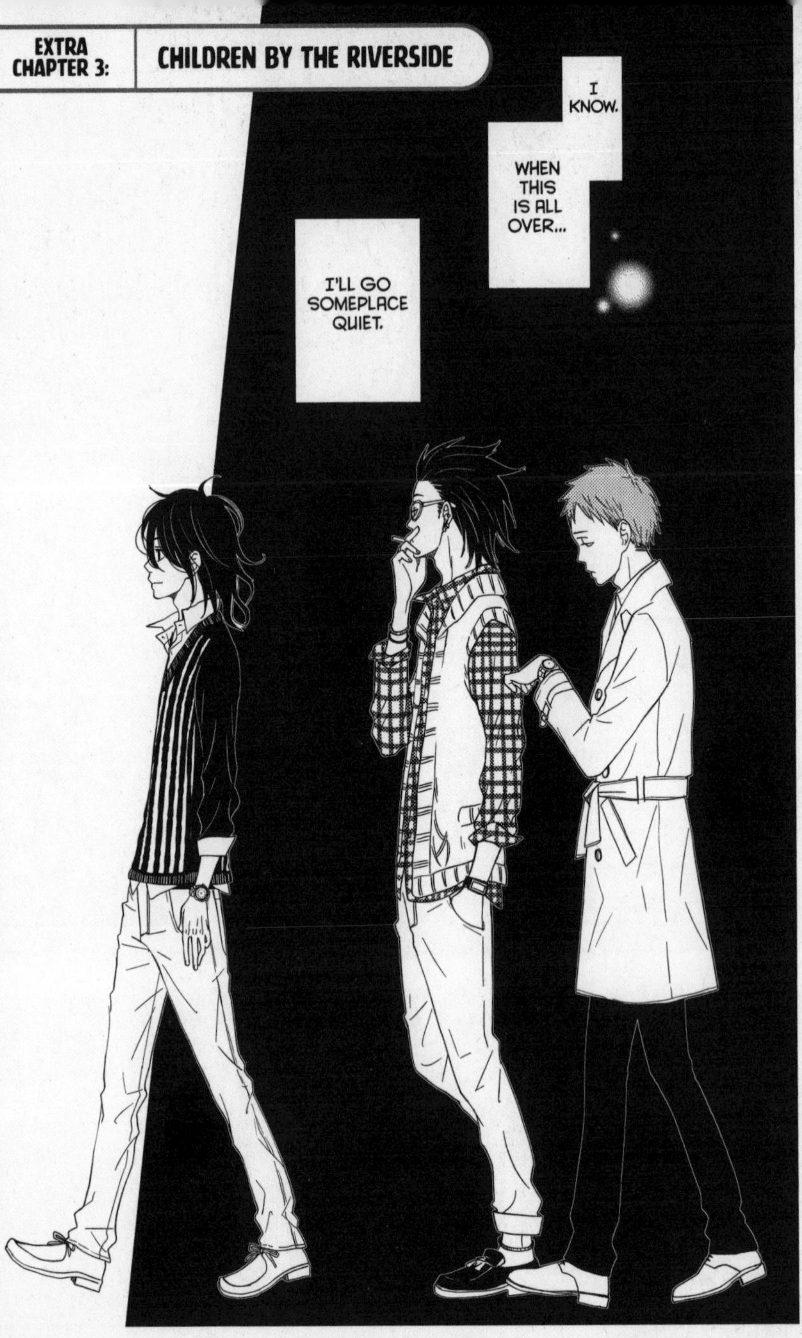
I KNOW.
WHEN THIS IS ALL OVER...
I'LL GO SOMEPLACE QUIET.

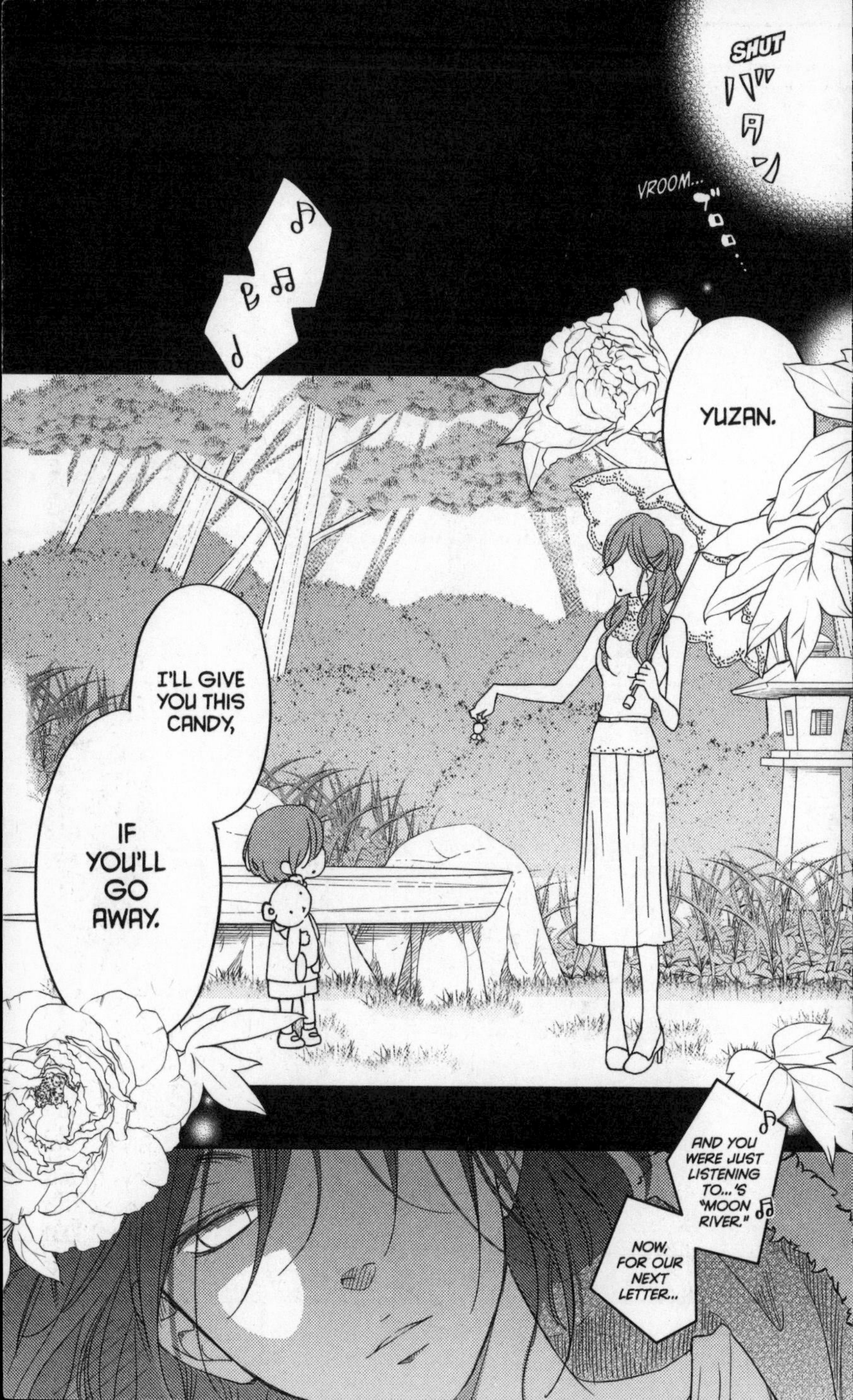
SHUT
VROOM...
YUZAN.
I'LL GIVE YOU THIS CANDY,
IF YOU'LL GO AWAY.
AND YOU WERE JUST LISTENING TO...'S "MOON RIVER."
NOW, FOR OUR NEXT LETTER...

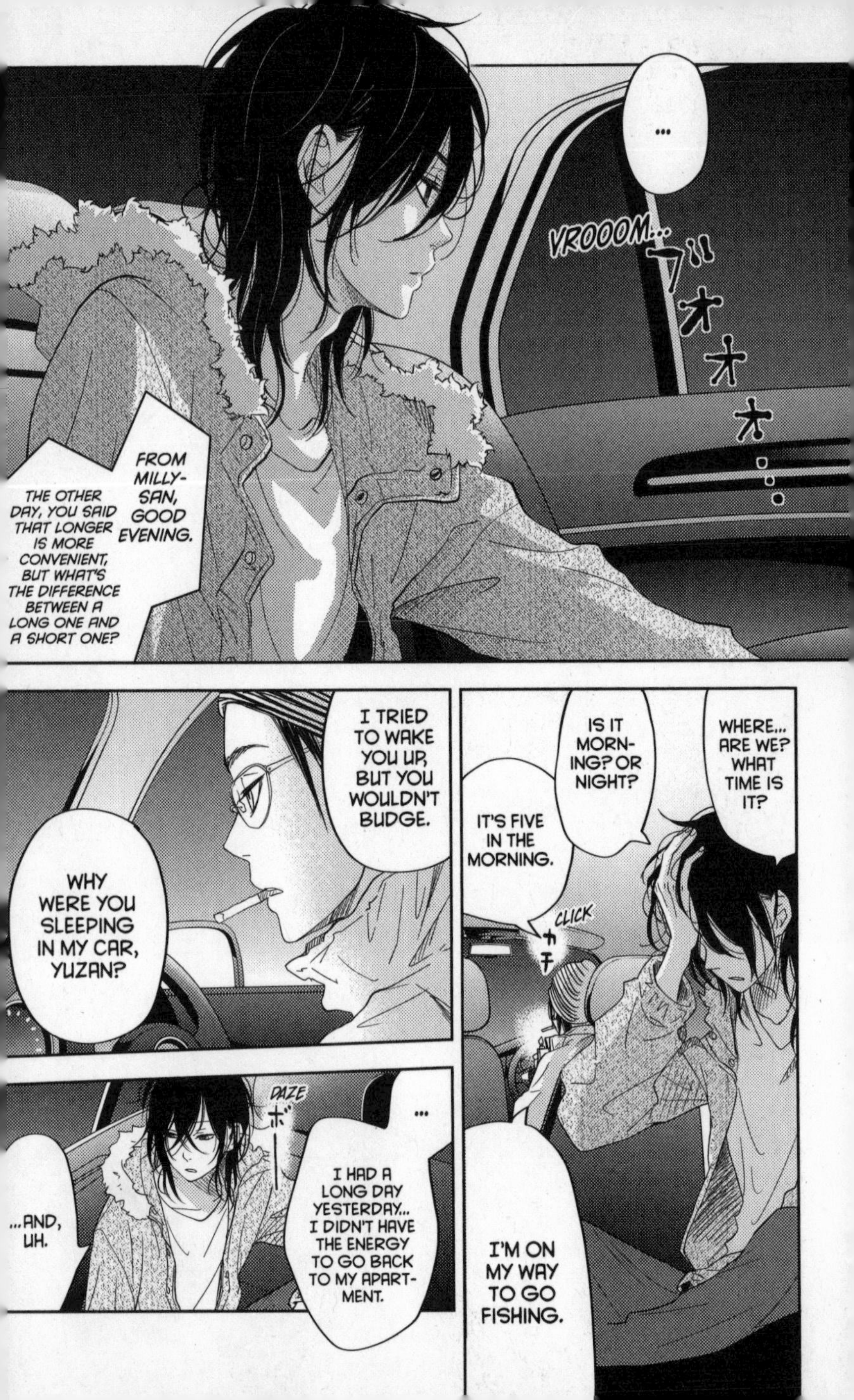
...
VROOOM...
ブオォォ...
FROM MILLY-SAN, GOOD EVENING.
THE OTHER DAY, YOU SAID THAT LONGER IS MORE CONVENIENT, BUT WHAT'S THE DIFFERENCE BETWEEN A LONG ONE AND A SHORT ONE?
WHERE... ARE WE? WHAT TIME IS IT?
IS IT MORNING? OR NIGHT?
IT'S FIVE IN THE MORNING.
CLICK
カチ
I'M ON MY WAY TO GO FISHING.
I TRIED TO WAKE YOU UP, BUT YOU WOULDN'T BUDGE.
WHY WERE YOU SLEEPING IN MY CAR, YUZAN?
...
DAZE
ボー
I HAD A LONG DAY YESTERDAY... I DIDN'T HAVE THE ENERGY TO GO BACK TO MY APART-MENT.
...AND, UH.

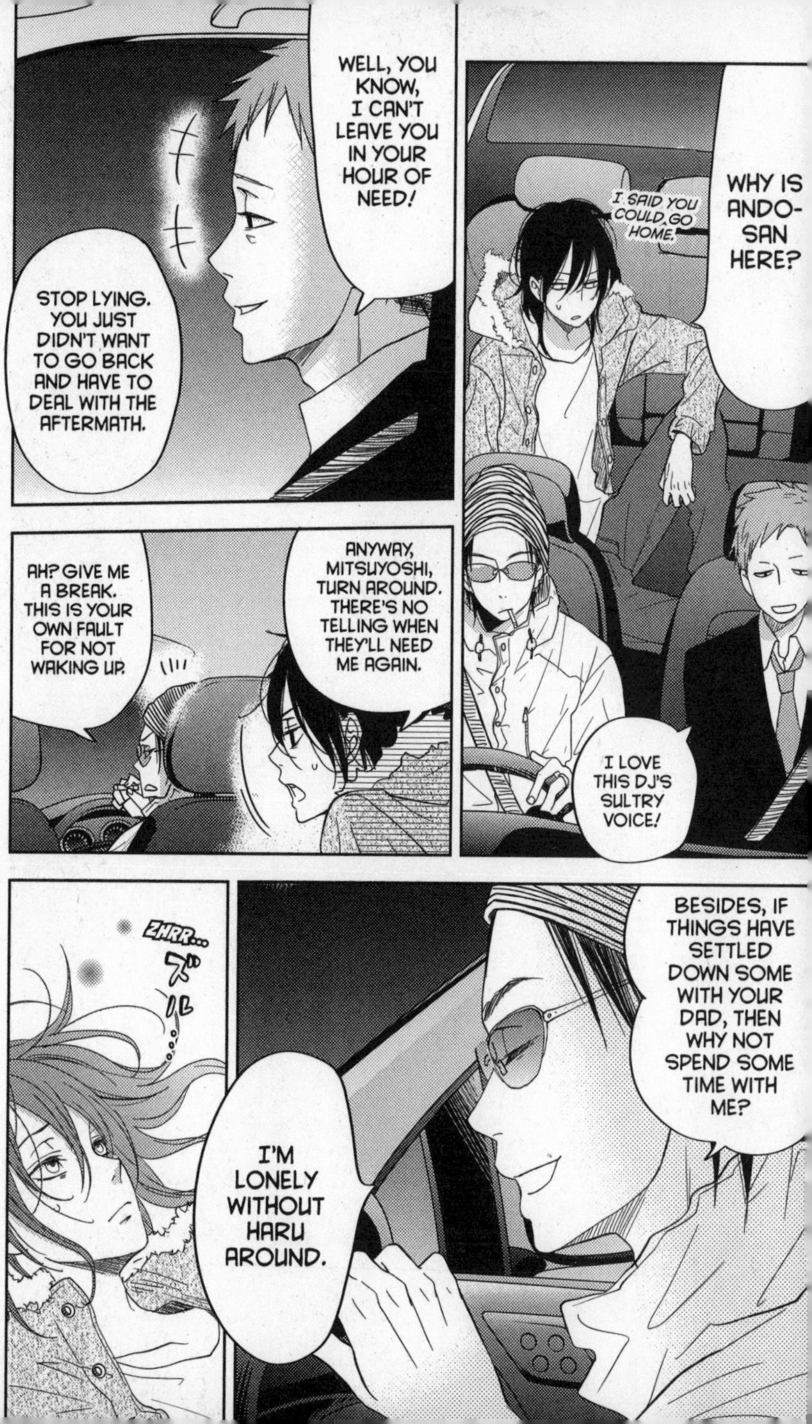
WHY IS ANDO-SAN HERE?
I SAID YOU COULD GO HOME.
I LOVE THIS DJ'S SULTRY VOICE!
WELL, YOU KNOW, I CAN'T LEAVE YOU IN YOUR HOUR OF NEED!
STOP LYING. YOU JUST DIDN'T WANT TO GO BACK AND HAVE TO DEAL WITH THE AFTERMATH.
ANYWAY, MITSUYOSHI, TURN AROUND. THERE'S NO TELLING WHEN THEY'LL NEED ME AGAIN.
AH? GIVE ME A BREAK. THIS IS YOUR OWN FAULT FOR NOT WAKING UP.
BESIDES, IF THINGS HAVE SETTLED DOWN SOME WITH YOUR DAD, THEN WHY NOT SPEND SOME TIME WITH ME?
I'M LONELY WITHOUT HARU AROUND.
ZHRR...
ズル

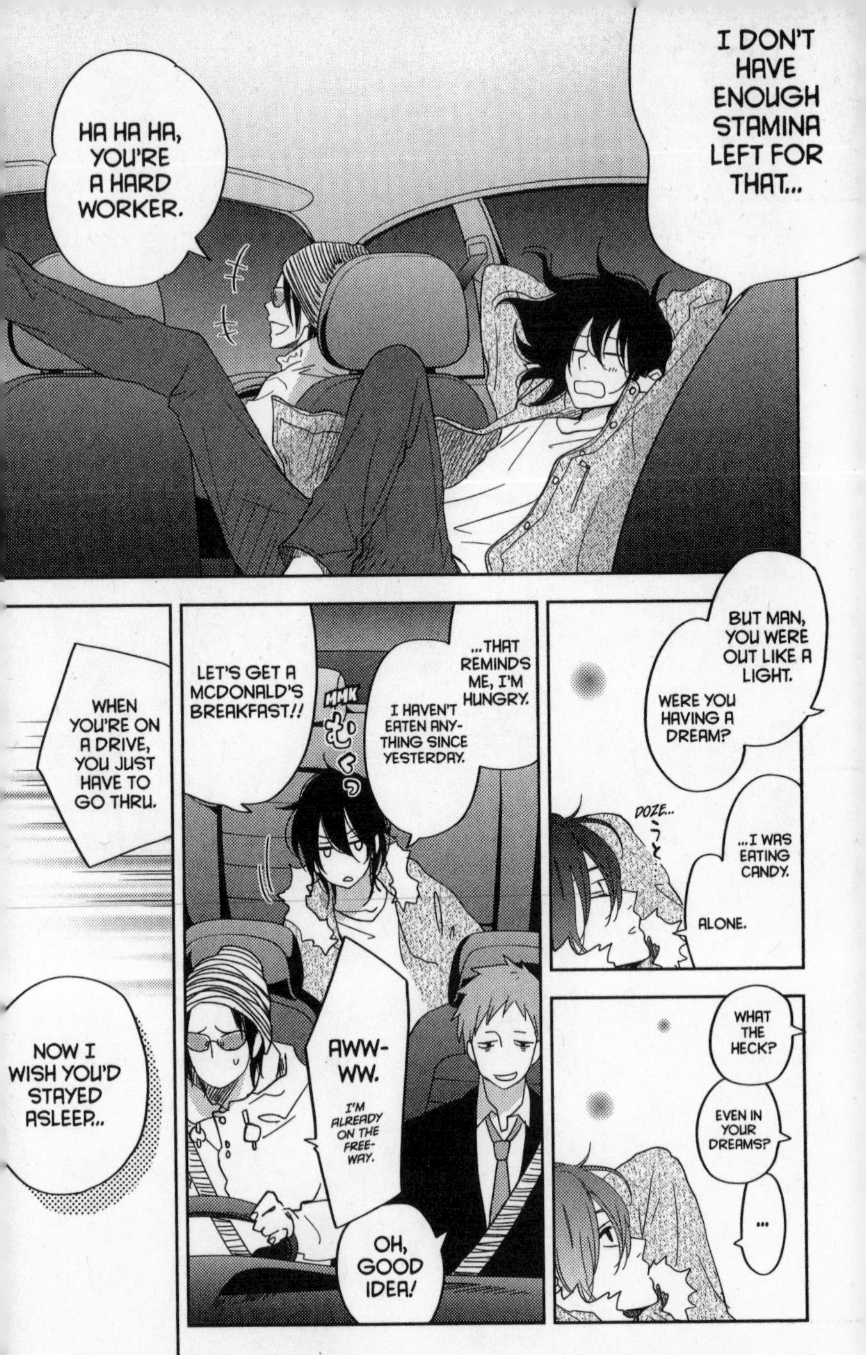
I DON'T HAVE ENOUGH STAMINA LEFT FOR THAT...
HA HA HA, YOU'RE A HARD WORKER.
BUT MAN, YOU WERE OUT LIKE A LIGHT.
WERE YOU HAVING A DREAM?
DOZE...
...I WAS EATING CANDY.
ALONE.
WHAT THE HECK?
EVEN IN YOUR DREAMS?
...
...THAT REMINDS ME, I'M HUNGRY.
I HAVEN'T EATEN ANY-THING SINCE YESTERDAY.
MMK
LET'S GET A MCDONALD'S BREAKFAST!!
AWWW-WW.
I'M ALREADY ON THE FREE-WAY.
OH, GOOD IDEA!
WHEN YOU'RE ON A DRIVE, YOU JUST HAVE TO GO THRU.
NOW I WISH YOU'D STAYED ASLEEP...

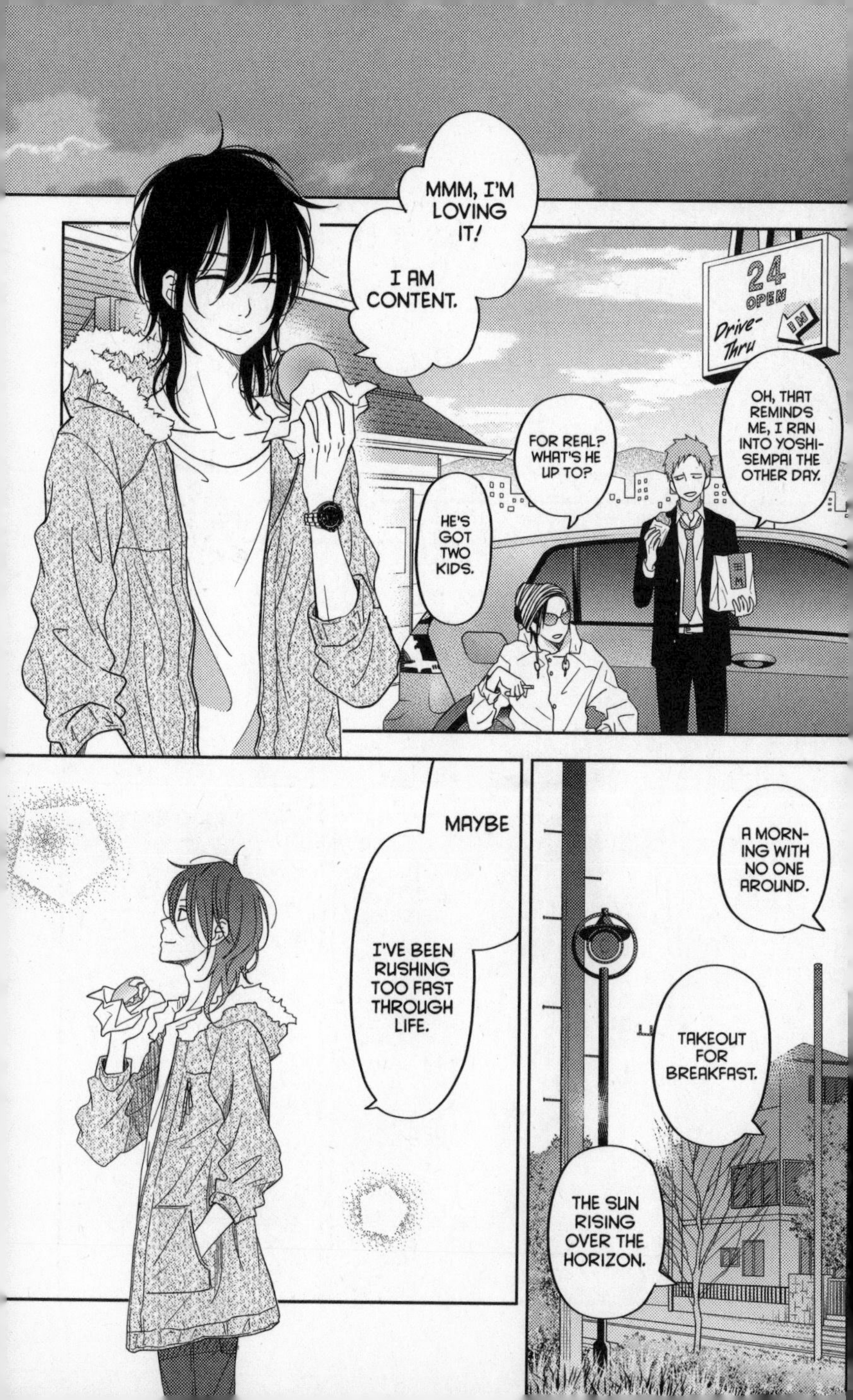
24
OPEN
Drive-Thru
IN
OH, THAT REMINDS ME, I RAN INTO YOSHI-SEMPAI THE OTHER DAY.
FOR REAL? WHAT'S HE UP TO?
HE'S GOT TWO KIDS.
MMM, I'M LOVING IT!
I AM CONTENT.
A MORNING WITH NO ONE AROUND.
TAKEOUT FOR BREAKFAST.
THE SUN RISING OVER THE HORIZON.
MAYBE
I'VE BEEN RUSHING TOO FAST THROUGH LIFE.

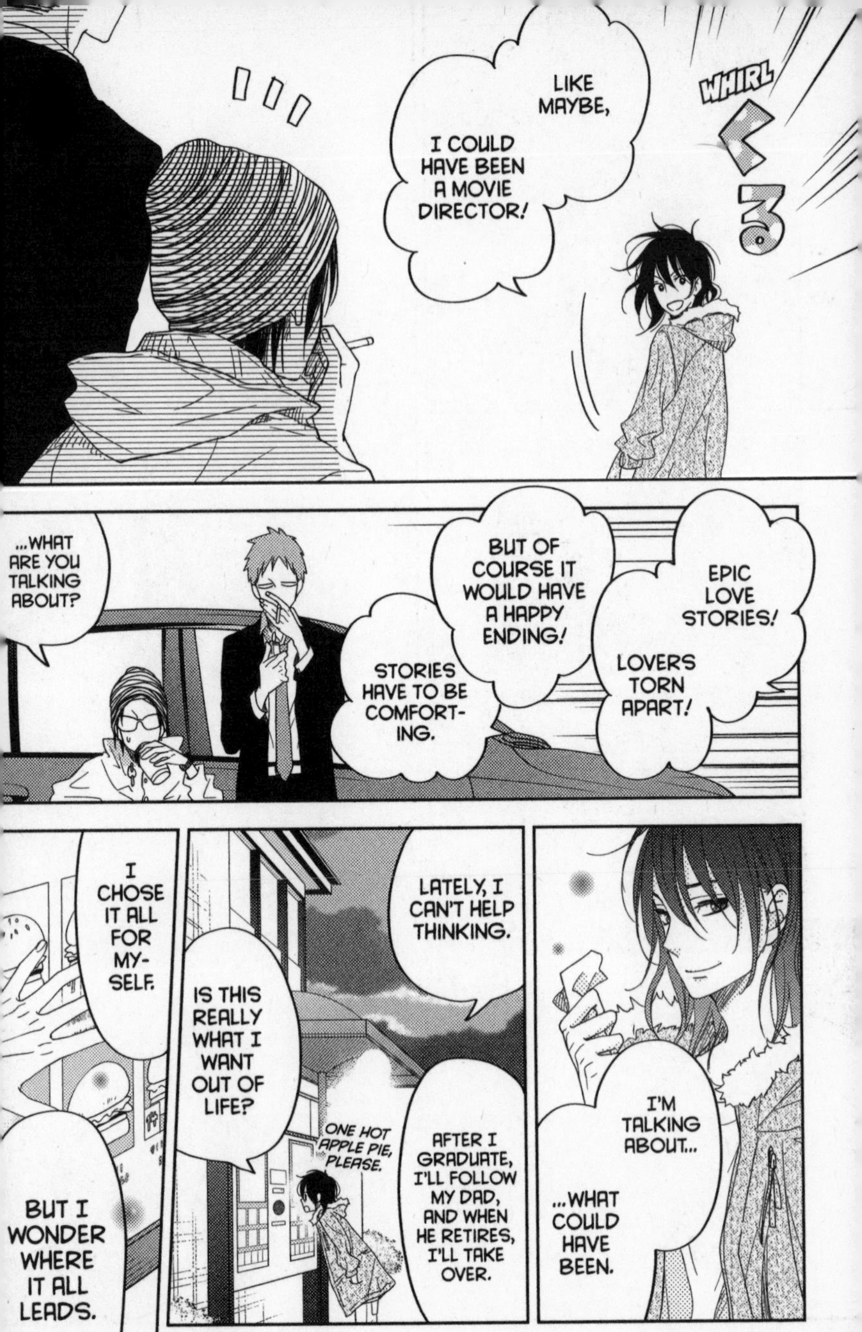
WHIRL
くる
LIKE MAYBE, I COULD HAVE BEEN A MOVIE DIRECTOR!
EPIC LOVE STORIES!
LOVERS TORN APART!
BUT OF COURSE IT WOULD HAVE A HAPPY ENDING!
STORIES HAVE TO BE COMFORTING.
...WHAT ARE YOU TALKING ABOUT?
I'M TALKING ABOUT...
...WHAT COULD HAVE BEEN.
LATELY, I CAN'T HELP THINKING.
AFTER I GRADUATE, I'LL FOLLOW MY DAD, AND WHEN HE RETIRES, I'LL TAKE OVER.
IS THIS REALLY WHAT I WANT OUT OF LIFE?
ONE HOT APPLE PIE, PLEASE.
I CHOSE IT ALL FOR MYSELF.
BUT I WONDER WHERE IT ALL LEADS.

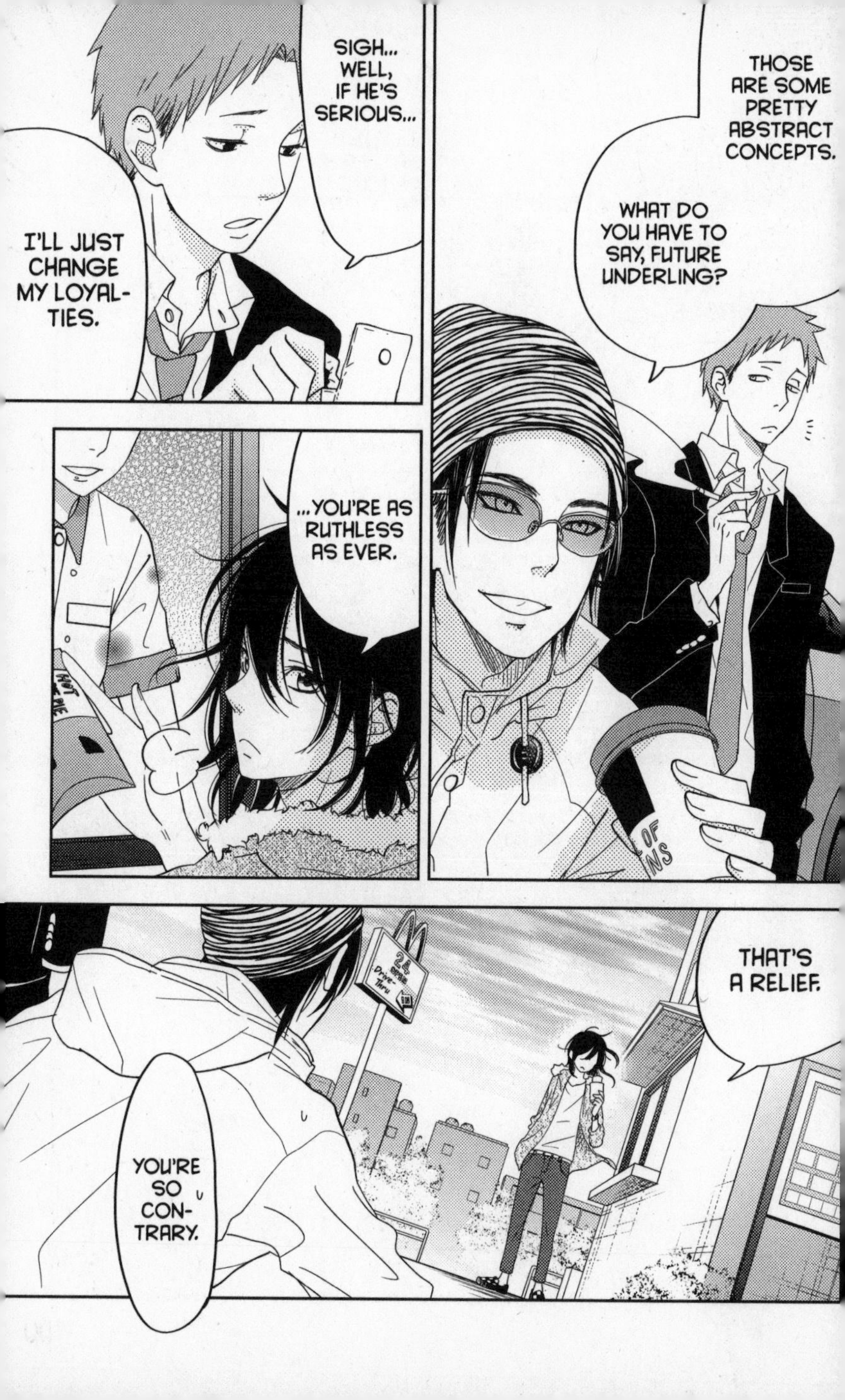
THOSE ARE SOME PRETTY ABSTRACT CONCEPTS.
WHAT DO YOU HAVE TO SAY, FUTURE UNDERLING?
SIGH... WELL, IF HE'S SERIOUS...
I'LL JUST CHANGE MY LOYAL-TIES.
...YOU'RE AS RUTHLESS AS EVER.
THAT'S A RELIEF.
YOU'RE SO CON-TRARY.

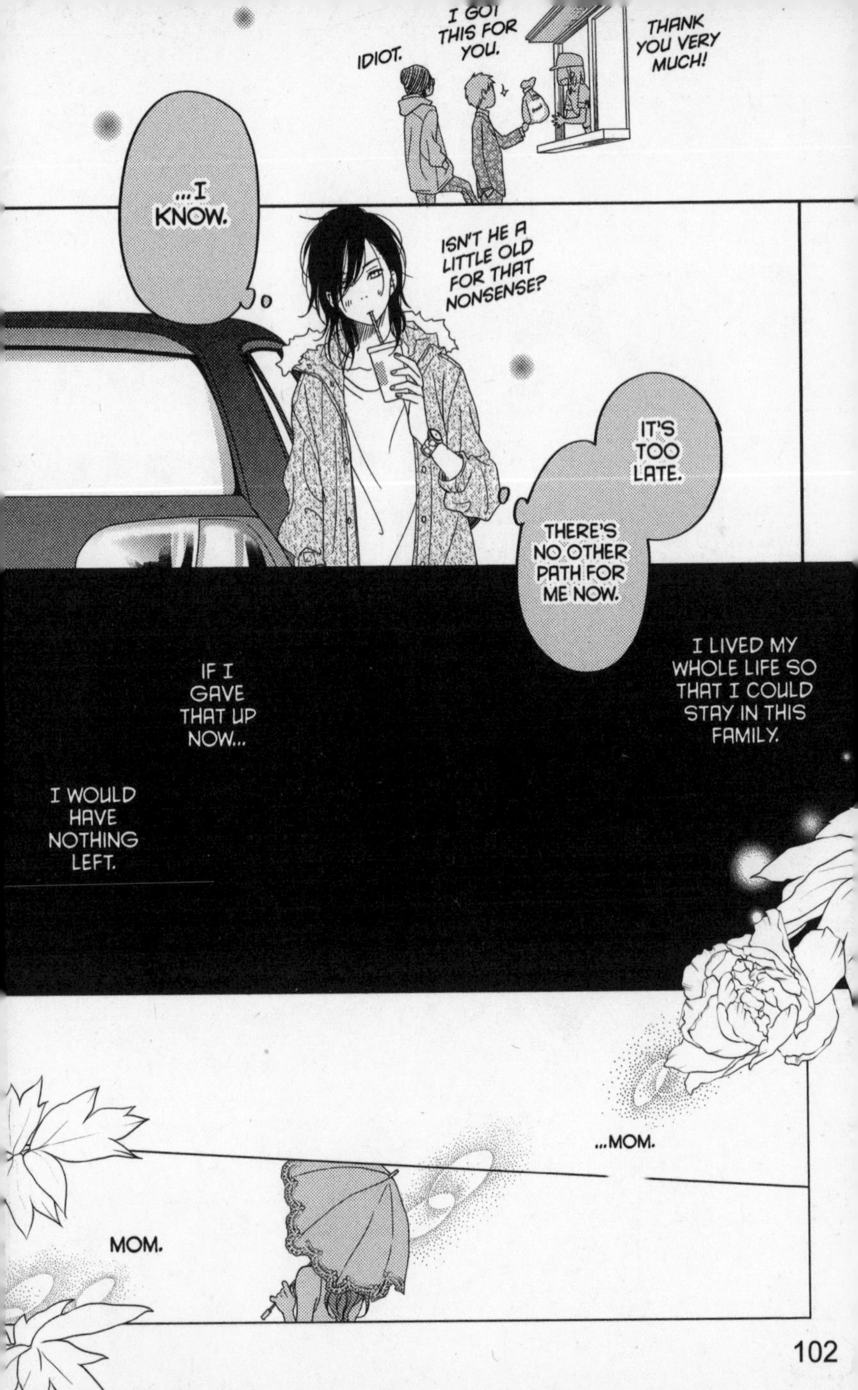
I GOT THIS FOR YOU.
THANK YOU VERY MUCH!
IDIOT.
ISN'T HE A LITTLE OLD FOR THAT NONSENSE?
...I KNOW.
IT'S TOO LATE.
THERE'S NO OTHER PATH FOR ME NOW.
I LIVED MY WHOLE LIFE SO THAT I COULD STAY IN THIS FAMILY.
IF I GAVE THAT UP NOW...
I WOULD HAVE NOTHING LEFT.
...MOM.
MOM.

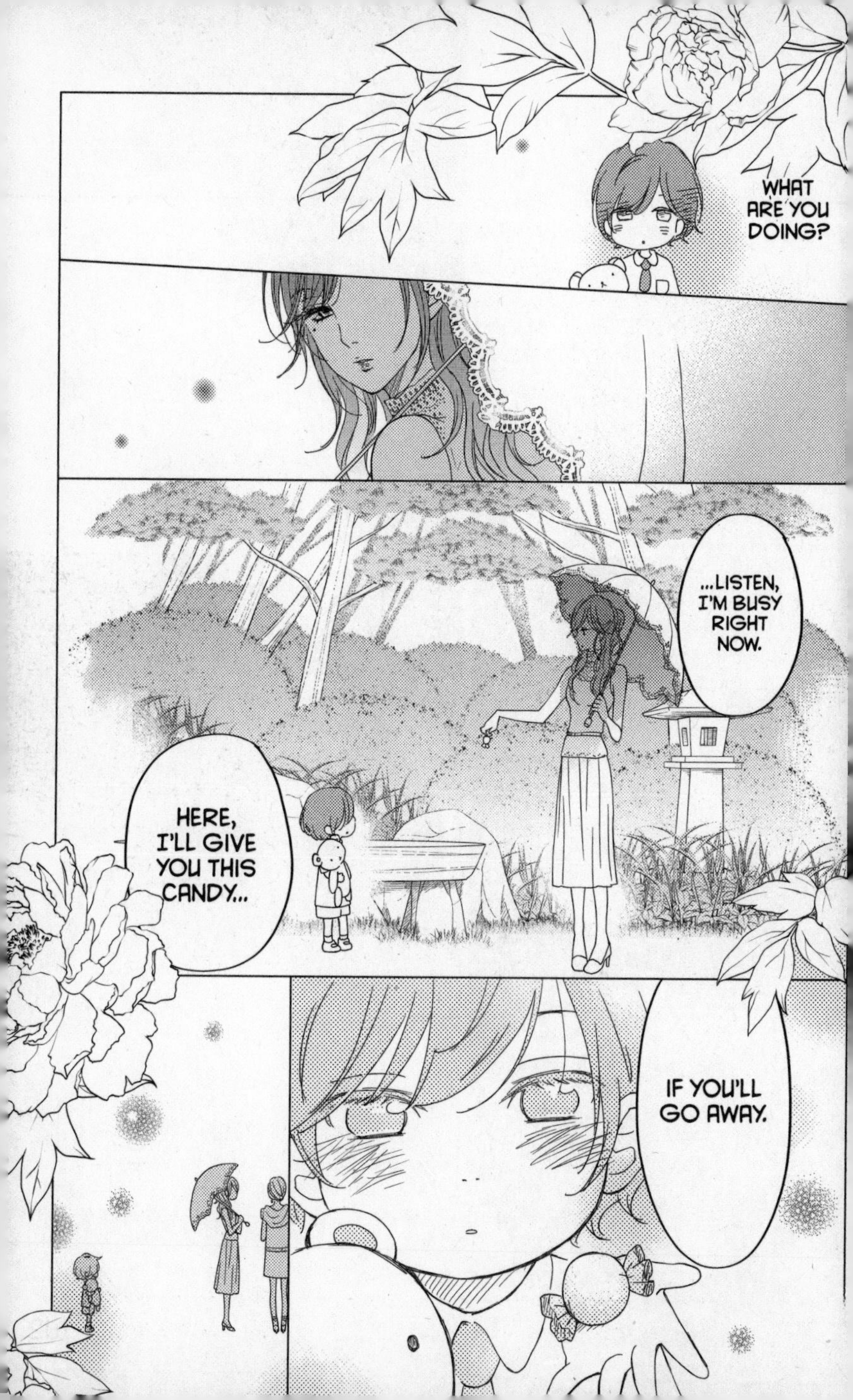
WHAT ARE YOU DOING?
...LISTEN, I'M BUSY RIGHT NOW.
HERE, I'LL GIVE YOU THIS CANDY...
IF YOU'LL GO AWAY.

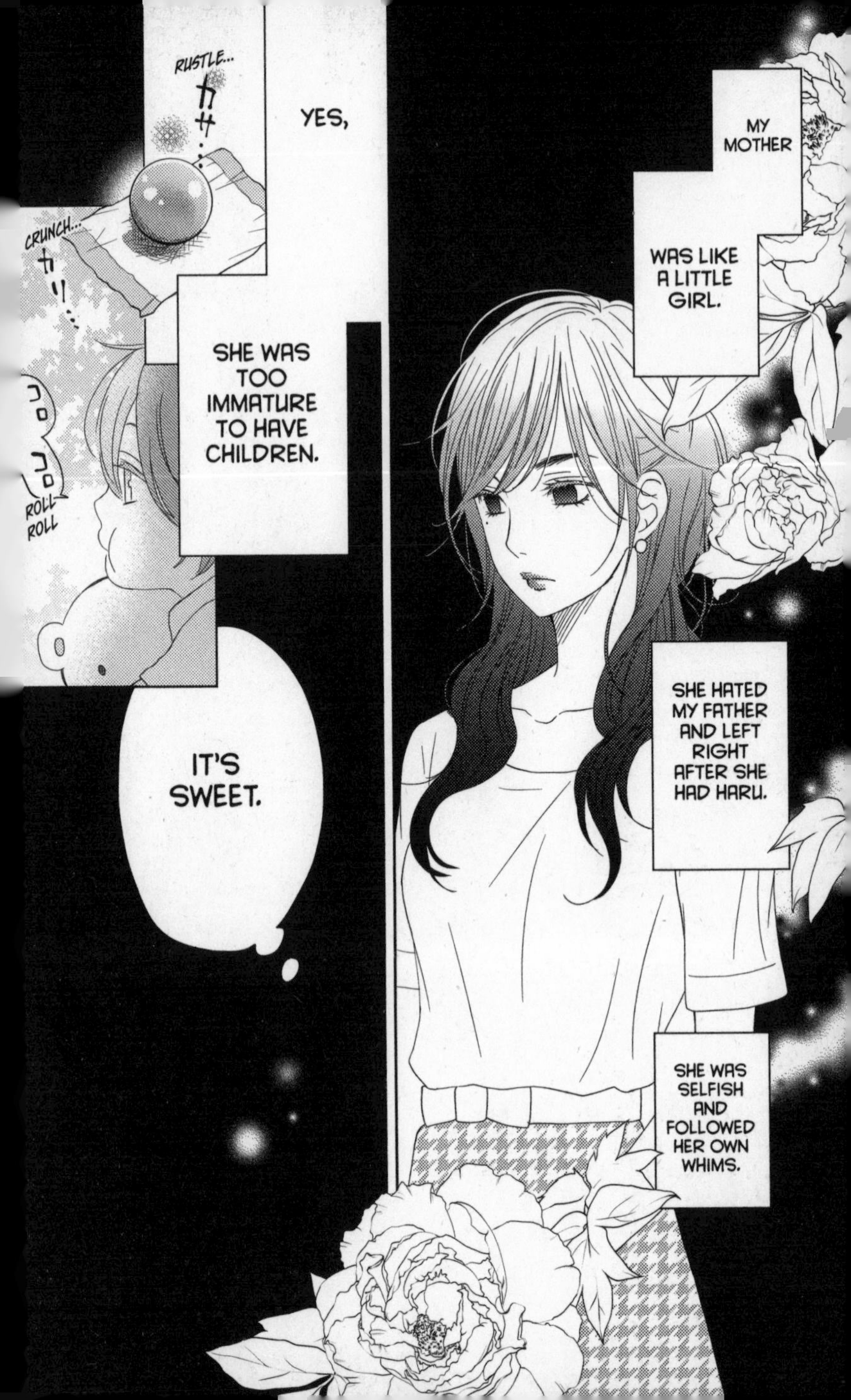
MY MOTHER
WAS LIKE A LITTLE GIRL.
SHE HATED MY FATHER AND LEFT RIGHT AFTER SHE HAD HARU.
SHE WAS SELFISH AND FOLLOWED HER OWN WHIMS.
YES,
RUSTLE... ガサ…
CRUNCH... カリ…
SHE WAS TOO IMMATURE TO HAVE CHILDREN.
コロコロ ROLL ROLL
IT'S SWEET.

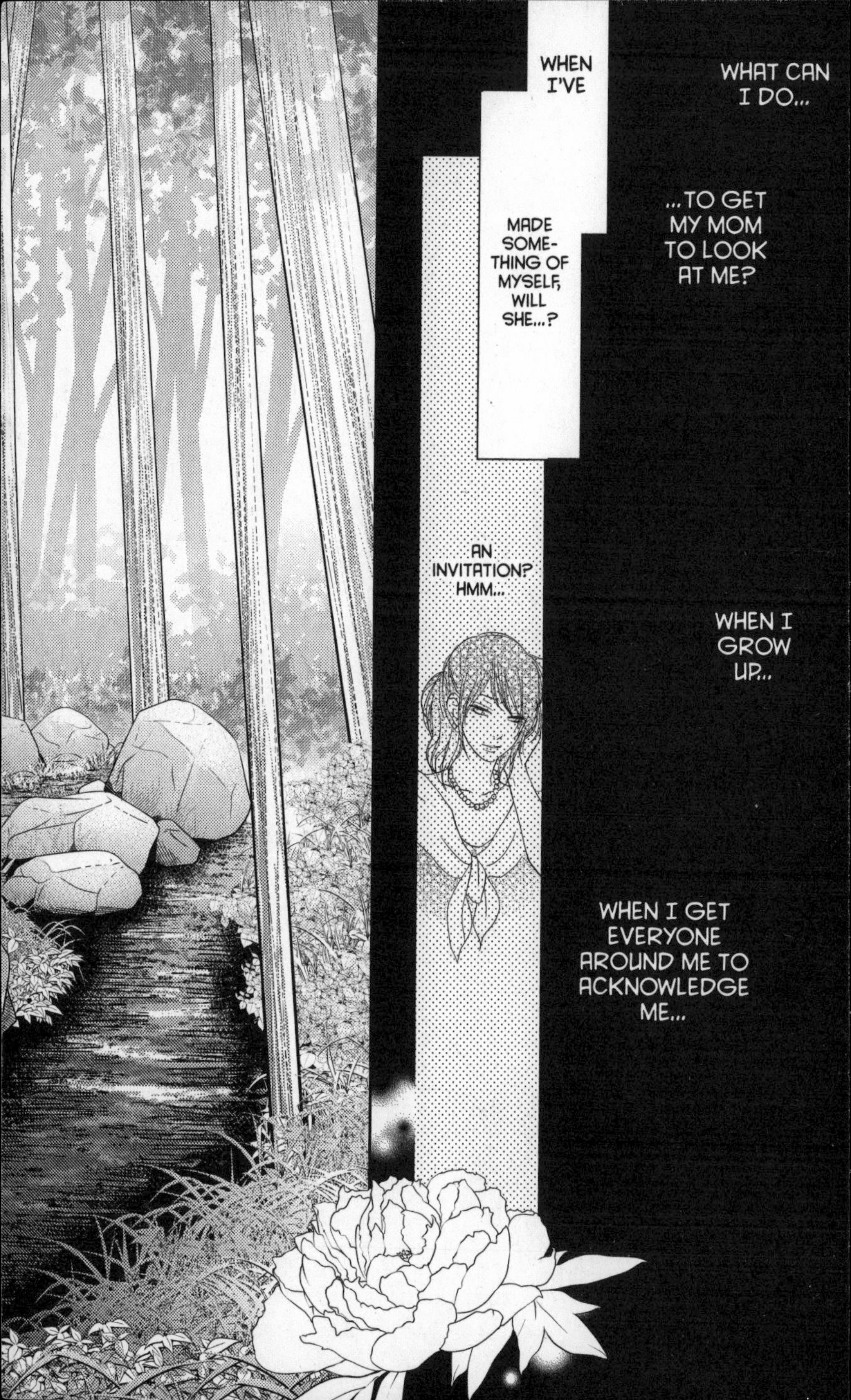
WHAT CAN I DO...
WHEN I'VE
...TO GET MY MOM TO LOOK AT ME?
MADE SOME-THING OF MYSELF, WILL SHE...?
AN INVITATION? HMM...
WHEN I GROW UP...
WHEN I GET EVERYONE AROUND ME TO ACKNOWLEDGE ME...

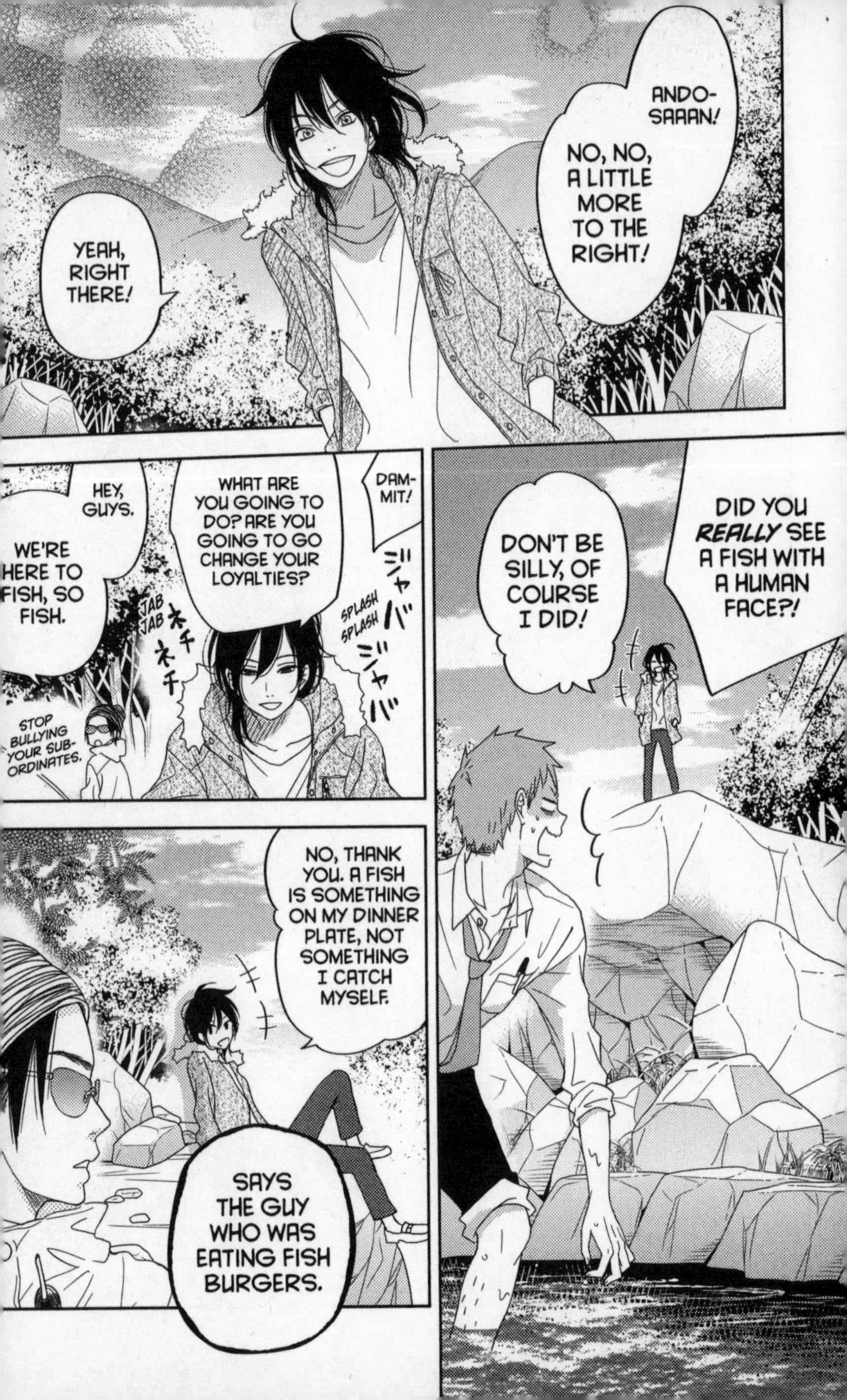
ANDO-SAAAN!
NO, NO, A LITTLE MORE TO THE RIGHT!
YEAH, RIGHT THERE!
DID YOU *REALLY* SEE A FISH WITH A HUMAN FACE?!
DON'T BE SILLY, OF COURSE I DID!
DAM-MIT!
WHAT ARE YOU GOING TO DO? ARE YOU GOING TO GO CHANGE YOUR LOYALTIES?
ジャバ ジャバ
SPLASH SPLASH
HEY, GUYS.
WE'RE HERE TO FISH, SO FISH.
ネチ ネチ
JAB JAB
STOP BULLYING YOUR SUB-ORDINATES.
NO, THANK YOU. A FISH IS SOMETHING ON MY DINNER PLATE, NOT SOMETHING I CATCH MYSELF.
SAYS THE GUY WHO WAS EATING FISH BURGERS.

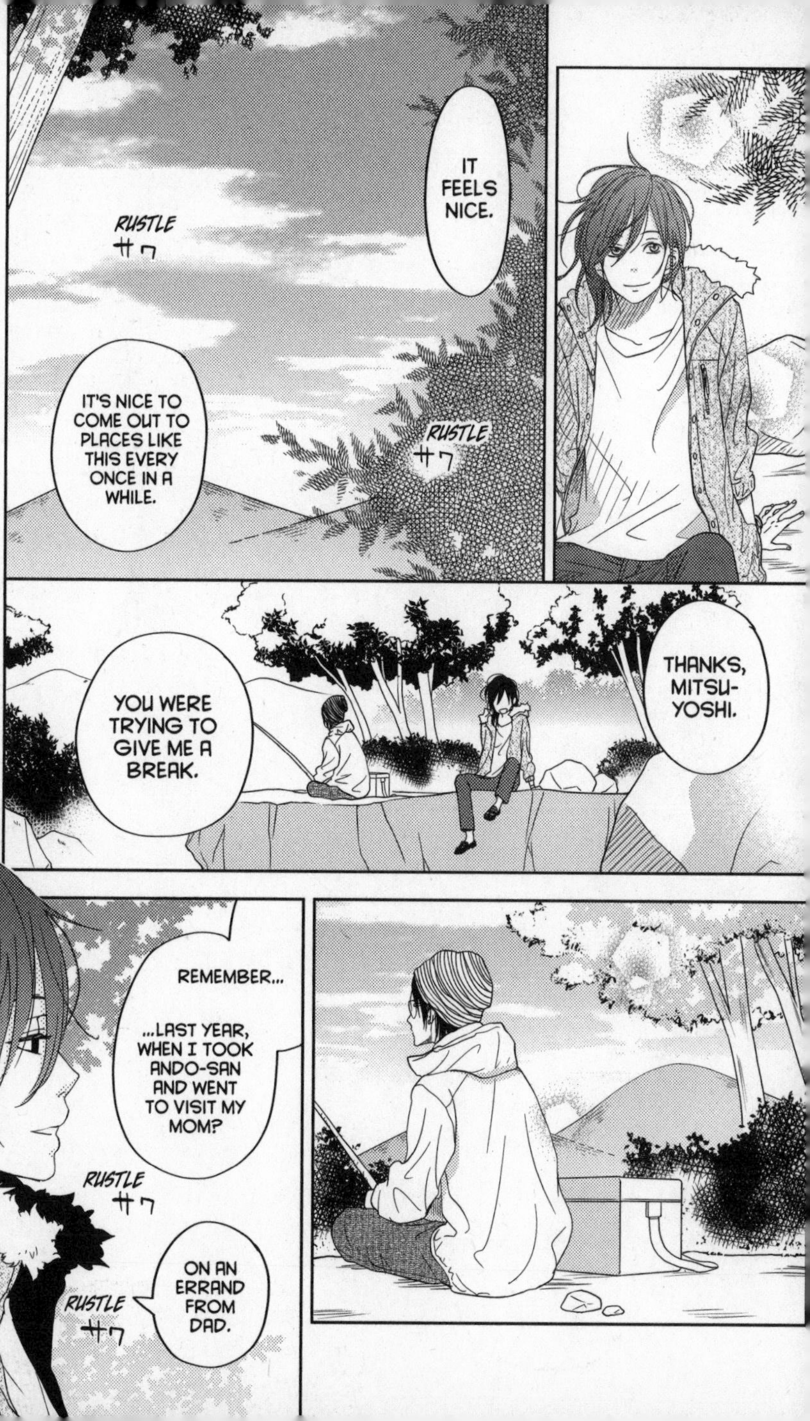
IT FEELS NICE.
RUSTLE
サワ
IT'S NICE TO COME OUT TO PLACES LIKE THIS EVERY ONCE IN A WHILE.
RUSTLE
サワ
THANKS, MITSU-YOSHI.
YOU WERE TRYING TO GIVE ME A BREAK.
REMEMBER...
...LAST YEAR, WHEN I TOOK ANDO-SAN AND WENT TO VISIT MY MOM?
RUSTLE
サワ
ON AN ERRAND FROM DAD.
RUSTLE
サワ

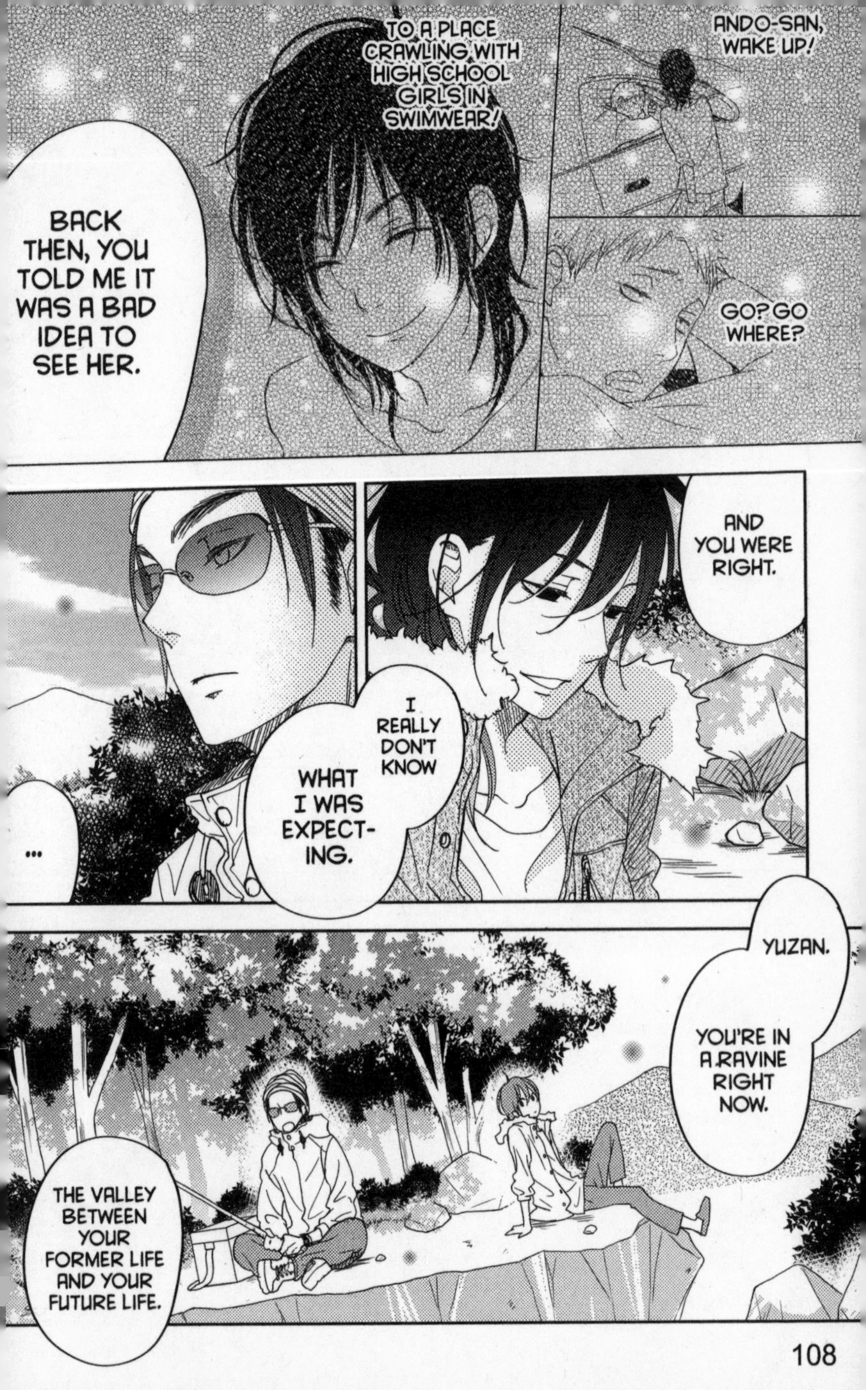
ANDO-SAN, WAKE UP!
GO? GO WHERE?
TO A PLACE CRAWLING WITH HIGH SCHOOL GIRLS IN SWIMWEAR!
BACK THEN, YOU TOLD ME IT WAS A BAD IDEA TO SEE HER.
AND YOU WERE RIGHT.
I REALLY DON'T KNOW
WHAT I WAS EXPECT-ING.
...
YUZAN.
YOU'RE IN A RAVINE RIGHT NOW.
THE VALLEY BETWEEN YOUR FORMER LIFE AND YOUR FUTURE LIFE.

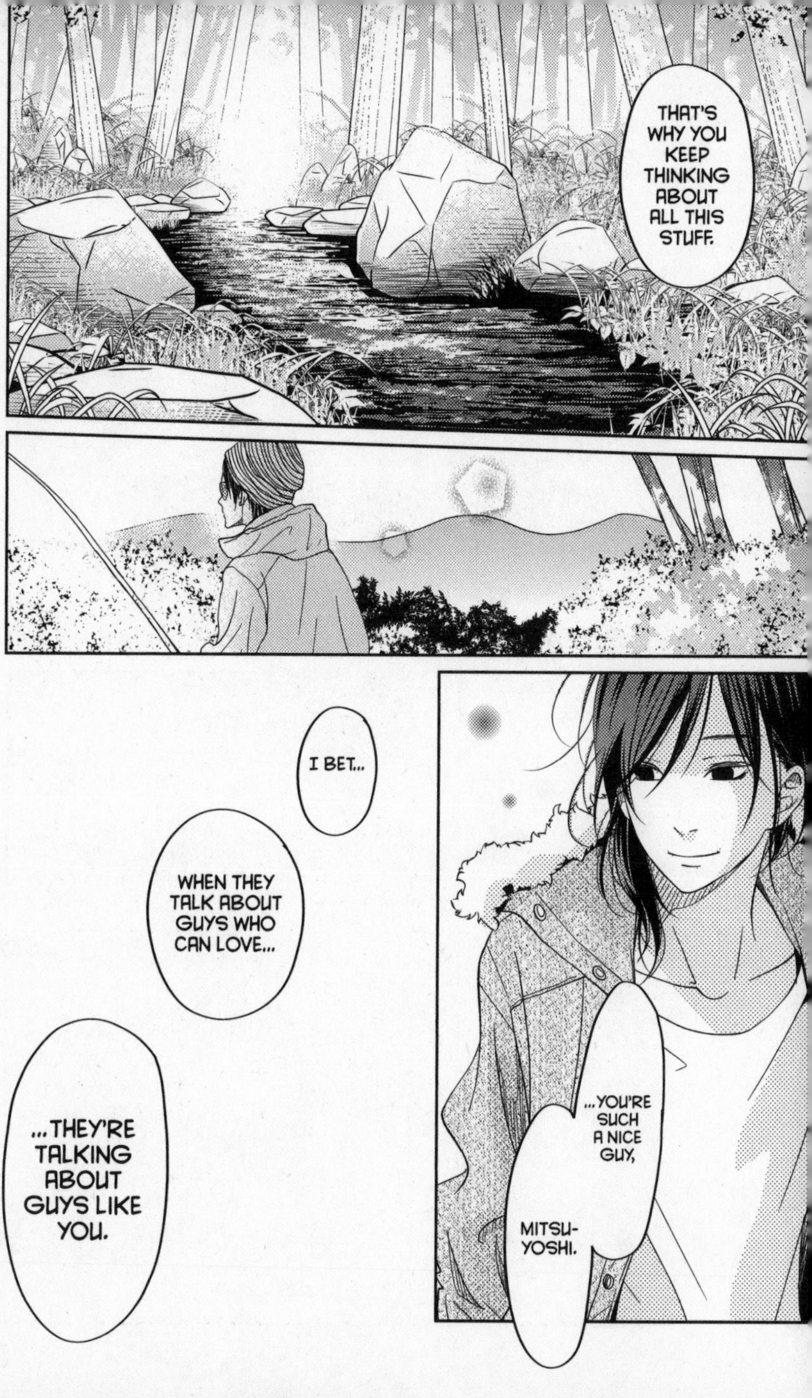
THAT'S WHY YOU KEEP THINKING ABOUT ALL THIS STUFF.
I BET...
WHEN THEY TALK ABOUT GUYS WHO CAN LOVE...
...THEY'RE TALKING ABOUT GUYS LIKE YOU.
...YOU'RE SUCH A NICE GUY,
MITSU-YOSHI.

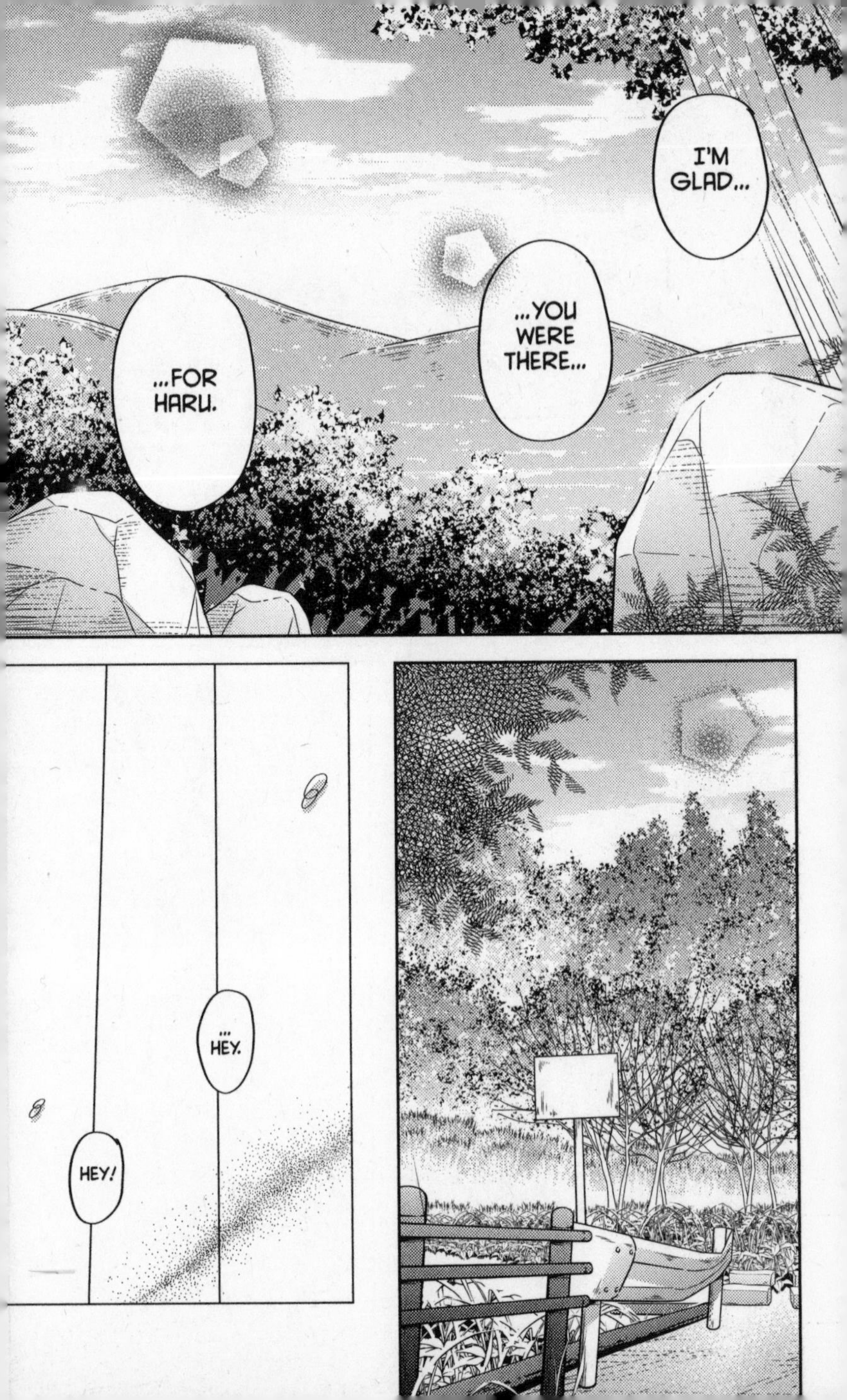
I'M GLAD...
...YOU WERE THERE...
...FOR HARU.
...HEY.
HEY!

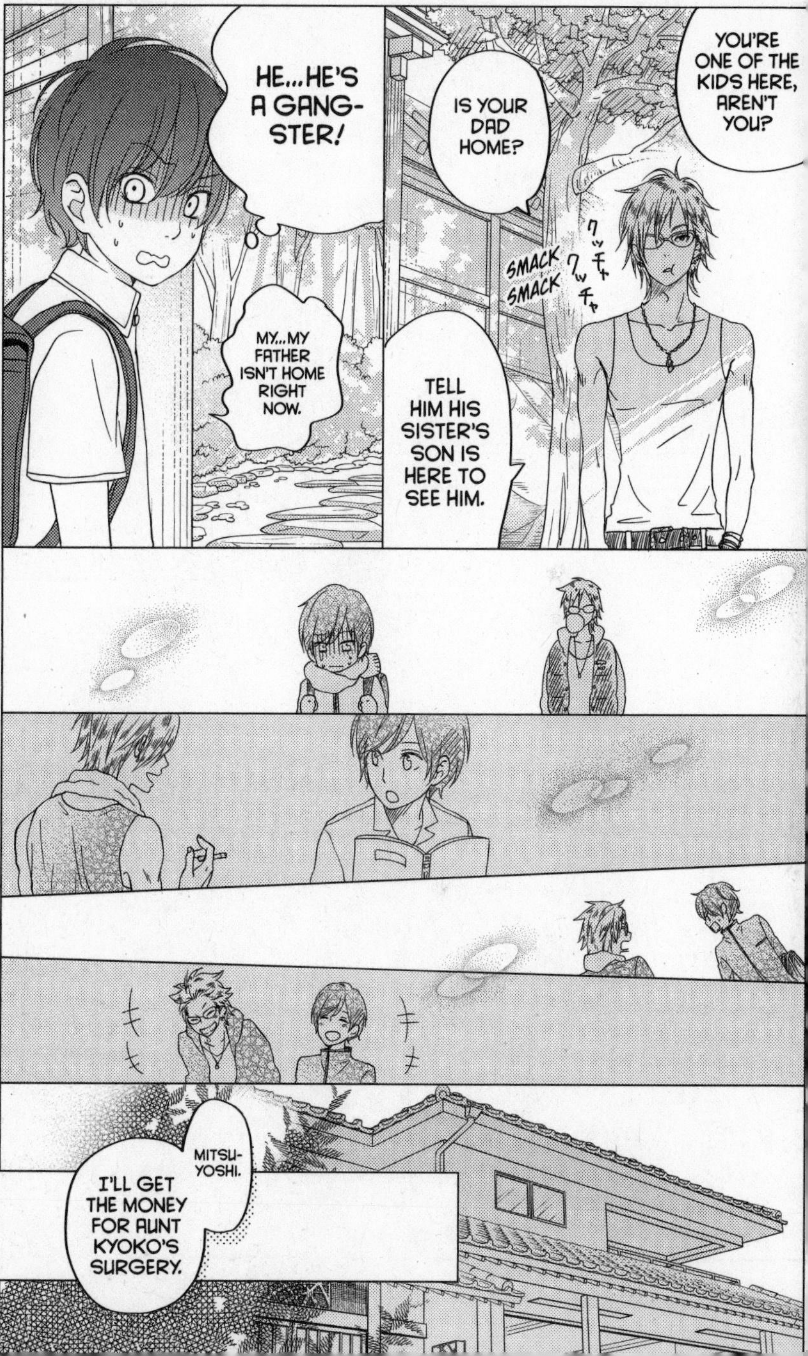
YOU'RE ONE OF THE KIDS HERE, AREN'T YOU?
SMACK SMACK
クッチャ クッチャ
IS YOUR DAD HOME?
TELL HIM HIS SISTER'S SON IS HERE TO SEE HIM.
HE...HE'S A GANG-STER!
MY...MY FATHER ISN'T HOME RIGHT NOW.
MITSU-YOSHI.
I'LL GET THE MONEY FOR AUNT KYOKO'S SURGERY.

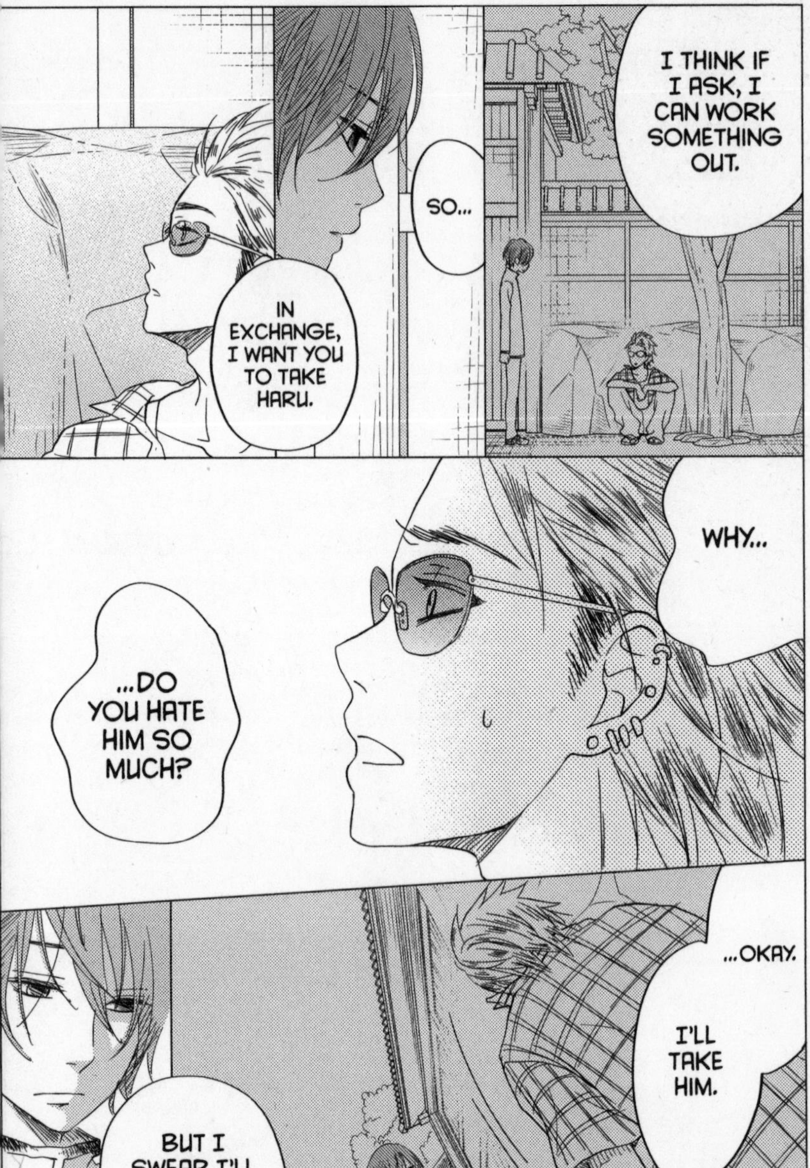
I THINK IF I ASK, I CAN WORK SOMETHING OUT.
SO...
IN EXCHANGE, I WANT YOU TO TAKE HARU.
WHY...
...DO YOU HATE HIM SO MUCH?
...OKAY.
I'LL TAKE HIM.
BUT I SWEAR I'LL PAY YOU BACK.

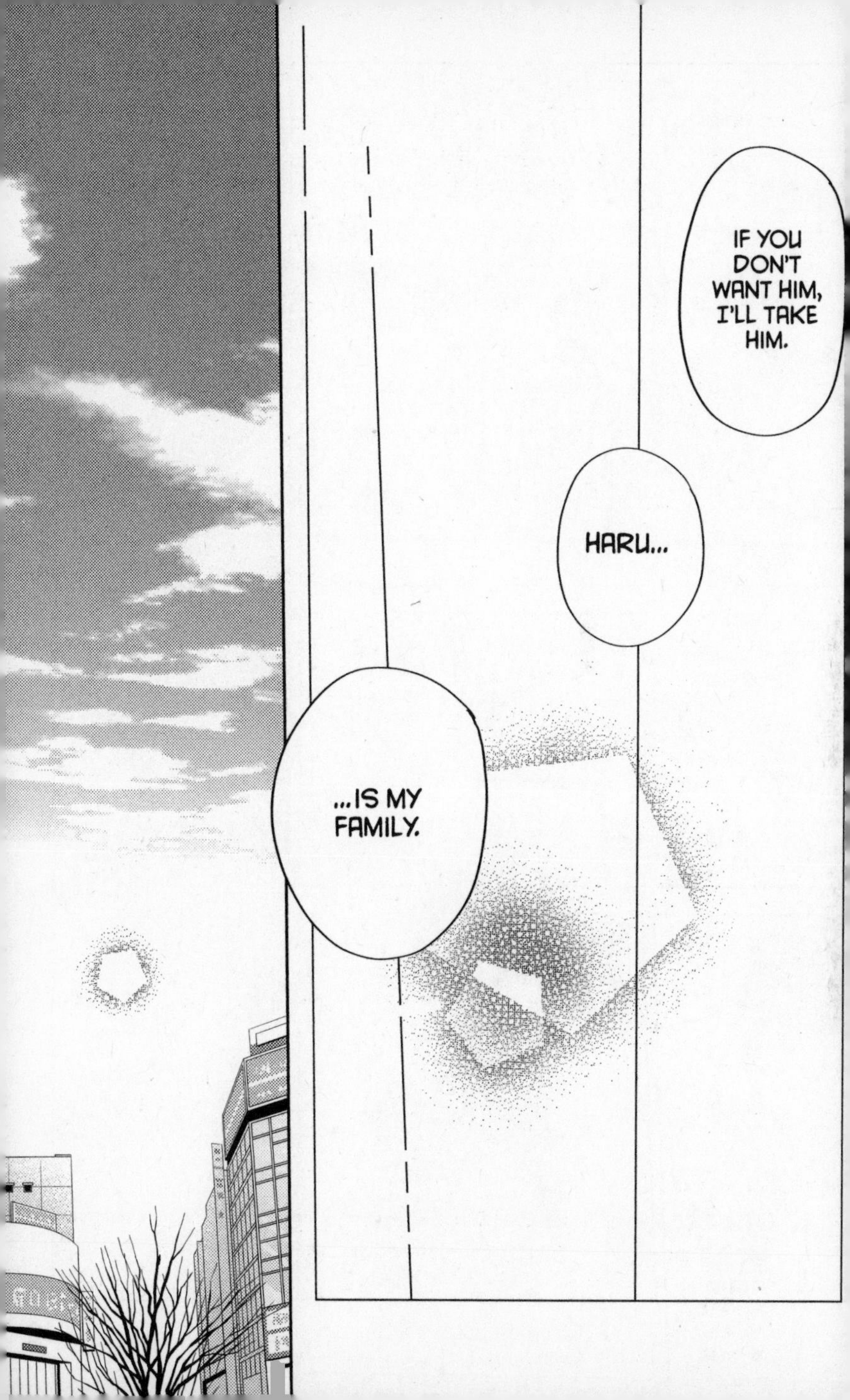
IF YOU DON'T WANT HIM, I'LL TAKE HIM.
HARU...
...IS MY FAMILY.

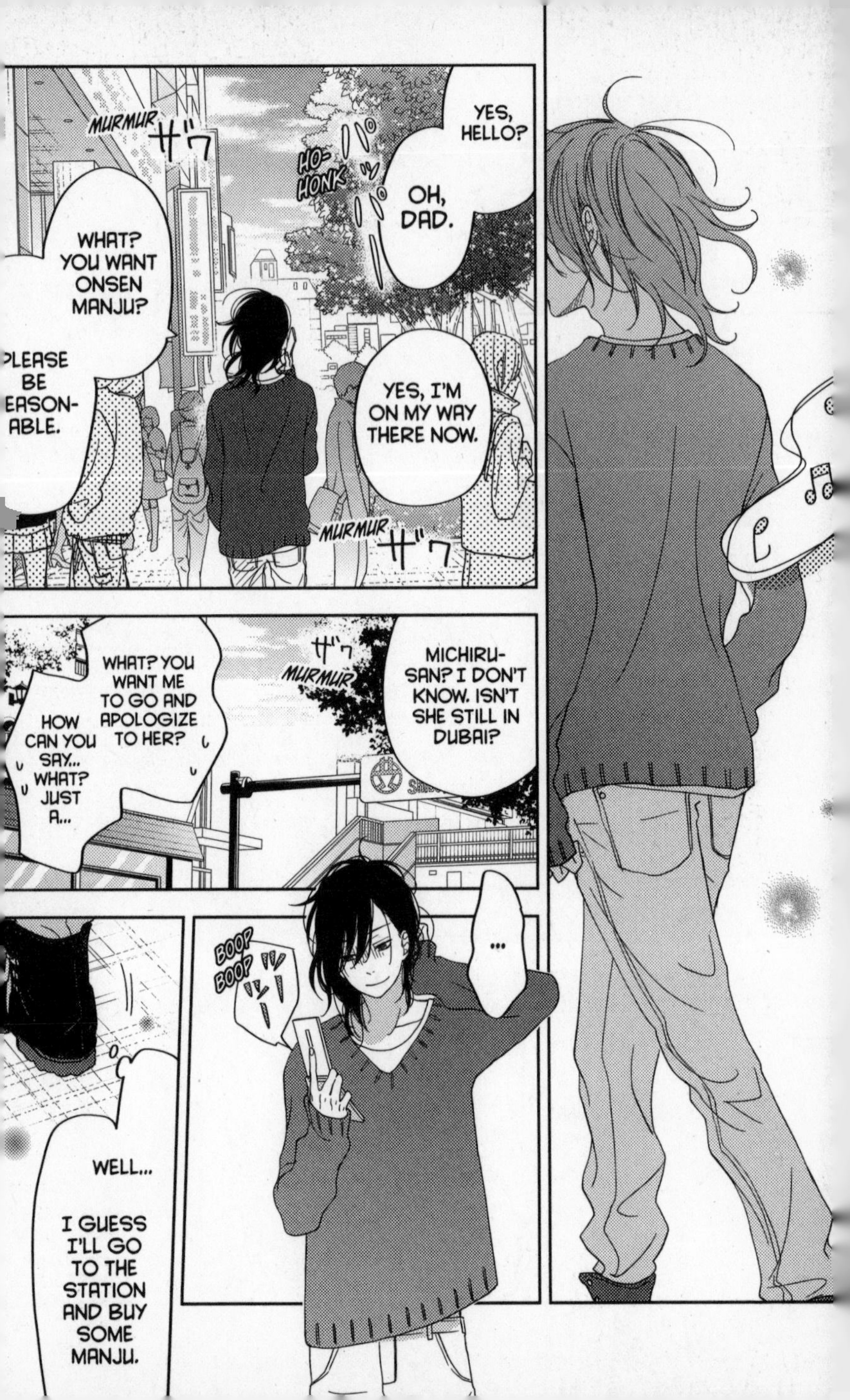
YES, HELLO?
OH, DAD.
HO-HONK
MURMUR
ザワ
WHAT? YOU WANT ONSEN MANJU?
PLEASE BE REASONABLE.
YES, I'M ON MY WAY THERE NOW.
MURMUR
ザワ
MICHIRU-SAN? I DON'T KNOW. ISN'T SHE STILL IN DUBAI?
ザワ
MURMUR
WHAT? YOU WANT ME TO GO AND APOLOGIZE TO HER?
HOW CAN YOU SAY... WHAT? JUST A...
...
BOOP BOOP
WELL...
I GUESS I'LL GO TO THE STATION AND BUY SOME MANJU.

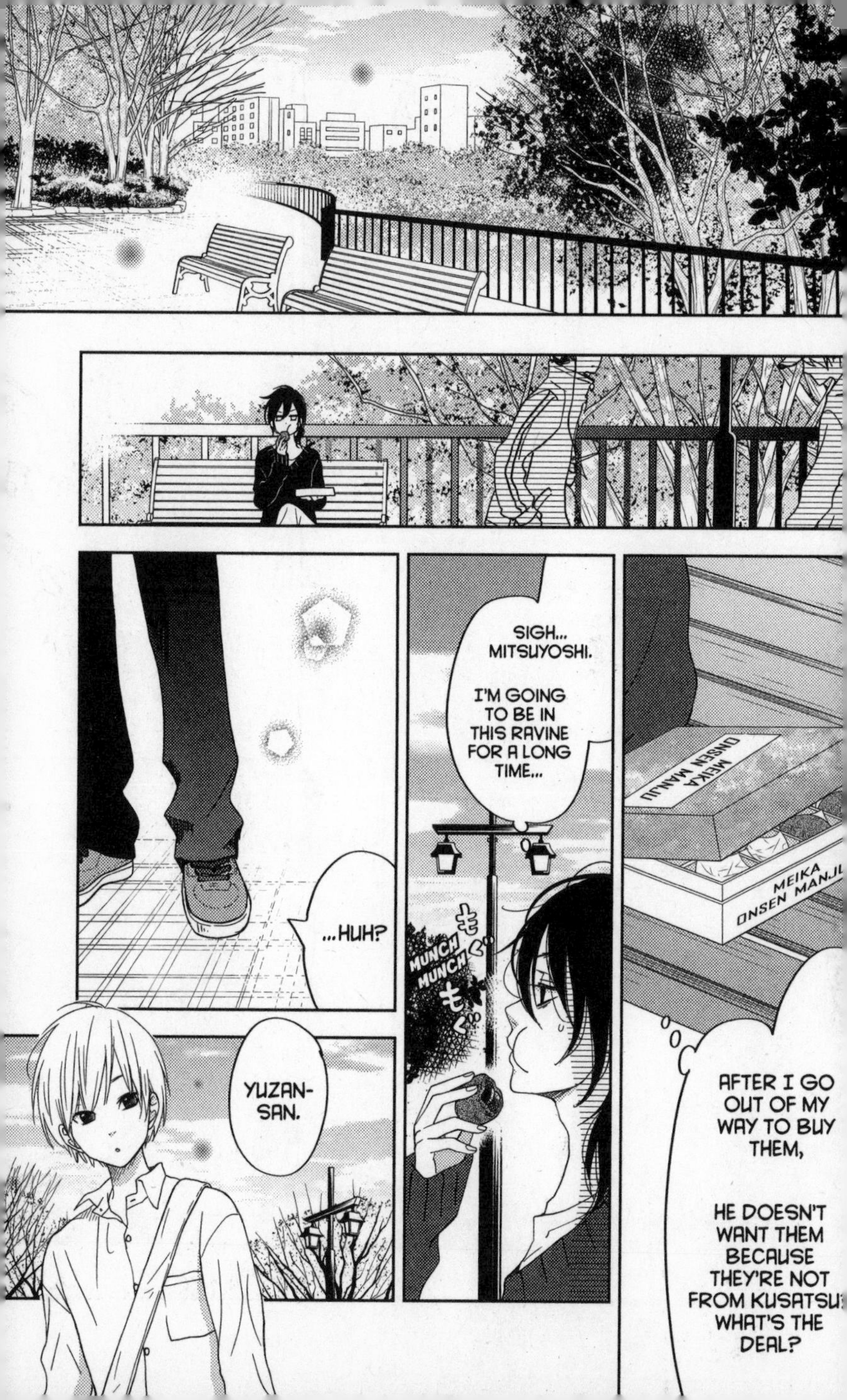
MEIKA ONSEN MANJU
MEIKA ONSEN MANJU
AFTER I GO OUT OF MY WAY TO BUY THEM,
HE DOESN'T WANT THEM BECAUSE THEY'RE NOT FROM KUSATSU? WHAT'S THE DEAL?
SIGH... MITSUYOSHI.
I'M GOING TO BE IN THIS RAVINE FOR A LONG TIME...
MUNCH MUNCH
...HUH?
YUZAN-SAN.

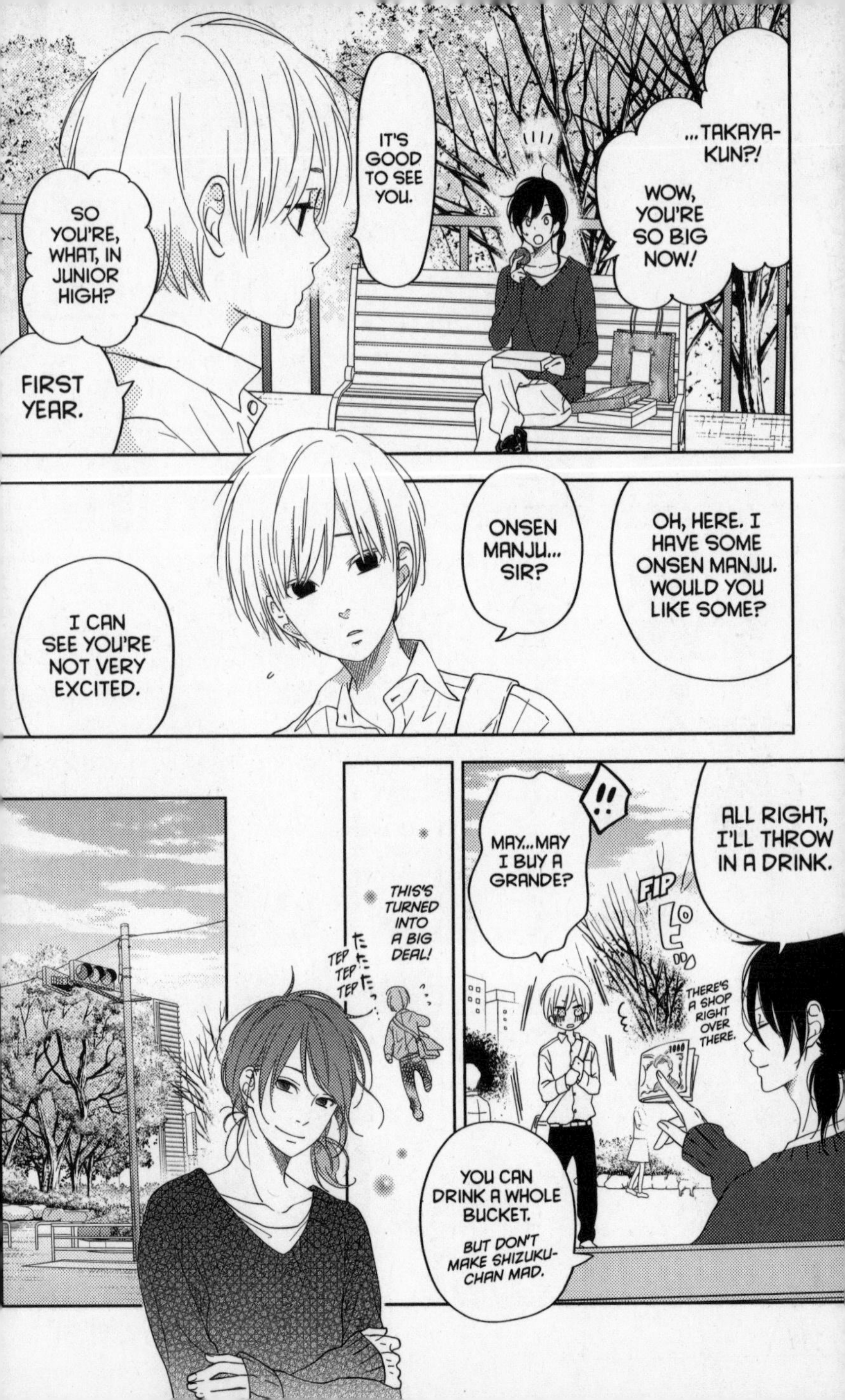
...TAKAYA-KUN?!
WOW, YOU'RE SO BIG NOW!
IT'S GOOD TO SEE YOU.
SO YOU'RE, WHAT, IN JUNIOR HIGH?
FIRST YEAR.
OH, HERE. I HAVE SOME ONSEN MANJU. WOULD YOU LIKE SOME?
ONSEN MANJU... SIR?
I CAN SEE YOU'RE NOT VERY EXCITED.
ALL RIGHT, I'LL THROW IN A DRINK.
!!
MAY...MAY I BUY A GRANDE?
FIP
THERE'S A SHOP RIGHT OVER THERE.
YOU CAN DRINK A WHOLE BUCKET.
BUT DON'T MAKE SHIZUKU-CHAN MAD.
THIS'S TURNED INTO A BIG DEAL!
たたたっ…
TEP TEP TEP

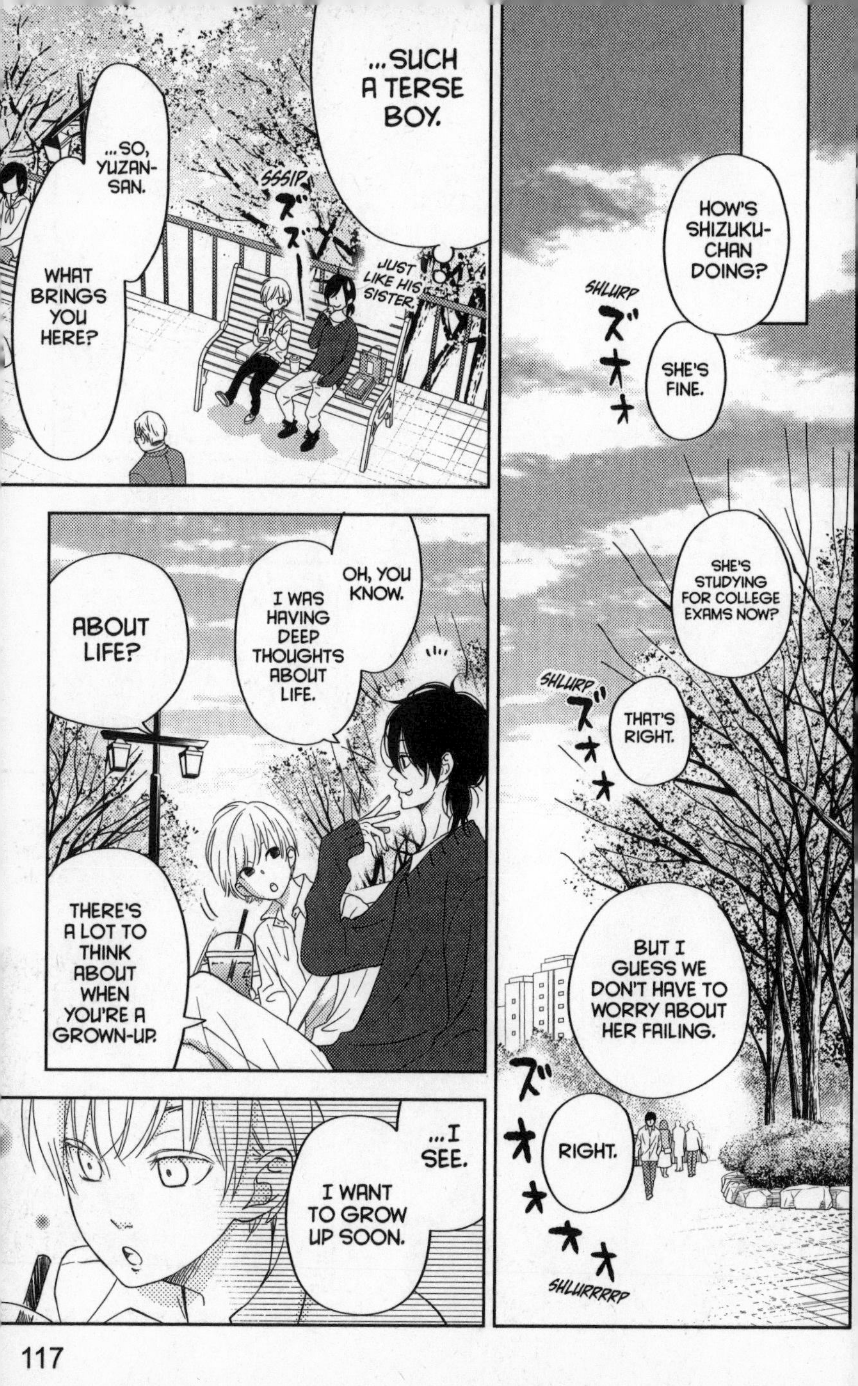
HOW'S SHIZUKU-CHAN DOING?
SHLURP
ズォォ
SHE'S FINE.
SHE'S STUDYING FOR COLLEGE EXAMS NOW?
SHLURP
ズォォ
THAT'S RIGHT.
BUT I GUESS WE DON'T HAVE TO WORRY ABOUT HER FAILING.
ズォォォォ
RIGHT.
SHLURRRRP
...SUCH A TERSE BOY.
SSSIP
ズズー
JUST LIKE HIS SISTER.
...SO, YUZAN-SAN.
WHAT BRINGS YOU HERE?
OH, YOU KNOW.
I WAS HAVING DEEP THOUGHTS ABOUT LIFE.
ABOUT LIFE?
THERE'S A LOT TO THINK ABOUT WHEN YOU'RE A GROWN-UP.
...I SEE.
I WANT TO GROW UP SOON.

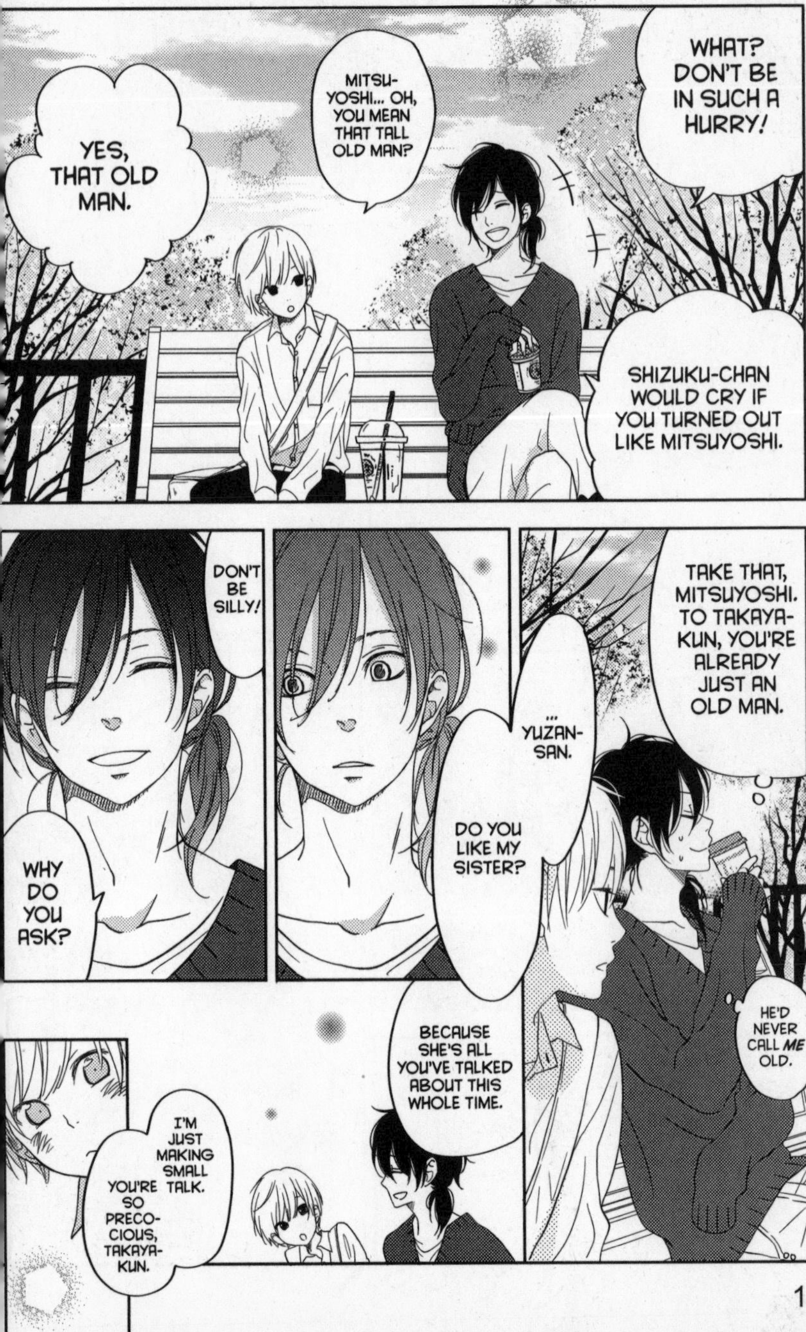
WHAT? DON'T BE IN SUCH A HURRY!
SHIZUKU-CHAN WOULD CRY IF YOU TURNED OUT LIKE MITSUYOSHI.
MITSU-YOSHI... OH, YOU MEAN THAT TALL OLD MAN?
YES, THAT OLD MAN.
TAKE THAT, MITSUYOSHI. TO TAKAYA-KUN, YOU'RE ALREADY JUST AN OLD MAN.
HE'D NEVER CALL *ME* OLD.
... YUZAN-SAN.
DO YOU LIKE MY SISTER?
DON'T BE SILLY!
WHY DO YOU ASK?
BECAUSE SHE'S ALL YOU'VE TALKED ABOUT THIS WHOLE TIME.
I'M JUST MAKING SMALL TALK.
YOU'RE SO PRECO-CIOUS, TAKAYA-KUN.

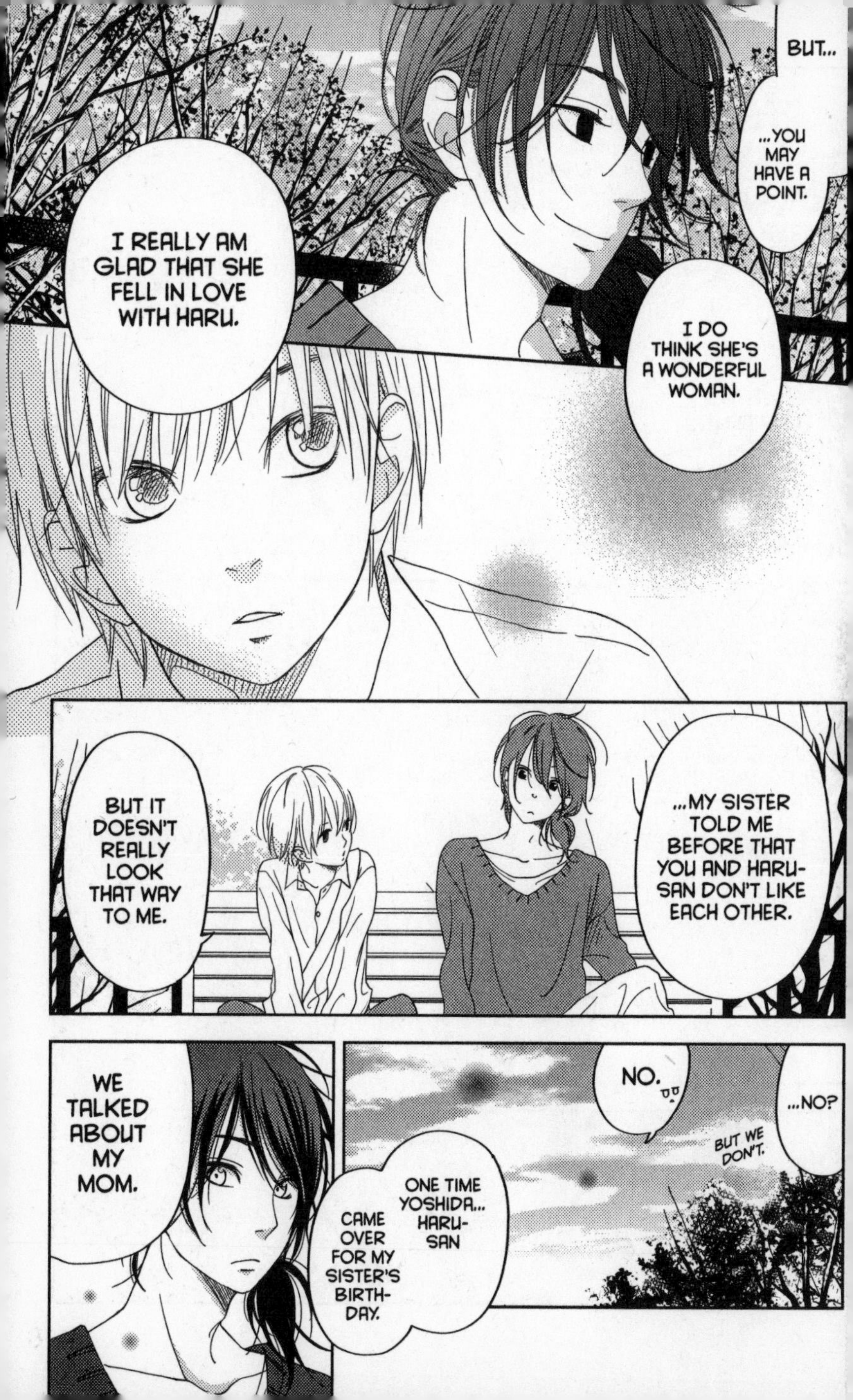
BUT...
...YOU MAY HAVE A POINT.
I DO THINK SHE'S A WONDERFUL WOMAN.
I REALLY AM GLAD THAT SHE FELL IN LOVE WITH HARU.
...MY SISTER TOLD ME BEFORE THAT YOU AND HARU-SAN DON'T LIKE EACH OTHER.
BUT IT DOESN'T REALLY LOOK THAT WAY TO ME.
...NO?
NO.
BUT WE DON'T.
ONE TIME YOSHIDA... HARU-SAN
CAME OVER FOR MY SISTER'S BIRTHDAY.
WE TALKED ABOUT MY MOM.

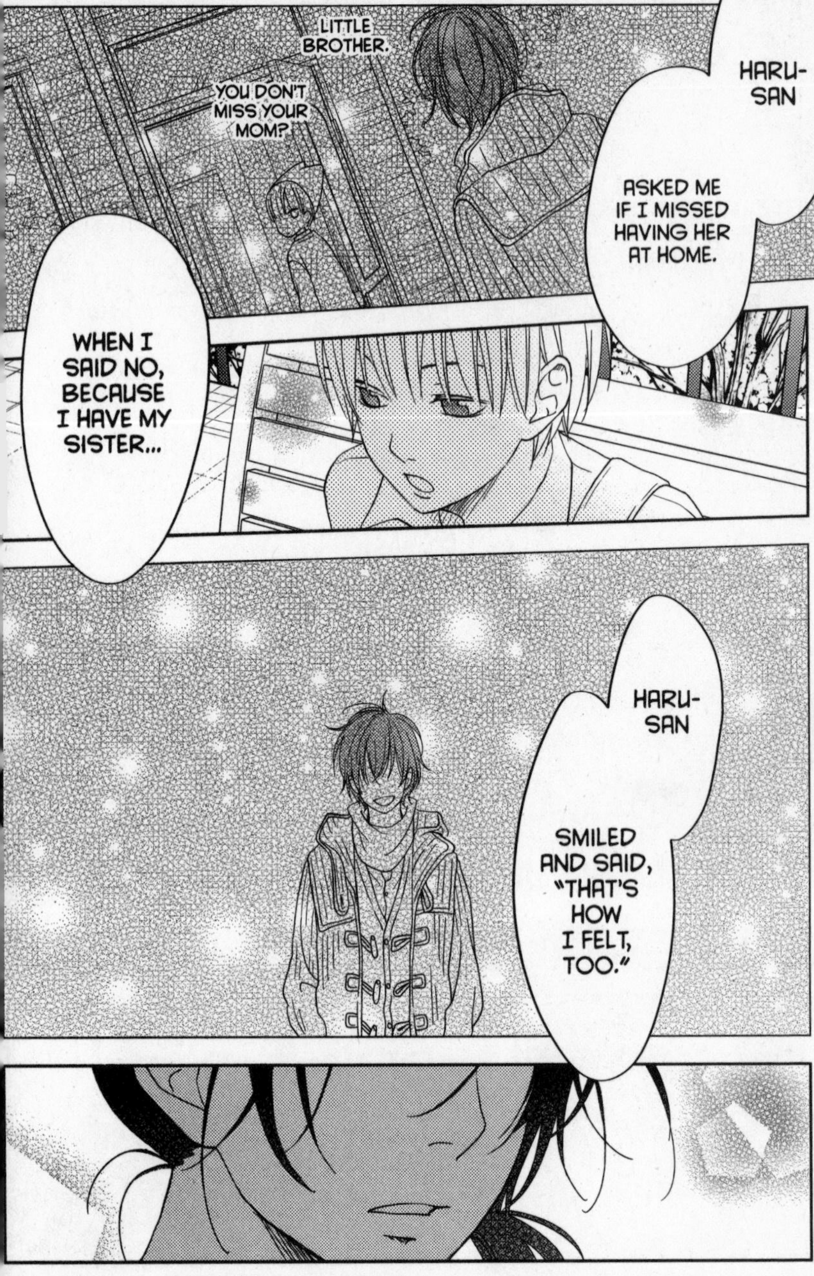
HARU-SAN
ASKED ME IF I MISSED HAVING HER AT HOME.
LITTLE BROTHER.
YOU DON'T MISS YOUR MOM?
WHEN I SAID NO, BECAUSE I HAVE MY SISTER...
HARU-SAN
SMILED AND SAID, "THAT'S HOW I FELT, TOO."

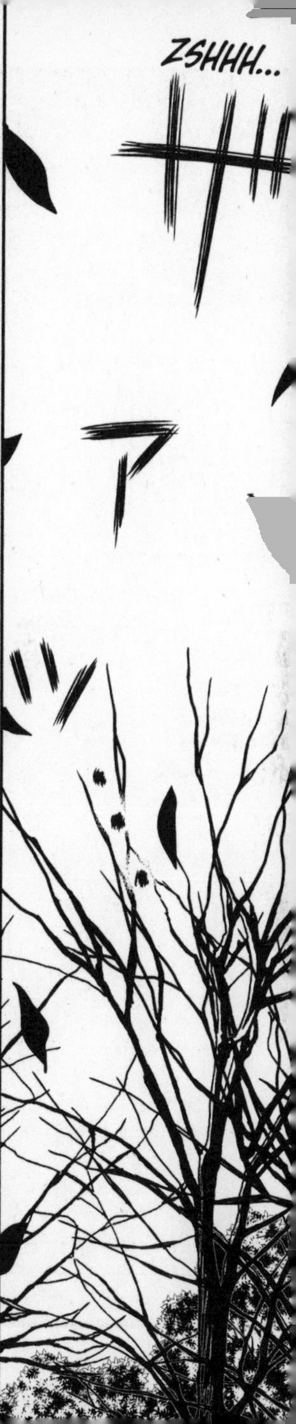
ZSHHH...

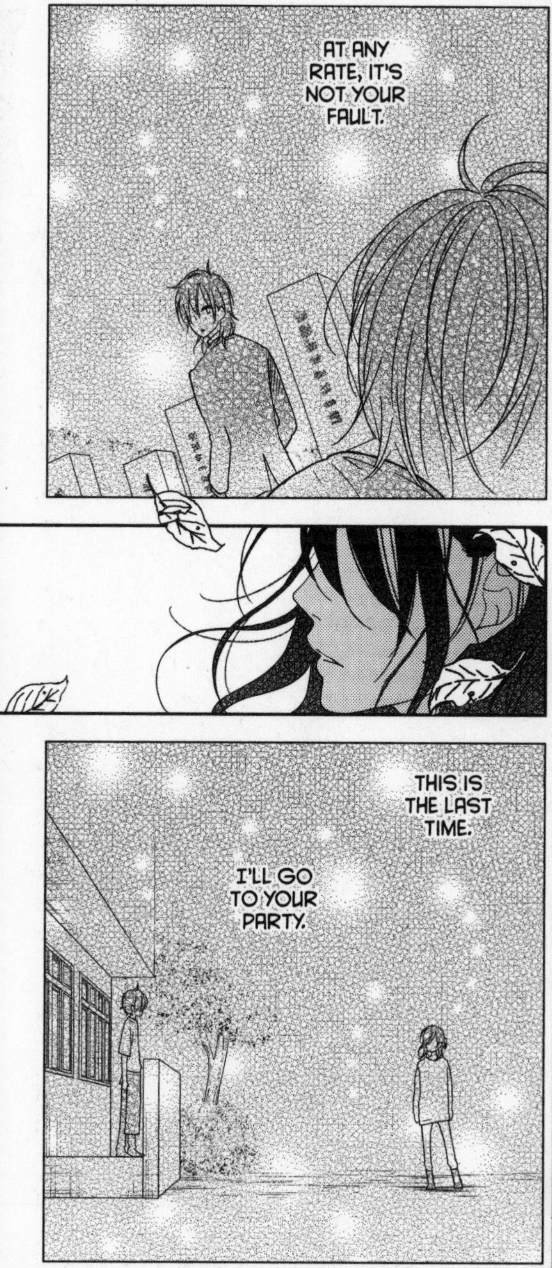
AT ANY RATE, IT'S NOT YOUR FAULT.
THIS IS THE LAST TIME.
I'LL GO TO YOUR PARTY.

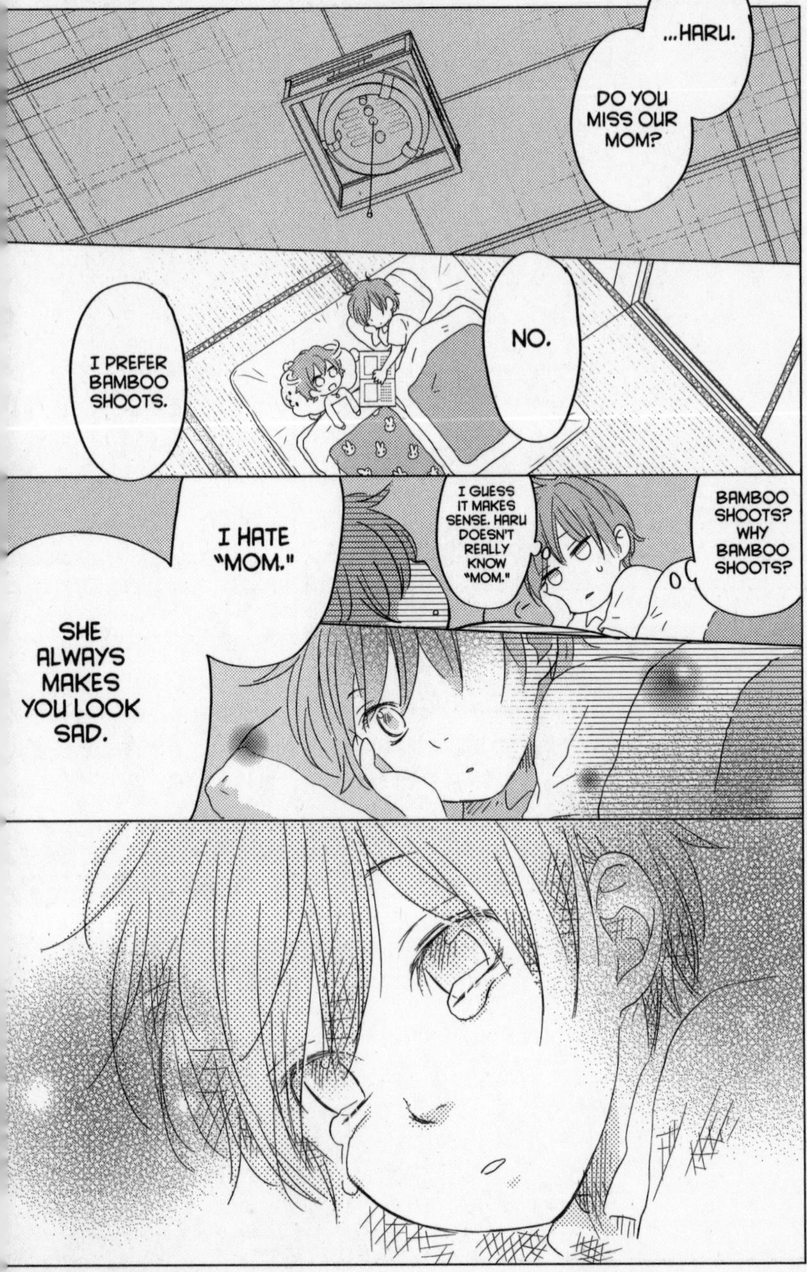

...HARU.
DO YOU MISS OUR MOM?
NO.
I PREFER BAMBOO SHOOTS.
BAMBOO SHOOTS? WHY BAMBOO SHOOTS?
I GUESS IT MAKES SENSE. HARU DOESN'T REALLY KNOW "MOM."
I HATE "MOM."
SHE ALWAYS MAKES YOU LOOK SAD.

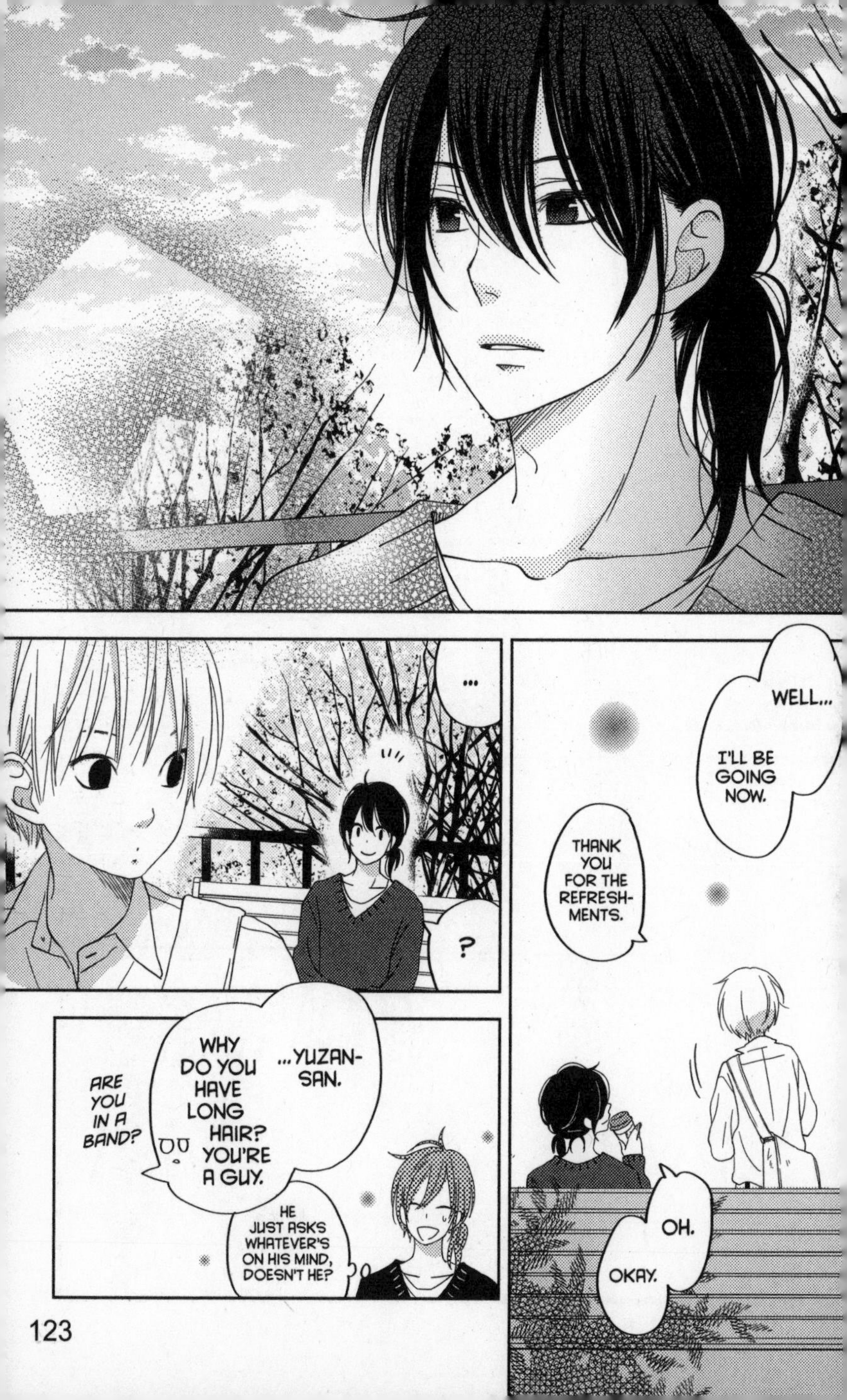
WELL...
I'LL BE GOING NOW.
THANK YOU FOR THE REFRESHMENTS.
OH.
OKAY.
...
?
...YUZAN-SAN.
WHY DO YOU HAVE LONG HAIR? YOU'RE A GUY.
ARE YOU IN A BAND?
HE JUST ASKS WHATEVER'S ON HIS MIND, DOESN'T HE?

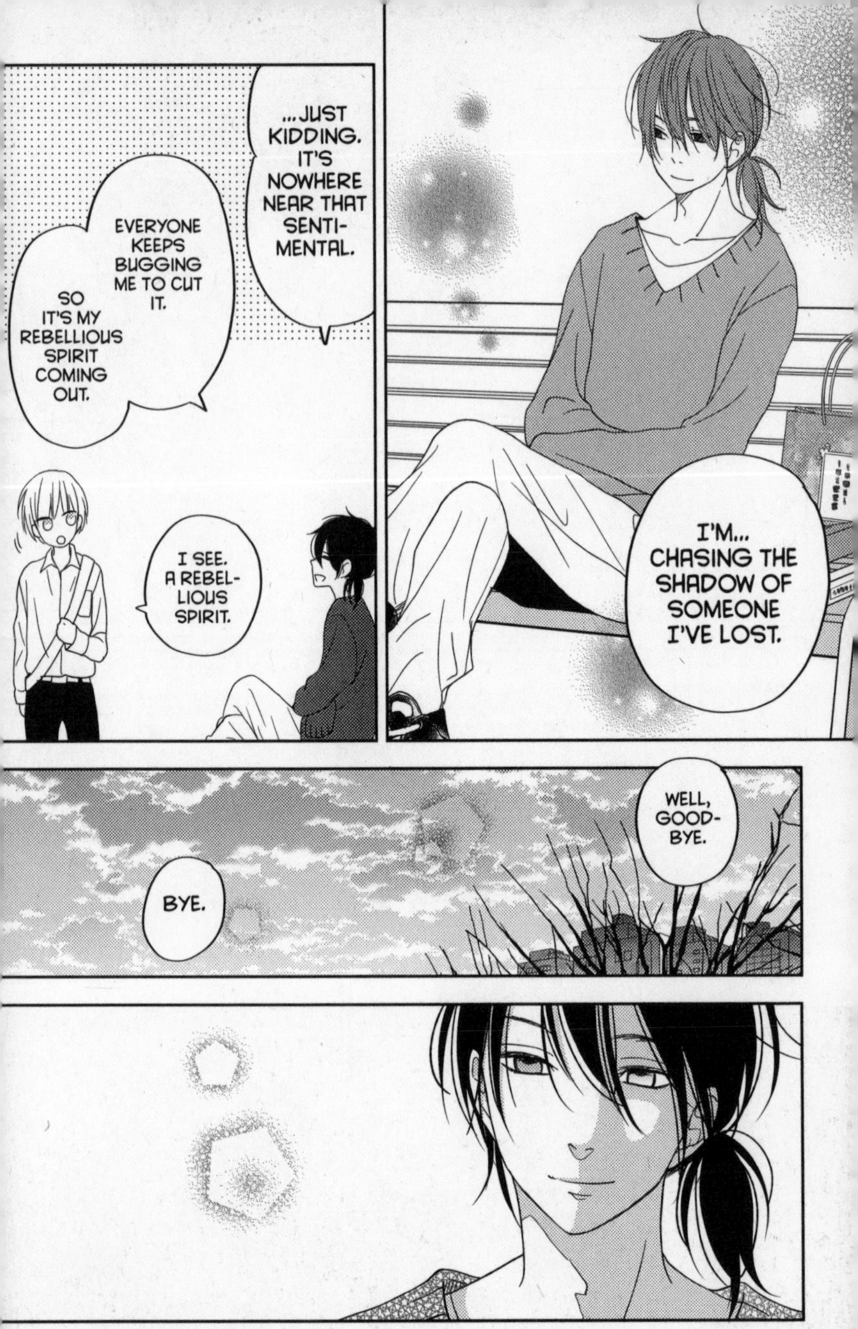
I'M... CHASING THE SHADOW OF SOMEONE I'VE LOST.
...JUST KIDDING. IT'S NOWHERE NEAR THAT SENTI-MENTAL.
EVERYONE KEEPS BUGGING ME TO CUT IT.
SO IT'S MY REBELLIOUS SPIRIT COMING OUT.
I SEE. A REBEL-LIOUS SPIRIT.
WELL, GOOD-BYE.
BYE.

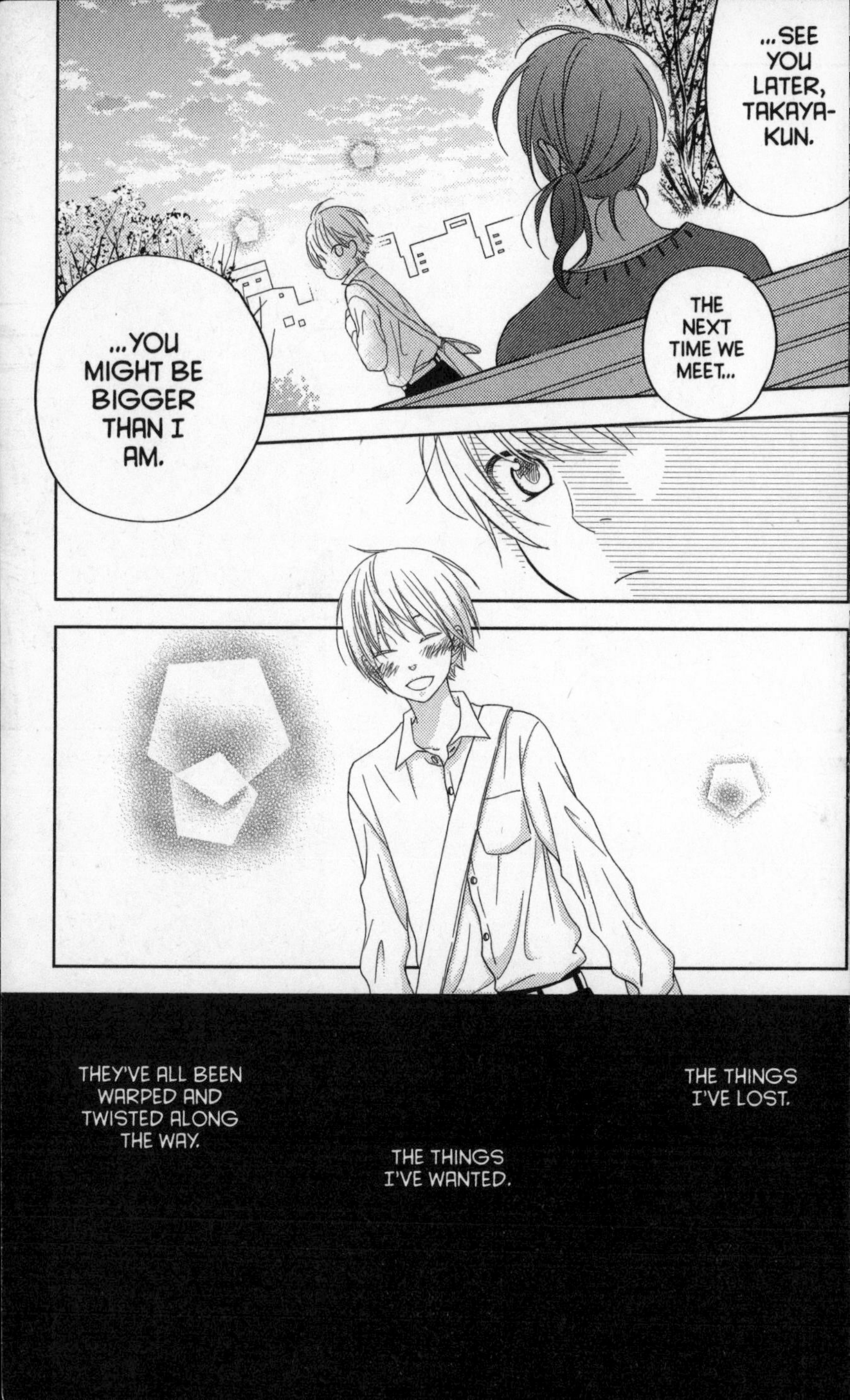
...SEE YOU LATER, TAKAYA-KUN.
THE NEXT TIME WE MEET...
...YOU MIGHT BE BIGGER THAN I AM.
THE THINGS I'VE LOST.
THE THINGS I'VE WANTED.
THEY'VE ALL BEEN WARPED AND TWISTED ALONG THE WAY.

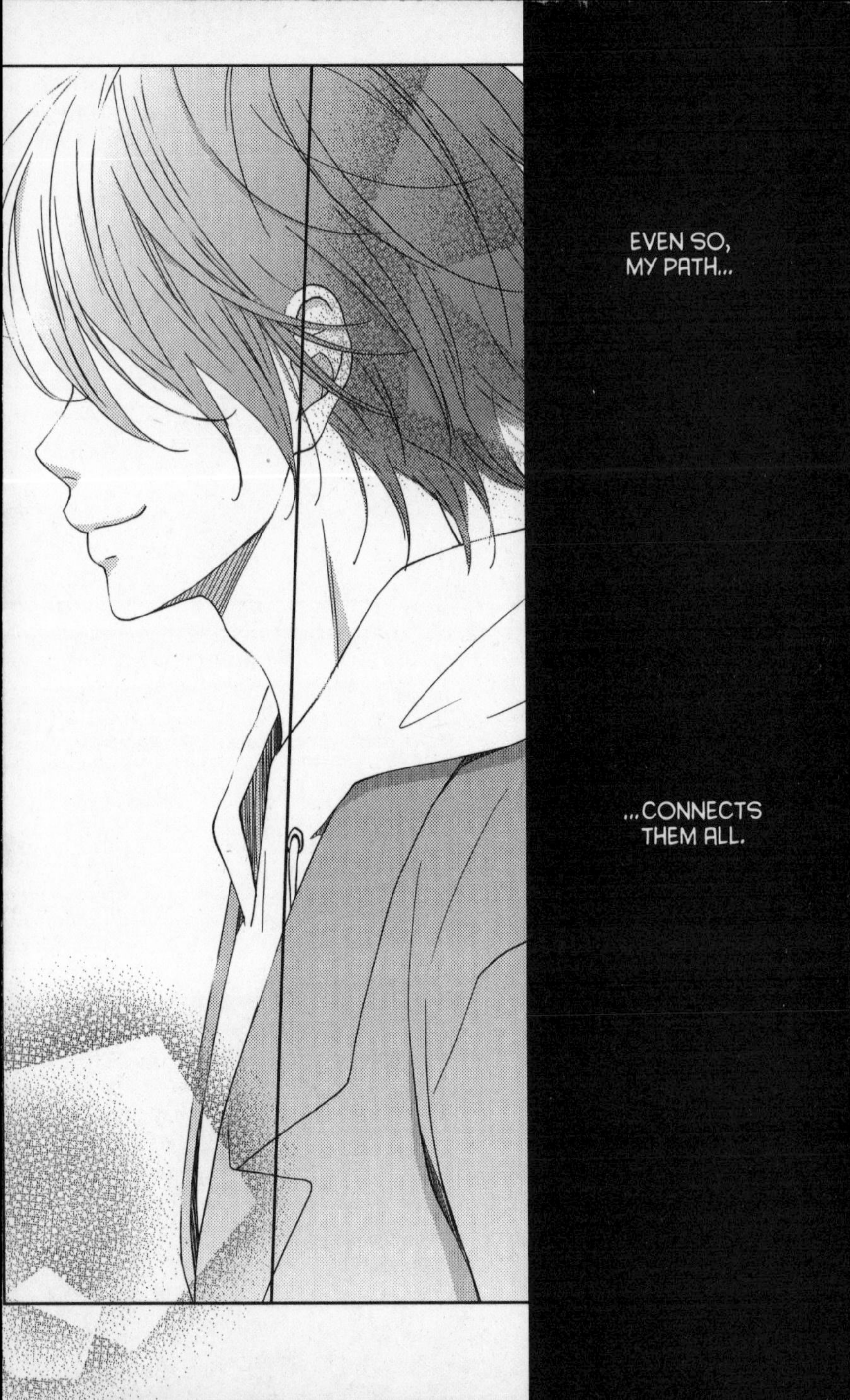
EVEN SO, MY PATH...
...CONNECTS THEM ALL.

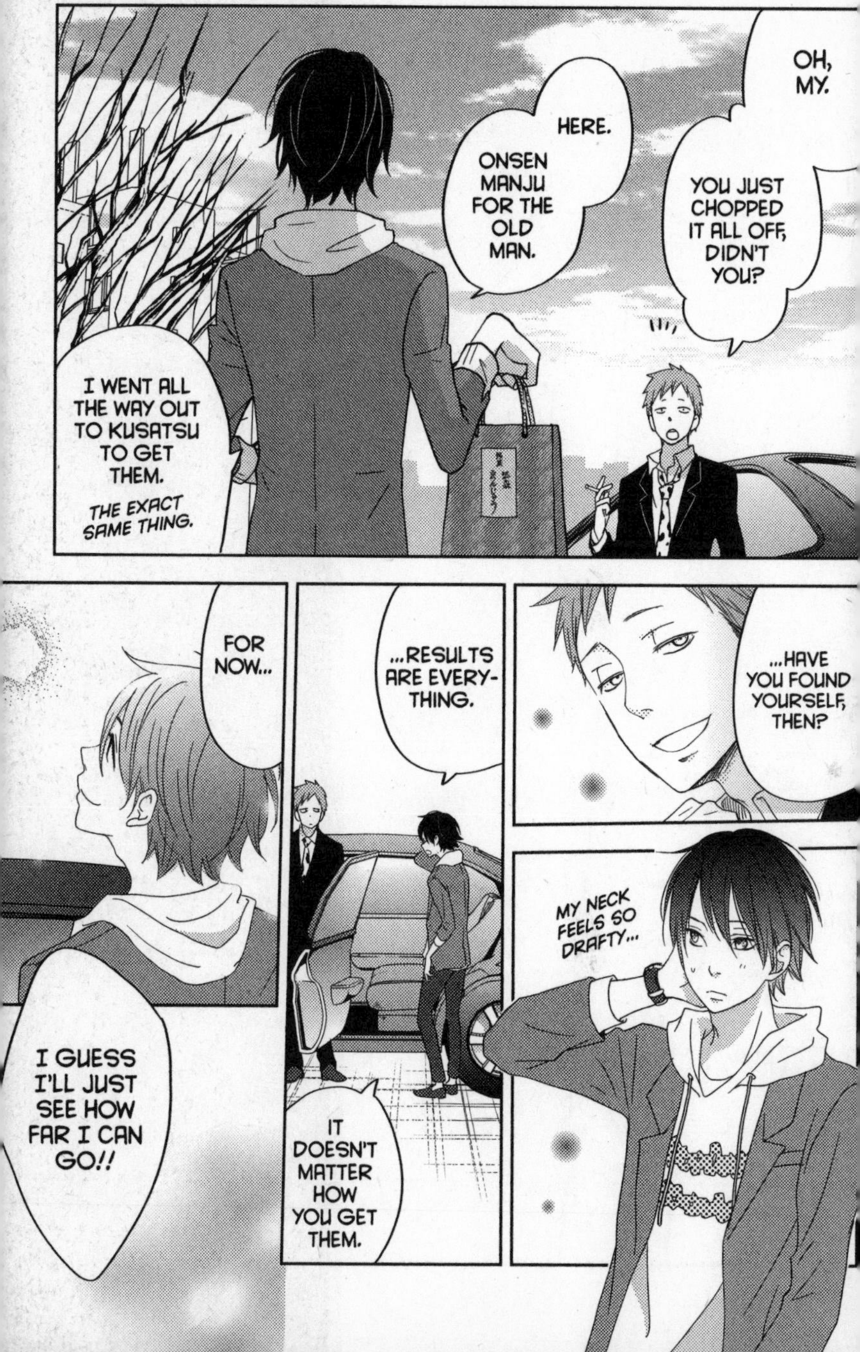
OH, MY.
YOU JUST CHOPPED IT ALL OFF, DIDN'T YOU?
HERE.
ONSEN MANJU FOR THE OLD MAN.
I WENT ALL THE WAY OUT TO KUSATSU TO GET THEM.
THE EXACT SAME THING.
...HAVE YOU FOUND YOURSELF, THEN?
MY NECK FEELS SO DRAFTY...
...RESULTS ARE EVERY-THING.
IT DOESN'T MATTER HOW YOU GET THEM.
FOR NOW...
I GUESS I'LL JUST SEE HOW FAR I CAN GO!!

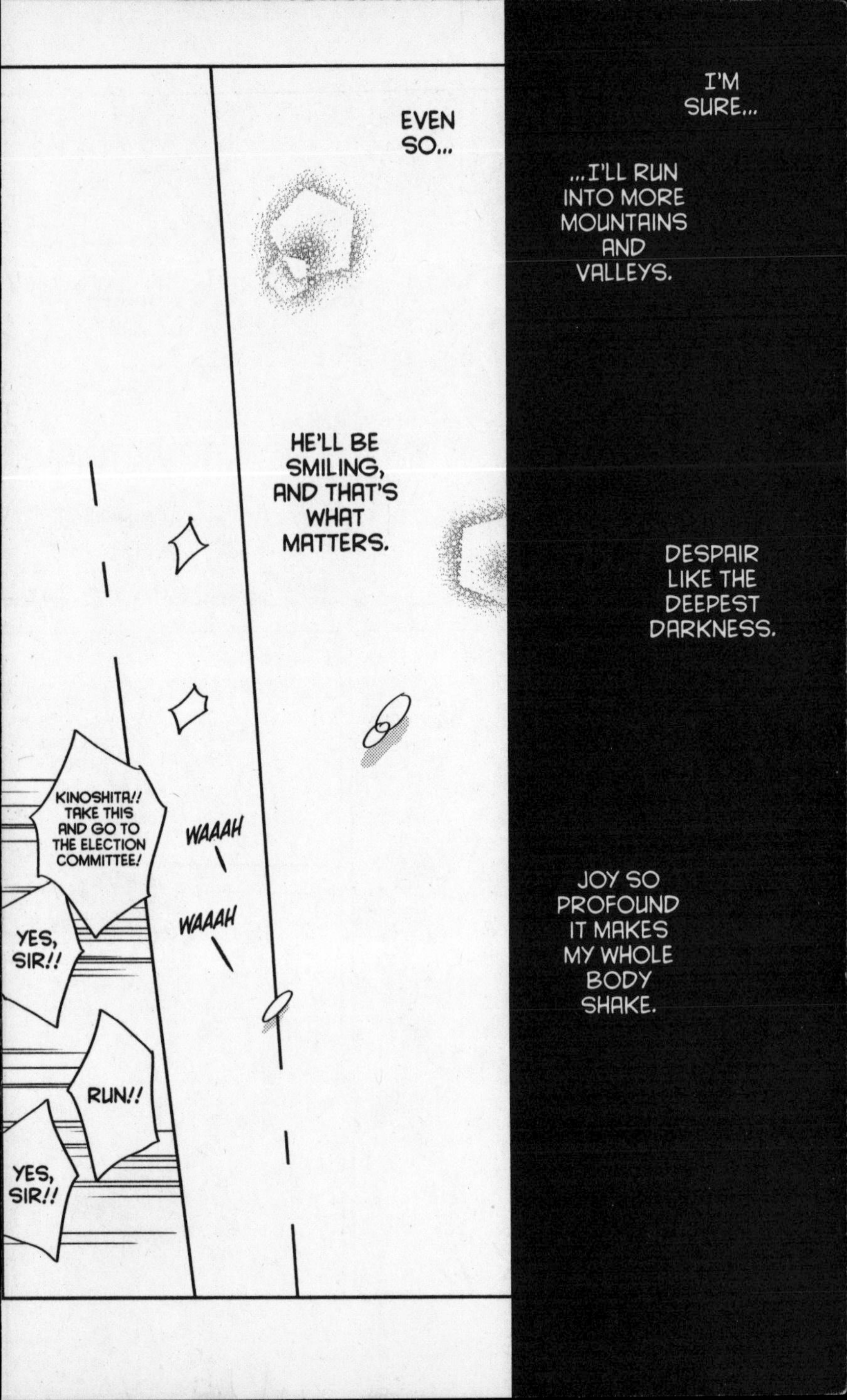
I'M SURE...
...I'LL RUN INTO MORE MOUNTAINS AND VALLEYS.
DESPAIR LIKE THE DEEPEST DARKNESS.
JOY SO PROFOUND IT MAKES MY WHOLE BODY SHAKE.
EVEN SO...
HE'LL BE SMILING, AND THAT'S WHAT MATTERS.
WAAAH
WAAAH
KINOSHITA!! TAKE THIS AND GO TO THE ELECTION COMMITTEE!
YES, SIR!!
RUN!!
YES, SIR!!

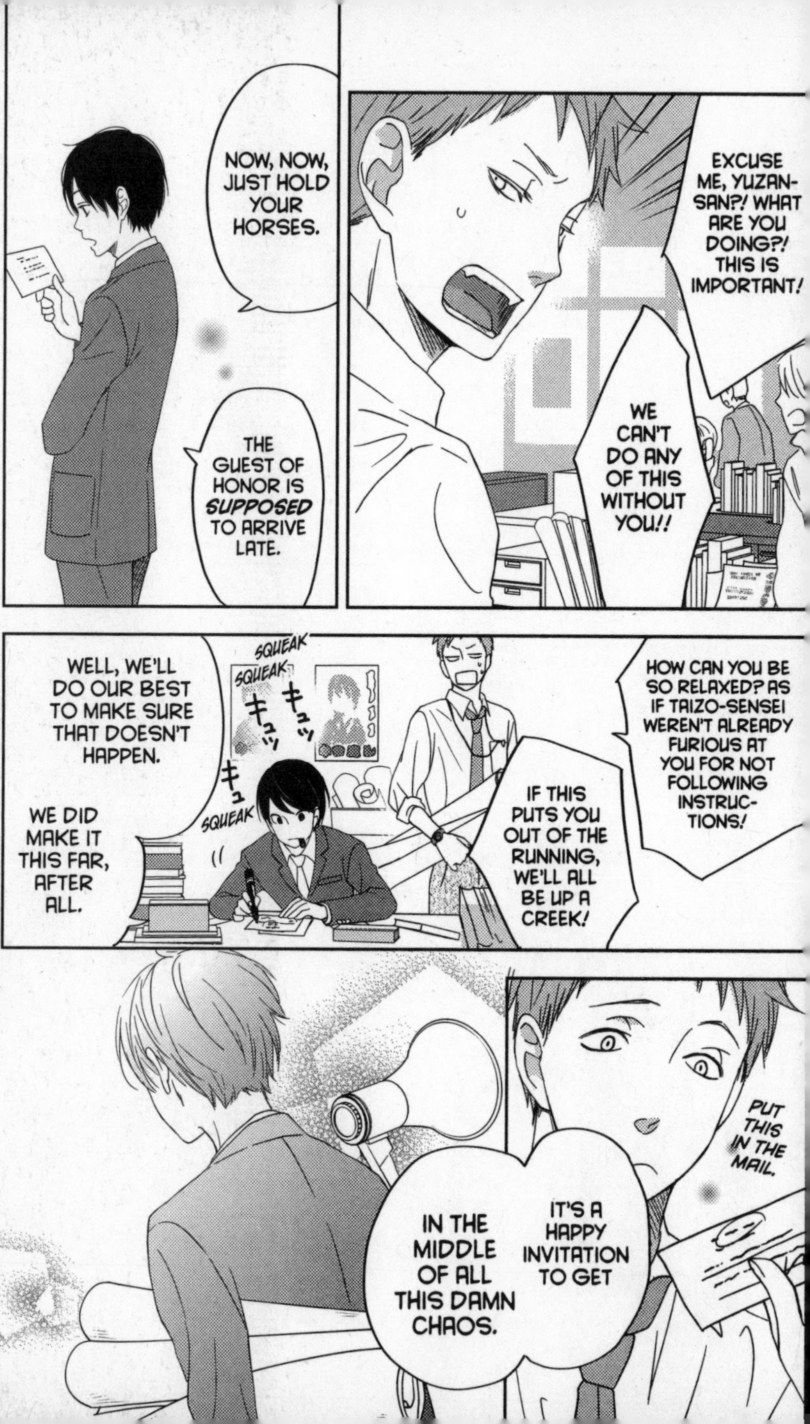
EXCUSE ME, YUZAN-SAN?! WHAT ARE YOU DOING?! THIS IS IMPORTANT!
WE CAN'T DO ANY OF THIS WITHOUT YOU!!
NOW, NOW, JUST HOLD YOUR HORSES.
THE GUEST OF HONOR IS ***SUPPOSED*** TO ARRIVE LATE.
HOW CAN YOU BE SO RELAXED? AS IF TAIZO-SENSEI WEREN'T ALREADY FURIOUS AT YOU FOR NOT FOLLOWING INSTRUC-TIONS!
IF THIS PUTS YOU OUT OF THE RUNNING, WE'LL ALL BE UP A CREEK!
SQUEAK
SQUEAK
キュッ
キュッ
キュ
SQUEAK
WELL, WE'LL DO OUR BEST TO MAKE SURE THAT DOESN'T HAPPEN.
WE DID MAKE IT THIS FAR, AFTER ALL.
PUT THIS IN THE MAIL.
IT'S A HAPPY INVITATION TO GET
IN THE MIDDLE OF ALL THIS DAMN CHAOS.

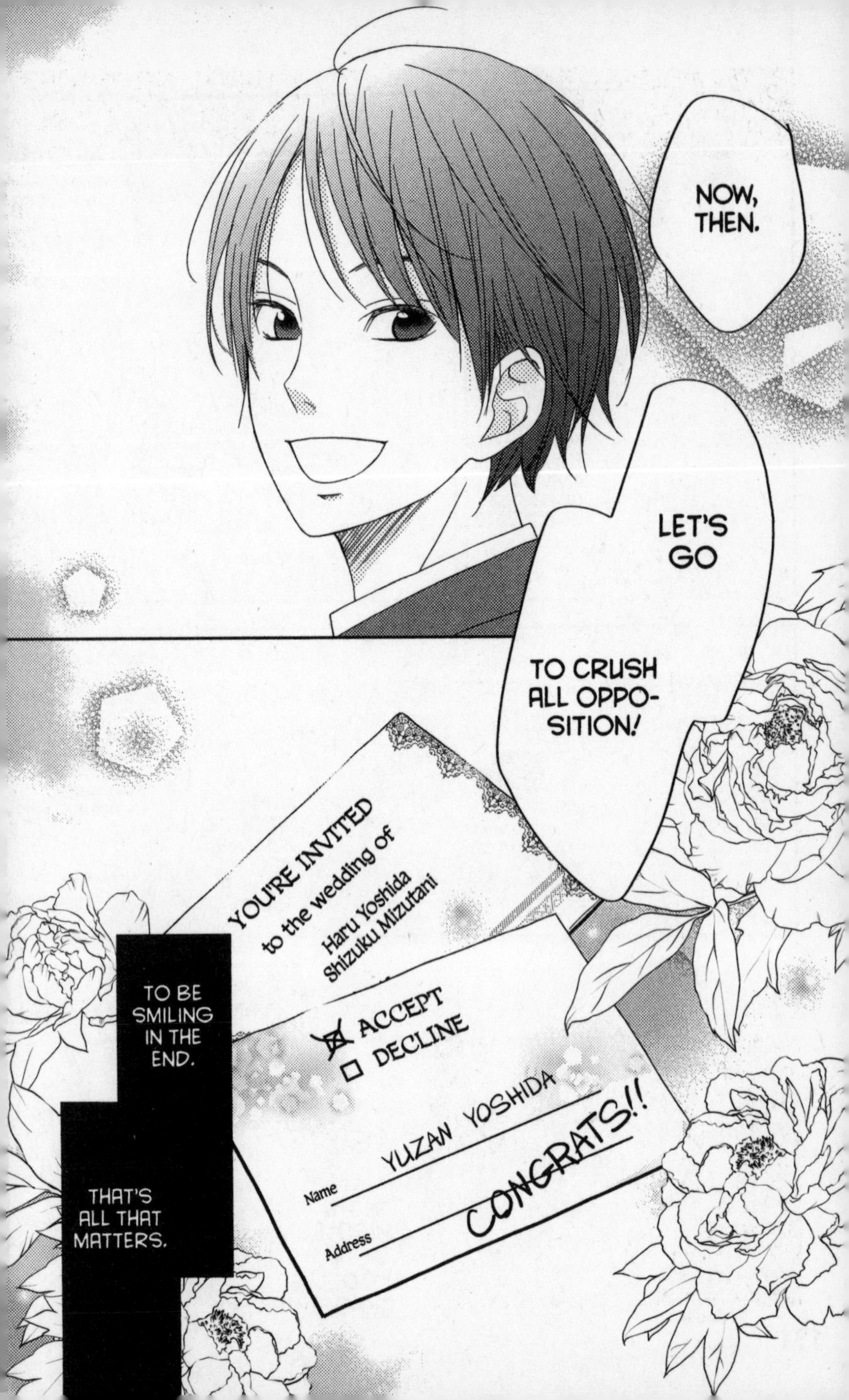
NOW, THEN.
LET'S GO
TO CRUSH ALL OPPO-SITION!
YOU'RE INVITED
to the wedding of
Haru Yoshida
Shizuku Mizutani
ACCEPT
DECLINE
Name YUZAN YOSHIDA
Address CONGRATS!!
TO BE SMILING IN THE END.
THAT'S ALL THAT MATTERS.

GROWNUP AND CHILD

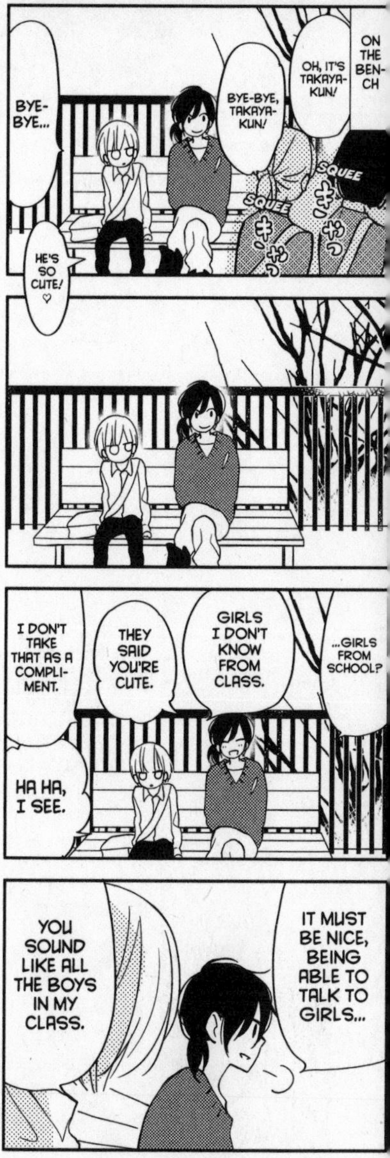
ON THE BEN-CH
OH, IT'S TAKAYA-KUN!
BYE-BYE, TAKAYA-KUN!
BYE-BYE...
SQUEE
SQUEE
HE'S SO CUTE! ♡
...GIRLS FROM SCHOOL?
GIRLS I DON'T KNOW FROM CLASS.
THEY SAID YOU'RE CUTE.
I DON'T TAKE THAT AS A COMPLI-MENT.
HA HA, I SEE.
IT MUST BE NICE, BEING ABLE TO TALK TO GIRLS...
YOU SOUND LIKE ALL THE BOYS IN MY CLASS.

EASY FOR YOU TO SAY

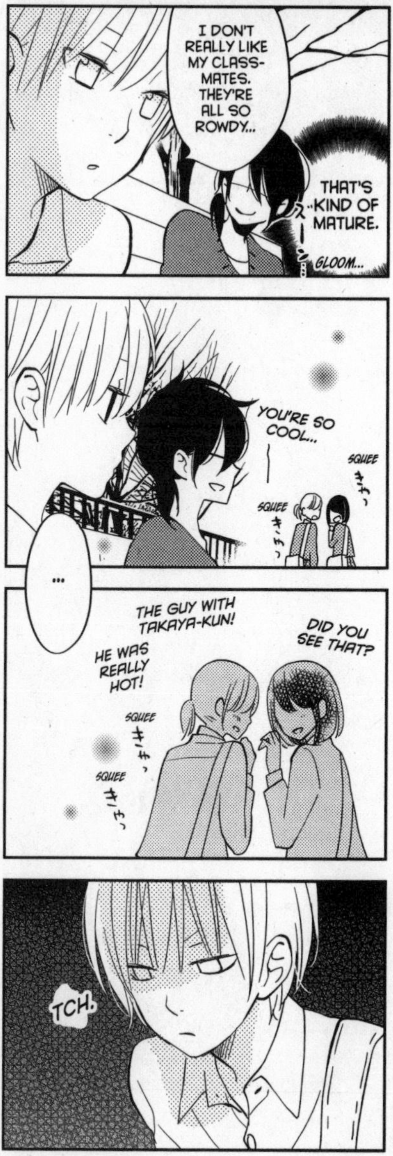
I DON'T REALLY LIKE MY CLASS-MATES. THEY'RE ALL SO ROWDY...
THAT'S KIND OF MATURE.
GLOOM...
YOU'RE SO COOL...
SQUEE
SQUEE
...
DID YOU SEE THAT?
THE GUY WITH TAKAYA-KUN!
HE WAS REALLY HOT!
SQUEE
SQUEE
TCH.

★EXTRA CHAPTER 3 BONUS MANGA★ "CHILDREN BY THE RIVERSIDE, EPILOGUE"

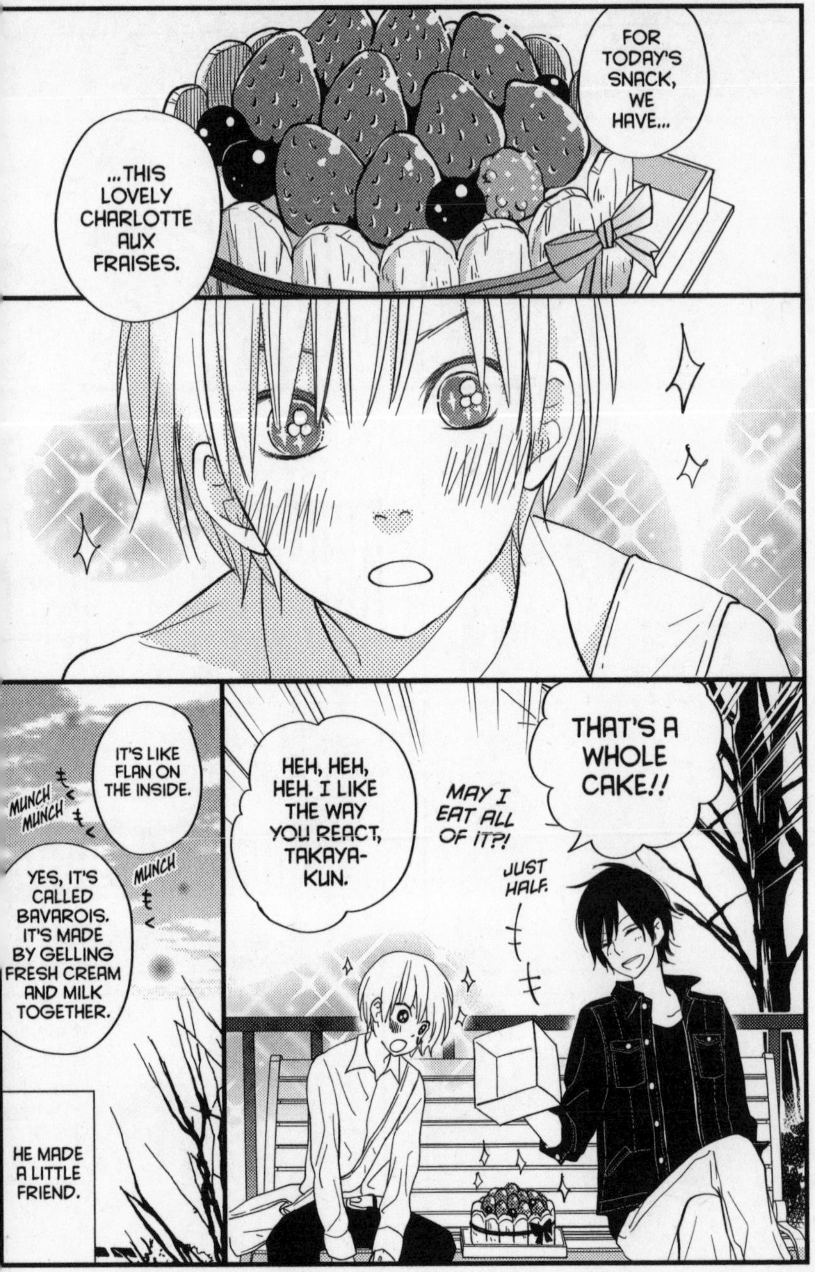
FOR TODAY'S SNACK, WE HAVE...
...THIS LOVELY CHARLOTTE AUX FRAISES.
THAT'S A WHOLE CAKE!!
MAY I EAT ALL OF IT?!
HEH, HEH, HEH. I LIKE THE WAY YOU REACT, TAKAYA-KUN.
JUST HALF.
IT'S LIKE FLAN ON THE INSIDE.
MUNCH MUNCH
YES, IT'S CALLED BAVAROIS. IT'S MADE BY GELLING FRESH CREAM AND MILK TOGETHER.
MUNCH
HE MADE A LITTLE FRIEND.

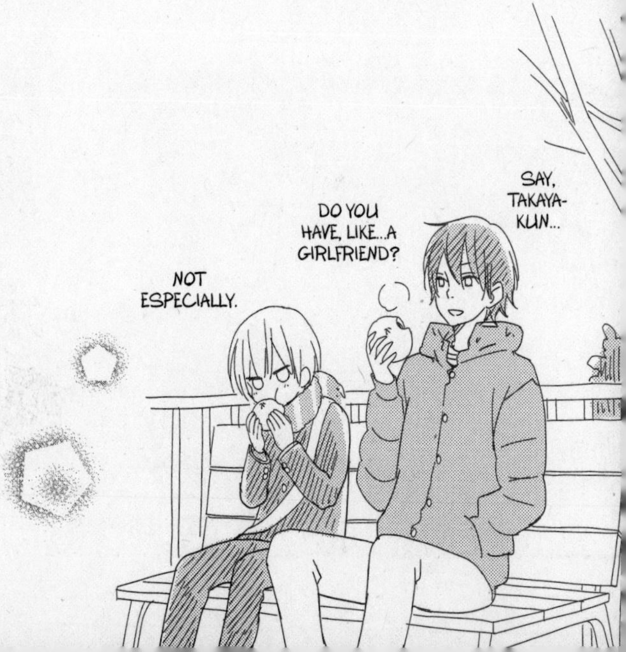
SAY, TAKAYA-KUN...
DO YOU HAVE, LIKE...A GIRLFRIEND?
NOT ESPECIALLY.

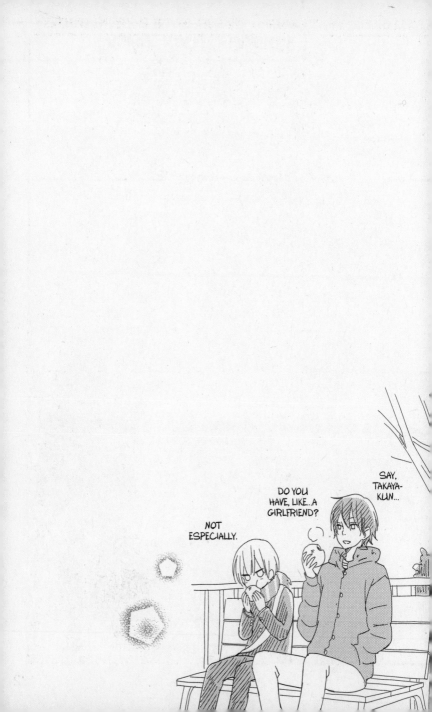

EXTRA CHAPTER 4: NEVER ENDING

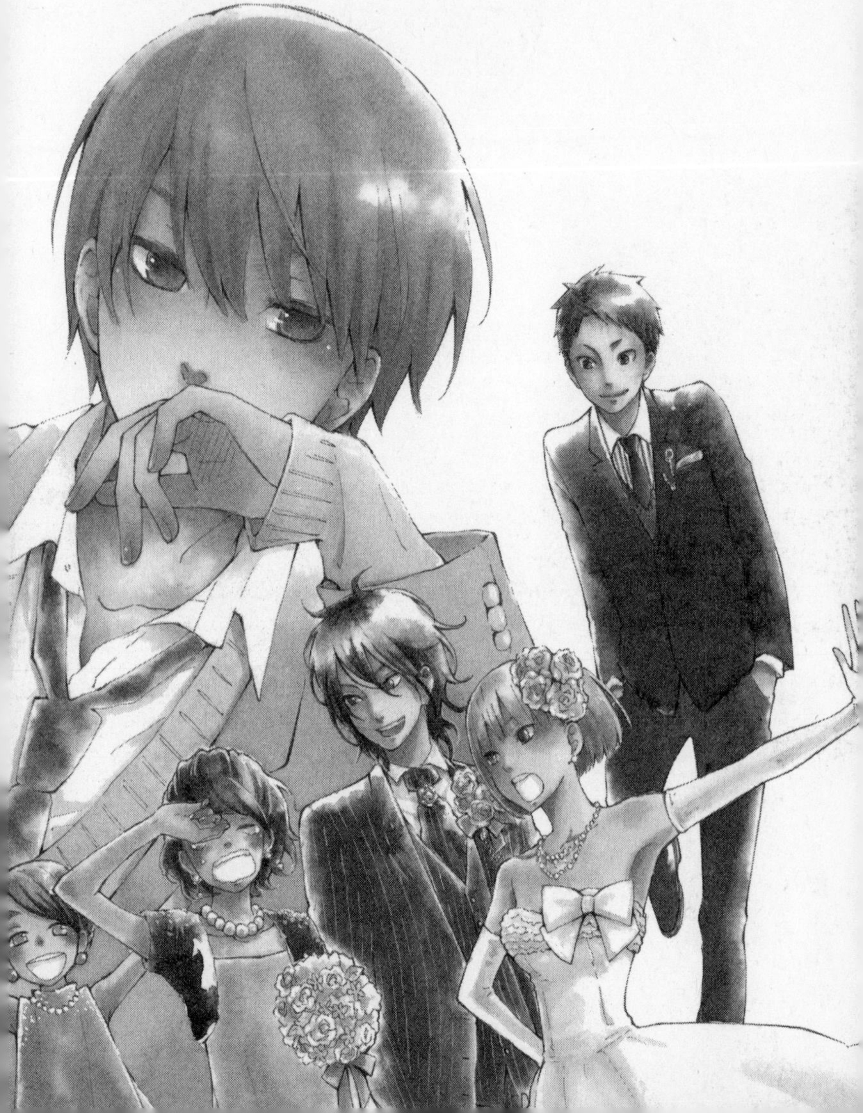

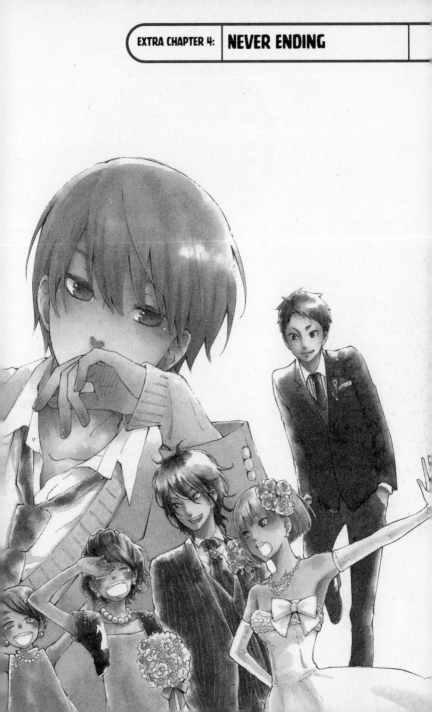

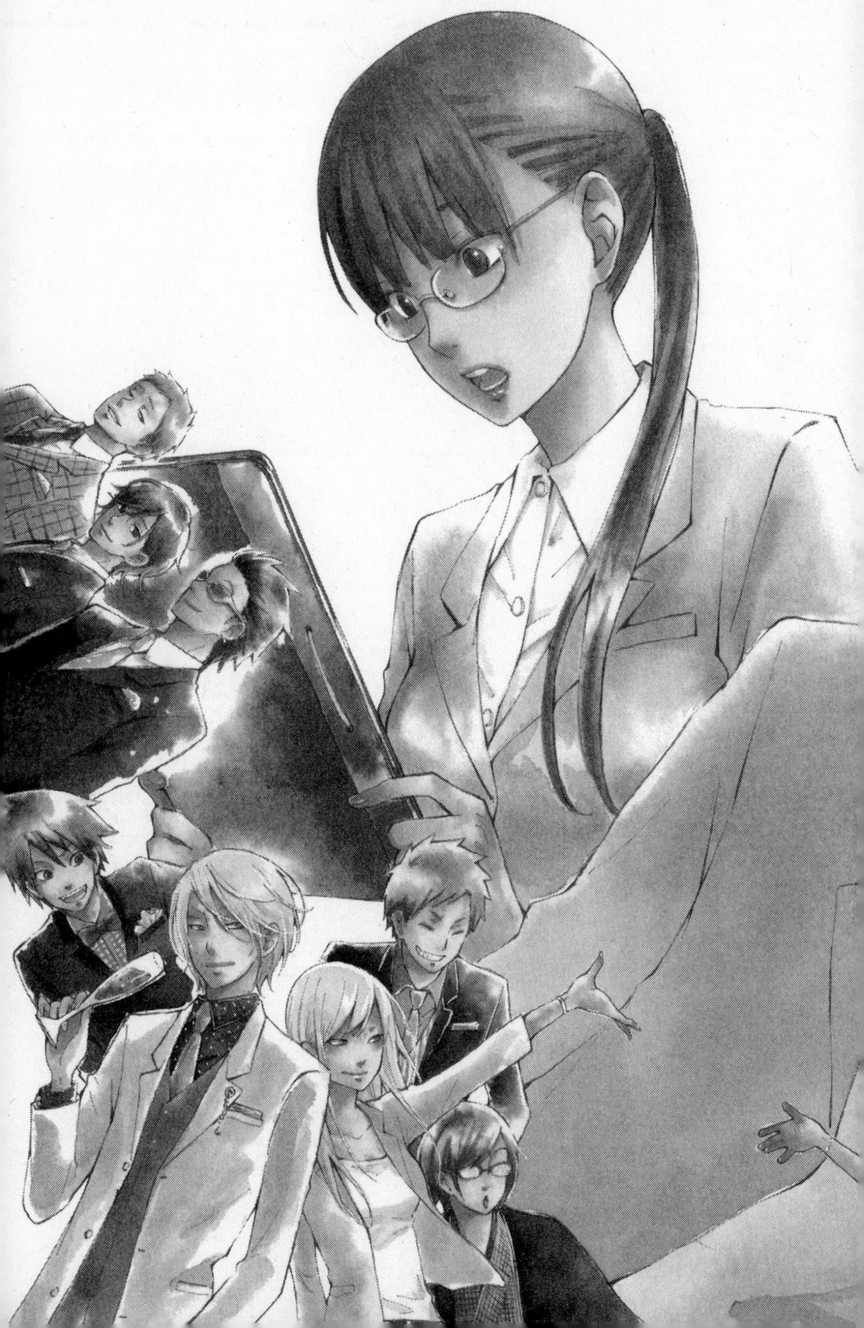

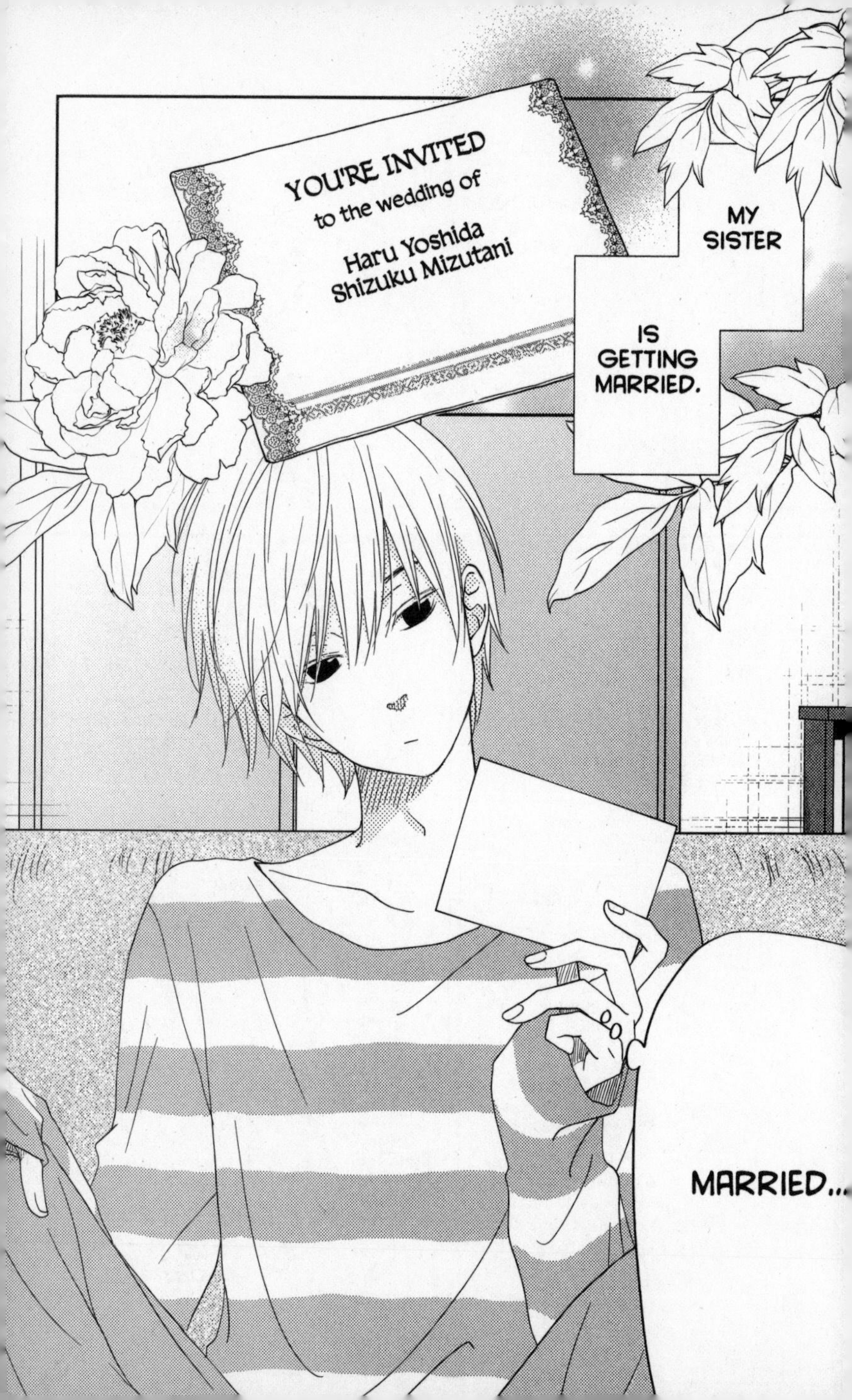
MY SISTER
IS GETTING MARRIED.
YOU'RE INVITED
to the wedding of
Haru Yoshida
Shizuku Mizutani
MARRIED...

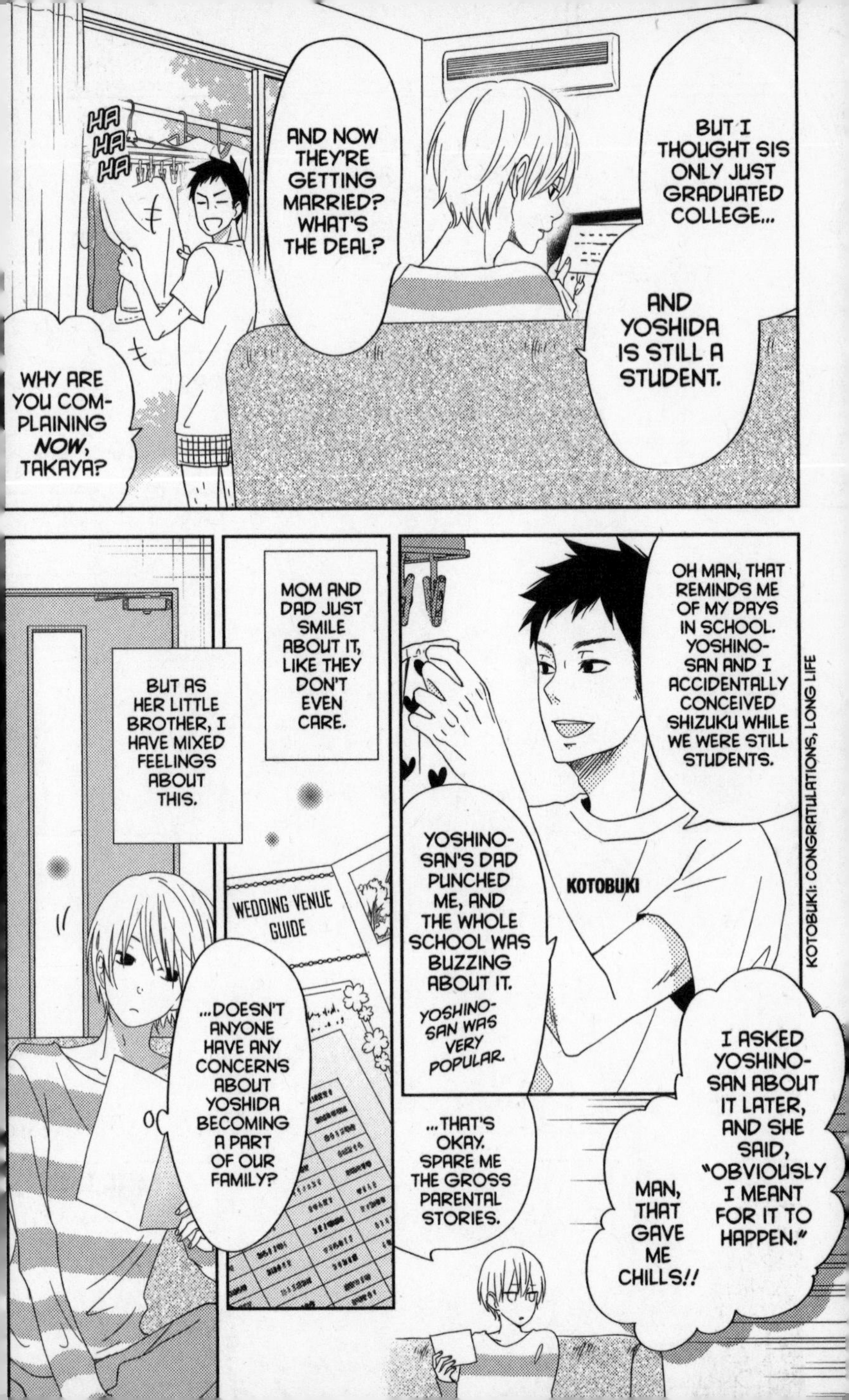
BUT I THOUGHT SIS ONLY JUST GRADUATED COLLEGE...
AND YOSHIDA IS STILL A STUDENT.
AND NOW THEY'RE GETTING MARRIED? WHAT'S THE DEAL?
HA HA HA
WHY ARE YOU COMPLAINING *NOW*, TAKAYA?
OH MAN, THAT REMINDS ME OF MY DAYS IN SCHOOL. YOSHINO-SAN AND I ACCIDENTALLY CONCEIVED SHIZUKU WHILE WE WERE STILL STUDENTS.
KOTOBUKI
YOSHINO-SAN'S DAD PUNCHED ME, AND THE WHOLE SCHOOL WAS BUZZING ABOUT IT.
YOSHINO-SAN WAS VERY POPULAR.
KOTOBUKI: CONGRATULATIONS, LONG LIFE
I ASKED YOSHINO-SAN ABOUT IT LATER, AND SHE SAID, "OBVIOUSLY I MEANT FOR IT TO HAPPEN."
MAN, THAT GAVE ME CHILLS!!
...THAT'S OKAY. SPARE ME THE GROSS PARENTAL STORIES.
MOM AND DAD JUST SMILE ABOUT IT, LIKE THEY DON'T EVEN CARE.
BUT AS HER LITTLE BROTHER, I HAVE MIXED FEELINGS ABOUT THIS.
WEDDING VENUE GUIDE
...DOESN'T ANYONE HAVE ANY CONCERNS ABOUT YOSHIDA BECOMING A PART OF OUR FAMILY?

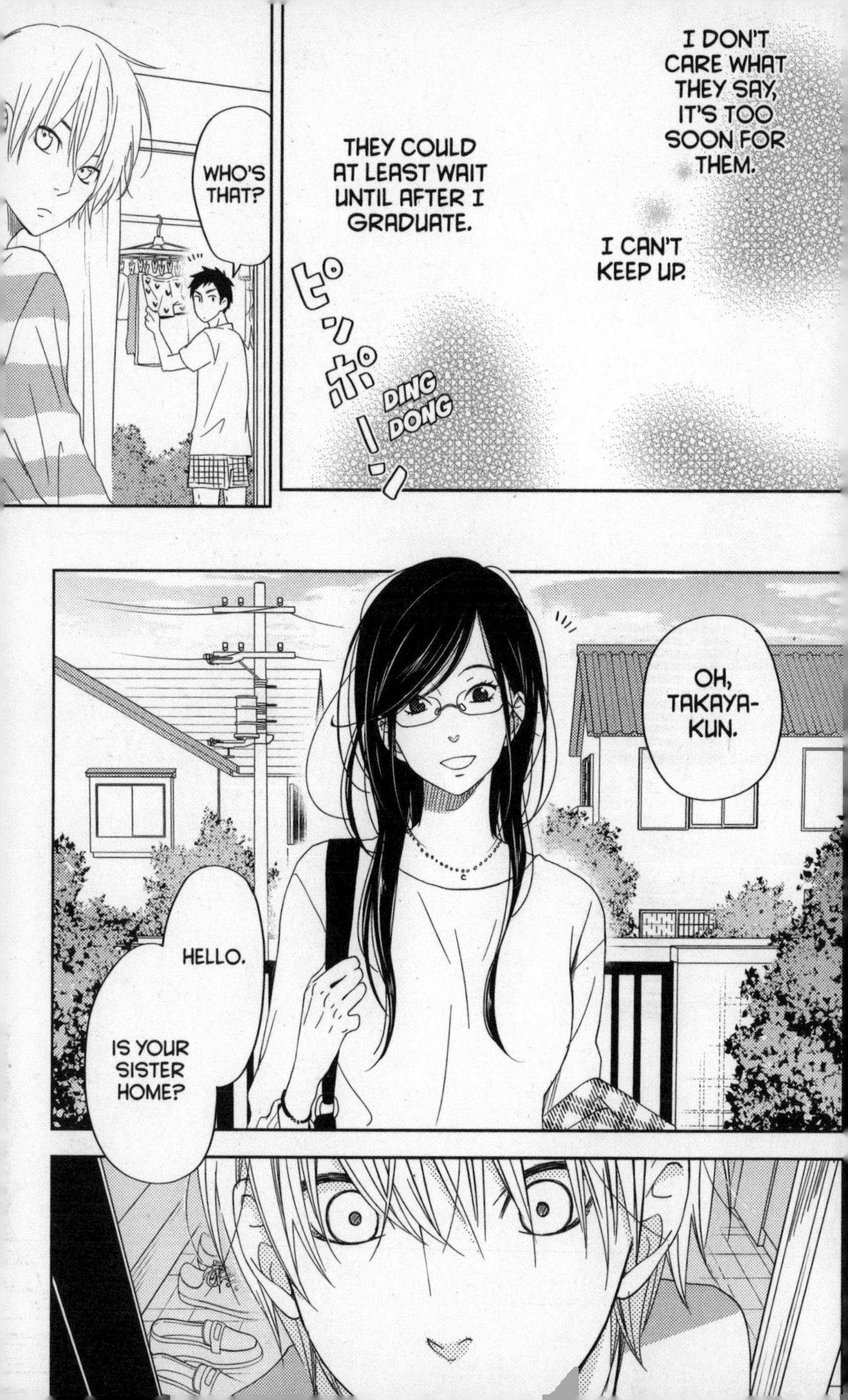
I DON'T CARE WHAT THEY SAY, IT'S TOO SOON FOR THEM.
THEY COULD AT LEAST WAIT UNTIL AFTER I GRADUATE.
I CAN'T KEEP UP.
ピッポーン
DING DONG
WHO'S THAT?
OH, TAKAYA-KUN.
HELLO.
IS YOUR SISTER HOME?

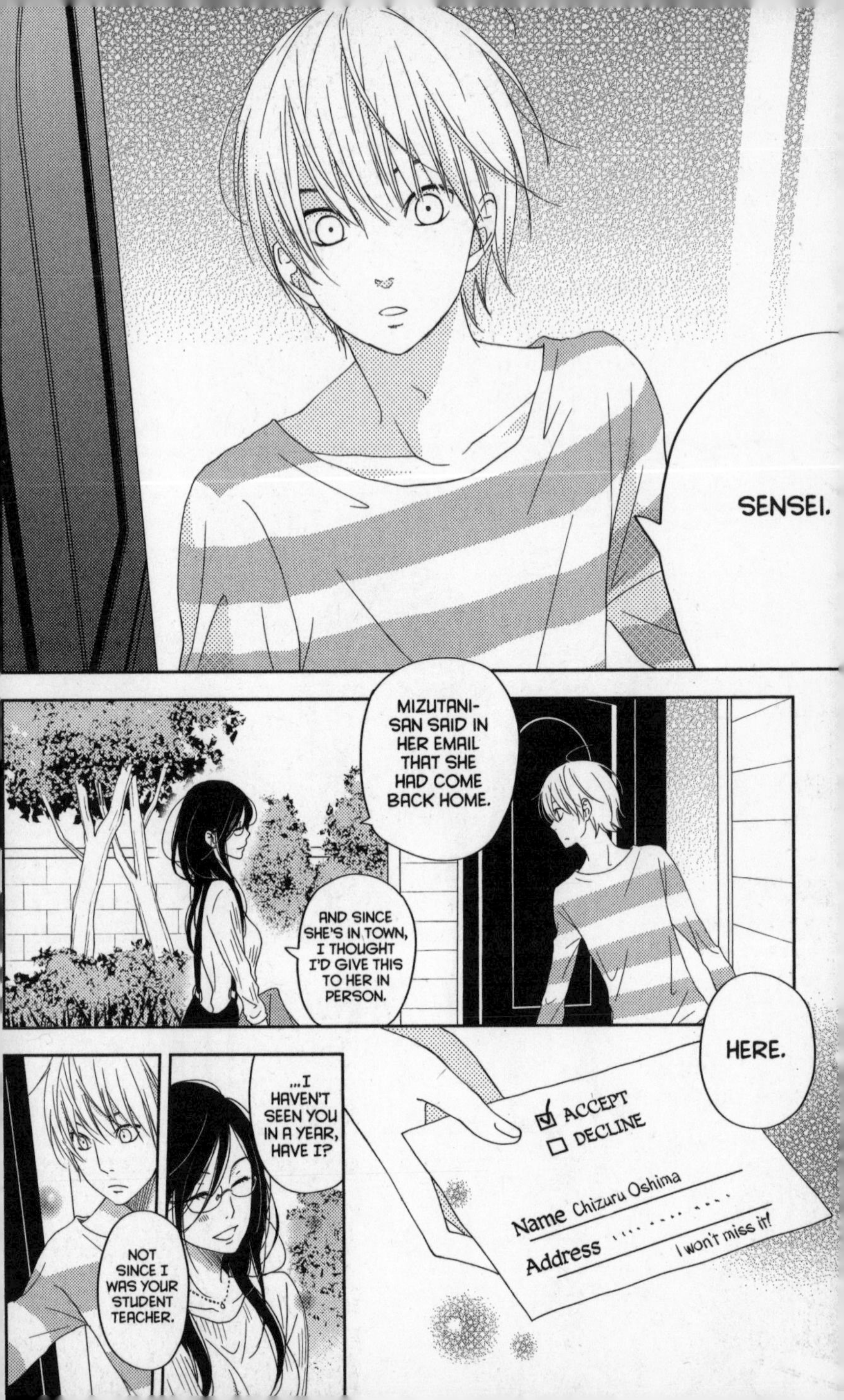
SENSEI.
MIZUTANI-SAN SAID IN HER EMAIL THAT SHE HAD COME BACK HOME.
AND SINCE SHE'S IN TOWN, I THOUGHT I'D GIVE THIS TO HER IN PERSON.
HERE.
ACCEPT
DECLINE
Name Chizuru Oshima
Address
I won't miss it!
...I HAVEN'T SEEN YOU IN A YEAR, HAVE I?
NOT SINCE I WAS YOUR STUDENT TEACHER.

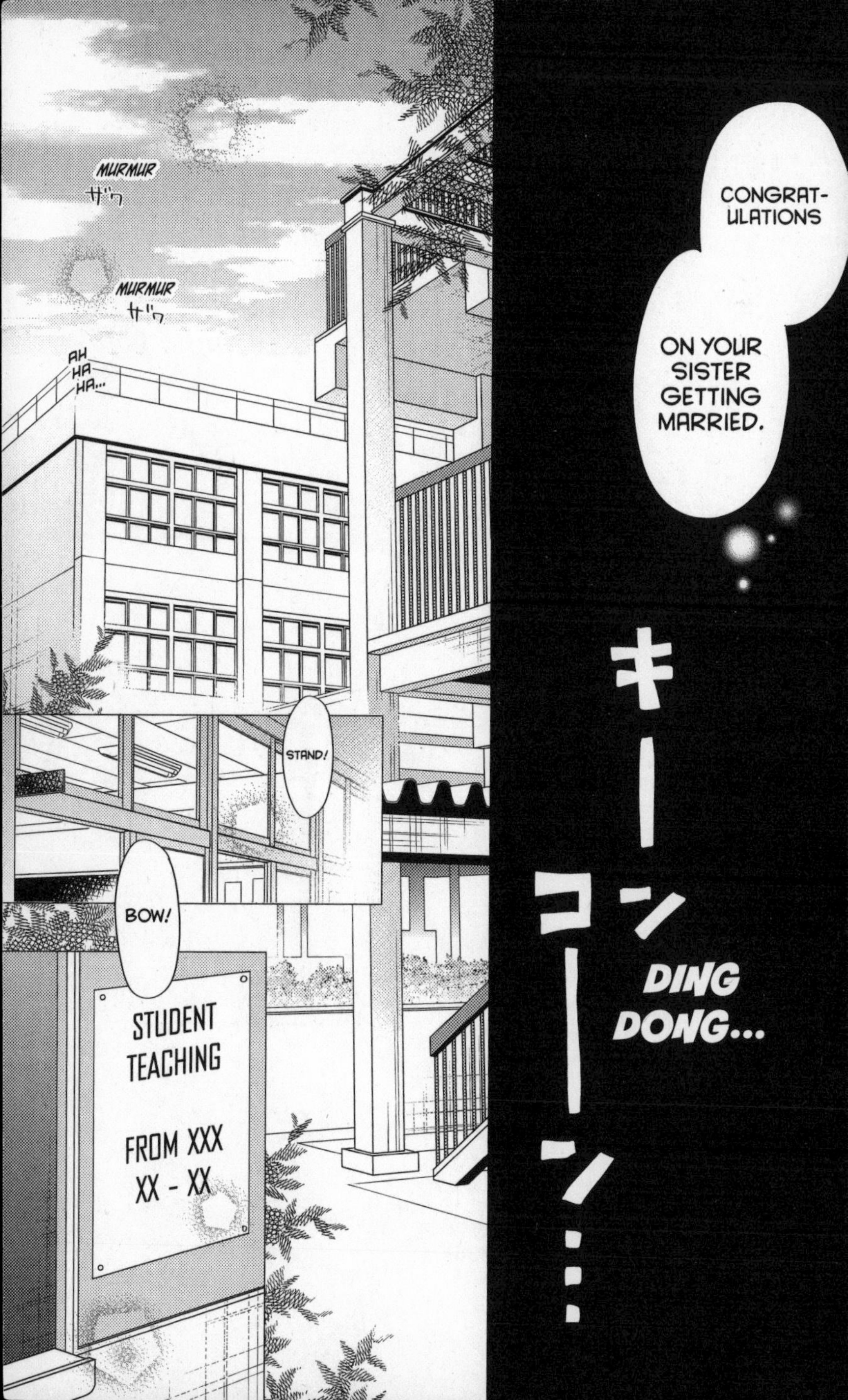
CONGRAT-
ULATIONS
ON YOUR SISTER GETTING MARRIED.
キーンコーン…
DING DONG...
MURMUR
ザワ
MURMUR
ザワ
AH HA HA...
STAND!
BOW!
STUDENT TEACHING
FROM XXX XX - XX

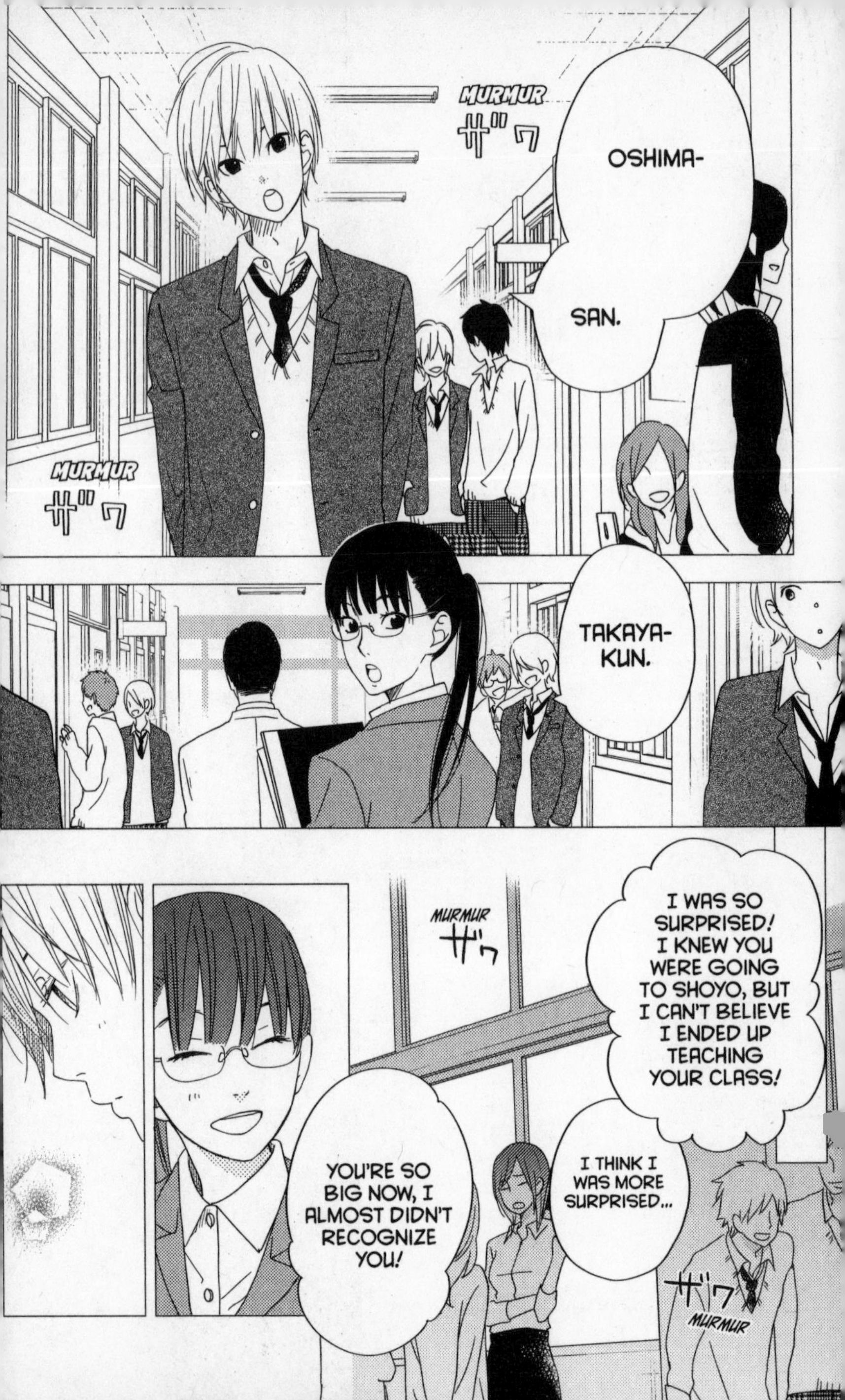
OSHIMA-
SAN.
MURMUR
ザワ
MURMUR
ザワ
TAKAYA-KUN.
I WAS SO SURPRISED! I KNEW YOU WERE GOING TO SHOYO, BUT I CAN'T BELIEVE I ENDED UP TEACHING YOUR CLASS!
MURMUR
ザワ
YOU'RE SO BIG NOW, I ALMOST DIDN'T RECOGNIZE YOU!
I THINK I WAS MORE SURPRISED...
ザワ
MURMUR

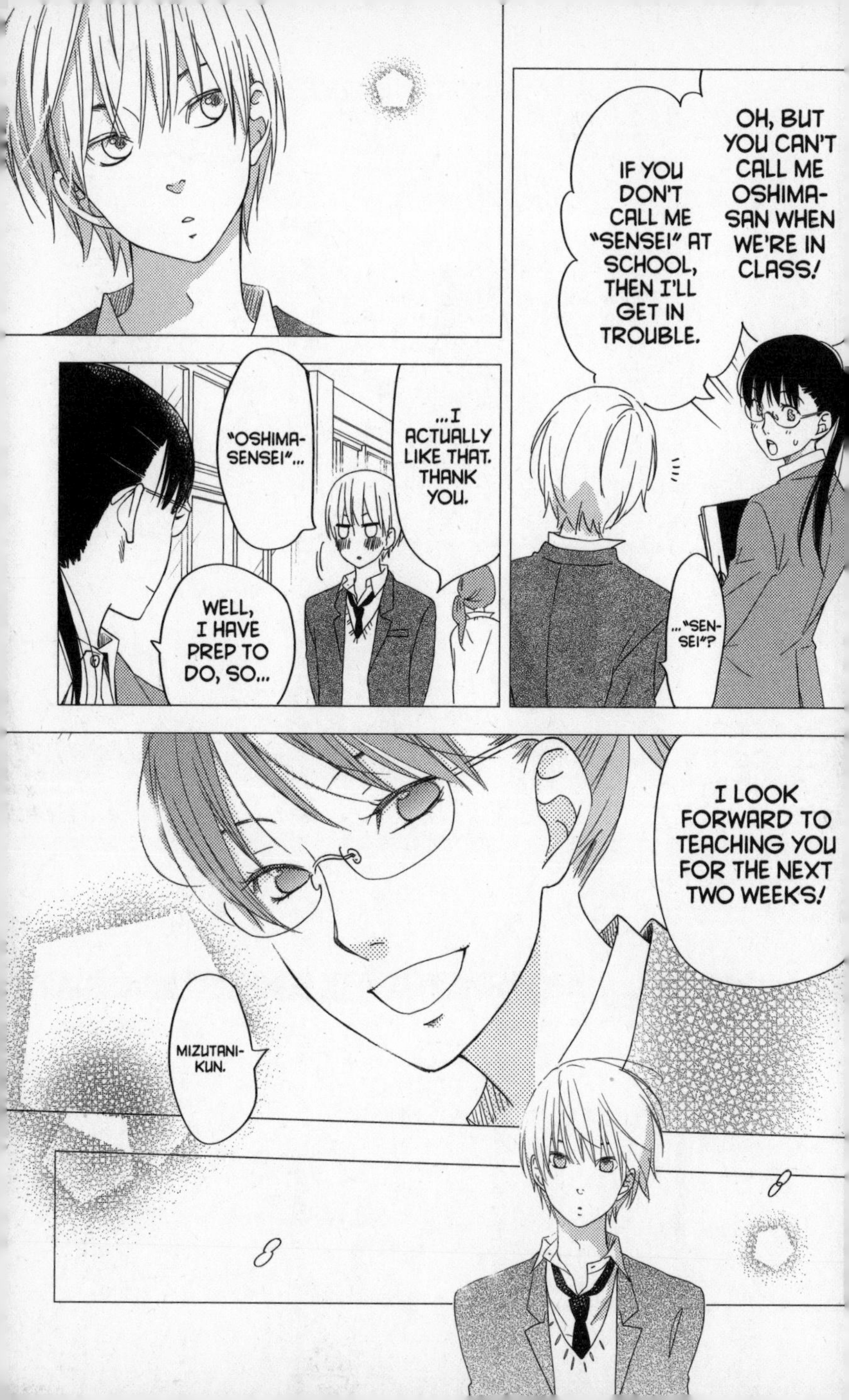
OH, BUT YOU CAN'T CALL ME OSHIMA-SAN WHEN WE'RE IN CLASS!
IF YOU DON'T CALL ME "SENSEI" AT SCHOOL, THEN I'LL GET IN TROUBLE.
..."SEN-SEI"?
...I ACTUALLY LIKE THAT. THANK YOU.
"OSHIMA-SENSEI"...
WELL, I HAVE PREP TO DO, SO...
I LOOK FORWARD TO TEACHING YOU FOR THE NEXT TWO WEEKS!
MIZUTANI-KUN.

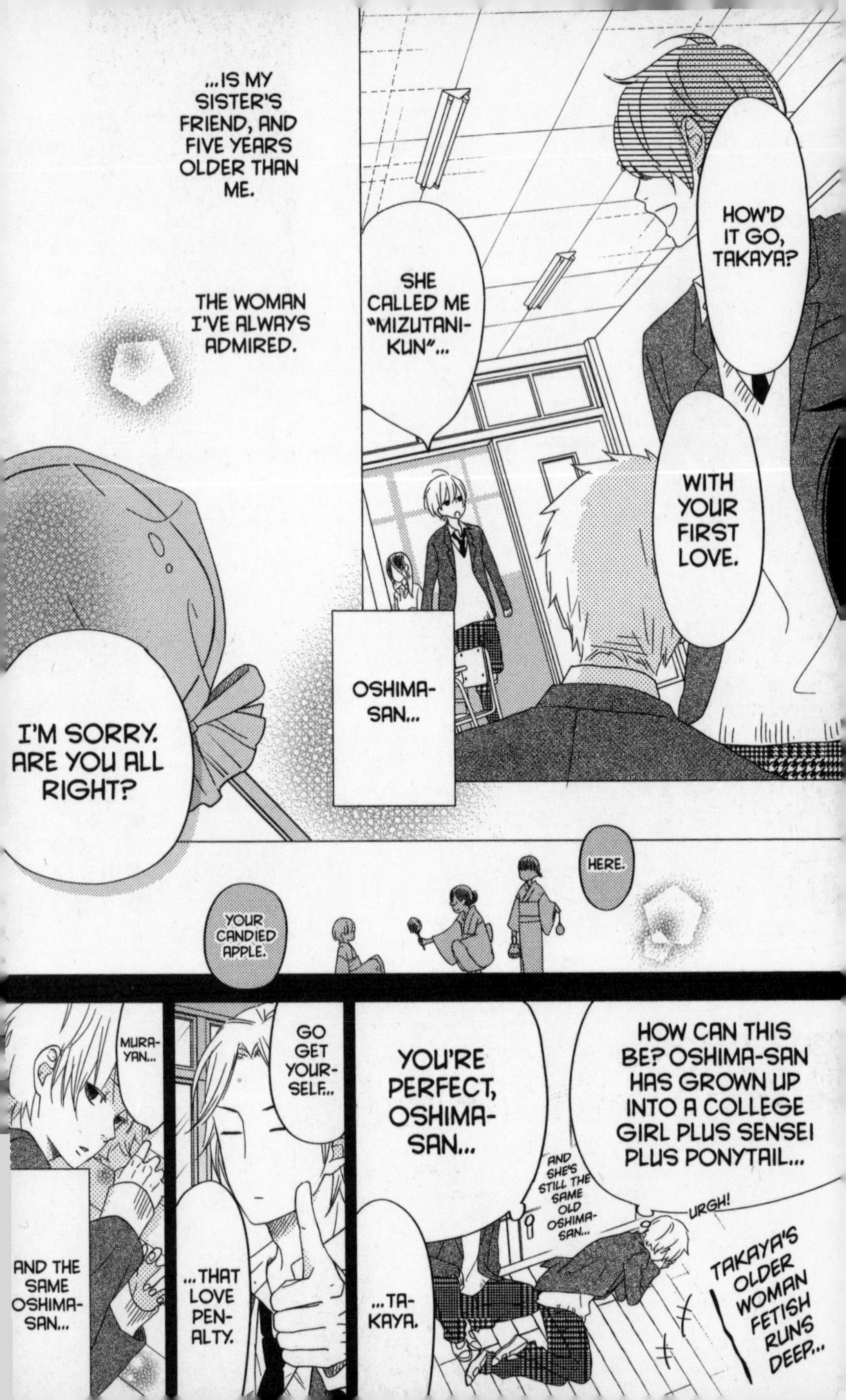
HOW'D IT GO, TAKAYA?
WITH YOUR FIRST LOVE.
SHE CALLED ME "MIZUTANI-KUN"...
OSHIMA-SAN...
...IS MY SISTER'S FRIEND, AND FIVE YEARS OLDER THAN ME.
THE WOMAN I'VE ALWAYS ADMIRED.
I'M SORRY. ARE YOU ALL RIGHT?
HERE.
YOUR CANDIED APPLE.
HOW CAN THIS BE? OSHIMA-SAN HAS GROWN UP INTO A COLLEGE GIRL PLUS SENSEI PLUS PONYTAIL...
AND SHE'S STILL THE SAME OLD OSHIMA-SAN...
URGH!
TAKAYA'S OLDER WOMAN FETISH RUNS DEEP...
YOU'RE PERFECT, OSHIMA-SAN...
...TA-KAYA.
GO GET YOUR-SELF...
...THAT LOVE PEN-ALTY.
MURA-YAN...
AND THE SAME OSHIMA-SAN...

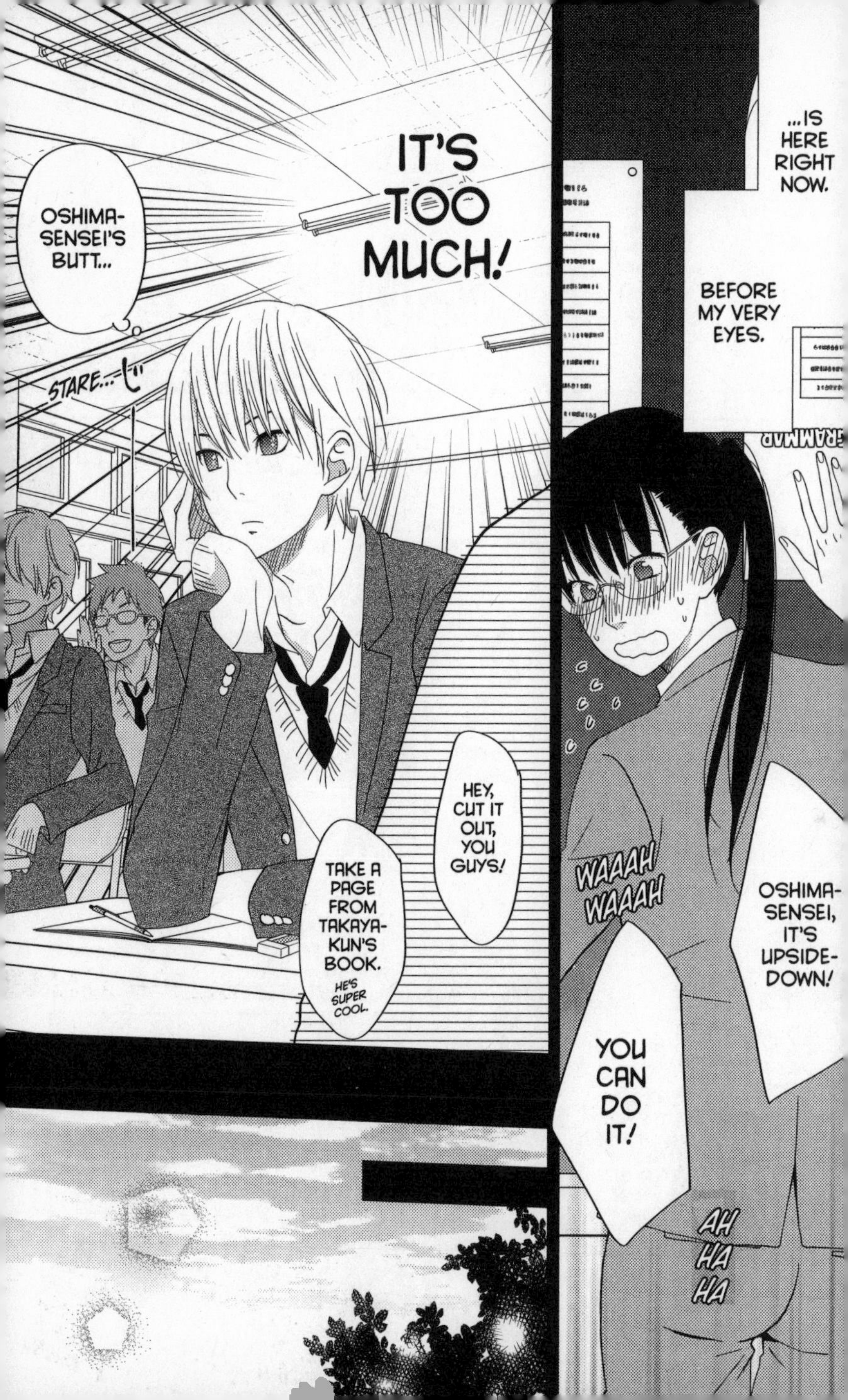

...IS HERE RIGHT NOW.
BEFORE MY VERY EYES.
OSHIMA-SENSEI, IT'S UPSIDE-DOWN!
WAAAH WAAAH
YOU CAN DO IT!
AH HA HA
IT'S TOO MUCH!
OSHIMA-SENSEI'S BUTT...
STARE... じ
HEY, CUT IT OUT, YOU GUYS!
TAKE A PAGE FROM TAKAYA-KUN'S BOOK.
HE'S SUPER COOL.

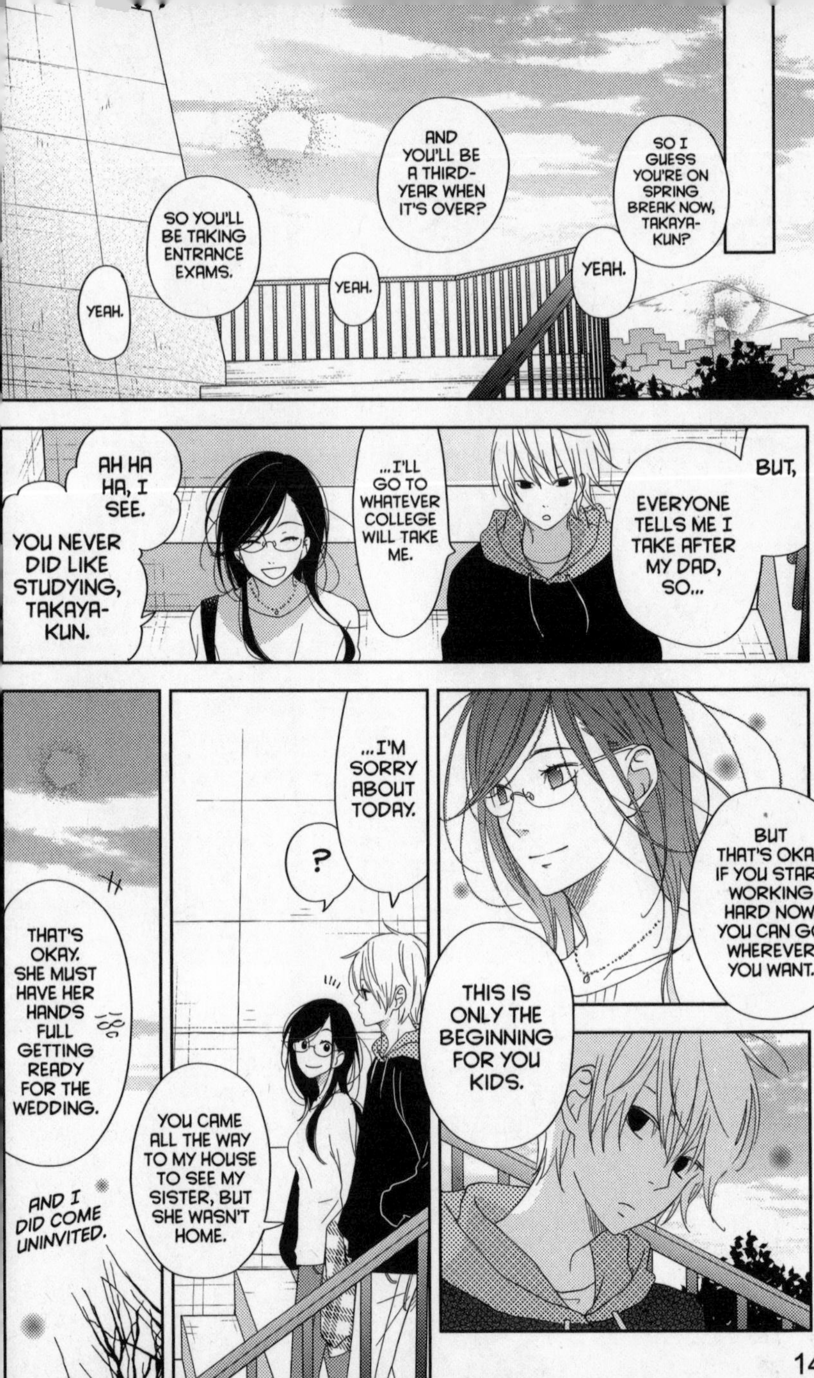
SO I GUESS YOU'RE ON SPRING BREAK NOW, TAKAYA-KUN?
YEAH.
AND YOU'LL BE A THIRD-YEAR WHEN IT'S OVER?
YEAH.
SO YOU'LL BE TAKING ENTRANCE EXAMS.
YEAH.
BUT,
EVERYONE TELLS ME I TAKE AFTER MY DAD, SO...
...I'LL GO TO WHATEVER COLLEGE WILL TAKE ME.
AH HA HA, I SEE.
YOU NEVER DID LIKE STUDYING, TAKAYA-KUN.
BUT THAT'S OKAY. IF YOU START WORKING HARD NOW, YOU CAN GO WHEREVER YOU WANT.
THIS IS ONLY THE BEGINNING FOR YOU KIDS.
...I'M SORRY ABOUT TODAY.
?
YOU CAME ALL THE WAY TO MY HOUSE TO SEE MY SISTER, BUT SHE WASN'T HOME.
THAT'S OKAY. SHE MUST HAVE HER HANDS FULL GETTING READY FOR THE WEDDING.
AND I DID COME UNINVITED.

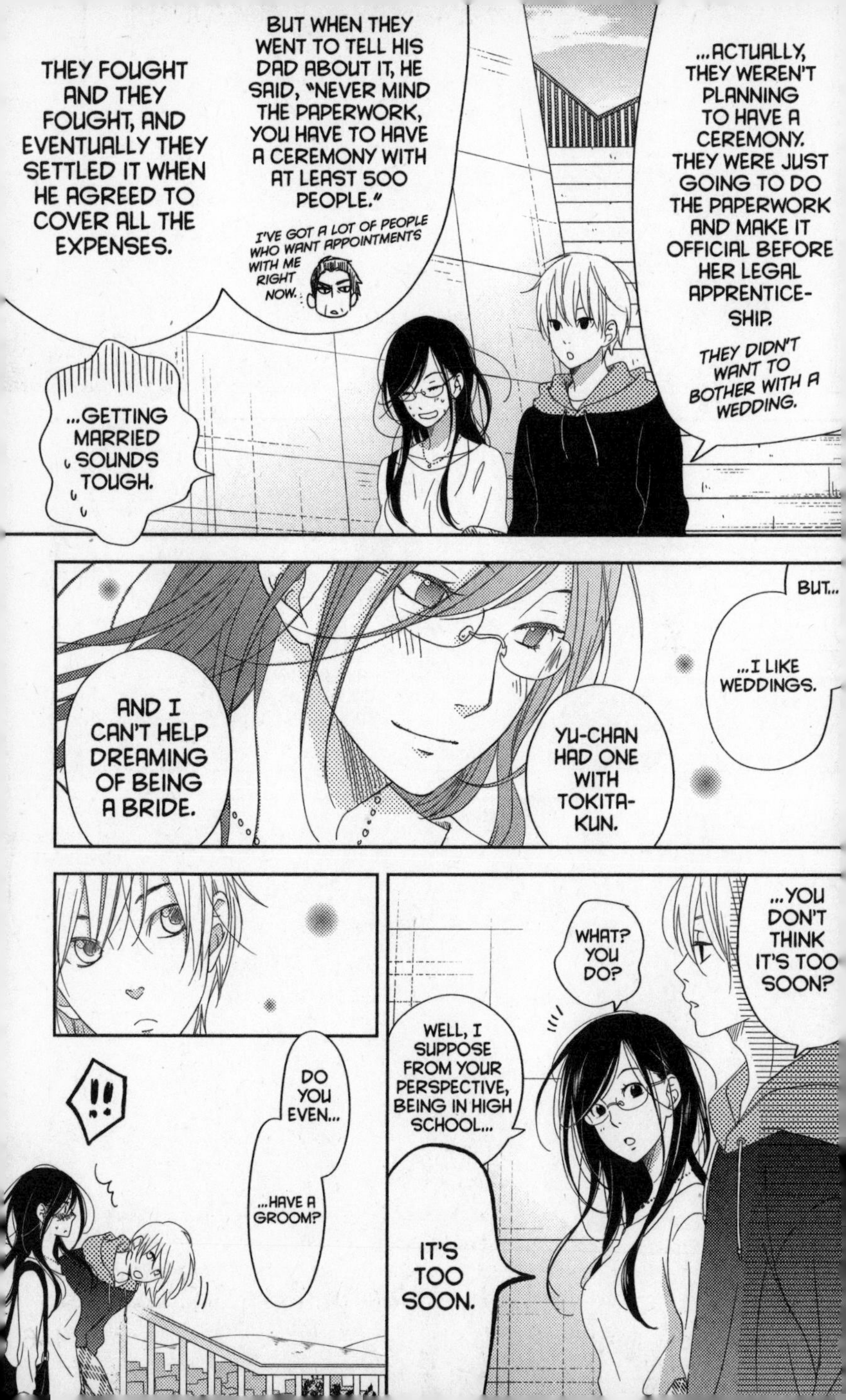
...ACTUALLY, THEY WEREN'T PLANNING TO HAVE A CEREMONY. THEY WERE JUST GOING TO DO THE PAPERWORK AND MAKE IT OFFICIAL BEFORE HER LEGAL APPRENTICE-SHIP.
THEY DIDN'T WANT TO BOTHER WITH A WEDDING.
BUT WHEN THEY WENT TO TELL HIS DAD ABOUT IT, HE SAID, "NEVER MIND THE PAPERWORK, YOU HAVE TO HAVE A CEREMONY WITH AT LEAST 500 PEOPLE."
I'VE GOT A LOT OF PEOPLE WHO WANT APPOINTMENTS WITH ME RIGHT NOW.
THEY FOUGHT AND THEY FOUGHT, AND EVENTUALLY THEY SETTLED IT WHEN HE AGREED TO COVER ALL THE EXPENSES.
...GETTING MARRIED SOUNDS TOUGH.
BUT...
...I LIKE WEDDINGS.
YU-CHAN HAD ONE WITH TOKITA-KUN.
AND I CAN'T HELP DREAMING OF BEING A BRIDE.
...YOU DON'T THINK IT'S TOO SOON?
WHAT? YOU DO?
WELL, I SUPPOSE FROM YOUR PERSPECTIVE, BEING IN HIGH SCHOOL...
IT'S TOO SOON.
DO YOU EVEN...
...HAVE A GROOM?
!!

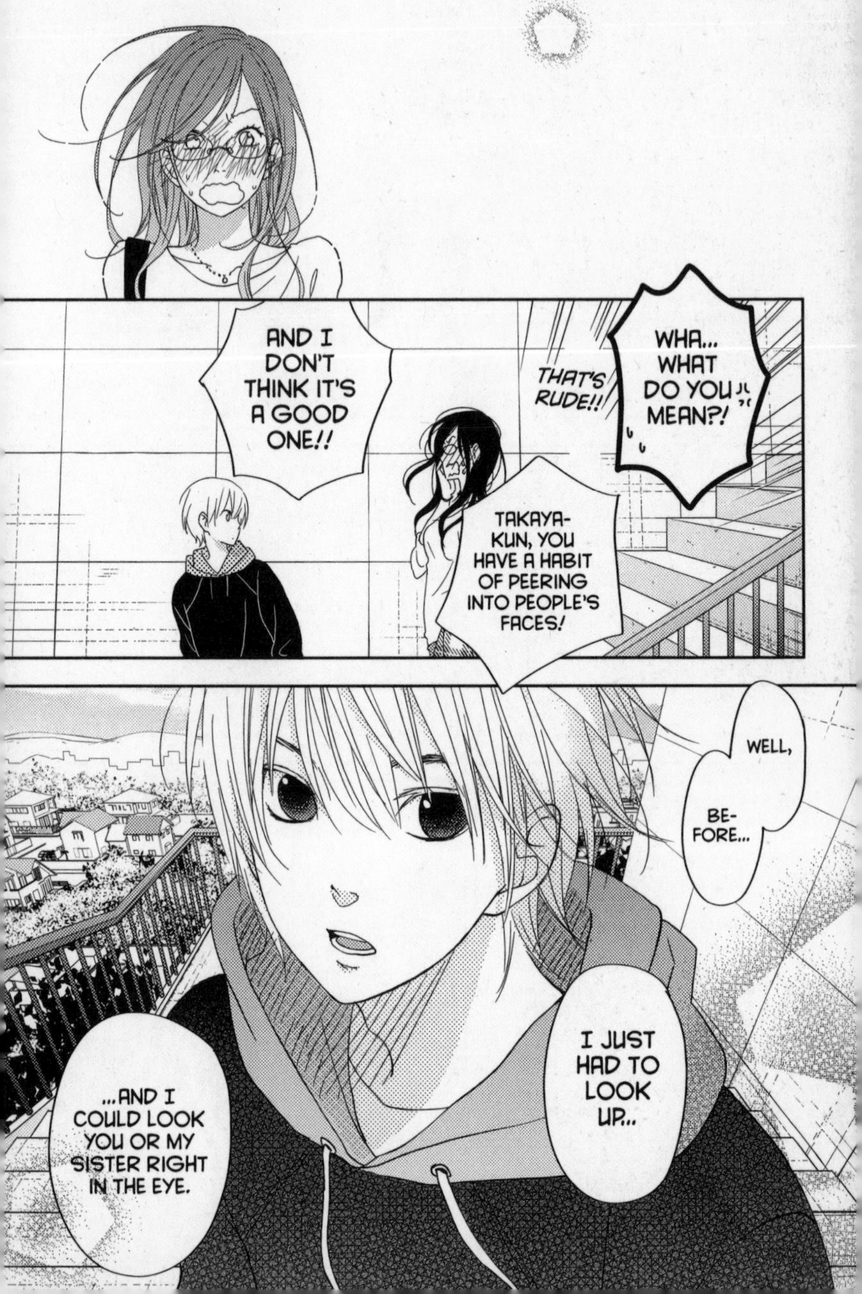
WHA... WHAT DO YOU MEAN?!
THAT'S RUDE!!
TAKAYA-KUN, YOU HAVE A HABIT OF PEERING INTO PEOPLE'S FACES!
AND I DON'T THINK IT'S A GOOD ONE!!
WELL,
BE-FORE...
I JUST HAD TO LOOK UP...
...AND I COULD LOOK YOU OR MY SISTER RIGHT IN THE EYE.

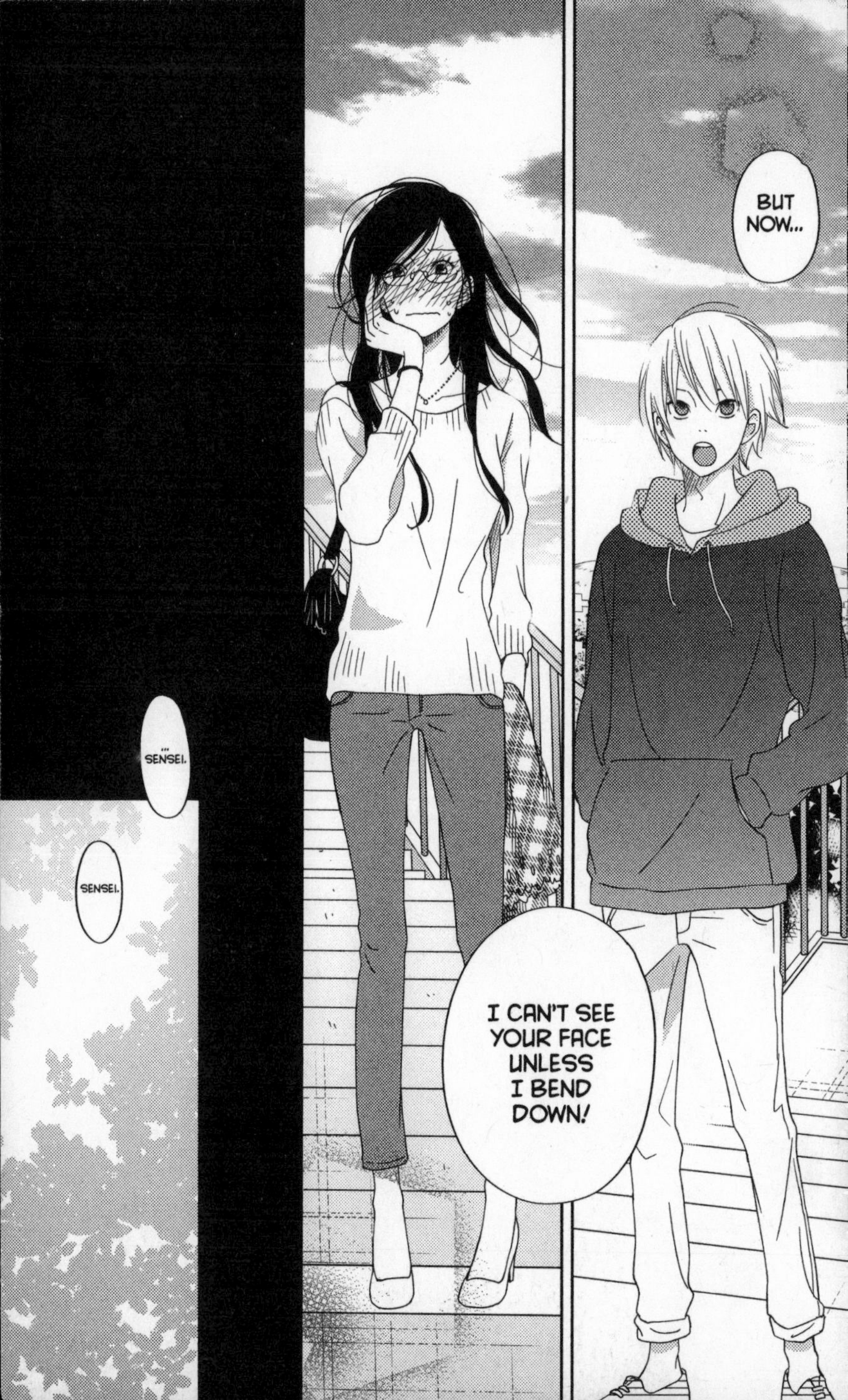
BUT NOW...
I CAN'T SEE YOUR FACE UNLESS I BEND DOWN!
...SENSEI.
SENSEI.

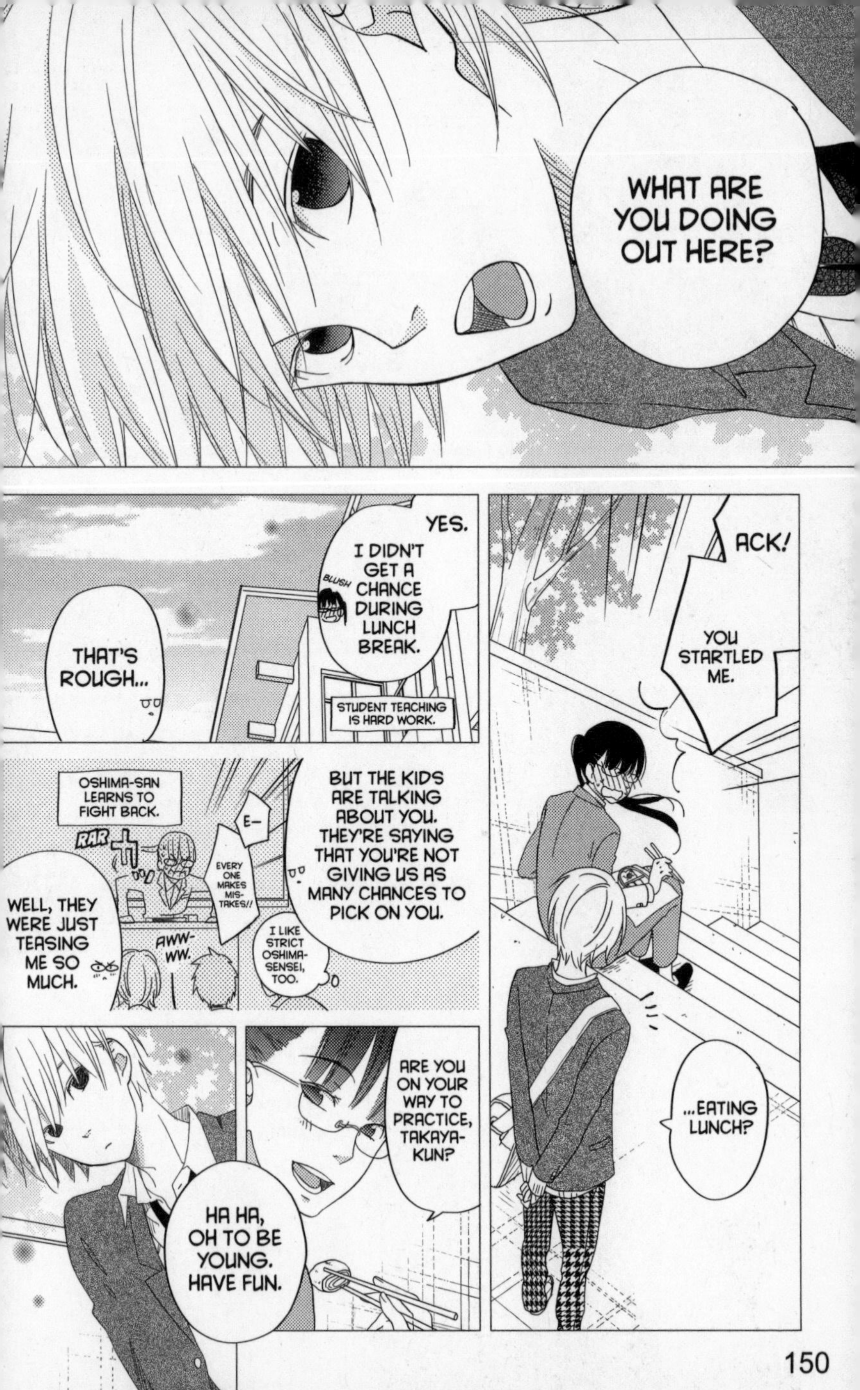
WHAT ARE YOU DOING OUT HERE?
ACK!
YOU STARTLED ME.
...EATING LUNCH?
YES.
I DIDN'T GET A CHANCE DURING LUNCH BREAK.
BLUSH
THAT'S ROUGH...
STUDENT TEACHING IS HARD WORK.
BUT THE KIDS ARE TALKING ABOUT YOU. THEY'RE SAYING THAT YOU'RE NOT GIVING US AS MANY CHANCES TO PICK ON YOU.
E—
OSHIMA-SAN LEARNS TO FIGHT BACK.
RAR
EVERY ONE MAKES MIS-TAKES!!
I LIKE STRICT OSHIMA-SENSEI, TOO.
AWW-WW.
WELL, THEY WERE JUST TEASING ME SO MUCH.
ARE YOU ON YOUR WAY TO PRACTICE, TAKAYA-KUN?
HA HA, OH TO BE YOUNG. HAVE FUN.

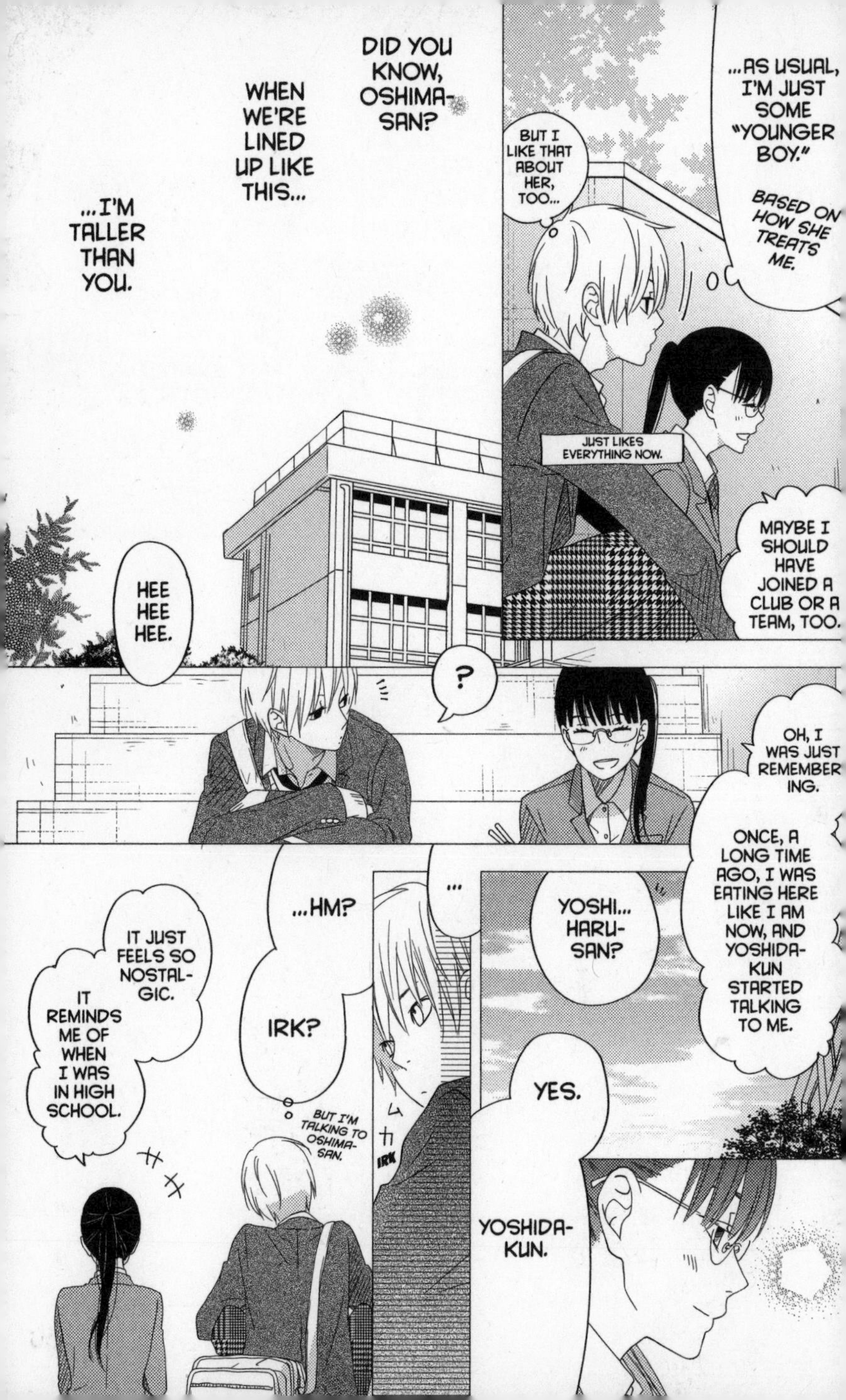

...AS USUAL, I'M JUST SOME "YOUNGER BOY."
BASED ON HOW SHE TREATS ME.
BUT I LIKE THAT ABOUT HER, TOO...
JUST LIKES EVERYTHING NOW.
MAYBE I SHOULD HAVE JOINED A CLUB OR A TEAM, TOO.
DID YOU KNOW, OSHIMA-SAN?
WHEN WE'RE LINED UP LIKE THIS...
...I'M TALLER THAN YOU.
HEE HEE HEE.
?
OH, I WAS JUST REMEMBERING.
ONCE, A LONG TIME AGO, I WAS EATING HERE LIKE I AM NOW, AND YOSHIDA-KUN STARTED TALKING TO ME.
YOSHI... HARU-SAN?
YES.
YOSHIDA-KUN.
...
IRK
...HM?
IRK?
BUT I'M TALKING TO OSHIMA-SAN.
IT JUST FEELS SO NOSTALGIC.
IT REMINDS ME OF WHEN I WAS IN HIGH SCHOOL.

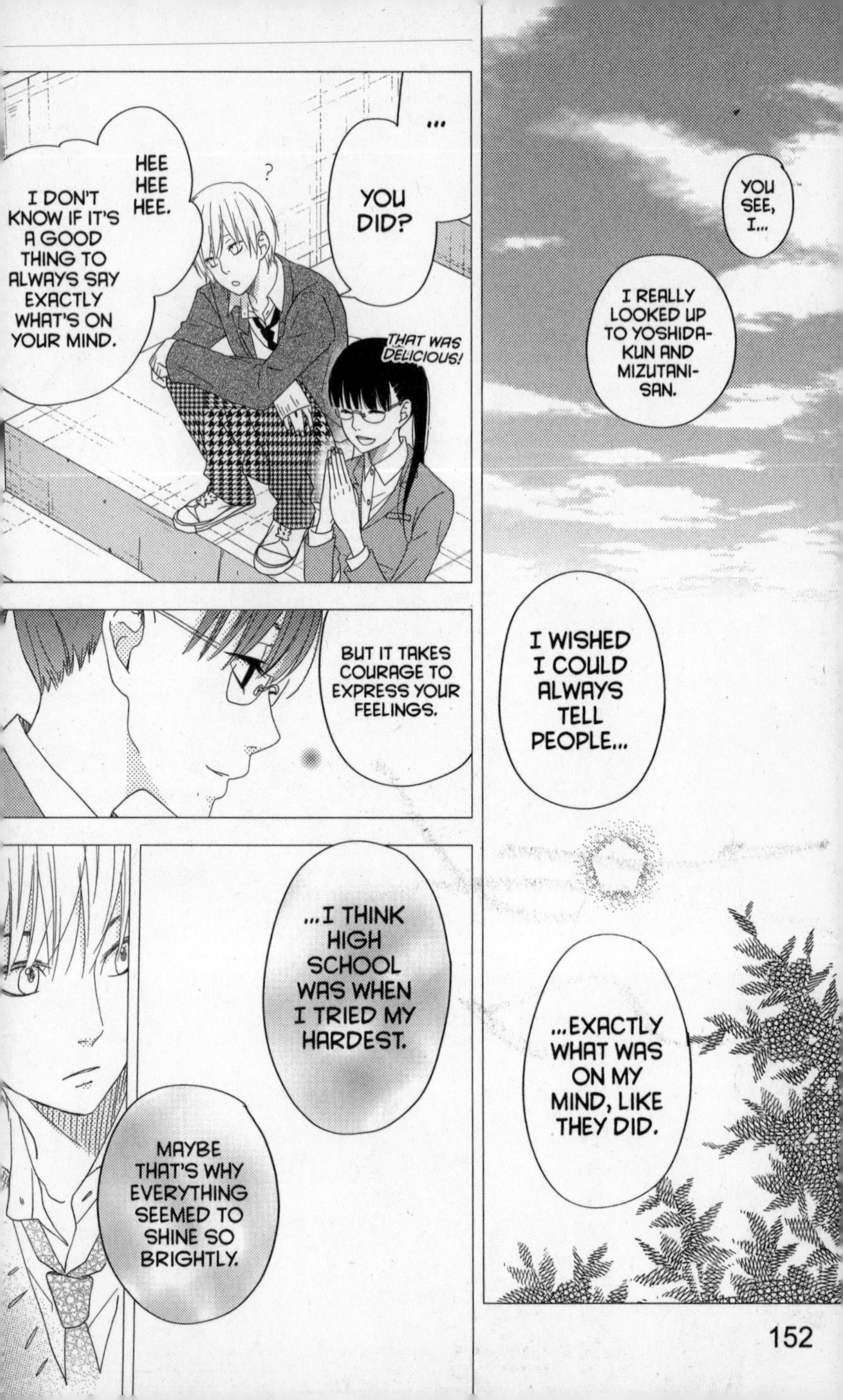
YOU SEE, I...
I REALLY LOOKED UP TO YOSHIDA-KUN AND MIZUTANI-SAN.
I WISHED I COULD ALWAYS TELL PEOPLE...
...EXACTLY WHAT WAS ON MY MIND, LIKE THEY DID.
...
YOU DID?
?
HEE HEE HEE.
I DON'T KNOW IF IT'S A GOOD THING TO ALWAYS SAY EXACTLY WHAT'S ON YOUR MIND.
THAT WAS DELICIOUS!
BUT IT TAKES COURAGE TO EXPRESS YOUR FEELINGS.
...I THINK HIGH SCHOOL WAS WHEN I TRIED MY HARDEST.
MAYBE THAT'S WHY EVERYTHING SEEMED TO SHINE SO BRIGHTLY.

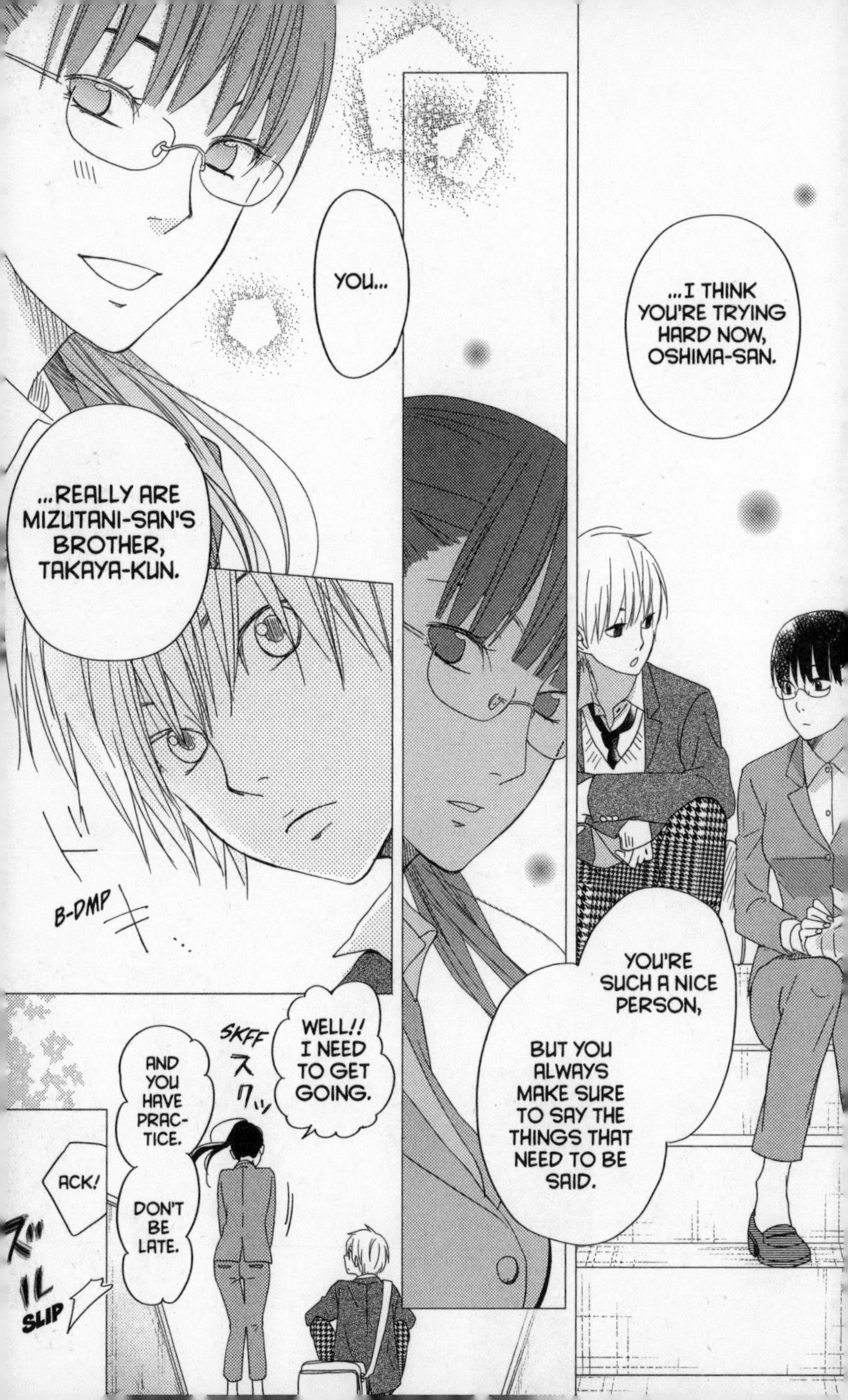
...I THINK YOU'RE TRYING HARD NOW, OSHIMA-SAN.
YOU'RE SUCH A NICE PERSON,
BUT YOU ALWAYS MAKE SURE TO SAY THE THINGS THAT NEED TO BE SAID.
YOU...
...REALLY ARE MIZUTANI-SAN'S BROTHER, TAKAYA-KUN.
B-DMP
WELL!! I NEED TO GET GOING.
SKFF
AND YOU HAVE PRAC-TICE.
DON'T BE LATE.
ACK!
SLIP

PLEASE BE CARE- FUL.

THAT NIGHT...

...I-I'M SORRY.

"... IT'S OKAY.

AND AFTER I WAS ACTING SO AUTHOR- ITATIVE...

BLUSH

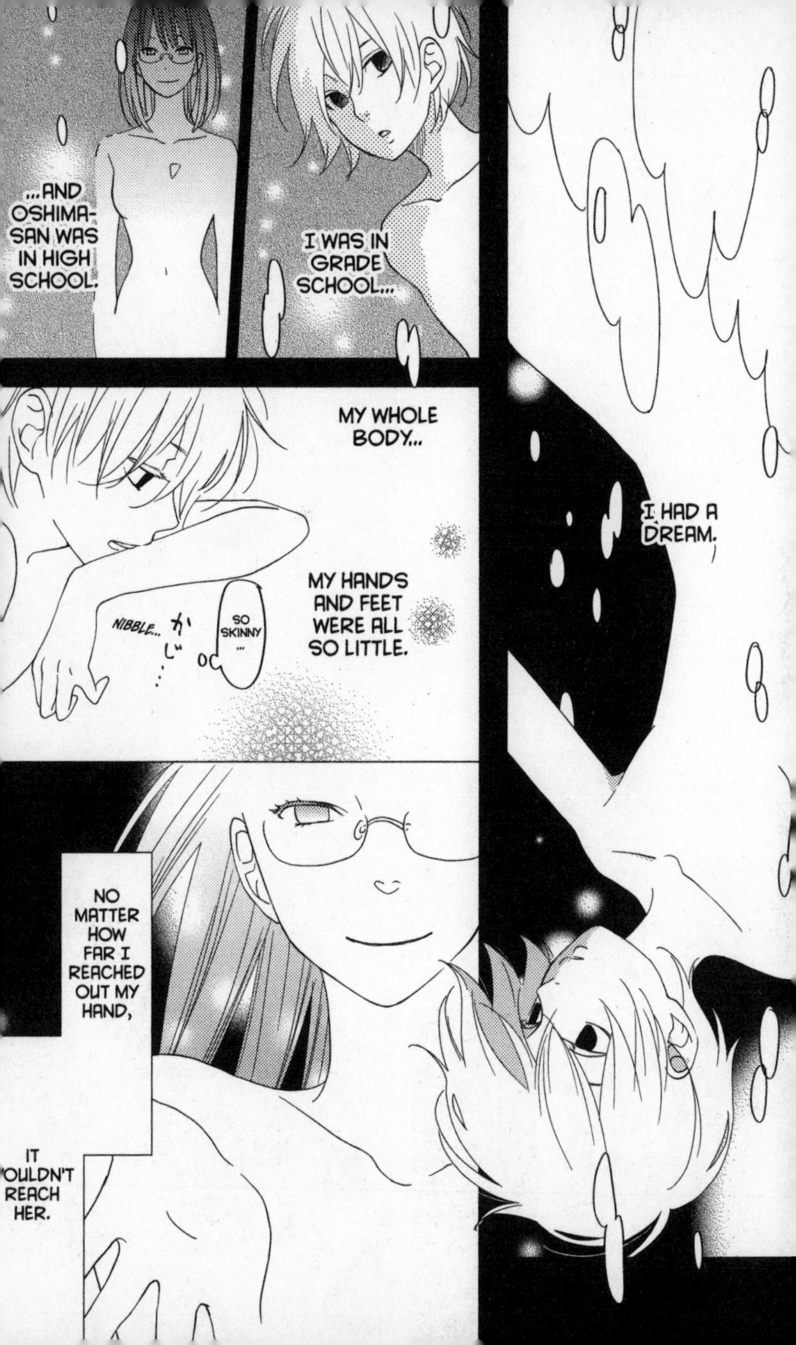
I HAD A DREAM.
I WAS IN GRADE SCHOOL...
...AND OSHIMA-SAN WAS IN HIGH SCHOOL.
MY WHOLE BODY...
MY HANDS AND FEET WERE ALL SO LITTLE.
SO SKINNY ...
NIBBLE... かじ...
NO MATTER HOW FAR I REACHED OUT MY HAND,
IT OULDN'T REACH HER.

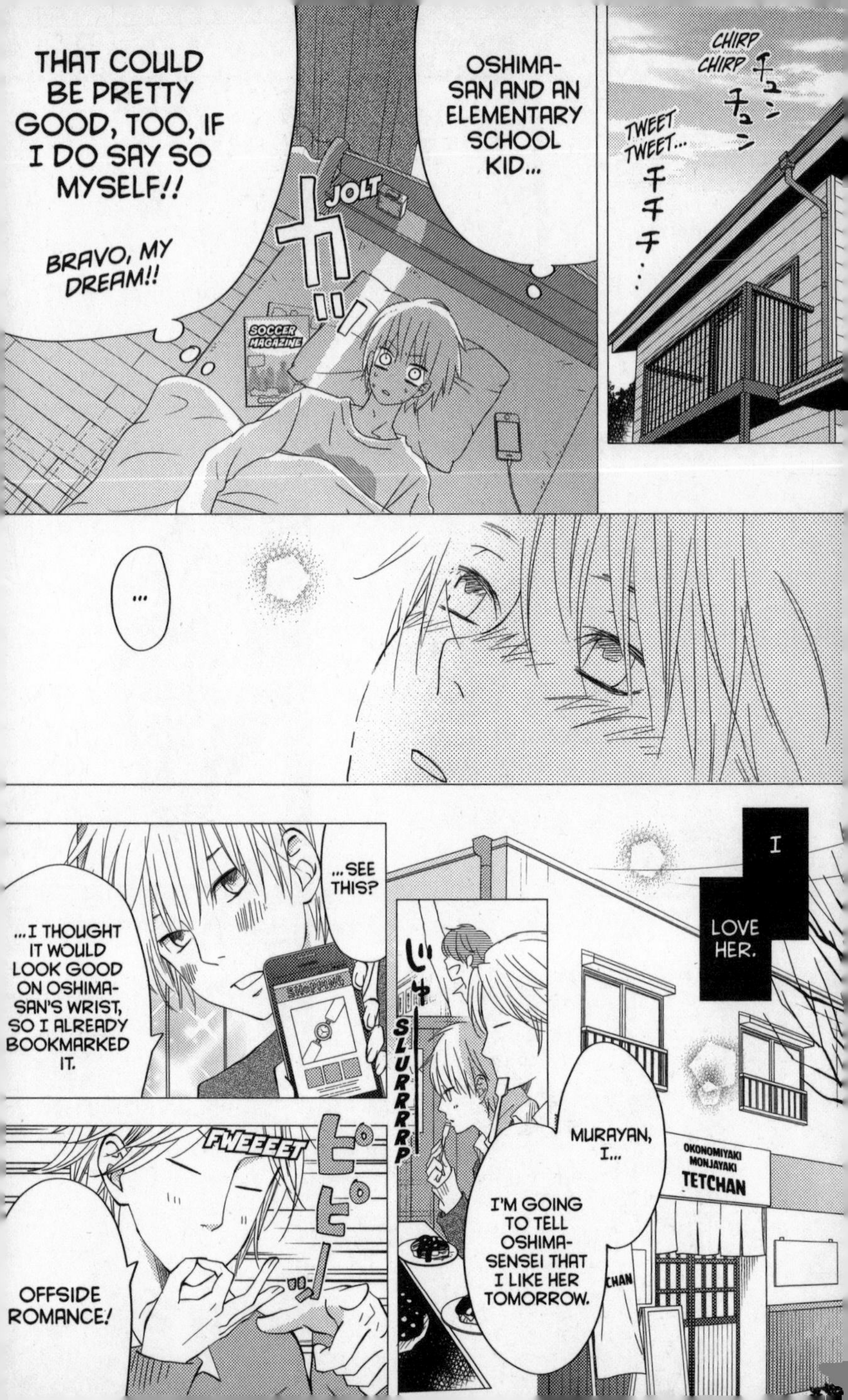
CHIRP CHIRP
チュン チュン
TWEET TWEET...
チチチ...
OSHIMA-SAN AND AN ELEMENTARY SCHOOL KID...
THAT COULD BE PRETTY GOOD, TOO, IF I DO SAY SO MYSELF!!
BRAVO, MY DREAM!!
JOLT
カッ
SOCCER MAGAZINE
...
I
LOVE HER.
OKONOMIYAKI MONJAYAKI
TETCHAN
MURAYAN, I...
I'M GOING TO TELL OSHIMA-SENSEI THAT I LIKE HER TOMORROW.
じゅ
SLURRRRP
...SEE THIS?
...I THOUGHT IT WOULD LOOK GOOD ON OSHIMA-SAN'S WRIST, SO I ALREADY BOOKMARKED IT.
SHOPPING
FWEEEEET
ピーピー
OFFSIDE ROMANCE!

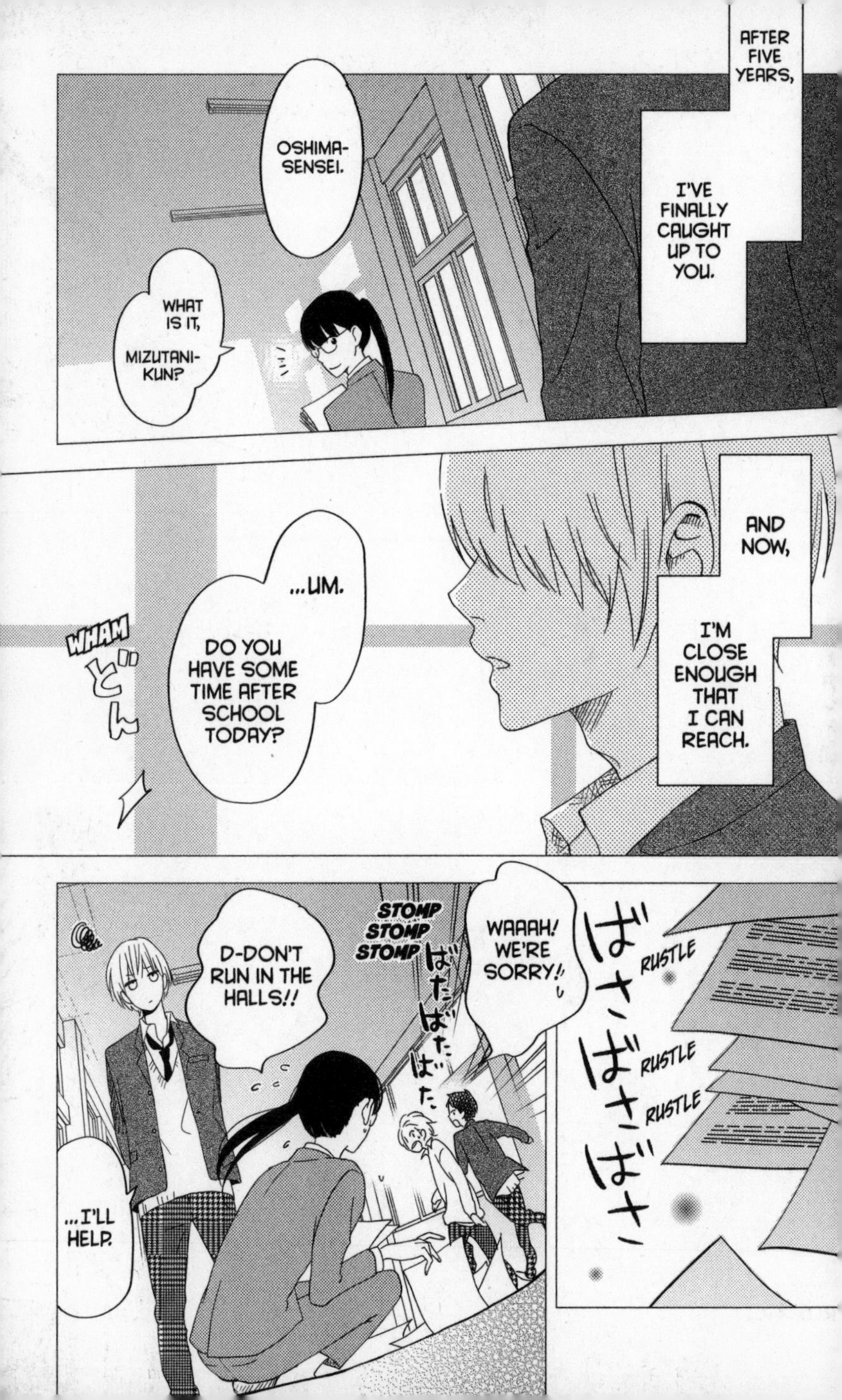
AFTER FIVE YEARS,
I'VE FINALLY CAUGHT UP TO YOU.
OSHIMA-SENSEI.
WHAT IS IT, MIZUTANI-KUN?
AND NOW,
I'M CLOSE ENOUGH THAT I CAN REACH.
...UM.
DO YOU HAVE SOME TIME AFTER SCHOOL TODAY?
WHAM
どん
ばさばさばさ
RUSTLE
RUSTLE
RUSTLE
WAAAH! WE'RE SORRY!!
STOMP STOMP STOMP
ばたばたばた
D-DON'T RUN IN THE HALLS!!
...I'LL HELP.

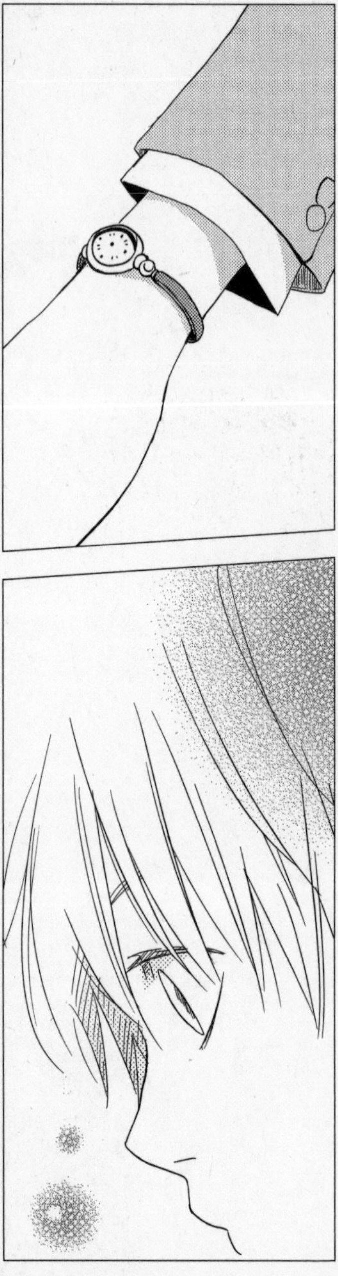

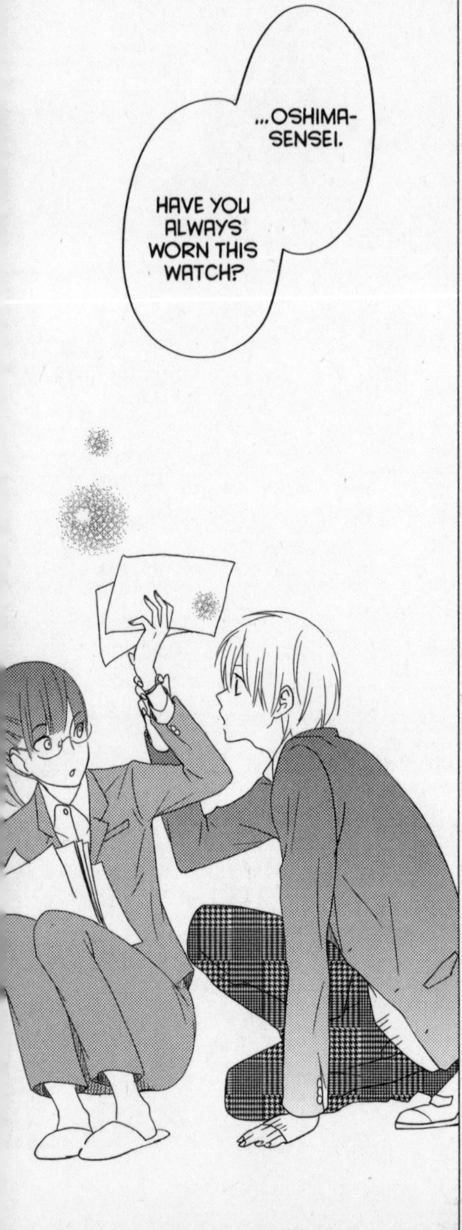
...OSHIMA-SENSEI.
HAVE YOU ALWAYS WORN THIS WATCH?

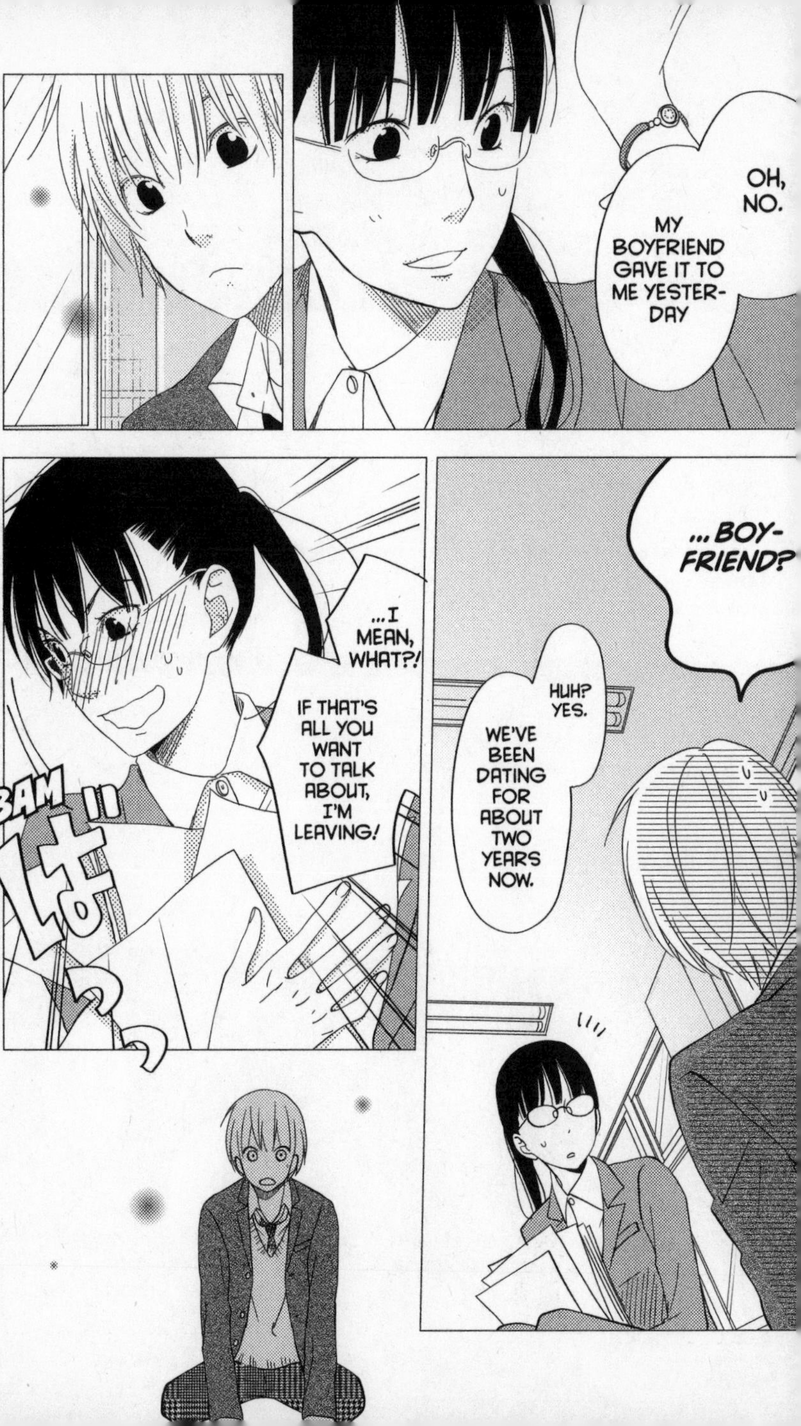
OH, NO.
MY BOYFRIEND GAVE IT TO ME YESTER-DAY
...BOY-FRIEND?
HUH? YES.
WE'VE BEEN DATING FOR ABOUT TWO YEARS NOW.
...I MEAN, WHAT?!
IF THAT'S ALL YOU WANT TO TALK ABOUT, I'M LEAVING!
BAM
ばっ

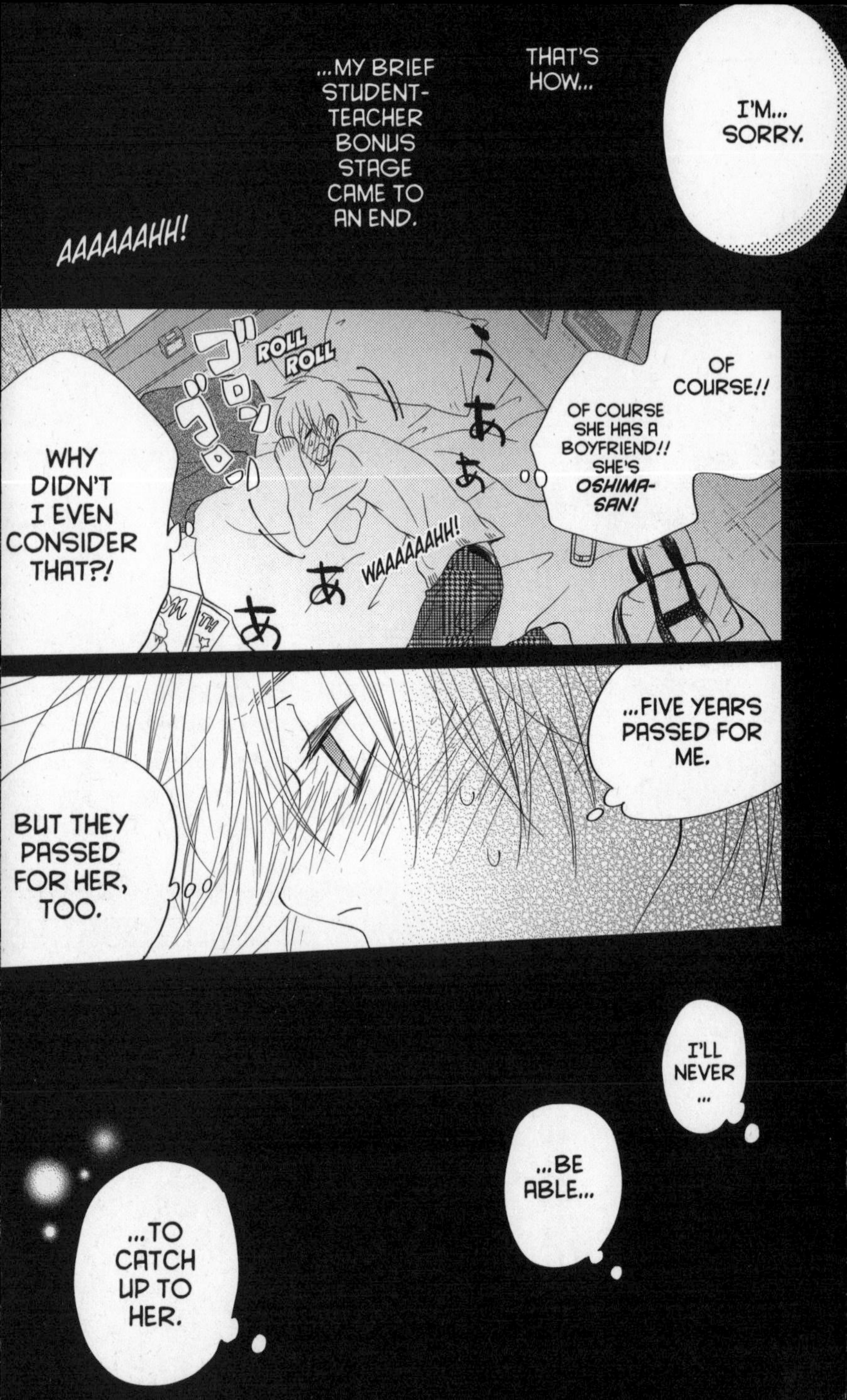
I'M... SORRY.
THAT'S HOW...
...MY BRIEF STUDENT-TEACHER BONUS STAGE CAME TO AN END.
AAAAAAHH!
OF COURSE!!
OF COURSE SHE HAS A BOYFRIEND!! SHE'S OSHIMA-SAN!
うああああ
WAAAAAAHH!
ゴロンゴロン
ROLL ROLL
WHY DIDN'T I EVEN CONSIDER THAT?!
...FIVE YEARS PASSED FOR ME.
BUT THEY PASSED FOR HER, TOO.
I'LL NEVER...
...BE ABLE...
...TO CATCH UP TO HER.

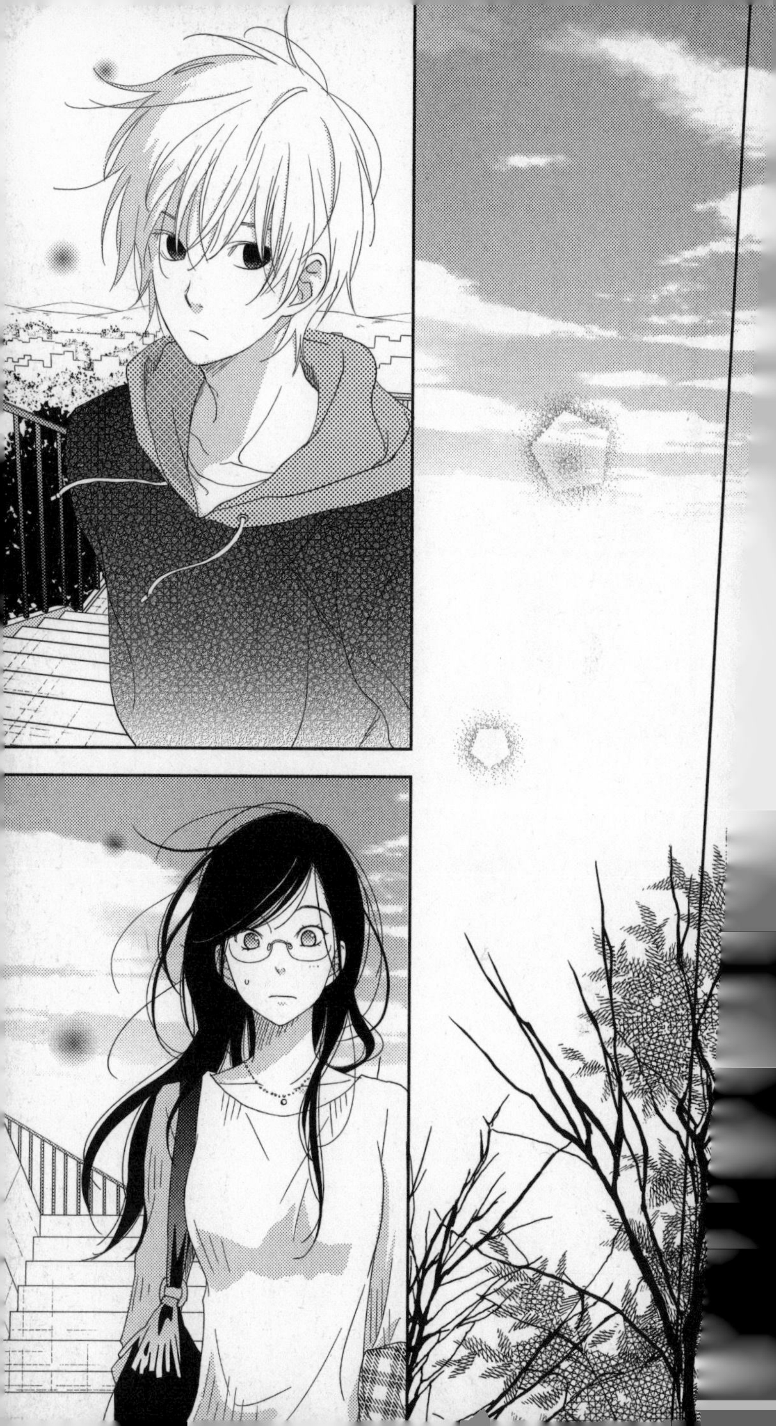

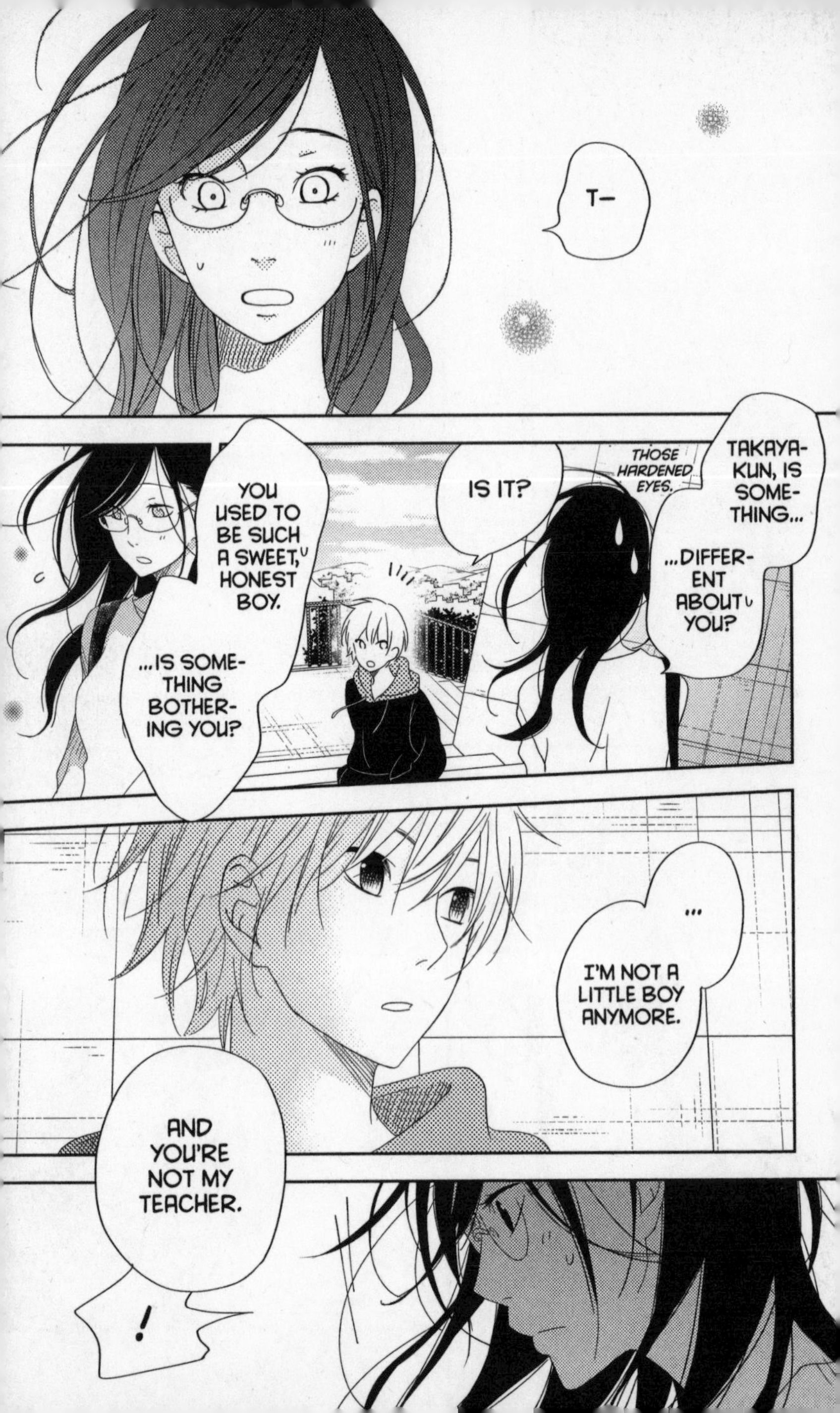
T—
TAKAYA-KUN, IS SOMETHING...
THOSE HARDENED EYES.
...DIFFERENT ABOUT YOU?
IS IT?
YOU USED TO BE SUCH A SWEET, HONEST BOY.
...IS SOMETHING BOTHERING YOU?
...
I'M NOT A LITTLE BOY ANYMORE.
AND YOU'RE NOT MY TEACHER.
!

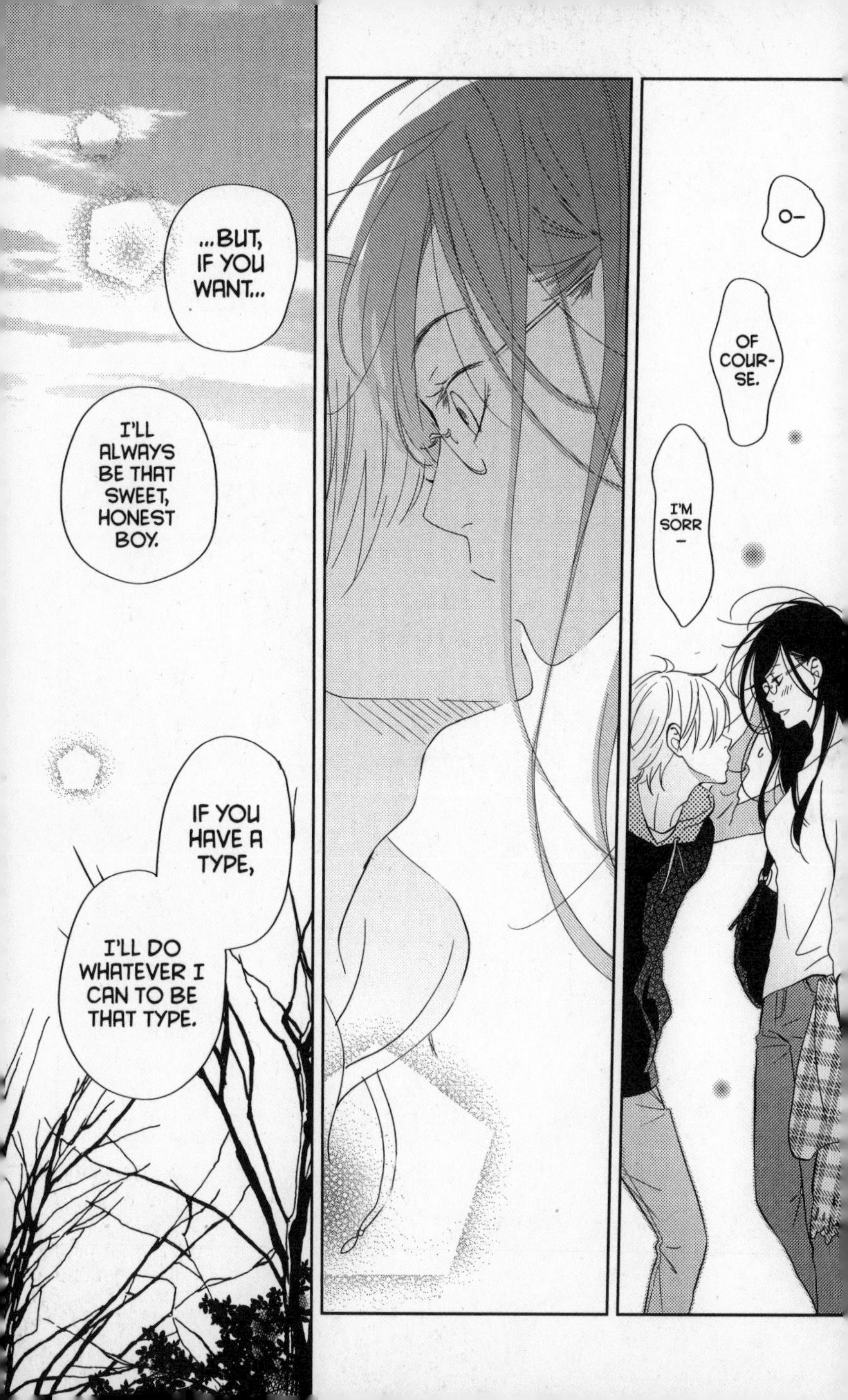
O—
OF COUR-SE.
I'M SORR—
...BUT, IF YOU WANT...
I'LL ALWAYS BE THAT SWEET, HONEST BOY.
IF YOU HAVE A TYPE,
I'LL DO WHATEVER I CAN TO BE THAT TYPE.

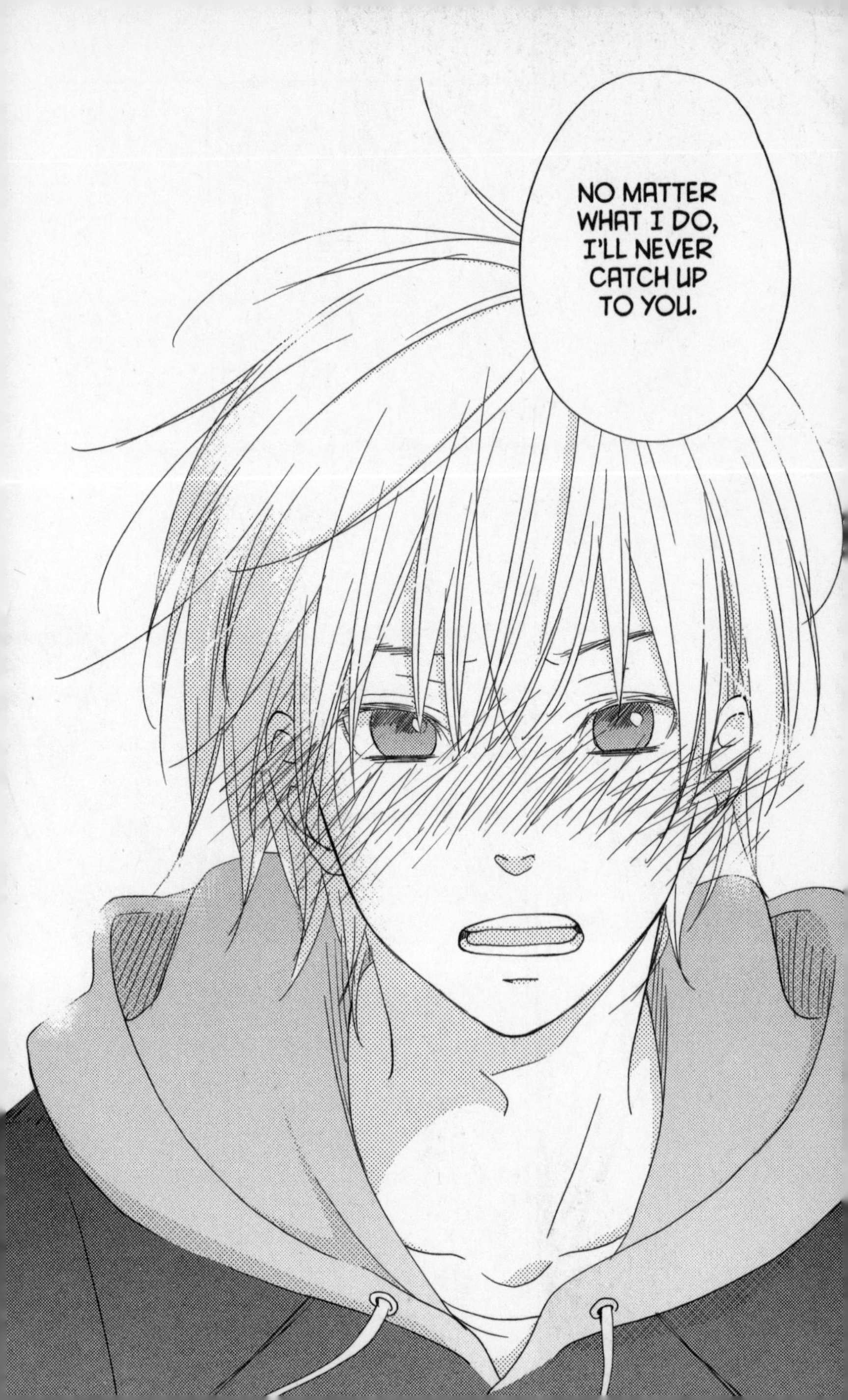
NO MATTER WHAT I DO, I'LL NEVER CATCH UP TO YOU.

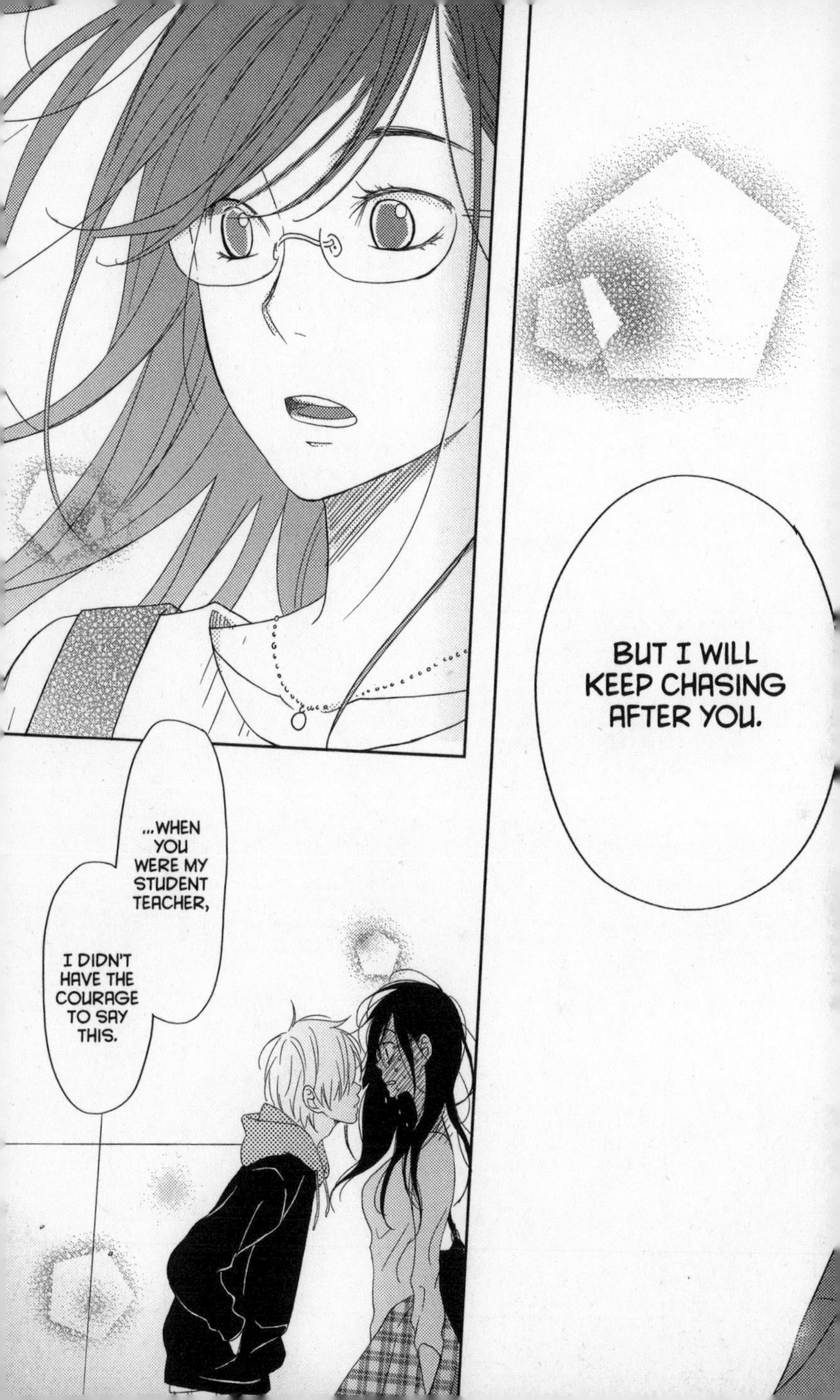
BUT I WILL KEEP CHASING AFTER YOU.
...WHEN YOU WERE MY STUDENT TEACHER,
I DIDN'T HAVE THE COURAGE TO SAY THIS.

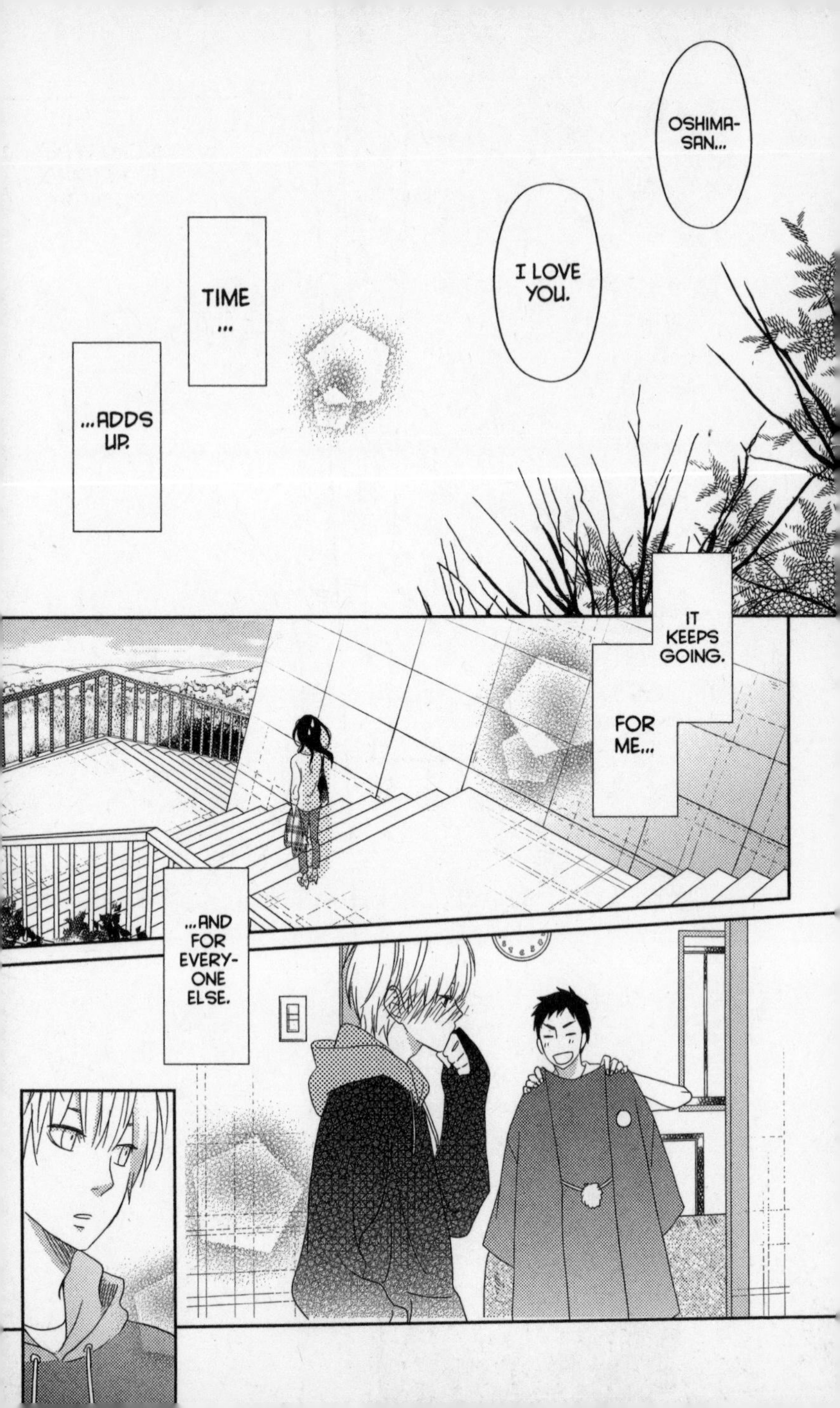
OSHIMA-SAN...
I LOVE YOU.
TIME...
...ADDS UP.
IT KEEPS GOING.
FOR ME...
...AND FOR EVERY-ONE ELSE.

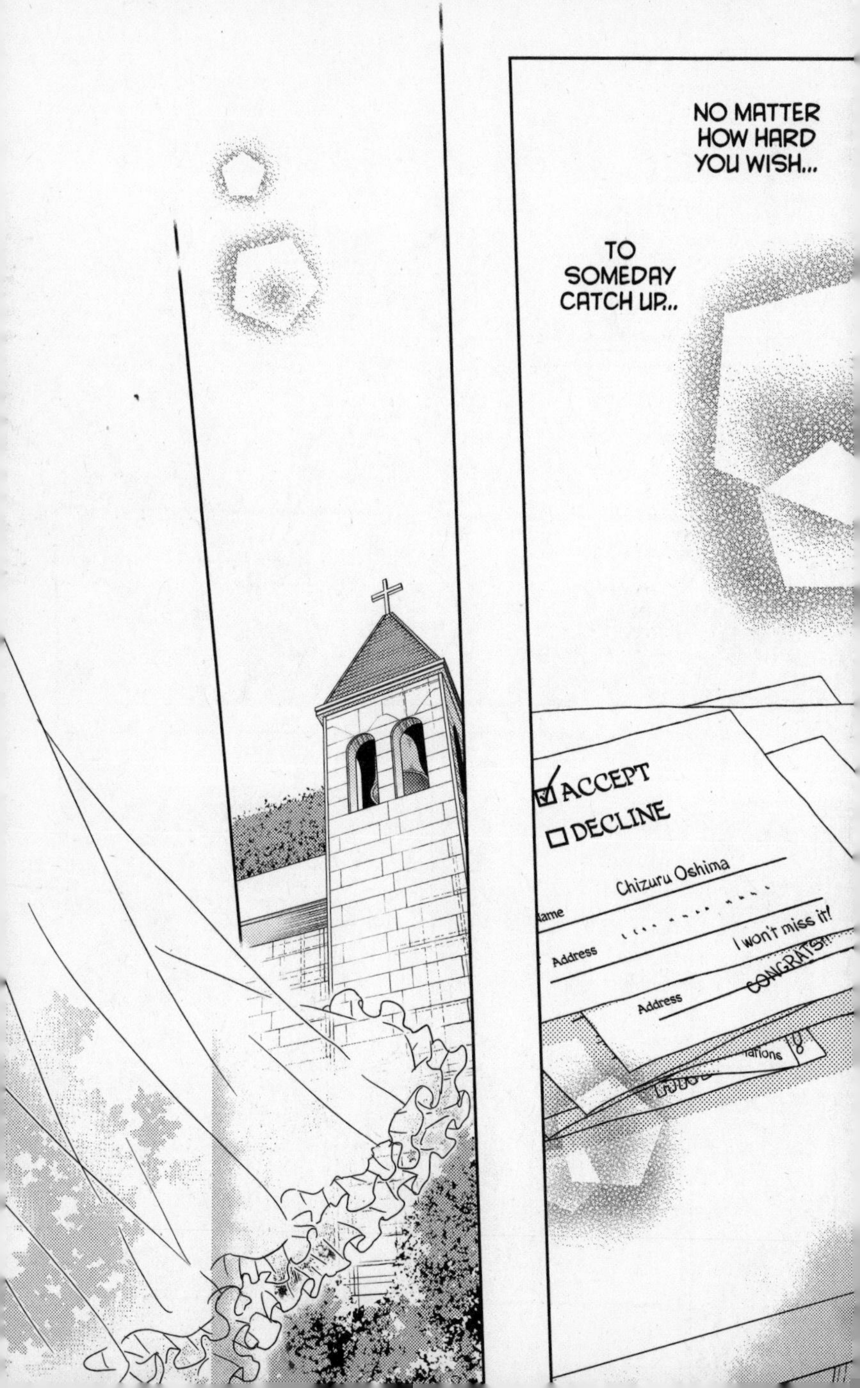
NO MATTER HOW HARD YOU WISH...
TO SOMEDAY CATCH UP...
ACCEPT
DECLINE
Chizuru Oshima
Address
I won't miss it!
Address
CONGRATS!!

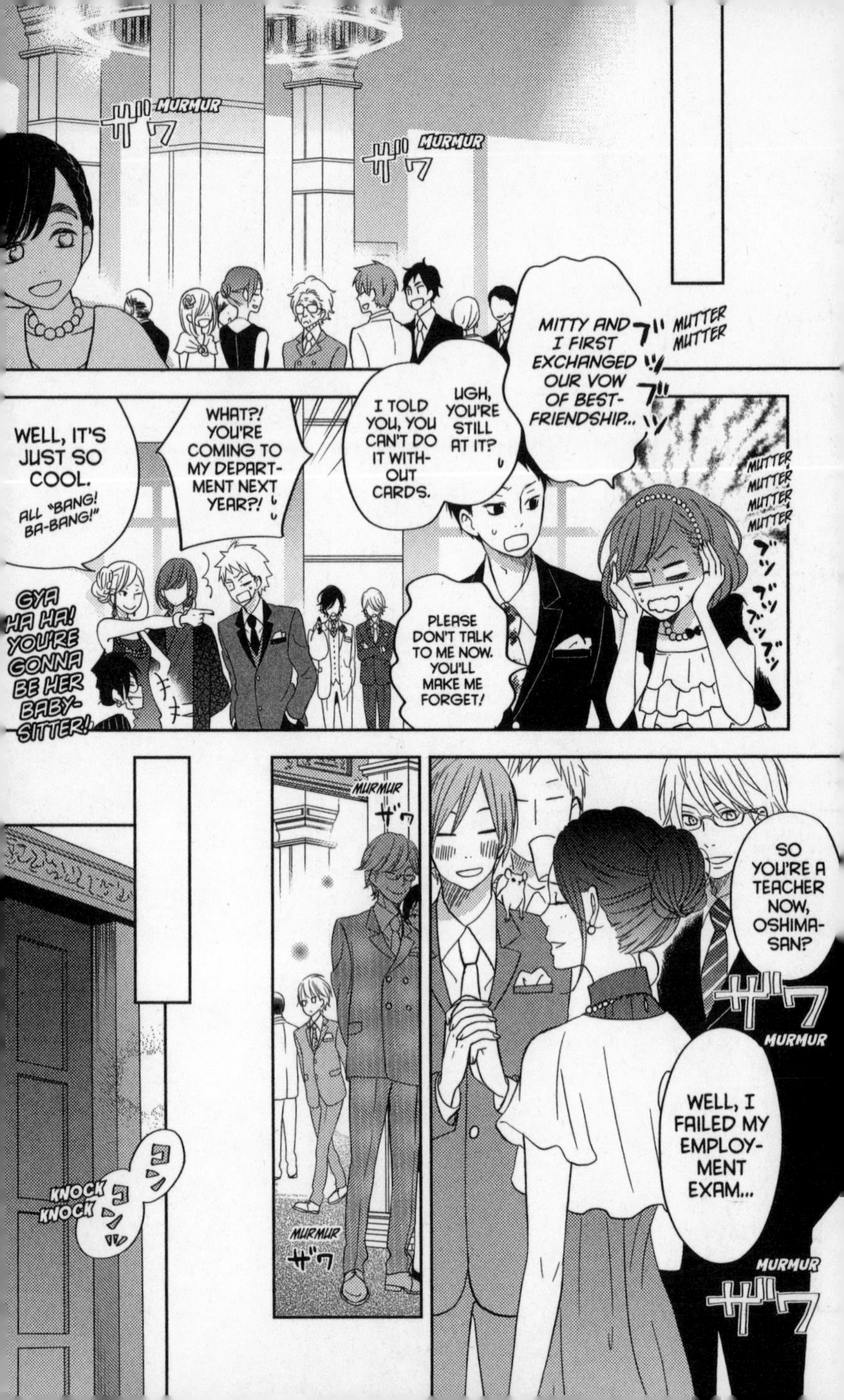
MURMUR
MURMUR
MITTY AND I FIRST EXCHANGED OUR VOW OF BEST-FRIENDSHIP...
MUTTER MUTTER
MUTTER, MUTTER MUTTER MUTTER
UGH, YOU'RE STILL AT IT?
I TOLD YOU, YOU CAN'T DO IT WITH-OUT CARDS.
PLEASE DON'T TALK TO ME NOW. YOU'LL MAKE ME FORGET!
WHAT?! YOU'RE COMING TO MY DEPART-MENT NEXT YEAR?!
WELL, IT'S JUST SO COOL.
ALL "BANG! BA-BANG!"
GYA HA HA! YOU'RE GONNA BE HER BABY-SITTER!
SO YOU'RE A TEACHER NOW, OSHIMA-SAN?
MURMUR
WELL, I FAILED MY EMPLOY-MENT EXAM...
MURMUR
MURMUR
MURMUR
KNOCK KNOCK

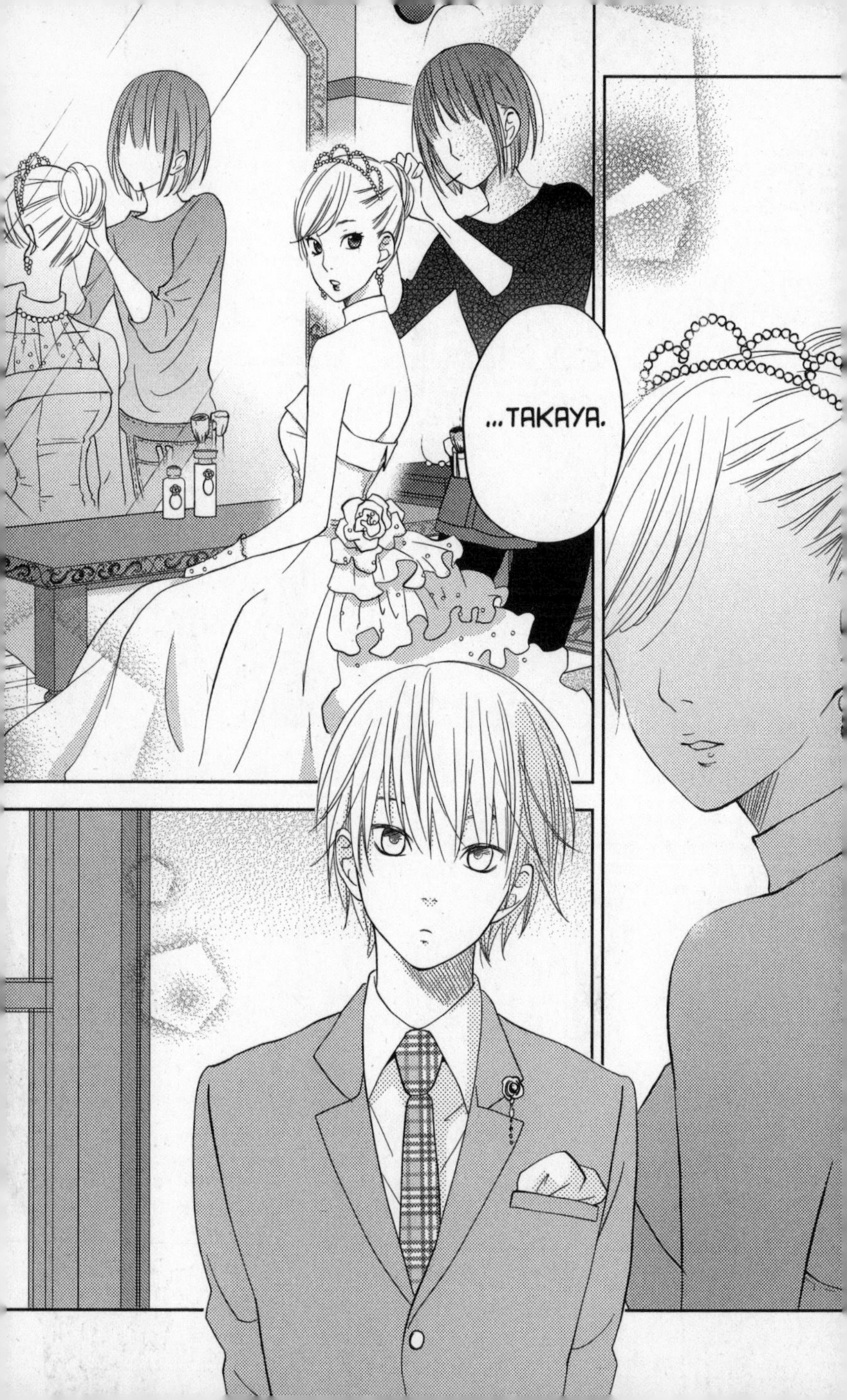
...TAKAYA.

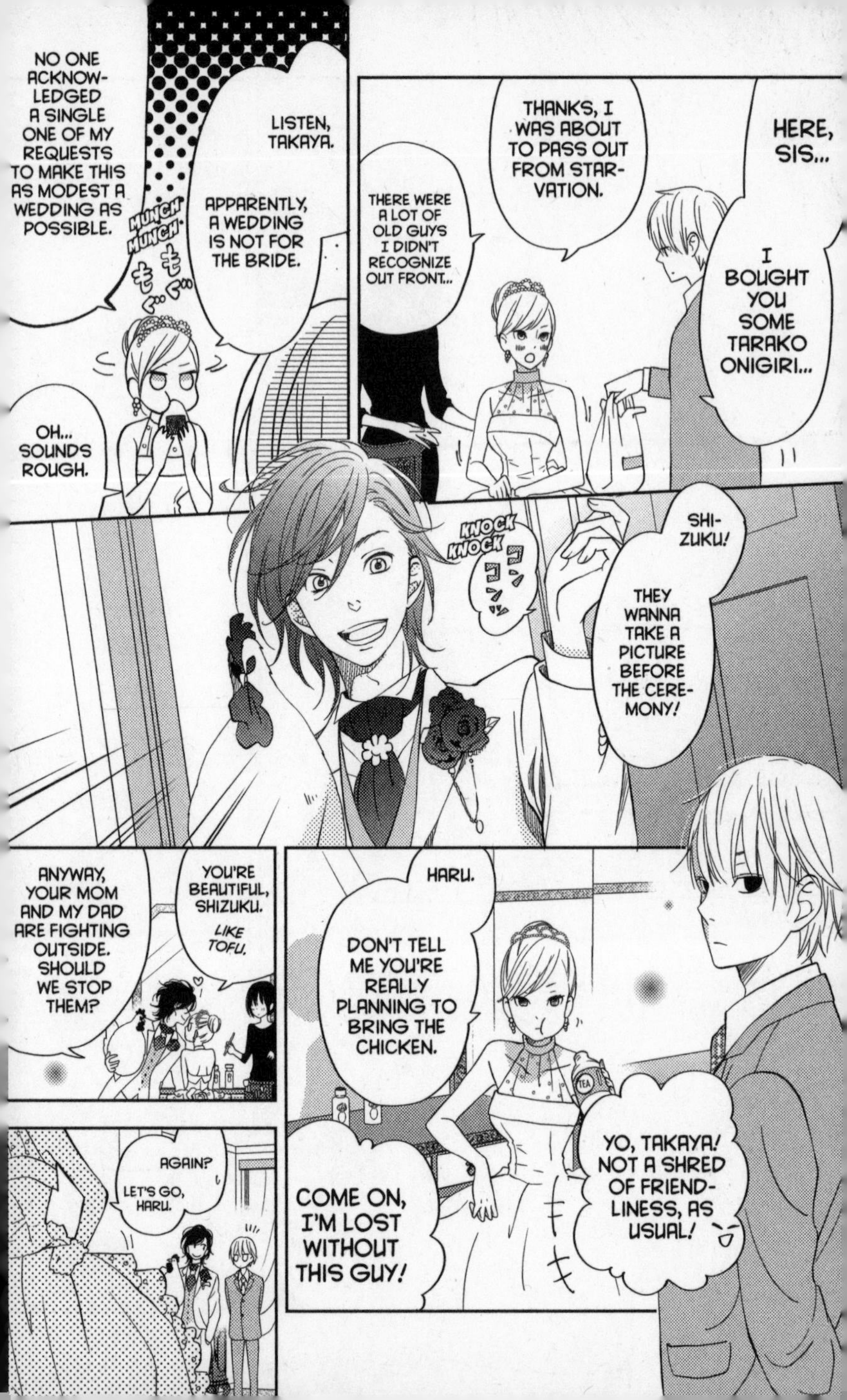
HERE, SIS...
THANKS, I WAS ABOUT TO PASS OUT FROM STAR-VATION.
I BOUGHT YOU SOME TARAKO ONIGIRI...
THERE WERE A LOT OF OLD GUYS I DIDN'T RECOGNIZE OUT FRONT...
LISTEN, TAKAYA.
APPARENTLY, A WEDDING IS NOT FOR THE BRIDE.
NO ONE ACKNOW-LEDGED A SINGLE ONE OF MY REQUESTS TO MAKE THIS AS MODEST A WEDDING AS POSSIBLE.
MUNCH MUNCH
OH... SOUNDS ROUGH.
SHI-ZUKU!
THEY WANNA TAKE A PICTURE BEFORE THE CERE-MONY!
KNOCK KNOCK
HARU.
DON'T TELL ME YOU'RE REALLY PLANNING TO BRING THE CHICKEN.
YO, TAKAYA! NOT A SHRED OF FRIEND-LINESS, AS USUAL!
COME ON, I'M LOST WITHOUT THIS GUY!
YOU'RE BEAUTIFUL, SHIZUKU.
LIKE TOFU.
ANYWAY, YOUR MOM AND MY DAD ARE FIGHTING OUTSIDE. SHOULD WE STOP THEM?
AGAIN?
LET'S GO, HARU.

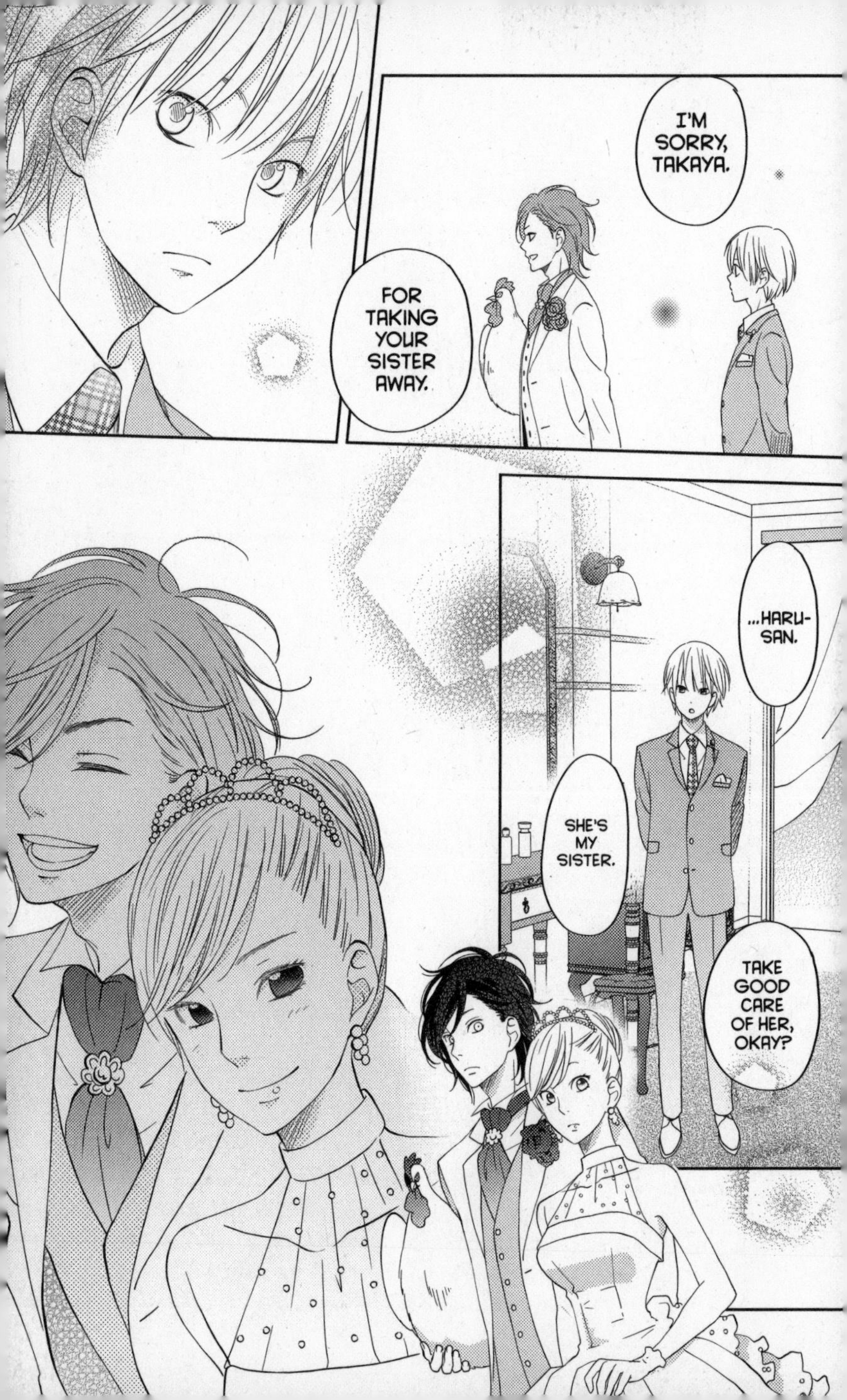
I'M SORRY, TAKAYA.
FOR TAKING YOUR SISTER AWAY.
...HARU-SAN.
SHE'S MY SISTER.
TAKE GOOD CARE OF HER, OKAY?

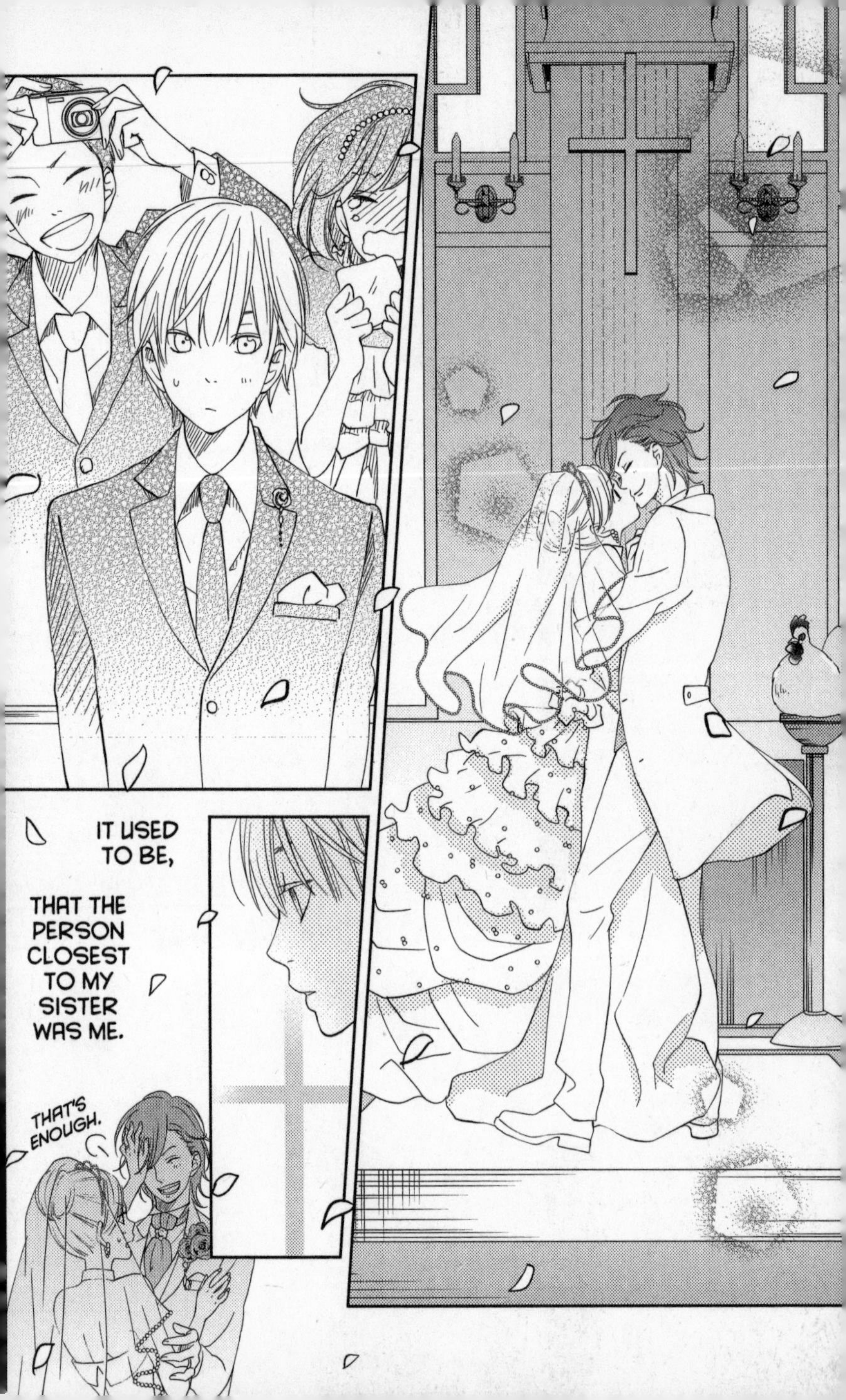
IT USED TO BE,
THAT THE PERSON CLOSEST TO MY SISTER WAS ME.
THAT'S ENOUGH.

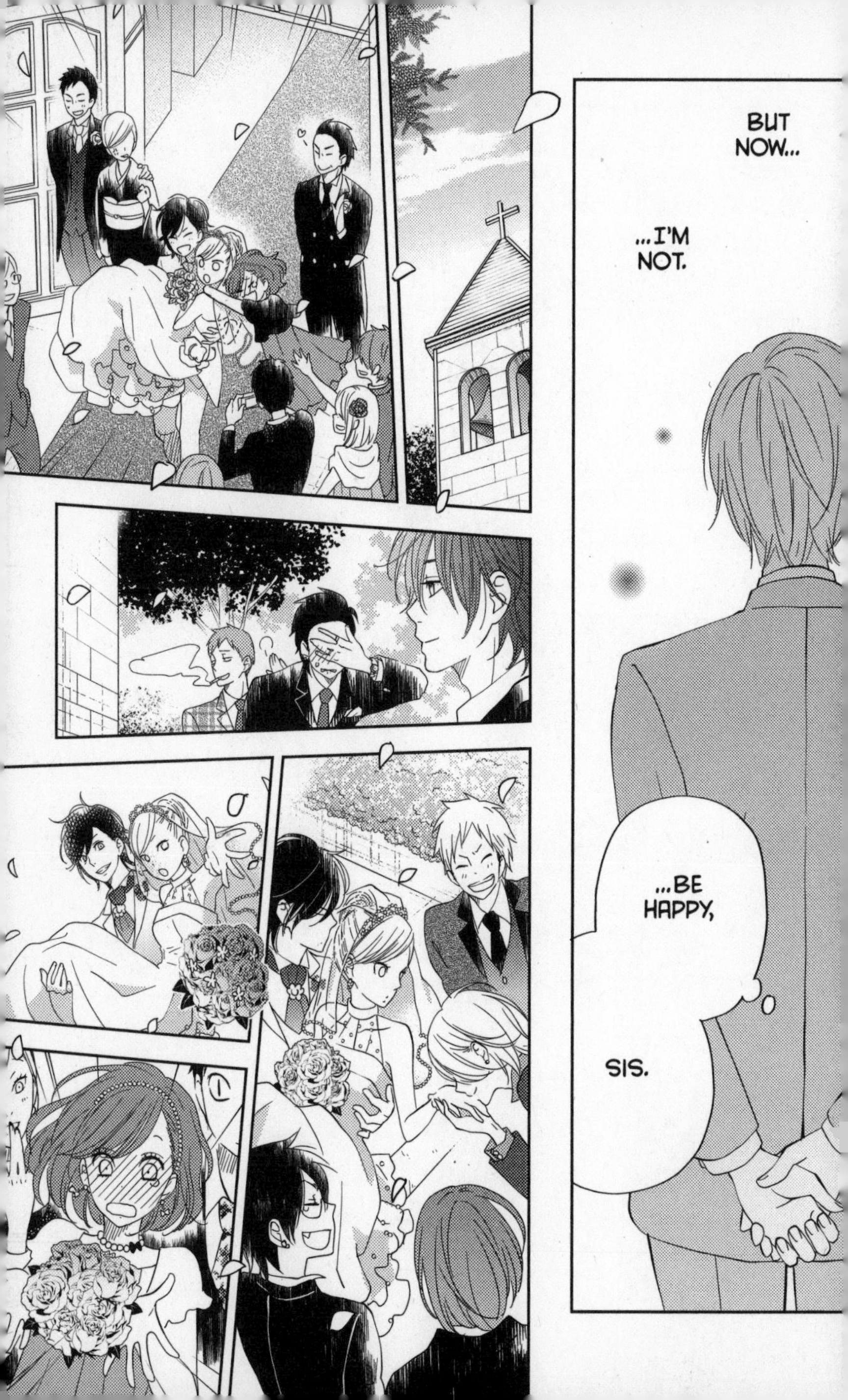
BUT NOW...
...I'M NOT.
...BE HAPPY,
SIS.

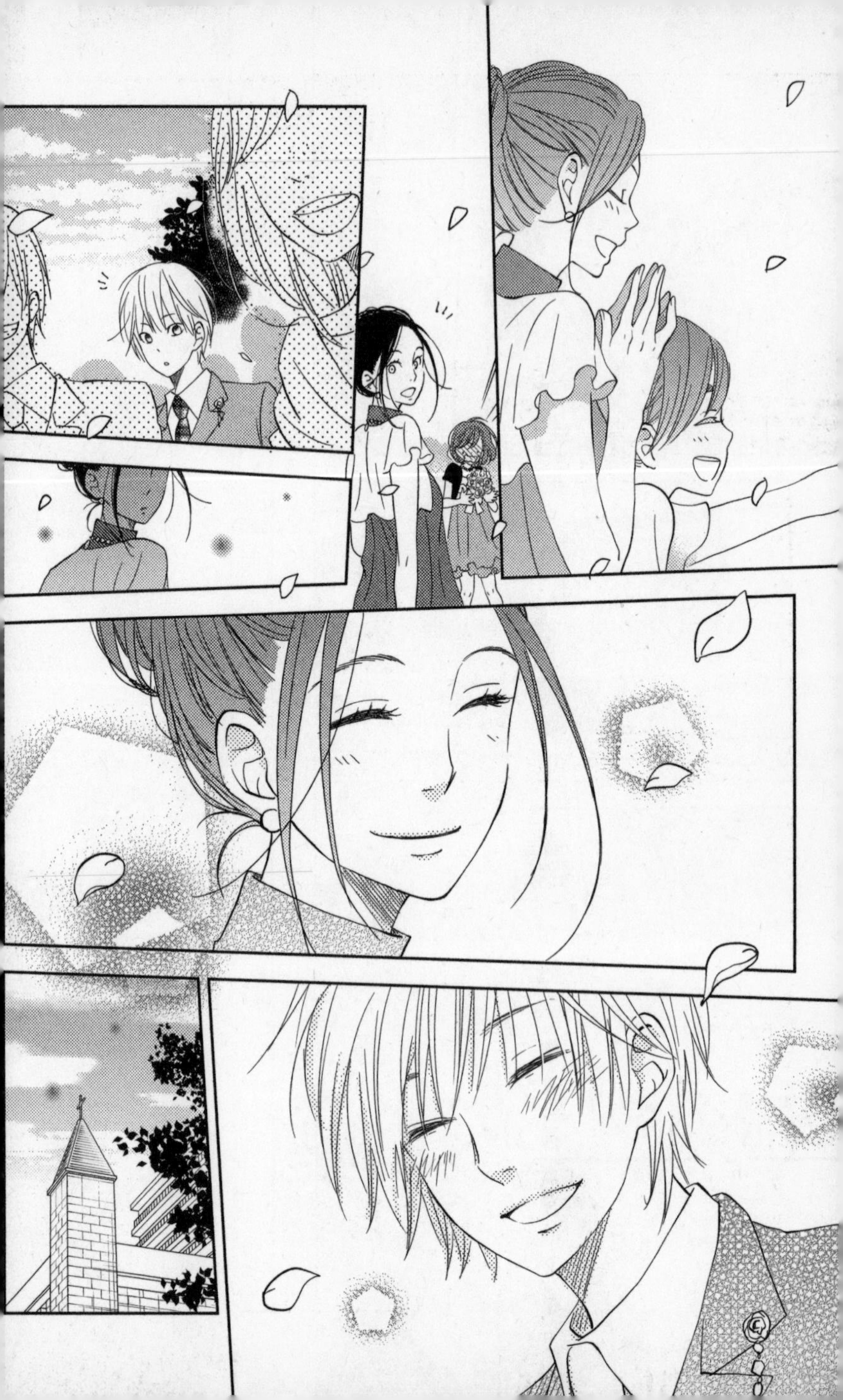

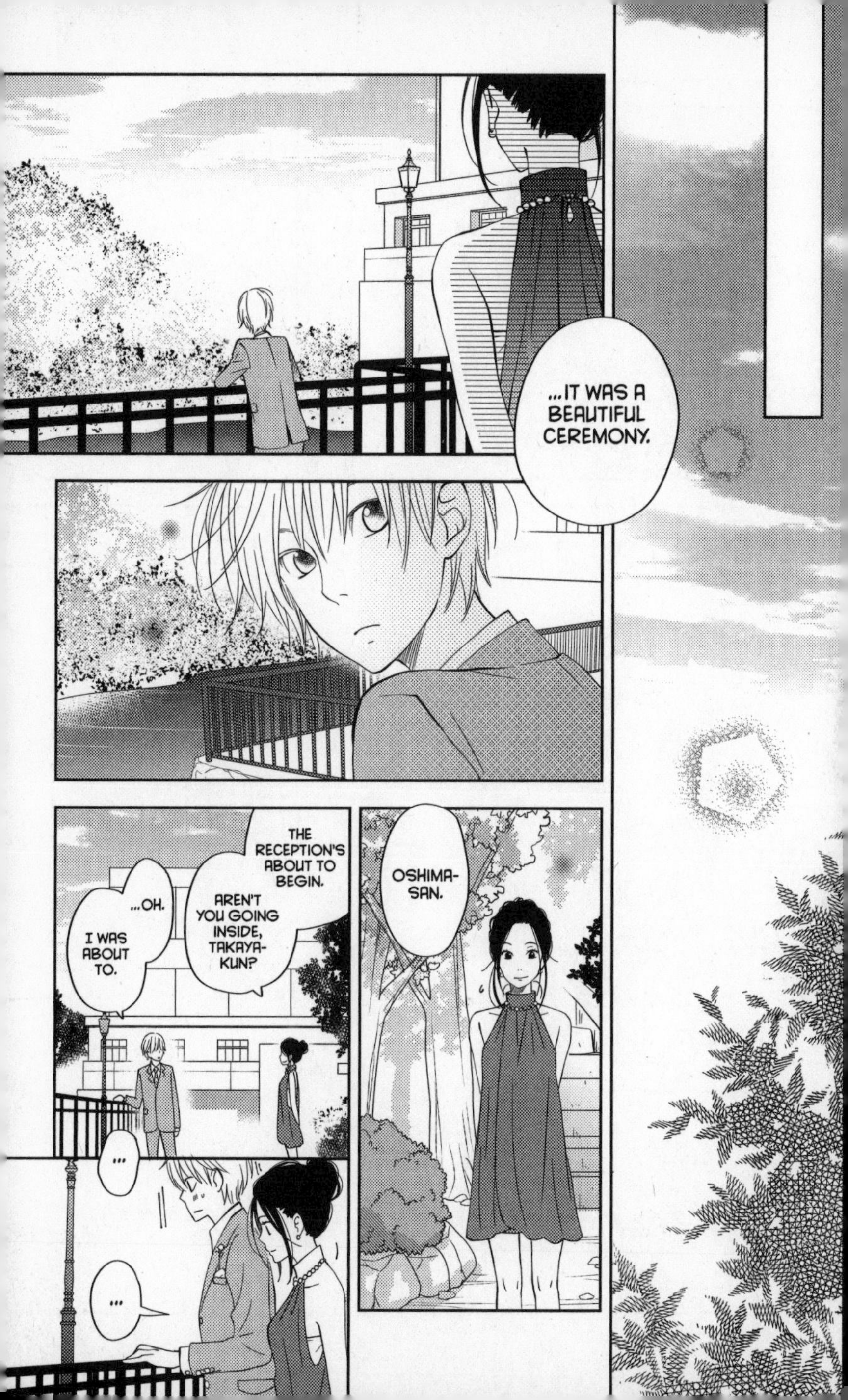
...IT WAS A BEAUTIFUL CEREMONY.
OSHIMA-SAN.
THE RECEPTION'S ABOUT TO BEGIN.
AREN'T YOU GOING INSIDE, TAKAYA-KUN?
...OH.
I WAS ABOUT TO.
...
...

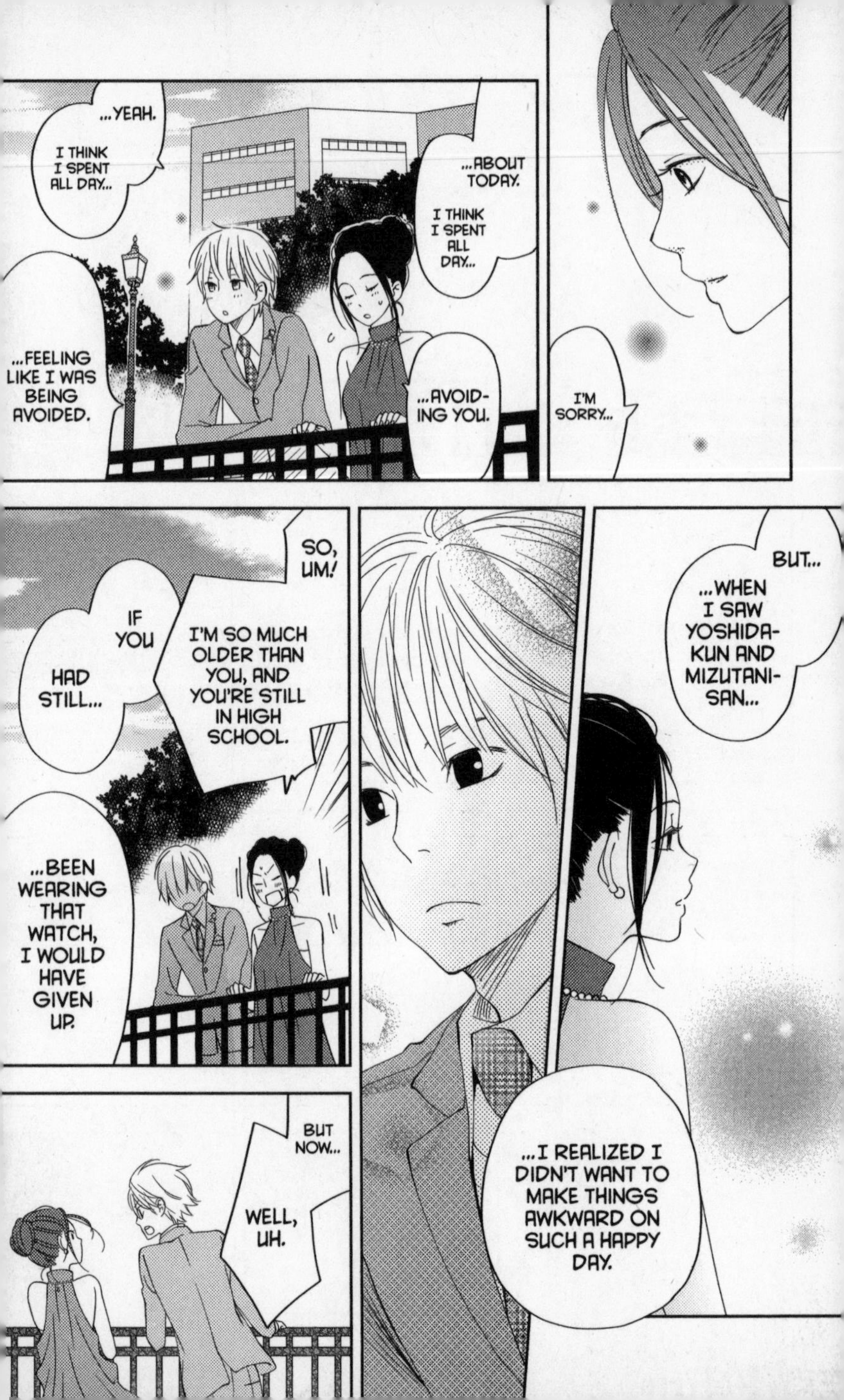
I'M SORRY...
...ABOUT TODAY.
I THINK I SPENT ALL DAY...
...AVOIDING YOU.
...YEAH.
I THINK I SPENT ALL DAY...
...FEELING LIKE I WAS BEING AVOIDED.
BUT...
...WHEN I SAW YOSHIDA-KUN AND MIZUTANI-SAN...
...I REALIZED I DIDN'T WANT TO MAKE THINGS AWKWARD ON SUCH A HAPPY DAY.
SO, UM!
I'M SO MUCH OLDER THAN YOU, AND YOU'RE STILL IN HIGH SCHOOL.
IF YOU HAD STILL...
...BEEN WEARING THAT WATCH, I WOULD HAVE GIVEN UP.
BUT NOW...
WELL, UH.

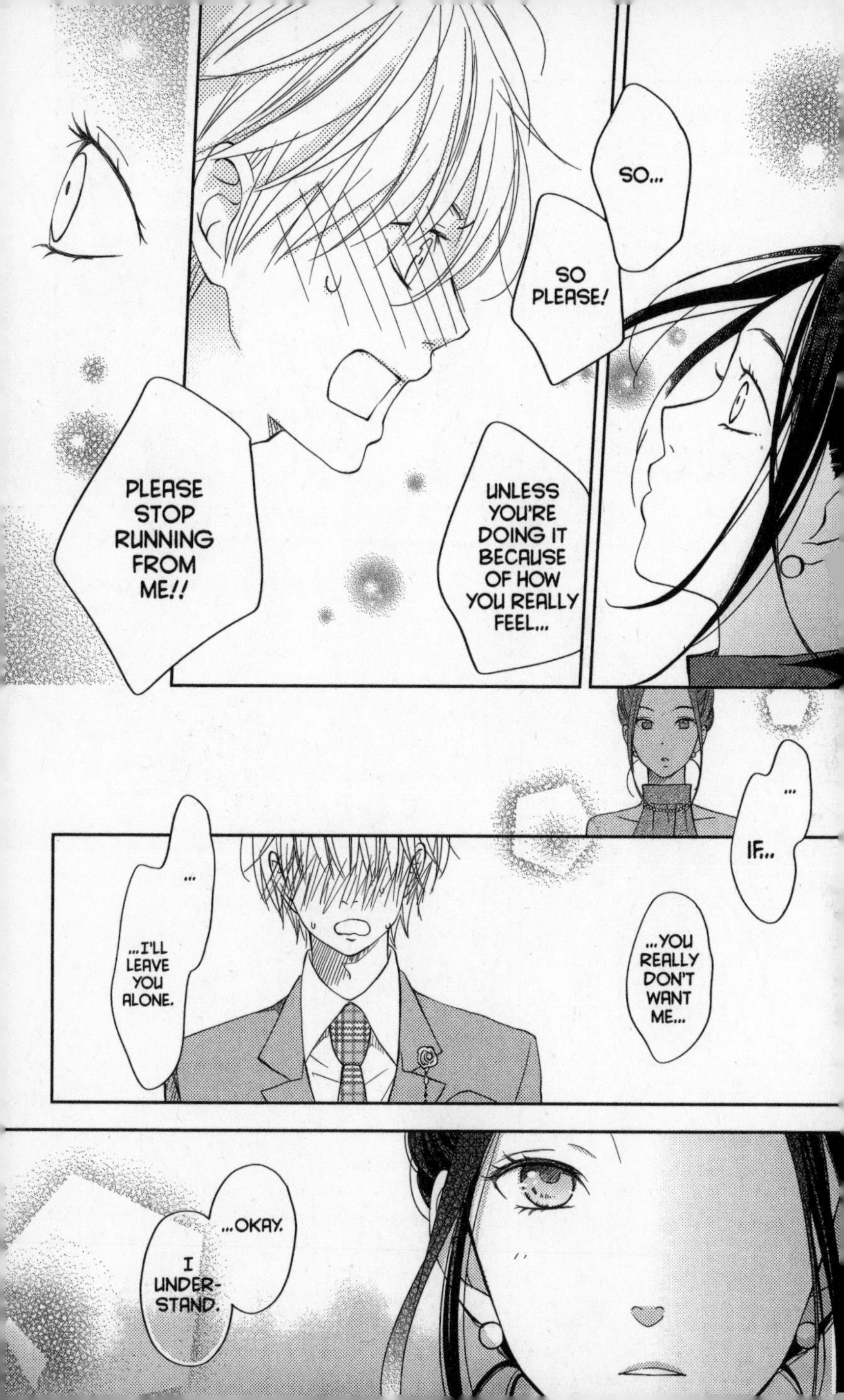
SO...
SO PLEASE!
UNLESS YOU'RE DOING IT BECAUSE OF HOW YOU REALLY FEEL...
PLEASE STOP RUNNING FROM ME!!
...
IF...
...YOU REALLY DON'T WANT ME...
...
...I'LL LEAVE YOU ALONE.
...OKAY.
I UNDER-STAND.

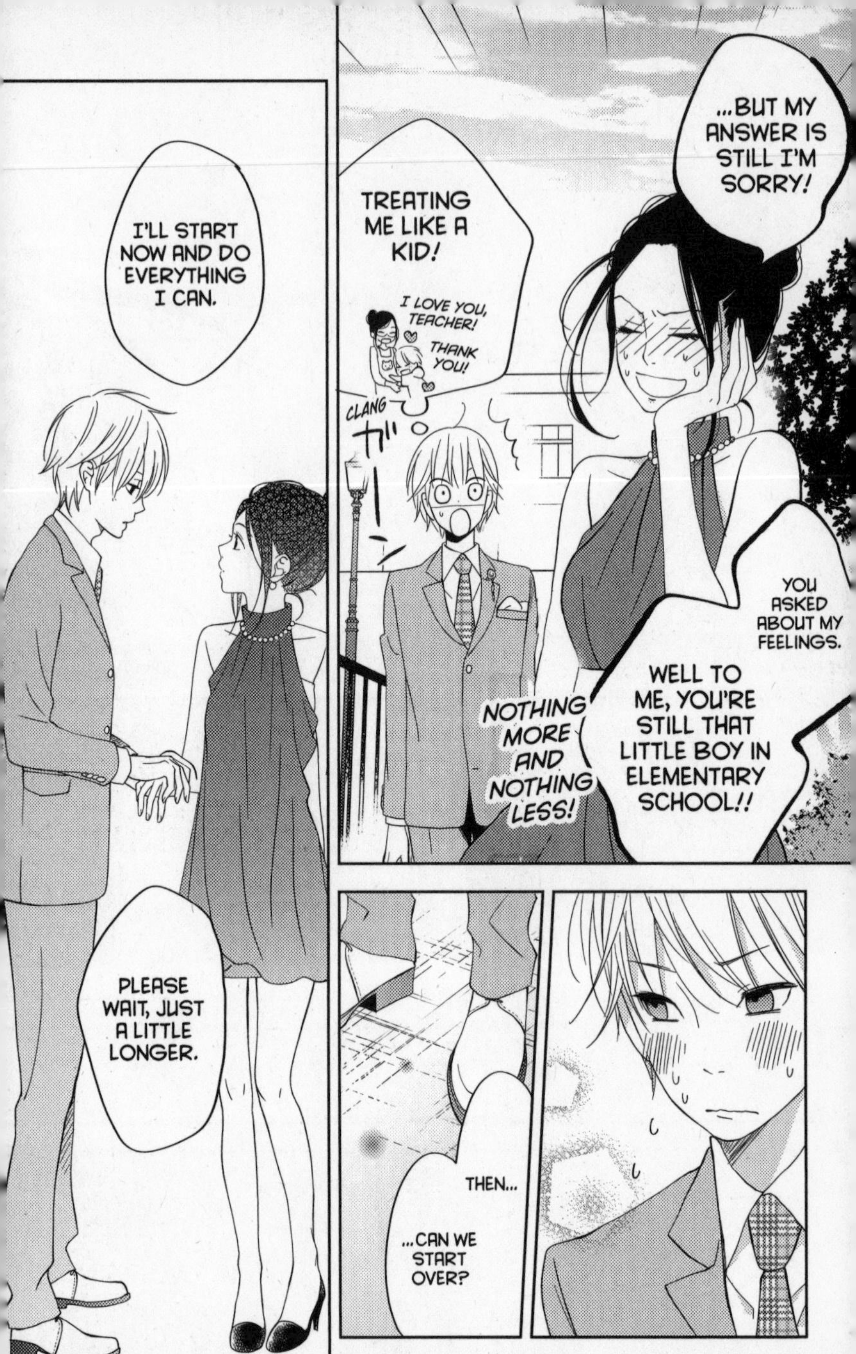
...BUT MY ANSWER IS STILL I'M SORRY!
YOU ASKED ABOUT MY FEELINGS.
WELL TO ME, YOU'RE STILL THAT LITTLE BOY IN ELEMENTARY SCHOOL!!
NOTHING MORE AND NOTHING LESS!
TREATING ME LIKE A KID!
I LOVE YOU, TEACHER!
THANK YOU!
CLANG
THEN...
...CAN WE START OVER?
I'LL START NOW AND DO EVERYTHING I CAN.
PLEASE WAIT, JUST A LITTLE LONGER.

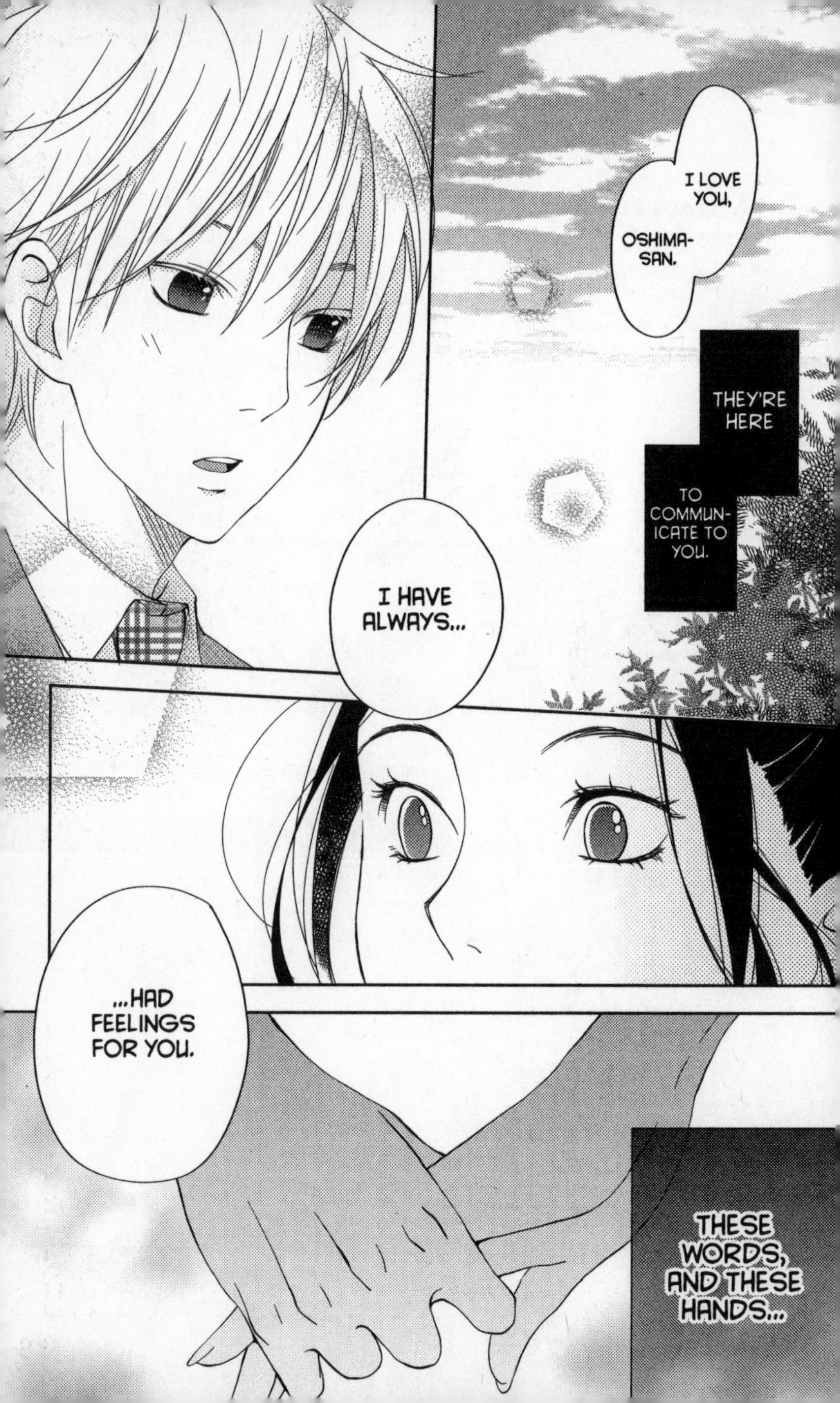
I LOVE YOU,
OSHIMA-SAN.
THEY'RE HERE
TO COMMUNICATE TO YOU.
I HAVE ALWAYS...
...HAD FEELINGS FOR YOU.
THESE WORDS, AND THESE HANDS...

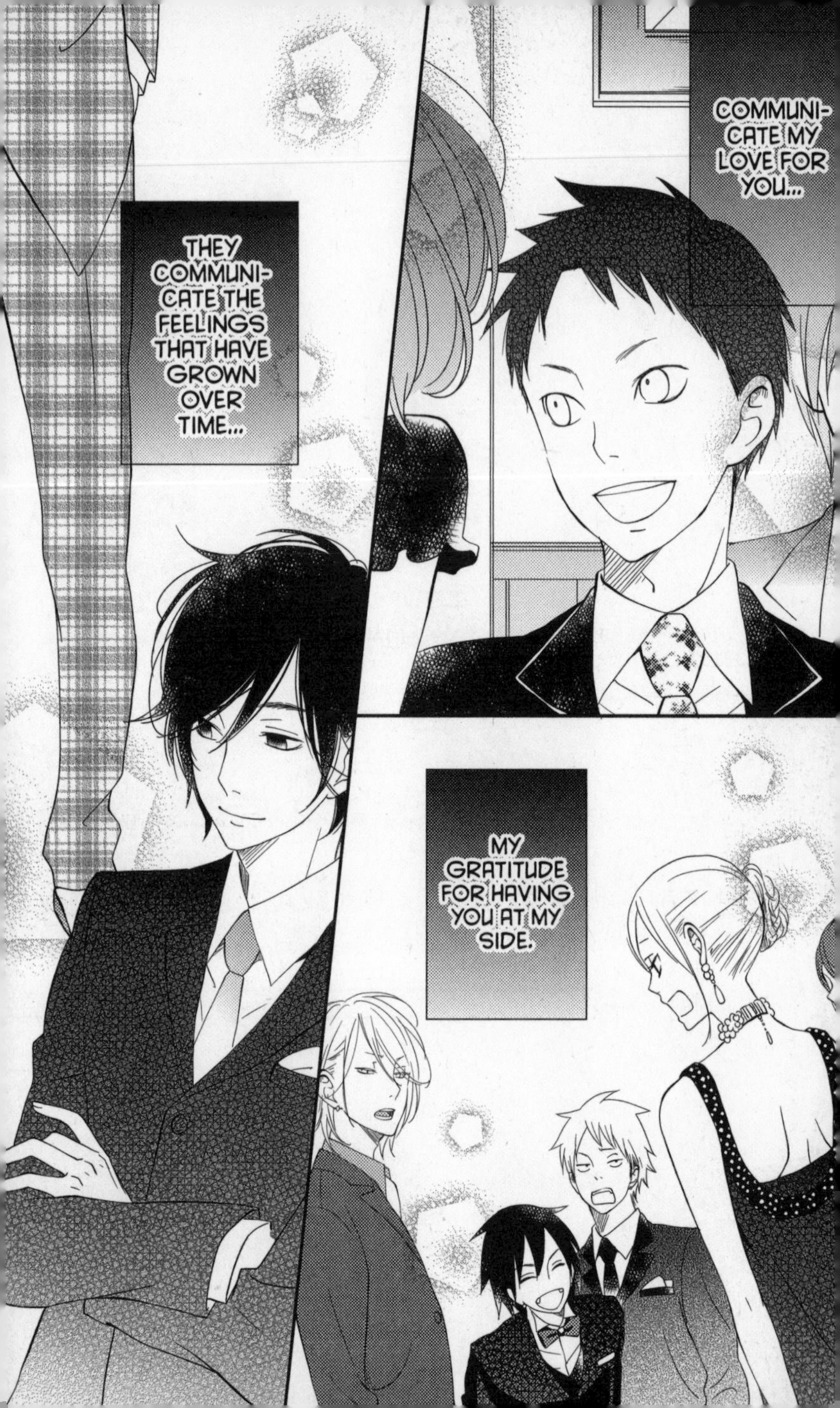
COMMUNI-CATE MY LOVE FOR YOU...
MY GRATITUDE FOR HAVING YOU AT MY SIDE.
THEY COMMUNI-CATE THE FEELINGS THAT HAVE GROWN OVER TIME...

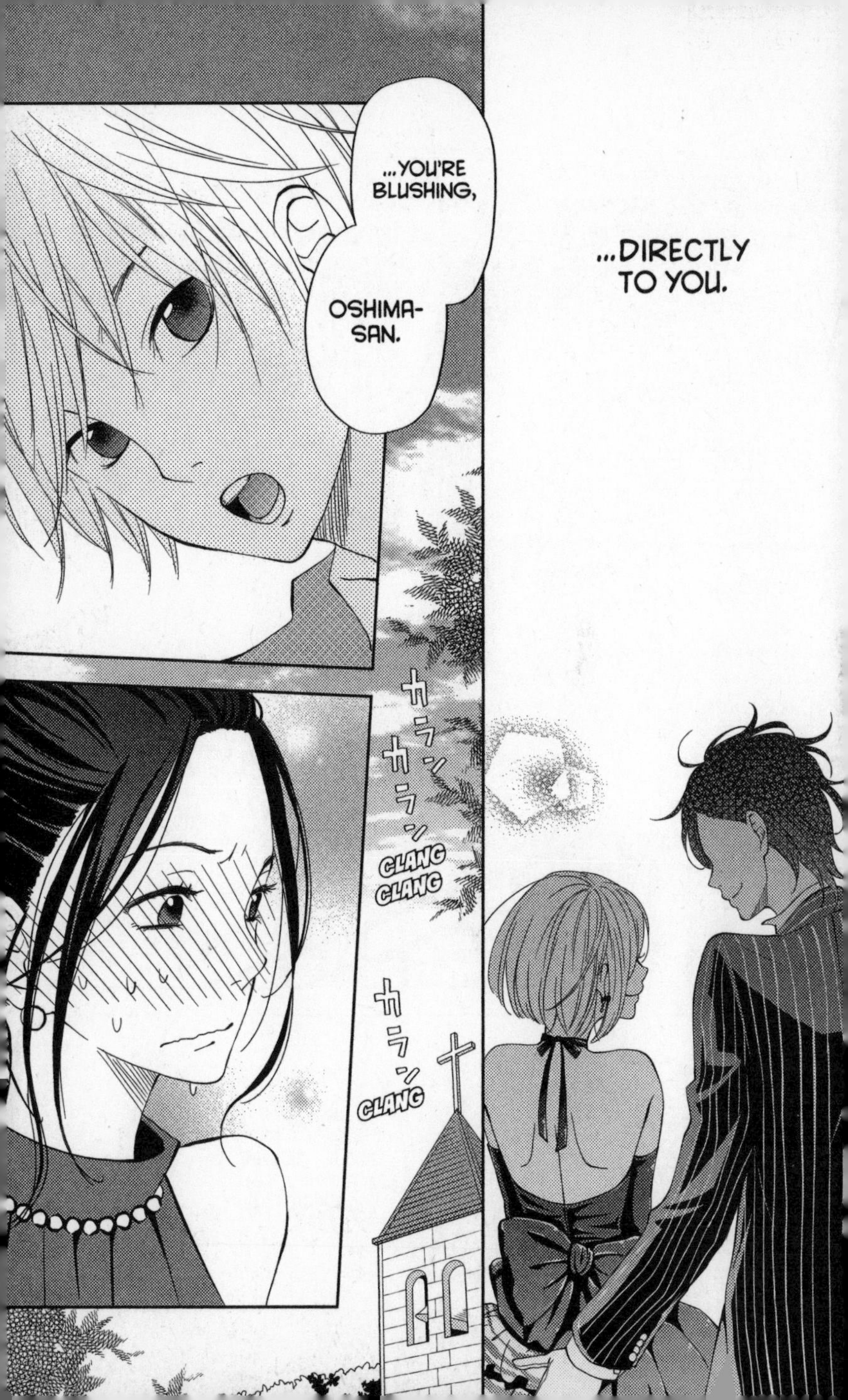
...DIRECTLY TO YOU.
...YOU'RE BLUSHING,
OSHIMA-SAN.
カランカラン
CLANG CLANG
カラン
CLANG

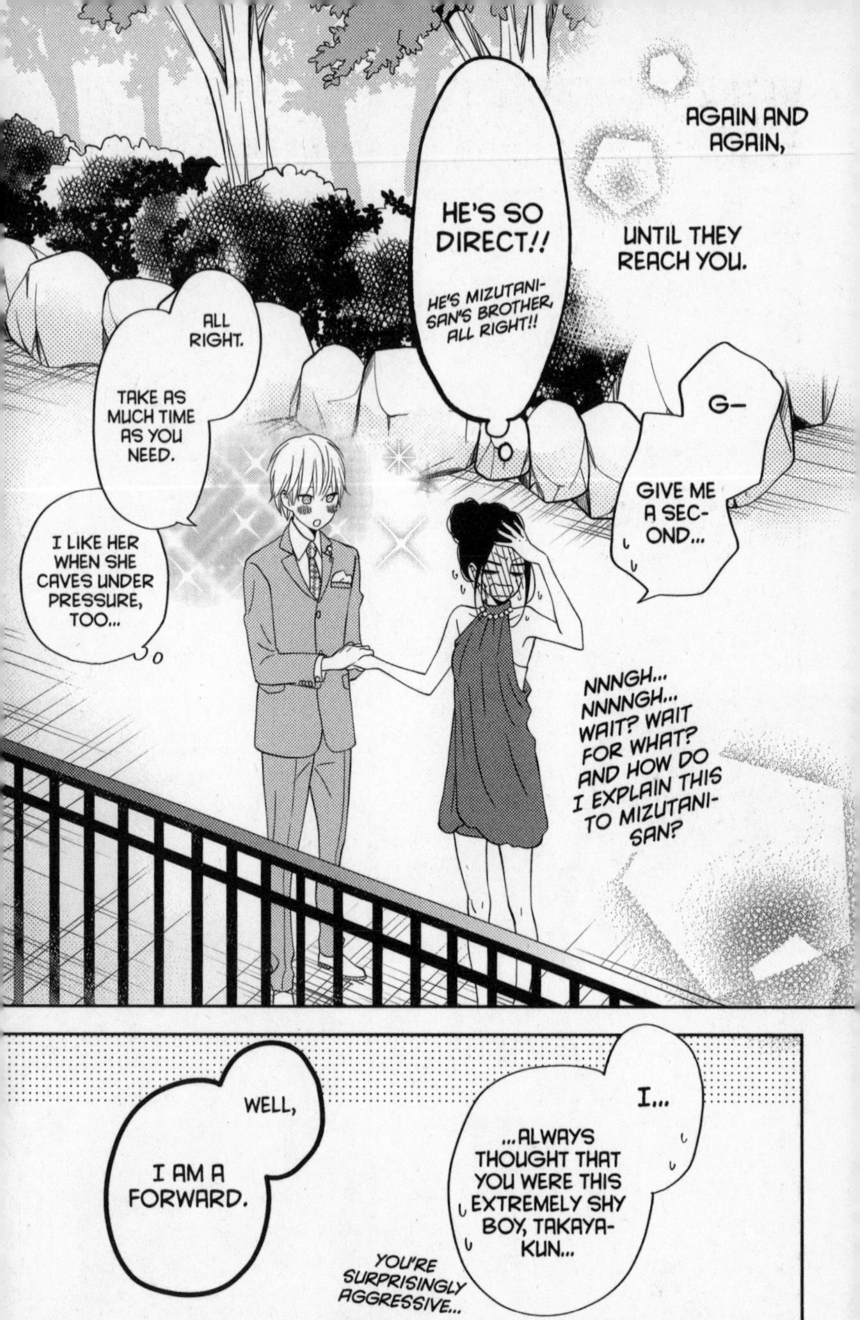
AGAIN AND AGAIN,
UNTIL THEY REACH YOU.
HE'S SO DIRECT!!
HE'S MIZUTANI-SAN'S BROTHER, ALL RIGHT!!
G—
GIVE ME A SEC-OND...
NNNGH... NNNNGH... WAIT? WAIT FOR WHAT? AND HOW DO I EXPLAIN THIS TO MIZUTANI-SAN?
ALL RIGHT.
TAKE AS MUCH TIME AS YOU NEED.
I LIKE HER WHEN SHE CAVES UNDER PRESSURE, TOO...
I...
...ALWAYS THOUGHT THAT YOU WERE THIS EXTREMELY SHY BOY, TAKAYA-KUN...
YOU'RE SURPRISINGLY AGGRESSIVE...
WELL,
I AM A FORWARD.

THE END

THE RECEPTION

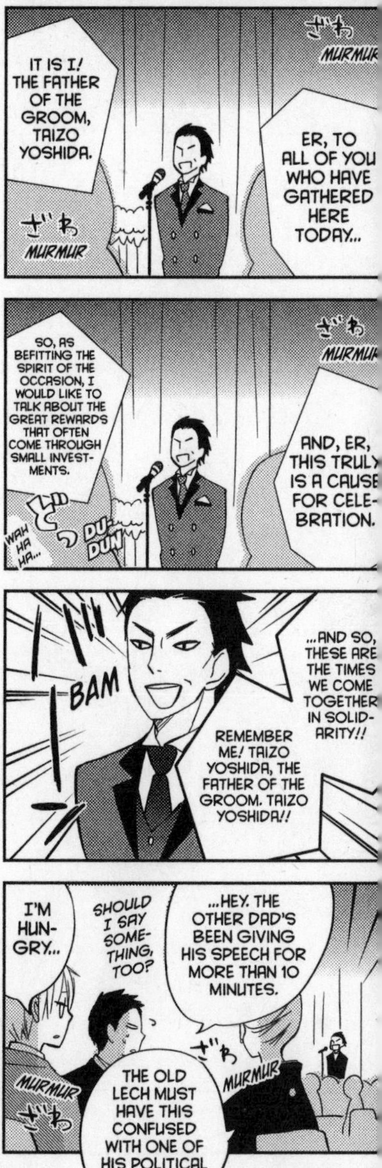
MURMUR
ER, TO ALL OF YOU WHO HAVE GATHERED HERE TODAY...
IT IS I! THE FATHER OF THE GROOM, TAIZO YOSHIDA.
MURMUR
MURMUR
AND, ER, THIS TRULY IS A CAUSE FOR CELEBRATION.
SO, AS BEFITTING THE SPIRIT OF THE OCCASION, I WOULD LIKE TO TALK ABOUT THE GREAT REWARDS THAT OFTEN COME THROUGH SMALL INVESTMENTS.
DU-DUN
WAH HA HA...
...AND SO, THESE ARE THE TIMES WE COME TOGETHER IN SOLIDARITY!!
REMEMBER ME! TAIZO YOSHIDA, THE FATHER OF THE GROOM. TAIZO YOSHIDA!!
BAM
...HEY. THE OTHER DAD'S BEEN GIVING HIS SPEECH FOR MORE THAN 10 MINUTES.
SHOULD I SAY SOMETHING, TOO?
I'M HUNGRY...
MURMUR
THE OLD LECH MUST HAVE THIS CONFUSED WITH ONE OF HIS POLITICAL RALLIES.
MURMUR

ENTER THE HAPPY COUPLE

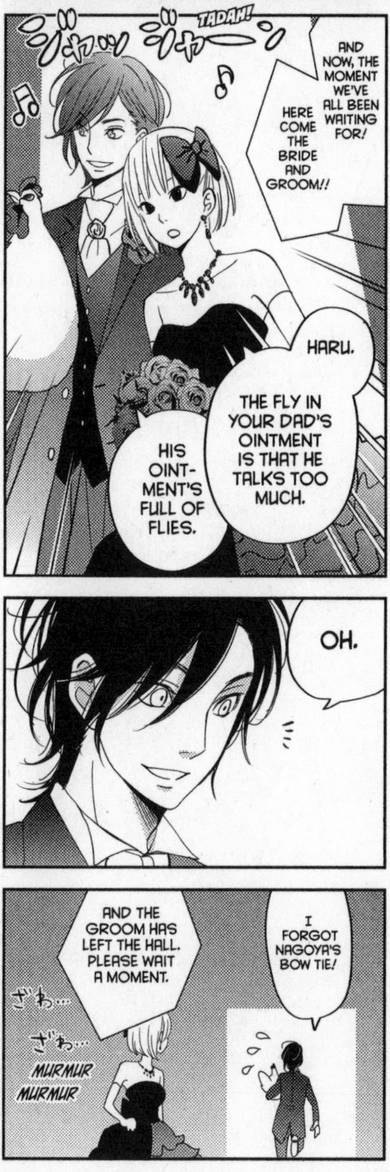
TADAH!
AND NOW, THE MOMENT WE'VE ALL BEEN WAITING FOR!
HERE COME THE BRIDE AND GROOM!!
HARU.
THE FLY IN YOUR DAD'S OINTMENT IS THAT HE TALKS TOO MUCH.
HIS OINTMENT'S FULL OF FLIES.
OH.
I FORGOT NAGOYA'S BOW TIE!
AND THE GROOM HAS LEFT THE HALL. PLEASE WAIT A MOMENT.
MURMUR
MURMUR

SPEECH

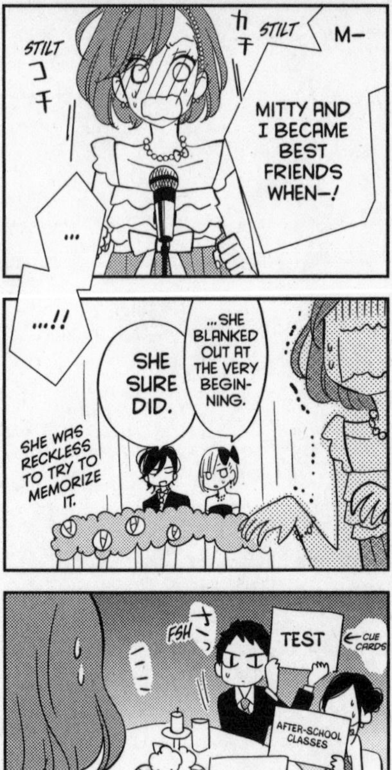
M—
STILT
カチ
MITTY AND I BECAME BEST FRIENDS WHEN—!
STILT
コチ
...
...SHE BLANKED OUT AT THE VERY BEGIN-NING.
SHE SURE DID.
...!!
SHE WAS RECKLESS TO TRY TO MEMORIZE IT.
←CUE CARDS
TEST
FSH
さっ
AFTER-SCHOOL CLASSES
FAIL
...BE-CAUSE
I WAS TOO STUPID!!
DU-DUN
どっ
AFTER THAT, SHE POWERED THROUGH WITH IMPROV-ISATION.

TAKAYA

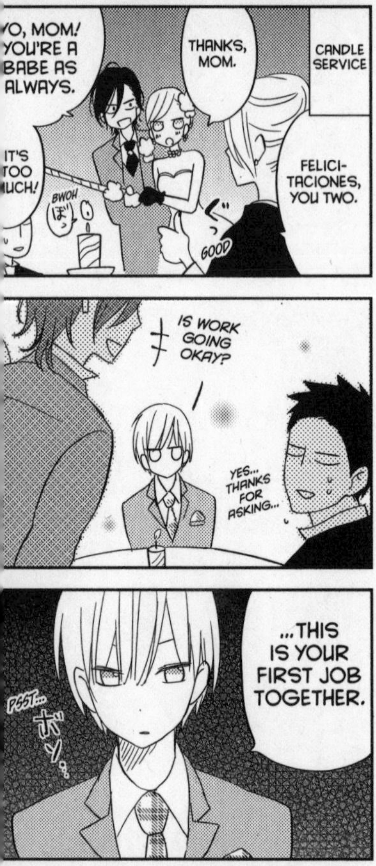
CANDLE SERVICE
FELICI-TACIONES, YOU TWO.
GOOD
ぐっ
THANKS, MOM.
O, MOM! YOU'RE A BABE AS ALWAYS.
IT'S TOO UCH!
BWOH
ぼっ
IS WORK GOING OKAY?
キ
YES... THANKS FOR ASKING...
...THIS IS YOUR FIRST JOB TOGETHER.
PSST...
ボソ...
IT'S BURNING HOT AND HEAVY... GETTING READY FOR LATER TONIGHT.
WHAT DID YOU SAY, TAKAYA? I COULDN'T HEAR IT.

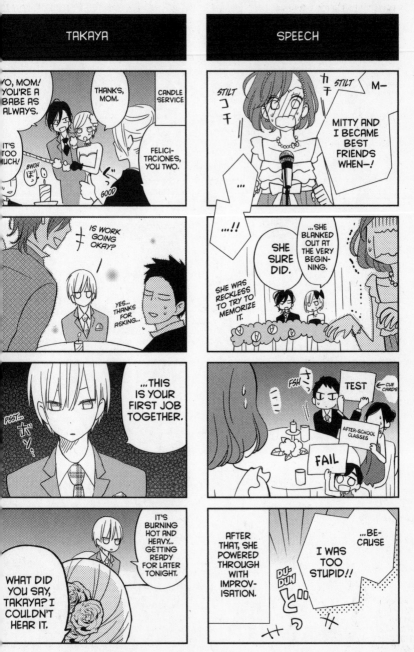

★END-OF-THE-VOLUME BONUS MANGA★ "FIFTH PARTY OF THE DAY: THEY CAN DRINK BECAUSE THEY'RE PAST 20"

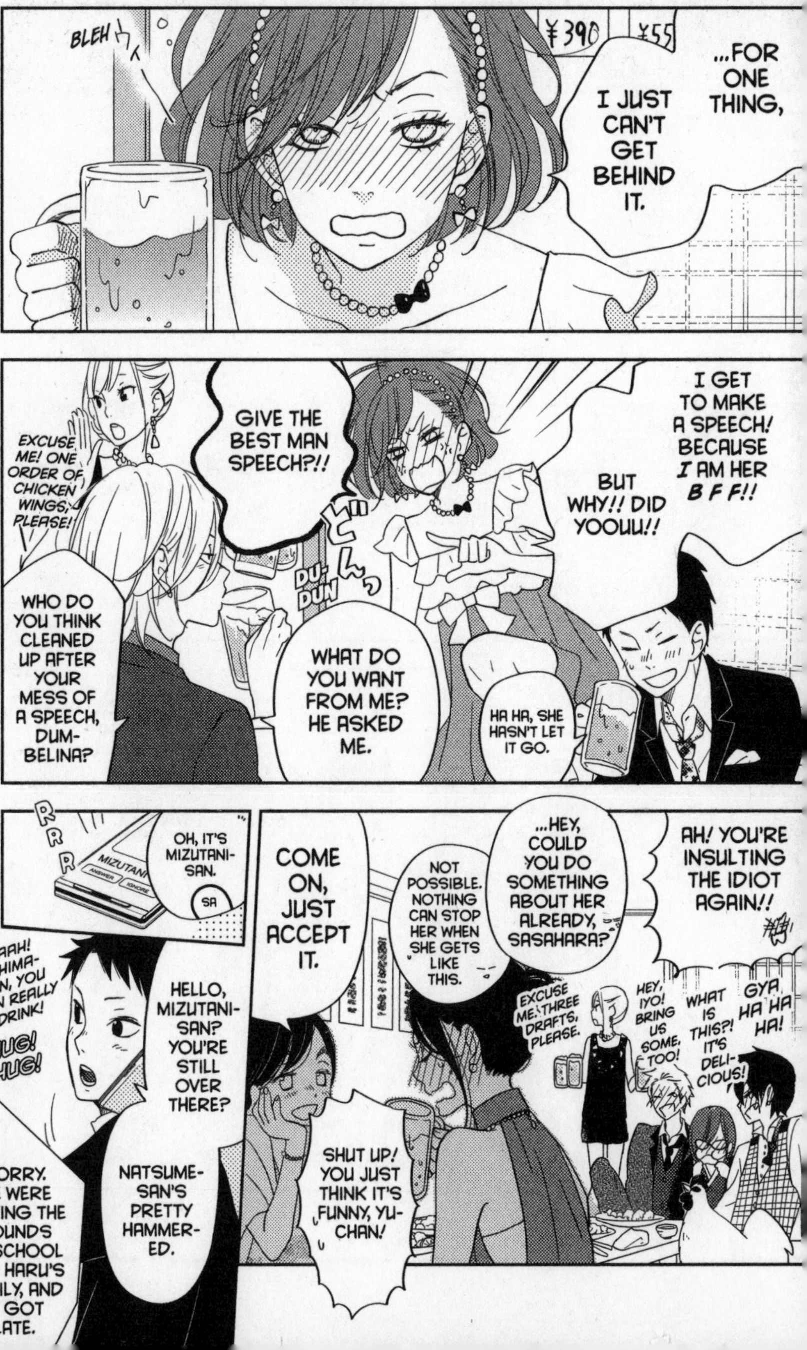

...FOR ONE THING,
I JUST CAN'T GET BEHIND IT.
¥55
¥390
BLEH
I GET TO MAKE A SPEECH! BECAUSE I AM HER BFF!!
BUT WHY!! DID YOOUU!!
GIVE THE BEST MAN SPEECH?!!
EXCUSE ME! ONE ORDER OF CHICKEN WINGS, PLEASE!
DU-DUN
HA HA, SHE HASN'T LET IT GO.
WHAT DO YOU WANT FROM ME? HE ASKED ME.
WHO DO YOU THINK CLEANED UP AFTER YOUR MESS OF A SPEECH, DUM-BELINA?
AH! YOU'RE INSULTING THE IDIOT AGAIN!!
...HEY, COULD YOU DO SOMETHING ABOUT HER ALREADY, SASAHARA?
NOT POSSIBLE. NOTHING CAN STOP HER WHEN SHE GETS LIKE THIS.
COME ON, JUST ACCEPT IT.
GYA HA HA HA!
WHAT IS THIS?! IT'S DELICIOUS!
HEY, IYO! BRING US SOME, TOO!
EXCUSE ME. THREE DRAFTS, PLEASE.
SHUT UP! YOU JUST THINK IT'S FUNNY, YU-CHAN!
R R R
MIZUTANI
ANSWER
IGNORE
OH, IT'S MIZUTANI-SAN.
SA
HELLO, MIZUTANI-SAN? YOU'RE STILL OVER THERE?
AAAAH! OSHIMA-SAN, YOU CAN REALLY DRINK!
CHUG! CHUG!
NATSUME-SAN'S PRETTY HAMMER-ED.
SORRY. WE WERE MAKING THE ROUNDS AT SCHOOL AND HARU'S FAMILY, AND IT GOT LATE.

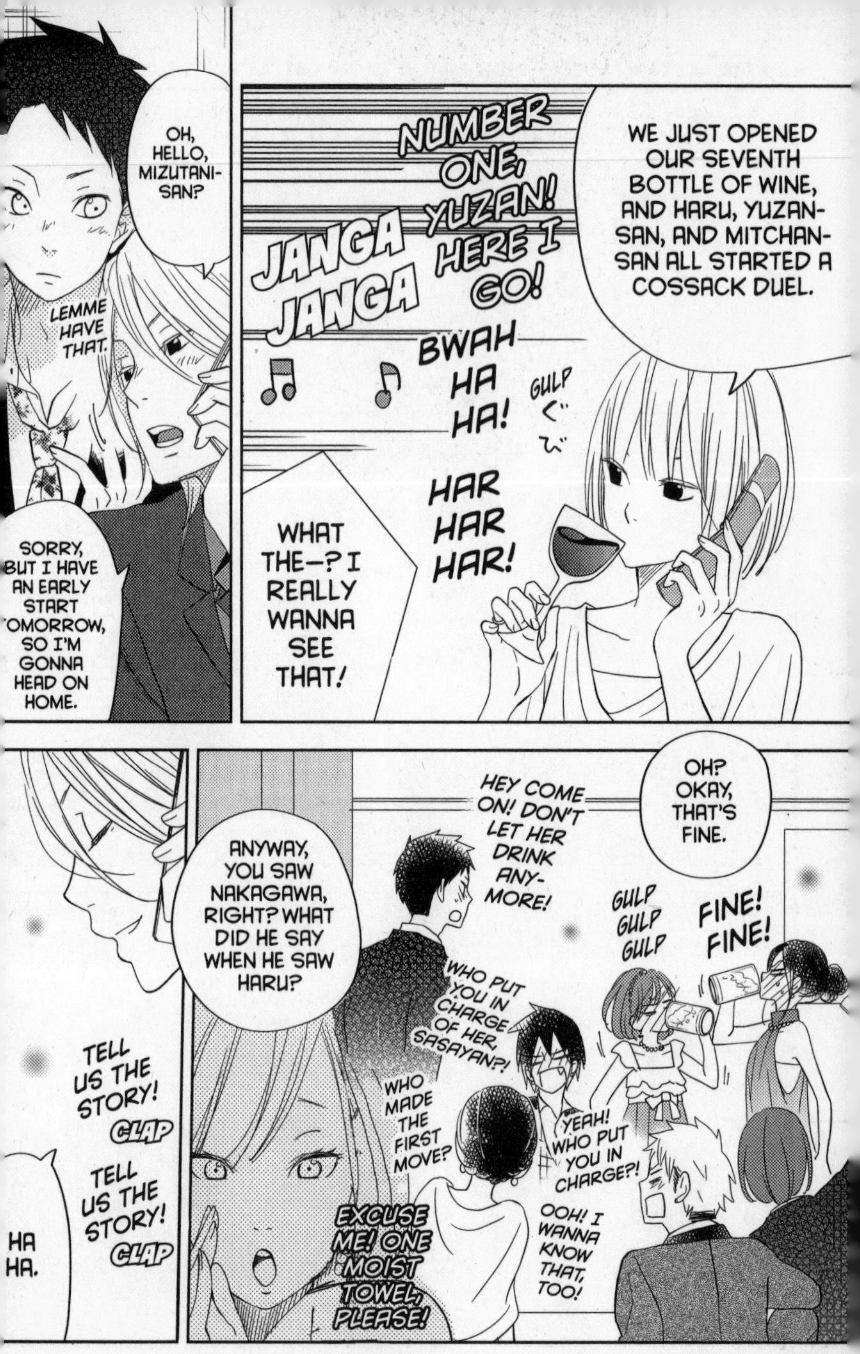
WE JUST OPENED OUR SEVENTH BOTTLE OF WINE, AND HARU, YUZAN-SAN, AND MITCHAN-SAN ALL STARTED A COSSACK DUEL.
NUMBER ONE, YUZAN! HERE I GO!
JANGA JANGA
BWAH HA HA!
GULP ぐび
HAR HAR HAR!
WHAT THE—? I REALLY WANNA SEE THAT!
OH, HELLO, MIZUTANI-SAN?
LEMME HAVE THAT.
SORRY, BUT I HAVE AN EARLY START TOMORROW, SO I'M GONNA HEAD ON HOME.
OH? OKAY, THAT'S FINE.
HEY COME ON! DON'T LET HER DRINK ANYMORE!
FINE! FINE!
GULP GULP GULP
WHO PUT YOU IN CHARGE OF HER, SASAYAN?!
YEAH! WHO PUT YOU IN CHARGE?!
OOH! I WANNA KNOW THAT, TOO!
WHO MADE THE FIRST MOVE?
ANYWAY, YOU SAW NAKAGAWA, RIGHT? WHAT DID HE SAY WHEN HE SAW HARU?
EXCUSE ME! ONE MOIST TOWEL, PLEASE!
TELL US THE STORY! CLAP
TELL US THE STORY! CLAP
HA HA.

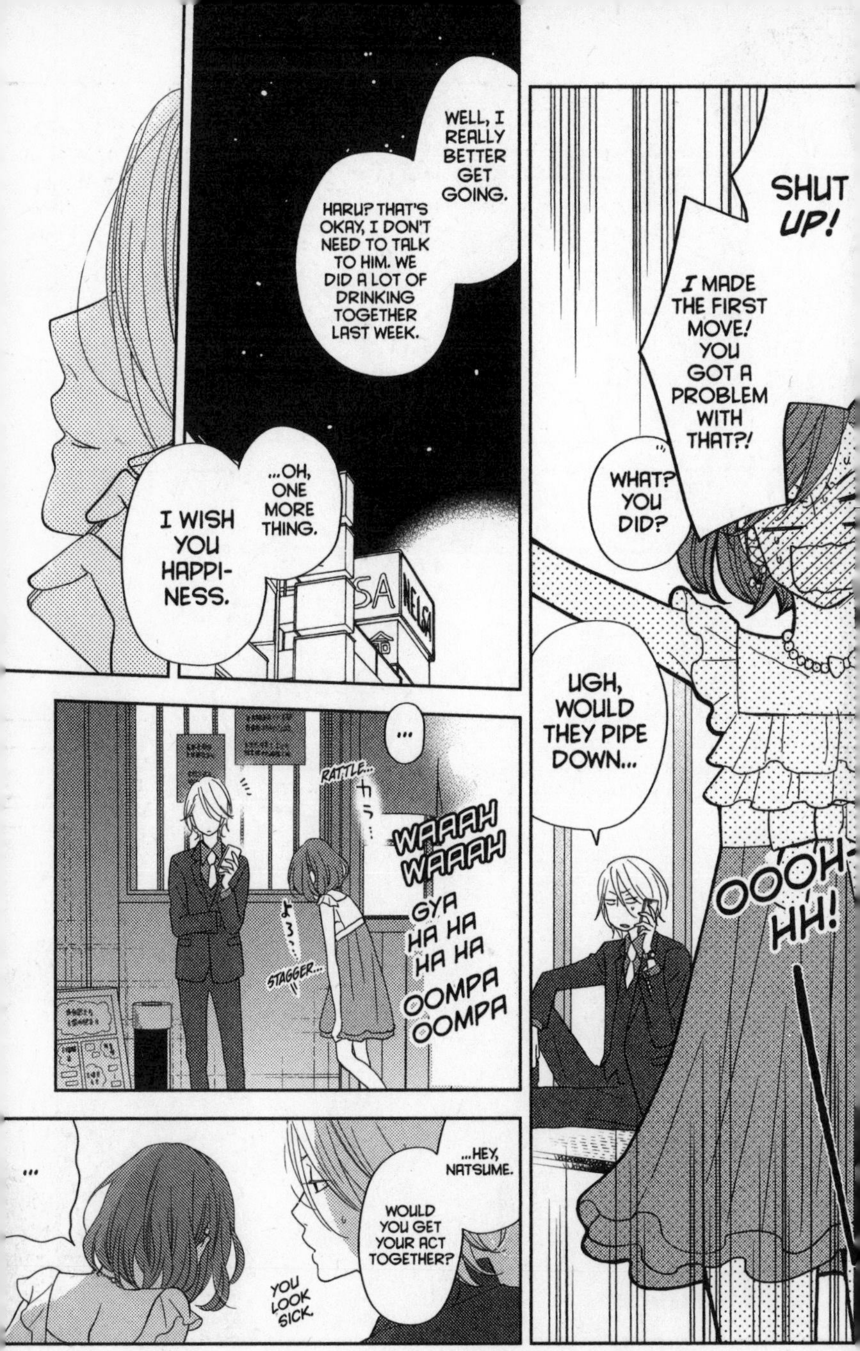
SHUT UP!
I MADE THE FIRST MOVE! YOU GOT A PROBLEM WITH THAT?!
WHAT? YOU DID?
UGH, WOULD THEY PIPE DOWN...
OOOH-HH!
WELL, I REALLY BETTER GET GOING.
HARU? THAT'S OKAY, I DON'T NEED TO TALK TO HIM. WE DID A LOT OF DRINKING TOGETHER LAST WEEK.
...OH, ONE MORE THING.
I WISH YOU HAPPINESS.
SA
MELSA
...
RATTLE...
カラ...
WAAAH WAAAH
GYA HA HA HA HA
OOMPA OOMPA
よろ...
STAGGER...
...HEY, NATSUME.
WOULD YOU GET YOUR ACT TOGETHER?
YOU LOOK SICK.
...

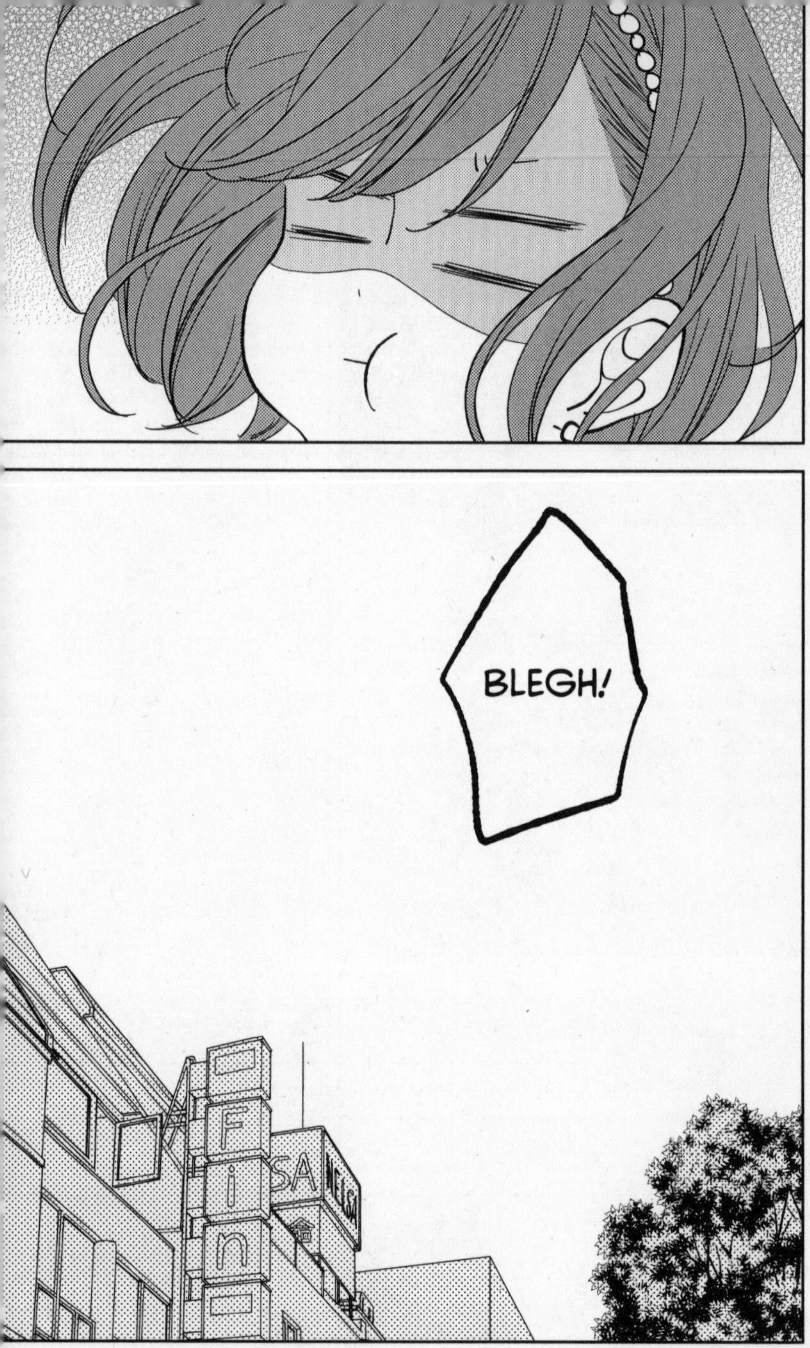
BLEGH!

Translation Notes

Japanese is a tricky language for most Westerners, and translation is often more art than science. For your edification and reading pleasure, here are notes on some of the places where we could have gone in a different direction in our translation of the work, or where a Japanese cultural reference is used.

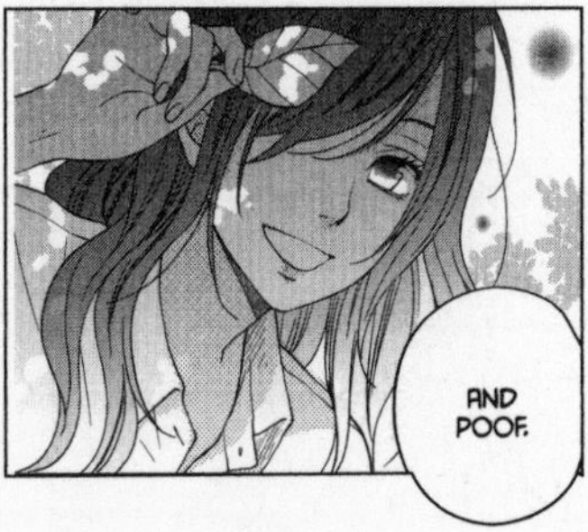
AND POOF.

And poof, page 23
According to Japanese folklore, certain creatures, such as foxes and tanuki, have shape-shifting powers. In order to transform, they'll put a leaf on their head. If the leaf falls off, they change back. "Poof" is a translation of the Japanese sound effect *doron*, which has been used in kabuki plays for centuries as the sound of a ghost or apparition appearing or disappearing, and has come to be the sound effect used when a fox or tanuki transforms.

Kanipan, page 25
With no visual or written context, it's difficult to ascertain what Asako is cackling over. She may be referring to an anime series translated as *Inventor Boy Kanipan*, about a boy who must save his planet from an evil robot clone. On the other hand, kanipan means "crab bread," so she might be talking about bread in the shape of a crab.

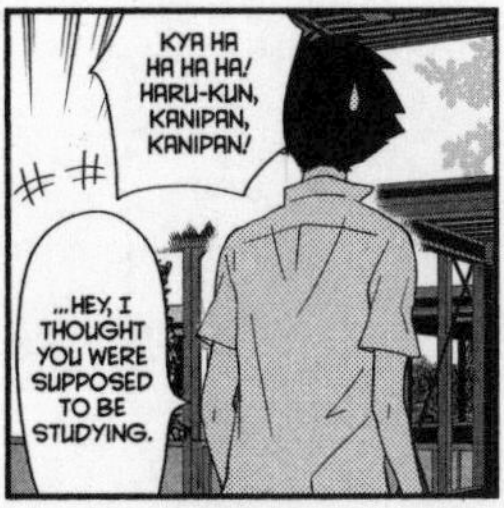
KYA HA HA HA HA! HARU-KUN, KANIPAN, KANIPAN!
...HEY, I THOUGHT YOU WERE SUPPOSED TO BE STUDYING.

The red string of destiny, page 56
The red string of destiny, or red string of fate, is an East Asian belief that originated in China. The idea is that a man and a woman who are destined to be married are tied together by an invisible red string or thread. It's similar to the concept of soul mates.

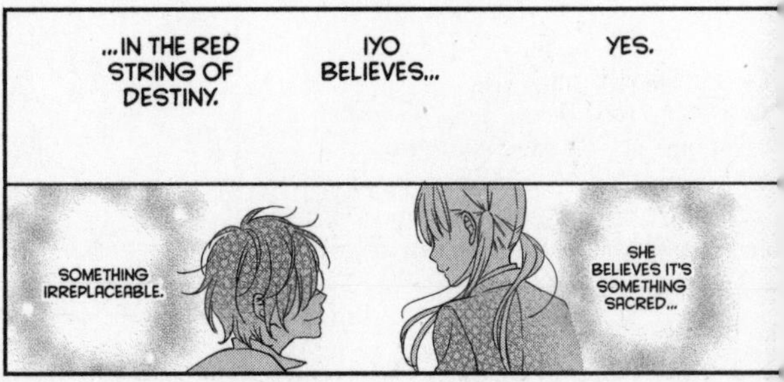
YES.
IYO BELIEVES...
...IN THE RED STRING OF DESTINY.
SHE BELIEVES IT'S SOMETHING SACRED...
SOMETHING IRREPLACEABLE.

"Zundoko-Bushi," page 73

"Zundoko-Bushi" is a Japanese song of unknown origin that has been remade many times over. One popular variation was performed by a rock band/comedy group known as The Drifters. They sang this song as part of a TV sketch comedy show in the 1970s. Iyo's affinity for comedy accounts for her attraction to the song.

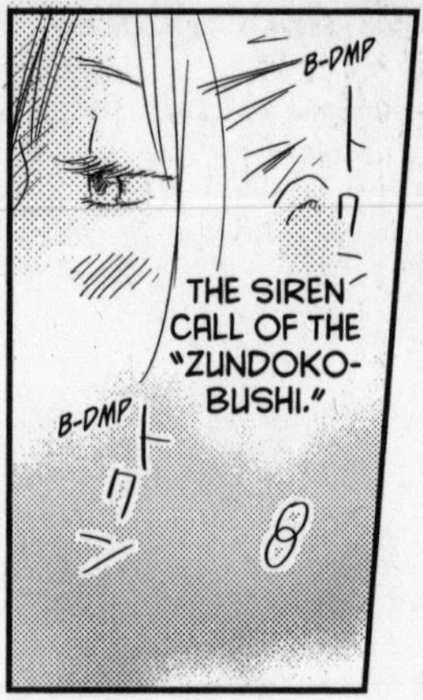
B-DMP
THE SIREN CALL OF THE "ZUNDOKO-BUSHI."
B-DMP

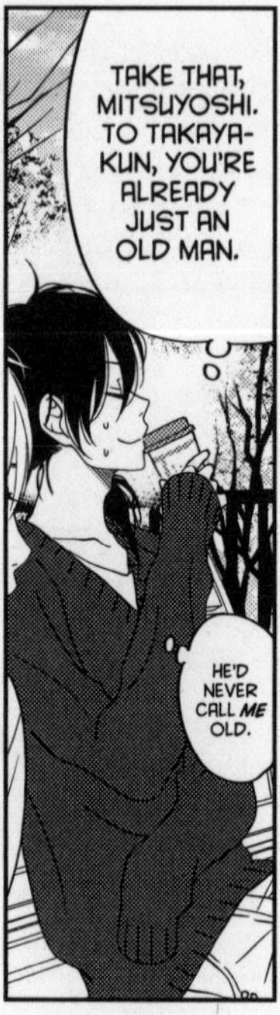
TAKE THAT, MITSUYOSHI. TO TAKAYA-KUN, YOU'RE ALREADY JUST AN OLD MAN.
HE'D NEVER CALL *ME* OLD.

He'd never call me old, page 118

Although Yuzan's theory seems baseless in English, there is a reason for him to believe it. When Takaya first addresses him earlier in this scene, he actually uses the honorific *oniisan*, which literally means "older brother," but is also used as a friendly way of addressing someone older, but not too much older, than the speaker. On the other hand, he calls Mitsuyoshi an *ojisan*, which means "uncle" and is used for addressing middle-aged men.

Candle Service, page 184

Japanese wedding receptions have many traditions, including this one. After the bride and groom have changed into their reception clothes, they will go around to each table, lighting the candle in the center.

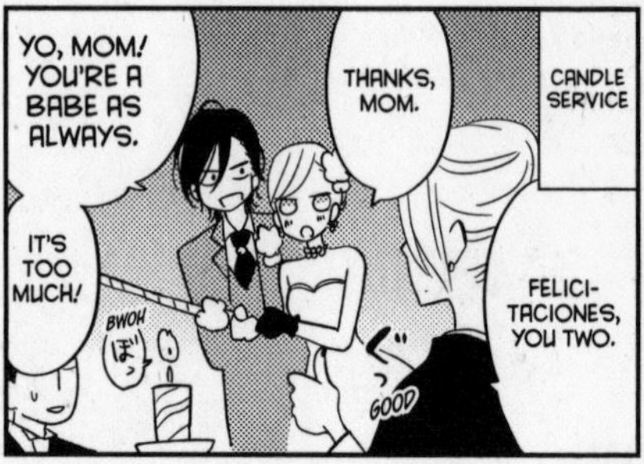
CANDLE SERVICE
FELICI-TACIONES, YOU TWO.
GOOD
THANKS, MOM.
YO, MOM! YOU'RE A BABE AS ALWAYS.
IT'S TOO MUCH!
BWOH

EXTRAS!

My Little Monster

Robico

For the final book of *My Little Monster*, we've included tons of bonus material! Join Haru and his friends on a typical(?) day off, see how the Yamaken gang got together, check out the profiles of your favorite characters (including what Natsume would bring to a desert island!), and more!

This material was published in Japan as part of the *My Little Monster Fan Book*.

FANBOOK EXTRAS!

From *My Little Monster Fan Book*

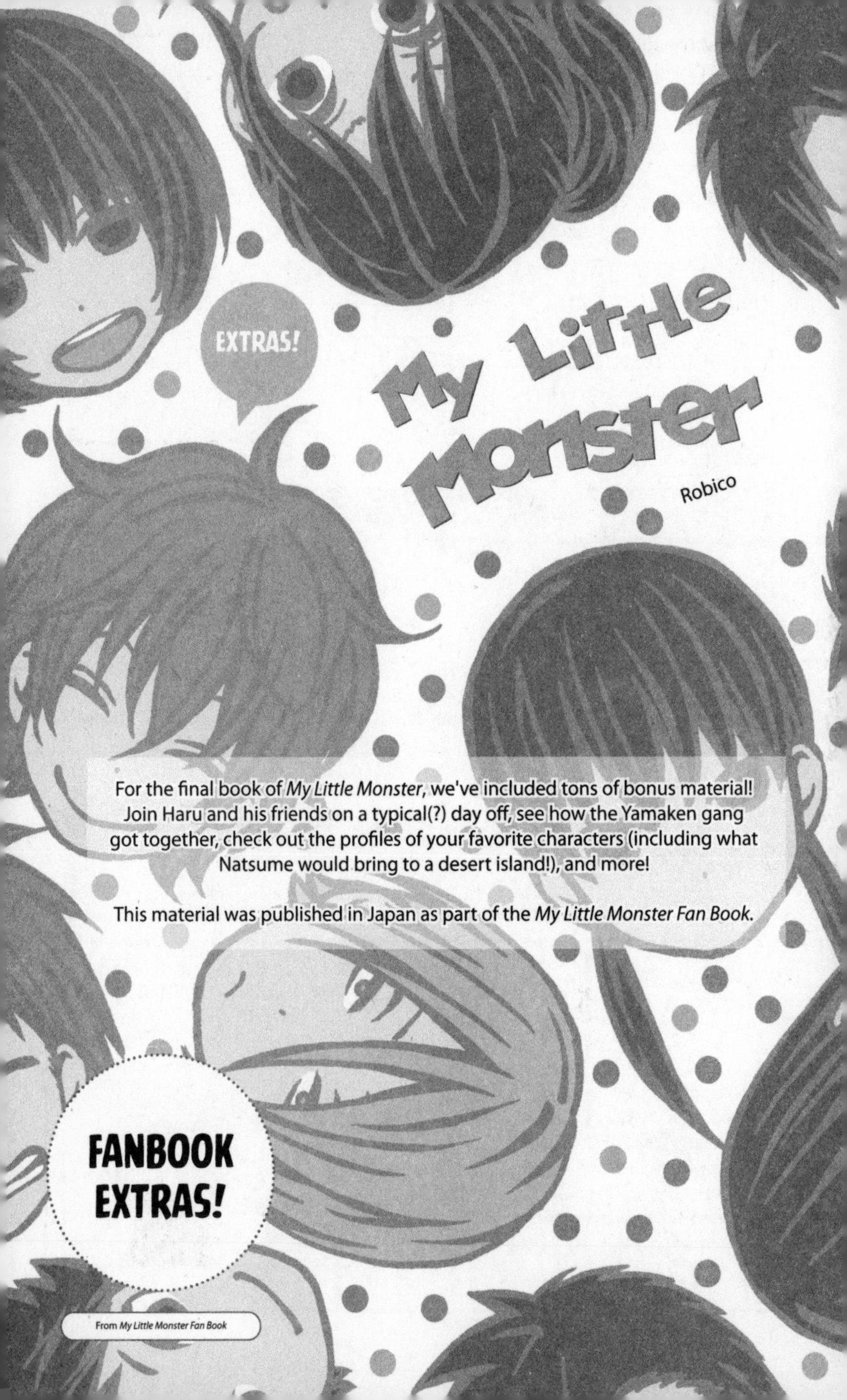

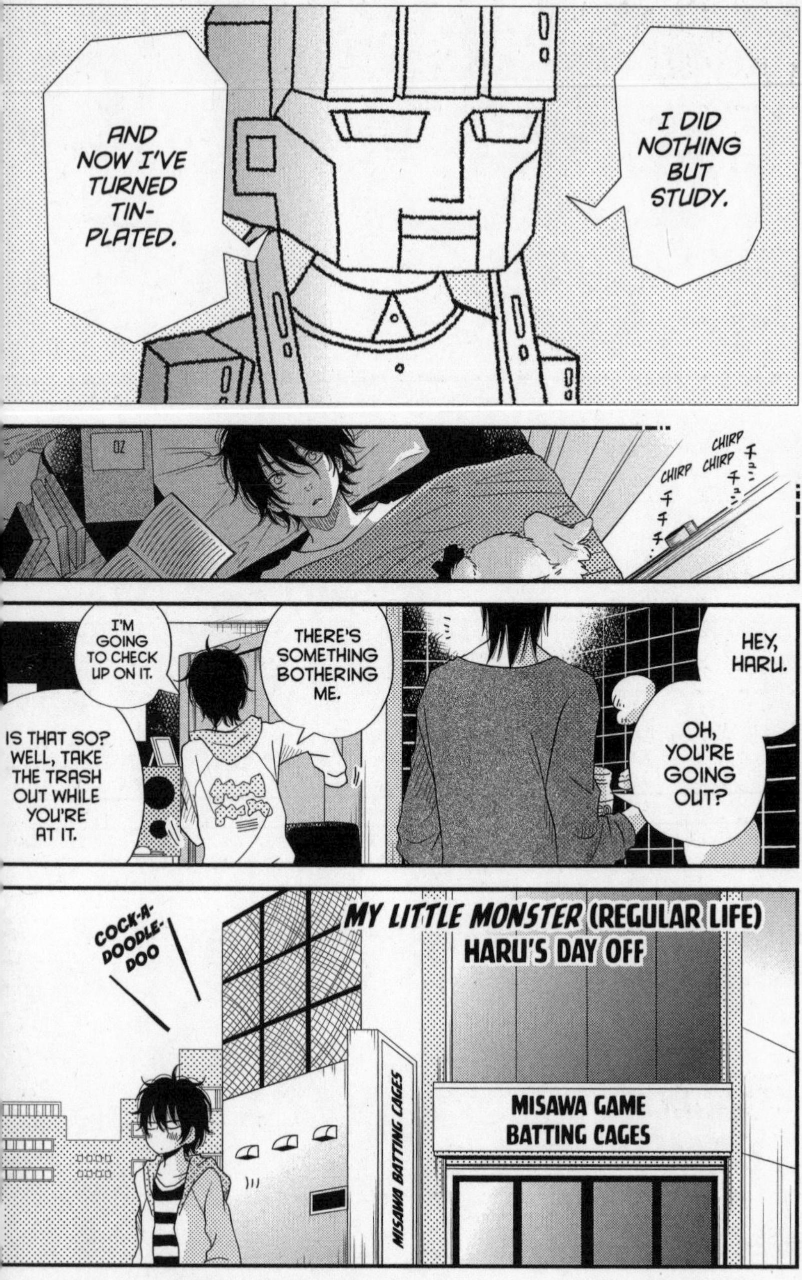
I DID NOTHING BUT STUDY.
AND NOW I'VE TURNED TIN-PLATED.
CHIRP CHIRP
チュンチュン
CHIRP
チチチ…
HEY, HARU.
OH, YOU'RE GOING OUT?
THERE'S SOMETHING BOTHERING ME.
I'M GOING TO CHECK UP ON IT.
IS THAT SO? WELL, TAKE THE TRASH OUT WHILE YOU'RE AT IT.
MY LITTLE MONSTER (REGULAR LIFE)
HARU'S DAY OFF
COCK-A-DOODLE-DOO
MISAWA GAME BATTING CAGES
MISAWA BATTING CAGES

ENCOUNTER WITH NATSUME-SAN

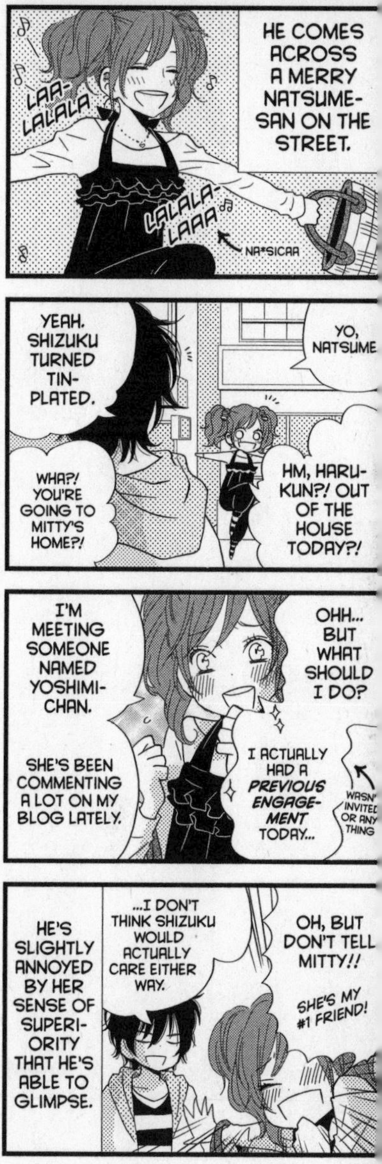
HE COMES ACROSS A MERRY NATSUME-SAN ON THE STREET.
LAA-LALALA
LALALA-LAAA
NA*SICAA
YO, NATSUME
HM, HARU-KUN?! OUT OF THE HOUSE TODAY?!
YEAH. SHIZUKU TURNED TIN-PLATED.
WHA?! YOU'RE GOING TO MITTY'S HOME?!
OHH... BUT WHAT SHOULD I DO?
I'M MEETING SOMEONE NAMED YOSHIMI-CHAN.
I ACTUALLY HAD A PREVIOUS ENGAGEMENT TODAY...
WASN' INVITED OR ANY THING
SHE'S BEEN COMMENTING A LOT ON MY BLOG LATELY.
OH, BUT DON'T TELL MITTY!!
SHE'S MY #1 FRIEND!
...I DON'T THINK SHIZUKU WOULD ACTUALLY CARE EITHER WAY.
HE'S SLIGHTLY ANNOYED BY HER SENSE OF SUPERIORITY THAT HE'S ABLE TO GLIMPSE.

EXPLANATION

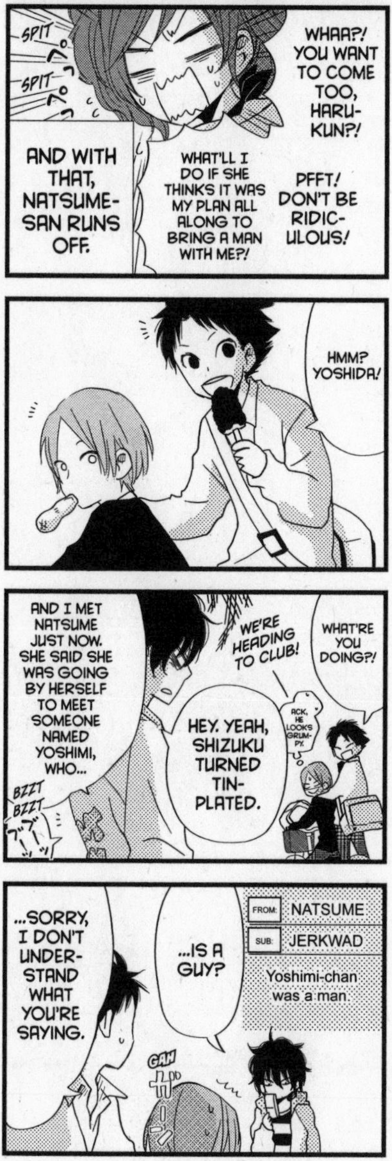
WHAA?! YOU WANT TO COME TOO, HARU-KUN?!
PFFT! DON'T BE RIDICULOUS!
WHAT'LL I DO IF SHE THINKS IT WAS MY PLAN ALL ALONG TO BRING A MAN WITH ME?!
SPIT
SPIT
AND WITH THAT, NATSUME-SAN RUNS OFF.
HMM? YOSHIDA!
WHAT'RE YOU DOING?!
WE'RE HEADING TO CLUB!
ACK, HE LOOKS GRUMPY.
HEY. YEAH, SHIZUKU TURNED TIN-PLATED.
AND I MET NATSUME JUST NOW. SHE SAID SHE WAS GOING BY HERSELF TO MEET SOMEONE NAMED YOSHIMI, WHO...
BZZT BZZT
FROM: NATSUME
SUB: JERKWAD
Yoshimi-chan was a man.
...IS A GUY?
...SORRY, I DON'T UNDERSTAND WHAT YOU'RE SAYING.
GAH

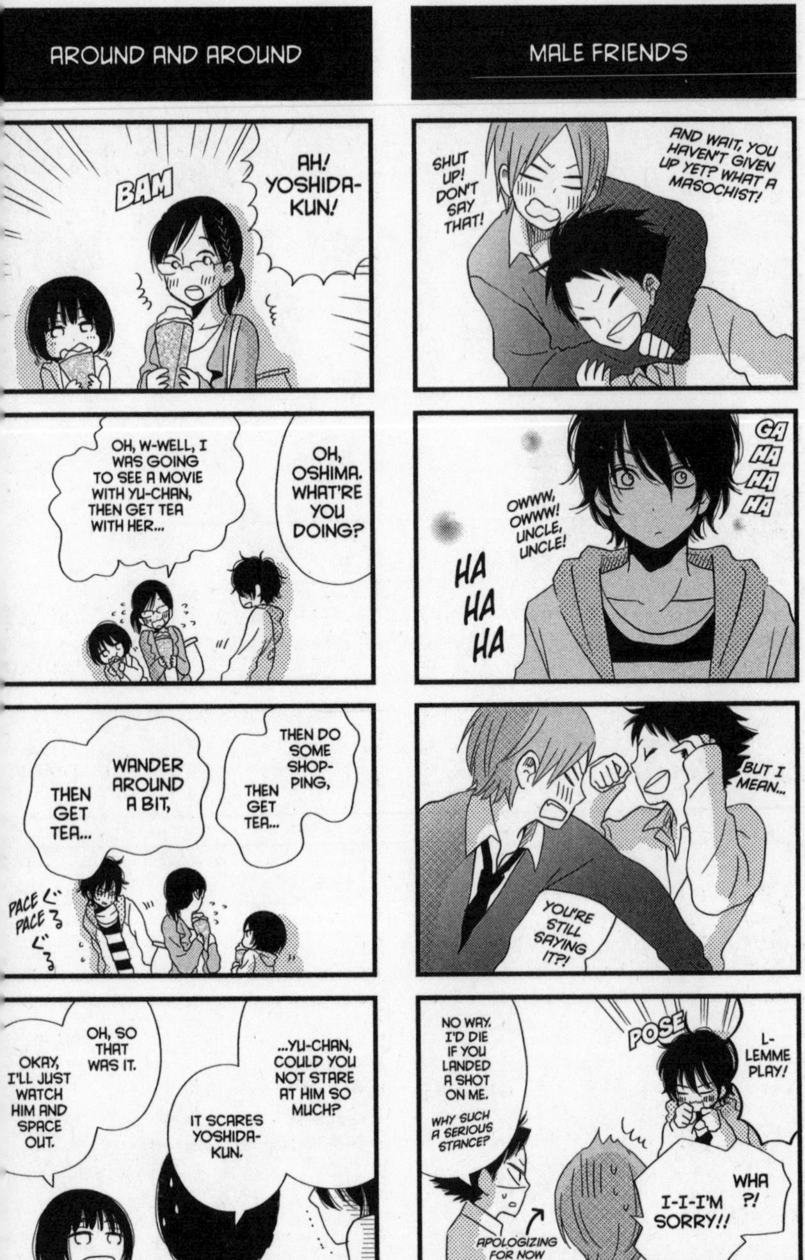
MALE FRIENDS
AND WAIT, YOU HAVEN'T GIVEN UP YET? WHAT A MASOCHIST!
SHUT UP! DON'T SAY THAT!
GA HA HA HA
OWWW, OWWW! UNCLE, UNCLE!
HA HA HA
BUT I MEAN...
YOU'RE STILL SAYING IT?!
L-LEMME PLAY!
POSE
NO WAY. I'D DIE IF YOU LANDED A SHOT ON ME.
WHY SUCH A SERIOUS STANCE?
WHA?!
I-I-I'M SORRY!!
APOLOGIZING FOR NOW
AROUND AND AROUND
AH! YOSHIDA-KUN!
BAM
OH, OSHIMA. WHAT'RE YOU DOING?
OH, W-WELL, I WAS GOING TO SEE A MOVIE WITH YU-CHAN, THEN GET TEA WITH HER...
THEN DO SOME SHOPPING, THEN GET TEA...
WANDER AROUND A BIT, THEN GET TEA...
PACE PACE
ぐるぐる
...YU-CHAN, COULD YOU NOT STARE AT HIM SO MUCH?
IT SCARES YOSHIDA-KUN.
OH, SO THAT WAS IT.
OKAY, I'LL JUST WATCH HIM AND SPACE OUT.

NEXT UP...

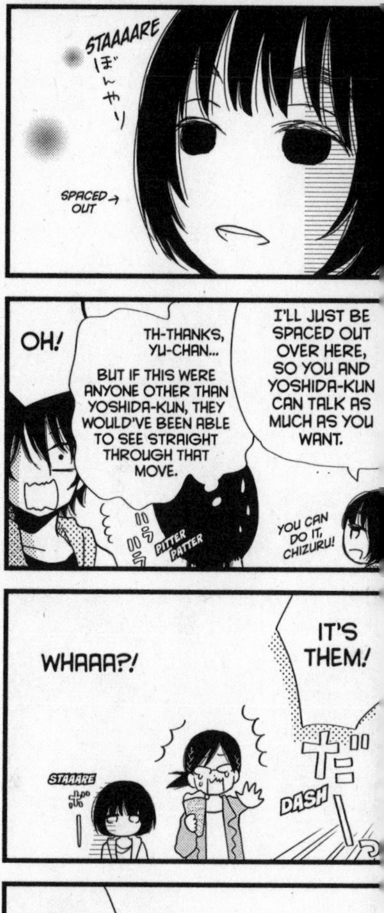
STAAAARE
ぼんやり
SPACED OUT
I'LL JUST BE SPACED OUT OVER HERE, SO YOU AND YOSHIDA-KUN CAN TALK AS MUCH AS YOU WANT.
TH-THANKS, YU-CHAN...
BUT IF THIS WERE ANYONE OTHER THAN YOSHIDA-KUN, THEY WOULD'VE BEEN ABLE TO SEE STRAIGHT THROUGH THAT MOVE.
OH!
YOU CAN DO IT, CHIZURU!
PITTER PATTER
IT'S THEM!
DASH
WHAAA?!
STAAARE
...
YOU'RE NOT SUPPOSED TO BE SPACED OUT, TOO.
STAAARE

TOP FIGHTER

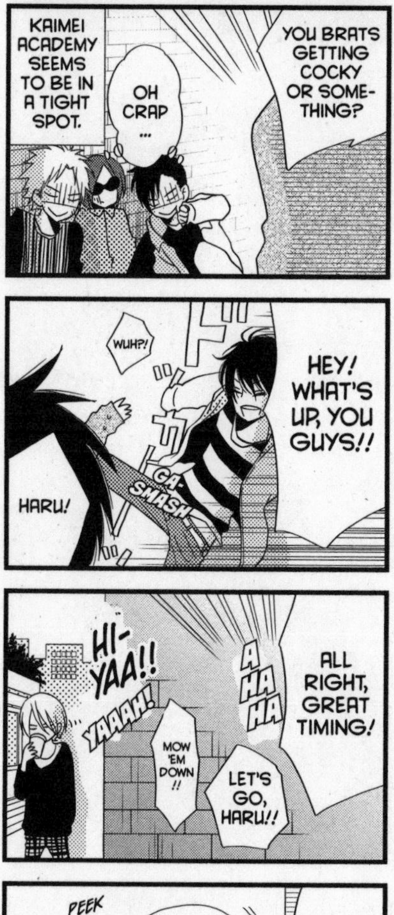
YOU BRATS GETTING COCKY OR SOME-THING?
OH CRAP ...
KAIMEI ACADEMY SEEMS TO BE IN A TIGHT SPOT.
HEY! WHAT'S UP, YOU GUYS!!
WUH?!
GA-SMASH
HARU!
ALL RIGHT, GREAT TIMING!
AHAHA
LET'S GO, HARU!!
MOW 'EM DOWN!!
HI-YAA!!
YAAAH!
YOU DONE?
PEEK ひょい
YOU USE-LESS PUNK!!

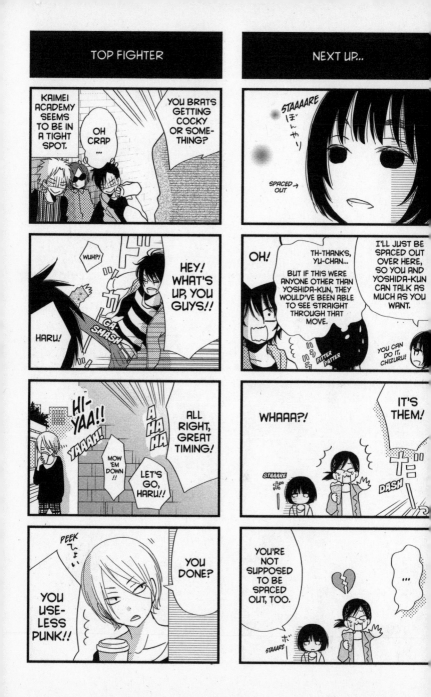

MALE FRIENDS 2

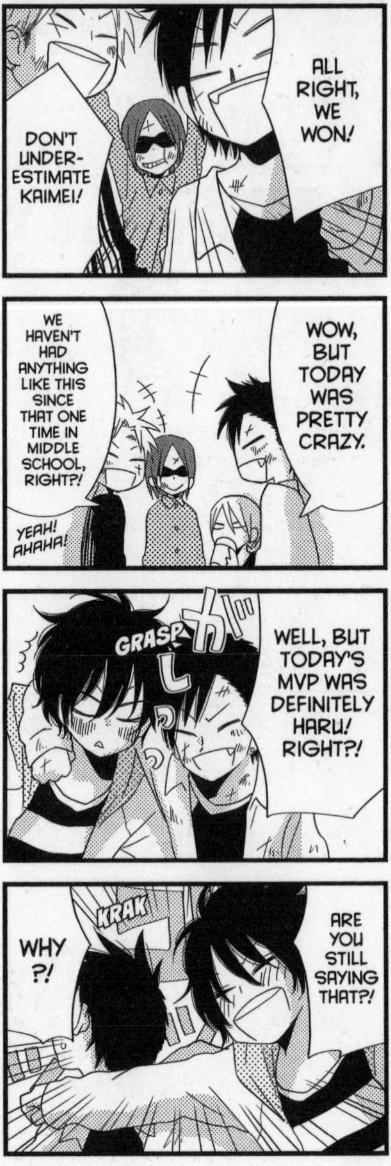
ALL RIGHT, WE WON!
DON'T UNDER-ESTIMATE KAIMEI!
WOW, BUT TODAY WAS PRETTY CRAZY.
WE HAVEN'T HAD ANYTHING LIKE THIS SINCE THAT ONE TIME IN MIDDLE SCHOOL, RIGHT?!
YEAH! AHAHA!
WELL, BUT TODAY'S MVP WAS DEFINITELY HARU! RIGHT?!
GRASP
ARE YOU STILL SAYING THAT?!
KRAK
WHY?!

REASONS

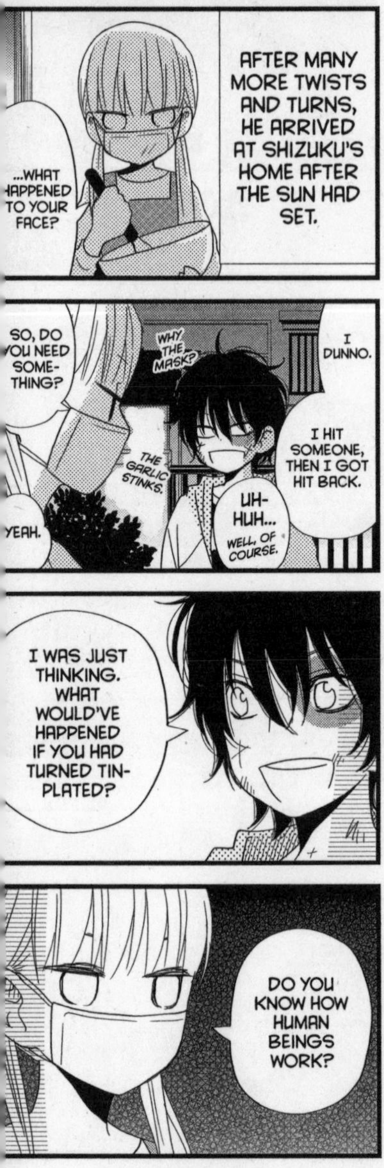
AFTER MANY MORE TWISTS AND TURNS, HE ARRIVED AT SHIZUKU'S HOME AFTER THE SUN HAD SET.
...WHAT HAPPENED TO YOUR FACE?
I DUNNO.
WHY THE MASK?
SO, DO YOU NEED SOMETHING?
I HIT SOMEONE, THEN I GOT HIT BACK.
UH-HUH...
WELL, OF COURSE.
THE GARLIC STINKS.
YEAH.
I WAS JUST THINKING. WHAT WOULD'VE HAPPENED IF YOU HAD TURNED TIN-PLATED?
DO YOU KNOW HOW HUMAN BEINGS WORK?

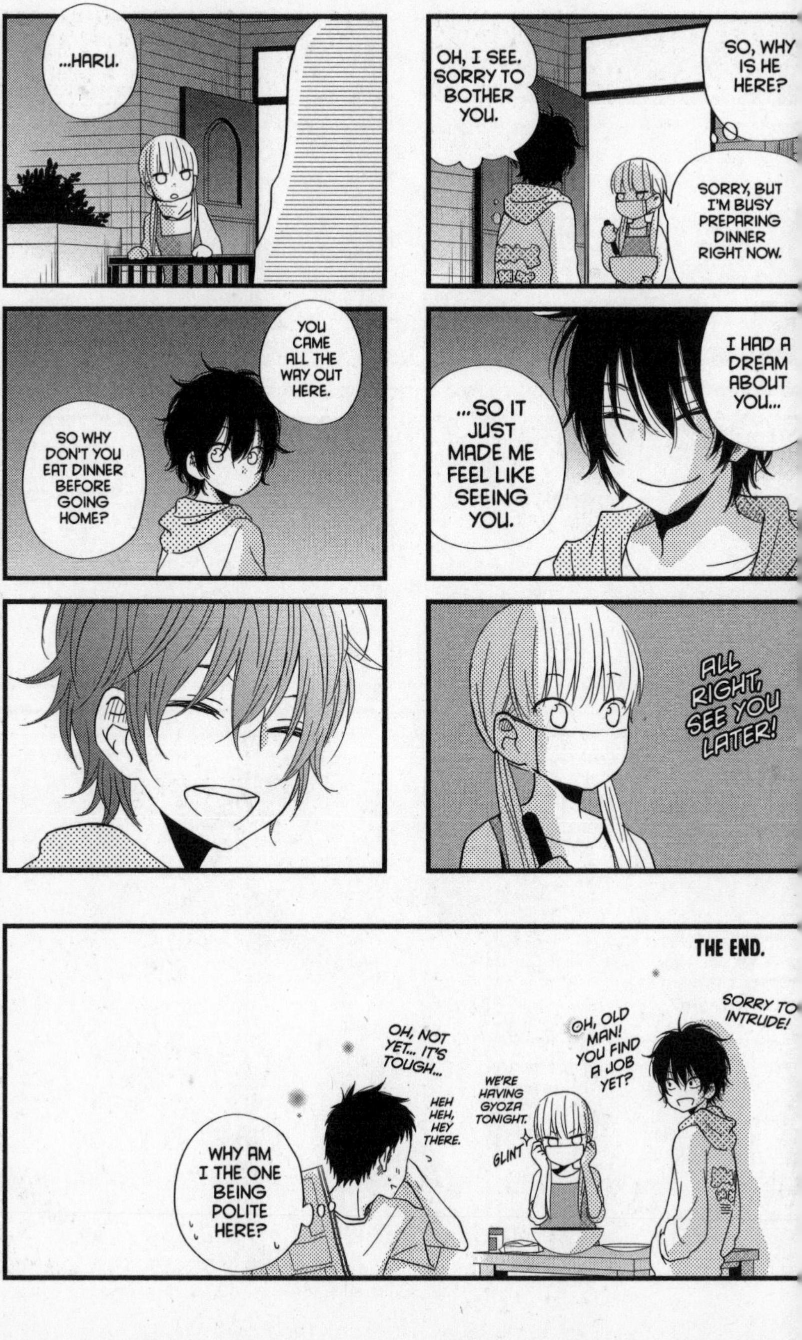
SO, WHY IS HE HERE?
SORRY, BUT I'M BUSY PREPARING DINNER RIGHT NOW.
OH, I SEE. SORRY TO BOTHER YOU.
...HARU.
I HAD A DREAM ABOUT YOU...
...SO IT JUST MADE ME FEEL LIKE SEEING YOU.
YOU CAME ALL THE WAY OUT HERE.
SO WHY DON'T YOU EAT DINNER BEFORE GOING HOME?
ALL RIGHT, SEE YOU LATER!
THE END.
SORRY TO INTRUDE!
OH, OLD MAN! YOU FIND A JOB YET?
WE'RE HAVING GYOZA TONIGHT.
GLINT
OH, NOT YET... IT'S TOUGH...
HEH HEH, HEY THERE.
WHY AM I THE ONE BEING POLITE HERE?

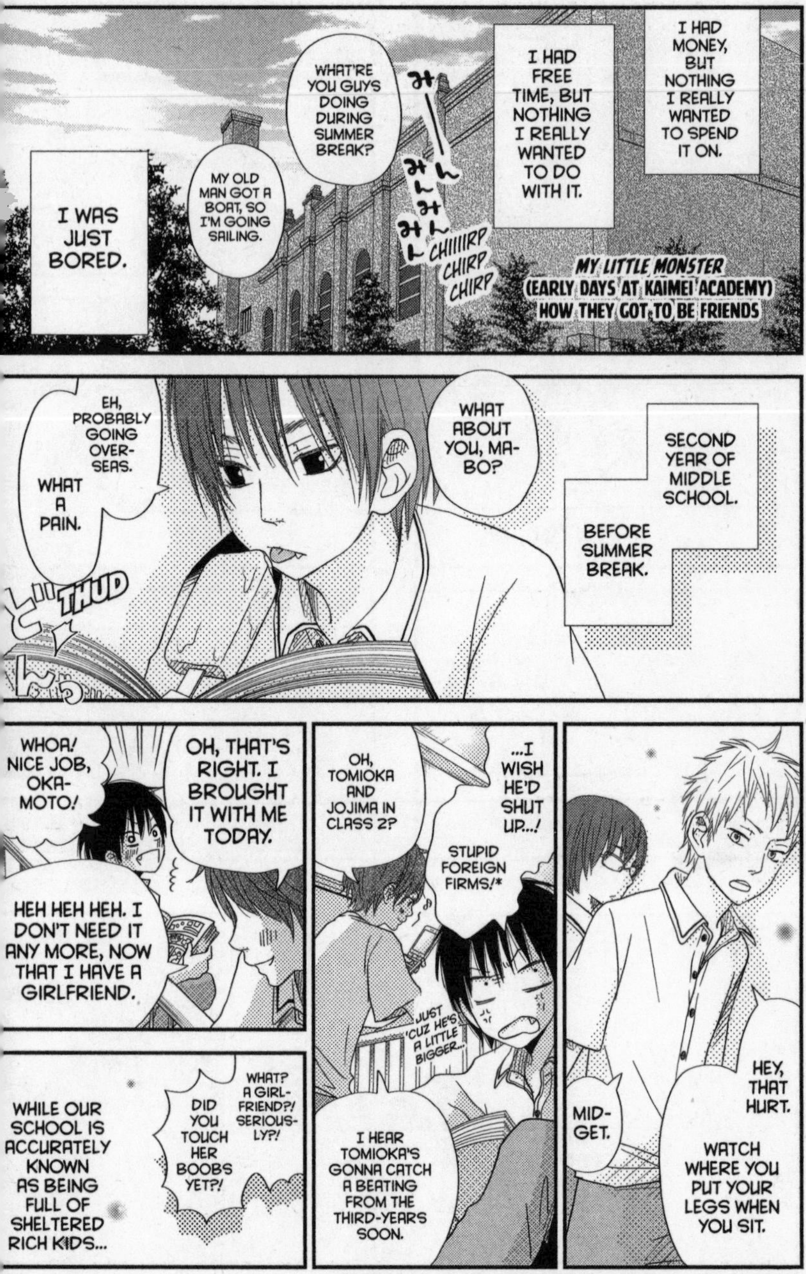
I HAD MONEY, BUT NOTHING I REALLY WANTED TO SPEND IT ON.
I HAD FREE TIME, BUT NOTHING I REALLY WANTED TO DO WITH IT.
MY LITTLE MONSTER (EARLY DAYS AT KAIMEI ACADEMY) HOW THEY GOT TO BE FRIENDS
WHAT'RE YOU GUYS DOING DURING SUMMER BREAK?
みーみんみんみん
CHIIIIRP CHIRP CHIRP
MY OLD MAN GOT A BOAT, SO I'M GOING SAILING.
I WAS JUST BORED.
SECOND YEAR OF MIDDLE SCHOOL.
BEFORE SUMMER BREAK.
WHAT ABOUT YOU, MA-BO?
EH, PROBABLY GOING OVER-SEAS.
WHAT A PAIN.
どん THUD
HEY, THAT HURT.
WATCH WHERE YOU PUT YOUR LEGS WHEN YOU SIT.
MID-GET.
...I WISH HE'D SHUT UP...!
OH, TOMIOKA AND JOJIMA IN CLASS 2?
STUPID FOREIGN FIRMS!*
JUST 'CUZ HE'S A LITTLE BIGGER...
I HEAR TOMIOKA'S GONNA CATCH A BEATING FROM THE THIRD-YEARS SOON.
OH, THAT'S RIGHT. I BROUGHT IT WITH ME TODAY.
WHOA! NICE JOB, OKA-MOTO!
HEH HEH HEH. I DON'T NEED IT ANY MORE, NOW THAT I HAVE A GIRLFRIEND.
WHAT? A GIRL-FRIEND?! SERIOUS-LY?!
DID YOU TOUCH HER BOOBS YET?!
WHILE OUR SCHOOL IS ACCURATELY KNOWN AS BEING FULL OF SHELTERED RICH KIDS...

*FOREIGN FIRMS = NEW STUDENTS JOINING FROM MIDDLE SCHOOL.

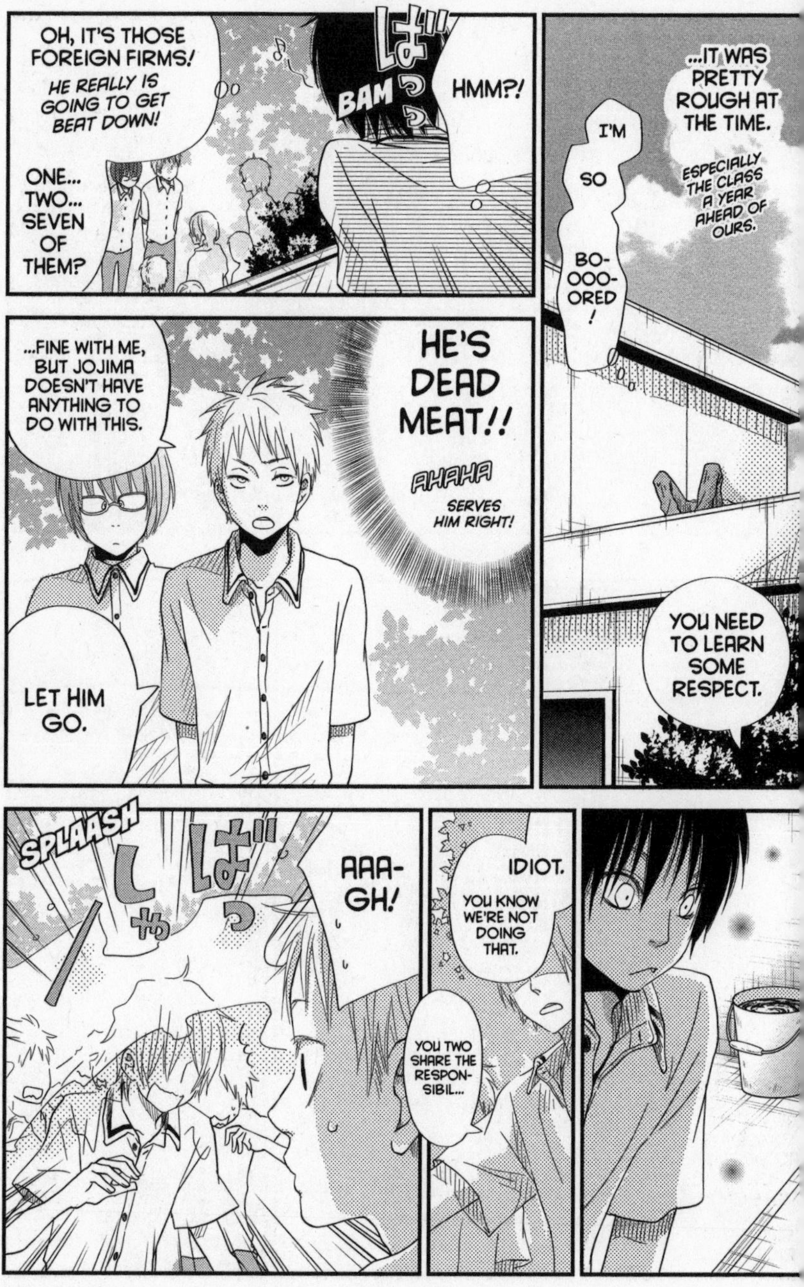
...IT WAS PRETTY ROUGH AT THE TIME.
ESPECIALLY THE CLASS A YEAR AHEAD OF OURS.
I'M SO BO-OOO-ORED!
YOU NEED TO LEARN SOME RESPECT.
HMM?!
BAM
OH, IT'S THOSE FOREIGN FIRMS!
HE REALLY IS GOING TO GET BEAT DOWN!
ONE... TWO... SEVEN OF THEM?
HE'S DEAD MEAT!!
AHAHA
SERVES HIM RIGHT!
...FINE WITH ME, BUT JOJIMA DOESN'T HAVE ANYTHING TO DO WITH THIS.
LET HIM GO.
IDIOT.
YOU KNOW WE'RE NOT DOING THAT.
YOU TWO SHARE THE RESPON-SIBIL...
AAA-GH!
SPLAASH

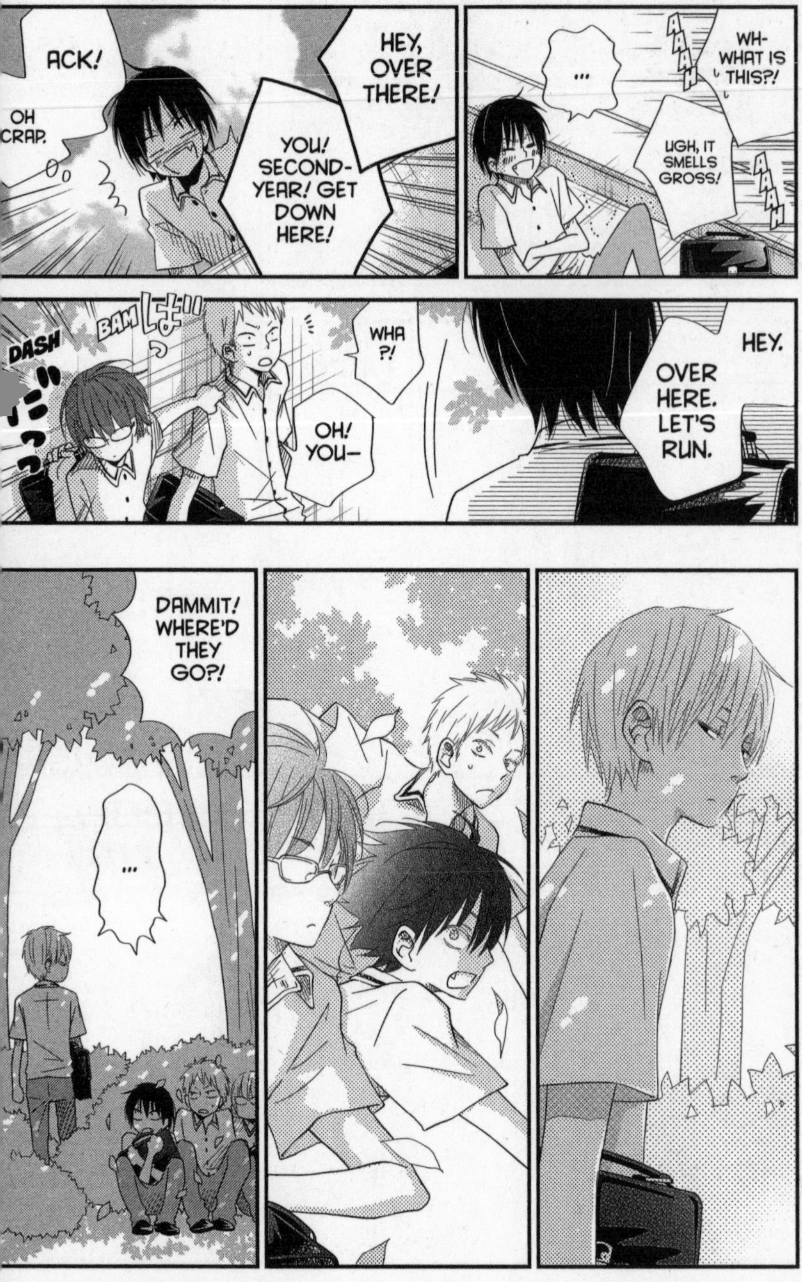
WH- WHAT IS THIS?!
AAAH
...
UGH, IT SMELLS GROSS!
AAAH
HEY, OVER THERE!
ACK!
YOU! SECOND-YEAR! GET DOWN HERE!
OH CRAP.
HEY.
OVER HERE. LET'S RUN.
WHA ?!
BAM
OH! YOU—
DASH
DAMMIT! WHERE'D THEY GO?!
...

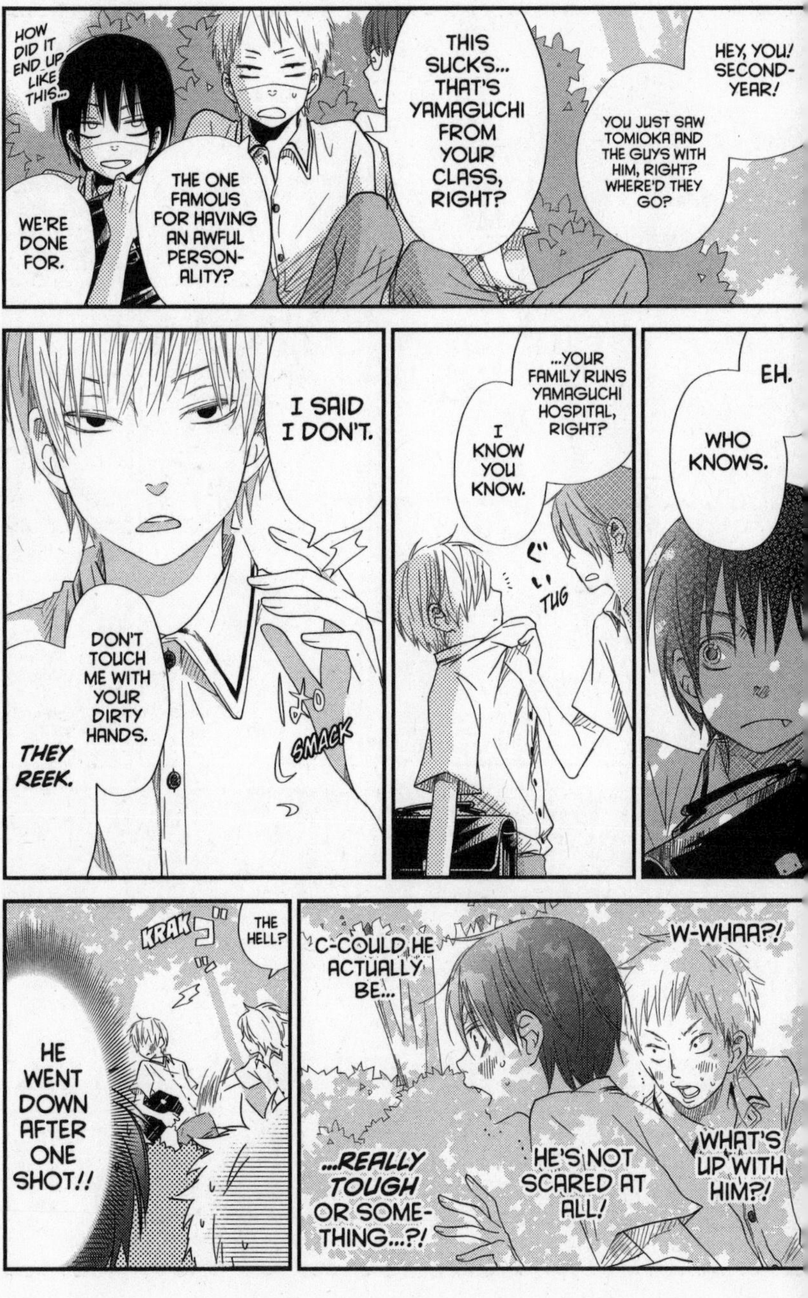
HEY, YOU! SECOND-YEAR!
YOU JUST SAW TOMIOKA AND THE GUYS WITH HIM, RIGHT? WHERE'D THEY GO?
THIS SUCKS... THAT'S YAMAGUCHI FROM YOUR CLASS, RIGHT?
THE ONE FAMOUS FOR HAVING AN AWFUL PERSON-ALITY?
HOW DID IT END UP LIKE THIS...
WE'RE DONE FOR.
EH.
WHO KNOWS.
...YOUR FAMILY RUNS YAMAGUCHI HOSPITAL, RIGHT?
I KNOW YOU KNOW.
TUG
I SAID I DON'T.
SMACK
DON'T TOUCH ME WITH YOUR DIRTY HANDS.
THEY REEK.
W-WHAA?!
C-COULD HE ACTUALLY BE...
WHAT'S UP WITH HIM?!
HE'S NOT SCARED AT ALL!
...REALLY TOUGH OR SOME-THING...?!
THE HELL?
KRAK
HE WENT DOWN AFTER ONE SHOT!!

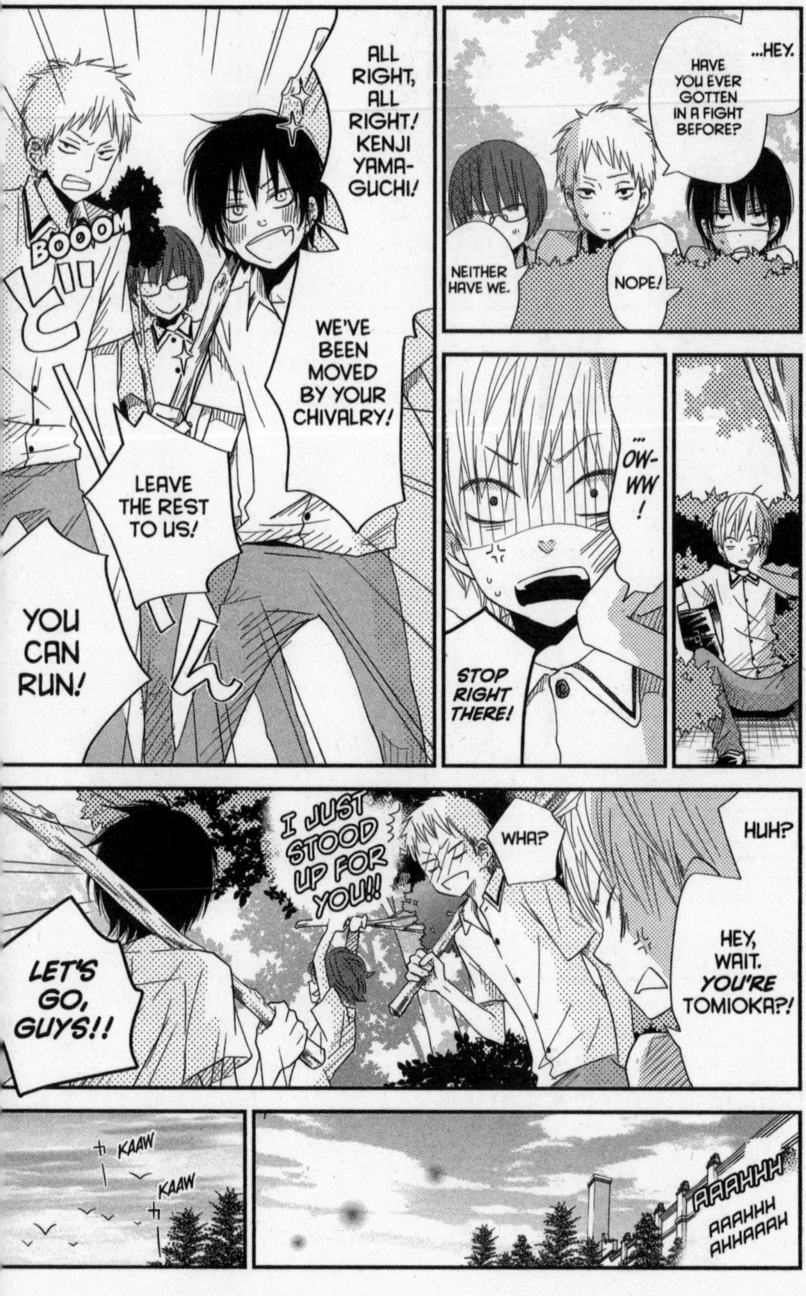
...HEY.
HAVE YOU EVER GOTTEN IN A FIGHT BEFORE?
NOPE!
NEITHER HAVE WE.
...OW-WW!
STOP RIGHT THERE!
ALL RIGHT, ALL RIGHT! KENJI YAMAGUCHI!
BOOOM
WE'VE BEEN MOVED BY YOUR CHIVALRY!
LEAVE THE REST TO US!
YOU CAN RUN!
HUH?
HEY, WAIT. *YOU'RE* TOMIOKA?!
WHA?
I JUST STOOD UP FOR YOU!!
LET'S GO, GUYS!!
AAAHHH
AAAHHH AHHAAAH
KAAW
KAAW

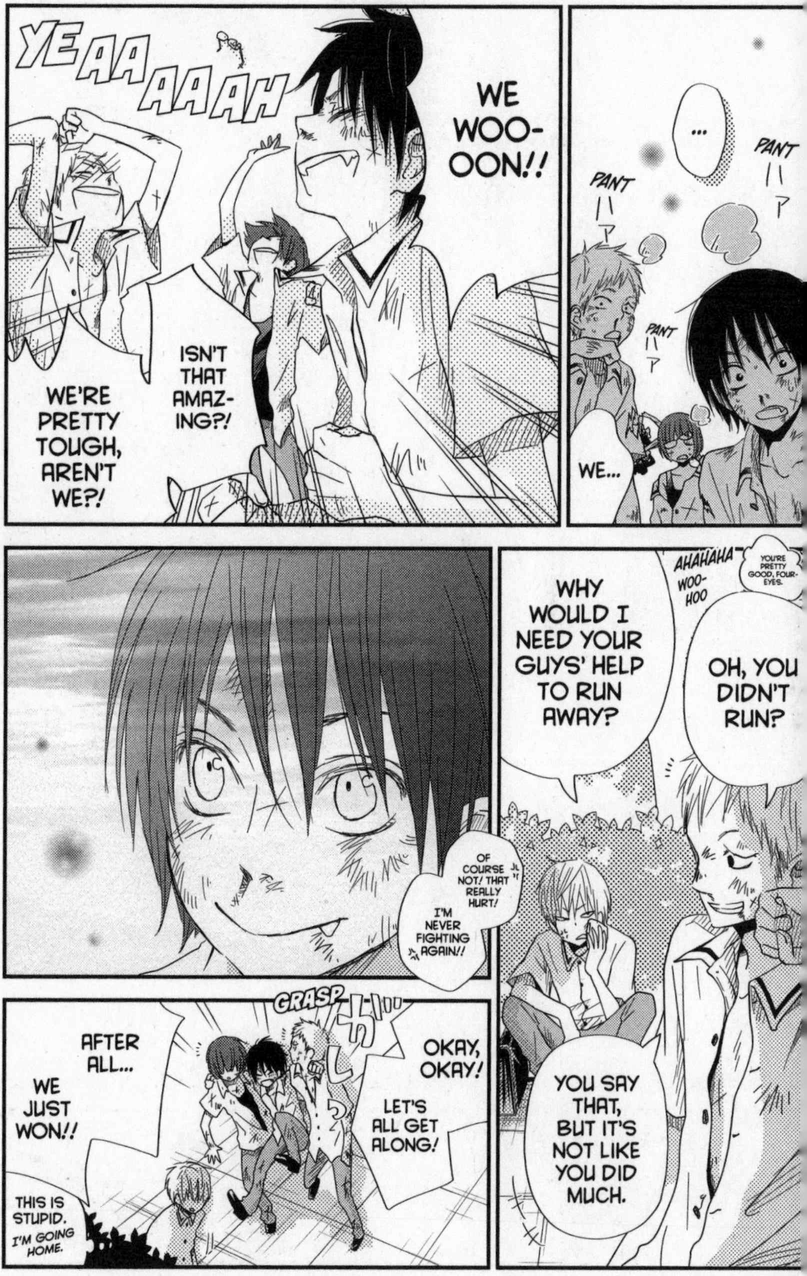

...
PANT ハア
PANT ハア
PANT ハア
WE...
YEAAAAAH
WE WOOO-OON!!
ISN'T THAT AMAZ-ING?!
WE'RE PRETTY TOUGH, AREN'T WE?!
AHAHAHA
WOO-HOO
YOU'RE PRETTY GOOD, FOUR-EYES.
OH, YOU DIDN'T RUN?
WHY WOULD I NEED YOUR GUYS' HELP TO RUN AWAY?
YOU SAY THAT, BUT IT'S NOT LIKE YOU DID MUCH.
OF COURSE NOT! THAT REALLY HURT!
I'M NEVER FIGHTING AGAIN!!
GRASP
OKAY, OKAY!
LET'S ALL GET ALONG!
AFTER ALL...
WE JUST WON!!
THIS IS STUPID.
I'M GOING HOME.

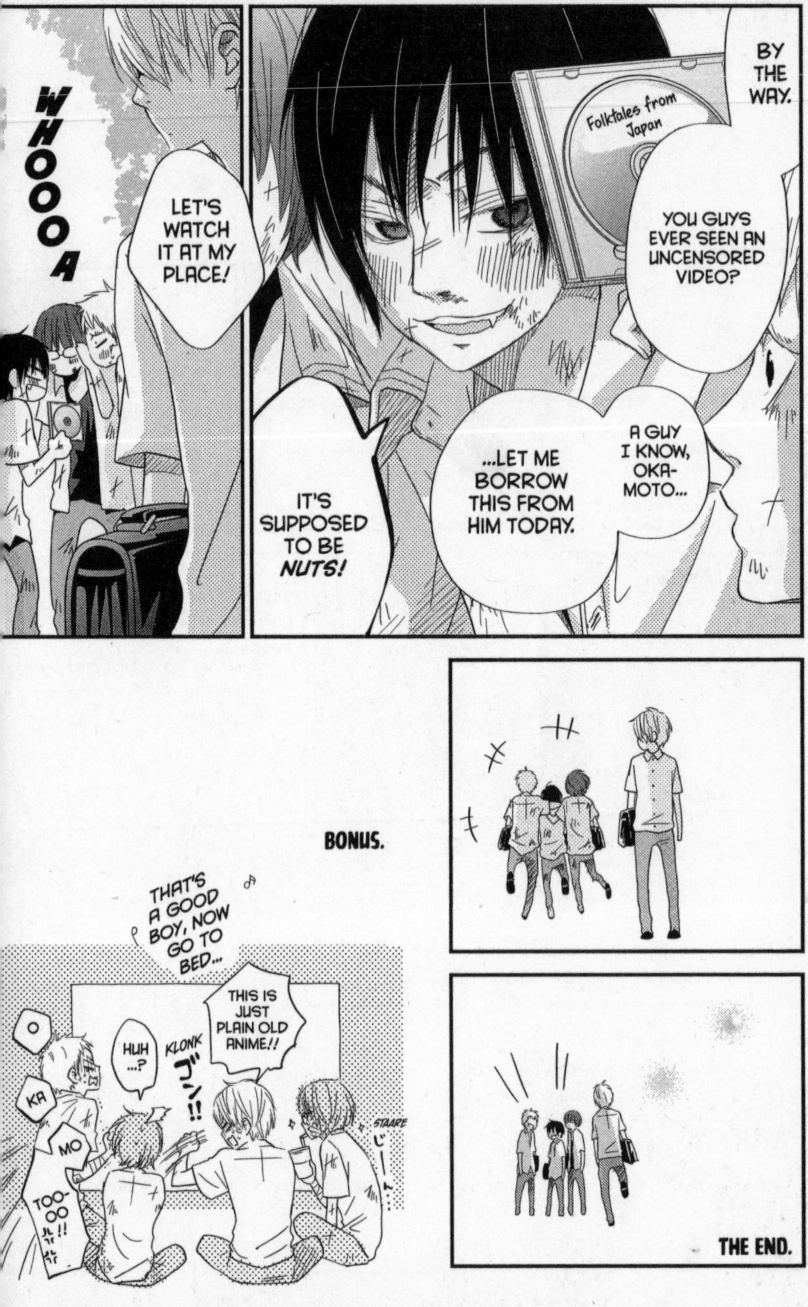
BY THE WAY.
Folktales from Japan
YOU GUYS EVER SEEN AN UNCENSORED VIDEO?
A GUY I KNOW, OKA-MOTO...
...LET ME BORROW THIS FROM HIM TODAY.
IT'S SUPPOSED TO BE *NUTS!*
WHOOOA
LET'S WATCH IT AT MY PLACE!
THE END.
BONUS.
THAT'S A GOOD BOY, NOW GO TO BED...
THIS IS JUST PLAIN OLD ANIME!!
KLONK
ゴン!!
HUH ...?
STAARE
じーん...
O
KA
MO
TOO-OO!!

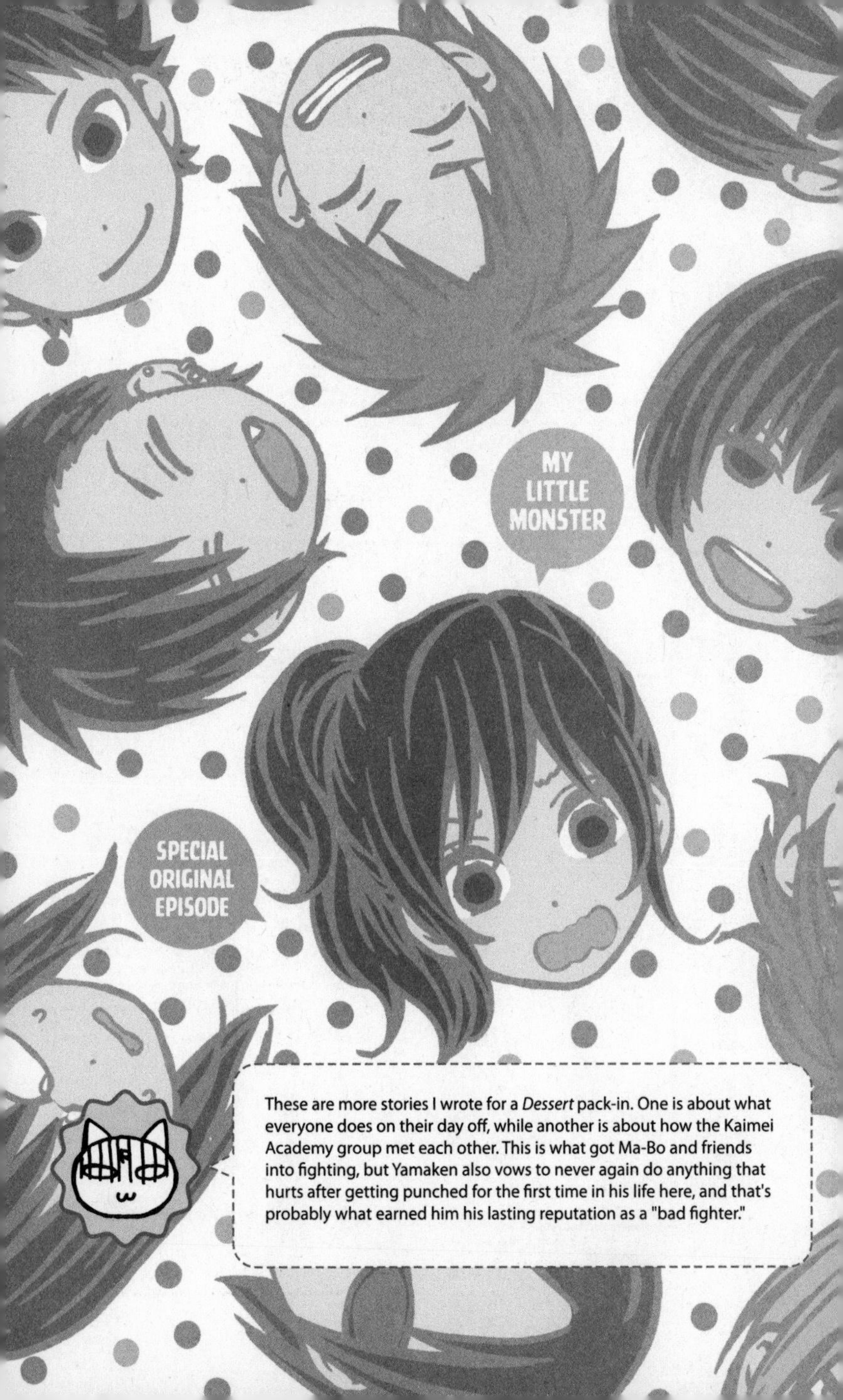
MY LITTLE MONSTER
SPECIAL ORIGINAL EPISODE

These are more stories I wrote for a *Dessert* pack-in. One is about what everyone does on their day off, while another is about how the Kaimei Academy group met each other. This is what got Ma-Bo and friends into fighting, but Yamaken also vows to never again do anything that hurts after getting punched for the first time in his life here, and that's probably what earned him his lasting reputation as a "bad fighter."

HARU'S DESSERT
(I'M SORRY IT'S SO STRAIGHTFORWARD)

FAIR-ONLY STRIP

ORIGINAL FOUR-PANEL STRIP GIVEN OUT AS A FAIR BONUS

THIS IS A FOUR-PANEL STRIP I DREW FOR THE DESSERT HARUKOI (SPRING LOVE) FAIR. I DREW IT OUT OF PURE MOMENTUM AND NOTHING ELSE, AND LOOKING BACK ON IT, I CAN STILL TELL THAT WAS THE CASE. BUT FOR SOME REASON, I DO LIKE THIS STRIP.

DESSERT HARUKOI FAIR 2012

HARUKOI ♡

Robico

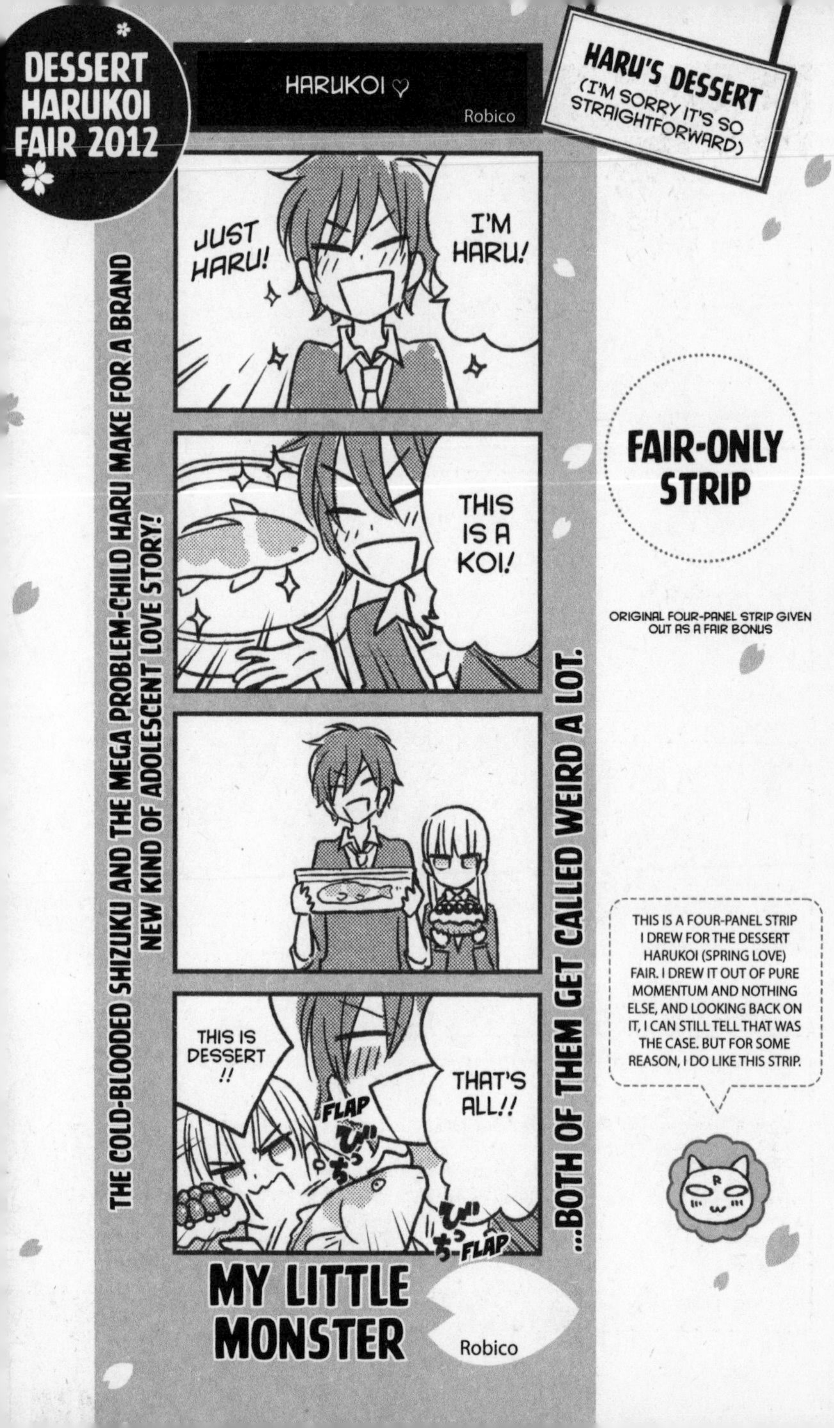
I'M HARU!
JUST HARU!
THIS IS A KOI!
THIS IS DESSERT !!
THAT'S ALL!!
FLAP
FLAP

THE COLD-BLOODED SHIZUKU AND THE MEGA PROBLEM-CHILD HARU MAKE FOR A BRAND NEW KIND OF ADOLESCENT LOVE STORY!

...BOTH OF THEM GET CALLED WEIRD A LOT.

MY LITTLE MONSTER

Robico

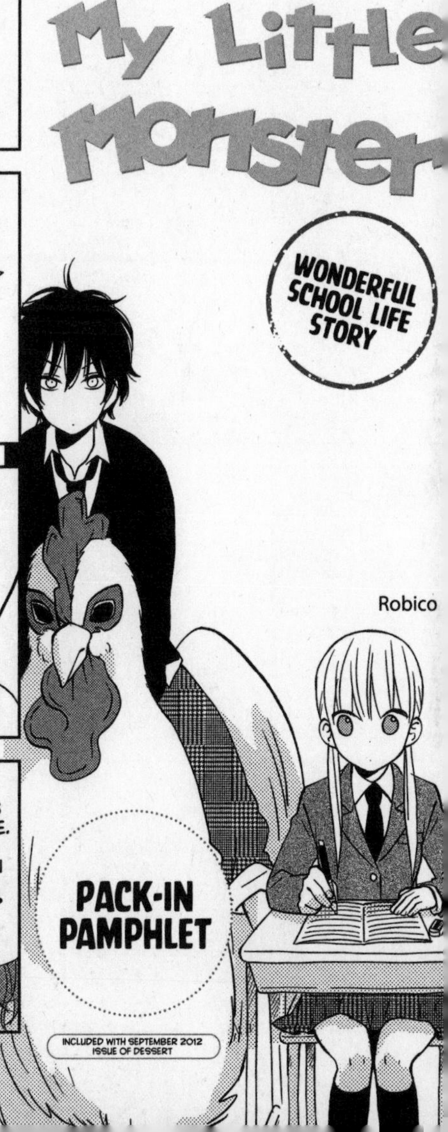
My Little Monster
WONDERFUL SCHOOL LIFE STORY
Robico
PACK-IN PAMPHLET
INCLUDED WITH SEPTEMBER 2012 ISSUE OF DESSERT

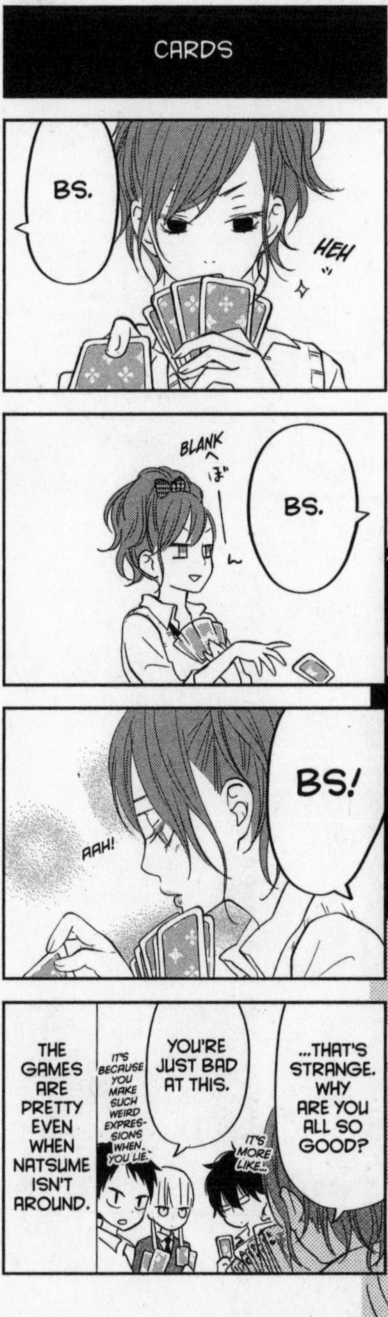
CARDS
BS.
HEH
BS.
BLANK
BS!
AAH!
...THAT'S STRANGE. WHY ARE YOU ALL SO GOOD?
IT'S MORE LIKE...
YOU'RE JUST BAD AT THIS.
IT'S BECAUSE YOU MAKE SUCH WEIRD EXPRES-SIONS WHEN YOU LIE.
THE GAMES ARE PRETTY EVEN WHEN NATSUME ISN'T AROUND.

OLD MAID

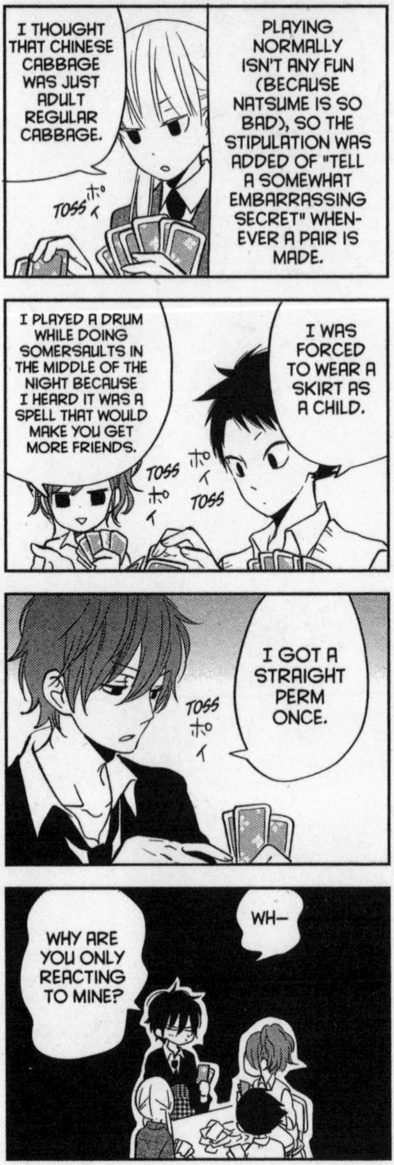

PLAYING NORMALLY ISN'T ANY FUN (BECAUSE NATSUME IS SO BAD), SO THE STIPULATION WAS ADDED OF "TELL A SOMEWHAT EMBARRASSING SECRET" WHENEVER A PAIR IS MADE.
I THOUGHT THAT CHINESE CABBAGE WAS JUST ADULT REGULAR CABBAGE.
TOSS ポイ
I WAS FORCED TO WEAR A SKIRT AS A CHILD.
I PLAYED A DRUM WHILE DOING SOMERSAULTS IN THE MIDDLE OF THE NIGHT BECAUSE I HEARD IT WAS A SPELL THAT WOULD MAKE YOU GET MORE FRIENDS.
TOSS ポイ
TOSS ポイ
I GOT A STRAIGHT PERM ONCE.
TOSS ポイ
WH–
WHY ARE YOU ONLY REACTING TO MINE?

I WAS WONDERING

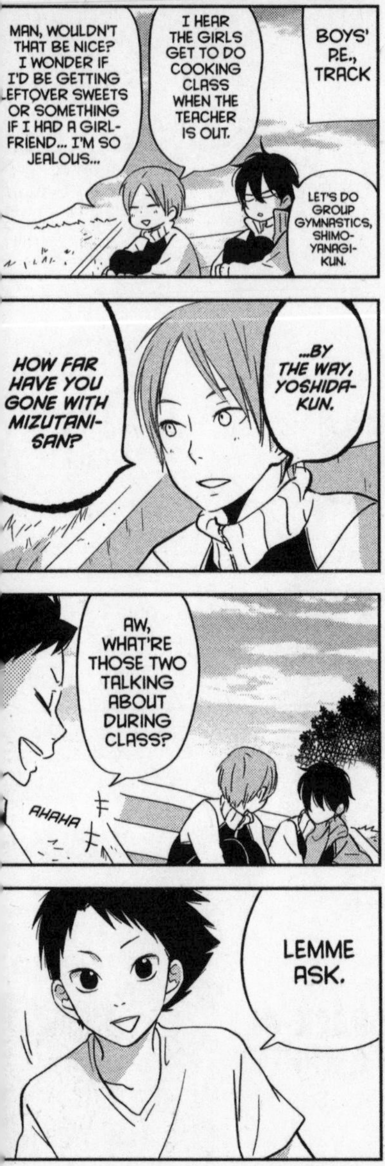

BOYS' P.E., TRACK
I HEAR THE GIRLS GET TO DO COOKING CLASS WHEN THE TEACHER IS OUT.
MAN, WOULDN'T THAT BE NICE? I WONDER IF I'D BE GETTING LEFTOVER SWEETS OR SOMETHING IF I HAD A GIRLFRIEND... I'M SO JEALOUS...
LET'S DO GROUP GYMNASTICS, SHIMO-YANAGI-KUN.
...BY THE WAY, YOSHIDA-KUN.
HOW FAR HAVE YOU GONE WITH MIZUTANI-SAN?
AW, WHAT'RE THOSE TWO TALKING ABOUT DURING CLASS?
AHAHA
LEMME ASK.

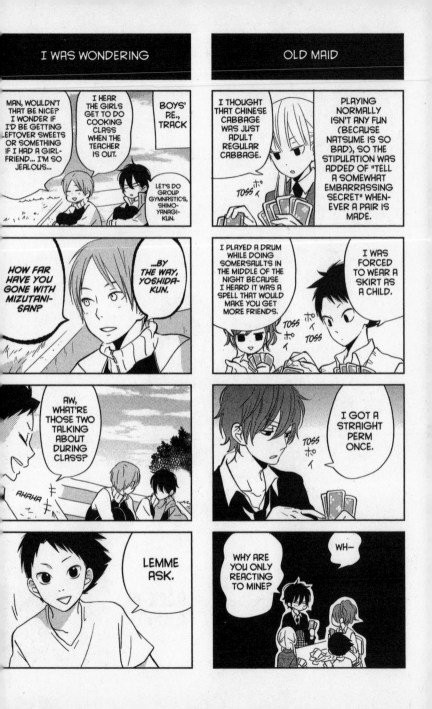

WELL, IT'S NOTHING

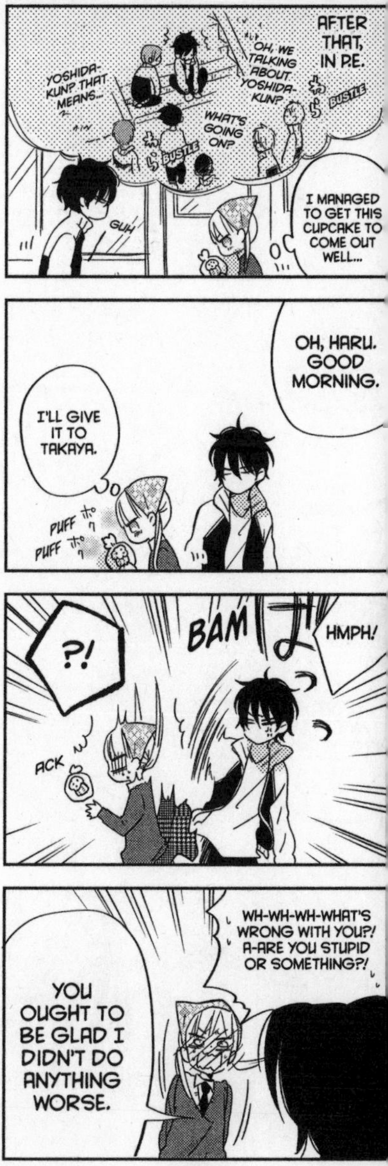
AFTER THAT, IN P.E.
OH, WE TALKING ABOUT YOSHIDA-KUN?
BUSTLE
WHAT'S GOING ON?
YOSHIDA-KUN? THAT MEANS...
BUSTLE
I MANAGED TO GET THIS CUPCAKE TO COME OUT WELL...
GUH
OH, HARU. GOOD MORNING.
I'LL GIVE IT TO TAKAYA.
PUFF
PUFF
HMPH!
BAM
?!
ACK
WH-WH-WH-WHAT'S WRONG WITH YOU?! A-ARE YOU STUPID OR SOMETHING?!
YOU OUGHT TO BE GLAD I DIDN'T DO ANYTHING WORSE.

TH-THUMP, TH-THUMP

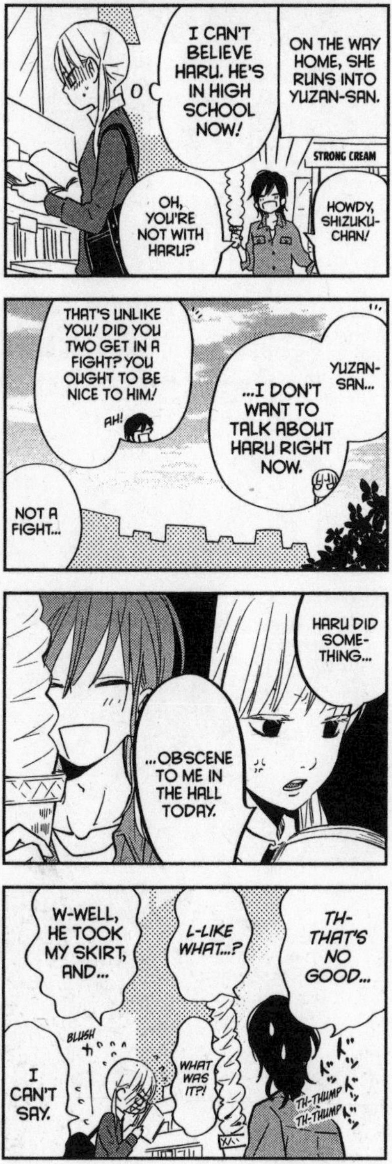
ON THE WAY HOME, SHE RUNS INTO YUZAN-SAN.
I CAN'T BELIEVE HARU. HE'S IN HIGH SCHOOL NOW!
STRONG CREAM
HOWDY, SHIZUKU-CHAN!
OH, YOU'RE NOT WITH HARU?
YUZAN-SAN...
...I DON'T WANT TO TALK ABOUT HARU RIGHT NOW.
THAT'S UNLIKE YOU! DID YOU TWO GET IN A FIGHT? YOU OUGHT TO BE NICE TO HIM!
AH!
NOT A FIGHT...
HARU DID SOMETHING...
...OBSCENE TO ME IN THE HALL TODAY.
TH-THAT'S NO GOOD...
L-LIKE WHAT...?
W-WELL, HE TOOK MY SKIRT, AND...
WHAT WAS IT?!
TH-THUMP
TH-THUMP
BLUSH
I CAN'T SAY.

EXCITEMENT

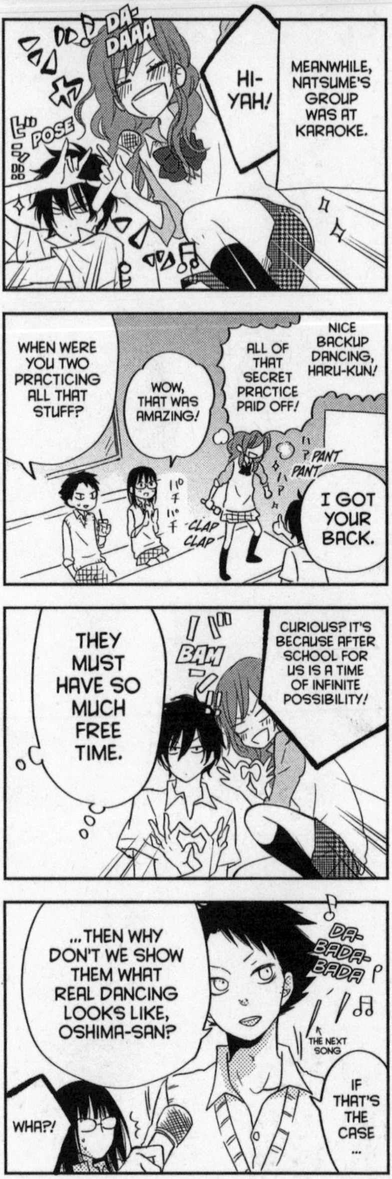
MEANWHILE, NATSUME'S GROUP WAS AT KARAOKE.
HI-YAH!
DA-DAAA
POSE
NICE BACKUP DANCING, HARU-KUN!
ALL OF THAT SECRET PRACTICE PAID OFF!
WOW, THAT WAS AMAZING!
WHEN WERE YOU TWO PRACTICING ALL THAT STUFF?
PANT PANT
I GOT YOUR BACK.
CLAP CLAP
CURIOUS? IT'S BECAUSE AFTER SCHOOL FOR US IS A TIME OF INFINITE POSSIBILITY!
BAM
THEY MUST HAVE SO MUCH FREE TIME.
DA-BADA-BADA
THE NEXT SONG
IF THAT'S THE CASE ...
...THEN WHY DON'T WE SHOW THEM WHAT REAL DANCING LOOKS LIKE, OSHIMA-SAN?
WHA?!

FOREVER

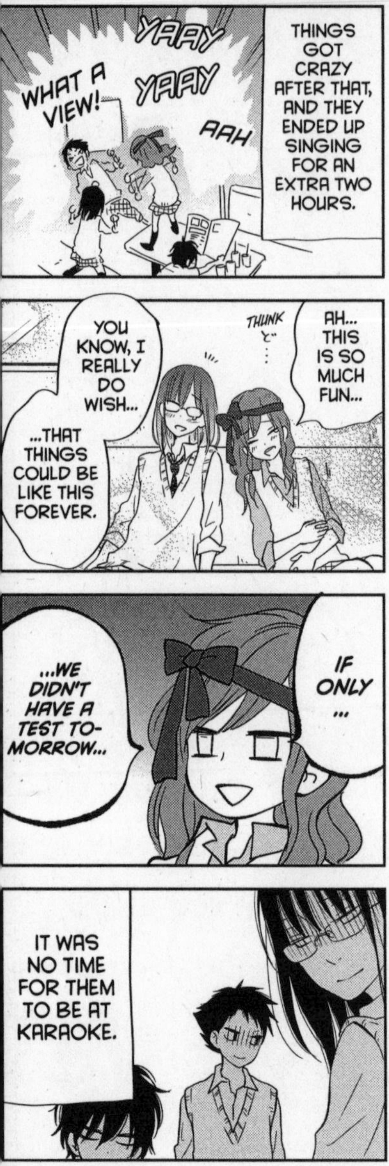
THINGS GOT CRAZY AFTER THAT, AND THEY ENDED UP SINGING FOR AN EXTRA TWO HOURS.
YAAY
YAAY
WHAT A VIEW!
AAH
AH... THIS IS SO MUCH FUN...
THUNK
YOU KNOW, I REALLY DO WISH...
...THAT THINGS COULD BE LIKE THIS FOREVER.
IF ONLY ...
...WE DIDN'T HAVE A TEST TO-MORROW...
IT WAS NO TIME FOR THEM TO BE AT KARAOKE.

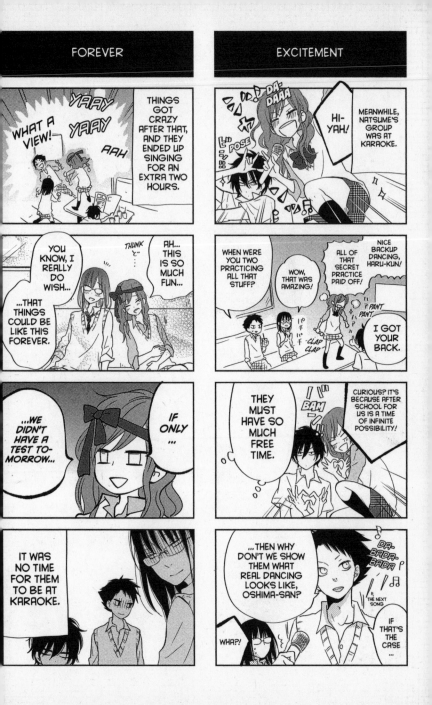

SPOT THE *MY LITTLE MONSTER* DIFFERENCES!

Shizuku and the others have come to the beach for some swimming over summer break. Look carefully and you might find differences between the top and bottom pictures. Try to find them all!

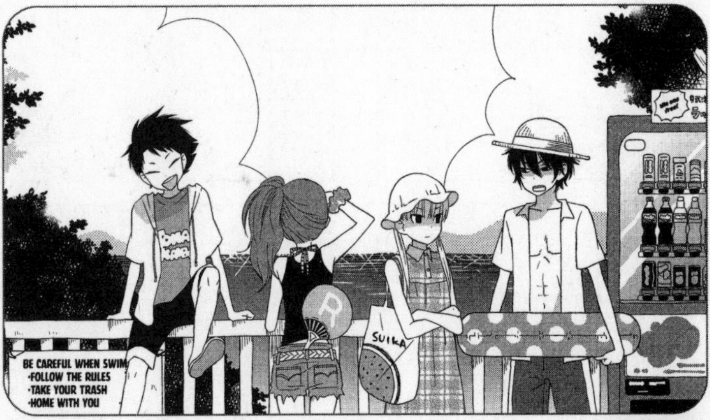
SUIKA
BE CAREFUL WHEN SWIM
•FOLLOW THE RULES
•TAKE YOUR TRASH
•HOME WITH YOU

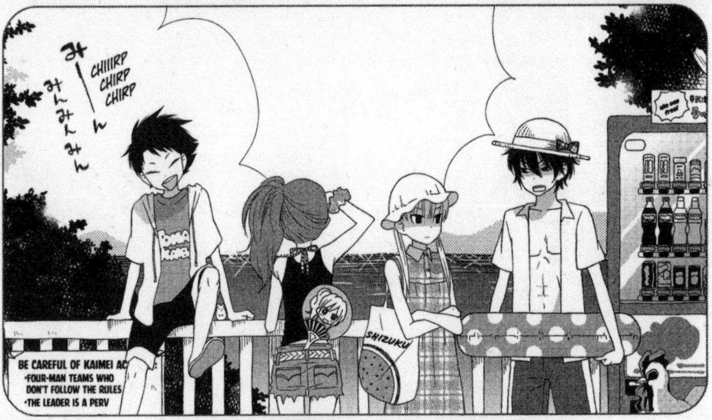
CHIIIRP CHIRP CHIRP
みーん
みんみんみん
SHIZUKU
BE CAREFUL OF KAIMEI AC
•FOUR-MAN TEAMS WHO DON'T FOLLOW THE RULES
•THE LEADER IS A PERV

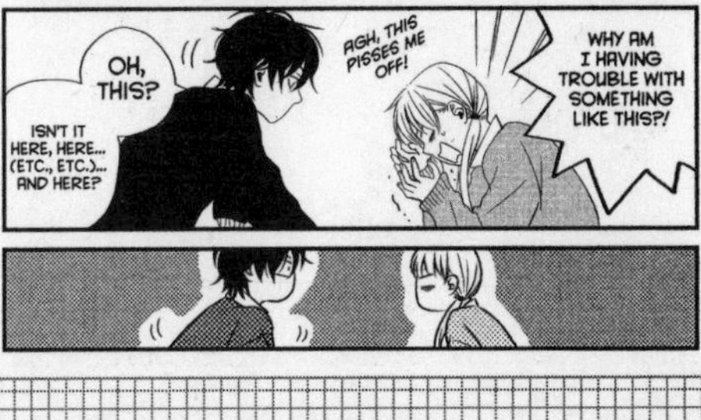
WHY AM I HAVING TROUBLE WITH SOMETHING LIKE THIS?!
AGH, THIS PISSES ME OFF!
OH, THIS?
ISN'T IT HERE, HERE... (ETC., ETC.)... AND HERE?

FOR ANSWERS, CHECK THE NEXT PAGE.

SPECIAL

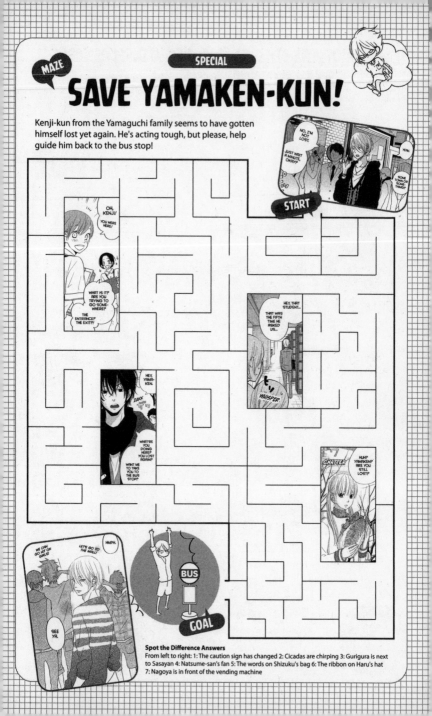

MAZE

SAVE YAMAKEN-KUN!

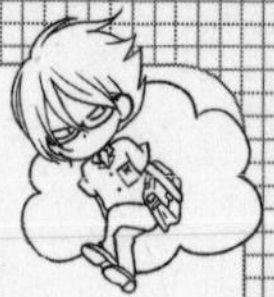

Kenji-kun from the Yamaguchi family seems to have gotten himself lost yet again. He's acting tough, but please, help guide him back to the bus stop!

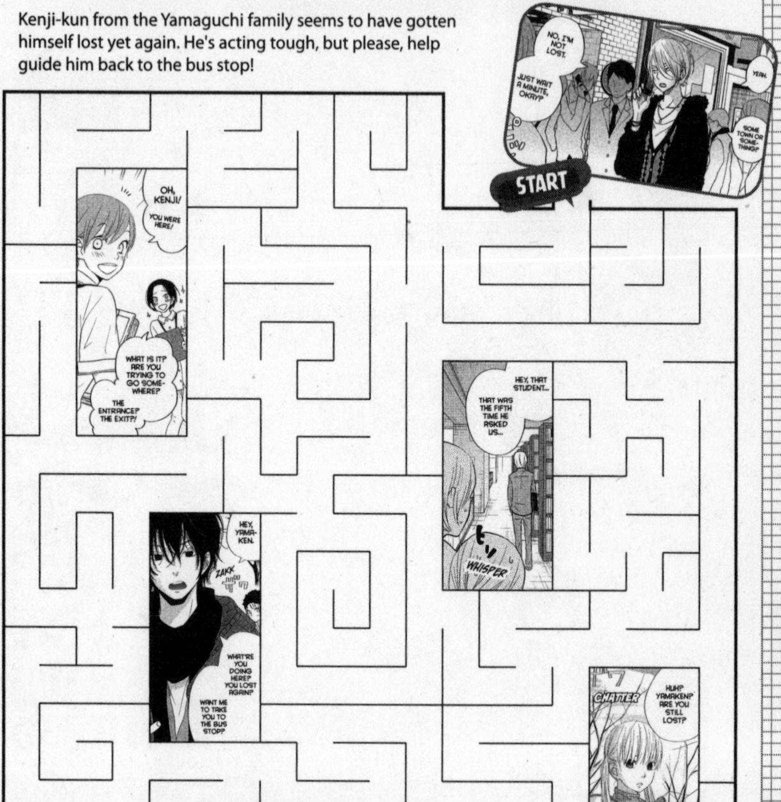
NO, I'M NOT LOST.
JUST WAIT A MINUTE, OKAY?
YEAH.
SOME TOWN OR SOME-THING?
START
OH, KENJI!
YOU WERE HERE!
WHAT IS IT? ARE YOU TRYING TO GO SOME-WHERE?
THE ENTRANCE? THE EXIT?
HEY, THAT STUDENT...
THAT WAS THE FIFTH TIME HE ASKED US...
WHISPER
HEY, YAMA-KEN.
ZAKK
WHAT'RE YOU DOING HERE? YOU LOST AGAIN?
WANT ME TO TAKE YOU TO THE BUS STOP?
CHATTER
HUH? YAMAKEN? ARE YOU STILL LOST?
BUS
GOAL

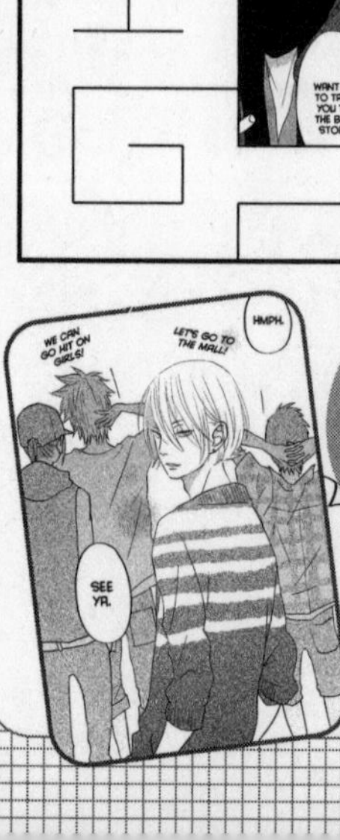
HMPH.
LET'S GO TO THE MALL!
WE CAN GO HIT ON GIRLS!
SEE YA.

Spot the Difference Answers

From left to right: 1: The caution sign has changed 2: Cicadas are chirping 3: Gurigura is next to Sasayan 4: Natsume-san's fan 5: The words on Shizuku's bag 6: The ribbon on Haru's hat 7: Nagoya is in front of the vending machine

No.

Date

RELEASED FOR THE FIRST TIME EVER!

CHARACTER PROFILES!

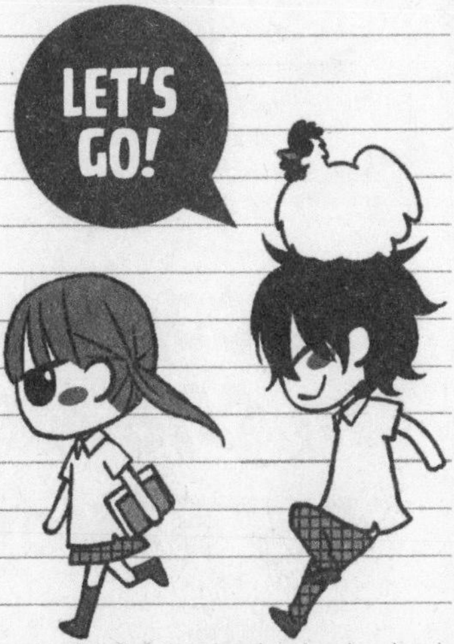
LET'S GO!

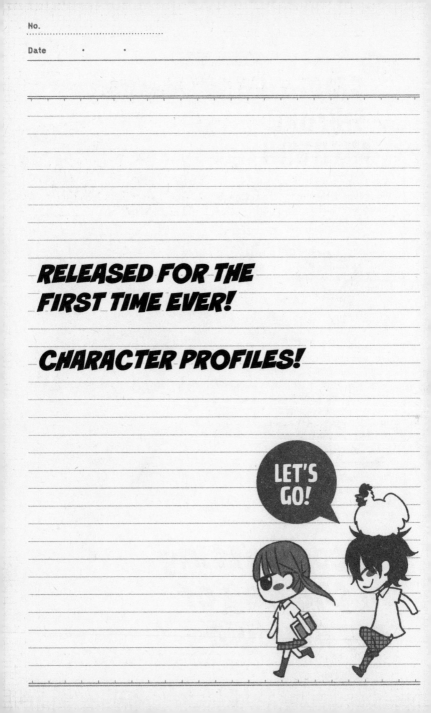

SHIZUKU MIZUTANI

Age: 16 **Birthday:** 2/14 Aquarius
Blood Type: B **Height:** 158 cm (approx. 5'2")
Family Structure: Father, mother, younger brother

*All ages listed in this section are the characters' starting ages when the main characters are second-years.

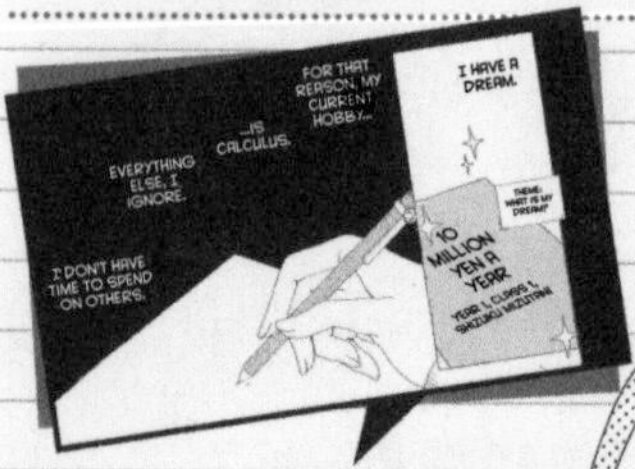
I HAVE A DREAM.
THEME: WHAT IS MY DREAM?
10 MILLION YEN A YEAR
YEAR 1, CLASS 1, SHIZUKU MIZUTANI
FOR THAT REASON, MY CURRENT HOBBY...
...IS CALCULUS.
EVERYTHING ELSE, I IGNORE.
I DON'T HAVE TIME TO SPEND ON OTHERS.

A girl whose goal in life is to get better grades and whose dream is a yearly income of 10 million yen.* Seen as cold-blooded because she thinks she doesn't need friends and she doesn't like animals. Her life changes when she gives Haru handouts in order to earn money for study guides.

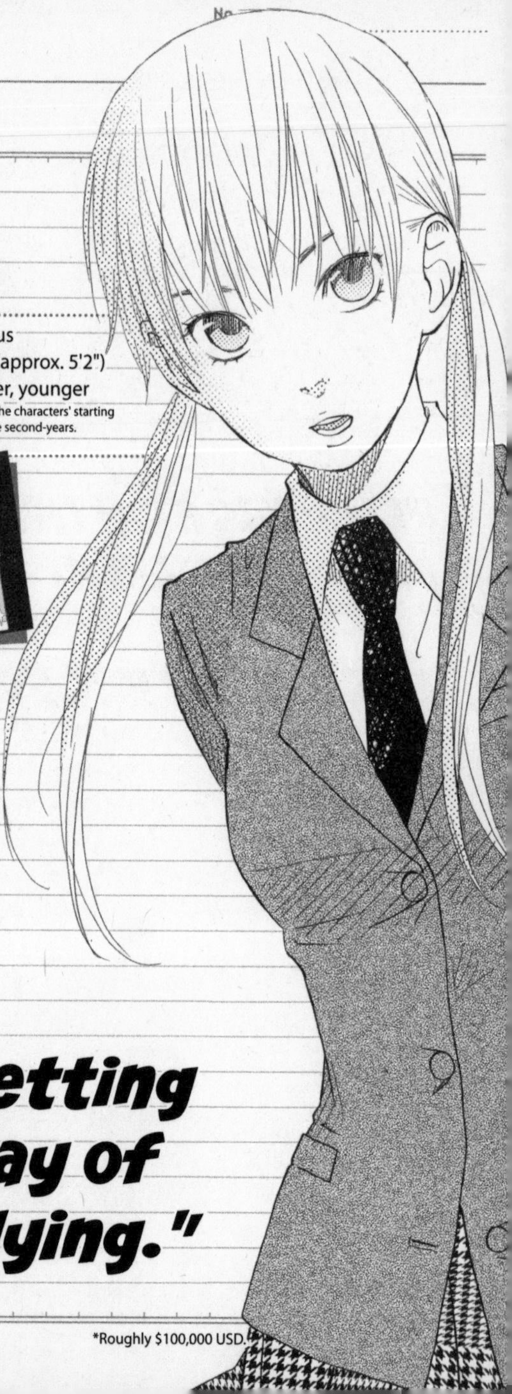

"Stop getting in the way of my studying."

*Roughly $100,000 USD.

No.

Date

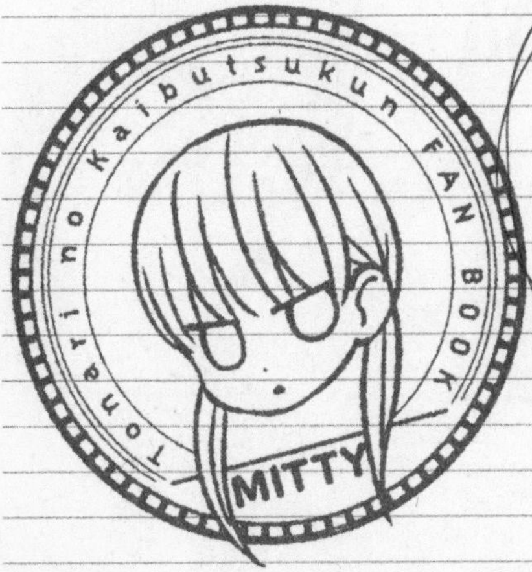
Tonari no Kaibutsukun FAN BOOK
MITTY

Taste in the opposite sex: Strong finances, smart, and rational (the opposite of her father)

Favorite Foods: None in particular

Likes: Eliminating waste

Hobbies: Studying, sewing

Check!!

★ ABOUT THIS CHARACTER ★

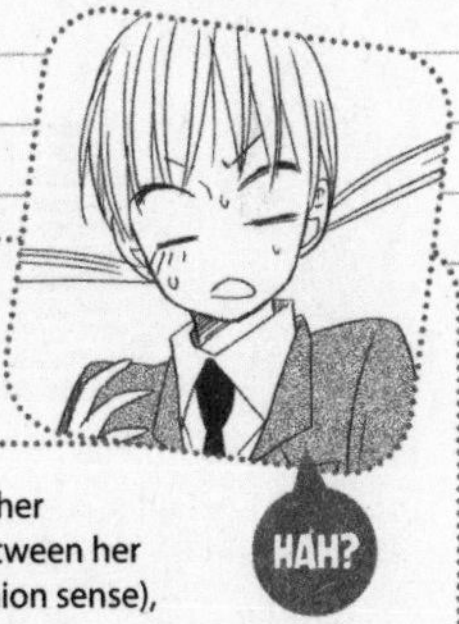
HAH?

Studying in order to become a lawyer like her mother. In the story, her seemingly cold demeanor earns her the nickname "dry ice," but between her skills as a chef and her love of looking girly (though she has no fashion sense), she's a surprisingly domestic and feminine girl.

Dotes on her little brother Takaya, and chose the closest school to her home in order to do housework. Takaya plays soccer, so whenever he has matches or goes on field trips, she makes him lunches. It could be that everything Shizuku does for Takaya, she wishes her parents had done for her.

Easily gets cold, so she wears wool panties in the winter. Hates needless spending (as the result of her father's influence), so she continues to wear the same clothes she wore in elementary and high school. All of the books she reads are borrowed from the library, too.

Poor at sports. Due to her theoretical approach she's able to understand what she needs to do, but her body can't do it.

Note from Robico: Shizuku is always reading while walking around. That's a dangerous thing to do, you know.

No.

Date

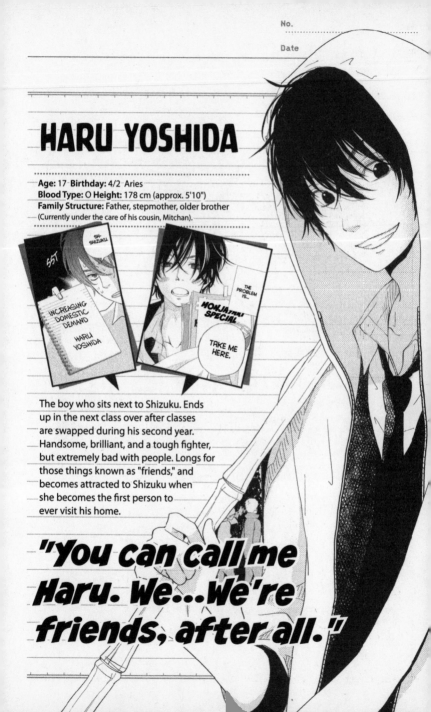

HARU YOSHIDA

Age: 17 **Birthday:** 4/2 Aries
Blood Type: O **Height:** 178 cm (approx. 5'10")
Family Structure: Father, stepmother, older brother
(Currently under the care of his cousin, Mitchan).

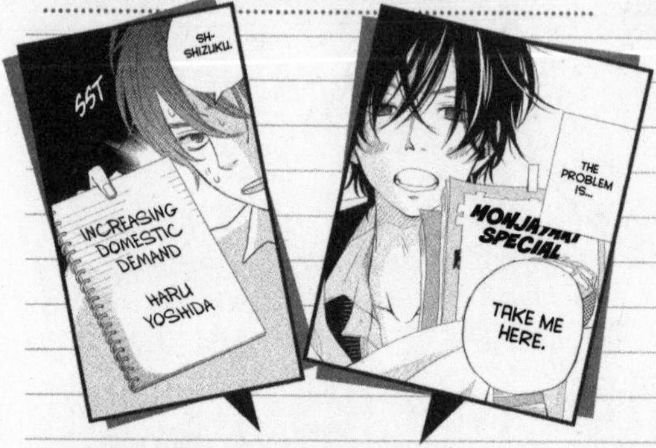
THE PROBLEM IS...
MONJAYAKI SPECIAL
TAKE ME HERE.
SH-SHIZUKU.
SST
INCREASING DOMESTIC DEMAND
HARU YOSHIDA

The boy who sits next to Shizuku. Ends up in the next class over after classes are swapped during his second year. Handsome, brilliant, and a tough fighter, but extremely bad with people. Longs for those things known as "friends," and becomes attracted to Shizuku when she becomes the first person to ever visit his home.

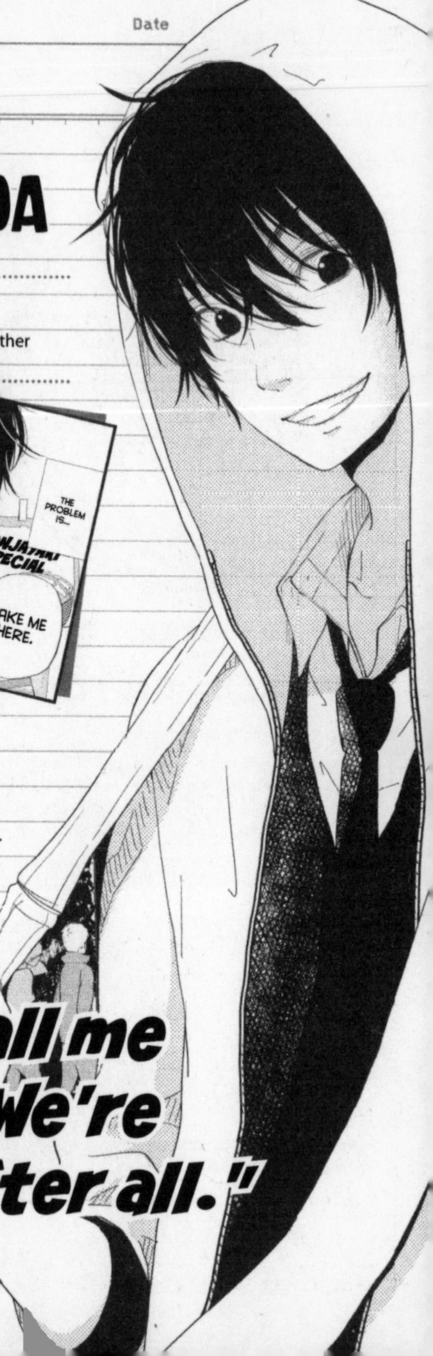

"You can call me Haru. We...We're friends, after all."

No.

Date

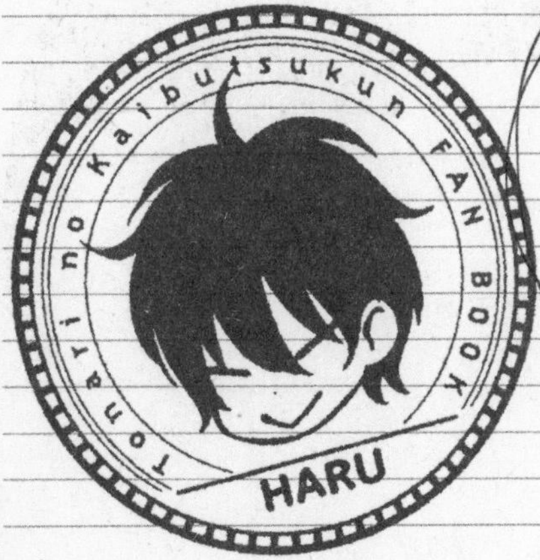
Tonari no Kaibutsukun FAN BOOK
HARU

Taste in the opposite sex: Warm and fluffy

Favorite Foods: Takoyaki

Likes: Shigaraki-ware tanuki

Hobbies: Shooting games

Check!!

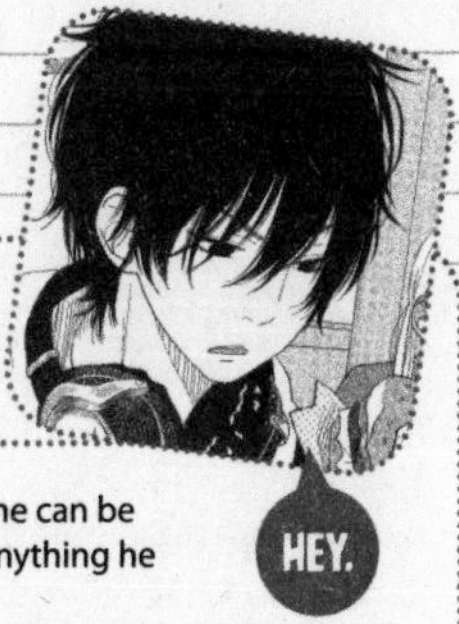
HEY.

★ ABOUT THIS CHARACTER ★

People can never tell what Haru is thinking. While he is as bad as one can be at communicating with others, he's able to succeed at just about anything he finds himself interested in.

As one can see by the kinds of people he becomes emotionally attached to, such as Shizuku, his aunt Kyoko-san, and his earth sciences teacher Oga-sensei, Haru generally likes those who are quiet, calm, and not overly emotional.

As Haru was often alone from an early age, he's very good at keeping himself amused, and particularly likes activities that keep both his mind and hands occupied, such as the Rubik's Cube and origami.

He sometimes acts as pure as a child, whether it's staying at Shizuku's house because he says he doesn't want to go home (though it is also very much like Shizuku to take him in), or finding something he calls a treasure before trying to give it away. It could be that both he and Shizuku are attempting to regain the experiences they never got the chance to have.

Has a habit of putting seasoning on everything.

Note from Robico: Even I'm surprised at times by what Haru does.

No.

Date

ASAKO NATSUME

Age: 16 **Birthday:** 7/2 Cancer
Blood Type: O **Height:** 157 cm (approx. 5'2")
Family Structure: Mother

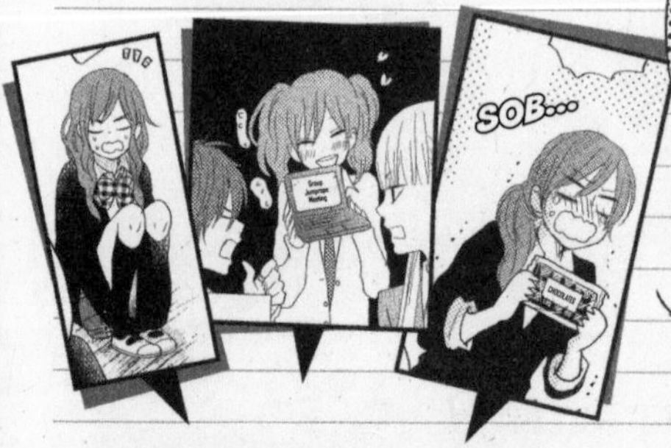
SOB...

A popular girl in the same class as Shizuku. Bad at homework and at making friends, so the Internet is everything to her. Doesn't like boys because of all the times she lost female friends when boys fell in love with her. Becomes friends with Shizuku and Haru when they study with her and save her from having to take supplemental exams. Like Haru, she longs to have friends.

"You can find all the answers online."

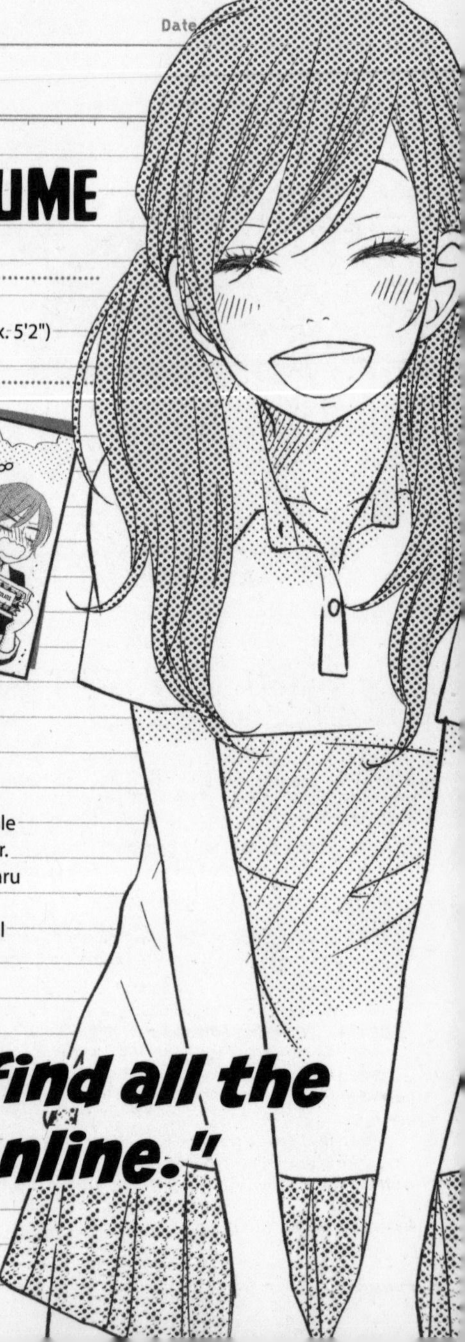

No.

Date

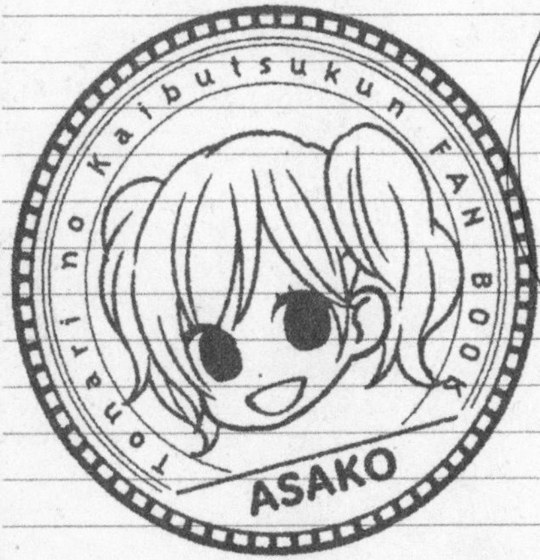
Tonari no Kaibutsukun FAN BOOK
ASAKO

Taste in the opposite sex:

A tolerant 42-year-old man

Favorite Drink: Banana milk

Hobbies: Looking at advice message boards

If she could only take one thing to a remote island:

Laptop

Check!!

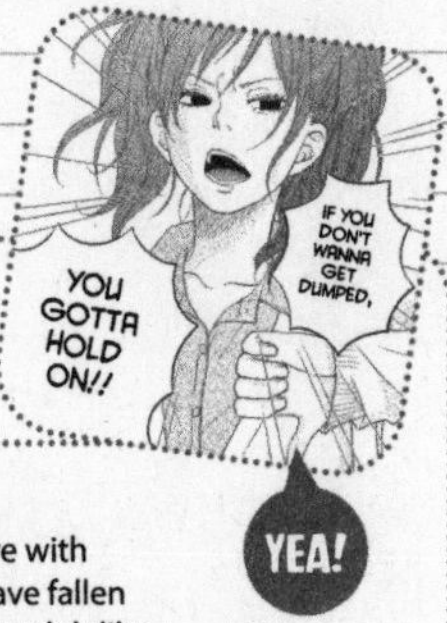
IF YOU DON'T WANNA GET DUMPED,
YOU GOTTA HOLD ON!!
YEA!

★ ABOUT THIS CHARACTER ★

A daddy's girl raised in relative affluence, she enters a dark period once adolescence begins and she starts to attract boys. Because she was in love with her father to begin with, it can't be said that she dislikes men. She may have fallen in love with Mitchan because she was attracted to the fatherliness that an adult like him possesses.

Likes cute things as well as being fashionable, but stopped dressing up for a time in middle school because she was concerned with what others would think of her, picking up some strange other interests instead.

In order to start her life over in high school, she wholeheartedly wanted to apply to a school where she was sure no one from her middle school would go, leading her to apply to Shoyo High. As a result, though, she lives the furthest from school.

Gets into school through the admissions office exam, rather than through test scores alone. Programming is her hobby, and she uploads the simple games and programs she creates to the Internet.

Also, while Shizuku has yet to notice, Natsume seems to be confessing her love to her three times a month.

Note from Robico: As an obstinate clean freak, dating boys her age might have been tough for her.

SOHEI SASAHARA (SASAYAN)

Age: 16 **Birthday:** 10/16 Libra
Blood Type: A **Height:** 164 cm (approx. 5'5")
Family Structure: Grandmother, father, mother, three older brothers

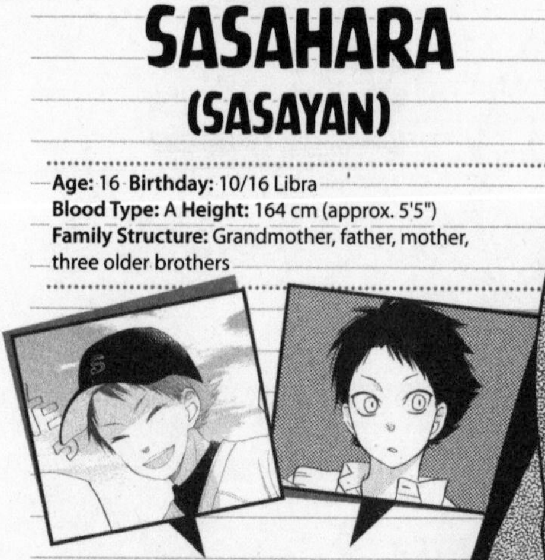

A member of the Baseball Club and in the same class as Shizuku, he gets along with everybody. He has a bright and refreshing personality, and is able to immediately open up to anyone, something that both Haru and Natsume are jealous of. From the same middle school as Haru, and seems to owe him because of something that happened back then.

"Why don't you just act normal?"

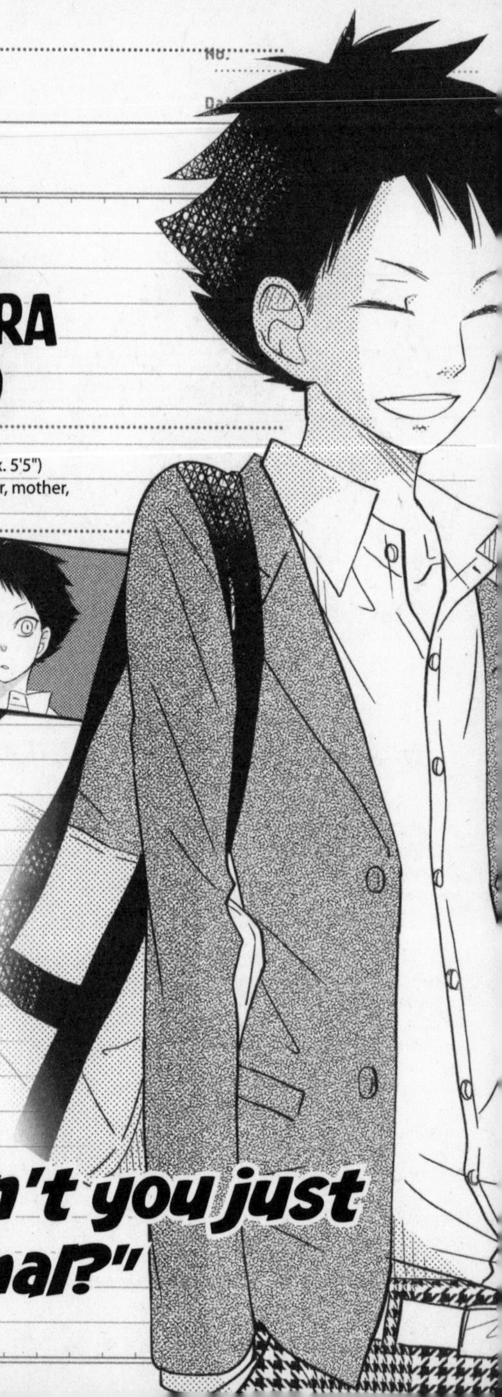

No.

Date

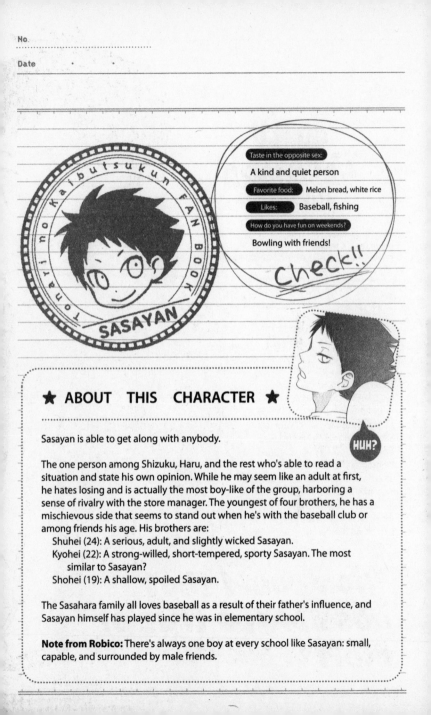

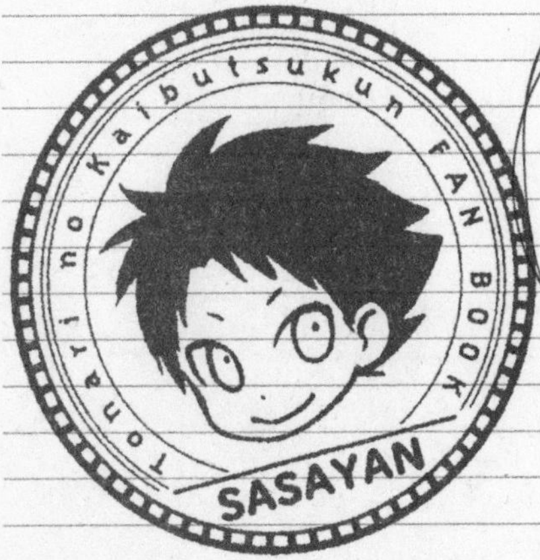
Tonari no Kaibutsukun FAN BOOK
SASAYAN

Taste in the opposite sex:
A kind and quiet person

Favorite food: Melon bread, white rice

Likes: Baseball, fishing

How do you have fun on weekends?
Bowling with friends!

Check!!

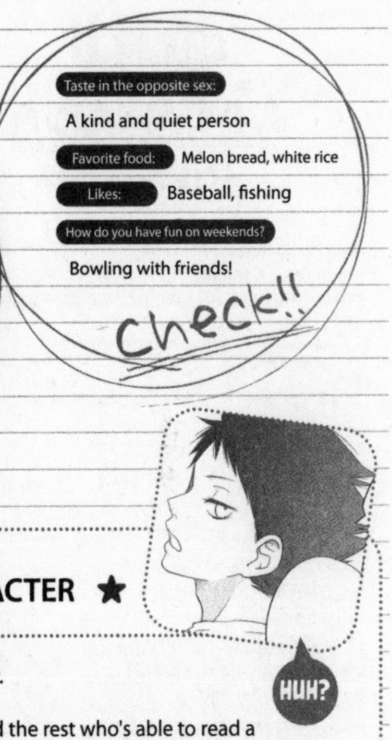
HUH?

★ ABOUT THIS CHARACTER ★

Sasayan is able to get along with anybody.

The one person among Shizuku, Haru, and the rest who's able to read a situation and state his own opinion. While he may seem like an adult at first, he hates losing and is actually the most boy-like of the group, harboring a sense of rivalry with the store manager. The youngest of four brothers, he has a mischievous side that seems to stand out when he's with the baseball club or among friends his age. His brothers are:

Shuhei (24): A serious, adult, and slightly wicked Sasayan.
Kyohei (22): A strong-willed, short-tempered, sporty Sasayan. The most similar to Sasayan?
Shohei (19): A shallow, spoiled Sasayan.

The Sasahara family all loves baseball as a result of their father's influence, and Sasayan himself has played since he was in elementary school.

Note from Robico: There's always one boy at every school like Sasayan: small, capable, and surrounded by male friends.

No.

KENJI YAMAGUCHI (YAMAKEN)

Age: 16 **Birthday:** 5/9 Taurus
Blood Type: A **Height:** 177 cm (approx. 5'10")
Family Structure: Grandfather, grandmother, father, mother, little sister

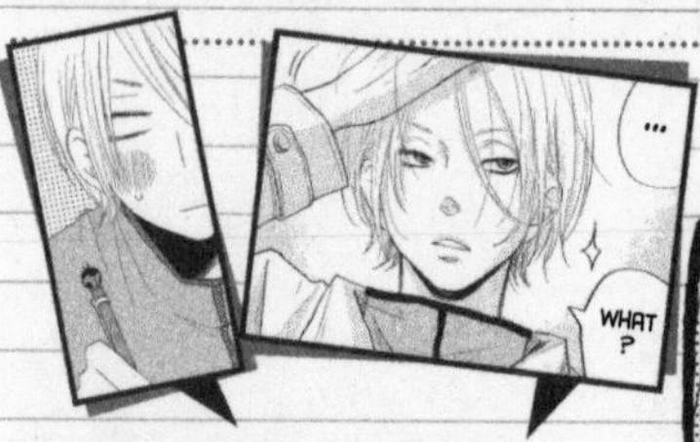
...
WHAT ?

A student at Kaimei Academy, a school for sheltered rich boys. Prideful, with no sense of direction. Meets Haru, a former classmate, again in high school for the first time since Haru left Kaimei after elementary school. Becomes interested in Shizuku because she was able to change Haru, and while he secretly begins to be attracted to her, his pride gets in the way of him being honest about his feelings. And?

"How could that possibly be true of me?!"

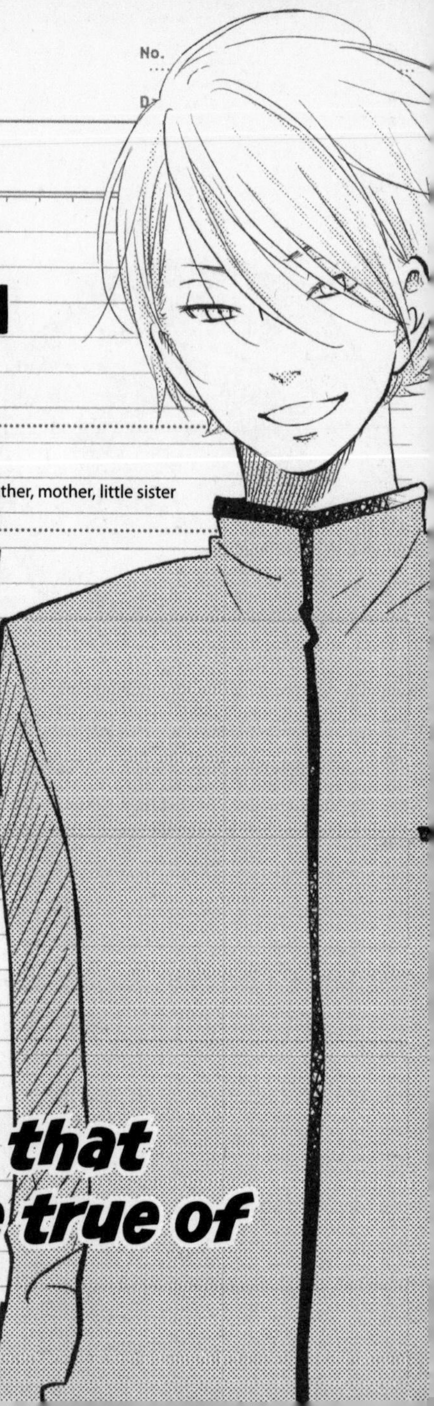

No.

Date

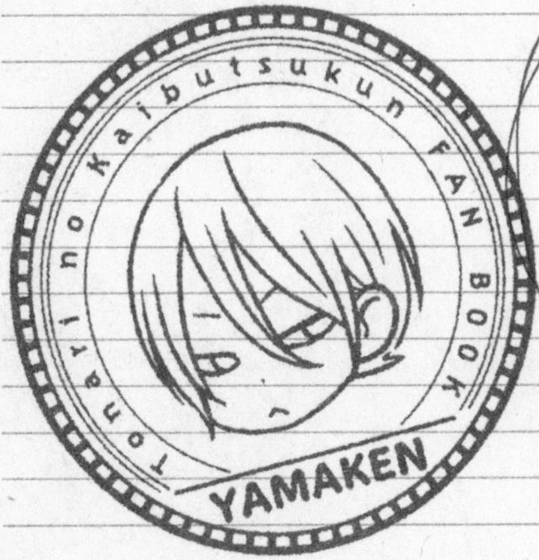
Tonari no Kaibutsukun FAN BOOK
YAMAKEN

Taste in the opposite sex:

A girl I can go on a walk with

Favorite vehicle: Taxis

Least favorite food:

Carrots, Chinese cabbage (New!!)

Most frequently used app:

Maps

Check!!

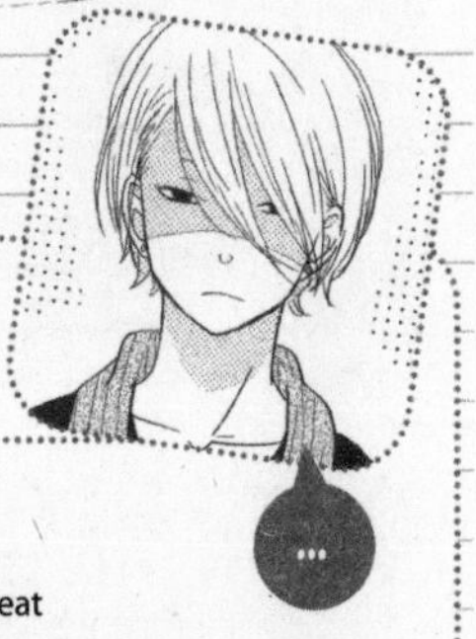
...

★ ABOUT THIS CHARACTER ★

The successor to Yamaguchi General Hospital.

One of the characters of his name, Kenji, is taken from that of his great grandfather, the daunting founder of the hospital.

A prideful boy who refuses to lose or yield to Shizuku or Haru. He makes no attempts to hide his excessive confidence and narcissism from Shizuku and the others as he talks down to them in a half-mocking manner. He understands how to act in order to attract women, and his good looks, gentlemanly ways, and kindness towards girls makes him popular with them.

As he never had a chance to eat plebian food, such as food from stalls or beef bowls (less because he's wealthy and more because his mother made sure to cook all the time), he seems to crave them somewhat when he sees them. While he does understand that he has a poor sense of direction and makes sure to leave the house early when meeting others, he never apologizes if he's late.

Note from Robico: I never imagined that Yamaken would grow this much. When you go back and look at him in Volume 1 now, it's kind of funny, isn't it? He doesn't even appear in my rough drafts.

No.

Date . .

CHIZURU OSHIMA

Age: 16 **Birthday:** 1/19 Capricorn
Blood Type: A **Height:** 165 cm (approx. 5'5")
Family Structure: Father, mother, older sister

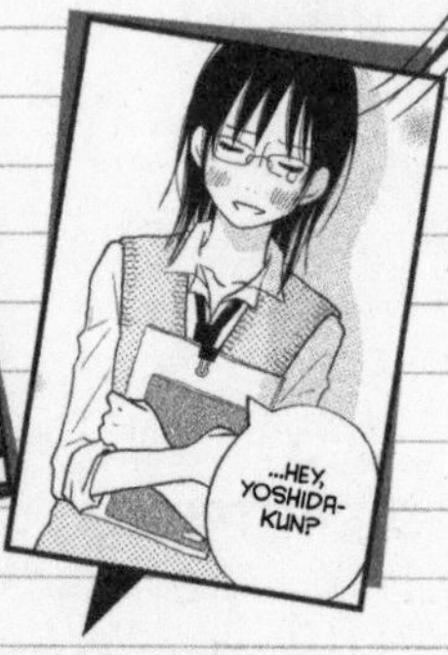
...HEY, YOSHIDA-KUN?

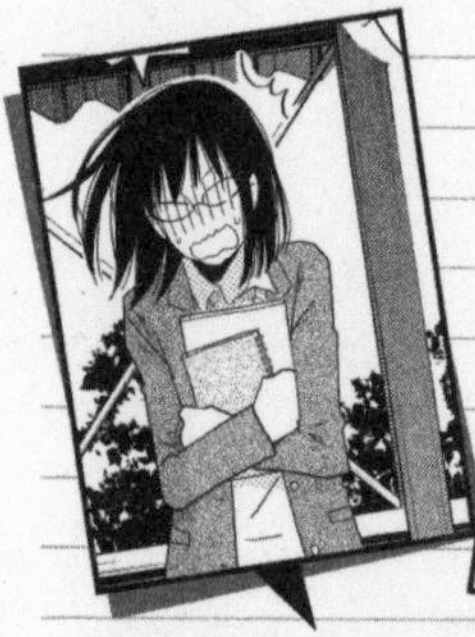

The class president of the class next door who wasn't able to make friends because of the bad cold she came down with shortly after beginning school. Becomes attracted to Haru after he protects her at the baseball tournament, but with his feelings toward Shizuku so obvious, she had no choice but to lose heart. It didn't take much to make her feel negative, you know?

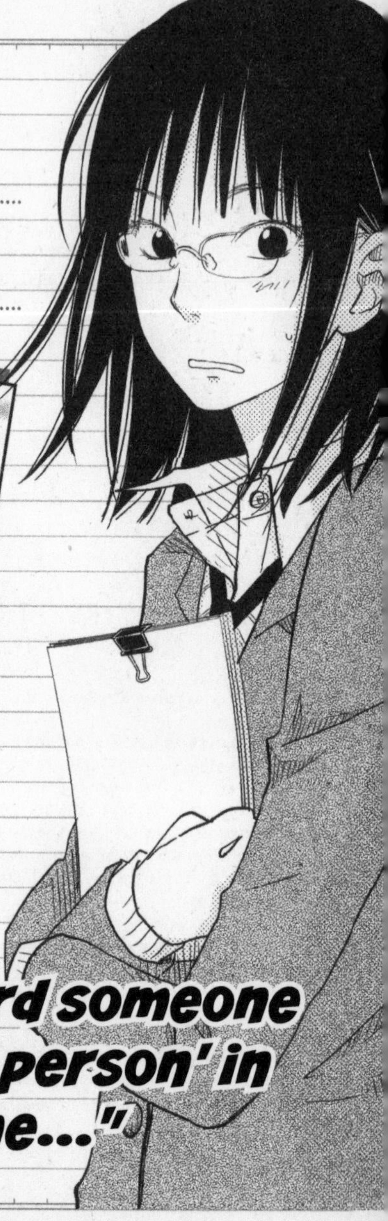

"I haven't heard someone call me a 'good person' in such a long time..."

No.

Date

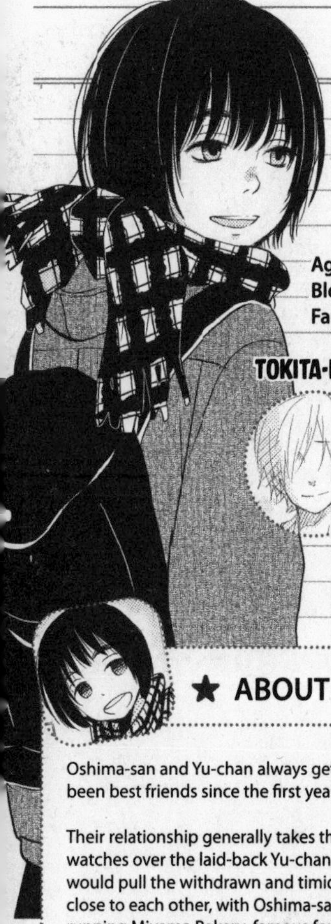

YU MIYAMA
(YU-CHAN)

Age: 16 **Birthday:** 12/10 Sagittarius
Blood Type: O **Height:** 146 cm (approx. 4'9")
Family Structure: Father, mother, little brother, little sister

TOKITA-KUN

Close friends with Oshima-san since middle school. Goes to Otowa Girls' School. Goes to see Haru when she hears from Oshima-san that there is "someone she likes," and soon becomes friends with everyone. Has a habit of staring at people, and is strangely sharp. Has a long-distance relationship with someone named Tokita-kun.

"You can do it, Chizuru. You can do it."

★ ABOUT THESE CHARACTERS ★

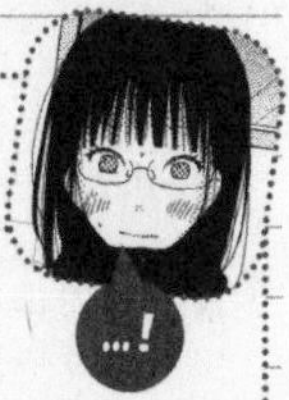
...!

Oshima-san and Yu-chan always get along with each other so well. The two have been best friends since the first year of middle school.

Their relationship generally takes the form of Oshima-san running around as she watches over the laid-back Yu-chan, but in middle school it was more the case that Yu-chan would pull the withdrawn and timid Oshima-san forward with her energy. The two also live close to each other, with Oshima-san's family running a textiles store and Yu-chan's family running Miyama Bakery, famous for its delicious white bread.

Oshima-san's phrase, "Do you even have balls?" is actually something she picked up from her father, and it's something over which she's held a mild grudge toward him ever since. She grew up watching her foul-mouthed father and sister and never wanted to turn out like them, but as a result, she now struggles with being so serious that people see her as uninteresting.

Yu-chan has a long-distance relationship with Tokita-kun, her classmate in middle school. She might have the most respectable and proper romantic relationship of anyone in this title.

Note from Robico: Oshima-san is such a serious and good girl that Yu-chan was born out of my desire to cheer her on. I think they turned out to be a good pair.

No.

Date

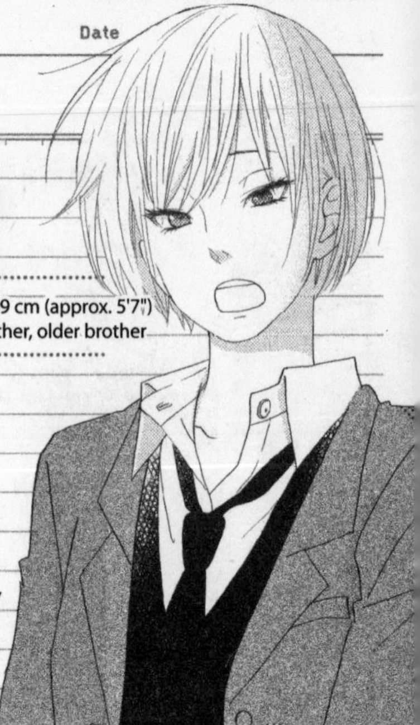

IYO YAMAGUCHI

Age: 15 **Birthday:** 9/21 Virgo **Blood Type:** A **Height:** 169 cm (approx. 5'7")
Family Structure: Grandfather, grandmother, father, mother, older brother

Yamaken's little sister who entered Shizuku and Haru's school. An extremely confident and self-conscious traveler of love. In utter fear of her brother.

"Iyo's cuter!"

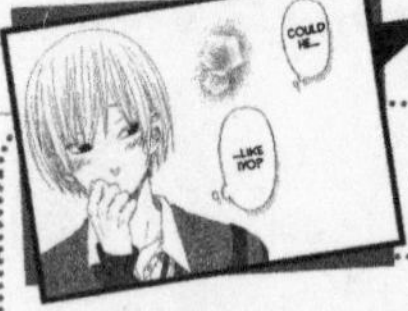
COULD HE—
—LIKE IYO?

★ ABOUT THIS CHARACTER ★

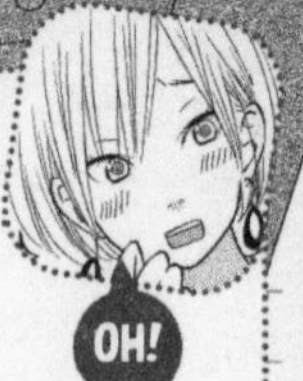
OH!

A girl who is self-obsessed and overly confident, just like her brother, but even compared to him, she's more focused on no one but herself. Conceited, but because she was raised in the patriarchal Yamaguchi family, she generally follows the orders of those above her. Because of this, she adheres to the rules of etiquette set out for her as a junior to her rival, Shizuku, pouring her tea first and always using polite language to her, making her a surprisingly dutiful girl. Her older brother has received all the attention since they were young, which has given Iyo a strong desire to be seen. This, combined with her overactive imagination, gives rise to Mishuran. While they don't appear in this series, she seems to have secretly been following the visual rock band Moebius since she was in middle school. She has no friends she's particularly close to, but she doesn't seem to mind that.

Has a brother complex.

Note from Robico: The one and only standard Iyo uses to judge others is looks. That's why she respects Natsume-san, who she has accepted as cuter than herself, and why she feels above the plain-looking Shizuku and the beautiful yet quiet Oshima-san. Iyo seems to maintain this kind of hierarchy inside of her head. It's not out of any particular malice, though.

No.

Date

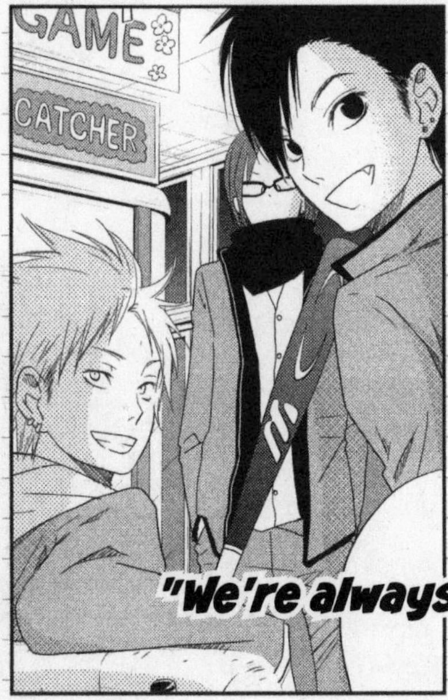
GAME
CATCHER

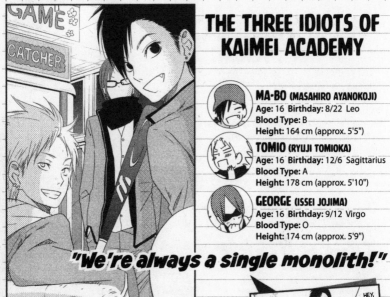

THE THREE IDIOTS OF KAIMEI ACADEMY

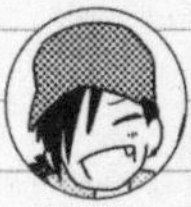

MA-BO (MASAHIRO AYANOKOJI)
Age: 16 **Birthday:** 8/22 Leo
Blood Type: B
Height: 164 cm (approx. 5'5")

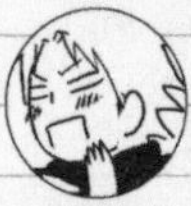

TOMIO (RYUJI TOMIOKA)
Age: 16 **Birthday:** 12/6 Sagittarius
Blood Type: A
Height: 178 cm (approx. 5'10")

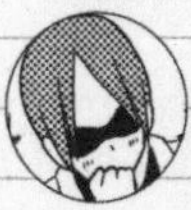

GEORGE (ISSEI JOJIMA)
Age: 16 **Birthday:** 9/12 Virgo
Blood Type: O
Height: 174 cm (approx. 5'9")

"We're always a single monolith!"

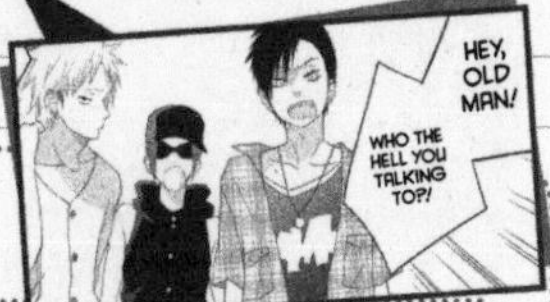
HEY, OLD MAN!
WHO THE HELL YOU TALKING TO?!

★ABOUT THESE CHARACTERS★

Famous troublemakers, even within Kaimei Academy. Ma-Bo and Yamaken have attended since elementary school, while Tomio and George joined in middle school.

Ma-Bo: The most hot-headed and quickest to fight.
Tomio: Actually very passionate about friends. Mature, relative to the others.
George: Seems to be a clever guy.

Each of them comes from quite a good pedigree, but Ma-Bo hails from a particularly wealthy family with a famous conglomerate.

The three of them have too much spare time on their hands and enjoy fighting. It generally begins when 1: Ma-Bo picks a fight or has a fight picked with him, causing 2: Tomio's temper to flare and him to join in and 3: George to make the situation even bigger (whether on purpose or by nature).

Note from Robico: While Yamaken acts like the leader of the group when dealing with others, he coolly backs off when a fight actually breaks out. Tomio will occasionally stop Ma-Bo and George, but he tends to be the most militaristic of the group.

No.

Date

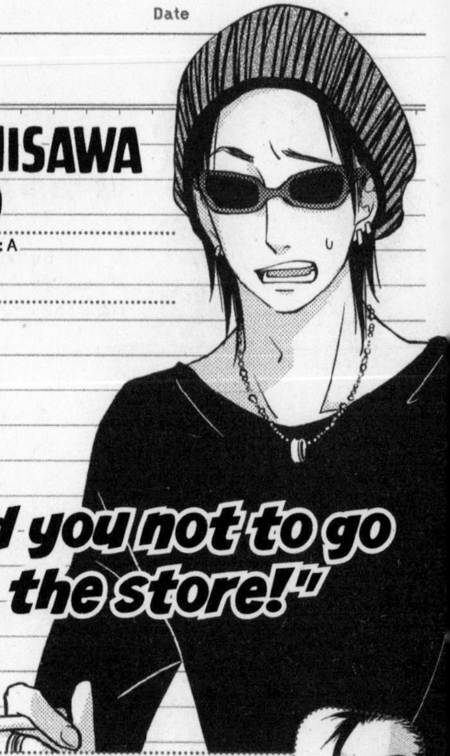

MITSUYOSHI MISAWA (MITCHAN)

Age: 25 **Birthday:** 6/18 Gemini **Blood Type:** A
Height: 185 cm (approx. 6')
Family Structure: Lives with Haru

Cousin of Haru and Yuzan, and Haru's caretaker. The store manager of the Misawa Batting Center. After his mother, who took care of Haru, dies, the two begin to live with each other.

"Haru! I told you not to go crazy inside the store!"

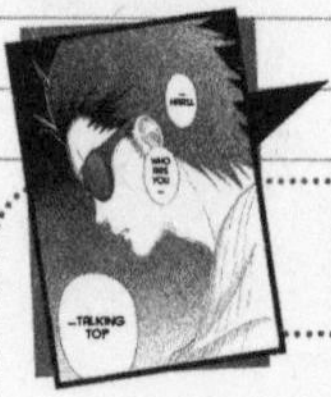

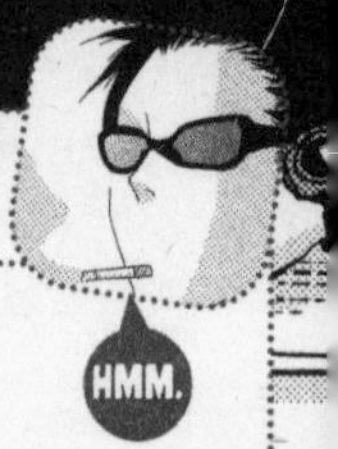
HMM.

★ ABOUT THIS CHARACTER ★

Takes Haru in after Kyoko-san passes away, and has lived with him ever since. Got in his fair share of trouble as a teen, and seems to have lived on his own for a while.

While he had his complaints about his research-obsessed mother, Kyoko-san, the two seemed to have been gradually interacting more after she took Haru in.

Currently in debt to Yuzan and has decided not to take any specific lovers until he finishes paying his debts. Always wears a necklace with a ring on it. He looks exactly like Haru and Yuzan's father behind his glasses, which is apparently why he can't take them off.

Note from Robico: Speaking of which, Mitchan was originally going to be an older guy with a big, thick beard, but my editor told me, "Unless you have good reason, this is a shojo manga, so could you make him handsome?"...which is how he ended up being his current cool self. Looking back on it, I'm truly glad I made that decision. Many thanks to my editor.

No.

Date

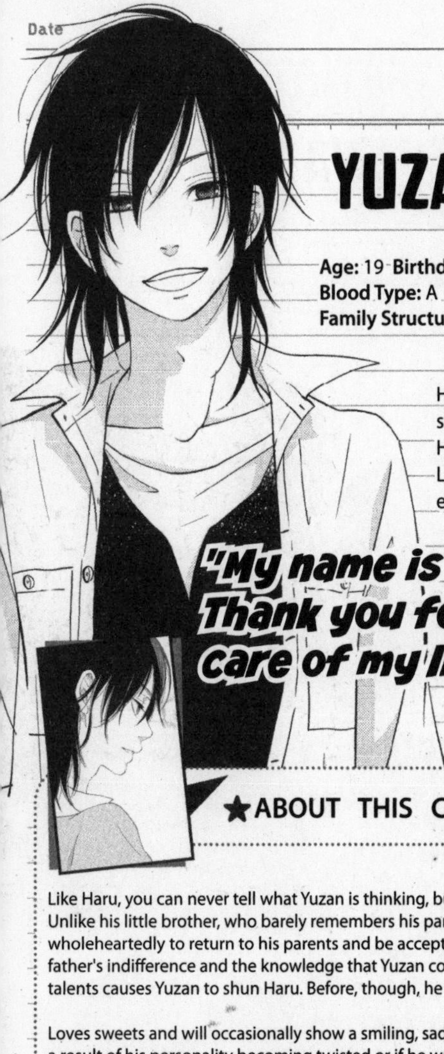

YUZAN YOSHIDA

Age: 19 **Birthday:** 11/5 Scorpio
Blood Type: A **Height:** 176 cm (approx. 5'9")
Family Structure: Father, stepmother, little brother

Haru's older brother and a college student. Seems to have a long past with Haru that has caused Haru to hate him. Loves sweet things and is always seen eating tons of snacks.

"My name is Yuzan Yoshida. Thank you for always taking care of my little brother."

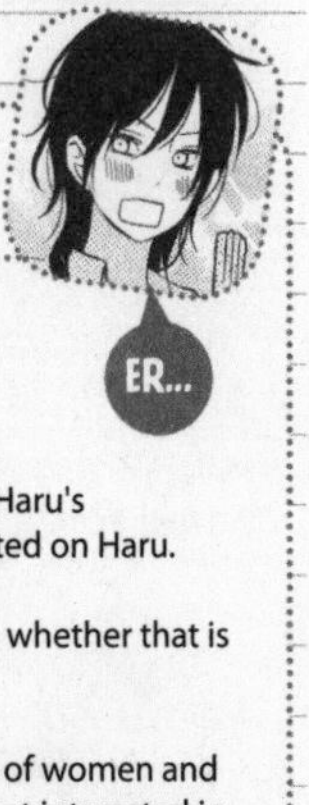
ER...

★ABOUT THIS CHARACTER★

Like Haru, you can never tell what Yuzan is thinking, but in a different way. Unlike his little brother, who barely remembers his parents' faces, Yuzan worked wholeheartedly to return to his parents and be accepted by them. However, his father's indifference and the knowledge that Yuzan could only return because of Haru's talents causes Yuzan to shun Haru. Before, though, he was a kind brother who doted on Haru.

Loves sweets and will occasionally show a smiling, sadistic side, but it isn't known whether that is a result of his personality becoming twisted or if he was simply born that way.

Always acts calm and collected toward everyone, but actually has a strong dislike of women and will run away if a woman gets close to him. That doesn't seem to mean that he's not interested in them, though.

Note from Robico: I think that if Haru and Yuzan had stayed in the countryside and continued to be brought up there, both of them would have been completely different people.

No.

Date · ·

THE MIZUTANI FAMILY

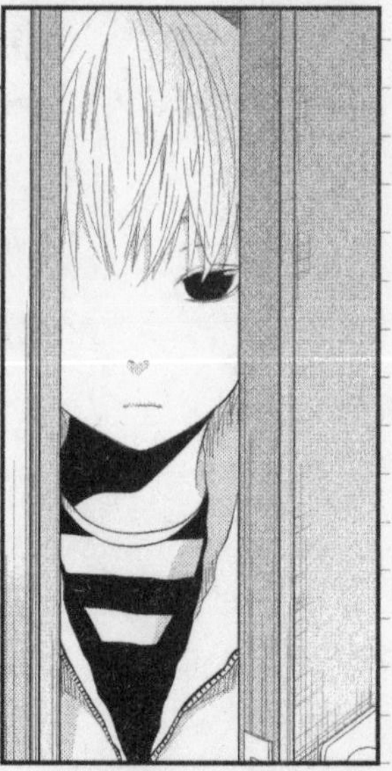

TAKAYA MIZUTANI

Age: 11 **Birthday:** 3/20 Pisces **Blood Type:** B
Height: 138 cm (approx. 4'6")

Shizuku's little brother. Doted on by Shizuku.

"Are you head-over-heels for Haru-san?"

★ ABOUT THIS CHARACTER ★

Like his older sister, Takaya is calm and rarely shows his expressions. However, one can occasionally see his boyish side, such as when he's allowed to have a soft drink on a special day, or when he gets to eat as many snacks as he wants. He plays soccer at school, and unlike his sister, he is reasonably social.

He seems to like pretty, older girls.

The only member of the Mizutani family to have his own computer. He seems to have a bunch of bookmarks saved, but his father and sister are both so bad with technology that they never open the folder...

Note from Robico: I wonder what kind of boy he's going to turn out to be.

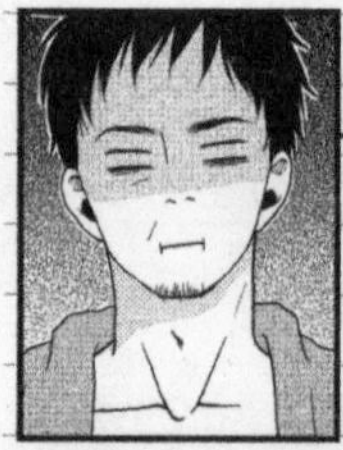

TAKASHI MIZUTANI

Age: 39 **Blood Type:** O
Height: 180 cm (approx. 5'11")

Shizuku's dad. In the field of business since Shizuku was a child, but is unsuccessful. A kind, cheerful, and unreliable father.

"Huh? Are we going to tell her? Are we telling Yoshino-san?"

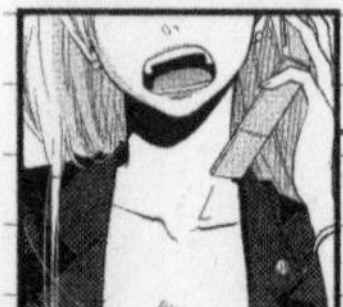

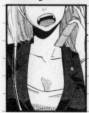

YOSHINO MIZUTANI

Age: 39 **Blood Type:** B
Height: 164 cm (approx. 5'5")

Shizuku's mom. Constantly running all over for her work in order to support the family's finances.

"If you want two, then you just have to work twice as hard!!"

★ ABOUT THESE CHARACTERS ★

While the mother of the family was a talented enough student that she passed the civil service exam, her dream was to become a wife, and so she got married when she graduated. However, her husband's debts forced her to begin working, and before long, she was shooting up the ladder.

As Yoshino is even more ambitious than her daughter, she is constantly demanding that her husband become a first-rate man. He seems to have a pointlessly long resume, and he can often be heard saying, "Your father may look this way, but he actually used to be a (XYZ)." How the two fell in love is the greatest mystery of the Mizutani family.

No.

Date

THE YOSHIDA FAMILY

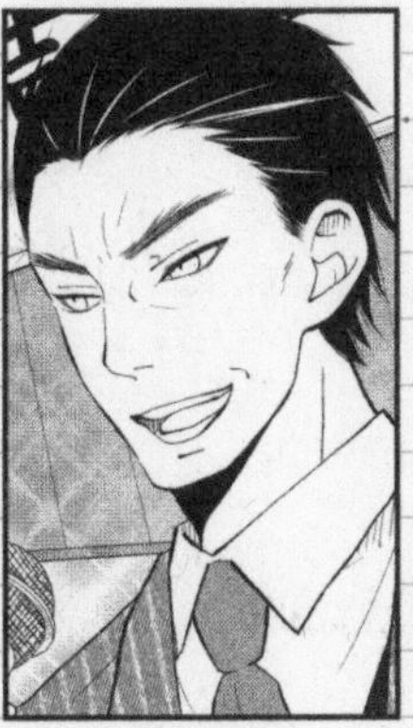

TAIZO YOSHIDA

Age: 53 **Blood Type:** A **Height:** 176 cm (approx. 5'9")

Yuzan and Haru's father. Seems to have a strong interest in women. A prominent politician. Has a second wife named Michiru-san.

"A little too young!"

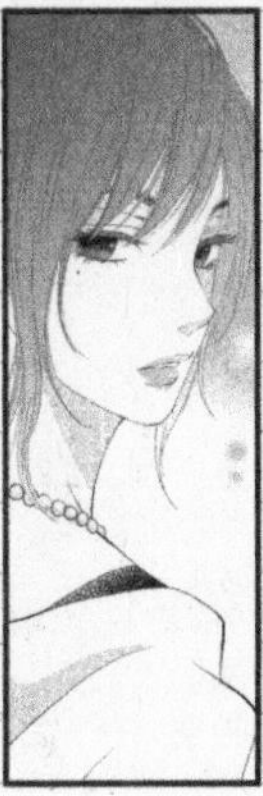

YUZAN AND HARU'S MOM

Age: 41 **Blood Type:** O
Height: 162 cm (approx. 5'4")

Currently divorced. Seems to have been a fairly selfish woman. Looks exactly like a female version of Yuzan.

★ ABOUT THESE CHARACTERS ★

A charming and arrogant father whose nickname is "Hasta la Romeo," and an otherworldly, girlish mother. She seems to have hated him and his womanizing quite a bit.

Yuzan seems to want to meet her, but...

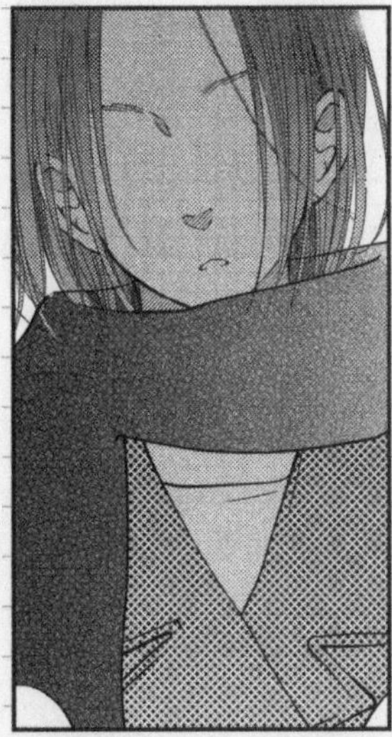

KYOKO MISAWA

Age at Death: 49 **Blood Type:** A **Height:** 170 cm (approx. 5'7")

Haru's aunt and Mitchan's mother. An assistant professor at a university. Took care of Haru from the time he was in middle school.

"Haru-kun. I'm going to cast a magic spell on you."

★ ABOUT THIS CHARACTER ★

Mitsuyoshi's mother, as well as Haru and Yuzan's father's little sister. Deceased. A researcher, she hated being tied to her home. One day, she found herself pregnant with Mitsuyoshi and was disinherited. The father is unknown. Misawa is the family name of Haru's grandmother (Kyoko-san's mother). A biology researcher, she would frequently take Haru to her lab. According to Oga-sensei, who knew her, she was talented as a student but had her problems as a person.

No. ....

Date . .

THE PEOPLE OF SHOYO HIGH SCHOOL

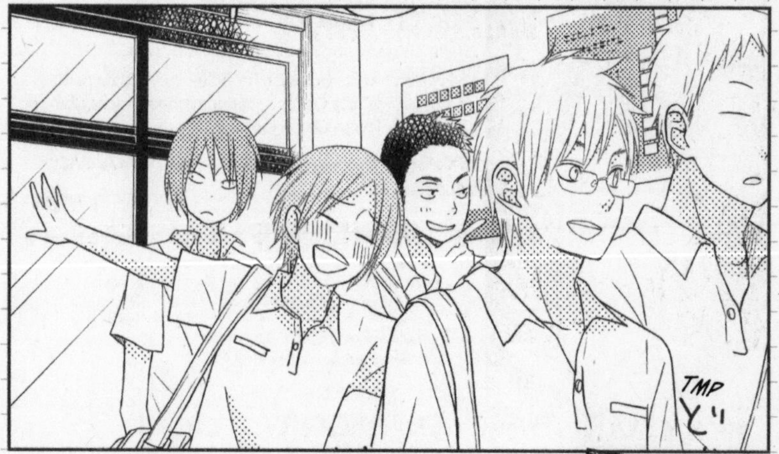
TMP

THE BASEBALL CLUB

"This is what's normal for us."

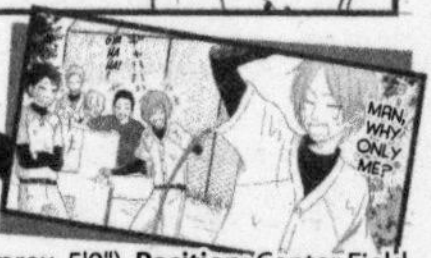
MAN, WHY ONLY ME?

From the left ....

Terajima-kun Age: 16 **Birthday:** 11/29 Sagittarius **Blood Type:** O **Height:** 174 cm (approx. 5'9") **Position:** Center Field

Shimoyanagi-kun Age: 16 **Birthday:** 6/2 Gemini **Blood Type:** A **Height:** 168 cm (approx. 5'6") **Position:** Right Field

Seri-kun Age: 16 **Birthday:** 8/15 Leo **Blood Type:** A **Height:** 172 cm (approx. 5'8") **Position:** First Base (Cleanup Hitter)

Shiota-kun Age: 16 **Birthday:** 12/22 Capricorn **Blood Type:** A **Height:** 170 cm (approx. 5'7") **Position:** Catcher

Murakami-kun Age: 16 **Birthday:** 2/19 Pisces **Blood Type:** B **Height:** 176 cm (approx. 5'9") **Position:** Pitcher

*Sasayan is Shortstop

★ ABOUT THESE CHARACTERS ★

The boys of the Shoyo High School Baseball Club who Sasayan can always be found hanging out with. This year, the team was defeated in the high school tournament's second round.

To quickly describe the personality of each member:

Shimoyanagi-kun: Weak-spirited and indecisive; often messed with by the rest of the Baseball Club.
Seri-kun: Cheerful and not very careful, but can always be counted on when it matters.
Terajima-kun: Determined and sometimes insensitive, he looks up to strong men. Likes manga about delinquents.
Shiota-kun: Calm and brotherly, Shiota-kun brings the group together.
Murakami-kun: Laid back and a bit high-strung in certain ways.

Shiota-kun will probably be captain of the team next year. Murakami-kun has a little brother who is friends with Shizuku's little brother Takaya. Seri-kun and Terajima-kun are constantly messing with Shimoyanagi-kun, something he truly dislikes by the time he enters his second year.

No.

Date

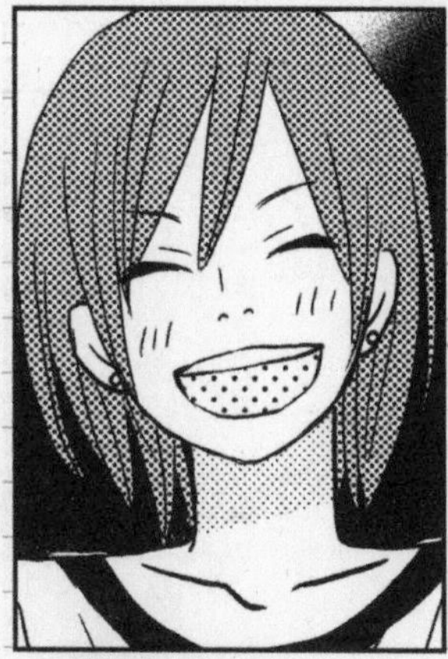

SAEKO NINOMIYA (SAEKO-SENSEI)

Age: 25 **Blood Type:** A **Height:** 162 cm (approx. 5'4")

Shizuku and Haru's homeroom teacher during their first year of high school. Currently the homeroom teacher for Haru's class. Teaches Japanese language classes.

"Yoshida-kun, you can't bring roosters to school!"

★ ABOUT THIS CHARACTER ★

As she is still a fairly new teacher, she was unable to refuse teaching the class containing Haru, the mega problem-child (for two years in a row, at that). However, when Haru begins to blend in at school, her stock rises among the other teachers, who now call her "GTS" (Great Teacher Saeko) behind her back.

OGA-SENSEI

Age: 66 **Blood Type:** O **Height:** 163 cm (approx. 5'4")

An earth sciences teacher idolized by Haru. Seems to have known Haru's aunt, Kyoko-san, as well.

"You have so much potential, if only you would reach for it."

★ ABOUT THIS CHARACTER ★

After finishing his life as a university researcher, he is asked by his old high school to come and teach earth sciences. Takes an interest in his old colleague Kyoko-san's nephew, Haru, and begins to watch over him.

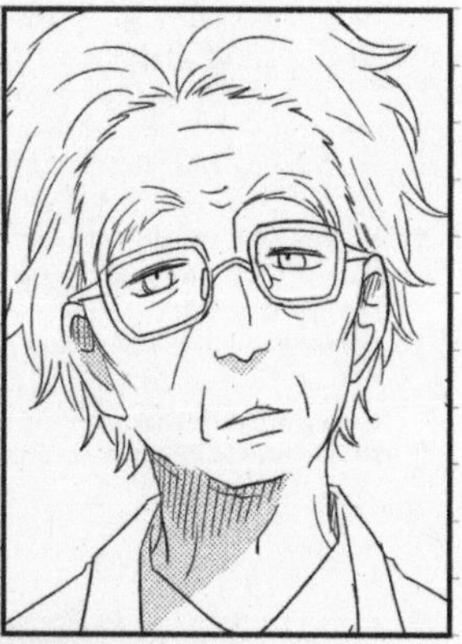

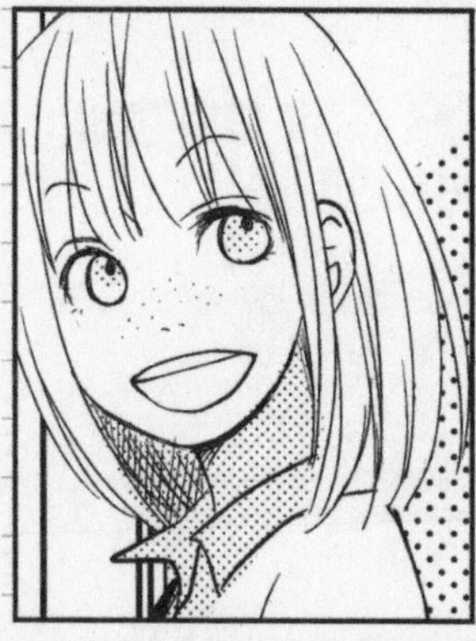

HACHIGASAKI-SAN

Age: 16 **Blood Type:** A **Height:** 158 cm (approx. 5'2")

A hardworking girl in the same class as Haru, starting their second year.

"I'm Hachigasaki, captain of Class A!"

★ ABOUT THIS CHARACTER ★

Friends with Oshima-san.

Note from Robico: I wanted to draw a girl with freckles. I like her quite a bit.

OTHER CHARACTERS

TAKUMA ANDO

Age: 25 **Birthday:** 7/29 Leo
Blood Type: AB **Height:** 178 cm (approx. 5'10")
Family Structure: Unknown

The Yoshida family's driver. Likes high school girls.

"There's some cool guys over there. Want to have some fun?"

★ ABOUT THIS CHARACTER ★

Originally the third private secretary for the Yoshida family, but is basically just Yuzan's driver. He has known Mitchan for a long time, and it seems like that is how he was hired at his current job, though it's uncertain. Appears to be a lover of high school girls, and will frequently do things like bring dating sims into Mitchan's house without permission while Yuzan is taking classes. Whether he's messing with Haru or calmly deflecting Yuzan's caustic remarks, it's hard to tell if he's being serious or not. It does seem like he takes his job seriously, at the very least. Doesn't drink.

Note from Robico: I really did mean to make him a more serious character at first.

PROFESSOR KIRITANI & GOTODA-SAN

★ ABOUT THESE CHARACTERS ★

Haru's aunt Kyoko-san's former colleagues. They seem to still ask Haru if he wants to come to their lab.

Gotoda-san is Professor Kiritani's assistant, as well as a fairly extreme woman.

No.

Date

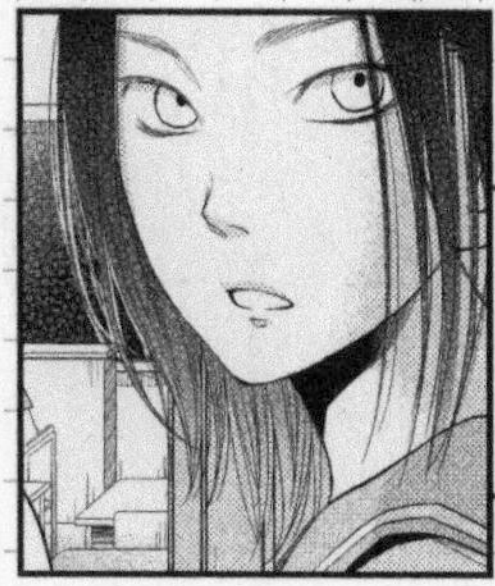

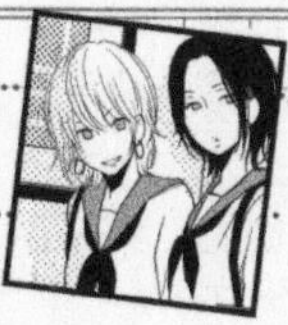

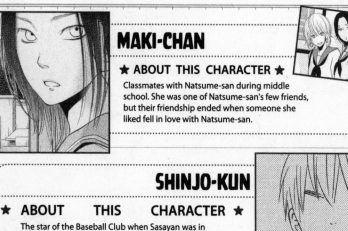

MAKI-CHAN

★ ABOUT THIS CHARACTER ★

Classmates with Natsume-san during middle school. She was one of Natsume-san's few friends, but their friendship ended when someone she liked fell in love with Natsume-san.

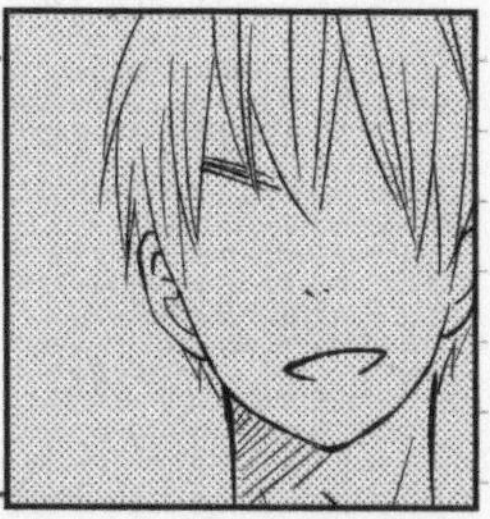

SHINJO-KUN

★ ABOUT THIS CHARACTER ★

The star of the Baseball Club when Sasayan was in middle school. It seems to have been his fault that Sasayan's team wasn't allowed to compete. Haru saves him when he's getting beaten up by his seniors.

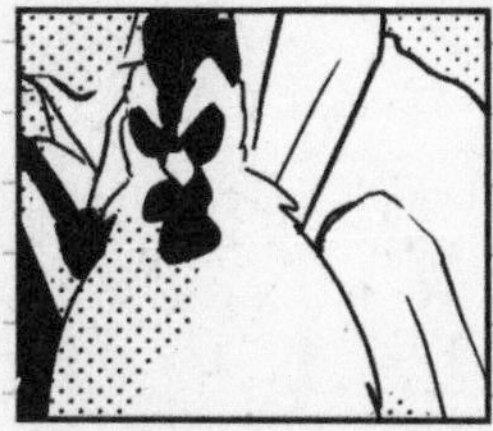

NAGOYA

A rooster that Haru picked up and eventually raises at school.

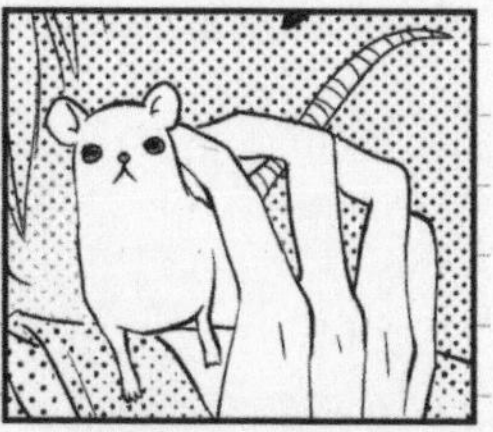

GURIGURA

A mouse that Shimoyanagi from the Baseball Club takes care of.

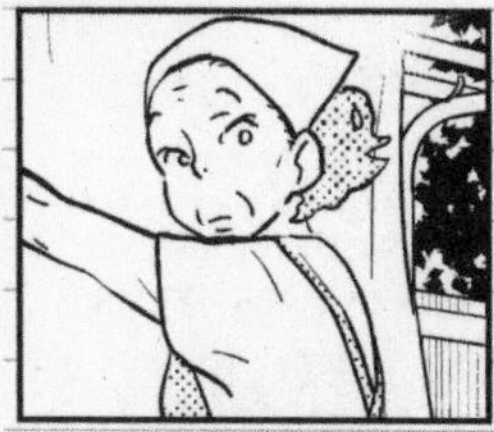

TONE-SAN

An older housekeeper who took care of the separate residence Haru and Yuzan lived in when they were young.

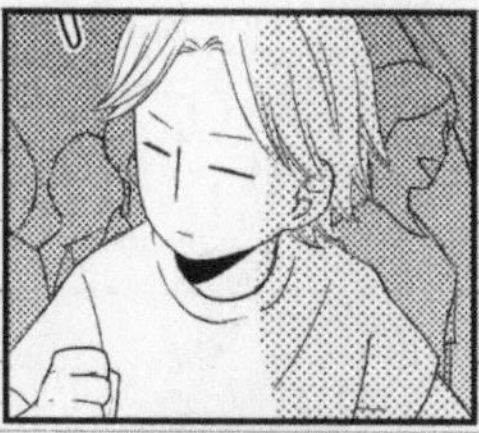

MURAYAN

The little brother of Murakami-kun from the Baseball Club, and classmates with Takaya. His haircut is apparently fashionable.

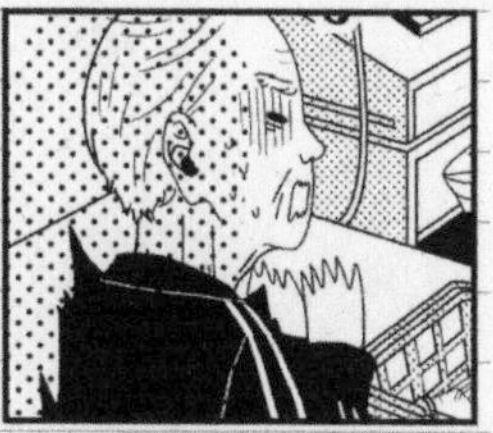

SAMEJIMA-SAN

A frequent customer at the mini-market previously run by Shizuku's father. His purpose in life is to buy items on discount in order to be praised by his wife.

SPECIAL

HOW MY LITTLE MONSTER IS MADE!

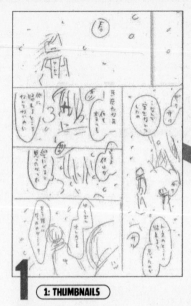

This section will show how a page of *My Little Monster* is created. This page is from Haru's flashback in chapter 40.

1: THUMBNAILS

While Robico's manuscripts are drawn digitally, the thumbnails for these are written with pencil and paper. These thumbnails are scanned after they are finished, and panel lines and word bubbles are then added.

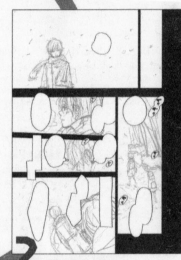

2: ROUGH DRAFT

A rough draft is drawn after panel lines and word bubbles are completed. While it depends on mood, Robico's regular pace is ten pages a day.

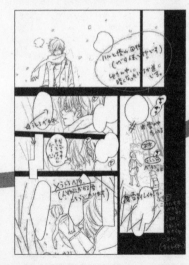

3: INKING & CHOOSING BACKGROUNDS

After drawing the rough draft, Robico begins to ink the lines while adding instructions for assistants regarding backgrounds. As this work is conducted using digital files, the files are sent with instructions written on them like this.

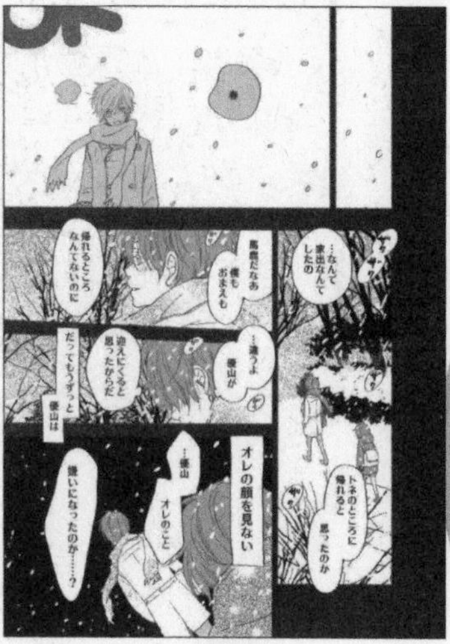
…なんて家出なんてしたの
馬鹿だなぁ 俺もおまえも
帰れるところなんてないのに
…違うよ 優山が
迎えにくると思ったからだ
だってもうずっと
優山は
トネのところに帰れると思ったのか
オレの顔を見ない
…優山 オレのこと
嫌いになったのか……?

6: FINISHED!!

The images are cleaned up and the dialogue is inserted to finish the page. This sample data is sent together with image-only data, and the dialogue is replaced with the font that will be used in the printed page. Margins and other small touches are added to make it the completed page seen by readers.

REVEALED FOR THE FIRST TIME EVER!

ROBICO'S SCREEN WHILE WORKING ON A PAGE!

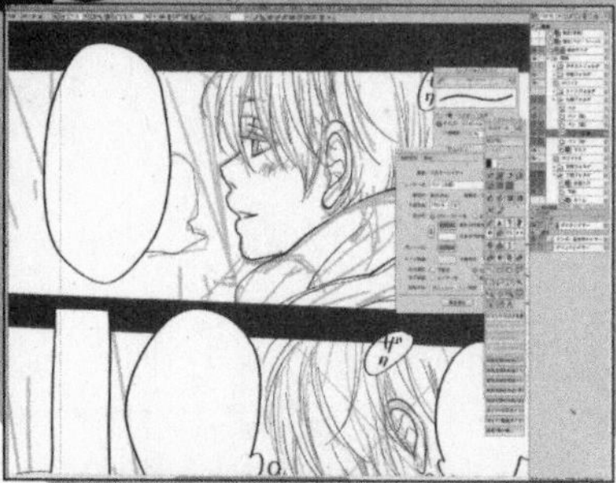

This is a special screen capture we received of Robico's computer during the production process. This manuscript is being drawn in a program known as Comic Studio, but it seems as though various custom pen settings, tool palettes, and more have been added for ease of use.

4: BACKGROUNDS COMPLETED

This is the page after inking and backgrounds are complete. This is a preliminary file that has yet to be adjusted, and it's amusing to see the backgrounds laid over the characters.

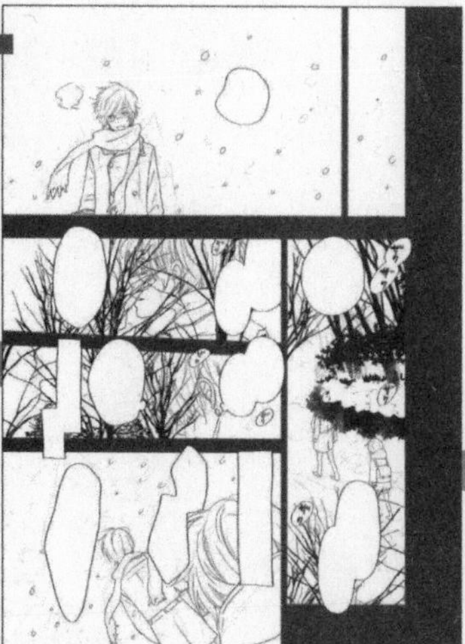

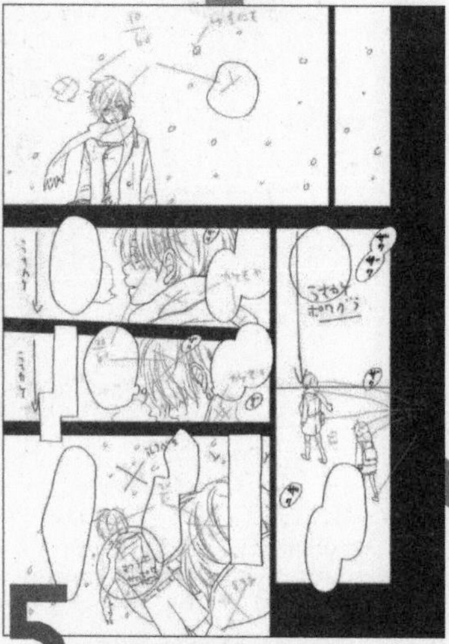

5: SELECT TONES

This is the same page after selecting which screentones to use. "10/60" means a 60-line tone at 10%, while other instructions, such as "usukake" and "powagura," seem to be the names of tone patterns.

No.

SPECIAL ORIGINAL MANGA: ASAKO NATSUME'S DAILY LIFE

Natsume Asako no Nichijo

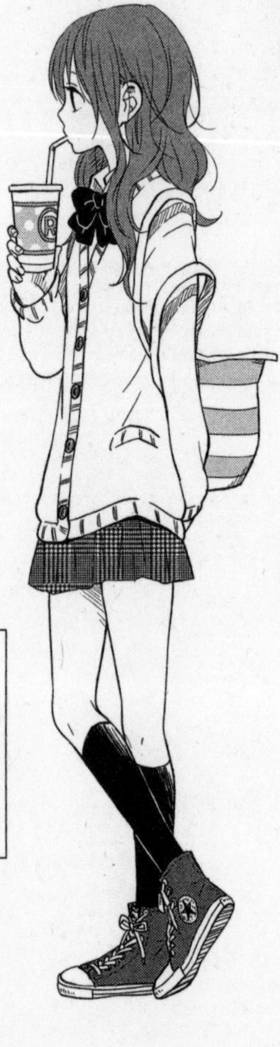

*IMAGINE THIS TAKES PLACE AROUND THE TIME SHE'S A FIRST-YEAR.

PART 1: FRIENDS

PART 2: NATURAL ENEMIES

PART 3: IRL MEETUP

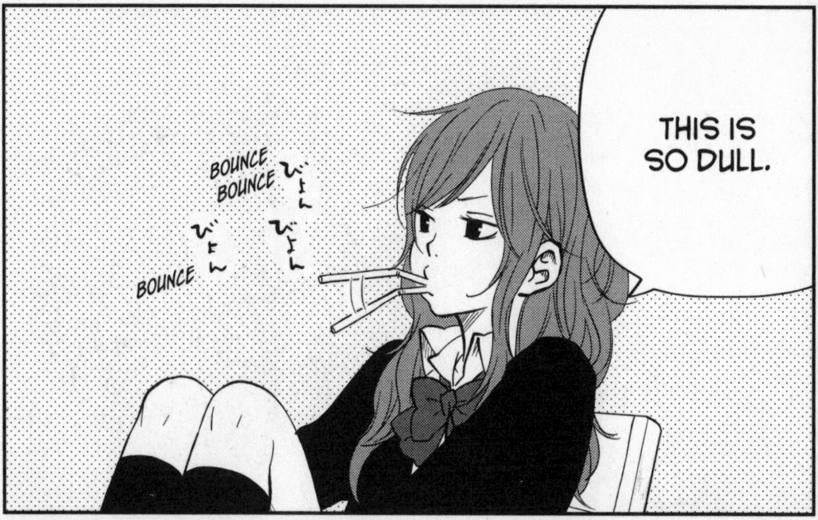
THIS IS SO DULL.
BOUNCE
BOUNCE
びよん びよん
びよん
BOUNCE

PART 1: FRIENDS

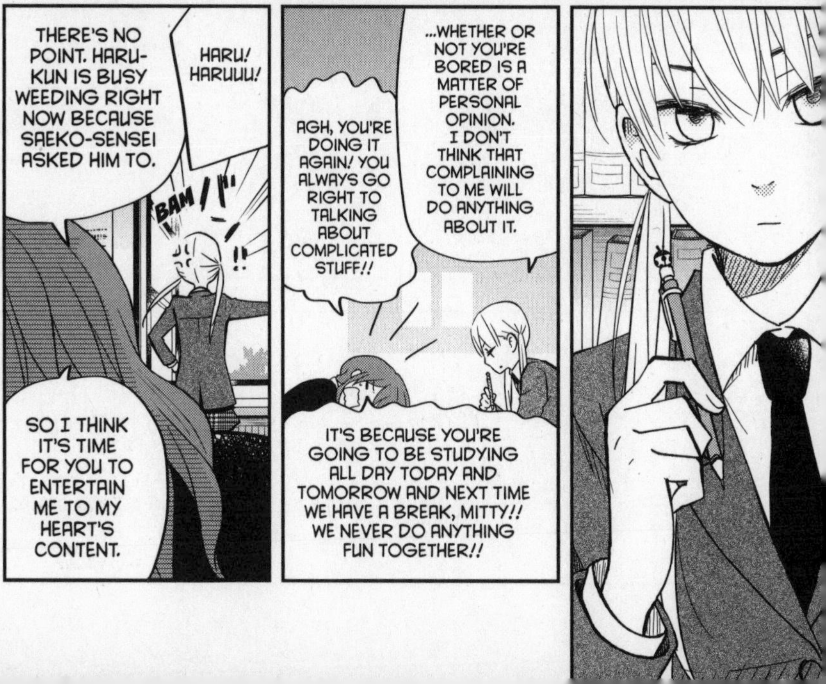
...WHETHER OR NOT YOU'RE BORED IS A MATTER OF PERSONAL OPINION. I DON'T THINK THAT COMPLAINING TO ME WILL DO ANYTHING ABOUT IT.
AGH, YOU'RE DOING IT AGAIN! YOU ALWAYS GO RIGHT TO TALKING ABOUT COMPLICATED STUFF!!
IT'S BECAUSE YOU'RE GOING TO BE STUDYING ALL DAY TODAY AND TOMORROW AND NEXT TIME WE HAVE A BREAK, MITTY!! WE NEVER DO ANYTHING FUN TOGETHER!!
HARU! HARUUU!
THERE'S NO POINT. HARU-KUN IS BUSY WEEDING RIGHT NOW BECAUSE SAEKO-SENSEI ASKED HIM TO.
BAM
!!
SO I THINK IT'S TIME FOR YOU TO ENTERTAIN ME TO MY HEART'S CONTENT.

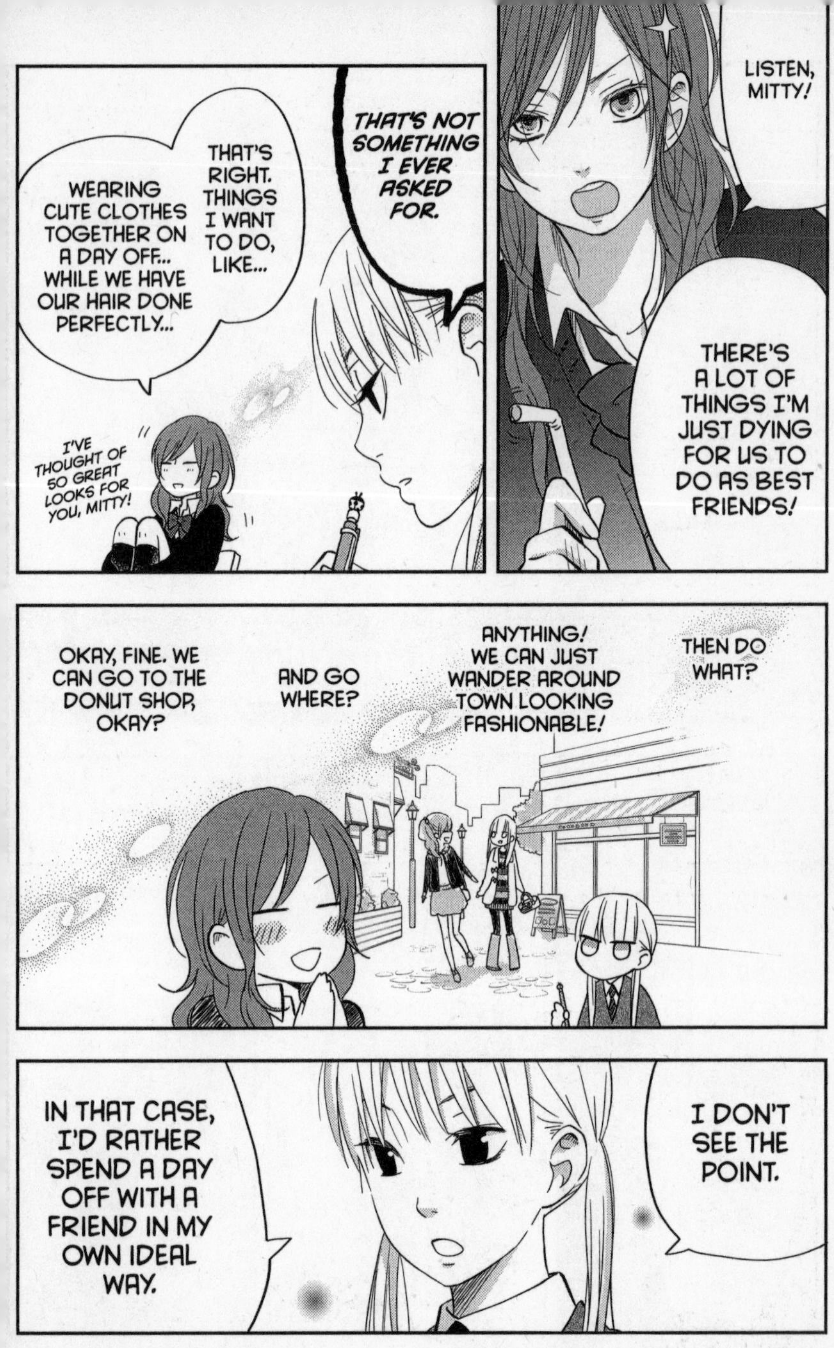
LISTEN, MITTY!
THERE'S A LOT OF THINGS I'M JUST DYING FOR US TO DO AS BEST FRIENDS!
THAT'S NOT SOMETHING I EVER ASKED FOR.
THAT'S RIGHT. THINGS I WANT TO DO, LIKE...
WEARING CUTE CLOTHES TOGETHER ON A DAY OFF... WHILE WE HAVE OUR HAIR DONE PERFECTLY...
I'VE THOUGHT OF SO GREAT LOOKS FOR YOU, MITTY!
THEN DO WHAT?
ANYTHING! WE CAN JUST WANDER AROUND TOWN LOOKING FASHIONABLE!
AND GO WHERE?
OKAY, FINE. WE CAN GO TO THE DONUT SHOP, OKAY?
I DON'T SEE THE POINT.
IN THAT CASE, I'D RATHER SPEND A DAY OFF WITH A FRIEND IN MY OWN IDEAL WAY.

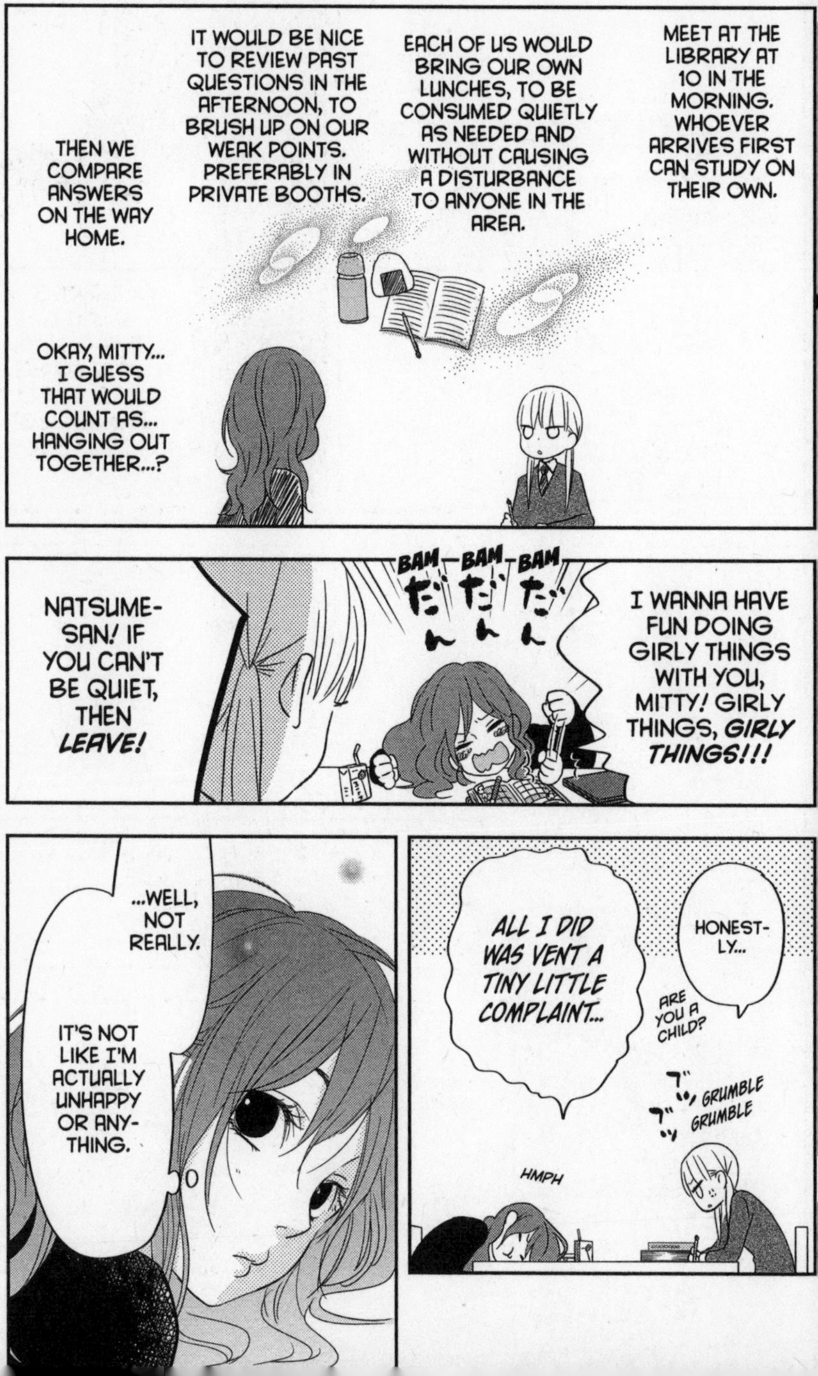
MEET AT THE LIBRARY AT 10 IN THE MORNING. WHOEVER ARRIVES FIRST CAN STUDY ON THEIR OWN.
EACH OF US WOULD BRING OUR OWN LUNCHES, TO BE CONSUMED QUIETLY AS NEEDED AND WITHOUT CAUSING A DISTURBANCE TO ANYONE IN THE AREA.
IT WOULD BE NICE TO REVIEW PAST QUESTIONS IN THE AFTERNOON, TO BRUSH UP ON OUR WEAK POINTS. PREFERABLY IN PRIVATE BOOTHS.
THEN WE COMPARE ANSWERS ON THE WAY HOME.
OKAY, MITTY... I GUESS THAT WOULD COUNT AS... HANGING OUT TOGETHER...?
I WANNA HAVE FUN DOING GIRLY THINGS WITH YOU, MITTY! GIRLY THINGS, GIRLY THINGS!!!
BAM だん BAM だん BAM だん
NATSUME-SAN! IF YOU CAN'T BE QUIET, THEN LEAVE!
HONEST-LY...
ARE YOU A CHILD?
ALL I DID WAS VENT A TINY LITTLE COMPLAINT...
ブツ GRUMBLE ブツ GRUMBLE
HMPH
...WELL, NOT REALLY.
IT'S NOT LIKE I'M ACTUALLY UNHAPPY OR ANY-THING.

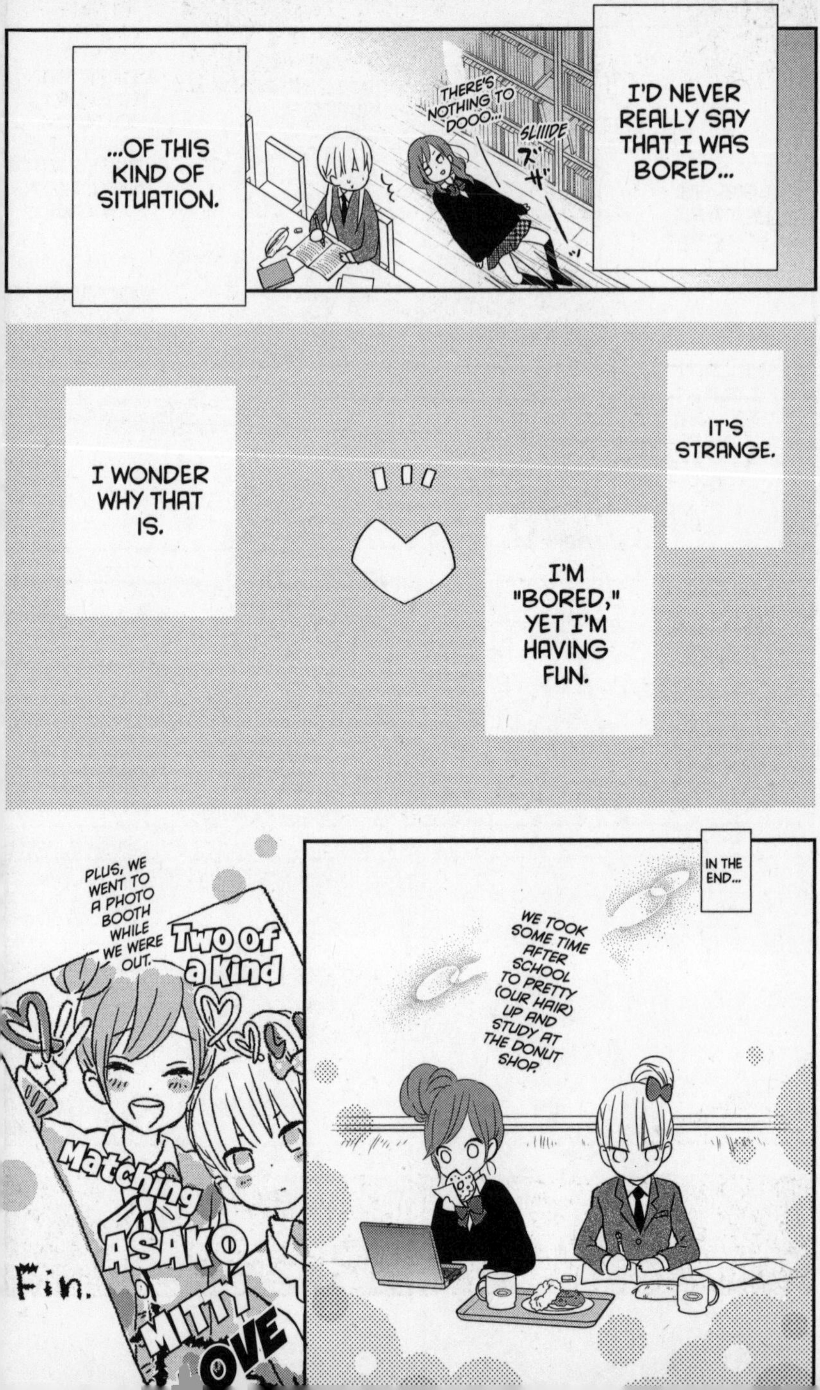
I'D NEVER REALLY SAY THAT I WAS BORED...
THERE'S NOTHING TO DOOO...
SLIIIDE
ズザ
...OF THIS KIND OF SITUATION.
IT'S STRANGE.
I'M "BORED," YET I'M HAVING FUN.
I WONDER WHY THAT IS.
IN THE END...
WE TOOK SOME TIME AFTER SCHOOL TO PRETTY (OUR HAIR) UP AND STUDY AT THE DONUT SHOP.
PLUS, WE WENT TO A PHOTO BOOTH WHILE WE WERE OUT.
Two of a Kind
Matching
ASAKO
MITTY
LOVE
Fin.

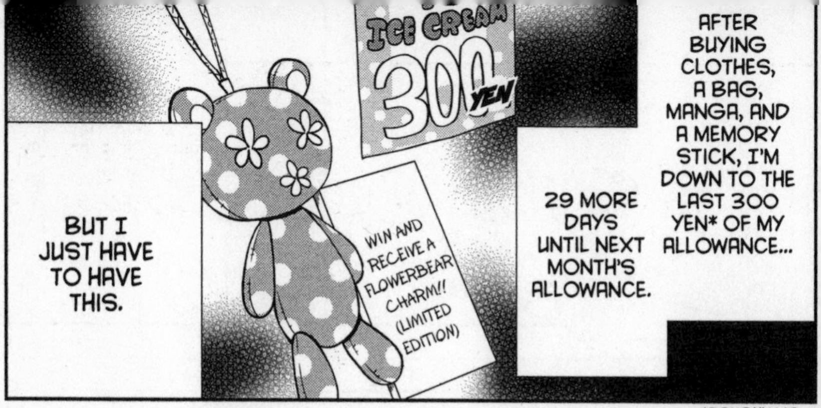
AFTER BUYING CLOTHES, A BAG, MANGA, AND A MEMORY STICK, I'M DOWN TO THE LAST 300 YEN* OF MY ALLOWANCE...
29 MORE DAYS UNTIL NEXT MONTH'S ALLOWANCE.
ICE CREAM 300 YEN
WIN AND RECEIVE A FLOWERBEAR CHARM!! (LIMITED EDITION)
BUT I JUST HAVE TO HAVE THIS.

*ROUGHLY $3.

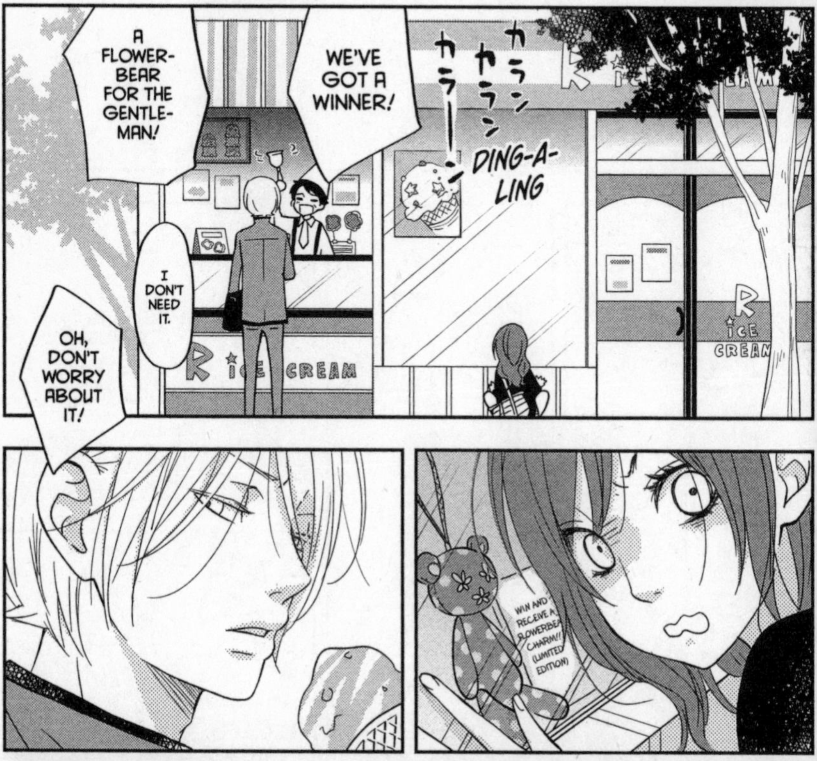
カラン
カラン
カラーン
DING-A-LING
WE'VE GOT A WINNER!
A FLOWER-BEAR FOR THE GENTLE-MAN!
I DON'T NEED IT.
OH, DON'T WORRY ABOUT IT!
ICE CREAM
WIN AND RECEIVE A FLOWERBEAR CHARM!! (LIMITED EDITION)

PART 2: NATURAL ENEMIES

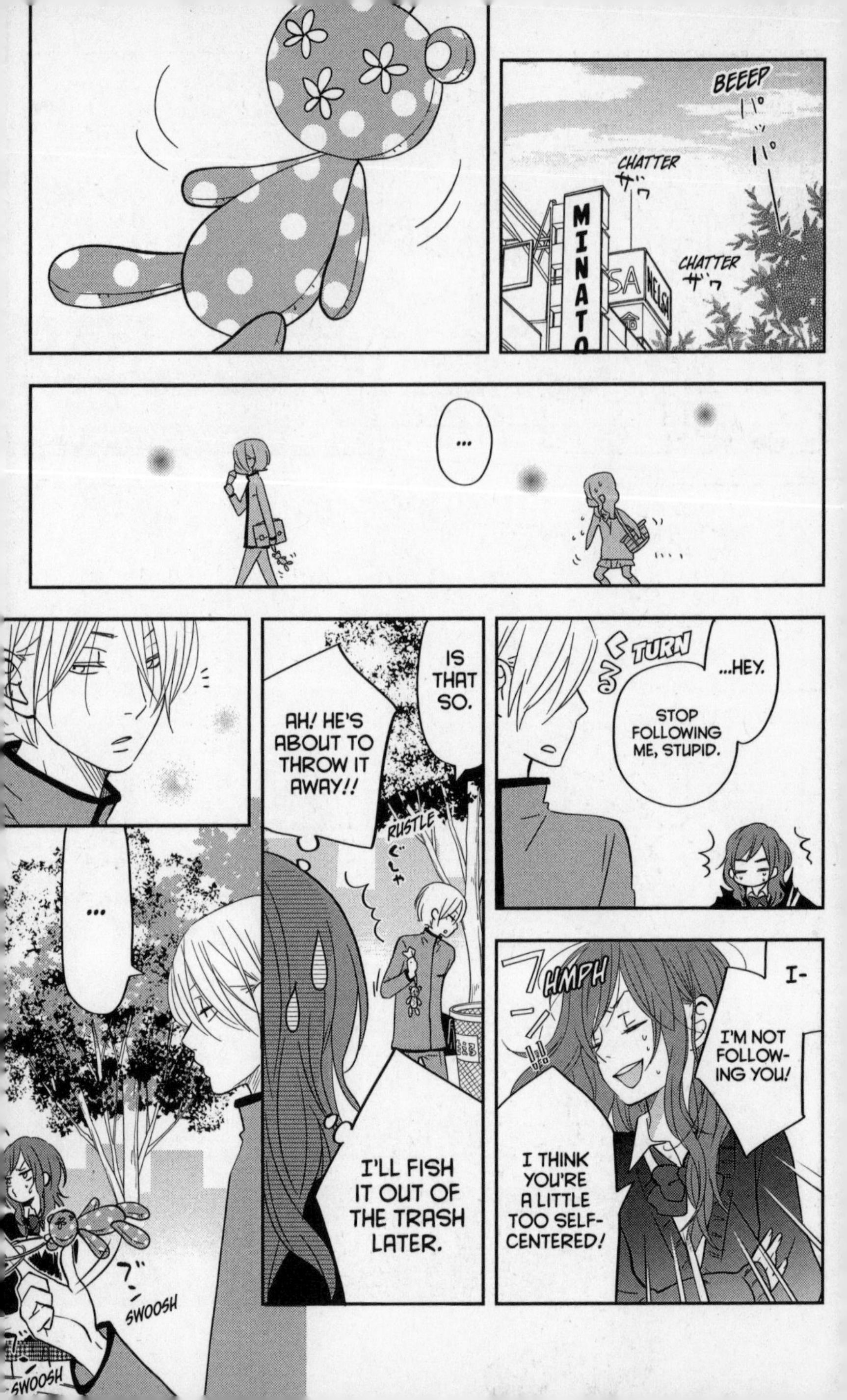
BEEEP
パッパー
CHATTER
ザワ
MINATO
SA
MELSA
CHATTER
ザワ
...
....
TURN
...HEY.
STOP FOLLOWING ME, STUPID.
I-
I'M NOT FOLLOW-ING YOU!
HMPH
I THINK YOU'RE A LITTLE TOO SELF-CENTERED!
IS THAT SO.
AH! HE'S ABOUT TO THROW IT AWAY!!
RUSTLE
I'LL FISH IT OUT OF THE TRASH LATER.
...
SWOOSH
SWOOSH

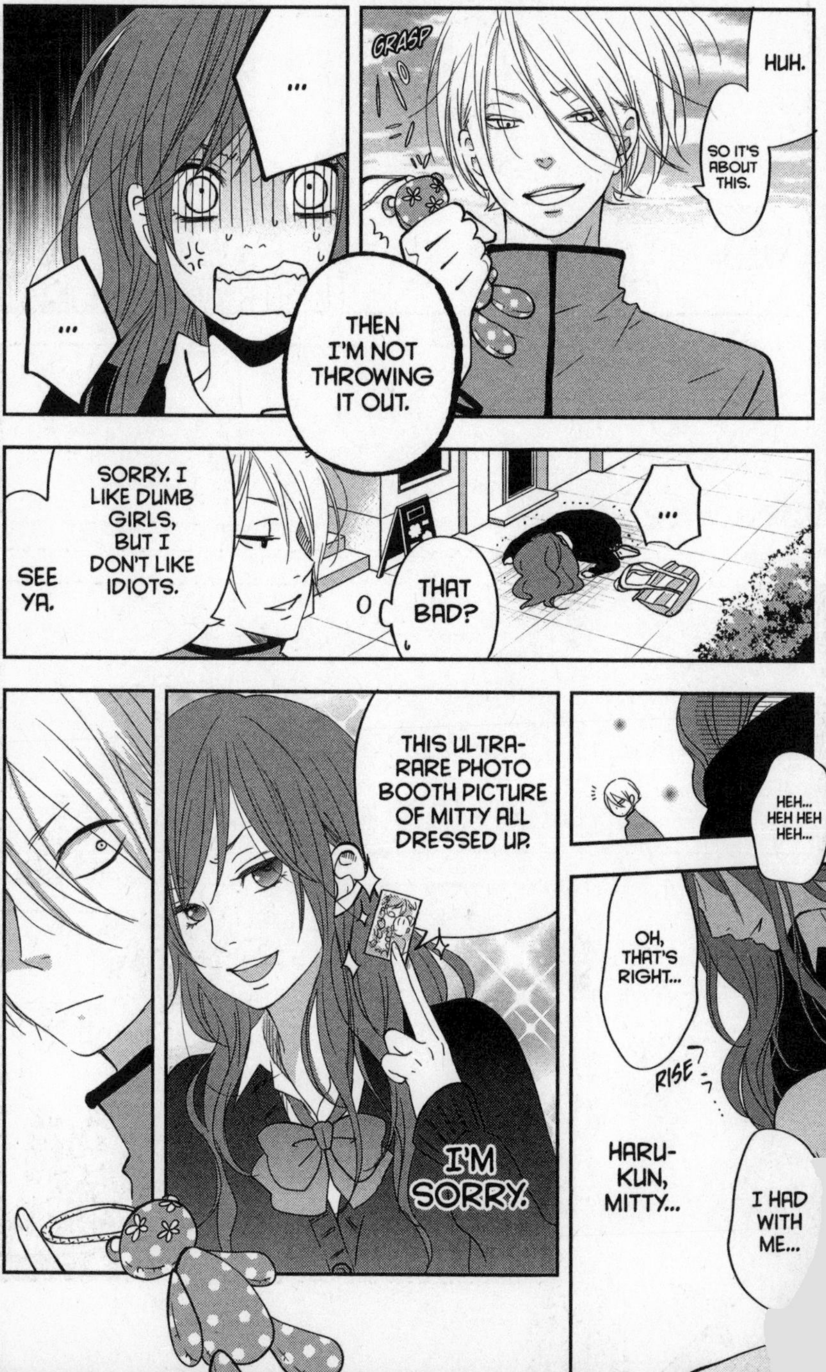
GRASP
HUH.
SO IT'S ABOUT THIS.
THEN I'M NOT THROWING IT OUT.
...
...
...
THAT BAD?
SORRY. I LIKE DUMB GIRLS, BUT I DON'T LIKE IDIOTS.
SEE YA.
HEH... HEH HEH HEH...
OH, THAT'S RIGHT...
RISE
HARU-KUN, MITTY...
I HAD WITH ME...
THIS ULTRA-RARE PHOTO BOOTH PICTURE OF MITTY ALL DRESSED UP.
I'M SORRY.

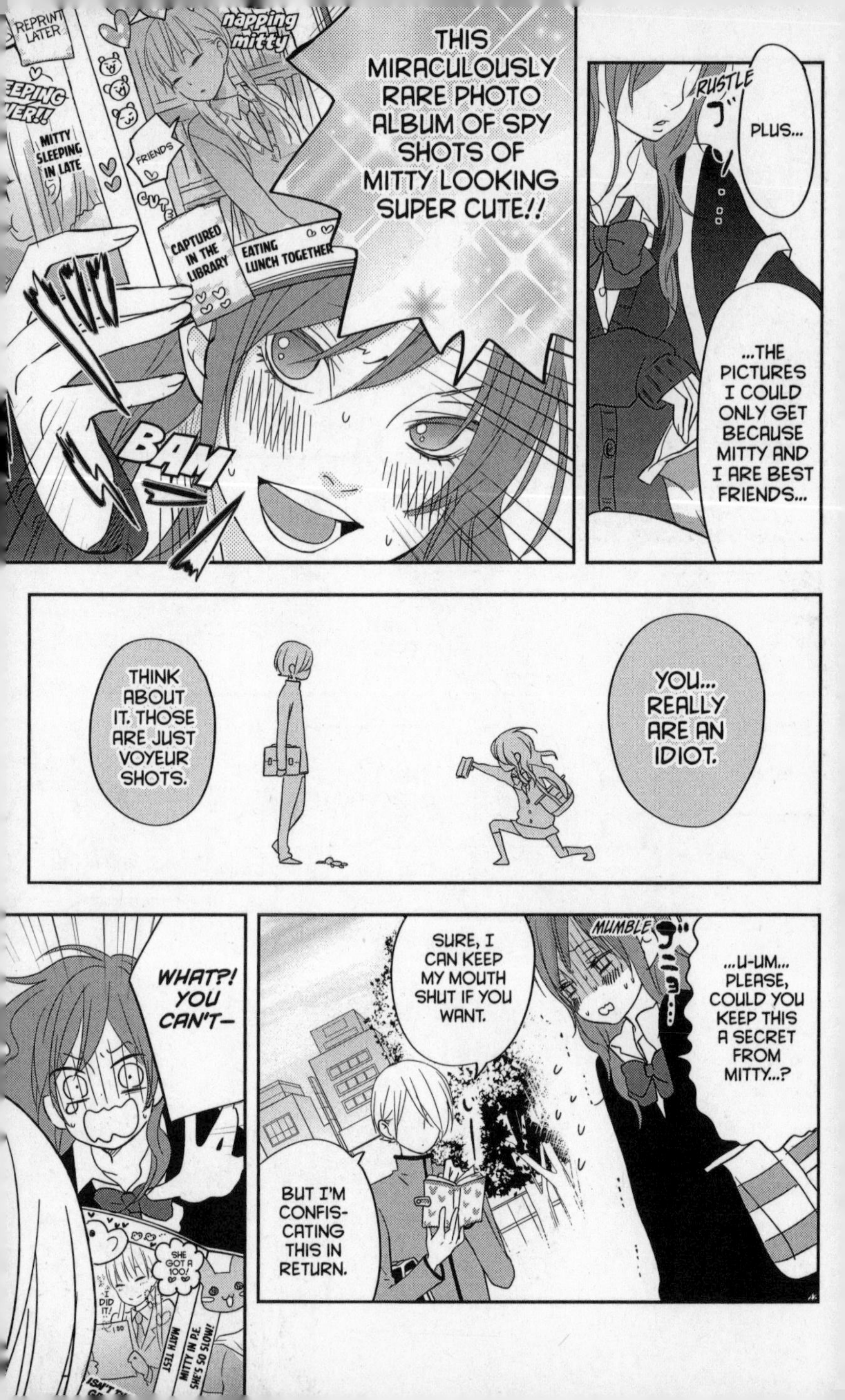
RUSTLE
PLUS...
...THE PICTURES I COULD ONLY GET BECAUSE MITTY AND I ARE BEST FRIENDS...
THIS MIRACULOUSLY RARE PHOTO ALBUM OF SPY SHOTS OF MITTY LOOKING SUPER CUTE!!
napping mitty
REPRINT LATER
MITTY SLEEPING IN LATE
FRIENDS
CUTE
CAPTURED IN THE LIBRARY
EATING LUNCH TOGETHER
BAM
YOU... REALLY ARE AN IDIOT.
THINK ABOUT IT. THOSE ARE JUST VOYEUR SHOTS.
MUMBLE
...U-UM... PLEASE, COULD YOU KEEP THIS A SECRET FROM MITTY...?
SURE, I CAN KEEP MY MOUTH SHUT IF YOU WANT.
BUT I'M CONFIS-CATING THIS IN RETURN.
WHAT?! YOU CAN'T—
SHE GOT A 100!
I DID IT!
MATH TEST
MITTY IN P.E. SHE'S SO SLOW!

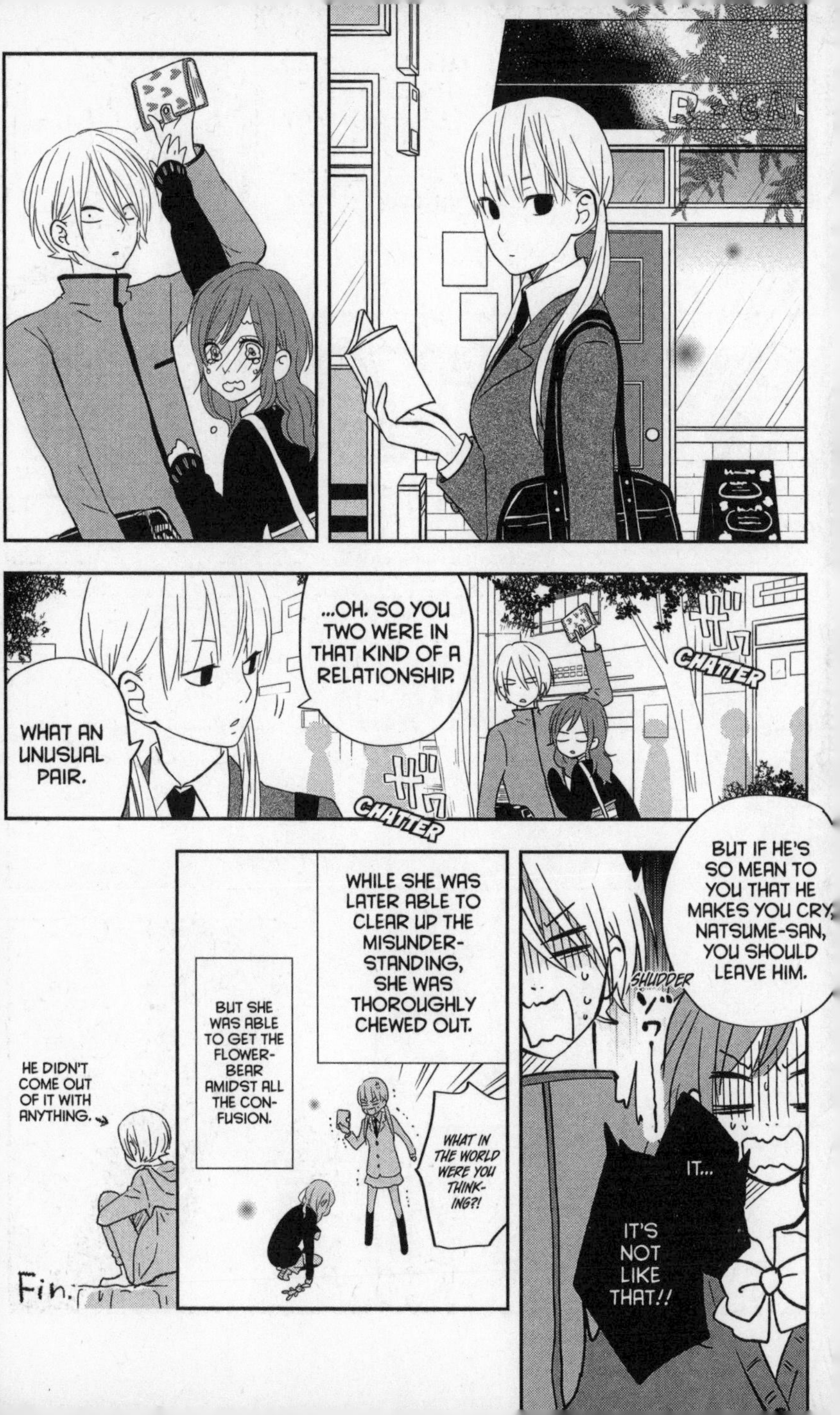
CHATTER
...OH. SO YOU TWO WERE IN THAT KIND OF A RELATIONSHIP.
WHAT AN UNUSUAL PAIR.
CHATTER
BUT IF HE'S SO MEAN TO YOU THAT HE MAKES YOU CRY, NATSUME-SAN, YOU SHOULD LEAVE HIM.
SHUDDER
IT...
IT'S NOT LIKE THAT!!
WHILE SHE WAS LATER ABLE TO CLEAR UP THE MISUNDER-STANDING, SHE WAS THOROUGHLY CHEWED OUT.
BUT SHE WAS ABLE TO GET THE FLOWER-BEAR AMIDST ALL THE CON-FUSION.
WHAT IN THE WORLD WERE YOU THINK-ING?!
HE DIDN'T COME OUT OF IT WITH ANYTHING.
Fin.

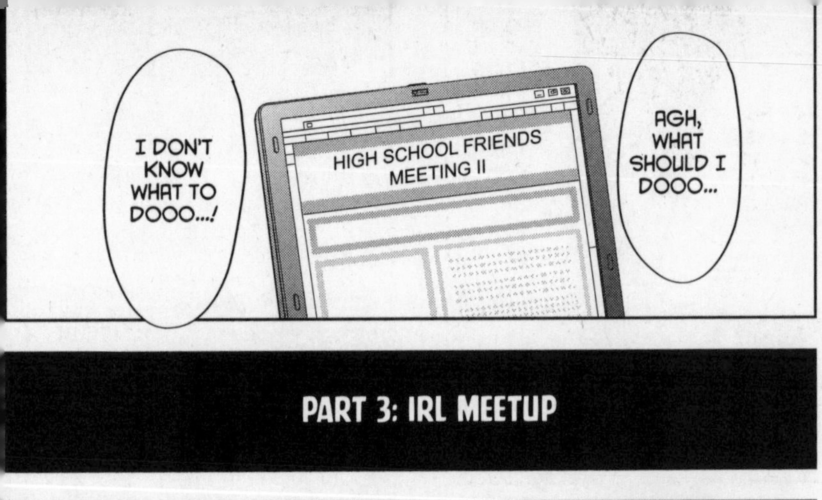
AGH, WHAT SHOULD I DOOO...
HIGH SCHOOL FRIENDS MEETING II
I DON'T KNOW WHAT TO DOOO...!

PART 3: IRL MEETUP

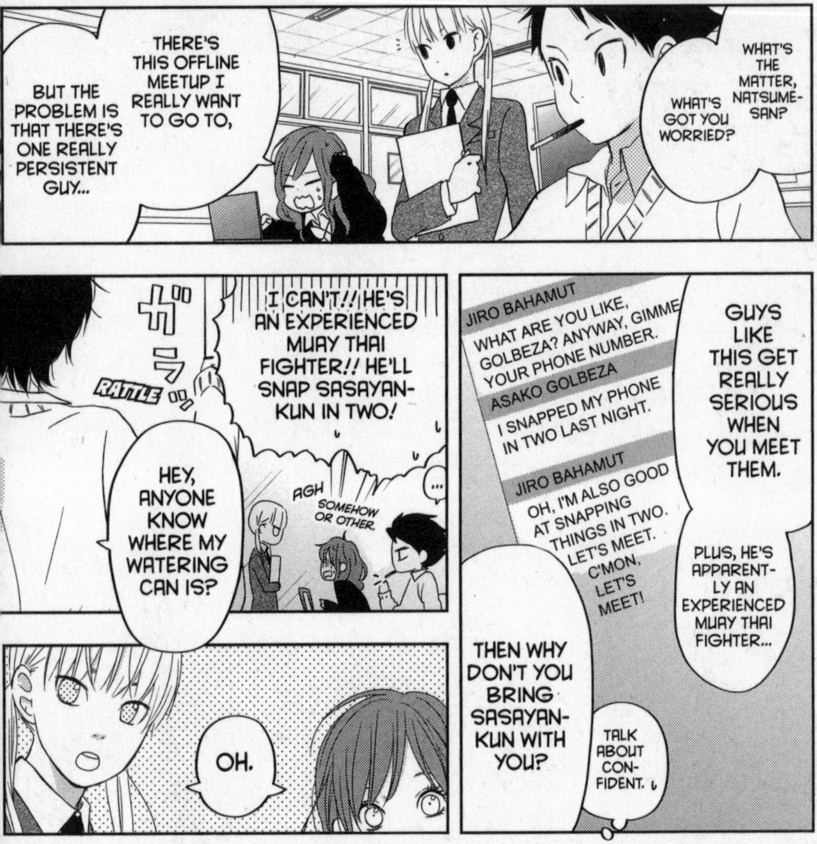
WHAT'S THE MATTER, NATSUME-SAN?
WHAT'S GOT YOU WORRIED?
THERE'S THIS OFFLINE MEETUP I REALLY WANT TO GO TO,
BUT THE PROBLEM IS THAT THERE'S ONE REALLY PERSISTENT GUY...
JIRO BAHAMUT
WHAT ARE YOU LIKE, GOLBEZA? ANYWAY, GIMME YOUR PHONE NUMBER.
ASAKO GOLBEZA
I SNAPPED MY PHONE IN TWO LAST NIGHT.
JIRO BAHAMUT
OH, I'M ALSO GOOD AT SNAPPING THINGS IN TWO. LET'S MEET. C'MON, LET'S MEET!
GUYS LIKE THIS GET REALLY SERIOUS WHEN YOU MEET THEM.
PLUS, HE'S APPARENTLY AN EXPERIENCED MUAY THAI FIGHTER...
THEN WHY DON'T YOU BRING SASAYAN-KUN WITH YOU?
TALK ABOUT CONFIDENT.
I CAN'T!! HE'S AN EXPERIENCED MUAY THAI FIGHTER!! HE'LL SNAP SASAYAN-KUN IN TWO!
ガラ
RATTLE
HEY, ANYONE KNOW WHERE MY WATERING CAN IS?
...
AGH
SOMEHOW OR OTHER.
OH.

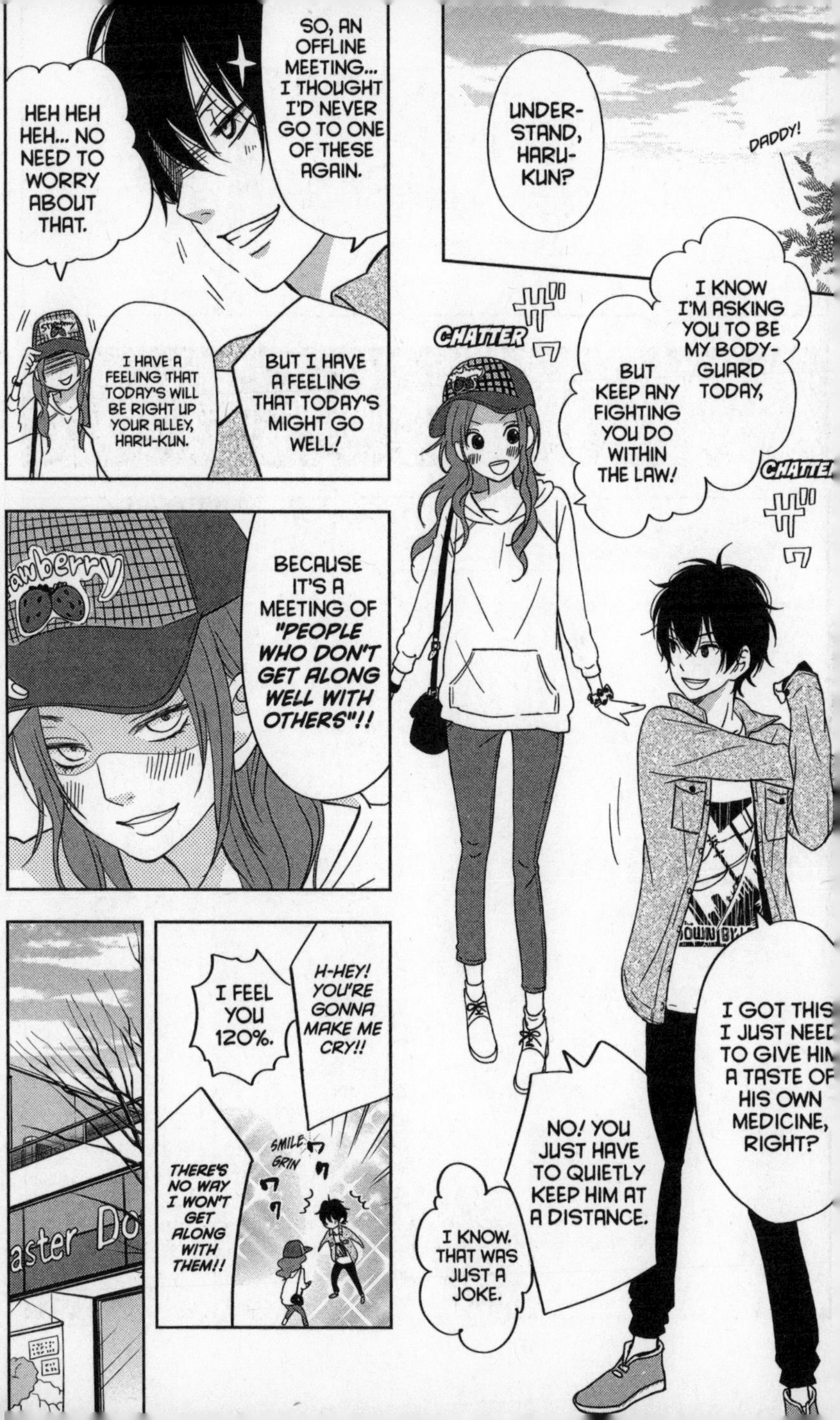
UNDER-STAND, HARU-KUN?
DADDY!
ザワ
CHATTER
I KNOW I'M ASKING YOU TO BE MY BODY-GUARD TODAY,
BUT KEEP ANY FIGHTING YOU DO WITHIN THE LAW!
CHATTE
ザワ
I GOT THIS I JUST NEED TO GIVE HIM A TASTE OF HIS OWN MEDICINE, RIGHT?
NO! YOU JUST HAVE TO QUIETLY KEEP HIM AT A DISTANCE.
I KNOW. THAT WAS JUST A JOKE.
SO, AN OFFLINE MEETING... I THOUGHT I'D NEVER GO TO ONE OF THESE AGAIN.
HEH HEH HEH... NO NEED TO WORRY ABOUT THAT.
BUT I HAVE A FEELING THAT TODAY'S MIGHT GO WELL!
I HAVE A FEELING THAT TODAY'S WILL BE RIGHT UP YOUR ALLEY, HARU-KUN.
BECAUSE IT'S A MEETING OF "PEOPLE WHO DON'T GET ALONG WELL WITH OTHERS"!!
H-HEY! YOU'RE GONNA MAKE ME CRY!!
I FEEL YOU 120%.
SMILE GRIN
THERE'S NO WAY I WON'T GET ALONG WITH THEM!!

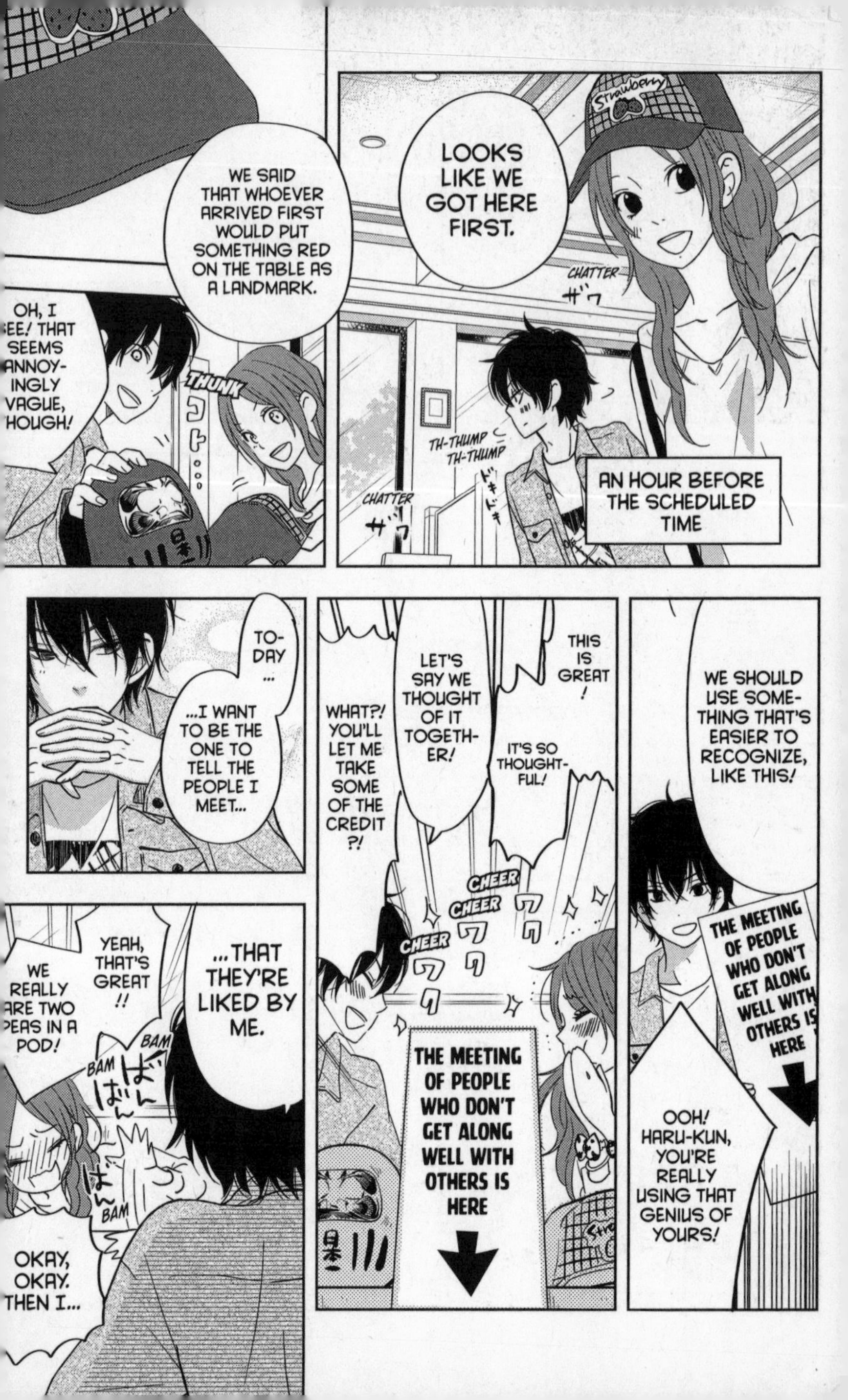
LOOKS LIKE WE GOT HERE FIRST.
CHATTER
TH-THUMP TH-THUMP
CHATTER
AN HOUR BEFORE THE SCHEDULED TIME
WE SAID THAT WHOEVER ARRIVED FIRST WOULD PUT SOMETHING RED ON THE TABLE AS A LANDMARK.
OH, I EE! THAT SEEMS NNOY- INGLY VAGUE, HOUGH!
THUNK
WE SHOULD USE SOME- THING THAT'S EASIER TO RECOGNIZE, LIKE THIS!
THE MEETING OF PEOPLE WHO DON'T GET ALONG WELL WITH OTHERS IS HERE
OOH! HARU-KUN, YOU'RE REALLY USING THAT GENIUS OF YOURS!
THIS IS GREAT!
IT'S SO THOUGHT- FUL!
LET'S SAY WE THOUGHT OF IT TOGETH- ER!
WHAT?! YOU'LL LET ME TAKE SOME OF THE CREDIT?!
CHEER CHEER CHEER
THE MEETING OF PEOPLE WHO DON'T GET ALONG WELL WITH OTHERS IS HERE
TO- DAY...
...I WANT TO BE THE ONE TO TELL THE PEOPLE I MEET...
...THAT THEY'RE LIKED BY ME.
YEAH, THAT'S GREAT!!
WE REALLY RE TWO EAS IN A POD!
BAM BAM
BAM
OKAY, OKAY. THEN I...

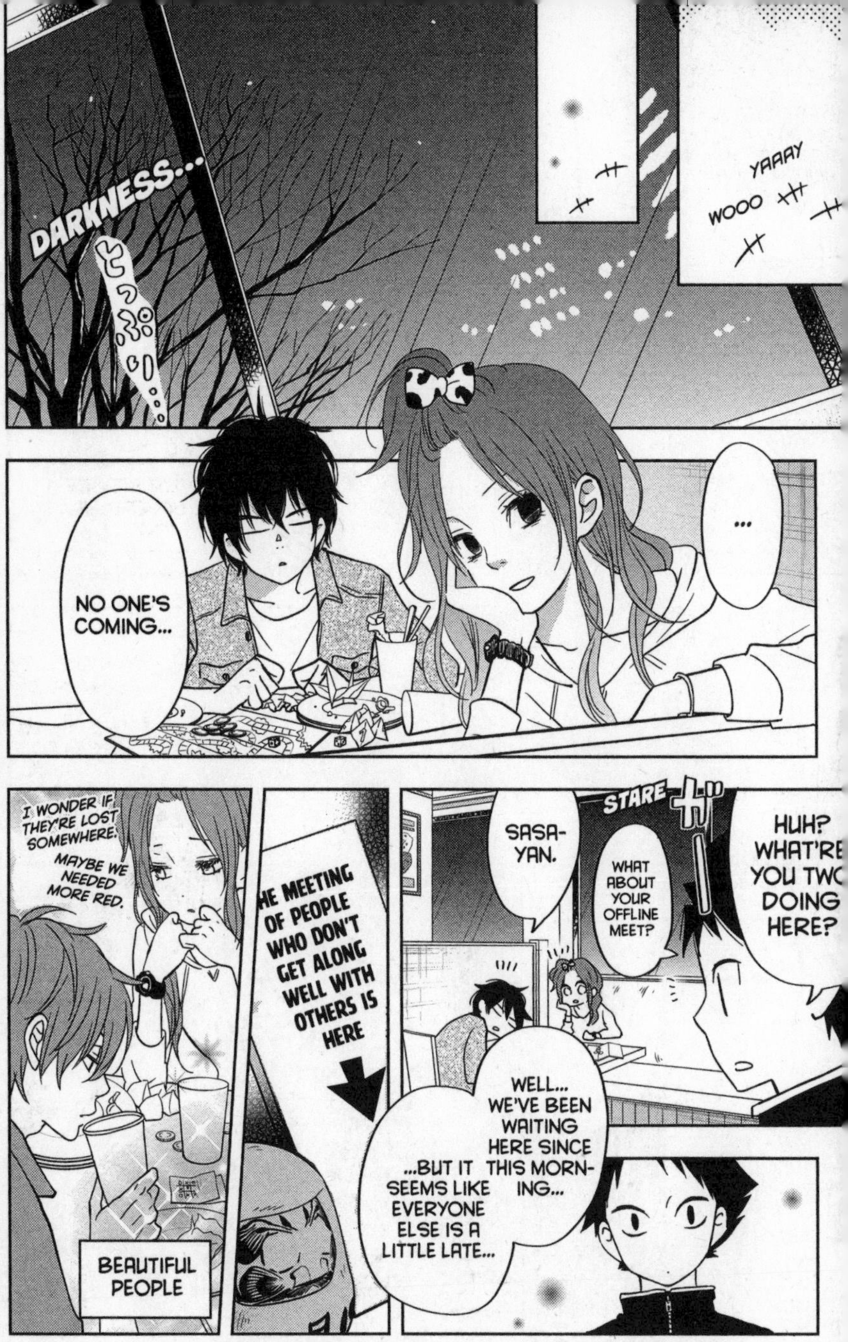
YAAAY
WOOO
DARKNESS...
...
NO ONE'S COMING...
HUH? WHAT'RE YOU TWO DOING HERE?
STARE
SASA-YAN.
WHAT ABOUT YOUR OFFLINE MEET?
WELL... WE'VE BEEN WAITING HERE SINCE THIS MORN-ING...
...BUT IT SEEMS LIKE EVERYONE ELSE IS A LITTLE LATE...
HE MEETING OF PEOPLE WHO DON'T GET ALONG WELL WITH OTHERS IS HERE
I WONDER IF THEY'RE LOST SOMEWHERE.
MAYBE WE NEEDED MORE RED.
BEAUTIFUL PEOPLE

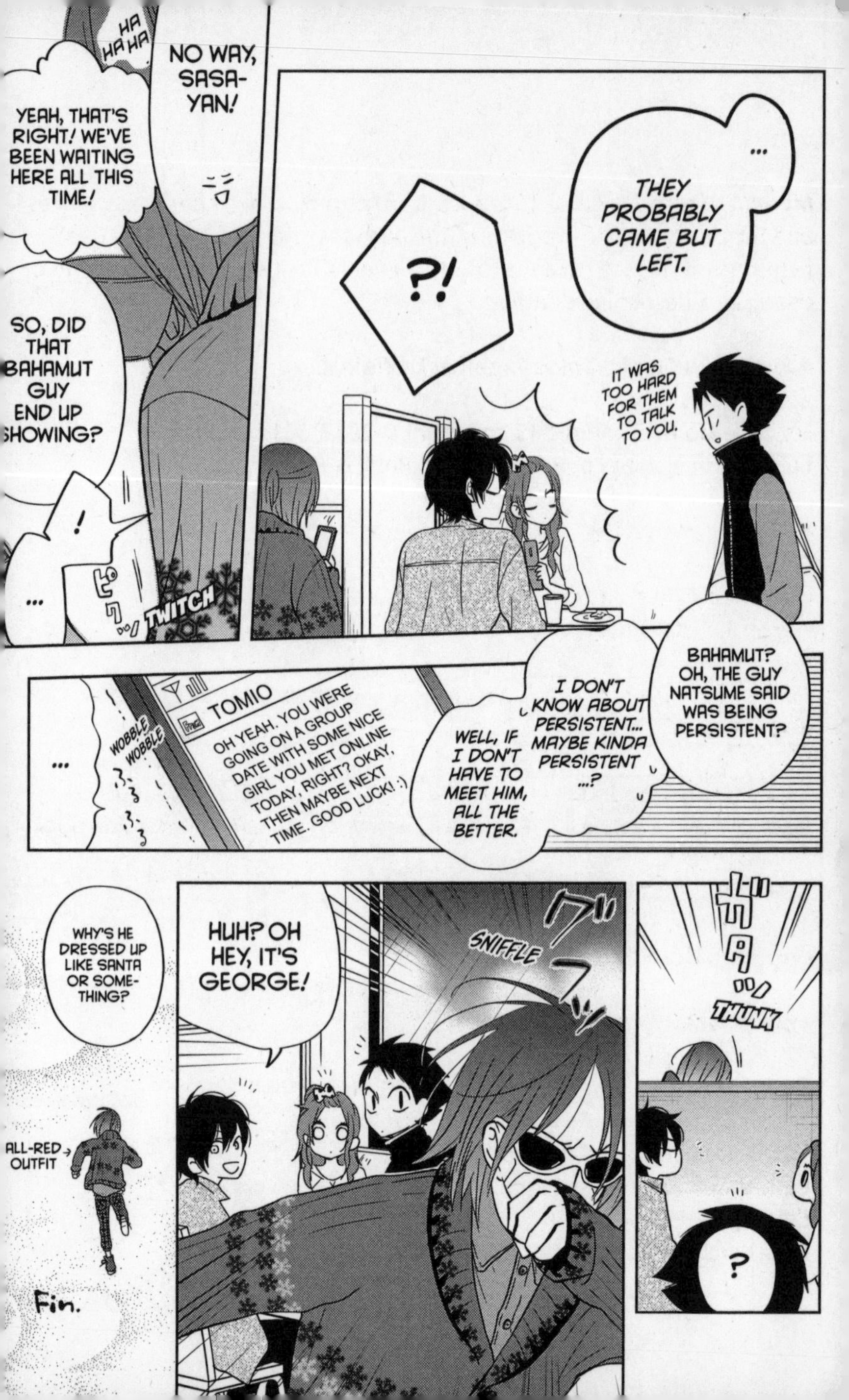
...
THEY PROBABLY CAME BUT LEFT.
?!
IT WAS TOO HARD FOR THEM TO TALK TO YOU.
HA HA HA
NO WAY, SASA-YAN!
YEAH, THAT'S RIGHT! WE'VE BEEN WAITING HERE ALL THIS TIME!
SO, DID THAT BAHAMUT GUY END UP SHOWING?
!
...
TWITCH
BAHAMUT? OH, THE GUY NATSUME SAID WAS BEING PERSISTENT?
I DON'T KNOW ABOUT PERSISTENT... MAYBE KINDA PERSISTENT ...?
WELL, IF I DON'T HAVE TO MEET HIM, ALL THE BETTER.
TOMIO
OH YEAH. YOU WERE GOING ON A GROUP DATE WITH SOME NICE GIRL YOU MET ONLINE TODAY, RIGHT? OKAY, THEN MAYBE NEXT TIME. GOOD LUCK! :)
WOBBLE WOBBLE
...
THUNK
?
SNIFFLE
HUH? OH HEY, IT'S GEORGE!
WHY'S HE DRESSED UP LIKE SANTA OR SOME-THING?
ALL-RED OUTFIT
Fin.

My Little Monster volume 13 is a work of fiction. Names, characters, places, and incidents are the products of the author's imagination or are used fictitiously. Any resemblance to actual events, locales, or persons, living or dead, is entirely coincidental.

A Kodansha Comics Trade Paperback Original.

Published in the United States by Kodansha Comics, an imprint of Kodansha USA Publishing, LLC, New York.

Publication rights for this English edition arranged through Kodansha Ltd., Tokyo.

First published in Japan by Kodansha Ltd., Tokyo, in 2014 as *Tonari no Kaibutsu-kun*, volume 13, and in 2012 as *Tonari no Kaibutsu-kun Fan Book*.

ISBN 978-1-63236-208-7

Printed in the United States of America.

www.kodanshacomics.com

9 8 7 6 5 4 3 2 1

Translation: Alethea Nibley & Athena Nibley
Lettering: Paige Pumphrey
Editing: Lauren Scanlan
Kodansha Comics edition cover design: Phil Balsman

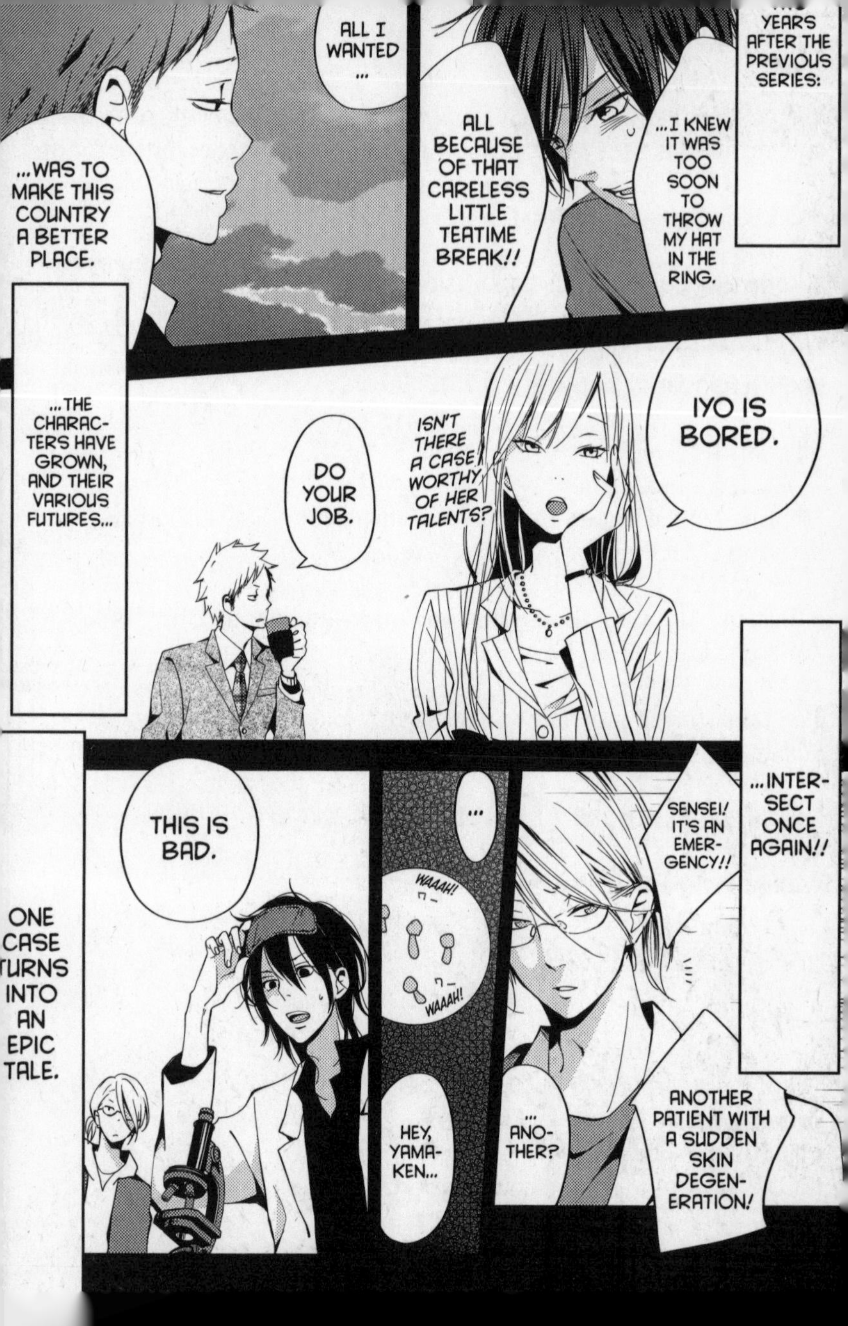
YEARS AFTER THE PREVIOUS SERIES:
...I KNEW IT WAS TOO SOON TO THROW MY HAT IN THE RING.
ALL BECAUSE OF THAT CARELESS LITTLE TEATIME BREAK!!
ALL I WANTED ...
...WAS TO MAKE THIS COUNTRY A BETTER PLACE.
IYO IS BORED.
ISN'T THERE A CASE WORTHY OF HER TALENTS?
DO YOUR JOB.
...THE CHARAC-TERS HAVE GROWN, AND THEIR VARIOUS FUTURES...
...INTER-SECT ONCE AGAIN!!
SENSEI! IT'S AN EMER-GENCY!!
ANOTHER PATIENT WITH A SUDDEN SKIN DEGEN-ERATION!
... ANO-THER?
...
WAAAH!
WAAAH!
HEY, YAMA-KEN...
THIS IS BAD.
ONE CASE TURNS INTO AN EPIC TALE.

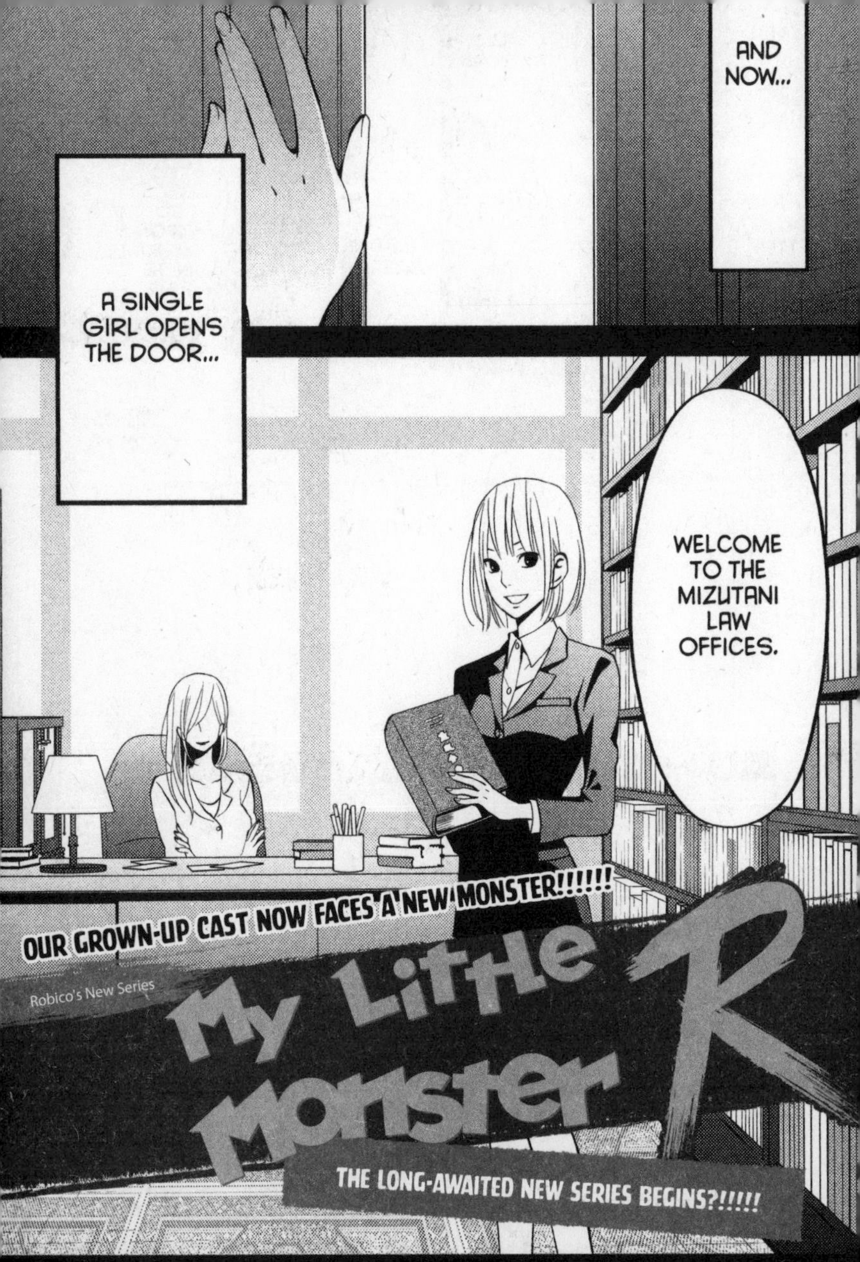
AND NOW...
A SINGLE GIRL OPENS THE DOOR...
WELCOME TO THE MIZUTANI LAW OFFICES.
OUR GROWN-UP CAST NOW FACES A NEW MONSTER!!!!!!
Robico's New Series
My Little Monster R
THE LONG-AWAITED NEW SERIES BEGINS?!!!!!

THE FUTURE OF MANKIND DEPENDS ON THEM.

Stop

Japanese manga is written and drawn from right to left, which is the opposite of the way American graphic novels are composed. To preserve the original orientation of the art, and maintain the proper storytelling flow, this book has retained the right to left structure. Please go to what would normally be the last page and begin reading, right to left, top to bottom.